Freedom's Journey

African American Voices of the Civil War

EDITED BY

DONALD YACOVONE

Lawrence Hill Books

Library of Congress Cataloging-in-Publication Data

Freedom's journey : African American voices of the Civil War / edited by
Donald Yacovone.—1st ed.
    p. cm.
Includes bibliographical references (p. 553) and index.
ISBN 1-55652-511-7 (cloth)—ISBN 1-55652-521-4 (pbk.)
1. United States—History—Civil War, 1861–1865—African Americans.
2. United States—History—Civil War, 1861–1865—Personal narratives.
3. African Americans—Biography. 4. Slaves—United States—Biography.
5. African American soldiers—Biography. 6. African American political
activists—Biography. I. Yacovone, Donald.

E540.N3F73 2004
973.7'092'396073—dc22

2003018583

Cover art: Jacob Lawrence (1917–2000); *The Life of Harriet Tubman,*
no. 27, 1940; casein tempera on hardboard,12 × 17$^{7}/_{8}$;
Hampton University Museum, Hampton, VA. Reproduced with the
permission of The Jacob and Gwendolyn Lawrence Foundation.
Jacket design by: Joan Sommers Design
Interior design by: Peirce Graphic Services

Published by Lawrence Hill Books
an imprint of Chicago Review Press, Incorporated
814 North Franklin Street
Chicago, Illinois 60610
1-55652-511-7 (cloth)
1-55652-521-4 (paper)

Printed in the United States of America
5 4 3 2 1

*For
My Friends*

Contents

Part II: Memory's Battlefield

Abbreviations

AME Church
  African Methodist Episcopal Church

AMEZ Church
  African Methodist Episcopal Zion Church

Berlin et al., *Freedom: The Destruction of Slavery*
  Ira Berlin et al., eds. *Freedom: A Documentary History of Emancipation, 1861–1867: The Destruction of Slavery*. Series 1, volume 1. Cambridge, England: Cambridge University Press, 1986.

Berlin et al., *Freedom: The Wartime Genesis of Free Labor: The Upper South*
  Ira Berlin et al., eds. *Freedom: A Documentary History of Emancipation, 1861–1867: The Wartime Genesis of Free Labor: The Upper South*. Series 1, volume 2. Cambridge, England: Cambridge University Press, 1994.

Berlin et al., *Freedom: The Black Military Experience*
  Ira Berlin et al., eds. *Freedom: A Documentary History of Emancipation, 1861–1867: The Black Military Experience*. Series 2. Cambridge, England: Cambridge University Press, 1982.

Emilio, *A Brave Black Regiment*
  Luis F. Emilio. *A Brave Black Regiment: History of the Fifty-fourth Regiment of Massachusetts Volunteer Infantry, 1863–1865*. 2nd edition, Boston, 1894. Reprint, New York: Johnson Reprint, 1968.

Faust, *Historical Times Illustrated Encyclopedia of the Civil War*
  Patricia Faust, ed. *Historical Times Illustrated Encyclopedia of the Civil War*. New York: HarperCollins, 1986.

McPherson, *Battle Cry of Freedom*
James M. McPherson, *Battle Cry of Freedom: The Civil War Era*. New York: Oxford University Press, 1988.

Official Records
The War of the Rebellion: A Compilation of the Official Records of the Union and Confederate Armies. 128 vols. Washington, DC: Adjutant General's Office, 1880–1901.

RG
Record Group, National Archives

Ripley et al., *The Black Abolitionist Papers*
C. Peter Ripley et al., eds. *The Black Abolitionist Papers*. 5 vols. Chapel Hill, NC: University of North Carolina Press, 1985–1992.

Sifakis, *Who Was Who in the Civil War*
Stewart Sifakis, ed. *Who Was Who in the Civil War*. New York: Facts on File, 1988.

Trudeau, *Like Men of War*
Noah Andre Trudeau. *Like Men of War: Black Troops in the Civil War, 1862–1865*. Boston: Little, Brown and Co., 1998.

USCC
United States Colored Cavalry

USCHA
United States Colored Heavy Artillery

USCT
United States Colored Troops

Warner, *Generals in Blue*
Ezra J. Warner. *Generals in Blue: Lives of the Union Commanders*. Baton Rouge, LA: Louisiana State University Press, 1964.

Wilson, *The Black Phalanx*
Joseph T. Wilson. *The Black Phalanx: African American Soldiers in the War of Independence, the War of 1812 & the Civil War*. Hartford, CT, 1880. Reprint: New York: DaCapo Press, 1994.

Yacovone, *A Voice of Thunder*
Donald Yacovone, ed. *A Voice of Thunder: A Black Soldier's Civil War*. Urbana, IL: University of Illinois Press, 1998.

Foreword

"The Negro is the key of the situation—the pivot upon which the whole rebellion turns." These words of Frederick Douglass that begin *Freedom's Journey*, Donald Yacovone's excellent collection of Civil War and post–Civil War documents, are at the heart of the material you are about to read. Unlike other texts that describe the road to war, its consequences, and the aftermath through the work of abolitionists, politicians, soldiers, slaveholders, slaves, and freedmen and freedwomen from various regions of the country, this collection is wholly devoted to the attitudes and voices of black people. For black people were indeed "the pivot," as it were, at the center of these extraordinary events. As such this book represents not only a unique opportunity to explore the feelings of the people for whom the war was fought, but it also resurrects their involvement in the war and allows us a clearer picture of the democratic ideals that precipitated it.

These ideals have, I am sorry to say, been lost in many instances, through the historical re-coloring of the events to reflect not the fight against the horror of slavery, but some idealized nonsense about Southern chivalry and the "Lost Cause." Too often we are eased into forgetting that the Southern states of the Confederacy were in *rebellion* against the lawful authority of the United States, that they hoped through secession to retain the institution of slavery, and hold in bondage 4 million African Americans against their will. At the root of all the myriad histories of the period of the Civil War and its aftermath is this unassailable fact.

Yet, as Donald Yacovone tells us in his introduction, blacks and whites, Northerners and Southerners held and still hold entirely different views of the War, its meaning, and its residual effects. How is this possible?

The major reasons are the extraordinary volume of history written about the Civil War and its aftermath, the color of its content, and who wrote it. There is another, less obvious factor, however. An example is Edward King's book, *The Great South*. Originally published as a series of articles by *Scribners Monthly* during 1873 and 1874, and described by its editors as "presenting a remarkably sensitive and vivid picture of the American South in an important period of its history," as well as a work that "*encouraged* sectional reconciliation" [italics mine], one is struck by the contrasting images of whites and Negroes. King, a northeastern reporter for the *New York Times*, begins his first chapter with the words, "Louisiana to-day is Paradise Lost." Throughout his description of New Orleans and the South of his "today," he gently juxtaposes energetic whites with lazy blacks, and contrasts a faded South eager to retake its place in America against "the more odious carpet-baggers, who have arrayed the negro wrongfully against the principal property-holders" (p. 793). While not a history of the South or the war, it was the first widely read description of the post-war South, and largely contributed, I believe, to the germ of the idea of a "Lost Cause" and a *noble South*, which fought for honor and not to preserve slavery. The damage it did to Negroes in the North through stereotyping was incalculable. King encourages the vision of the soft, sweet South and the worthless, stupid Negro, unable to speak English and a drag on a region anxious to get started again. It is remarkable that so many historians of the nineteenth and early twentieth centuries downplay the effect popular articles like King's had on their own opinions about Reconstruction, and the life it gave to their extrapolations of who and what the people of the South were before and during the War.

The point I have tried to make above is that our differing racial views of the period may be as much the fault of the Edward Kings, the journalists sent into the South to report on its conditions, as that of the historians. Nowhere in *The Great South* is there a single instance of a Negro who could have, through education and learning, participated in or initiated the events surrounding the war. So little that is intelligent is attributed to Negroes that one wonders why the North expended so much energy and so many lives to free them. And while history books can describe battles and who won them, only the popular literature of the day can set the tone and color the content of what most people will or want to believe.

Freedom's Journey is an extraordinary step forward in dispelling the idea of the Negro as a humorous lazy fool "recumbent in a cart, with his eyes languidly closed, and one dirty foot sprawled on the sidewalk" (p. 29). While I cannot argue that books like *The Great South* were the cause of our differing views of the Civil War and Reconstruction, I do believe, long before anyone read a single history of these events, whole sections of the nation "tuned-in," as it were, to the monthly articles of King and other journalists like him. The *die* had been cast. The results continue in many ways even now, and *Freedom's Journey* will doubtless help to bring balance and intelligence to a greatly misunderstood period.

CHARLES FULLER

Preface

African Americans tell their story of the Civil War in *Freedom's Journey*. In their own words, black Americans recount their experiences and express themselves on every major issue that arose during the war—and after. They challenge us to rethink familiar events and give us a new appreciation for what they accomplished under unprecedented adversity. Most important, they compel us to rethink our understanding of this nation's greatest crisis. Their voices are clear. Rather than a mythological "brother's war," the Civil War represented a defining struggle for freedom and democracy.

As a sourcebook of the African American experience during the war, *Freedom's Journey* presents a comprehensive collection of documents. Some, such as Frederick Douglass's call for men to join the 54th Massachusetts Regiment, will be familiar. Others, such as those that touch on the troubled relationship between blacks and Lincoln and on criticism of the Emancipation Proclamation, will be strikingly new to many readers. All the documents are published in full, without modification or abbreviation on my part. This important principle respects the authors' intentions, even if they express opinions that do not ring comfortably to modern ears. I left unaltered as many nineteenth-century writing and publishing practices as possible, including appearance and spelling, to retain the flavor of the era. I have, however, for the sake of clarity silently corrected many misspellings and misprints, especially of proper names, when dealing with printed works. All other editorial insertions are enclosed by brackets.

The book's introduction sets the broadest framework for understanding the issues that African Americans confronted during the Civil War. Part I, Freedom's Battlefield, contains a comprehensive selection of letters, speeches, addresses, journal articles, book chapters, newspaper editorials, individual statements, and diary entries that trace the major social and political issues that African Americans confronted from 1860 until the end of the Civil War. Almost all of the selections were written during the war and convey the immediacy of the experience, unfiltered by time or shifting political priorities. I have also included documents composed by Civil War participants after the war. To recover the black female experience of the war, one is left with few alternatives but to use these items. Still, the selections by Susie King Taylor and Elizabeth Keckley, for instance, accurately reflect the experiences they portray, as supported by other contemporary documents.

While a few African American soldiers wrote about their combat experience, the overwhelming amount of the documentary record is devoted to issues related to race, rights, and slavery. Fortunately for us, the opinions and experiences of wartime African Americans are unequivocally and clearly expressed in these selections, preserving the role black Americans played in the nation's greatest crisis and in creating our modern democratic values.

Each chapter in Part I is organized around a specific theme, with notes that introduce each document or group of documents and supplement the general introduction with a more specific level of contextual information. In choosing these writings, I preferred texts that could largely stand on their own. Doing so permitted me to take a minimalist approach to document annotation and avoid cluttering the texts with heavy scholarly apparatus. The reader will find that the documents' notes focus on African American–related subjects and people. In some cases, however, the authors provided insufficient evidence to determine the identity of an individual, and in others, misspellings make identifications impossible. A number of references simply defied my ability to gather any information about them.

In Part II, Memory's Battlefield, readers will find selections written by men and women who experienced the Civil War, but who—with a few exceptions—recorded their reflections long after the surrender at Appomattox. I believe that the selections in Part II are essential to fully understand the black Civil War experience and the ways in which that experience shaped and was shaped by postwar imperatives. How Americans remembered the war during the Reconstruction era, for example, resulted in enormous implications for African Americans. The differing ways that people remember the past has become a vital part of the writing of American history. We should not be surprised that various interpretations of the meaning of the Civil War vied for public acceptance in the late nineteenth century, nor that African Americans sought to influence that debate through the publication of memoirs, histories, poetry, and fiction. Black writers struggled along with (but usually against) other Americans to forge a collective memory of the most traumatic experience in the nation's history. As whites of the North turned their backs on the promises of freedom and democracy amended to the U.S. Constitution after the war, and those of the South schemed to crush them, black writers, former soldiers, and former slaves raised a dissenting voice. They would not allow the war's cause, slavery, the unbroken chains of racial prejudice, or their sacrifices for freedom and the Union to be swept aside.

Together, the book's two sections form an interesting and even passionate mix of short and long, familiar and new, previously published and unpublished selections written by both men and women. The relatively large number of women represented in *Freedom's Journey* reflects not only their role in the war, but the reality that the Civil War amounted to far more than victory on the battlefield. In a contest that helped Americans define the meaning of freedom, the experiences of *all* free blacks and slaves mattered; indeed, they were central to the war.

This book includes several items, I am happy to say, that have not been published since the Civil War. Where gaps exist, such as black-authored documents relating to the thousands of African American workers and slaves who dug the trenches, repaired the railroad lines, and built the fortifications for both armies during the war, it is not for want of searching for them. While I could have included white-authored documents that shed light on these experiences, I have adhered strictly to the policy of offering only unmediated black voices.

To assist the reader, I have included a list of abbreviations used throughout the book, and I've closed this collection with a selected reading list for anyone seeking additional information about the black Civil War experience.

Acknowledgments

Without the indispensable volumes of *Freedom: A Documentary History of Emancipation* and *The Black Abolitionist Papers*, this book could not have been written. Anyone studying the African American role in the Civil War must consult the books in these two collections. Walt Whitman once warned that the real Civil War was not getting into the history books. *Freedom* and *BAP* have proved him wrong, although perhaps not in ways that he would have imagined. I have borrowed heavily from both project's volumes, as the notes and source citations reveal.

I am very much indebted to the Massachusetts Historical Society. The society's council, its president, and its director, William M. Fowler, Jr., granted me both paid and unpaid leave to complete this project. From the beginning, the MHS has supported and encouraged my work, and I could not be more grateful. My colleagues in the publications department, Conrad Wright, Ondine LeBlanc, Melissa Pino, and Seth Vose, bore additional burdens because of my absence, and I want to thank them for their patience. The MHS senior cataloger Mary Fabiszewski helped countless times, and, with her usual alacrity and accuracy, *never* failed to find the right answer.

My former Florida colleague Roy Finkenbine, now at the University of Detroit Mercy and head of the university's Black Abolitionist Archives, graciously provided assistance many times and never objected to my seemingly endless requests. I have been fortunate to benefit from his vast knowledge and comradeship. Scholars who study African Americans in the North prior to 1865 must use the collections managed by Roy if they expect to render a full account of that community's history. Joseph P. Reidy at Howard University helped me considerably with the role of African Americans in the Union Navy. Richard

Blackett at Vanderbilt University is the reason I have edited this collection. He is, however, absolved of all responsibility for the results. This has been a great undertaking, and Richard's confidence in me is very much appreciated. I want to acknowledge the work of series editor Yuval Taylor, whose many suggestions are reflected throughout the book.

I also want to thank Kathy Olsen and Richard J. Sommers at the United States Military Institute, George Graf, serials librarian at Trinity College, Francis Bremer and Dennis Downey at Millersville University, James Oliver Horton at George Washington University, James Hunn, reenactor in the 12th USCHA who takes on the role of Elijah P. Marrs, and Margaret Roberts, film and video producer—the angel of Venice Beach—whose commitment to the history of blacks in the military and on film has no peer. C. Douglas Alves, Jr., director of the Calvert County Marine Museum and my friend for more years than either of us want to admit, for the second time assisted me with Maryland history. David Gordon, historian, lawyer, and gourmet, always gives expert legal opinion and reminders to get finished. My friends have helped me weather especially difficult ordeals as I completed this project, and I will be forever thankful for their support. I prefer not to contemplate life without them; sad absences already abound. Frank and Dennis offered ready ears and reminders of the benefits of faith and persistence; Doug and Mary gave me the love and understanding of a brother and a sister; and David provided a calm and well-reasoned voice. I wish I could have shared the experience of writing this book with Natasha, who, while I pecked at the keyboard, shocked me by changing from a wiry little girl with a ponytail into an adolescent. "Her wings unfurled/ like a long story foretold/ in heaven/or a flag of a just cause." Every tear holds a rainbow, I remind myself. I want her to know that all love is not fleeting.

Introduction

The "Negro is the key of the situation—the pivot upon which the whole rebellion turns."[1] Most white Northerners did not accept Frederick Douglass's view of the Civil War, and before 1863 their interest in the contest did not extend much beyond a desire to preserve the Union. Even when abolitionists, who had been agitating since the 1820s, compelled whites to consider the problem of slavery, they did not view African Americans as an exploited people. Northerners distinguished between the institution of slavery, which they feared, and its victims, which they disdained. They came to see slavery as a looming threat to free labor, material prosperity, and their white "race." Rather than condemning the peculiar institution as a crime or a sin, Northerners opposed slavery because it increased the power of the South and, most menacingly of all, increased the number of African Americans.

The Southern understanding of the war, ironically, more closely mirrored Douglass's view. Despite what later apologists for the "Lost Cause" might assert, prior to 1865 little disagreement existed in the South over the root cause of its conflict with the North. Differing views regarding secession existed, and many Southerners only reluctantly cooperated with the "national" government in Richmond, at times seeing it as onerous and as aggrandizing as the one in Washington. But no disagreement existed over the source of their conflict with the North. To every supporter of the Confederate cause, their survival as a people and as a nation were inextricably bound up with slavery.[2]

After the Compromise of 1820 was enacted, Southern fears of Northern aggression and capitalist exploitation, shifting power, and antislavery agitation grew. In the thirty years before the Civil War, abolitionists increased in numbers; they appeared strident and well organized. Their incendiary publications, many directed at the South, appeared calculated to incite slave rebellions. Despite their clamor, they never became a majority in the North and before 1863 remained widely despised, even in liberal Boston. Nevertheless, Southerners perceived them as representing Northern views, and the louder their cries for slavery's end, the more anxiety coursed through the South. In the end, all Southern calls for secession, which multiplied after 1850, centered upon preserving a social structure that depended upon the forced labor of about four million Americans of African descent.

Southerners perceived blacks as inherently unsuited for independent life, incapable of higher learning, and either too servile to survive on their own or too violent to trust unless subjugated. As Southerners said countless times, blacks represented a race fit "naturally" and only for slavery. The peculiar institution was not evil; indeed, Southerners—and their Northern allies—maintained that the slave trade had brought great benefits to Africans. Who could doubt, they asked, that blacks were better off as slaves in a Christian America than as free "savages" in "pagan" Africa? Any deviation from these ironclad principles, Southerners believed, would lead to the destruction of the country and the white race. William L. Harris, the Confederate commissioner from Mississippi who was charged with the task of convincing Georgia to leave the Union, put the case for slavery and secession in the starkest terms: Mississippi would rather "see the last of her race, men, women and children, immolated in one common funeral pile, than see them subjected to the degradation of civil, political, and social equality with the negro race."[3]

As long as Southerners, or Southern interests, dominated the federal government, the legislative and executive branches, and the federal courts—especially the Supreme Court—the South felt a measure of security. Southerners perceived Northern abolitionists as intolerable threats who openly (or secretly) plotted slave revolts. For every Nat Turner, Southerners saw a John Brown lurking in the background. By controlling the federal government and African Americans, Southerners felt confident that inflammatory abolitionists would be stymied and human bondage would endure.

But between 1850 and 1860, the North came to fear *Southern* aggression. The 1850 Fugitive Slave Law, with its suspension of habeas corpus and requirement that all citizens aid in returning an accused fugitive to bondage, threatened the very foundation of liberty. More ominous, the South's insistence that masters possessed the legal right to take their "property" anywhere they pleased appeared to be a harbinger of slavery's unlimited growth. Abraham Lincoln and the Republican party, pledging to bar the spread of slavery into the West, emerged victorious in the 1860 election and signaled the end of Southern political dominance. Despite Republican assurances that the new government would respect "Southern institutions," meaning that they would not challenge slavery where it existed, the South could not help but perceive Lincoln's election as a lethal threat to the institution of slavery. Southern states hotly debated secession and many came reluctantly to a final decision, but one after another they severed the "mystic cords of union" and left the United States. And the war came.[4]

Although the blue and gray armies stopped fighting in 1865, Americans have been fighting about the meaning of the war ever since. Thomas Beer, a popular author and cultural critic in the 1920s, observed that the military aspects of the Civil War ended in 1865, but "its political end may be reasonably expected about the year 3000."[5] Given the nation's continued fascination with the Civil War, there is little reason to doubt Beer's prediction. When Ken Burns's eleven-hour epic appeared on public television in the fall of 1990 it attracted about fourteen million viewers—a population larger than that of all the Confederate states. Countless more Americans saw the film in rebroadcasts or purchased the bestselling companion book. Interest alone, regardless of intensity, says nothing about the nature of that interest, and we have not always recognized the contrasting opinions that still thrive on the subject of the Civil War. The recent public controversies over display of the Confederate battle flag on state capitol buildings, a monument to President Lincoln in Richmond, and unsupported assertions of widespread use of black troops by the Confederacy reveal deep cultural fissures over the legacy of the war. Whether in rural Kentucky or in downtown Atlanta, one can still readily hear declarations of loyalty to the Confederate past that assume religious ferocity. "My husband was a Yankee and I converted him to a rebel and I'm damn proud of it!" one woman declared at a school board meeting in Todd County, Kentucky. "I will not compromise my values and equal rights to satisfy a minority. God bless America, God bless our rebel flag!"[6] Most declarations of devotion to the "Lost Cause" either skirt the issue of race or deny that slavery had anything to do with the conflict. No one, however, disputes the centrality of the war to American history.

Robert Penn Warren, one of the original Southern agrarian dissenters of *I'll Take My Stand* (1930), underwent his own transformation on the subject of race. He did not, however, lose his appreciation for the meaning of the Civil War to American identity and mythology. "The Civil War is, for the American imagination, the great single event of our history. Without too much wrenching," he wrote in 1961, "it may, in fact, be said to *be* American history. . . . The Civil War is our only 'felt' history—history lived in the national imagination. This is not to say that the War is always, and by all men, felt in the same way. Quite the contrary. But this fact is an index to the very complexity, depth, and fundamental significance of the event. It is an overwhelming and vital image of human, and national, experience." Warren believed that (white) men, like the hallowed leader of the 54th Massachusetts Regiment, Col. Robert Gould Shaw—immortalized by Augustus Saint-Gaudens—had created an American "Homeric period." Such heroes "loom up only a little less than gods, but even so," Warren believed, "we recognize the lineaments and passions of men, and by that recognition of common kinship share in their grandeur." Thus, the bravery of Civil War soldiers lent a kind of holy meaning to the lives of their descendants. Men like Robert Penn Warren did not consider what the war meant to African Americans, nor how *their* understanding of the struggle might alter the way all Americans understood the conflict.

Warren's criticism, by extension a kind of self-criticism, focused on the South and its delusional "Great Alibi," which both explained and excused all things. "Lost Cause" mythology permitted white Southerners to retain their pride and their dominance of African Americans. "Heritage, not hate," is the current cliché for defenders of the "Old South." Southerners, Warren wrote, managed the spectacular feat of transforming the legacy of slavery and racism into a glorious cause with saintly military heroes. The white North, on the other hand, ignored its own hypocrisy (especially on the subject of race) by imaging its role in the war as constituting what Warren termed a "Treasury of Virtue." Each section suffered its own delusions and each bore responsibility for bringing on the nation's most horrible of wars. Warren acknowledged the importance of slavery to the war, but discounted its terrors and never included African Americans in his pantheon of Homeric gods. The first white man to give his life for black freedom, John Brown, would, for Warren, always be a terrorist who deserved his fate. Still, Warren believed that Virginia erred in executing the determined man, which only turned him into a martyr, and should have confined him to an insane asylum. African Americans saw history differently.[7]

With few exceptions, modern professional historians have generally reached a consensus on the origins of the Civil War and put slavery in the causal center. Differences of emphasis remain, but none that approach the profound chasm that split the profession prior to the 1960s, when historians avoided or de-emphasized the issue of slavery and instead blamed a "blundering" generation of politicians for leading the nation into an avoidable war.[8] Popular culture, on the other hand, has not experienced this transformation of opinion. It continues to battle over the causes and meaning of the Civil War in a conflict that began the moment the guns fell silent in 1865. So long as Americans find their identity in the Civil War, as Robert Penn Warren wrote over forty years ago, the war and related issues, especially race, will remain an open wound.[9]

The Civil War is contested ground. Our appreciation for the African American role in the war is a recent phenomenon, and to a disappointing degree is far from universally known or understood. While the number of books—and Web sites—about black participation in the war have increased in recent years, this growth represents a mere trickle compared to the deluge of books on the Civil War that monthly gush from publishers north and south. Rather than an analysis of causes or consequences, the majority of this literature amounts to little more than sentimentalized battle glory. Perhaps not by design, but certainly in effect, this flood of words overwhelms other voices that are indispensable to understanding the causes, conduct, and full meaning of the Civil War. The documentary record offered in *Freedom's Journey* seeks to resist the relentless blue and gray tide of military valor that has yet to reach full flood stage. In bringing African American perspectives of the war to the broadest possible audience, we refocus our attention on the larger issues of freedom and liberty that lay at the heart of the conflict.

For African Americans, the Civil War was all about slavery. From the opening guns at Fort Sumter to the surrender of arms at Appomattox Court House, the war was framed and defined by issues of slavery and freedom. Blacks' participation in the war as soldiers, sailors, spies, stevedores, and scouts was an extension of their role in the antislavery movement that began in earnest after formation of the hated American Colonization Society in 1816. Their fight for freedom fit into a centuries-long struggle for freedom and democracy, from 1776 to the abandonment of Reconstruction in 1876 and beyond. Even those who could not tolerate American racism and advocated emigration or strident black nationalist ideas saw themselves as the Americans they were; their ancestors had arrived in North America before the Pilgrims; the Founding Fathers were their Founding Fathers; they read the same Bible, Plato, Jefferson, Scott, Tennyson, and Dickens as other Americans, whatever their nationality. Assertions that blacks should return to Africa where they "belonged," or that they could not live in freedom with whites, as President Lincoln publicly declared, affronted their dignity and ignored the historical record. They needed no "education," as Lincoln and most Northerners required, as to the true issues at stake in the conflict. Indeed, they became the educators, like Frederick Douglass or the great black New York editor Robert Hamilton, who reflected black opinion and helped realign the debate over war aims for whites toward freedom.

Black Americans fought valiantly for independence, shed their blood before the Old State House in Boston, at Bunker Hill, and at Red Bank, New Jersey. They provided Andrew Jackson and Oliver Hazard Perry victories in the War of 1812, as the Medal of Honor winner Christian A. Fleetwood emphasizes in this book's second half. Although blacks had established a long record of military service in the army *and* navy, white Americans did not want their assistance in the Civil War. As Samuel Sewall, the author of the nation's first antislavery tract, had written in 1700, whites never stopped viewing African Americans as "extravasat Blood" in the "Body Politick."[10] When rebels forced Robert Anderson to haul down the American flag at Fort Sumter in April 1861, thousands of African Americans rushed to defend that flag. But from Capitol Hill to Beacon Hill, from governors' offices to city halls, the same message rang in the ears of black Americans: "This is a white man's war." The idea of a black man in a blue uniform offended the racial pride and masculinity of white Americans. The appropriately-named Ohio Congressman Chilton A. White exclaimed, "This is a government of white men, made by white men for white men, to be administered, protected, defended, and maintained by white men." Yankees simply would not permit black men to fight.[11]

"Practical Abolitionists," Robert Hamilton asserted in 1861, "can afford to wait for a while." As editor of the North's leading black newspaper, the New York *Weekly Anglo-African*, Hamilton counseled patience to his spurned brethren. "The nation is doing our work with more force than we can. The slaves are not ready either. Their masters must exhaust themselves by preparation and struggle. Then the long-expected moment will come."[12] Indeed, before the close of 1862, Union regiments of former slaves began appearing on the battlefield. In halting efforts and amid howling protests, African Americans in blue uniforms began fighting their Southern masters. As Hamilton predicted, the war proved a swift educator. Desperate for more soldiers, a reluctant federal government allowed the "experiment" of black recruitment to begin.

Black Union troops in Kansas, Louisiana, and South Carolina stunned Union commanders with their bravery under fire. After the fighting at Port Hudson, Louisiana, in May 1863, Union generals on the scene, such as Nathaniel P. Banks, could not avoid the conclusion that "the manner in which they [black troops] encountered the enemy, leaves upon my mind no doubt of their ultimate success." Gen. Daniel Ullman announced that the "brilliant conduct of the colored regiments at Port Hudson, on the 27th has silenced cavilers and changed sneers into eulogizers. There is no question but that they behaved with dauntless courage."[13] Col. Thomas Wentworth Higginson, a defiant Massachusetts supporter of John Brown, sent a stream of letters to the daily press detailing the solid conduct of his soldiers in the 1st South Carolina Volunteers. They had faced rebel infantry, cavalry, and artillery and in each case came off "not only with unblemished honor, but with undisputed triumph." Higginson's reputation as a clearheaded abolitionist went far to convince some doubters; as far as the Boston *Daily Advertiser* was concerned, if he said black troops fought well, that was "in our opinion conclusive."[14]

The same could not be said of the Union army or the rest of the North. In part, military prowess defined white manhood and the possibility of a black man fighting in uniform alongside white men provoked rage. White Union soldiers wanted no part of black troops: "We think we are too superior a race for that." One Pennsylvania soldier announced that he wouldn't mind if "the niggers be sent here to use the pick and shovel in the boiling sun," but white men should use a real soldier's tools, the gun and bayonet. One black scout who had worked for a white regiment heard the men repeatedly swear that "they would shoot the negro that would shoot a white man, even if he was a rebel." Another Yankee, who claimed to have witnessed Higginson's 1st South Carolina Volunteers in combat, said that when attacked the blacks threw down their guns and ran. The only thing they willingly assaulted, he alleged, were "innocent white women."[15]

Thus, the importance of the 54th Massachusetts Regiment. Formed of free blacks from across the North and organized in the spring of 1863 by Gov. John A. Andrew and the commonwealth's abolitionist elite, the 54th would determine the future of black recruitment. Upon this one regiment rested the hopes of every free African American and, to whites, the character of the race. The one thousand men of the 54th felt the eyes of the entire North, indeed "the eyes of the whole world" on them, waiting to see if they would "prove ourselves men." Led by Col. Robert Gould Shaw, the son of fervent abolitionists, the 54th Massachusetts took only handpicked white officers who enthusiastically backed the cause of black recruitment and could pass an examination to prove it. The best black men the North could muster readied themselves in about three months to become one of the most efficient and disciplined regiments in the Union army. Success on the battlefield would affirm black worth to skeptical whites and lead to widespread recruitment of African Americans. Failure would bring a speedy halt to the enlistment of blacks—jeopardizing the course of the war—and would destroy black hopes for equal citizenship in the postwar world.[16]

They did not disappoint. On the evening of July 18, 1863, 600 men of the 54th Massachusetts Regiment led a Union assault on Fort Wagner, a sand and palmetto-log bastion straddling the hot sands of Morris Island at the mouth of Charleston Harbor. To reach the fort's parapets, the men withstood a storm of shot and shell. Colonel Shaw died on the fort's wall, and about half of the regiment's attacking force was killed, wounded, or captured. Sgt. William H. Carney, who suffered several wounds, carried the national flag back to Union lines—heroism that later won him the Medal of Honor. Despite the 54th Massachusetts's courage and sacrifice that night, the fort remained in rebel hands. Only a siege of over a month's time compelled the rebels to abandon the post and give up the hundreds of Union dead they had hastily buried in mass graves.

Shortly after the failed attack on July 18, a correspondent for the New York Evening Post went to the Union hospitals at Port Royal, South Carolina, to visit the 54th's wounded and shattered men. Standing over them, he said, "Well, boys, this was not a part of the program, was it?" Much to his surprise one man replied, "Oh yes indeed, we expected to take all that comes." The reporter then asked the men if the army honorably discharged them now, "how many would enlist again?" With eagerness, many lifted themselves from their beds, and all announced, "Oh, yes, yes." Others exclaimed: "Oh, never give it up, till the last rebel be dead," when "the last brother breaks his chains," and "If all our people get their freedom, we can afford to die."[17]

The bravery and sacrifice displayed by the 54th Massachusetts at Fort Wagner changed Northern opinion about black recruitment almost overnight. "Open opposition to colored soldiers has ceased both in the States and in the army, many of their fiercest enemies have become their fastest friends. . . ." Massachusetts's adjutant general even predicted that, as a result of the 54th's bravery, "the time will come when they will be commanded by officers of their own color and race." Newspapers that had previously opposed the idea of a black man in uniform now sung the praises of black valor and reprinted the story of Carney's heroism again and again. Such bravery "has never been exceeded in any battle," one paper pronounced. As a result, full-scale recruitment of African Americans began, ultimately totaling 178,975 men in nearly 150 different infantry, cavalry, and artillery regiments, and led to a Union victory.[18]

The Union achieved this victory at an enormous cost. As one officer in the 54th Massachusetts Regiment remarked, "We pay a high price in our young men, for the sin of slavery."[19] Black soldiers paid that price and more. When they faced the enemy, they understood that if captured they would either be killed or enslaved. Lincoln's General Order #233, which threatened to execute one rebel soldier for each Union man "killed in violation of the laws of war," was never enforced, and perhaps could not have been enforced given the Confederacy's determination to treat black soldiers as outlaws. Summary executions took place wherever black soldiers fell into rebel hands. The infamous massacre at Fort Pillow may have been the most egregious example of official rebel policy, but it typified what black soldiers could expect from their enemies. As one black soldier declared, "We will ask no quarter, and rest satisfied that we will give none."[20]

The few black soldiers who did end up in Confederate prison camps received the harshest treatment. Rebel guards gave them the worst food and the most repulsive camp jobs, including handling the steady stream of emaciated corpses that the camps produced. Those black prisoners confined in city jails were compelled to regularly clean out the piles of filth that accumulated there. Black prisoners who spoke out of line or did anything to draw attention to themselves, such as search for water, could be shot. One 54th Massachusetts Regiment prisoner confined at Camden, South Carolina, became embroiled in an argument with a white Union deserter. As a result, Dr. R. C. Todd, Mary Todd Lincoln's brother, ordered the black soldier whipped. Another Union prisoner "heard the screams as they lashed him" forty times.[21]

Black soldiers willingly endured all this danger and hardship for the sake of freedom and liberty. But the racial prejudice and hatred that they suffered from the white senior officers and from the Lincoln administration proved more galling than anything they might have expected from rebel troops. Those black soldiers raised by the federal government and organized into the division of United States Colored Troops (USCT) often received inferior weapons (many exploded when fired), poor training, and inadequate medical care, were relegated to fatigue duty, and were presided over by some of the most racist officers in the Union army. Although promised the same pay and benefits as white soldiers, all black soldiers, regardless of rank, received about half the pay that was given to a white private.[22]

For eighteen months many of the black regiments, especially those raised in the North, refused all pay until the government lived up to its promises. Lincoln refused to intervene, and the War Department claimed that all black soldiers were enrolled under provisions of the 1862 Militia Act, which legally determined their inferior pay rate. The pay strike caused endless misery among the soldiers and their families and left many black regiments on the verge of mutiny. The army executed several soldiers for their opposition to unequal pay, and if the War Department had not changed its position, widespread mutiny may well have resulted. For the black soldiers, the issue did not revolve around money, but honor, respect, and recognition of their rights as American citizens. If the soldiers had capitulated on this point, they would have abandoned all claim to equal rights after the war. Thus, the troops determined to endure whatever hardships resulted until they won their point. Their victory, in the late summer and fall of 1864, on the issue of equal pay represented a greater triumph than anything they had achieved on the battlefield.

Valor on the battlefield and defense of their rights as American citizens laid the groundwork for black insistence on equal rights after the war. After the 54th Massachusetts's heroism at Fort Wagner, many saw that the fate of the South was sealed. Much blood and treasure would be lost to finally subdue the South, but few Unionists doubted that victory would ultimately come. To some insightful newspaper editors in the North, once blacks had proved their worth in battle and won the right to serve their country, the next important question the nation had to face was "the position and treatment of the black races." Massachusetts's diminutive *Charlestown Advertiser* cut through the debris of war and racist propaganda to clearly identify the issue facing the country once the fighting came to a halt. "The nation—that is, the individuals who compose the nation—must learn to treat the blacks on the simplest principle of even justice. They are to be treated neither with harshness nor with softness; not as a servile class, not as natural inferiors, not as a degraded race,—but simply as men."[23]

The successful conclusion of the war completely altered the nation's political terrain. To African Americans, adoption of the Thirteenth Amendment to the Constitution meant more than just the end of slavery. They believed that the final destruction of the institution of slavery empowered them as equal citizens, automatically giving them full civil rights, including the right to testify in court, to sign contracts, and most important of all, to vote. Whether white or black, one California black newspaper asserted, each man is "endowed with the requisite qualifications of an elector." Civilians, soldiers, former slaves, and free blacks unanimously demanded the same thing: "We want the privilege of voting."[24]

The soldiers, sailors, and slaves who had helped the North defeat the South and destroy slavery carried the principles of the antislavery movement with them into the war. As the documents in this collection reveal, their cry for freedom did not stop at the slave's door. They fought against slavery *and* racial prejudice. In February 1865 John S. Rock became the first African American to win the right to argue cases before the United States Supreme Court. Only a few years earlier, the Court had declared that Rock, and all other blacks, possessed no rights that white men were bound to respect. The same month, Henry Highland Garnet, who had advocated slave insurrections and African emigration, addressed the United States House of Representatives, standing between portraits of Washington and Lafayette. Until that moment, "a colored man would not be allowed in the Capitol unless he had a dust-pan and broom in his hand."[25] The elation and hope felt real. But the sense of joy that swept through African American communities proved short-lived.

President Lincoln's assassination deeply disturbed and worried blacks, in both the North and the South. While the murder came as no surprise, given the South's hatred for the North's "emancipator," the horrifying act struck African Americans in ways that few whites fully appreciated. The pistol John Wilkes Booth had pointed at Abraham Lincoln, clearly, was aimed at them. By killing Lincoln, African Americans held, the South sought to destroy the idea of "human freedom" for all. Although still critical of Lincoln's reconstruction policies, after the president's death former slaves and free blacks together portrayed the fallen president as their "Moses," their "Father Abraham." The act of uniting behind the image of the "martyred president" represented blacks' most powerful strategy to rally Northern support for black rights, especially in the South, where real threats to national peace remained. Would the new president abandon Lincoln's tentative and forgiving reconstruction policies? Many blacks and whites called for a "liberal but judicious hanging" of rebel leaders to prevent a revival of treason and to guarantee black freedom. African Americans had fought for their race and their country; they deserved full rights, not to "be treated like a dog," as one former soldier lamented.[26]

One black Mississippian wrote to President Andrew Johnson in 1865, reminding him that "we stood by the government when it needed help. Now. . . will it stand by us?" Although a portion of the Republican Party eagerly supported full equality for blacks, the president fought it with unseemly vigor and resolutely opposed black voting rights. To help ensure that African Americans would never gain political dominance in the South, Johnson began a policy of liberal and injudicious pardoning of former Confederates. Why, African Americans wondered? They could not possibly "send worse men to Congress than have been sent from the South during the last fifteen years," as one black newspaper explained.[27] The answer became clear soon enough.

Hopes for a thorough reconstruction of the former Confederate states faded by the 1870s, and whites drove African Americans from any political offices they held. Confederate and Union veterans began publishing their recollections of the war, ensuring that only interpretations that buttressed white social and political priorities gained public acceptance. Having lost the political ground to "redeemers," Democrats, and white supremacists, African Americans refused to cede the cultural ground as well. They used their postwar memoirs, poems, and writings about slavery and the Civil War to celebrate the material, economic, and educational progress of former slaves and to condemn the Ku Klux Klan's atrocities and racial oppression in general.

Susie King Taylor, usually recalled for her work in the 1st South Carolina Volunteers, used the memoir of her days in the war—reprinted in part here—to remind her readers that "All men are born free and equal" in the sight of God. While touring the South, she saw firsthand how whites used their economic power to control black life. Taylor recoiled at the lynchings and murders that whites visited upon blacks with impunity. For speaking to a white man in Shreveport, Louisiana, one hapless black was shot dead in his tracks. "I was surprised at this," she wrote, "but I was told by several white and colored persons that this was a common occurrence, and the persons were never punished if they were white, but no mercy was shown to negroes."[28] Elijah P. Marrs, Louis Hughes, Alexander H. Newton, Frances Ellen Watkins Harper, and countless others who also wrote about their Civil War days recorded similar events. They detailed their escapes from slavery, their combat in the black regiments, the successes they achieved in the postwar years, and the crimes that continued against their brethren. While white authors glorified "lost causes" and military valor, African American writers warned that "the sting of the serpent of slavery" remained "in the hearts of the people." Slavery had died. The convictions that had given it life lived on.[29]

1. Frederick Douglass quoted in Ripley et al., *The Black Abolitionist Papers*, 5:57.

2. Charles B. Dew, *Apostles of Disunion: Southern Secession Commissioners and the Causes of the Civil War* (Charlottesville, VA: University Press of Virginia, 2001).

3. *Address of Hon. W. L. Harris, Commissioner from the State of Mississippi, delivered before the General Assembly of the State of Georgia, on Monday, Dec. 17th, 1860* (Milledgeville, GA, 1860) in Dew, *Apostles of Disunion*, 89.

4. The literature on the coming of the Civil War is voluminous. Some texts that represent excellent starting points for understanding the issues that eventually drove the nation apart are: Allan Nevins, *The Ordeal of the Union*, 8 vols. (New York: Charles Scribner's Sons, 1947–1971); William R. Taylor, *Cavalier & Yankee: The Old South and American National Character* (New York: George Braziller, 1961); David Potter, *The Impending Crisis, 1848–1861* (New York: Harper & Row, 1976); William W. Freehling, *Prelude to Civil War: The Nullification Controversy in South Carolina, 1816–1836* (New York: Harper & Row, 1968); William W. Freehling, *The Road to Disunion: Secessionists at Bay, 1776–1854* (New York: Oxford University Press, 1990); Kenneth M. Stampp, *And the War Came: The North and the Secession Crisis, 1860–1861* (Baton Rouge, LA: Louisiana State University Press, 1970); William J. Cooper. Jr., *The South and the Politics of Slavery, 1828–1856* (Baton Rouge, LA: Louisiana State University Press, 1978); John McCardell, *The Idea of a Southern Nation: Southern Nationalists and Southern Nationalism, 1830–1860* (New York: W. W. Norton, 1979); Eric H. Walther, *The Fire-Eaters* (Baton Rouge, LA: Louisiana State University Press, 1992); Michael A. Morrison, *Slavery and the American West: The Eclipse of Manifest Destiny and the Coming of the Civil War* (Chapel Hill, NC: University of North Carolina Press, 1997); George B. Forgie, *Patricide in the House Divided: A Psychological Interpretation of Lincoln and His Age* (New York: W. W. Norton, 1979).

5. Beer quoted in Daniel Aaron, *The Unwritten War: American Writers and the Civil War* (New York: Oxford University Press, 1973), xiii.

6. Jim Cullen, *The Civil War in Popular Culture: A Reusable Past* (Washington, DC: Smithsonian Institution Press, 1995), 9; Tony Horwitz, *Confederates in the Attic: Dispatches from the Unfinished Civil War* (New York: Pantheon Books, 1998), quoted, 102. Also see the essays by David W. Blight and Kathy Stanton and Stephen Belyea in Martin H. Blatt, Thomas J. Brown, and Donald Yacovone, eds., *Hope & Glory: Essays on the Legacy of the 54th Massachusetts Regiment* (Amherst, MA: University of Massachusetts Press, 2001), 79–93, 253–274. David Blight's *Race and Reunion: The Civil War in American Memory* (Cambridge, MA: Harvard University Press, 2001) is the most trenchant pre-1920 exploration of the battle Americans waged over the memory and meaning of the war.

7. Robert Penn Warren, *The Legacy of the Civil War* (Cambridge, MA: Harvard University Press, 1961), quoted, 3–4, 82; Louis D. Rubin, ed., *I'll Take My Stand: The South and the Agrarian Tradition* (New York, 1930; reprint, Baton Rouge, LA: Louisiana State University Press, 1977), 246–264. For black views on John Brown, see Benjamin Quarles, *Allies for Freedom & Blacks on John Brown* (New York: Oxford University Press, 1974); and Paul Finkelman, ed., *His Soul Goes Marching On: Responses to John Brown and the Harpers Ferry Raid* (Charlottesville, VA: University Press of Virginia, 1995).

8. See for instance, Roy Franklin Nichols, *The Disruption of American Democracy* (Toronto: The Macmillan Co., 1948); Avery Craven, *The Coming of the Civil War* (New York, 1942; reprint, Chicago: University of Chicago Press, 1957); Edmund Wilson, *Patriotic Gore: Studies in the Literature of the American Civil War* (New York: Oxford University Press, 1962).

9. Horwitz, *Confederates in the Attic*, 386.

10. Samuel Sewall, *The Selling of Joseph, 1674–1729* (1700) in M. Halsey Thomas ed., *The Diary of Samuel Sewall*, 2 vols. (New York: Farrar, Straus and Giroux, 1973), 2:1118.

11. Quoted in Forrest G. Wood, *Black Scare: The Racist Response to Emancipation and Reconstruction* (Berkeley, CA: University of California Press, 1970), 43.

12. New York *Weekly Anglo-African*, May 11, 1861.

13. Quoted in Joseph T. Glatthaar, *Forged in Battle: The Civil War Alliance of Black Soldiers and White Officers* (New York: Free Press, 1990), 129–130.

14. Boston *Daily Evening Traveller*, February 11, 1863, quoted; Boston *Daily Advertiser*, February 13, 1863; Boston *Daily Courier*, February 21, 1863.

15. Boston *Daily Courier*, April 11, 1863; New York *Weekly Anglo-African*, April 11, 1863; Randall C. Jimerson, *The Private Civil War: Popular Thought During the Sectional Conflict* (Baton Rouge, LA: Louisiana State University Press, 1988), 93–94.

16. Yacovone, *A Voice of Thunder*, 30–31.
17. *Liberator*, July 31, 1863.
18. William Schouler, *Annual Report of the Adjutant-General . . . 1864* (Boston: State of Massachusetts, 1864), 62–63; Boston *Post*, August 4, 1863; Boston *Evening Transcript*, August 4, 1863; Philadelphia, *The Press*, July 31, 1863; New York *Tribune*, September 8, 1865; Berlin et al., *Freedom: The Black Military Experience*, 12.
19. John Whittier Messer Appleton letterbook, May 30, 1864, p. 231, West Virginia University Library.
20. *Liberator*, August 7, 1863; "Bay State" to Editor, April 10, 1864, New York *Weekly Anglo-African*, May 14, 1864; "A Soldier of the 55th Mass. Vols." to Editor, January 15, 1864, New York *Weekly Anglo-African*, June 30, 1864.
21. Congressional Report on the Treatment of Prisoners of War, in 54th Massachusetts Regiment records, vol. 2, 1008, 1090, Massachusetts Historical Society; Testimony of C. W. Brunt, Captain, 1st New York Cavalry, 54th Massachusetts Regiment records, vol. 3, Massachusetts Historical Society; Jean Baker, *Mary Todd Lincoln: A Biography* (New York: W. W. Norton, 1987), 223.
22. For a good summary of the treatment accorded to black Union soldiers, see Glatthaar, *Forged in Battle*.
23. Charlestown *Advertiser*, June 20, 1863.
24. San Francisco *Elevator*, December 29, 1865; New York *Weekly Anglo-African*, May 27, July 29, December 23, 1865.
25. Eric Foner, *Reconstruction: America's Unfinished Revolution, 1863–1877* (New York: Harper & Row, 1988), 28; New York *Weekly Anglo-African*, February 18, May 27, 1865.
26. New York *Weekly Anglo-African*, April 15, May 6, 13, 18, June 24, 1865.
27. Foner, *Reconstruction*, 115; San Francisco *Elevator*, June 2, 1865; New York *Weekly Anglo-African*, September 19, 1863.
28. Susie King Taylor, *Reminiscences of My Life in Camp with the 33rd United States Colored Troops Late 1st S.C. Volunteers* (Boston: by the Author, 1902), 65–66, 69–73.
29. New Orleans *Black Republican*, April 15, 1865.

PART I

Freedom's Battlefield

1

What Is at Stake: Black Abolitionism, Politics, and Lincoln's Election

"They differ only in the method"
Thomas Hamilton
MARCH 17, 1860

American politics offered few options to African Americans. Most blacks could not vote, and in some states, such as Pennsylvania, where they had exercised the franchise, whites took the privilege away from them. In New York, where the great journalists Thomas and Robert Hamilton spent their lives, property qualifications reduced the number of voting blacks. Despite these restrictions, African Americans took a keen interest in politics and participated wherever they could, even if that participation was restricted to the local level. They followed national politics closely and were careful to note how the principles and practices of the Democrats and Republicans affected black rights and the institution of slavery. Two decades of antislavery politics had taught blacks that they could not place their trust in a political party. Party principles and platforms certainly mattered, but the ability to advance abolitionism and equality mattered more. While black leaders like Thomas Hamilton might find some satisfaction in the rise of third party antislavery politics and be heartened by white political abolitionists such as Joshua Giddings in the House of Representatives or Charles Sumner in the Senate, in 1860 the progressive few were vastly outweighed by the intolerant many. The Democratic Party offered nothing for African Americans; it represented the slave power of the South and the bitterest racial prejudice of the North. The new Republican Party convinced some black leaders that it embodied the progressive force in the nation and held out the best "practical" hope of becoming a bulwark against the institution of slavery. But its racist campaigns, its insistence on enforcing the Fugitive Slave Law, its preference for colonizing blacks, and its limited commitment to opposing only the spread of slavery, proved inadequate for the hour. Only three years earlier, the Supreme Court of the United States had ruled that black men had no rights that whites were bound to respect. Republican states like Illinois offered no rights to blacks, not even to testify in court. What could African Americans expect from a man like Lincoln, who publicly declared his belief that blacks could never be the equal of whites? To many, his victory in the fall elections represented nothing more than the "fag end of a series of pro-slavery administrations."

Thomas Hamilton (1823–1865), son of William Hamilton (who believed he descended from Alexander Hamilton), began his career in reform and antislavery journalism in 1837, when he worked for the *Colored American.* He also worked for a variety of other papers before establishing his first newspaper, the *People's Press,* in 1841. One of New York's most important black leaders, he spoke out for temperance, black suffrage, equal rights, and resistence to the Fugitive Slave Law. He and his brother Robert published the *Anglo-African Magazine* and the New York *Weekly Anglo-African,* the leading black newspaper of the Civil War era, which ran from 1859 to the close of 1865. While Hamilton's views were decidedly pessimistic, many agreed with him that in 1860, "We have no hope from either [Democrats or Republicans] as political parties." Ripley et al., *The Black Abolitionist Papers,* 3:42–54, 359, 5:27–28; Yacovone, *Voice of Thunder,* 12–13.

THE TWO GREAT POLITICAL PARTIES

THE TWO GREAT POLITICAL parties separate at an angle of two roads, that they may meet eventually at the same goal. They both entertain the same ideas, and both carry the same burdens. They differ only in regard to the way they shall go, and the method of procedure. We, the colored people of this country, free and enslaved, who constitute the burthen that so heavily bears down both of these parties—we, who constitute their chief concern, their chief thought—we, who cause all their discord, and all their dissentions, and all their hates, and all their bitter prejudices—we, say both of these religious political parties, we, the blacks, must, in some form or other, be sacrificed to save themselves and the country—to save the country intact for the white race.

The Democratic party would make the white man the master and the black man the slave, and have them thus together occupy every foot of the American soil. Believing in the potency of what they term the superior race, they hold that no detriment can come to the Republic by the spread of the blacks in a state of servitude on this continent; that with proper treatment and shackles upon him, proper terrors over him, and vigorous operations for the obliteration of his mind, if he have any—that with these, and whatever else will brutify him, he can be kept in sufficient subjection to be wholly out of the pale of danger to the Republic; that he can never be so much as a consideration in any calculation of imminence to the government. On the contrary, it is held by this party that his presence, under these restrictions, is of incalculable benefit to the nation—the chief instrument in the development of her resources, and the cornerstone of her liberties. What the Democratic party complains of is that the Republican party—not for the negro's, but for their own political advancement—advocate the necessity for a check upon the spread of the blacks—not as free, but in chain, not as men, but as slaves; for in this—that the blacks, as free men, shall have neither their rights, footing, nor anything else, in common with the whites, in the land—both parties are agreed; and in looking at matters as they present themselves to us at this moment, we are not sure that if any of the many withheld rights were to be secured to us, they would not come from the Democratic side after all, notwithstanding the great excesses their leaders frequently carry them into. We mean the great body, acting, as it will some day, independent from the party leaders. The great masses, if left to themselves to act up to their true instincts, would always do much better in matters involving right and wrong than they do when operated upon by what are generally supposed to be intelligent leaders. These are generally great demagogues or great conservatives, neither of which have done the world any positive good. Whatever of worth it receives from them is the result of their negative position.

The Republican party today, though we believe in the minority, being the most intelligent, contains by far the greatest number of these two classes of men, and hence, though with larger professions for humanity, is by far its most dangerous enemy. Under the guise of humanity, they do and say many things—as, for example, they oppose the reopening of the slave trade. They would fain make the world believe it to be a movement of humanity; and yet the world too plainly sees that it is but a stroke of policy to check the spread, growth, and strength of the black masses on this continent. They oppose the progress of slavery in the territories, and would cry humanity to the world; but the world has already seen that it is but the same black masses looming up, huge, grim, and threatening, before this Republican party, and hence their opposition. Their opposition to slavery means opposition to the black man—nothing else. Where it is clearly in their power to do anything for the oppressed colored man, why then they are too nice, too conservative, to do it. They find, too often, a way to slip round it—find a method how not to do it. If too hard pressed or fairly cornered by the opposite party, then it is they go beyond said opposite party in their manifestations of hatred and contempt for the black man and his rights.

Such is the position of the two parties today, and it is yet to be seen whither they will drive in the political storm they are creating, and which is now raging round them. In their desire to "hem in" and crush out the black man, they form a perfect equation. They differ only in the method. We have no hope from either as political parties. We must rely on ourselves, the righteousness of our cause, and the advance of just sentiments among the great masses of the Republican people, be they Republicans or Democrats. These masses we must teach that it will not do for them to believe nor yet act upon the declaration of their party leaders that we are a naturally low and degraded race, and unfit to have or enjoy liberty and the rights of men and citizens, and hence must be crushed out of the land. We must teach these masses that all this is a fabrication, a great political lie, an abominable injustice to an outraged but honest and determined people, who cannot be crushed out—a people outraged by overpowering brute force, and then declared unfit to come within the pale of civilization. All this is our work, and rising by all the forces within our grasp high above the chicanery and vulgar policies of the day, we must perform fully and well our duty in these respects.

New York *Weekly Anglo-African*, March 17, 1860.

"every colored man in the community is an anti-slavery speech"
H. Ford Douglas
OCTOBER 6, 1860

H. Ford Douglas (1831–1865) escaped from slavery in 1846. He fled Virginia for the relative safety of Cleveland, Ohio. He became a barber and provided himself an education, becoming remarkably conversant in the Bible, history, classical literature, and the popular literature of the day. He quickly became a force in the Ohio black community. After the adoption of the Fugitive Slave Law he moved to Chicago, participated in various black state and national conventions, and organized protests against the state's discriminatory laws. During the 1860 political campaign Douglas lectured throughout the North and took the opportunity to voice his hatred of slavery and his willingness to use any means necessary to destroy it.

In his speech before an antislavery gathering in Salem, Ohio, Douglas, like Hamilton, denounced the major American political parties as subservient to the slave power and enemies of blacks. Douglas took a "political purist" position, not caring for parties but insisting that those who vote should be voting only for true antislavery men—not just the best of a bad lot. If American politics had sunk to new depths, Douglas believed that the voters ultimately bore responsibility for it. Nevertheless, he recognized that either Abraham Lincoln or Stephen A. Douglas would become president. Rethinking his previous cynical preference, he now determined that Lincoln's election would at least bring the antislavery element of the party into prominence. Perhaps in time that element would grow. In this, H. Ford Douglas represented many African Americans who clearly saw the shortcomings of the Republican party, but feared the Democrats even more. Douglas's political ambivalence drew him toward John Brown. While Douglas would not directly praise Brown's attack on Harpers Ferry, he saw a purity in Brown's motives that placed him on the same level as the Founding Fathers. "If Washington and his associates of the Revolution were right,

so was John Brown." American politics provided men like Douglas with
few alternatives and even fewer heroes. Ultimately, Douglas and Hamilton voiced the same sentiment: we must rely on ourselves. One can
understand, then, why Douglas became one of the first African Americans to serve in the army, enlisting in 1862 and ironically becoming one
of the few blacks to serve in a white regiment. Ripley, et al., *The Black
Abolitionist Papers*, 4:78–79.

MR. CHAIRMAN:[1]

The difference between my distinguished namesake [Stephen A.
Douglas], to whom you have referred, and myself, is this. He is seeking
his mother; I am not. I feel but little, just now, like making a speech.
We have just been listening to the very able report of your Executive
Committee, and I fear I can add nothing to the interest of the occasion
by any poor words that I may utter.

We have listened to a recital of the imminent dangers which
threaten the liberties of the people; and I am sure none of us can go away
from this meeting without feeling that we all have much to do—that
our mission is not fulfilled till slavery shall cease to exist in every portion of our widely extended country.

Thirty-five years ago, when the abolitionists began their labor, they
supposed all that was necessary was to let the people know the true
character of slavery—to hold the hateful system up to the scorn and indignation of the world, and the work would be done. But we have lived
to learn that slavery is no weak and impotent thing, but a giant power,
so fortified by potent influences, social, political and religious, that it
can be rooted out only by uncompromising and untiring effort. We have
proved it true, as was said by Benjamin Franklin, that "a nation may lose
its liberty in a day and be a century in finding it out." When the people
of this country consented to a union with slaveholders—when they
consented to strike out, at the bidding of South Carolina, from the original draft of the Declaration of Independence, the clause condemning
the King of Great Britain for bringing Africans into this land, and
dooming them to slavery—at that moment they sold their own liberties. If there was ever any doubt of this, we can doubt it no longer, now
that the rights of the white man, as well as the black, are so ruthlessly
stricken down.

I do not mean to assert, at present, that the Constitution of the United States is not susceptible of an anti-slavery interpretation. I believe if I was a Supreme judge, and there was in the country a public sentiment that would sustain me in it, I would find no difficulty in construing that instrument in favor of the freedom of all men. But that is not now the question. You have decided upon the character of the Constitution, and I must accept your own interpretation; and with that rendering, I repudiate the instrument, and the government and the institutions which it is made to sustain.[2] I will not stand connected with a government that steals away the black man's liberties, that has corrupted our best political leaders, by leading them to the support of the greatest crimes, the vilest of all institutions. Even William H. Seward has lately declared that this is to be the white man's government. Ten years ago he would have been thought incapable of such a declaration; but such is the influence of slavery.[3] Hence the necessity of attacking the system now, in a deadly warfare; otherwise, our people will be—if they are not now—wholly and hopelessly lost.

Yes! we must do as John Brown[4] did, not necessarily in the *way* he did it, but we must labor with the sure determination to effect, in some way, the complete overthrow of slavery. I am not an advocate for insurrection; I believe the world must be educated into something better and higher than this before we can have perfect freedom, either for the black man or the white. In the present moral condition of the people, no true liberty can be established, either by fighting slavery down, or by voting it down. Hence our object is not to put anybody into office, as a means of abolishing slavery, or to keep anybody out. I care not for the success or defeat of any party, so far as the interests of freedom are concerned. The failure or success of any of the present political parties can neither injure nor aid us. Our business must be to educate the people to the highest sentiment that shall make them recognize the white man, the black man, the red man, *all* men, to the rights of manhood. There is not to be, as your noblest statesman seems to imagine, a government for the *white* man alone. What merit is there in your boasted liberty or the christianity you profess to adopt, unless they recognize the brotherhood of all men, in all time? Till we have protected the rights of all, we have secured the liberties of none—that government is no government which fails to protect the freedom of its meanest subject. I will put the rights of the meanest slave against the greatest government of the world—for liberty is more than any institution, or any government.

But the idea that man is superior to institutions finds no favor in this country. The principles of justice are forgotten. The question is not what is right; but rather, "how shall we accomplish our selfish ends?" And all parties make success a foregone conclusion. Under no circumstances must the government be endangered, to give the black man his rights; yet, let me tell you, my liberty is more to me, and more in fact, than all the glory of your government. I have it from God, and you have no more right to compromise my freedom for the sake of the success of your party, than you have to take my life. For what is my life worth to me, when you take away all that makes it worth the living?

As I said I am not advocate for revolution. I would only resort to it after all other means have failed. I believe in the right of self-defence; it was given us at the creation. I believe it a duty, as well as a right, and no man has a *right* to become a slave for a single hour, if by defending himself he can prevent it. If you can take away the freedom of one man, you strike at the liberty of all. The same means required to prepare the white man for enslaving the black, prepares the black man to enslave the white; and the master and the slave are alike in chains. "Man never fastens a chain upon the limbs of a slave, but God, in his divine justice, fastens the other end around his own neck."[5]

So in this country we have four political parties, all talking of liberty, yet all in chains! Stephen A. Douglas said, yesterday, at Cleveland, that he would stop this slavery agitation; he would put the slave question outside of Congress. They had nothing to do with it, and he did not care whether slavery was voted up or voted down.[6] He did not know, when he thus sneered at liberty, that he was himself a slave! So of W. H. Seward; when he talks of a government of white men, he may think he is free, but he is not, and cannot be. And when Abraham Lincoln opposes the rights of the free colored people, even in his own state—when he shuts them out from the courts of justice, he does not know that he makes himself a slave.[7] When you have made me a slave, no white man is free. Strike down my liberty, if you will, but when you do it, you can no longer enjoy your own.

Hence this struggle interests not one class alone, but all classes of the people. While the colored people are bowed down by slavery, they can accomplish nothing great or noble; nor can you, while you oppress

them. They are men as you are, demoralized by slavery. Often they oppose anti-slavery lectures, just as you do. I find many of them in New
York and New England opposing anti-slavery. All classes are alike degraded, and if anything is done for freedom, we must make this question
of slavery, not a colored question, but a white question as well. Thus
you see where the Republican party stands when it calls itself the white
man's party—it stands arrayed against the freedom of all, white or black.
I have said sometimes, in view of the fact that the Republican party fell
so far short of its professions, and was deceiving so many honest anti-
slavery men, that I would rather hear of its defeat than of its success. I
have said I would rather Douglas would be elected President of the
United States than Lincoln. But I have changed my feelings on that
matter; and now my choice would be to see Douglas and his party, with
all their arrogance and impudence, overthrown, and Lincoln elected,
rather than any other of the candidates. Not that I suppose there is any
essential difference between the two men, or would be any in their action. But there is in the Republican party a strong anti-slavery element.
And though the party will do nothing for freedom now, that element
will increase; and before long—I trust—springing up from the ruins of
the Republican party will come a great anti-slavery party that will be
true to freedom, and recognize the rights of all men. But while I thus declare my desire to see the Republican party succeed, I must say that as
a party, I regard it false to freedom and in no higher position than the
Democratic party. And in its pres[ent] position it can do nothing for the
salvation of the nation, notwithstanding the noble anti-slavery men
who are in it. For God has made it certain that the truth cannot be advanced by the telling of lies. I believe that in giving the enemy the one
half, you cannot save the other; for as somebody has said, every compromise with the devil weakens the man that makes it.

The Republicans say they are bringing the Government back to the
policies of the fathers. I do not desire to do this; the policy of the fathers
was not uncompromising opposition to oppression; and nothing less
than a position far higher than they occupied will ever make us worthy
of the name of freemen. If we cannot succeed by the force of ideas, then
I go for a policy far different from that of the fathers, if you refer to their
policy in the management of the government; for in that case this
blood-stained despotism must be overthrown. But all peaceful means
must first be exhausted. And for one, though I cannot accomplish what

many others can, I am disposed to do everything I can by moral and pacific means to educate the people into true ideas of their duty—to eradicate the mean spirit of selfishness that makes almost everyone in the country look upon himself, his color, his race, as alone worthy of consideration.

This is the most wicked and the meanest kind of infidelity; yet it is in all your churches, even your professors of religion do not know the A B C of the Bible, or of christianity, do not know that God is no respecter of persons, and has made of one blood all the nations of man, do not know that colored men have the rights of humanity. They condemn John Brown as the vilest of criminals, yet laud the Revolutionary fathers for doing what John did. If Washington and his associates of the Revolution were right, so was John Brown. I know that Henry Ward Beecher preached a sermon in which he argued that John Brown was in the wrong, in doing as he did, because there was no prospect of success; thus making success the test of the matter.[8] But if John Brown was wrong in defeat, would he have been right in success? If our Revolutionary fathers had failed, would they, therefore, have been the greatest of criminals?

What the age wants is a confidence in justice and a determination to do it. We are in fellowship with slaveholders, and so long as we remain in this position we are no better than they. The receiver is as bad as the thief. When you consent to carry out the fugitive slave law, you do as badly as to hold slaves. What difference does it make to me whether you hold me in bondage yourself, or deliver me up to the man who will. Anthony Burns[9] could feel as much respect—and far more—for his master, than for those Boston minions of slavery who gave him up to bondage. Yet Abraham Lincoln will carry out the fugitive slave law, and you will carry him into office! He will be the bloodhound to catch the slave, and send him back to his life of toil, and you by sustaining him, will make yourselves as guilty as he. I want to see the day when no slaveholder will dare to come here for his slave. But that day cannot come so long as you are willing to exalt to the presidency men who endorse the Dred Scott decision.[10] And all your Presidential candidates do this. I know this has been denied of the Republican candidate. But does anyone who hears me deny that Abraham Lincoln endorses the worst features of that infamous decision, "that the black man has no rights which the white man is bound to respect"? If anyone denies or doubts it, let him speak. In the state of Illinois, I cannot testify against a white man in any court of justice. Any villain may enter my house at Chicago and outrage my family, and unless a white man stands by to see it done, I have no redress. Now, I went to Abraham Lincoln, personally, with a petition for the repeal of this infamous law, and asked him to sign it, and he refused to do it. I went also to Lyman Trumbull,[11] with the same petition, and he also refused; and he told me, if I did not like the laws of Illinois, I had better leave the State! This is the doctrine of the Dred Scott decision in its most odious form. It is declaring, not only in words, but in action, the infamous principle that colored people have no rights which you are bound to respect. And yet, you tell me, you are anti-slavery men, while you support such men as these for the highest offices of the nation! Surely, you will not expect me to regard you as in favor of freedom, when you will not recognize me as a free man, or protect me on your own soil. Your anti-slavery should begin at home, or it is not to be trusted. There is too much of this hypocritical abolitionism. You pro-fess to be in favor of freedom, and then allow the slaveholder to come among you and carry away your citizens. You allow it, and you agree to it, if you do not *approve* it, and you have no right thus to sacrifice prin-ciple and practice, to save any political party. To elevate men to office is not an object for which a man should barter away his manhood. Let us act nobly and justly—do right, and leave the consequences to God.

But you may inquire, who shall we vote for? I answer, vote for an anti-slavery man, or do not vote at all. God put you here to do your duty and be true to your own souls. He never commanded you to tell a lie, and violate principle, even to break the fetters from the slave. And you can-not break the slave's fetters by thus trampling on every righteous prin-ciple. You gain no power for good by sacrificing principles to gain num-bers. God and one true man, are in a majority over all the hosts of error and falsehood; and we never can, as anti-slavery men, do the work we have to do, till we make our own hands clean.

Garrisonians have been denounced as disorganizers, and the enemies of all Government.[12] But what is the object of Government? Is it to make money—the rich richer and the poor poorer? Is it merely to raise wheat and corn and rye? No; it is to make men; and if it fails in this—as your government has done—it fails in everything and is no govern-ment. Man, as I have said, is above and will survive all governments. Garrisonians desire to be true to humanity; and will respect no government that tramples upon it. But you are sacrificing *man* to the government, humanity to success. An ancient king decreed that all the male children born in his kingdom should die to save his government; and you are following his example—sacrificing a whole race to sustain an iniquitous tyranny. And this nation should go away to Judea and dig up the rotten bones of Herod, and should seek for the bones of Captain Kidd the pirate, collect them together and build monuments over them, instead of seeking for the remains of Sir John Franklin in the frozen regions.[13] Why should you not meet together to glorify the bloody Herod and the pirate Kidd? You have dethroned God, and enthroned the devil, and why not go to work and have a devilish good time.

Three hundred years ago, your English ancestors were opposed by the bloody Stuarts. You said the king had no right to violate your rights and trample on all law and justice. Charles the First replied that he would have his will, that the king could do no wrong. So you beheaded Charles the First and established the government of 1678. Afterward your fathers came to New England, and again made battle against the despotism of these same despotic kings of England. And you rose up against the power of George III and established the government of 1776. Then you thought you had done something worthy of the friends of freedom. But what has been the result? You have today Freedom only in name. You are no better than the worst governments of the Old World. I would rather live in the most tyrannical government in Europe, so far as freedom is concerned, than in yours, which atheistically declares itself to be the white man's country, and has not risen above the lowest despotism. You have no true ideas of government or of law. No conception, with all your boasts, of the true ideas of liberty.

I do not come among you, as a colored man, to ask any special favor at the hands of the white people; I ask only that my manhood be recognized before the law—only that you shall repeal your unjust enactments against the colored race. I do not ask you to invite me into your parlors; I ask not to be recognized, socially, by any man in the world. We are not demanding social equality. All we ask is the same rights, legally, as yourselves, and to grant this is as necessary to your own well-being as to ours. When our rights are recognized, and let our merits decide the rest.

I see colored men before me; and I would say to them, that every colored man in the community is an anti-slavery speech. Let us try to do our duty, and so conduct ourselves as to convince the white man that we are capable of liberty. Let us, by improving the few opportunities we have, show ourselves worthy of the rights we demand, and so live and act as to leave the world better than we found it.

Salem, Ohio, *Anti-Slavery Bugle*, October 6, 1860.

---

1. Marius Robinson, a member of the Western Anti-Slavery Society, edited the organization's newspaper, the *Anti-Slavery Bugle*. Ripley et al., *The Black Abolitionist Papers*, 4:185.

2. Many reformers—especially those allied with William Lloyd Garrison—repudiated the Constitution and the Founding Fathers as fatally stained by slavery. Between 1840 and the beginning of the Civil War, the abolitionist community bitterly divided over the question of slavery and the Constitution, with many refusing to relinquish an antislavery interpretation of the document. Most black abolitionists refused to go as far as Garrison and reject the constitution as a "covenant with death and an agreement with hell." Their quest for equal rights and the vote, ultimately, was founded on a progressive interpretation of the nation's founding document. William M. Wiecek, *The Sources of Antislavery Constitutionalism in America, 1760–1848* (Ithaca, NY: Cornell University Press, 1977).

3. William H. Seward (1801–1872), Lincoln's secretary of state, had been governor of New York and a U.S. senator. While governor, Seward won the admiration of African Americans for his support of their civil rights and opposition to the Fugitive Slave Law. But during the 1860 campaign, he and many other Republicans sought to distance themselves from abolitionists and blacks by appealing to white voters' racial prejudice. Faust, *Historical Times Illustrated Encyclopedia of the Civil War*, 668–669; James M. McPherson, *The Struggle for Equality: Abolitionists and the Negro in the Civil War and Reconstruction* (Princeton, NJ: Princeton University Press, 1964), 24–25.

4. John Brown (1800–1859) led his band of twenty-one warriors, including five African Americans, against the federal arsenal at Harpers Ferry, Virginia, on October 16, 1859. His attempt at freeing slaves ended on the gallows on December 2. Benjamin Quarles, *Allies for Freedom: Blacks and John Brown* (New York: Oxford University Press, 1974).

5. Paraphrased from Ralph Waldo Emerson, "Compensation," in *Essays: First Series* (1841), "If you put a chain around the neck of a slave, the other end fastens itself around your own." Brooks Atkinson, ed., *The Selected Writings of Ralph Waldo Emerson* (New York: The Modern Library, 1968), 179.

6. Stephen A. Douglas (1813–1861), on September 22, 1860, repeated his position in the famed debates with Lincoln in the 1858 Illinois senatorial campaign that "popular sovereignty"—not politicians—should decide the status of slavery in the territories. Robert W. Johannsen, *Stephen A. Douglas* (New York: Oxford University Press, 1973), 795; Harry Jaffa, *Crisis of the House Divided: An Interpretation of the Issues in the Lincoln–Douglas Debates* (Chicago: University of Chicago Press, 1982).

7. Abraham Lincoln (1809–1865) believed in the racial inferiority of African Americans and, thus, considered them unqualified to serve as witnesses or jurors in a court, to vote or hold elected office, or to intermarry with whites: "I will say in addition to this that there is a physical difference between the white and black races which I believe will for ever forbid the two races living together on terms of social and political equality." McPherson, *The Struggle for Equality*, 23–24.

8. Henry Ward Beecher (1813–1887) served as pastor of New York City's Plymouth Congregational Church, was an ardent abolitionist, and after the Civil War became the nation's most popular preacher. After the Harpers Ferry raid and again after Brown's execution, Beecher expressed his admiration for Brown's bravery, but deplored his actions and even paradoxically declared that the slave must be "an obedient servant." Milton Rugoff, *The Beechers: An American Family in the Nineteenth Century* (New York: Harper & Row, 1981), 383–384.

9. Anthony Burns (1834–1862) fled from his Virginia owners in February 1854. He worked as a cook and in a clothing store until his former owner seized him in March under the 1850 Fugitive Slave Law. Boston abolitionists led a violent attempt to free him but failed, and Burns was returned to slavery. Members of Boston's Twelfth Baptist Church purchased Burns's freedom, and a sponsor supported his studies at Oberlin College and the Fairmont Theological Seminary near Cincinnati. Burns later moved to Canada and served in the ministry there until his death. Ripley et al, *Black Abolitionist Papers*, 4:397; Albert J. Von Frank, *The Trials of Anthony Burns: Freedom and Slavery in Emerson's Boston* (Cambridge, MA: Harvard University Press, 1998).

10. In the Supreme Court's most notorious decision, *Dred Scott v. Sandford* (1857), Chief Justice Roger B. Taney declared that the due process clause of the Constitution's Fifth Amendment protected slavery, and he denied Congress's right to determine the fate of slavery in the territories. Equally important, and in words that would be repeated derisively for years to come, Taney declared that African Americans had no rights "which a white man was bound to respect." Don Fehrenbacher, *The Dred Scott Case:*

Its Significance in Law and Politics (New York: Oxford University Press, 1978).

11. Lyman Trumbull (1813–1896), U.S. senator from Illinois, firmed opposed slavery but preferred that all blacks be removed from the United States. Illinois sought to prevent free blacks from settling in the state, barred racial intermarriage, restricted the testimony of blacks in court, and in 1862, by a 5 to 1 majority, continued the state's ban on black suffrage and office holding. Faust, *Historical Times Illustrated Encyclopedia of the Civil War*, 763–764; V. Jacque Voegeli, *Free But Not Equal: The Midwest and the Negro during the Civil War* (Chicago: University of Chicago Press, 1967), 18–19, 23–24, 27, 170, 178.

12. William Lloyd Garrison (1805–1879), leader of the most radical antislavery reformers, espoused a form of Christian nonresistance that rejected government as a form of coercion designed to support slavery and immorality and was, thus, illegitimate. Lewis Perry, *Radical Abolitionism: Anarchy and the Government of God in Antislavery Thought* (Ithaca, NY: Cornell University Press, 1973).

13. Sir John Franklin (1786–1847), an English explorer, led a disastrous expedition to the Arctic in 1846–1847.

2

Where We Stand

"revolutions never go backward"
Frederick Douglass
MAY 5, 1861

No one brought more authority to the antislavery lecture platform than Frederick Douglass (1818–1895). A former slave and freedom's most eloquent spokesman, Douglass had no peer. Through twenty years of speeches, letters, and three different newspapers, Douglass warned the nation against the evils of slavery and racial hatred. While many important and articulate black leaders emerged during the thirty years before the Civil War, none could rival Douglass's influence. When the war began in the spring of 1861, he sought to ensure that the North correctly understood the causes of the conflict that had engulfed the nation. Not federalism, not sectional power, not land, and certainly not tariffs caused the horrors that had only just begun. Let there be no mistake, Douglass declared, "For all the woes of this terrible civil war, we have to thank the foul slave system. Treason, rebellion, and every abomination, spring out of its pestilential atmosphere, like weeds from a dunghill, and but for the existence of slavery, this country would to-day be enjoying all the blessings of peace and security. . . ."

"We want Nat Turner—not speeches; Denmark Vesey—not resolutions; John Brown—not meetings," exclaimed black abolitionists. The war seized the imaginations of African Americans in the North and brought hope to the slaves of the South. Although few whites in the North believed that the conflict would last for long, and in 1861 even fewer fought to end slavery, Douglass confidently predicted the outcome. The real causes of the war propelled the combatants into the future and the result, to Douglass, was inevitable. "It will go on," he told the packed crowd at the Spring Street African Methodist Episcopal Zion Church (AMEZ Church) in his home of Rochester, New York, on May 5, 1861. "It cannot stop." A whirlpool had begun that would drag slavery down. Since the early days of the republic, African Americans had pleaded for the end of slavery; they had tried every means, made every argument, but still the nation would not listen. John Brown had given them hope, but now the South itself was bringing on the only conditions that would lead to slavery's demise: war. Moreover, Douglass predicted, that war would not end until "the iron arm of the black man" was called into service. New York *Weekly Anglo-African*, April 27, 1861; John Blassingame et al., eds., *The Frederick Douglass Papers*, series I, *Speeches, Debates, and Interviews* (New Haven, CT: Yale University Press, 1985), 3:428.

I PROPOSE AGAIN TO throw out a few thoughts on the great crisis through which the country is now passing. On many accounts it would be pleasant to me to vary the character of these Sunday afternoon lectures; but I find it impossible to do so at present. Like the rod of Moses which swallowed up all the petty creations of the Eastern magicians, the awful and sublime crisis in our national affairs, swallows up all other subjects. I must either speak of that which engages all minds and fills all hearts at this moment, or speak as one who beateth the air. The solemn departure of the troops from this city only a few days ago, composed of the sons, brothers, husbands and fathers of some, perhaps, of those who hear me, is fitted to bring this subject before us more impressively than anything else. That departure was a thrilling spectacle. I witnessed it with feelings that I cannot describe. And I saw the tears, and heard the mournful sobs of mothers, as they parted from their sons; wives, as they parted from their husbands; sisters, as they parted from their brothers, my very soul said in the depths of its bitterness, let Slavery, the guilty cause of all this sorrow and sighing, be accursed and destroyed forever—and so I say to-day.

For all the woes of this terrible civil war, we have to thank the foul slave system. Treason, rebellion, and every abomination, spring out of its pestilential atmosphere, like weeds from a dunghill, and but for the existence of slavery, this country would to-day be enjoying all the blessings of peace and security, and the hearts of your wives and daughters would not be tossed with the bitter anguish which now rends them. I

wish the cause of your national troubles, which has thus snatched your
own flesh and blood from you to be exposed to all the dangers, horrors
and hardships of civil war, to be constantly borne in mind.

It is not the sturdy farmer of the west, who tills his broad acres with
his own hard but honest hands, who eats his bread in the sweat of his
own honest brow, that has plotted and conspired for the overthrow of
this Government. It is not the skilful mechanic of New England, who
by his daily toil supports his wife and children by his skill and industry,
that has risen against the peace and safety of the Republic. It is not the
hardy laborer of the North, nor of the South, who has treacherously
conceived this hell-black conspiracy to destroy the Government and
the Liberties of the American people. No! Oh, no! We owe our present
calamity to the existence among us of a privileged class, who are permitted to live by stealing. We owe it to the existence of a set of respectable robbers and murderers, who work their fellow men like beasts
of burden, and keep back their wages by fraud.

It was once a favorite maxim of Daniel O'Connell,[1] "that England's
extremity was Ireland's opportunity." Another proverb, somewhat trite,
is, that when "rogues fall out, honest men get their rights." To both sayings there have been many exceptions, and there will be many more.

The Irish people could never be brought to adopt or to act upon
O'Connell's maxim, and there have been many quarrels among dishonest men, which have only ended in further compacts and combina-
tions of dishonesty. One thing, however, I think we may all venture to
assert, the present war between slaveholding traitors and the legitimate
American Government, affords much rational ground for the hope of
the abolition of slavery.

A favorite maxim among the slaveholders a few years ago, was that
revolutions never go backward. They quote this saying with enthusiastic exultation. No doubt while doing so, the stately halls of Washington flit before them, and they see in the not distant future, Jeff. Davis
and his brother traitors, the masters of the great American government,
and enjoying all the luxury, grandeur and magnificence of the national
capital.

This weapon is two-edged. It cuts both ways. It is as good for one section, as for the other. If revolutions never go backward, they are of
course as likely to go forward in one section as the other—in the North,
as in the South. The slaveholders have resolved to battle for slavery,

and the people of the Free States will yet come forth to battle for freedom. The end is clearly foreshadowed.

Freedom's battle once begun,
Bequeathed from bleeding sire to son,
Tho' baffled oft is ever won.[2]

At present, as all know, the North only strikes for government, as against anarchy. She strikes only for loyalty, as against treason and rebellion. The slaveholders strike for absolute independence, and total separation. The North strikes for the absolute supremacy of the Constitution, the Union, and the laws. Her loyal sons have buckled on their armor, with the full determination that not one of the thirty-four stars shall fall from the blue ground of our national flag.

But this is, after all, but the surface of this war. It will, and must, if continued, take on a broader margin. The law of its life is grown. The rallying cry of the North now is: "Down with treason, down with secession, down with rebellion." And until this trio of social monsters are completely crushed out, the war is not to cease. Herein is my hope for the slave. The war cannot cease; the battle must go on. The Government must die in the first century of its existence, or it must now strike a blow which shall set it in safety for centuries to come. For let this rebellion be subdued, let the chief conspirators and traitors be hanged, or made to flee the country, let the country, let the Government in this instance fully assert its power, and the lesson will last for ages.

It was said that the first gun fired at Bunker Hill, was heard round the world. The first gun which was fired upon Sumter, will be heard ringing through the dome of a thousand years, as a warning to rebels and traitors.

It is not more true, that this irrepressible conflict must go on, until one of the parties to it is ground to powder, than it is, that the elements that enter into it, will widen and deepen the longer it lasts.

What would have been gladly accepted by the Government at Washington, one little month ago, would be rejected with scorn to-day; and what might possibly be accepted to-day, will a few weeks hence, be looked upon as a mockery and insult.

Already, there is a visible change in the bearing of the Government at Washington. Two weeks ago, they asked Baltimore to graciously grant permission to American soldiers to pass through her streets to defend and protect the American capital. Now they take possession, not only of Baltimore, and subject her to a rigorous blockade, but take possession of any and every part of the State, they have any use for.[3] Two weeks ago, the President was concerned for the safety of his soldiers. It will not be long before he will be concerned for the safety of the now persecuted loyal men and women in the State of Maryland. The President will, by and by, see that the United States Congress gives him the right, and makes it his duty to take care that none are deprived of life or liberty, without due process of law; and that the citizens of each State shall enjoy all the rights and immunities of citizens of the several States. The first Proclamation of Mr. Lincoln was received with derision at the South. It is said that the cabinet of Jeff. Davis read it amid roars of laughter. They were intoxicated with their victory at Charleston. "Whom the Gods would destroy, they first make mad."[4]

Nero fiddled while Rome was on fire, and men have danced over the jaws of an earthquake. But those who have been merry in the morning have wept and howled in the evening.

This conflict can never be reduced to narrower limits than now by either party. It can be extended, and probably will be extended, but it cannot be limited. Neither party can limit the issues involved in it. They would not if they could, and they could not if they would.

The only thing that could have prevented or postponed this mighty conflict was compromise. But now this has entirely vanished from the field of possibilities, and the work must go on. The leaders of secession first asked the right of States to secede—to go out in peace; next it seized and appropriated arsenals; next it sent traitorous emissaries to corrupt the loyal States, and to organize treason within their borders; next it fired on the American Flag; next it rained balls and bombshells upon Sumter; next it collected an army to capture all the national defences within one section of the Confederacy; and next it marched its army for the destruction of the National Capital.

It will go on. It cannot stop. It has at last got on the much coveted seven mile boots. It is in the nature of things to go on. One success begets another. Once on the outer circle of the whirlpool, you are sure of being drawn in due time to the centre. The slaveholding rebels can stop their war upon the Government only when their men and money have gone. They must be starved out, broken down, overpowered and totally exhausted, before they can consent, after their high sounding threat, to sue for peace.

I am quite free to say, aside from any direct influence this war is to have towards liberating my enslaved fellow countrymen, I should regret the sudden and peaceful termination of this conflict.

The mission of the revolution would be a failure were it to stop now. It would, in that case, only have lived long enough to do harm, and not long enough to do any good.

One most important element of this war on the part of the North is to teach the South a lesson which it has been slow to learn.

The people of the North have long borne a bad reputation at the South. They have borne the reputation of being mean spirited and cowardly. All the bravery and manliness has been monopolized by the South. This is one of the many evils arising out of our connection with slavery. In all our wars the North has furnished the men and the money, and the South has furnished the officers, and, therefore received the largest measure of the glory.

Now, I take it that no people are safe from attack who bear such a reputation as we have borne in the Southern States. No people can be long respected who bear any such reputation. A reputation for cowardice is a constant invitation to abuse and insult. He is always whipt oftenest who is whipt easiest. The coward my be pitied and protected by the magnanimous and brave, but there will always be mean men, and even cowards themselves, who will abuse and insult those whom they can abuse and insult with impunity.

We of the North may have learning, industry and wealth without end—with every other advantage, but so long as we are considered as destitute of manly courage, as too limited to defend ourselves, freedom and our country, we shall be the victims of insult and outrage, whenever we venture among the rapacious and ferocious Slave-drivers of the South.

Now instead of looking upon the present war as an unmitigated evil, you and I, and all of us, ought to welcome it as a glorious opportunity for imparting wholesome lessons to the southern soul-drivers.

The first of these lessons, is to demonstrate before all, and especially before the people of the South, that they have been entirely, and most dangerously deceived.

We have got to show them that they have mistaken our forbearance for cowardice, and our love of peace, only for a selfish love of ease, and unwillingness to suffer for an idea, or a principle.

The only condition upon which we can reasonably hope to live with them in peace, and goodfellowship hereafter, is that we entirely undeceive them at this very important point.

They have need of the lesson as well as ourselves. We need it that we may have our rights respected and secure.

They need it to make them respectful of the rights of northern men.

The case is a plain one. The slave-holding rebels tell us to our teeth, that they do not love us. They acknowledge a feeling of infernal animosity towards all men who hate Slavery. All our past efforts to make them love us have proved abortive, and all such are likely to prove so in the future.

Now, the next best thing, if we cannot make them love us, is to make them fear us.

The opportunity for doing this is providential, and we should embrace it with a determination to make the best of it.

The doctrine of submission to injustice, has its limits, and those limits have been fully reached.

What I have been now saying applies with even more force to the man of sable hue. We have been everywhere despised as cowards, as wanting in manly spirit, as tamely submitting to the condition of Slavery. A time is at hand, I thrust, when this reproach will be wiped out.

If this conflict shall expand to the grand dimensions which events seem to indicate, the iron arm of the black man may be called into service.

Rochester *Evening Express*, May 8, 1861, and *Douglass' Monthly*, June 1861. Reprinted in Blassingame et al., *The Frederick Douglass Papers*, 3:428–435.

---

1. Daniel O'Connell (1775–1847) was a member of Parliament, an Irish nationalist, and Ireland's most outspoken critic of slavery. Noel Ignatiev, *How the Irish Became White* (New York & London: Routledge, 1995), 6–9, 11–14, 16–31.

2. A slight variation from lines in Lord Byron's *The Giaour* (London: John Murray, 1813).

3. On April 19, 1861, rioters attacked the federal troops of the 6th Massachusetts Regiment as they attempted to pass through Baltimore to defend

Washington, D.C. Four soldiers were killed, along with a number of civilian rioters. As a result of Baltimore's Confederate sympathies, federal troops
rigorously occupied the city. McPherson, *Battle Cry of Freedom*, 285–287.

4. "Whom God would destroy He first sends mad," probably originated with
James Duport (1606–1679), the well known English Classic scholar, who
gained some renown for his *Homeri Gnomologia* (1660), a collection of
aphorisms and quotations from classical sources, the Bible, and literature.

"Well, I am a negro, and I was not contented"
J. Sella Martin
OCTOBER 27, 1865

Northern whites scorned slaves. They did not approve of the institution
of slavery, but they hated the slave even more. Much of their disdain
rested on the notion that masters were good, benevolent caretakers of
their "property," and that the typical slave lived a simple, happy life. The
stereotype of the "contented slave" proved an enduring myth among
whites despite the testimony of scores of slaves including Frederick
Douglass, William Wells Brown, and William and Ellen Craft. It also survived the scores of slave narratives that appeared before the Civil War
and graphically depicted the barbarism that whites inflicted on their
black "property." Despite the eruption caused by Harriet Beecher
Stowe's *Uncle Tom's Cabin* in 1852, the idea of the contented slave persisted well into the Civil War. Such prejudices prevented the North
from fully understanding the conflict that tore the nation apart.

Between 1836 and 1856, Southern slave traders had sold a young J.
Sella Martin (1832–1876) eight different times. He escaped in 1856
while working as a boatman on the Mississippi River and traveled to
Chicago. He moved to Detroit the next year and began lecturing on
the antislavery circuit. Martin believed that his birth on the day that Virginians executed Nat Turner represented a harbinger of his mission to
end slavery. It fueled his passion; he taught himself to read, and then
prepared for the ministry. He filled a variety of pulpits, and when war
broke out in 1861 he was ministering to Boston's famed Joy Street
Church. The next year, he took over a church in London, England. He

spent much of the war raising funds to free his sister and her two children from slavery and speaking out against Confederate influence in Great Britain.

Few speakers could match Martin's commanding presence, and his condemnations of slavery came with the authority of personal experience. His speech on October 27, 1865, in Bristol, England, expressed the sentiments that former slaves had been preaching for over thirty years. Born the property of another man, Martin understood the feelings and desires of slaves and represented them with powerful credentials. To whites who believed that slavery represented no crime because slaves lived in blissful contentment, Martin thundered defiance. "Well, I am a Negro, and I was not contented. The white man was not in slavery; I was, and I know where the shoe pinched; and I say I was not contented." Ripley et al, *The Black Abolitionist Papers,* 1:565; R. J. M. Blackett, *Beating Against the Barriers: The Lives of Six Nineteenth-Century Afro-Americans* (Ithaca, NY: Cornell University Press, 1986), 185–285.

WHAT THE SLAVES THINK

MEN ENTER INTO CONVERSATION with me in railway carriages, and they say, "We are as much opposed to slavery as you are; but then, after all slavery ought to have been gradually abolished, and not immediately." Well now, suppose it ought, it was not. (Laughter.) It would cost just as much blood and treasure to get the negroes back into slavery as it has cost to get them out, and if these people really meant to criticize where they can remedy, and not to find fault merely in a querulous spirit, they would accept the state of facts as they present themselves and make the best of it. (Hear, hear.) I will tell you what is the fact. The people that find fault with abolition generally do not want it, gradual or immediate. They say that the negroes were very well contented when they were in slavery. "I have seen them," some will say, "and heard them say they were contented." They have told me that frequently, and there was never a greater mistake in the world. Here a white man says that the negroes were contented. Well, I am a negro, and I was not contented. (Loud applause.) The white man was not in slavery; I was, and I know where the shoe pinched; and I say I was not contented. But then, Mr. Chairman, suppose it were the fact that the black man was contented in bondage, suppose he was contented to see his wife sold on the auction-block, or his daughter violated, or his children separated from him, or having his own manhood crushed out of him, I say that is the heaviest condemnation of the institution, that slavery should blot out a man's manhood so as to make him contented to accept this degradation, and such an institution ought to be swept from the face of the earth. (Loud applause.) While there is an irresponsible power committed to the hands of the slaveholder, and while human nature remains as it is, it is impossible to talk about treating slaves kindly. You cannot do it. I was once on a plantation—I went there accidentally—and I saw a lot of negroes gathered by the side of the water. In the middle of the stream there stood a stalwart negro with an axe on his shoulder. The overseer was trying to urge the negroes on the bank to go in and make him come out, but the boys all knew him, and he said, "Do not approach me, for I will brain the first one that does, and die in this water." The boys knew that he would do it, and they would not approach him. Finally, the overseer had to send for the young master, who came down and said to the negro, "Jim, you must come out of the water." Jim said, "I will come out if you promise that I shall not be flogged. I have done nothing to be flogged for. I do my work faithfully. You sold away my wife. I have made up my mind never to be flogged, and I will not come out of the water." The young master appealed to him by all the feelings connected with their boyhood, all the reminiscences and associations of their early life, but the negro still refused; and at last the young master said to the negro-driver, who was standing by, "You must shoot him down: there is no help for it." The negro-driver then raised his rifle, and in a moment the sharp crack of the rifle sent the poor corpse floating down the stream, his blood staining all the water. Now, that I saw. It was not because the man who did it was bloodthirsty, or tyrannical, or ferocious, or more cruel than many of us might be here, but if the negro had been successful in resisting his authority that day, another negro would have attempted it the next, and so on until all discipline would have been at an end in the plantation. When I have talked about the inherent cruelty of the institution, men have said, "Why do you talk so? Don't you know that I would not kill my horse?" Ah, but people do not remember that there is this great difference between a man and a horse: if you beat a horse, the other horses go on; if a horse is punished for rebellion, another horse will eat his oats just as well. But if one negro becomes successful, another negro becomes successful, and if one is shot down, the others are deterred. Therefore I say the institution of slavery is so bitter in itself that it sours everything it comes in contact with. It is no use talking about the majority of slaves having been kindly treated or anything like contented. Not one in ten thousand was contented, and the fact is, that where they were well treated the more discontented they were. I was a slave until I was twenty-two years of age, and I know I suffered more acute anguish than most of the slaves around me, just because aspirations had been roused in me that were not aroused in them; because I was associated with gentlemen who were so near to liberty and brought me so near to it that I wanted it all the more.

London *Nonconformist*, November 8, 1865. Reprinted in Ripley et al., *The Black Abolitionist Papers*, 1:565–567.

"Is the war one for Freedom?"
James Madison Bell
MAY 24, 1862

The North had rejected black patriotism in the spring of 1861, refusing to permit African Americans, free or slave, to enlist in the army. Although denied this opportunity, the African American community in the North remained committed to influencing the public debate over the war. From the pulpit, the lecture platform, and in print, and from New England to California, black leaders filled the public arena with their insistence that the North's attention not stray from the issues of slavery and freedom. James Madison Bell (1826–1902), one of the most successful black poets of the nineteenth century, is best remembered for his epic poems *The Progress of Liberty* (1866) and *The Triumph of Liberty* (1870). Before the war, he had worked as a plasterer in Cincinnati, Ohio, and in 1854 he moved to the black community of Chatham, Canada West, where he established himself as an abolitionist leader and assisted in the resettlement of slaves who reached Canada via the Underground Railroad. Defiant and uncompromising, Bell raised funds for John Brown's 1859 raid against Harpers Ferry. He moved to San Francisco in 1860, and again quickly established himself as an antislavery activist and opponent of racial discrimination. He became a lay leader in the African Methodist Episcopal Church (AME Church) and frequently published in the city's two black newspapers, the *Elevator* and the *Pacific Appeal.*

Four million slaves lived in the South. A ready-made army for freedom lay within the North's grasp. Why would the government not let its natural allies help defeat the South? Bell and scores of black leaders across the North tried to shape the public response to this question and bend government policy toward freedom. The two confiscation acts adopted by Congress in 1861 and 1862 authorized the full utilization of all "contraband" captured in the war, including slaves. Thus, what, if anything, the North should do with Southern slaves became a central preoccupation of Congress and of the press in the North. For African Americans, the government's answer to the question "what should we do with the contraband" represented a test of Lincoln's and the North's commitment to freedom. The recruitment of the "contraband" into the army, Bell and other Northern blacks believed, was essential to the country's future and to their own. It would not only bring an end to slavery and restore the Union, but would regenerate the image of African Americans in the eyes of whites: "let them war in the van,/ Where each may confront with his merciless lord,/ And purge from their race, in the eyes of the brave,/ The stigma and scorn now attending the slave." Ripley et al., *The Black Abolitionist Papers,* 5:138–139; James Smethurst, "'The Noble Sons of Ham': Poetry, Soldiers, and Citizens at the End of Reconstruction," in Martin H. Blatt, Thomas J. Brown, Donald Yacovone, eds., *Hope & Glory: Essays on the Legacy of the 54th Massachusetts Regiment* (Amherst, MA: University of Massachusetts Press, 2001), 171–172.

WHAT SHALL WE DO WITH THE CONTRABANDS?

SHALL WE ARM THEM? Yes, arm them! give to each man
A rifle, a musket, a cutlass or sword;
Then on to the charge! let them war in the van,
Where each may confront with his merciless lord,
And purge from their race, in the eyes of the brave,
The stigma and scorn now attending the slave.

I would not have the wrath of the rebels to cease,
Their hope to grow weak nor their courage to wane,
Till the Contrabands join in securing a peace,
Whose glory shall vanish the last galling chain,
And win for their race an undying respect
In the land of their prayers, their tears and neglect.

Is the war one for Freedom? Then why, tell me why,
Should the wronged and oppressed be debarred from the fight?
Does not reason suggest, it were noble to die
In the act of supplanting a wrong for the right?
Then lead to the charge! for the end is not far,
When the Contraband host are enrolled in the war.

San Francisco *Pacific Appeal*, May 24, 1862. Reprinted in Ripley, et al., *The Black Abolitionist Papers*, 5:138.

3

Emigration and Colonization

"Hayti needs population"
Henry Highland Garnet
DECEMBER 22, 1860

No issue proved more divisive to Northern blacks than the question of emigration, and no issue united them more than their hatred of colonization. To its supporters, emigration represented hope and escape from grinding racial oppression in the United States. It signified solidarity with people of color in Africa, the Caribbean, or elsewhere in Latin or South America. Equally important, it fueled a fervent black nationalist pride, and many of its advocates believed that there could be no progress among American blacks unless they controlled their own country, preferably in Africa. Still others, such as the radical abolitionist and Presbyterian minister, Henry Highland Garnet (1815–1882), saw emigration as needed assistance to the struggling black republic of Haiti. An educator, publisher, and ceaseless advocate for black rights, Garnet led New York's black abolitionists and gained fame for his 1843 call for a slave insurrection.

Garnet supported black emigration to Haiti and to Africa. Just before he crafted the following letter, the Haytian Emigration Bureau named Garnet as an agent, and the African Civilization Society, which Garnet led, had sent three agents to Yoruba to determine if the organization should promote a settlement there. Haiti, with its great symbolism of black freedom and revolutionary success, appealed to some American blacks. The Haitian government's willingness to pay African Americans to settle there, and the support of black leaders including Garnet, William Wells Brown, and H. Ford Douglas, encouraged many, despite a long history of failed attempts by American blacks to resettle there. To Garnet, the forced colonization of American blacks in Liberia had nothing to do with his ventures. Ripley et al., *The Black Abolitionist Papers*, 3:336–337, 5:100–109; R. J. M. Blackett, *Building an Antislavery Wall: Black Americans in the Atlantic Abolitionist Movement, 1830–1860* (Ithaca, NY: Cornell University Press, 1983), 175–178.

NO CHANGE—A WORD TO MY FRIENDS AND FOES

IT HAS BEEN FEARED by some of my friends and rumored by my foes generally, that I, like a few of my former coadjutors, have turned my back upon the African cause, and have repudiated my former views, for the utterance of which I have so greatly and joyfully suffered. *This is entirely a mistake.* Thus far I have seen no occasion for a change in my views. I am more than ever confirmed in the opinions that I have cherished on this question from my youth. My approval of the Haytien emigration movement is not of a recent date, but has uniformly been incorporated—and that, too, very prominently—in all my humble advocacy of the general principles of emigration.

Hayti needs population to develope her agricultural and mineral resources and to fortify and defend her against the invasion of the slave power of the western world. She is capable of containing ten millions of inhabitants, and has only a little over one million in all her borders. She needs men and labor, and labor will be amply rewarded. Hayti therefore needs many, and both divine providence and the liberality of the Haytien Government conspire to point to that country as the wide field which is to be benefitted by the masses who may be disposed to emigrate from this land.

But with regard to Africa the case is far different. She does not need population, for that she already has in abundance. *She needs but a few to direct the labor,* the elements of which are on her soil, and to call them forth into systematic, productive, and economical activity. It is in the power of the colored men of America to supply the wants of both countries, and thus give the death blow to slavery, and bless our scattered race throughout the world. These are my views in brief, and I trust no one will trouble himself further about the probability of a change in my views. Both of these grand and stupendous schemes have entered so deeply into my heart and thoughts that they have become a part of my existence, and hence, while I live, there can be no change in my principles and opinions on this subject.

Had I opposed or dodged the question of Haytien emigration in its infancy, or given the cold shoulder to it when it was unpopular, my recent appointment by the chief of the bureau[1] would have filled me with astonishment. There is one class of men whom I greatly pity. They are those who are like sky-rockets: they go up with a blaze and whiz, and quickly come down worthless, blackened sticks. They have but one idea, and hold to that but a little while. In reference to human progress, they have but one eye, and see but poorly out of that. They move with the wind, whichever way it blows, and you cannot find them in the same place for the period of a lunar month. Let them read the first clause of the 4th verse of the 49th chapter of Genesis, and be profitted by the rebuke of the patriarch—*"Unstable as water, thou shalt not excel."*

HENRY HIGHLAND GARNET

New York *Weekly Anglo-African,* December 22, 1860. Courtesy of the Black Abolitionist Archives, University of Detroit Mercy.

---

1. The Haytian Emigration Bureau, created by the Haitian government to encourage African American resettlement, named the abolitionist editor James Redpath as its commissioner. With headquarters in Boston, a newspaper (the *Pine and Palm*), and a $20,000 budget, the bureau recruited a number of black leaders in the United States and Canada to convince blacks to emigrate. Garnet became an agent for the bureau in late 1860, but after the start of the war, he and others lost interest in the project. Ripley et al., *The Black Abolitionist Papers,* 5:108.

"the free blacks of the United States are wanted in the United States"
James McCune Smith to Henry Highland Garnet
JANUARY 5, 1861

James McCune Smith (1813–1865), Garnet's prime rival for leadership of New York blacks, had known Garent since their youth in the segregated schools of New York City. Denied educational opportunities in the United States, Smith went to the university at Glasgow, Scotland, where he earned three academic degrees, including a doctorate of medicine. He conducted a successful integrated practice in New York, which included his own pharmacy, the first black-owned one in the country. Smith, a great advocate of educational uplift, also became active in New York politics and helped lead the campaign to remove all restrictions on black suffrage in the state. In 1857 he ran unsuccessfully for secretary of state of New York. A prolific writer, he published many pamphlets and letters, sometimes written under the pseudonym "Communipaw," that reached thousands of African Americans across the North. Smith, a lifelong enemy of emigration, reflected mainstream Northern black opinion in condemning all emigrationist and colonizationist schemes. Anything that brought into question blacks' right to full equality in America raised Smith's ire. He sought full integration, and anything that diverted attention from that goal earned Smith's uncompromising opposition. His sarcastic reply to Henry Highland Garnet made clear the shortcomings of all emigration schemes and, with fatal aim, accused Garnet's projects of protecting slavery. Ripley et al., *The Black Abolitionist Papers,* 3:350–351; Craig Steven Wilder, *In the Company of Black Men: The African Influence on African American Culture in New York City* (New York: New York University Press, 2001), 131–132, 139–140, 150–152, 158–159, 174–175.

New York,
Jan 5th, 1861

REVEREND AND DEAR SIR:

Your schemes of emigration have neither the charm of novelty nor the prestige of success.

The African Civilization scheme[1] is a feeble attempt to do what the American Colonization Society has failed to do; witness Liberia. After forty years of incessant labor, at an expense of one hundred thousand dollars a year—to say nothing of the sacrifice of precious lives and the immolation of brilliant talents and acquirements—we have the admission, through a recent number of the *Liberia Herald,* that if the colonization funds were withheld, Liberia would be unable to support itself. And it is in consequence of their utter dependence on the Colonizationists of this land for their support that the Liberians are obliged to admit into their borders the thousands of recaptured Africans sent there by the United States Government.

I do not see in your African Civilization scheme anything different in character or at all equal in force and power to the American Colonization Society. Yes, there is this difference: the Liberians, by their Constitution, prohibit slavery and the slave trade within their borders; your commissioners—Messrs. Campbell and Delany[2]—in their treaty with the chiefs of Abbeokuta, agree in one of their articles to *"respect the domestic institutions of the country."* One of those institutions—I have it from Mr. Campbell's own lips—is "THE INSTITUTION OF SLAVERY." You, therefore, as president of an association, one professed object of which is to abolish slavery in America, are joined, without protest, in a league to respect the institution of slavery in Africa. Does your reverence see more than one face in this matter? It shines double to the world without you. Mr. Campbell mildly interposes the statement that the slavery of Abbeokuta "is of the mildest form," &c. Did you ever hear a slaveholder or his apologist admit of any other kind of slavery? But I forget. You have recently sent out pioneers in to the land of Abbeokuta. They may change the face of matters. Yet they must be mighty men to do so, being themselves, all told, two barbers and a poet! In the meantime, you owe it to your own fair fame to wash your hands of that treaty, which commits your association to "respect the institution" of domestic slavery.

In like manner, the Haytian emigration scheme is an attempt at an experiment which was made, and failed, thirty years ago. At that time the Haytian government sent to the United States one of its most honored citizens—M. Granville—who laid before the colored people proposals for their emigration.[3] Between two and four thousand of our people migrated to Hayti, and within six or ten months nearly all who survived or could get away from Hayti returned to the United States. The Haytian government was unwilling to allow them to leave, and the Rev. Peter Williams and another were obliged to go to Port-au-Prince to plead for the release of their disappointed, distressed, and dissatisfied brethren.[4]

I do not see any reason to believe that the present experiment will be any more successful, because—

1. While the Haytian government *then* gave emigrants six months' board and shelter, the same government *now* offers emigrants only eight days' board and lodging (see [James] Redpath's *Guide to Hayti*, p. 94).

2. Dissimilarity of language is the same now as in 1824. Our people do not understand the French; the Haytians do not speak English. "A knowledge of the French language," says Mr. Redpath (p. 131), "is

absolutely essential to every one who intends to reside in Hayti." He afterwards proves that a knowledge of Creole is equally necessary. How
many of the emigrants whom you prayerfully dismissed to Hayti the
other day knew anything of French? How many "text-books and dictionaries" were furnished them by the "Bureau of Emigration"?

3. Dissimilarity of manners and morals. Thirty years have made a vast
difference in the manners and morals of the free colored people of the
United States—especially in the now free States. We are almost exclusively of the Protestant faith, and live and believe according to that
faith. We believe, as you know, in the marriage relation, and are accustomed to the proprieties, the joys, and the responsibilities that spring
therefrom. Hayti, according to Mr. Redpath's own showing in his letters
to the [New York] *Tribune*, is half Romanist, half fetich; not only among
the masses, but even in the upper classes—reaching until recently to the
very head of the government—there is no such rule as marriage. There
are a few noble exceptions. Can there be, will there be, any cordial sympathy between such a people and ours? Will not our young women, married or single, ask to be delivered from such a contact?

4. In your manifesto you say that Hayti needs population, and that
you propose to remedy this want by sending thither our colored population. The bureau of emigration is happily located, with this view, in
Boston, where, among the colored people, in the year 1859 (see last
week's Boston letter in the *Weekly Anglo-African*), there were 326
deaths and only 183 births! How long would it take this class to popu-
late Hayti—or Hades? The true remedy for sparseness of population in
Hayti is, that the Haytians should become so far Christian as to respect
the marriage relation; and this, I take it, could be done by the preaching of one apostle (such as your reverence, speaking French) sooner
than by the landing of a few hundred emigrants, which will be the extent of your labors.

Your duty to our people is to tell them to aim higher. In advising
them to go to Hayti, you direct them to sink lower. You and those with
whom you are immediately identified—nay, the most, if not all, of our
people in the free States—believe themselves of equal force and ability
with the whites, come whence they may. We affirm by our lives and
conduct that, if degraded, it is not by our innate inferiority, but by the
active oppression of those who outnumber us. The Haytians have a

proverb, universal among the masses, "*Aprez bon Jo-blanc*"—"*Next to God is the white man.*" The Haytians, too, like the Liberians, further admit their inferiority by making it an article of their constitution that "no white man can become a Haytian (or Liberian) citizen."

No, my dear sir, the free blacks of the United States are wanted in the United States. The people of Maryland said so the other day when they voted that they should not be reduced to slavery. Even the people of Charleston, S.C., say that they cannot spare them as freemen, even to be converted into slaves. And our people want to stay, and will stay, at home; we are in for the fight, and will fight it out here. Shake yourself free from these migrating phantasms, and join us with your might and main. You belong to us, and we want your whole soul. We have lost [Alexander] Crummell, and we have lost [Samuel Ringgold] Ward, and Frederick Douglass's eyes appear dazzled with the mahogany splendor of the Boston "bureau."[5] Do not, I beseech you, follow their example, and leave an earnest and devoted people without a leader.

As the beloved pastor of a large and intelligent people in the centre of a metropolis which appreciates your talents and acknowledges your genius, you have ample room and verge enough for the marked abilities with which it has pleased God to endow you, without wasting your vigor in the vain attempt to people an island within the tropics. Sincerely and faithfully yours,

JAMES McCUNE SMITH

New York *Weekly Anglo-African*, January 12, 1861.

---

1. Founded in September 1858, the African Civilization Society pledged itself to the "civilization and evangelization" of Africa. The interracial body under the leadership of Garnet attracted some public support, particularly for its intent to teach Africans to raise cotton without slave labor. By doing so, they hoped to undercut the market for slave-grown cotton and lead to slavery's demise. The Society's popularity remained limited because its programs too closely paralleled the hated American Colonization Society—it even shared a building with the New York State Colonization Society. By 1862 the African Civilization Society largely abandoned its African emphasis and concentrated on educating the former slaves. Ripley et al., *The Black Abolitionist Papers*, 5:9–10.

2. Although Garnet and the African Civilization Society did from time to time refer to Martin R. Delany (1812–1885) and Robert Campbell (?–1884) as "our commissioners," their Niger Valley Exploring Party (1859) represented a separate effort to resettle American blacks in Africa. In December 1859 Delany and Campbell concluded a treaty with the king of Abeokuta, not far from Liberia, and agreed to respect "the laws of the Egba people." Delany was the period's most eloquent advocate of black nationalism. The Jamaica-born Campbell moved to New York, where he became a teacher. Both men concluded that blacks could flourish only in a black republic, free of white racism. Ripley et al., *The Black Abolitionist Papers*, 1:448–449, 5:106–107.

3. In 1824 the Haitian government sent Jonathan Granville (1785–1839) to the United States seeking emigrants. Between six and seven thousand blacks from a variety of cities emigrated to the island during the 1820s with the encouragement of prominent white leaders. Within a year many died and about a third returned to the states. Yacovone, *A Voice of Thunder*, 180.

4. Contrary to Smith's assertion, the Haitians allowed the Americans to leave. The New Jersey-born Peter Williams, Jr. (1780?–1840), became one of New York's most prominent black Episcopal ministers and founded St. Phillip's Episcopal Church. In April 1825, Williams traveled to Haiti to investigate conditions there, and he returned to the United States with fifty-six settlers. Ripley et al., *The Black Abolitionist Papers*, 3:224–225, 5:108.

5. Alexander Crummell (1819–1898), perhaps the era's most influential black Episcopal priest, filled the pulpit at New York's Church of the Messiah before removing to England for additional education. He then spent twenty years in Liberia, returning to the United States in 1873. Samuel Ringgold Ward (1817?–1866), a New York state congregational minister, filled pulpits in black and white churches, and he became an extremely effective abolitionist speaker. He fled the United States in 1851 after participating in a fugitive slave rescue and settled in Jamaica. Throughout his life, Frederick Douglass found inspiration in the Haitian Revolution. Although he opposed colonization and emigration of African Americans, in 1860 and 1861 he grew interested in Haiti and accepted an invitation from the Haitian government to visit the island. The attack on Fort Sumter prevented Douglass from visiting the island nation. Wilson J. Moses, *Alexander Crummell: A Study in Civilization and Discontent* (Oxford, England: Oxford University Press, 1988); Ripley et al., *The Black Abolitionist Papers*, 3:343–344; Benjamin Quarles, *Black Abolitionists* (New York: Oxford University Press, 1969), 222.

"His removal, even if possible, will not effect a cure"
George B. Vashon to Abraham Lincoln
SEPTEMBER 1862

Our understanding of the relationship between blacks and Abraham Lincoln has been distorted by the president's assassination and its legacy. Prior to 1865 blacks found little in Lincoln or the Republican Party that was very appealing. Even the Emancipation Proclamation, while welcomed, struck African Americans in the North as a reluctant move by an unwilling president who preferred the colonization of all blacks. On August 14, 1862, Lincoln met with a delegation of Washington, D.C., black leaders and told them that the two races could never live together in freedom. Thus, it would be necessary for all blacks to leave the country. To begin their exodus, Lincoln and the Congress had appropriated $600,000 for black resettlement in the Chiriqui region of Central America. Even more galling, Lincoln advised the visiting delegation that if it were not for African Americans and the institution of slavery, "the war could not have an existence." In words that found their way into every black community of the North, Lincoln had announced that African Americans should leave the United States and that they, not Southerners, were responsible for the war.

Two years into the Civil War, and the president of the United States wished to deport the country's most important ally! The shock was palpable. Even Frederick Douglass, who sought cooperation with Lincoln and the Republican Party, denounced Lincoln as "a genuine representative of American prejudice and Negro hate." George Boyer Vashon (1824–1878), a free black lawyer from Pittsburgh, spent several years in Haiti teaching, since racial prejudice would not permit him to practice law in Pennsylvania. Upon his return to the United States, he lived in New York for a time, teaching and running for election as the state's attorney general. A lifelong abolitionist, Vashon wrote for several anti-slavery newspapers and participated in Underground Railroad activities. His years in Haiti made Vashon suspect in some eyes, but he did oppose colonization and left the United States only when racism denied him the opportunity to practice his profession. His open letter to Lincoln, published by Frederick Douglass, recited the arguments that African Americans had been making against colonization since the formation of the American Colonization Society in 1816. Incensed by Lincoln's accusation that blacks bore any responsibility for the war, Vashon reminded the nation that the cause "must be sought in the wrongs inflicted upon him [i.e. blacks] by the white man." Yacovone, *A Voice of Thunder*, 18; Ripley et al., *The Black Abolitionist Papers*, 3:321–322.

To His Excellency ABRAHAM LINCOLN,
President of the United States of America
HIGHLY HONORED AND RESPECTED SIR:

The papers announce that on the 14th of August you had an interview with a committee of colored men, and addressed them in reference to the propriety of the expatriation of their class. As a colored man, I am deeply interested in this matter; and feel that under the circumstances, I ought to be excused for the liberty which I take in making answer to you personally.

In the first place, sir, let me say, that I do not put myself in opposition to the emigration of the Colored Americans, either individually, or in large masses. I am satisfied, indeed, that such as emigration will be entered upon, and that too, to no inconsiderable extent. Liberia, with the bright and continually growing promise for the regeneration of Africa, will allure many a colored man to the shores of his motherland. Haiti, with her proud boast, that, she alone, can present an instance in the history of the world, of a horde of despised bondmen becoming a nation of triumphant freeman, will by her gracious invitation, induce many a dark hued native of the United States to go and aid in developing the treasures stored away in her sun-crested hills and smiling savannahs. And, Central America, lying in that belt of empire which Destiny seems to promise to the blended races of the earth, will, no doubt, either with or without federal patronage, become the abiding place of a population made up, in great measure, of persons who will have taken refuge there from the oppression which they had been called upon to undergo in this country.

But, entertaining these views, and almost persuaded to become an emigrant myself, for the recollections of a thirty months' residence in Haiti still crowd pleasantly upon my memory, I am confident that, in thus feeling, I am not in sympathy with the majority of my class—not in sympathy either with the great body of them. Those men are doubt-less aware that many comforts and advantages which they do not now enjoy here, await them elsewhere. No feeling of selfishness, no dread of making sacrifices (as you intimate), detains them in the land of their birth. They are fully conscious of the hatred to which you have ad-verted, they endure its consequences daily and hourly; tremblingly too, perhaps, lest the utterances of their Chief Magistrate may add fuel to the fire raging against them, but buoyed up by the knowledge that they are undeserving of this ill usage, and sedulously endeavoring to perform the various duties that are incumbent upon them, they enjoy, amid all their ill, a species of content, and echo back, by their conduct, your own words, that "It is difficult to make a man miserable while he feels he is worthy of himself, and claims kindred to the great God who made him." Thus, they have schooled themselves "to labor and to wait," in the hope of the coming of a better time. And, this hope is based in the innermost convictions of their religious nature, in trust which is not to be shaken, that the God who rules the Universe is a God of fixed, and immutable justice, under whose dispensations the proud and defiant ones of today become invariably the peeled and broken ones of the morrow; while those who were despised and rejected, find themselves, in turn, the re-cipients of abundant and overflowing "mercies."

These men, too, have another reason for clinging to the land of their nativity; and that is, the gross injustice which inheres even in the slightest intimation of a request, that they should leave it, an injustice which must necessarily be, in the highest degree, revolting to their every sense of right. Who and what are these men? Their family records in this land, in almost every instance, antedate our revolutionary strug-gle, and you, sir, will read in your country's history, unlike the ignorant and rapid reporters, who, from time to time, in their marketless and pen free calumny of a race, detail from our camps the lie that "the negro will not fight"—you, sir, know that black Americans fighting shoulder to shoulder with white Americans, in the contest which confirmed our na-tionality, merited and received the approbation of Washington; and that the zealous and fleet-footed slave of that time did, for the partizan bands of Sumter and Marion,[1] the same kind of offices which the travel-worn and scarcely tolerated "contraband" of our days has done for the armies of [Gen. Ambrose E.] Burnside and [Gen. George B.] McClel-lan. And now, what reward is offered by republican gratitude? Now, forsooth, when the banquet of Freedom has been spread, when the descendants of the men who fought under [Gen. William] Howe and [Gen. Henry] Clinton, under [Gen. Charles] Cornwallis and [Gen. John] Burgoyne, have with ostentatious liberality been invited to the repast, the children of the patriotic blacks who periled their lives at Bunker Hill, at Red Bank, and on many another hard fought field, must be requested, not merely to take a lower seat, but to withdraw entirely from the table.

But setting aside the injustice of a policy which would expatriate black Americans, let us examine for a moment its expediency. Cicero has declared, in his principal ethical treatise, that, "no greater evil can happen to humanity than the separation of what is expedient from that which is right."[2] Let us suppose, however, that he was wrong in thus teaching; and that the antipathy existing between the white and black races—somewhat of a one-sided antipathy, by the by—would justify the removal of the latter one from this country. It might be, indeed, a matter for discussion, whether this antipathy is as extended and as exacting as you allege; whether, instead of being a permanent instinct, it is not rather a temporary sentiment which will gradually pass away, when once its cause—the slavery and wrong imposed upon the descendants of Africa—will have been removed. But, let that pass. Would it be wise, sir, when Denmark and France and England are looking with envious eyes upon our liberated slaves, and regarding them as important acquisitions to their West India possessions, to denude our southern States of that class of laborers? Has not the experience of our heart-stricken armies—an experience which has prompted the yielding up of the spade to the black man, while the musket is withheld from him—sufficiently indicated that negro cultivators are absolutely required for that portion of the Union?

But, sir, it is not enough that the policy which you suggest should be expedient. It must also be feasible. You have, doubtless, looked at this matter with the eye of a statesman. You have reflected, that to remove entirely this "bone of contention" demands the expatriation of nearly one-sixth portion of the Union. You have, after mature thought, settled the physical possibility of so large an expatriation; and calmly calculated the hundreds of millions of dollars which its accomplishment will add to our national liabilities—large now, and growing larger daily under the exigencies of our civil war. Have you also considered that the meagre handful of negroes under Federal rule constitutes, so to speak, only the periosteum, while "the bone" itself projects over into territory arrayed against your authority, and may yet be employed by unhallowed Rebellion, grown desperate in its extremity, as a vast and terrible weapon for the attainment of its ends? Whether this be a probability, or not, it is clear that the difficulties in the way of your suggested enterprise are such as entitle it to be termed Herculean. Herculean? I fear, sir, that we must glance at another of the pages of mythology to find an epithet with which to characterize it. Africa, in the days of your administration, as in those of the line of Belus, may be called upon to witness the retribution dealt out to wrong by the Eternal Powers. The States of this Union, having assassinated in the person of the negro all of the principles of right to which they were wedded, may, like the Danaides, be condemned to expiate their crime; and this scheme of expatriation may prove, for them, the vain essay to fill a perforated "cistern which will hold no water."[3]

President of the United States, let me say in conclusion that the negro may be "the bone of contention" in our present civil war. He may have been the occasion of it; but he has not been its cause. That cause must be sought in the wrongs inflicted upon him by the white man. The white man's oppression of the negro, and not the negro himself, has brought upon the nation the leprosy under which it groans. The negro may be the scab indicative of the disease, but his removal, even if possible, will not effect a cure. Not until this nation, with hands upon its lips, and with lips in the dust, shall cry repentantly, "Unclean! unclean!" will the beneficent Father of all men, of whatever color, permit its healing and purification.

I have the honor, sir, to be, with all the consideration due to your high office, Most Respectfully, Your Obedient Servant,

GEORGE B. VASHON

Rochester, N.Y. *Douglass' Monthly*, October 1862. Reprinted in Ripley et al., *The Black Abolitionist Papers*, 5:153–155.

---

1. Vashon draws a parallel between the African Americans who assisted the Revolutionary War patriot generals Thomas Sumter (1734–1832) and Francis Marion (1732?–1795) and the freed slaves who served indispensable roles as scouts, guides, and spies for Union forces during the Civil War.

Benjamin Quarles, *The Negro in the American Revolution* (orig., 1961, Chapel Hill, NC: University of North Carolina Press, 1996), 103–106, 108–110, 115, 123, 149.

2. From Cicero's (106–43 B.C.) third book of *On Duties*.

3. In the Greek myth of Belus, the Danaides, fifty daughters of Danaus, are condemned for eternity to carry water in containers that cannot hold water.

4

The Slavery of Racial Prejudice

*"The position of the colored man
today is a trying one"*
John S. Rock
MARCH 5, 1860

To many blacks, the American Revolution represented hope unfulfilled. To many others, it represented hopes betrayed. The history of democracy in America since the Revolution worked toward the benefit of whites and increasingly to the detriment of blacks. With each passing year, blacks lost ground, lost rights, and lost their property and lives to white rioters. The 1857 Supreme Court decision in *Dred Scott v. Sandford* put a capstone on the reality that African Americans had long understood: they had no rights that white men were bound to respect. The antislavery movement, at least for African Americans and their white allies, aimed at destroying slavery *and* racial prejudice. But on the eve of the most important election in American history, African Americans in 1860 suffered more oppression than any white man in 1776 ever could have imagined.

Since the infamous Dred Scott decision, Boston blacks, led by the historian and activist William C. Nell, celebrated the role of Crispus Attucks in bringing on the American Revolution. To Nell and other Boston blacks, Attucks's death in the "Boston Massacre" symbolized the African American contribution to the nation. They believed that such facts refuted the baseless accusations of black inferiority by racists. But to John S. Rock (1825–1866), the Boston physician and lawyer, African American participation in the Revolution had been a mistake, and celebrating Attucks's sacrifice only brought unwanted attention to a fool's errand. Blacks had fought for liberty but got slavery. They expected equality, but received hate. The Revolution had brought great benefits to whites, but mostly tragedy to blacks. Even in Boston, the cradle of the Revolution, African Americans suffered grinding racial oppression. Education brought them only frustration, since whites refused to hire them. Finding a decent home proved an exercise in futility since whites would not sell or rent to blacks. And the independent black businessman received "more respect and less patronage than in any other place" that Rock knew.

The New Jersey–born Rock earned a medical degree from the American Medical College in 1852 and one year later began his practice in Boston. Renowned for his abilities and intellectual gifts, Rock succeeded at teaching, medicine, and the law—becoming the first African American to win the right to try cases before the U.S. Supreme Court—and spoke French, German, and Spanish with fluency. With the beginning of the war, Rock helped recruit for the commonwealth's three black regiments. After the war, he offered legal assistance to ex-soldiers and their families. A supporter of John Brown, Rock declared, "I believe in insurrections." Clearly, the American Revolution was not the kind he had in mind. Ripley et al., *The Black Abolitionist Papers*, 5:66–67.

LADIES AND GENTLEMEN:

I have been invited by my friend, Mr. [William C.] Nell,[1] to say something to you on the occasion of this, the ninetieth anniversary of the birth of the American Revolution, and that, too, in the face of my recorded opinion that that event was ushered in by the rashness of one of our "noble, but misguided ancestors." If, under the circumstances, I should give you a little plain talk, differing somewhat from that which you have been accustomed to hear, on occasions like this, you need not be surprised. The times require us to speak out. I am free to confess that the remembrance of the details of the event which we are assembled here to celebrate are, by no means, dear to me. I am not yet ready to idolize the actions of Crispus Attucks, who was a leader among those who resorted to forcible measures to create a new government which has used every means in its power to outrage and degrade his race and posterity, in order to oppress them more easily, and to render their condition more hopeless in this country.

I am free to confess that I have strong attachments here, in this my native country, and desire to see it prosperous and happy; yet, situated and
outraged as I am, in common with a race whose lives have been one of
toil to make this country what it is, I would deny the manly promptings
of my own soul if I should not say that American liberty is a word which
has no charms for me. It is a name without meaning—a shadow without
substance, which retains not even so much as the ghost of the original.

The only events in the history of this country which I think deserve
to be commemorated are the organization of the Anti-Slavery Society
and the insurrections of Nat Turner and John Brown. (Applause.)[2]

I believe in insurrections (applause)—and especially those of the pen
and of the sword. Wm. Lloyd Garrison is, I think, a perfect embodiment
of the moral insurrection of thought, which is continually teaching the
people of this country that unjust laws and compacts made by fathers
are not binding upon the sons, and that the "higher law" of God, which
we are bound to execute, teaches us to do unto others as we would have
them do unto us. William H. Seward (the most prominent Republican
candidate for the Presidency), who has been a "Helper" in speeding on
the "irrepressible conflict" between freedom and slavery, has suddenly
lowered his moral standard, and dwindled from a great statesman to a
cunning politician. I agree with *Le Courrier des Etats-Unis* that "his recent speech had disappointed both his friends and his foes: the former
he has deceived, and the latter are authorized to look upon it as a snare."
Chicago and the Presidency have done this.[3] But when the crisis is
passed, I think you will agree with me, that while he has sinned, he has
not wholly fallen from grace.

John Brown was, and is, the representative of that potent power, the
sword, which proposes to settle at once the relation between master and
slave—peaceably if it can, forcibly if it must. This is, no doubt, the
method by which the freedom of the blacks will be brought about in this
country. It is a severe method; but to severe ills it is necessary to apply
severe remedies. Slavery has taken up the sword, and it is but just that
it should perish by it. (Applause.) The John Brown of the second Revolution is but the Crispus Attucks of the first. A few years hence, and
this assertion will be a matter of history.

Crispus Attucks was a brave man, and he fought with our fathers in
a good cause; but they were not victorious. They fought for liberty, but
they got slavery. The white man was benefitted, but the black man was

injured. I do not envy the white Americans the little liberty which they enjoy. It is their right, and they ought to have it. I wish them success, though I do not think they deserve it. I desire to see all men enjoy freedom and prosperity. (Applause.) But by this I do not mean to imply, that, should our country be again situated as it was then, we would be willing to recommit the errors of our Revolutionary fathers. The Scotch have a saying, "When a man deceives me once, shame on *him*; but when he deceives me twice, shame on *me*."

I see one thing in celebrating this day, which it would be well not to overlook, and that is, Crispus Attucks has demonstrated to us that insurrections, when properly planned, may lead to successful revolutions.

If the present aspect of things is an index to the future, then, indeed, our prospects are gloomy. Of the two great political parties in this country, one is openly hostile to us, and seeks to reduce us to the position of beasts of burden; and the other has evidently but little sympathy for us, only as we may serve to advance its interests. The only class who avow themselves openly as the friends of the black man are the Abolitionists; and it would be well for the colored people to remember this fact. (Applause.) I do not wish to be understood as saying that we have no friends in the Republican party, for I know that we have. But the most of those who sacrifice for our cause are among the Abolitionists. Next to them I place the Republicans, many of whom I have found more practically interested in our welfare than the rank and file of the Abolitionists. But I place no one before the leading Abolitionists in this country—they who have spoken for the dumb, and who have braved the storms in their fury. In this connection, I must not omit Gerrit Smith[4] (applause), the leader of the Liberty party, who is one of the most liberal and disinterested of nature's noblemen. He has done more for our race, pecuniarily, than any other man in this country. May a kind Providence preserve him! (Applause.)

It is the Anti-Slavery men and women who have made our cause a holy thing. I always feel proud of my humanity after an interview with any one of them. In the language of [Thomas] Moore, I can say:

Oh, there are looks and tones that dart
An instant sunshine through the heart;
As if the soul that minute caught
Some treasure it through life had sought.[5]

The position of the colored man today is a trying one; trying, because the whole country has entered into a conspiracy to crush him; and it is against this mighty power that he is forced to contend. Some persons think we are oppressed only in the South: this is a mistake. We are oppressed everywhere on this slavery-cursed land. To be sure, we are seldom insulted here by the vulgar passersby. We have the right of suffrage. The free schools are open to our children, and from them have come forth young men who have finished their studies elsewhere, who speak two or three languages, and are capable of filling any post of profit and honor. But there is no field for these men. Their education only makes them suffer the more keenly. The educated colored man meets, on the one hand, the embittered prejudices of the whites, and on the other the jealousies of his own race. Perhaps you may think that there are exceptions. This is true; but there are not enough of them in the whole United States to sustain, properly, a half dozen educated colored men. The colored man who educated his son, educates him to suffer. When [Alphonse Marie Louis de] Lamartine said to an Arminian chief at Damascus, "You should send your son to Europe, and give him that education you regret the want of yourself," the Arminian answered, "Alas! what service should I render to my son, if I were to raise him above the age and the country in which he is destined to live? What would he do at Damascus, on returning thither with the information, the manners, and the taste for liberty he has acquired in Europe? If one must be a slave, it is better never to have known anything but slavery. Woe to the men who precede their times: their times crush them."[6] And woe to the black man who is educated: there is not field for him.

The other day, when a man who makes loud anti-slavery pretensions, and who has the reputation of being the friend of the blacks, had it in his power to advance the interests of a colored man, and was asked to do so, he said, "Colored men have no business to aspire—the time has not come!" This gentleman no doubt regrets that he did not originate the ideas that "black men have no rights that white men are bound to respect," and that "a white skin is the only legitimate object of ambition." He has now only to sigh for a "plantation well stocked with healthy negroes," and his cup of pleasure will be full. Some men are ruined by success. I remember very well that about five years ago he was an active laborer with us, and I am certain he did not say, "the time has not yet come," when he asked us to elect him to the Legislature. (Applause.)

Nowhere in the United States is the colored man of talent appreciated. Even here in Boston, which has a great reputation for being anti-slavery, he is by no means treated like other talented men. Some persons think that because we have the right to vote, and enjoy the privilege of being squeezed up in an omnibus, and stared out of a seat in a horsecar, that there is less prejudice here than there is farther South. In some respects this is true, and in others it is not true. For instance, it is five times as hard to get a house in a good location in Boston as it is in Philadelphia, and it is ten times as difficult for a colored mechanic to get work here as it is in Charleston, where the prejudice is supposed to be very bitter against the free colored man. Colored men in business here receive more respect and less patronage than in any other place that I know of. In this city, we are proscribed in some of the eating houses, many of the hotels, and all of the theatres but one. Boston, though anti-slavery and progressive, supports, in addition to these places, two places of amusement, the sole object of which is to caricature us, and to perpetuate the existing prejudices against us! I now ask you, is Boston anti-slavery? Are not the very places that proscribe us sustained by anti-slavery patronage? Do not our liberal anti-slavery politicians dine at the Revere House, sup at the Parker House, and take their creams and jellies at Copeland's? We have several friends (whose tested anti-slavery is like gold tried in the fire which comes out purer every time it is tried), who speak occasionally upon platforms that are claimed to be anti-slavery, and which are dependent upon their eloquence for support, which have, up to this time, refused to give any colored man a hearing. The Boston Theatre, an institution which has been fighting death ever since it came into existence, could not survive a single year without anti-slavery patronage!

The friends of slavery are everywhere withdrawing their patronage from us, and trying to starve us out by refusing us employment even as menials. Fifteen or twenty years ago, colored men had more than an equal chance in menial employments; today, we are crowded out of almost everything, and we do not even get the patronage of our professed friends. The colored stevedores, who could once be found all along the wharves of Boston, may now be found only about Central wharf, where they meet with just encouragement enough to keep soul and body together. Such is the progress of the public sentiment and of humanity in Boston!

Last summer, a colored servant who was stopping at the Revere House, with a gentleman from New York, was maltreated by the Irish servants. He told his employer, who made complaint to Mr. [Paran] Stevens. Mr. Stevens replied that he would not interfere in anything that his servants should do to any colored man—that if gentlemen travel with colored servants, they must expect to be insulted, and he would rather that such gentlemen would stop somewhere else. That is the idea—colored men have no right to earn an honest living—they must be starved out.

Fifteen or twenty years ago, a Catholic priest in Philadelphia said to the Irish people in that city, "You are all poor, and chiefly laborers; the blacks are poor laborers, many of the native whites are laborers; now, if you wish to succeed, you must do everything that they do, no matter how degrading, and do it for less than they can afford to do it for." The Irish adopted this plan; they lived on less than the Americans could live upon, and worked for less, and the result is that nearly all the menial employments are monopolized by the Irish, who now get as good prices as anybody. There were other avenues open to American white men, and though they have suffered much, the chief support of the Irish has come from the places from which we have been crowded.

Now, while we are denied the humblest positions, is there anything higher open to us? Who is taking our boys into their stores at a low salary, and giving them a chance to rise? Who is admitting them into their workshops or their counting rooms? Who is encouraging those who have trades? With the exception of a handful of Abolitionists and a few black Republicans, there are none. If a few more of those who claim to be our friends would patronize us when they can, and in this manner stimulate us to be industrious, they would render us infinitely more service than all of their "bunkum" speeches.

You can have but a faint idea of the charm their friendship would carry with it, if they would spend a dollar or two with us occasionally. It will not do to judge men by what they say. Many speak kindly of us when their hearts are far from us. Or, as Shakespeare has it,

Words are easy like the wind,
Faithful friends are hard to find.[7]

This is our experience, and we have learned to appreciate the Spanish proverb, "He is my friend who grinds at my mill." In New England, we have many good mechanics who get very little patronage. Indeed, a trade appears to be of but little service to any of us, unless we can, like the tailor of Campillo, afford to work for nothing, and find thread.

I hope that our friends will look at these things, and receive my re-marks in the spirit in which they have been given. I do not mean to un-derrate the efforts of our friends, or to speak disparagingly of their labors; but I would discriminate between our real and our pretended friends. I differ, however, from many of our true friends, as to the means to be used to elevate our race. While I believe that anti-slavery speeches, whether political or otherwise, will do much to correct a cruel and wicked pub-lic sentiment, I am confident that such means alone can never elevate us. My opinion is that the only way by which we the free colored peo-ple can be elevated is through our own exertions, encouraged by our friends. Every colored man who succeeds is so much added to the cause. We have nothing to stimulate our young men. They see many of us struggling hard, and not appreciated, and they become discouraged. The success of such a man as Mr. [John Sella] Martin is worth more to us than a pile of resolutions and speeches as high as Tremont Temple.[8] (Applause.) All honor to Mr. [Isaac Smith] Kalloch, who had the courage and the *will* to give him a hearing in his pulpit, where he could and did do credit to himself and his race. (Applause.) I thank Mr. Kalloch and the immense congregation that assembles at his church every Sunday for the interest they have manifested in his welfare. I do this in behalf of a struggling people who seldom meet with such friends. Mr. Kalloch has done for Mr. Martin what the abolitionists have long been doing for others, and the enchanted audiences who have listened to the lively and witty speeches of Wm. Wells Brown,[9] the inimitable mimicry and pungent sarcasm of Frederick Douglass, and the burning eloquence of Charles Lenox Remond,[10] must agree with us that the abo-lition idea of human rights is the correct one. (Applause.)

It is in this manner that we ask our friends to help us open those thor-oughfares through which all others are encouraged to pass, and in this manner keep continually breathing into the Anti-Slavery movement the breath of life. Then will we become educated and wealthy, and then the roughest looking colored man that you ever saw or ever will see will be pleasanter than the harmonies of Orpheus, and black will be a very pretty color. (Laughter.) It will make our jargon, wit; our words, oracles; flattery will then take the place of slander, and you will find no preju-dice in the Yankee whatever. (Applause.)

The question whether freedom or slavery shall triumph in this country will no doubt be settled ere long, and settled in accordance with the eternal principles of justice. Whether the result is to be brought about by the gradual diffusion of an anti-slavery gospel, or the method introduced by Crispus Attucks, and seconded by John Brown, no one can tell. I hope it may be done peaceably; but if, as appears to be the case, there is no use in crying peace, then let us not shrink from the responsibility. My motto has always been, "Better die freemen than live to be slaves."[11] In case of a contest with our enemies, fifty negroes would take the State of Virginia without the loss of a man. Gov. [Henry] Wise, as a manner of course, would be the first to surrender. (Applause.) One thousand negroes would sweep the slave States from the Potomac to the Rio Grande, and the time and places that know the slaveholders now would shortly know them no more forever. It has been said that "Virginia was frightened by seventeen men and a cow"; but if I remember aright, Virginia, even when under arms, was frightened by a *cow*. (Laughter.) Verily, verily, I say unto you, the slaveholders are a base race of *cowards*. (Laughter and Applause.)

The slaveholders affect to despise the leaders of the Anti-Slavery cause, as you have a fair illustration in Gov. Wise's bombastic speech to the half-civilized southern medical students, who left Philadelphia for Philadelphia's good.[12] But we too well know that it is common for men to affect disdain, when in reality their only sentiment is fear. Metellus ridiculed Sertorius, and called him "fugitive" and "outlaw"; and yet he offered for the head of this "fugitive" and "outlaw" no less than one hundred talents of silver, and twenty thousand acres of land! The barbarous offers of large sums of money by the slaveholders for the heads of prominent Anti-Slavery men prove that the latter are a power that is not disdained. All efforts, thus far, to crush the pioneers in our cause have proved the most miserable failures. Our cause is of God, and cannot be overthrown. (Applause.) Governor Wise, the distinguished Virginia knight-errant, after his imaginary victory of driving Wendell Phillips[13] into Canada, might have quoted these lines from Homer:

I saw my shaft with aim unerring go,
And deemed it sent him to the shades below;
But still he lives; some angry god withstands,
Whose malice thwarts these unavailing hands.

And when he commences his raid upon the North, he will find it exceedingly difficult to drive a windmill with a pair of bellows. (Laughter.)

Our cause is moving onward. The driving of the free colored people from the slave States, and the laws preventing their ingress into the free States, is only the tightening of the already stranded cord that binds the slave; and I am daily looking for some additional force to sever it, and thereby annihilate forever the relation existing between master and slave. (Applause.)

Boston *Liberator*, March 16, 1860. Reprinted in Ripley et al., *The Black Abolitionist Papers*, 5:58–66.

---

1. William C. Nell (1816–1874), Boston-born black abolitionist leader, was a close ally of William Lloyd Garrison. He is best remembered for his indispensable study of black contributions to American freedom, *Colored Patriots of the American Revolution* (1855). In the 1850s he organized annual Crispus Attucks celebrations, and during the Civil War he recruited for the 54th Massachusetts Regiment. Ripley et al., *The Black Abolitionist Papers*, 3:307–308.

2. Rock refers to the founding of the American Anti-Slavery Society in 1833, the bloody Nat Turner revolt in Northampton, Virginia, in 1831, and John Brown's raid against Harpers Ferry, Virginia, in October 1859.

3. Rock alludes to Hinton Rowan Helper (1829–1909), a North Carolinian, whose book *The Impending Crisis of the South and How to Meet It* (1857) stimulated enormous anger in the South. Seward, the leader of the Republican party prior to Lincoln's election, gained notoriety for asserting, in reaction to the Fugitive Slave Law, that the North should obey a "higher law" than the Constitution. In 1858 he announced that an "irrepressible conflict" faced the North and the South. As the 1860 election approached, Seward came under attack by reformers for distancing himself from abolitionism to gain votes. Hinton Rowan Helper, *The Impending Crisis of the South and How to Meet It*, ed., George Frederickson (Cambridge, MA: Belknap Press of Harvard University Press, 1968); Thomas D. Morris, *Free Men All: The Personal Liberty Laws of the North, 1780–1861* (Baltimore: Johns Hopkins University Press, 1974), 135–136; George E. Baker, ed., *The Works of William H. Seward*, 5 vols. (Boston: Houghton, Mifflin and Co., 1884), 4:56.

4. Gerrit Smith (1797–1874), one of the wealthiest Americans of his time, committed himself to abolitionism and black rights. Only William Lloyd

Garrison had more support among black abolitionists. Smith, a congress-man and major force in the Liberty Party, also became one of John Brown's most generous contributors. John Stauffer, *The Black Hearts of Men: Radical Abolitionists and the Transformation of Race* (Cambridge, MA: Harvard University Press, 2002).

5. From Thomas Moore's *Lalla Rookh: An Oriental Romance* (London: Longman, Hurst, Rees, Orme, and Brown, 1817).

6. An adaptation from Alphonse Marie Louis de Lamartine's *Voyage en Orient, 1832–1833* (Paris: C. Grosselin, 1843), later published as *Travels in the East* (Edinburgh: Chambers, 1850).

7. Rather than Shakespeare, these lines came from Richard Barnfield's *Poems: In Divers Humors* (London: Iohn Iaggard, 1598).

8. Abolitionists and reformers frequently met at Boston's Tremont Temple, an interracial Baptist congregation. J. Sella Martin temporarily filled the church's pulpit in 1859 when its regular pastor, Isaac Smith Kalloch, moved to Kansas. Ripley et al., *The Black Abolitionist Papers*, 5:69–70.

9. William Wells Brown (1814?–1884), the nation's first African American novelist, spent twenty years in slavery before escaping and settling in Buffalo, New York. He became active in the antislavery movement and its most effective speaker next to Frederick Douglass. Sometime after 1847 he moved to Boston and continued his career as an author and antislavery speaker. Ripley et al., *The Black Abolitionist Papers*, 4:5–6.

10. Charles Lenox Remond (1810–1873), a Salem, Massachusetts–born black abolitionist, became a founding member of the American Anti-Slavery Society and successfully led the campaign to desegregate Salem's public schools. He became one of Garrison's most valuable traveling agents. During the Civil War he, like many Boston black leaders, helped recruit men for the state's black regiments. Ripley et al., *The Black Abolitionist Papers*, 3:318–319.

11. This expression, repeated countless times during the Civil War, was popularized by Henry Highland Garnet's radical speech advocating slave rebellion, which was presented at the 1843 Black National Convention.

12. Virginia's governor addressed a group of Southern medical students who had withdrawn from two Philadelphia medical schools in protest over the Harpers Ferry raid. In his remarks, Wise accused abolitionists of threatening the Union. Ripley et al., *The Black Abolitionist Papers*, 5:70.

13. Many abolitionists who had contact with John Brown fled the country after the attack on Harpers Ferry. Wendell Phillips (1811–1884), perhaps the greatest orator in the antislavery community on either side of the Atlantic Ocean, remained in the United States and praised Brown's heroism. James Brewer Stewart, *Liberty's Hero* (Baton Rouge, LA: Louisiana State University Press, 1986).

"truth shall yet triumph over error"
Robert Hamilton
JULY 14, 1864

The war was a swift educator. Whites exclaimed again and again that they wanted no help from African Americans in defeating the South. But realities inevitably compelled a change in policy. In the Revolution, Washington at first did not want to enroll African Americans in the army, although they had fought valiantly for the patriot cause since the Bunker Hill battle. The need for men changed Washington's official policy, and soon the Continental Army enlisted blacks, installing them alongside their white comrades in the same regiments. In the War of 1812, African Americans proved critical to Jackson's victories in the south and to Oliver Hazard Perry's victories on the Great Lakes. When Philadelphia was threatened, African Americans worked feverishly to build defenses. During the Civil War, the navy immediately turned to blacks for help and, in general, accorded its black personnel equality in pay, benefits, and conditions. Although blacks certainly encountered racial prejudice in the navy, it amounted to little compared to what the average black soldier endured in the army. But blacks who worked as laborers for the navy found that the old rules of racial hatred still applied.

The U.S. Navy, since its early days, had been accustomed to using slave labor to build its facilities. The economic advantages of slave labor over free labor proved irresistible. With the adoption of the Second Confiscation Act in 1862, the navy speedily sought to exploit the slave manpower that suddenly became available to it. It established thirteen camps of at least 8,000 men and their families, and from these facilities enlisted many new sailors and naval employees. Although the camps existed in the South, much of the manpower needs lay in the North. The navy sent hundreds of former slaves to its facilities in New York and even to New Hampshire, where the men encountered the hate and jealousy of local workers who feared losing their jobs to the temporary emigrants. As Robert Hamilton (1819?–?), the talented editor of the New York *Weekly Anglo-African* warned, when a crisis loomed, whites forgot their prejudices and welcomed the opportunity to work alongside blacks. But when the immediate threat passed, ingrained prejudice reasserted itself. The lessons that Hamilton learned about this in 1864 would prove instructive the next year when the guns fell silent.

Robert Hamilton, in addition to enjoying a brilliant editorial career along with his brother Thomas, earned wide respect for his work against the American Colonization Society and for black suffrage in New York State. He helped organize city blacks against the Fugitive Slave Law and in 1856 sat on the executive committee of the American League of Colored Laborers. His masterful handling of the New York Weekly Anglo-African during the Civil War offered a powerful forum for black soldiers and for the defense of black rights. His untimely death in November 1865 denied Northern blacks a thoughtful and influential voice. Ripley et al., *The Black Abolitionist Papers*, 5:27–29; Steven J. Ramold, *Slaves, Sailors, Citizens: African Americans in the Union Navy* (DeKalb, IL: Northern Illinois University Press, 2002), 23, 45–47.

Editorial Correspondence.
Washington, July 14, 1864.

AN OLD PICTURE IN A NEW FRAME

WHEN THE CITY WAS thought to be in imminent danger of capture, the employees of the Navy Yard were all taken to work in the trenches. They, both white and black, went with alacrity, nor did the white men stand upon the order of their going: they willingly took seats in the cars and wagons with black men, and not a murmur was heard. This was on Tuesday. On Thursday, the danger being over, the men were ordered home, and now the discovery was made by many of these whites that they could not and would not ride in the same car with "niggers." The Superintendent of the Yard reminded them of the fact that they had rode with them coming out, and worked with them in the trenches, and he did not intend to stand by and see the colored men insulted. If they would not ride with the colored men they might walk. He, at the same time, ordered the colored men to get in the cars. What others may think we know not, but it does appear to us that Southern rebels are a complete embodiment of honor when compared to these creatures. Is it any wonder that the South despises them, and is fighting to get rid of them? When we recollect that the Navy Yards, workshops, and other departments of government, including the Postmaster General's office, is filled with these haters of a portion of God's creation, because they are black, we are compelled to ask ourself the question: How can the God of justice give victory to the arms of such a people? We confess that it is a hard matter to wish and labor for the prosperity and perpetuity of a nation that fosters the sentiments which make the growth of such reptiles possible. But the goodness and mercy of God, as already manifested towards this nation, even against the designs of its rulers, makes us to feel and know that truth shall yet triumph over error, and the principles of the Declaration of Independence shall yet be a living reality in our land.

REBELS

This city is filled with rebels of the meanest kind. They have not the honesty of those in the South, but under the shadow of an oath of allegiance, they await the hour when they can assist in tearing out the heart of the nation, and handing it over to their superiors in the South.

They thought that the Southern army was coming into the city this week, and they manifested their joy in a thousand ways. The chuckle was in their throats, and the fire of revenge gleamed from their eyes; but, thank God, their anticipated carnival came not, and now they have slunk away to their hiding-places to abide their time.

SOLDIERS' AID SOCIETY

A society of this character has been formed in Asbury Church,[1] consisting of ladies and gentlemen. The officers have not been elected, but the Association has already done much for our wounded soldiers at Camp Barker.[2] This makes the third society of the kind now existing among the colored people in this city. Persons at a distance might wonder why so many societies of the same kind should exist here, but when it is recollected that the members of the different churches do not mingle much socially, the wonder why their action is isolated ceases. No joint action will ever take place until the good and true-hearted of all the churches become acquainted and seek each others society for noble purposes.

R. H.

New York *Weekly Anglo-African*, July 30, 1864.

1. The Asbury United Methodist Church was founded in 1836 by African Americans who withdrew from the Foundry Methodist Church because of white racial prejudice. The congregation constructed several buildings, all on the church's original site at the corner of Eleventh and K Streets, NW, in Washington, D.C. www.asburyumcdc.org.
2. Camp Barker was established for freedmen at Thirteenth Street and Vermont Avenue in Washington, D.C., on the current site of the Howard University Hospital. Elaine C. Everly, "Freedmen's Bureau Records: An Overview," *Prologue Magazine*, U.S. National Archives & Records Administration, www.archives.gov/publications/prologue.

"We need no compromise with traitors"
"Africano" to the *Weekly Anglo-African*
SEPTEMBER 2, 1864

The election of 1864 was anything but a foregone conclusion. Until Sherman's victory at Atlanta on the day that this anonymous soldier in the 5th Massachusetts Cavalry wrote to the *Weekly Anglo-African*, Lincoln believed that he would lose and that America's "Napoleon" would become president. Prior to September 1864 disgust with the war, the endless casualty lists, and the South's vexing ability to endure threatened Lincoln's political survival. Earlier in the year, Secretary of the Treasury Salmon P. Chase sought to replace him on the Republican ticket. Abolitionists harped on Lincoln's shortcomings, his deafness to the grievances of black soldiers, and his dreary reconstruction policies in Louisiana that portended much ill after the end of the war. They abhorred his unwillingness to directly attack slavery, and they favored either Chase or the party's 1856 presidential candidate, John C. Frémont, who possessed meaningful antislavery credentials.

But the prospect of a victory by George B. McClellan and the Democratic Party sent waves of fear into African Americans. McClellan, an avowed racist who had strong support even in liberal Boston, symbolized to Northern blacks the nation's legacy of racial injustice. He had pledged to end the war swiftly and to preserve all "Southern rights."

Phrases such as "the Union as it was," which fell from the lips of Democrats across the North, meant to blacks only the preservation of racial hatred and slavery. For a black soldier such as "Africano," who risked his life to preserve the Union and end slavery, the reality of a McClellan candidacy reminded him of the continued precariousness of Northern black life. Sherman's victory and Frémont's withdrawal from the race in mid-September guaranteed Lincoln's victory. But the meaning of McClellan's popularity could not be ignored. James McPherson, *The Struggle for Equality: Abolitionists and the Negro in the Civil War and Reconstruction* (Princeton, NJ: Princeton University Press, 1964), 260–286.

THE CHICAGO CONVENTION.

GEORGE B. MCCLELLAN—THE COUNTRY AND THE NEGRO

MR. EDITOR: THE SIGNS of the times leave no room for doubting the triumph of the Democratic party in the ensuing Presidential election. The most sceptical observer can no longer doubt the restoration of the Union on such a platform of peace as will naturally be adopted by McClellan and his peace-at-any-cost partisans, after the final achievement of their political trophy.

Should the Chicago Convention succeed in being the means of McClellan's political aggrandizement, the horrific enmity of the slave oligarchs will again spread its dire effects over the whole of the country, and black men will become, after the final settlement, the object of the unmitigated wrath of both *War* and *Peace* Democrats.

In all probability this state of things, coming from the stirring events of the past week, is liberty's funeral knell, the echo of which will reverberate from the Atlantic to the Pacific Ocean, racking the foundations of liberty's sanctum wherever established.

The slave trade, notwithstanding the solemn compact of the civilized world, will again be inaugurated regardless even of the principles of international law, and negroes will be at as high a demand as before the cannons of rebeldom belched their destructive missiles on the ramparts of Sumter. Forbid it, Muse! forbid it, Heaven!

Whatever visitations of Divine wrath McClellan's success may bring upon the country at large, there is to-day ground enough for the conviction that ere months elapse this most unnatural and destructive rebellion will be at an end—the *Union* and *Constitution* as it is was preserved—and, alas! the darkness of human bondage, from which the country was fast emerging, will again spread its gloominess with revivified strength in to the heart of the States made free even by Lincoln's "military necessity."

The Territories into which the non-extension of slavery has caused so much blood and treasure to flow, will be at the very mercy of liberty's assailants, who will not fail to carry out pre-eminently their preconcerted design. Why must the people submit to this triumph, which is conducive only to the country's dishonor, and pregnant with at least the temporary benefit of a few upstart politicians? Why should not the great mass of the loyal Union people of the North—and if there is any to be found in the South—rise in their strength, and like an earthquake of power, drive these Party entangling, Humanity and Justice degrading politicians from the arena, and nominate, in the Nation's name, a man more worthy of the Nation's gift, a man more capable of sustaining the national honor by enforcing submission upon traitors?

Is it to be conceded—is it to be thought consistent—that we are wrong and the South right?

Must we now have to confess, after having exhausted the country of its best blood and pecuniary resources, depopulated every hamlet, destroyed the peace of mothers and wives, and carried the country to the verge of bankruptcy and almost irretrievable ruin, that the rebellion was only an unintentional error, and that, on our part, that the South was upholding and defending her "State rights" *sanctioned by the Constitution,* and that *we* were indulging in a *frenzy founded on Abolitionism* and sanctioned only by public opinion and fanaticism in the North? Animadversion in this case would only exhibit the weak and annihilated side of the so-called *"rights"* of the South leaving them to liquify into nothingness.

We who are fighting our country's battles, without pay or without even being considered as prisoners of war, are not yet weary of the conflict and the late victories achieved by our Anglo-Saxon brethren who are, like us, in the same boat, do not evince any palpable evidence of the least weariness on their part. Would it not, therefore, be prudent that the politicians at home think well before they act? I would say surely they should. Their growing boldness may be the cause of a unit military effort, which, like a devastating hurricane, will sweep them forever from the shrine at which they so delight to adore.

Are we to have, now that on every battlefield slavery's banner has been crushed and liberty's unfurled to the breeze, a compromise with armed traitors by securing to them fresh guarantees in putting an arch-traitor at the head of our government at the expense of Liberty, Humanity and Justice? No! One hundred thousand more black freemen would leave their peaceful cots and freely give their lies as hecatombs for freedom's cause!

Hundreds of thousands of lives, as if concentrated in one, would be willing to share a soldier's grave, and then we should be for vigorously prosecuting this monstrous rebellion until we forced the traitors to submit to that flag which they so flagrantly insulted.

We need no compromise with traitors, for their rebellion has become so circumscribed that it can with justice be said to be in a *nutshell* and must soon be unkernelled.

[Gen. U. S.] Grant's unprevaricating arm is daily hovering around the little sphere in which its main strength is embodied; and when the nation least think, the glorious tidings will be made known, and the birds of the air, with their harmonious voices, will announce to the silent, grumbling, desponding and never-satisfied North the *"resurrexit libertas,"*[1] giving them to understand that Richmond, the proud and haughty rebel Capital, has fallen and is ours, and that peace, more lasting than ever, has decked the sky with her rosy fingers, pouring plenty into the nation's lap.

We have wandered from our subject, but like a rallying army we again return to the front.

It is true that George B. McClellan, has been an active war Democrat, but what did his activity accomplish for the furtherance of the Union cause? What did his war-like proclivities achieve? Carnage and famine, defeat and dishonor! We say that had he been animated with the least spark of patriotism he could have not only gained the nation's sympathies, but the applause of the world, for he could have [checked] the bloody stream by strangling the rebellion ere it attained its maturity. Instead of this we saw him when at the head of the grand army of the United States, pampering with treason; bartering human sinews, and enforcing the Fugitive Slave Law, by returning the negroes to their disloyal masters whose hands have just been plunged into the blood of those sustaining their country's flag.

Is this the worthiest of the Democratic party? Is this the only political horse that the Democratic stables afford? Is this, I would ask, the man on whose shoulders the chariot wheels of this great Republic is to rest? I pity the Democratic hostlers, if George B. McClellan is the only, the best, the fleetest and the strongest horse they have kept in reserve for a crisis on which the country's weal or woe depends. I pity the Nation, if he is the only man capable of avoiding the country's impending ruin by bringing out of chaos this once prosperous realm of commerce and uninterrupted prosperity.

O all ye true Democrats, consider the labyrinth into which your utter recklessness has plunged our common country, and cease to dispoil her of her few remaining jewels, cease now ere it to be too late to gratify your political greed. Are you going to give despotic Europe the proof of what has been so often asserted? Are you going to implore Divine Providence to hurl His thunderbolts on this already wrath-consumed country, that like the great Republic of old, she may perish by her own grandeur?

Has not God's accumulated wrath gone into the corners—into the hiding places of this land and nearly destroyed the wicked found therein?—Yes, the scum from all other climes has he destroyed; the oppressors of his people he has smitten as with the rod of his vengeance, and *you* silent lookers on, secret abettors of crime, of oppression and of man-stealing, he has purged ago, even to the loss of your once vaunted and proud nationality!

Must Slavery and the Union be now preserved after so many heart-rending sacrifices, or must Right, Freedom, Humanity and Justice be the corner-stones of this Republic? This is a question that I will not, under existing circumstances, undertake to answer.

Here is a question presenting itself worthy the attention of the clamorers for peace; are we to prostrate ourselves before a prostrate and nearly lifeless foe, by submitting to worn out and fallen politicians, who, like their treason hatching brethren, are fast degenerating into nothing—even into political insignificance?

The answer appropriate to this interrogatory concerns the integrity, the inviolability, the future well-being of our country, therefore in our next we will give it a little attention.

Africano

Regimental Hospital, Point Lookout, Md.
Sept. 2d, 1864.

New York *Weekly Anglo-African*, September 17, 1864.

---

1. Revival of liberty.

"Save us from our Friends (?)"
Paschal Beverly Randolph to the *Weekly Anglo-African*
NOVEMBER 5, 1864

A person's antislavery commitment did not necessarily reflect positive racial attitudes. As African Americans discovered with disturbing regularity, few of their white allies lived up to the highest ideals of the antislavery movement. John S. Rock made clear that even in Boston, the cradle of liberty and the home of the antislavery movement, racial prejudice still reigned. With few exceptions, black abolitionists encountered ugly manifestations of racism even among their closest white allies. Frederick Douglass broke with his white Boston colleagues because they could not abide his drive for leadership and independence. They wanted a black speaker whose voice still reflected a "little of the plantation," and they discouraged the publication of black newspapers which white leaders could not control. White abolitionists who owned businesses or who controlled job opportunities in antislavery offices either refused to hire African Americans or relegated them to inferior positions that exposed them to quick job loss when contributions fell.

The black abolitionist and popular spiritualist Paschal Beverly Randolph (1825–1875) and a colleague visited the offices of the National Freedmen's Relief Association in the fall of 1864. Randolph was one of the most unusual figures to emerge out of the nineteenth century. Born in New York's rugged "Five Points" district, he largely made his own way in the world after the death of his mother; his father, if he knew him at all, never assisted in the child's upbringing. Of mixed racial parentage and light skinned, Randolph lifted himself from the streets of New York and, through the assistance of an aunt, made his way as a cabin boy on a vessel that operated out of New Bedford, Massachusetts. During the 1840s he worked as a barber in upstate New York, somehow finding the time to educate himself along exceptional lines. In 1852 he dramatically announced himself as "Dr. Paschal Beverly Randolph, clairvoyant physician and psycho-phrenologist." He specialized in human sexual problems, mostly those of women, and spiritualism. As a self-trained "physician," he became the nation's most popular advocate of the use of hashish.

Racism and racial identity would dog Randolph all his life and at times he would claim Spanish heritage to escape the burdens of a black identity. But during the late 1850s and the Civil War, Randolph proudly identified himself with the black abolitionist cause. William Lloyd Garrison, Henry Ward Beecher, and especially Gerrit Smith offered him assistance and support. He became an effective and well-known advocate of black recruitment, and he delivered a much-admired address at the 1864 Black National Convention. He moved to New Orleans in 1864, became deeply immersed in local politics, and worked as an agent for the New York *Weekly Anglo-African.* In 1866 he toured Illinois, promoting black suffrage and winning praise as "a champion of the rights of man." But for most of his life, Randolph was a spiritualist and occultist who existed on the fringes of the legitimate medical profession. It is thought that he likely suffered from bipolar disorder or a similar malady. Randolph shot himself in the head in Toledo, Ohio, on July 29, 1875.

But in the fall of 1864, Beverly and his colleague wished to volunteer to go South and assist the newly freed slaves. Many Northern blacks traveled to the former slave states, both during and after the war, feeling it their particular duty to assist their brethren in the difficult transition to freedom. Randolph no doubt expected a warm reception from the father of Col. Robert Gould Shaw, the commander of the 54th Massachusetts Regiment who had died with so many of his black troops attacking Fort Wagner the previous year. But well-attuned to racial intolerance, Randolph came away from Shaw's office with an invaluable, if unexpected, lesson that he had learned many times before: "the black race must be its own deliverer." Jane H. Pease and William H. Pease, *They Who Would Be Free: Blacks' Search for Freedom, 1830–1861* (orig. 1974, Urbana, IL: University of Illinois Press, 1990), 76–78, 82–93; John Patrick Deveney, *Paschal Beverly Randolph: A Nineteenth-Century Black American Spiritualist, Rosicrucian, and Sex Magician* (Albany, NY: State University of New York Press, 1997); Philip S. Foner and George E. Walker, eds., *Proceedings of the Black National and State Conventions, 1865–1900* (Philadelphia: Temple University Press, 1986), I:248, 259, 274.

SAVE US FROM OUR FRIENDS

Mr. Editor: Another demonstrative proof that the black race must be its own deliverer, was presented to me to-day; and one too, so decisive as to leave no room to doubt in what light we are really and at bottom held by men who make philanthropy a business, and use the negro as either the stepping-stone to power, or the convenient black grindstone whereon to sharpen their axes.

Myself and Mr. Frank Potter having determined to go down South, and there aid the Freedmen, by establishing schools and organizing them, in and for which work we proposed to act entirely without cost to anyone—Mr. P. sustaining himself by his trade, and I by my profession—we learned that by applying to Mr. F. G. Shaw, President of the N. F. R. Association,[1] we might find out all we required to know relative to the field we proposed to labor in. Accordingly, we called on him, entered the office, and found Mr. S. at his desk, conversing very politely with several white men. As we entered, he looked up, and seeing our color, and before we had time to open our lips, rudely waved his hand; and ordered us to leave the room and stay in the hall till he got ready. Surprised at such treatment, I halted, when he twice repeated his order in the most offensive manner; whereon I indignantly left the room and building, positively assured that our color alone was the pretext for the insult, and feeling that if our cause is left to the care of such lovers of our race, it is quite time that we put our sole trust in God.

P. B. Randolph, M.D.

New York *Weekly Anglo-African*, November 5, 1864.

———

1. Francis George Shaw (1809–1882), an abolitionist and reformer originally from Boston, lived on Staten Island during the war and was president of the National Freedmen's Relief Association, the New York branch of the American Freedmen's Union Commission. The NFRA's offices were on lower Fourth Avenue in Manhattan. Joan Waugh, *Unsentimental Reformer: The Life of Josephine Shaw Lowell* (Cambridge, MA: Harvard University Press, 1997), 90, 186.

5

Race Riots

Hate in Detroit
John A. Warren to Elisha Weaver
MARCH 21, 1863

The infamous New York "draft riot" of July 1863 was not the first incident of its kind to mar the Civil War years. Blacks endured a persistent pattern of racial antagonism that stretched from the early nineteenth century to the mid-twentieth century. In Civil War Philadelphia, an African American could not walk the streets in safety, and "the very lowest and the most vulgar language that ever any human being uttered, is addressed to our wives and daughters." When race hate exploded in Detroit on March 6, 1863, whites had been whipped up for months by the city's popular newspaper, the *Free Press*. A racist enemy of the Lincoln administration and the war, the *Free Press* spewed immense amounts of bile warning against miscegenation and the threats that emancipated slaves posed to free white labor in the North. Labor strikes and the new draft law, published in the *Free Press* the day before the riot, only further inflamed Detroit whites.

On the afternoon of March 6, white rage centered on a saloon keeper named William Faulkner. Arrested on February 26 for the rape of two nine-year-old girls, Mary Brown and Ellen Hoover, Faulkner was thought to be a mulatto, although he claimed to be of mixed Spanish and Indian parentage. No evidence for the crime existed except for the testimony of the two girls who testified that Faulkner enticed them into his saloon, an "amalgamation den." The "black fiend, the monster Faulkner," the *Free Press* bellowed, deserved the "gibbet or the guillatine [sic]." The crowded courtroom seethed, and about 1,000 whites paced in front of city hall, which housed the court.

The trial lasted less than a day, and the jury decided Faulkner's fate after ten minutes of deliberation. "Guilty" hung in the air like the ringing of a giant firebell. When Faulkner, surrounded by an armed military guard, tried to make his way to the jail, rioters attacked with bricks and paving stones. The soldiers leveled their rifles, fixed with bayonets, at the rabble. Poor shots or unwilling to kill, they fired at the crowd but killed an innocent bystander. In the ensuing melee, the soldiers rushed Faulkner into the jail. The rioters, screaming "kill the niggers," plunged into Detroit's black neighborhood, wreaking havoc. They attacked one of the city's most successful black businesses, Whitney Reynolds's cooperage. Although Reynolds was away, his employees defended his factory and home. Joshua Boyd, an older employee, had just escaped from slavery in western Virginia and was working to buy the rest of his family from their owner. Their hopes for freedom ended when a rioter smashed open Boyd's skull with an ax. The mob then fired the building, chasing the Reynolds family from their home. Rioters grabbed a newborn infant and tossed it fifteen feet onto the pavement. By 8:00 that evening, when the 27th Michigan arrived to quell the violence, thirty black-owned buildings had been incinerated, and about 200 of Detroit's African Americans had been rendered homeless and destitute. Although only about two people lost their lives in the riot, scores were injured, and the financial losses were staggering.

John A. Warren (1815–1870), who composed the following account of the Detroit riot, was from Baltimore and became an active black abolitionist and a successful AME Church clergyman. He spent three years preaching in Detroit, and he served a variety of churches in the Midwest and in Canada. *Christian Recorder,* March 14, 1863; Frank B. Woodford, *Father Abraham's Children: Michigan Episodes in the Civil War* (Detroit, MI: Wayne State University Press, 1961), 63–70; John C. Schneider, "Detroit and the Problem of Disorder: The Riot of 1863," *Michigan History* 58 (1974): 4–24; Ripley et al., *The Black Abolitionist Papers,* 2:331; Benjamin Tanner, *An Apology for African Methodism* (Baltimore, MD: n.p., 1867), 264–269; *Pine and Palm,* October 5, 1861.

MOB LAW IN DETROIT

BRO. WEAVER[1]:—You have doubtless heard before this, through the public journals, that many of our brethren have become homeless, houseless, and penniless by a disgraceful riot which took place in our city on the 6th inst.

Allow me, through the columns of the Recorder, to give you a bird's eye view of the suffering of our people. I am aware that many of our people are anxiously looking and impatiently waiting for me to answer the many letters they have written me about the condition of their friends. I therefore seize the present moment to answer them, one and all, through the columns of our organ, in a summary manner. The first question generally asked is, what was the cause of the riot?

I answer. The immediate cause was <u>prejudice</u> and passion, brought on by the Democratic <u>Free Press,</u> the most reckless sheet that was ever issued from any press. Every crime perpetrated by a negro is magnified tenfold. If he steals a chicken, the Free Press reports it a horse. If he knocks down a "rough" in self-defence, the Free Press construes it into an attempt to murder. Thus he would have us killed all day long. Do you ask me why he persecutes the poor colored people, whose houses were sacked and burned, and whose lives were periled, to the disgrace of the city of Detroit [?] I answer, for political purposes. Let me say to that Editor, beware! for he that sows the wind, shall, in God's good time, reap the whirlwind. But, I must be brief. The white man, (they say colored man) [William] Falkner,[2] was arraigned before the court, found guilty of a diabolical outrage upon a white girl, also a colored girl, by the name of Ella Hoover. He was sentenced to prison for life. While on his way to prison, the mob attempted to arrest him from the hands of the officers. In this, they were disappointed, for the police were determined that the law should be obeyed, and the prisoner secured in the jail; before this was accomplished, however, one man was killed and several wounded. The mob at this moment became enraged, and one man, mounting a stump, cried out, "Gentlem[e]n, I am for killing all the negroes." "Kill the negroes, kill the negroes!" shouted five hundred, at the top of their voices. They came down Benden St., frantic, like so many devils. They made a halt at the Sumner House, kept by Mr. Buckner. They broke his windows. They proceeded on to Lafayette St., to the house of Edward Frease, Thomas Belton, Sarah Streets, Susan Biddle,

Mary Jones, Edward Pierce, and Mr. Fletcher. Brother Pierce kept a second-hand furniture store. His house, together with that of Mr. Brown, who kept the Sailor's boarding house, was all destroyed by fire, with their contents. Messrs. Pierce and Fletcher were seriously injured. The next place they attacked was Whitney Reynold's cooper-shop. This brother has truly distinguished himself by the many hands he employed, and the number of barrels he turned out weekly. Brother Reynolds was not home at the time of the riot. His hands fought like heroes to save his property. They never left his building until the house was set on fire; and in their retreat from the building, Solomon Houster, Lewis Houster, and Mr. Boyd were seriously injured—the latter has since died. Brother Reynolds['s] loss is great, but I am glad to say that the citizens are making every provision to relieve our suffering people, and our city is again restored to peace.

I almost forgot to mention that Father Evans, Bro. Williams, and Mr. Berley had lost all by fire. Father Evans, who is eighty years of age, was badly beaten. He was supposed to be dead when they stopped beating him. The old gentleman is still living, but suffering much from his injuries. He is an honest and upright old man, and has thus lived for forty years in the city of Detroit. He has a son, Mr. Evans, who has been head-waiter at the Biddle House a number of years.

Yours, faithfully,

JOHN A. WARREN.

Philadelphia *Christian Recorder*, March 21, 1863.

---

1. Elisha Weaver, born in North Carolina, left for Paoli, Indiana, where he attended Quaker schools. While living in Indianapolis, he founded schools for African Americans and became extremely active in abolitionism and the Underground Railroad. In 1849 he joined the AME Church and briefly attended Oberlin College before becoming a full-time laborer for the church. In 1857 he launched a monthly magazine devoted to literature and religion and served in a variety of AME Church publishing positions. From 1861 to 1867 he served as editor of the *Christian Recorder*. After the Civil War, Weaver filled pulpits in Buffalo, New York, and Newark, New Jersey. Benjamin Tanner, *An Apology for African Methodism* (Baltimore, MD: n.p., 1867), 175–177; Alexander W. Wayman, *My Recollections of African M.E. Ministers, or Forty Years' Experience in the African Methodist Episcopal Church*

(Philadelphia: A.M.E. Book Rooms, 1881), 77–100, 118–119; Alexander W. Wayman, *Cyclopaedia of African Methodism* (Baltimore, MD: Methodist Episcopal Book Depository, 1882), 177.

2. Faulkner, a Detroit saloon keeper, denied being black and claimed to be Spanish and American Indian. His two accusers later recanted their testimony and the city released him from prison. Some of Detroit's wealthier citizens reestablished Faulkner in a business, but the city refused to compensate Detroit's black citizens for their losses. Woodford, *Father Abraham's Children*, 65.

The New York Draft Riot
William P. Powell to William Lloyd Garrison
JULY 18, 1863

The nineteenth century's most devastating race riot took place in New York City on July 13–17, 1863. Fed by hate, fear, an incendiary press, and opposition to the war, white workers (many of whom were Irish) paralyzed the city and attempted to kill, maim, or injure as many African Americans as possible. They hung at least one black from a street lamp, lit a bonfire beneath him, and stripped flesh off his legs. The family of Sgt. Robert J. Simmons of the 54th Massachusetts Regiment, who gave up his life in the attack on Fort Wagner the day after the riot, lost their home, and his nephew was murdered. The rabble burned the Colored Orphan Asylum, although the children escaped uninjured. At least eleven blacks were killed and hundreds suffered injury or significant property losses.

William P. Powell (1807?–1879), a freeborn New Yorker of African and American Indian heritage and a founding member of the American Anti-Slavery Society, spent the early part of his career as a sailor. In 1839 he and his wife Mercy O. Haskins (1814–?) opened a home for sailors. They left for England after passage of the Fugitive Slave Law to avoid its consequences and to ensure the proper education of their five children. The Powells' daughter Sarah A. Powell (b. 1845) was an invalid who nevertheless worked as a wax-flower maker and as a teacher of needlework.

After returning to New York in 1861 Powell resumed his antislavery and reform activities. His Colored Seamen's Home, established in 1839, a financial success and an effective venue for disseminating antislavery literature, became a target of the rioters in 1863. Just as in Detroit four months earlier, white rioters singled out the symbols of black achievement and uplift and sought to destroy them. William P. Powell, whose son served as a surgeon in the Union army, had proven himself a solid citizen and a living rebuke of racist stereotypes. Nevertheless, his success did not shield Powell and his Seamen's Home from the mob. His disappointment was palpable. "What more could I do? What further evidence was wanting to prove my allegiance in the exigencies of our unfortunate country?" The riots ended only with the arrival of Union soldiers fresh from the Gettysburg battlefields. As many as a hundred people died in the mayhem, and the black community suffered devastating losses. City leaders later organized a drive to relieve those who suffered losses in the riots, and Powell reopened his Seamen's Home three months later. In the following letter to the famed radical abolitionist William Lloyd Garrison, written from the safety of New Bedford, Massachusetts, Powell detailed the attack on his property and family. Iver Bernstein, *The New York City Draft Riots: Their Significance for American Society and Politics in the Age of the Civil War* (New York: Oxford University Press, 1990); Ripley et al., *The Black Abolitionist Papers*, 3:302–303, 5:235–237.

New Bedford, [Massachusetts]
July 18, 1863

FRIEND GARRISON:

With a sorrowful heart, I write you a narrative of the outrages perpetrated upon myself and defenceless family by a lawless, infuriated New York mob. On the afternoon of the 18th inst., the Colored Sailors' Home, No. 2 Dover street, was invaded by a mob of half-grown boys. At this Home, established under the direction of the American Seamen's Friend Society,[1] boarded the last eleven months four hundred and fifty colored seamen. Founded on the strict principles of temperance, and the moral and religious elevation of my brethren of the sea, it was the only refuge where *they* could rest secure, when in port, from the snares and temptations which unhappily beset them on shore.

More than thirteen years ago, the anniversary meeting of the American Anti-Slavery Society was mobbed, and driven out of the Broadway

Tabernacle and other public buildings by the notorious Capt. [Isaiah] Rynders and his hellish crew. That was an outrage for which it was hoped New York had condoned for by confession, contrition and satisfaction, and had received absolution and remission of their sins, from the ghastly hands of our downtrodden humanity.

Dear Garrison, throughout the course of your eventful life, as the unflinching advocate of the suffering dumb of our enslaved race, in which you have never faltered, and have, from time to time, been mobbed, imprisoned, bruised, beaten, and dragged through the streets of Puritan Boston as a malefactor, you can well enter into my feelings. As a man of peace, I have religiously, and upon principles eternal as the heavens, never armed myself with deadly weapons of defence, and thus have been at the mercy of bloodthirsty Vandals. It was the wisdom of one insignificant man that once saved a besieged city. I thank God who has given me the victory—to rely wholly upon His all-protecting arm. It was better that all my property should be destroyed, as it has been, and my family stripped of everything except the clothing in which they escaped with their lives, than that one drop of blood should be shed in defence of their lives. Let us thank God that He still reigns, and that He will yet make the wrath of man to praise him.

From 2 P.M. till 8 P.M. myself and family were prisoners in my own house to *king mob,* from which there was no way to escape but over the roofs of adjoining houses. About 4 P.M., I sent a note to Superintendent [John A.] Kennedy for protection, but received none, from the fact that he had been seriously injured by the mob in another part of the city. Well, the mob commenced throwing stones at the lower windows until they had succeeded in making an opening. I was determined not to leave until driven from the premises. My family, including my invalid daughter (who is entirely helpless), took refuge on the roof of the next house. I remained till the mob broke in, and then narrowly escaped the same way. This was about 8½ P.M. We remained on the roof for an hour; still I hoped relief would come. The neighbors, anticipating the mob would fire my house, were removing their effects on the roof—all was excitement. But as the object of the mob was plunder, they were too busy engaged in carrying off all my effects to apply the torch. Add to this, it began to rain as if the very heavens were shedding tears over the dreadful calamity. "Hung be the heavens with black!"

How to escape from the roof of a five-story building with four females—and one a cripple—besides eight men, without a ladder, or any
assistance from outside, was beyond my *not* excited imagination. But
the God that succored Hagar in her flight came to my relief in the person of a little, deformed, despised Israelite—who, Samaritan-like, took
my poor helpless daughter under his protection in his house; there I presume she now is, until friends send her to me. He also supplied me with
a long rope. I then took a survey of the premises, and fortunately found
a way to escape; and though pitchy dark, I took *soundings* with the rope,
to see if it would touch the next roof, after which I took a clovehitch
around the clothesline which was fastened to the wall by pulleys, and
which led from one roof to the other over a space of about one hundred
feet. In this manner I managed to lower my family down to the next
roof, and from one roof to another, until I landed them in a neighbor's
yard. We were secreted in our friend's cellar till 11 P.M., when we were
taken in charge by the police, and locked up in the Station house for
safety. In this dismal place, we found upwards of *seventy* men, women
and children—some with broken limbs—bruised and beaten from head
to foot. We stayed in this place for twenty-four hours, when the police
escorted us to the New Haven boat, at 11 P.M. Thus we escaped from
an infuriated mob, leaving our invalid daughter in New York in the
hands of kind friends.

All my personal property, to the amount of $3000, has been scattered
to the four winds, which, "like the baseless fabric of a vision, leaves not
a wreck behind," except our lives; and so the Lord be praised.

As a devoted loyal Unionist, I have done all I could do to perpetuate and uphold the integrity of this free government. As an evidence of
this devotedness, my oldest son[2] is now serving my country as a surgeon
in the United States army, and myself had just received a commission
in the naval service. What more could I do? What further evidence was
wanting to prove my allegiance in the exigencies of our unfortunate
country? I am now an old man, stripped of everything which I once possessed, of all the comforts of life; but I thank God that He has yet spared
my life, which I am ready to yield in the defence of my country. I am,

Sir, yours, &c.,

WM. P. POWELL

Boston *Liberator*, July 24, 1863.

1. Powell established the Colored Seamen's Home in 1839 in New York City to assist black seamen and to promote abolitionism. His facility received finanicial support from the American Seamen's Friend Society, a Protestant mission society. Powell boasted of his success in using black seamen to disseminate David Walker's *Appeal* in the South, and he maintained a large antislavery library for the sailors' use. He reopened the facility in 1861 after a ten-year hiatus, and cooperated with several of his lodgers to organize the American Seamen's Protective Union Association. His considerable success and public role as an abolitionist made him a target for the racist rioters. Although Powell suffered both financially and emotionally for the 1863 riot, he reopened the Seamen's Home and continued operations until after the end of the war. Ripley et al., *The Black Abolitionist Papers*, 5:236.
2. William P. Powell, Jr. (b. 1836).

"not the first of its kind, and it may not be the last"
J. W. C. Pennington
August 24, 1863

James W. C. Pennington (1807–1870), a recipient of an honorary Doctor of Divinity degree from the University of Heidelberg, represented the talent and courage of Northern black leaders. Born in Queen Anne's County, Maryland, Pennington enjoyed much freedom in slavery, but witnessed enormous abuse, and in 1827, at age twenty, resolved to escape. An abolitionist Pennsylvania Quaker family provided him with shelter and taught Pennington to read and write. He moved on to Brooklyn, New York, and within a few years began speaking out against the hated American Colonization Society. He received additional education from local Sunday schools, and he also paid for his own tutors. Determined to become a clergyman, Pennington moved to New Haven, Connecticut, to attend Yale Divinity School, but was rejected because of his race. Nevertheless, the school allowed him to attend classes, and eventually he took over a Congregational church in Hartford.

Pennington fought for black education and attacked racism in all its many forms. He became a founding member of the Union Missionary

Society, and he acquired a national reputation for his antislavery and African missionary work. In the late 1840s he assumed the pulpit of New York's Shiloh Presbyterian Church, and in 1850 he published his very successful autobiography, *The Fugitive Blacksmith,* a story that emphasized the triumph of persistence and courage over adversity. At the time of his remarks about the 1863 New York riots, Pennington had fallen on hard times. He had lost his congregation, and likely taught school in Poughkeepsie to keep the wolf from the door. After the war he served as a missionary to the freedmen in Natchez, Mississippi, and in Jacksonville, Florida, where he died.

The anger in the following address needed no fuel from personal frustrations or disappointment. Pennington knew firsthand the injustices of slavery and racism, and he understood that the outrages inflicted on a hardworking black minority by a largely working-class Catholic mob possessed deep historical roots. While he believed that jealousy and religion played a major role in provoking the riot, he emphasized that black Americans suffered from a form of race hatred older than the republic. R. J. M. Blackett, *Beating Against the Barriers: The Lives of Six Nineteenth-Century Afro-Americans* (Ithaca, NY: Cornell University Press, 1986), 1–86; Ripley et al., *The Black Abolitionist Papers,* 3:477–478.

THE POSITION AND DUTIES OF THE COLORED PEOPLE

Or the great lessons to be learned from the late riotous attack
upon them in New York.
Notes of a Lecture given in Poughkeepsie, August 24, 1863.
BY J. W. C. PENNINGTON, D. D.

THE MOB AGAINST THE colored people of New York in July 1863, was not the first of its kind, and it may not be the last.

THE MOB OF 1740

IN THE YEAR 1740, when New York was a British, and a slaveholding city, it was the scene of one of the most curious and malignant attacks upon the colored people to be found on record. At that time the white population of the city was 10,000; and the colored population was

2,000. By a wicked trick of some evil minded persons, combined with the fears of the timid, a report was gotten up that the negroes of the city, along with a few whites, had entered into a conspiracy to burn the city, and murder all the white inhabitants, except a few of the females. It was charged, that this scheme embraced Long Island—then called "Nassau"—and extended even to South Carolina. The result was a legalized mob or public persecution which lasted for more than a year, during which time the entire colored population were subject to the most cruel and unheard of insults, abuses and injuries. There were 160 trials on charge of conspiracy with intent to commit arson and murder. Seventy-one were condemned to banishment, or to be sold to the West Indies, 18 were hanged; and 13 were BURNED at the stake. The remaining 58 being the slaves of influential owners were acquitted. The volume containing the account of this affair covers nearly 400 pages. It was compiled by the Supreme Court where the trials were held, and is falsely styled,

"THE NEGRO PLOT"

SHAME HAS BLUSHED THE book out of print. But the records of the old Provincial Supreme Court in the archives in the City Hall, contain all the facts, consisting of the indictment,* against Caesar, Quack, Cuffee, &c, &c. Proclamations of the Governor, charges to the juries, addresses to the prisoners, when sentenced, altogether forming a cabinet of curiosities. Time corrected the tongue of slander. It fully transpired, that

---

*The forms of these indictments is, "the King against Caesar" &c. The allegations embrace the charge of an intention to overthrow His Majesty's government, in the Province, and siege upon the whole country. At that early date, the colored men of New York had a society called the Geneva Club, which was supposed, by the whites, to be substantially a Masonic body. This gave offence to the white men of that fraternity; and the blacks were ordered to disband the society, and to abstain from meetings of any kind, either at night, on holiday, or Sundays. The magistrates throughout the city and province were strictly charged with the duty of breaking up all such gatherings. To add to the excitement, it was alleged that some colored enthusiast, had prophecied that Long Island, and York Island were to be sunk, about that time, so the people suffered, in part, for opinions' sake.

instead of it being a plot of the negroes against the lives and property of
the whites, it was a plot of the whites against the lives and liberties of
the negroes.

THE MOB OF 1863

AND, NOW, AFTER THE lapse of more than a hundred and twenty years,
we are called to witness a similar, but far more diabolical conspiracy and
riotous outrage against the lives and liberties of the descendants of the
same people, in the same city.

What shall we call the mob of July 1863? Although I am not now assuming the responsible task of giving it a full designation; yet, I may remark in passing, that intelligent colored men of studious minds, owe it
to themselves to record this mob in history by its right name. We should
let no mere considerations of present relief deter us from bringing out all
the facts, that will fasten the weight of responsibility where it belongs.

If it is an Irish Catholic mob prompted by American Protestant demagogues and negro haters, let it be thereafter know as such in history. If
it was a desperate effort to resurrect the old rabid and hateful spirit of
colonization, so let it be known to be. If it was an attempt of the southern rebels to plant the black flag of the slavery propagandist on the
banks of the Hudson, let future generations so read it. Ye living historians, record the truth, the whole truth and nothing but the truth.

ITS ANTECEDENTS

THE ELEMENTS OF THIS mob have been centering and gathering strength
in New York, for more than two years. And, as soon as the rebellion
broke out, prominent colored men in passing the streets, were often
hailed as "Old Abe," or "Jeff. Davis," evidently to feel their loyal pulse,
and as it become evident that our sympathies were with the Federal government, we became objects of more marked abuse and insult. From
many of the grocery corners, stones, potatoes, and pieces of coal, would
often be hurled, by idle young loafers, standing about, with the consent
of the keepers of those places, and very often by persons in their employ. The language addressed to colored men, not seemly to record on
paper, became the common language of the street, and even of some of

the fashionable avenues. The streets were made to ring with words, and sayings, the most filthy, and yet no effort was made by magistrates, the press, or authorities, to suppress these ebulitions of barbarism. In no other country in the world would the streets of refined cities be allowed to be polluted, as those of New-York have been, with foul and indecent language, without a word of rebuke from the press, the pulpit, or the authorities. Every loafer, from the little rebel, who could but just tussle over the curb stone, up to the lusty mutton fisted scamp who could throw a stone of half a pound's weight, across the street at a colored man's head, might anywhere about the city, on any day, and at any hour, salute colored persons with indecent language, using words surcharged with filth, malice, and brutal insult. And what has been the result? Why, just what we might have expected,—the engendering of a public feeling unfriendly toward colored people. This feeling, once created, might at any moment be intensified into an outbreak against its unoffending objects. We have, in this way, been made the victims of certain antagonisms.

OPPOSITION TO THE DRAFT

I. THE OPPOSITION TO the draft comes largely from that class of men of foreign birth who have declared their intention to become citizens, but who have not done so. They have been duly notified that they could leave the country within sixty days, or submit to the draft. As soon as the President's proclamation containing this notice was made public, men of foreign birth, of this class, began to speak openly against the draft. And for obvious cause. They do not wish to leave the country, and they do not wish to fight. They came to make money, and so far as the war interferes with their schemes, they oppose it.

Now, dishonest politicians aim to make these men believe that the war has been undertaken to abolish slavery; and so far as they believe so, their feelings are against colored people, of course.

From this class, there has been a very considerable mob element. Many of them are a little too shame-faced to be seen with a stone or brick-bat in their hands in the streets; but they have, in large numbers encouraged the mobbing of the colored people. It is known that they have allowed loafers to congregate in their places of business and concoct their plans. Yes, not a few of these men are among your grocery-men, and others that you deal with, and are extremely malignant in their feelings. They are fair to your face, and will take your money, but behind your back, *it is "nigger."* These men know perfectly well, that in the countries from which they come, conscription laws, of a far more strict, and severe character exist, and they also know that they would not dare to resist those laws, if they were there; and hence their opposition to the draft is ungrateful and revolutionary. Many of this class of men are not so ignorant as to believe that the war is carried on by the President to abolish slavery. They have other objects in view. They fall in with the cry against the negro, only for effect.

CATHOLICISM AND PROTESTANTISM

II. THE NEXT POINT OF antagonism which has developed itself in the recent attack upon us, is that between CATHOLICISM, and PROTESTANTISM.

Why have *Irish Catholics* led the way in the late murderous attack upon the *colored protestants*? It is not known that a single colored catholic family or individual suffered during the late riots, at the hands of the Irish, except by mistake. If the colored people, as a body, were Roman Catholic, there would be no attacks made upon them by Irish Catholics. During the Sabbaths of the riots, while colored protestant churches were closed; and colored protestant ministers had to take shelter out of the city of New York, colored members of Catholic churches were quietly worshipping in Catholic churches without insult, or molestation.

As to the color of the skin. Everybody knows, that Catholics consist of all colors in the known world. In other countries, black priests, officials, and members, are as common as the sun that shines.

As to the labor question. If colored mechanics, and laborers; and all our women and youth who earn wages, were Catholics, we should bear no objection from the Irish Catholics about their employment, because the wages would be good Catholic money, and would go to extend that church.

The Irish objection to us is then, not as colored laborers; but as *colored protestant* laborers.

The American people may take a lesson from this, and judge what may come next.

THE LABOR QUESTION

LET US LOOK AT the labor question a little more closely, and see what must be the greed of those who would have us believe that there is not room and labor enough in this country for the citizens of foreign birth, and the colored people of native growth. The legitimate territory of these United States, is about 3,306,863 acres. That is ten times larger than Great Britain and France together. Three times larger than Britain, France, Austria, Prussia, Spain, Portugal and Denmark; and only one-sixth less, in extent, than the fifty-nine, or sixty republics and empires of Europe put together. And yet there are those who would teach the British and other foreigners the selfish and greedy idea that there is not room enough in this country for them and the colored man. Such a notion is ridiculous.

LESSONS OF DUTY

THE FORGOING STATE OF fact suggests some lessons of duty.

1st. We must study the use of arms, for *self-defense*. There is no principle of civil, or religious obligation, that requires us to live on, in hazard, and leave our persons, property, and our wives and children at the mercy of barbarians. Self-defense is the first law of nature.

2nd. We must enter into a solemn free colored *protestant industrial or labor league*.

Let the greedy foreigner know that a part of this country BELONGS TO US; and that we assert the right to live and labor here: That in New York and other cities, we claim the right to buy, hire, occupy and use houses and tenements, for legal considerations; to pass and repass on the streets, lanes, avenues, and all public ways. Our fathers have fought for this country, and helped to free it from the British yoke. We are now fighting to help free it from the combined conspiracy of Jeff. Davis and Co.; we are doing so with the distinct understanding, that WE ARE TO HAVE ALL OUR RIGHTS AS MEN AND AS CITIZENS, and, that there are to be no side issues, no RESERVATIONS, either political, civil, or religious. In this struggle we know nothing but God, Manhood, and American Nationality, full and unimpaired.

The right to labor, earn wages, and dispose of our earnings for the support of our families, the education of our children, and to support religious institutions of our free choice, is inherent. No party, or power, in politics, or religion, can alienate this right.

No part of our influence has been used to prevent foreigners from coming to this country and enjoying its benefits. We have done them no wrong. What we ask in return is, NON-INTERVENTION. LET US ALONE.

3rd. Let us place our daughters, and younger sons in industrial positions, however humble; and secure openings where they may be usefully employed. Every father, and every mother may be of service, not only to their own children, but also to those of others. You will have many applications for "colored help." Be useful to applicants. Prepare your sons and daughters for usefulness, in all the branches of domestic labor and service.

4th. Let our able bodied men go into the United States service. There is no better place for them. If I had a dozen sons, I would rather have them in the United States army and navy, than to have them among our loose population. The army of the United States must, hereafter, be the great bulwark of our life, as a nation. The rebellion has rendered it necessary that we should have a powerful standing army. Colored men should enter the army in force, for the sake of the strength it will give them, the education they will obtain, the pay they will get; and the good service they will do for God, the country, and the race.

There are some among us, who still doubt whether we are in duty bound to take up arms in support of the Government; and whether the Government has a right to draft colored men.

The answer is obvious. NATURE AND CIVIL LAW HAS INSTITUTED a relation between colored men and the United States Government, which is mutually binding. We are BOUND to support the Government, and the Government is BOUND to protect us. Neither party has a right to ignore this duty. The plain and safe course for colored men, is to *do service and claim their rights*.

COLONIZATION INFLUENCES—EDUCATION

5TH. WE SHOULD RECONSTRUCT our Union against the insidious influences of colonization. It is a fact, that the time our present troubles began, colored men were very much divided, on the question of our continuance in the country. Hardly any two of our leading men were agreed about the matter. Some had squarely gone over to colonization, adopting the views of those who hold that a black man can never be a man, in this country. Many angry discussions had taken place. Old friendships were broken up, and a bitter spirit had been engendered among us. All this is to be traced to the insidious influences of colonizationists. It is a fact that, for several years past, any prominent colored man in the city of New York, who would not cave in, on *"the colored car[?]"* system, and go for some modified scheme of colonization, was sure to be marked; and special effort made to break him down. This influence has been most deadly. Years will not redeem us from its effects. At this moment, while the great and glorious southern field of usefulness is spreading and widening before us, there is no adequate plan, or movement on foot among us, for raising up proper agents to occupy the field. Why is this the case? What are we, ministers and teachers, doing? Why is there not some great movement going on, to bring forward young men and women of color for the southern field? These questions are to the point, and call for action, on the part of our ministers and teachers, who are in positions of influence.

We have no right to leave it to the government entirely, nor to any one denomination of whites, to supply this vast field, which is opening before us. Evil always grows out of monopoly. With the exception of what the Zion A. M. E., and the A. M. E. churches[1] have done in the way of supplying ministers and teachers for the South, the colored churches North, are doing nothing. Some years ago it was found that eighty, or one hundred thousand of the southern slaves were held as Presbyterian property. Doubtless the great mass of those are now on the freedman's list; but what are the northern Presbyterians doing for their freed brethren? Is there a single colored Congregational or Presbyterian Church in New England, New York, New Jersey, or Pennsylvania, that has a young man in course of training for a teacher, or minister, with reference to the southern field? And echo answers, is there one? Thirty years hard and self-denying labors among the Congregational and Presbyterian churches of color, entitles me to speak, at least to them, upon this subject of religious and educational commissions to the South. Those two wealthy bodies have a few semi-mission churches scattered about, in the North—for really not one of them is self-sustaining—but they have no plan for supplying the race with a sufficient number of instructors in this country. Would not some of our influential colored men do well to use an influence with a view to advance this cause, *or, will they continue to let the colonization influence neutralize their zeal for the advancement of home interests?* It is painful to notice, that among the most indifferent to the cause of education, are some, who in former years, have, themselves been the recipients of liberal aid, when they were seeking education; and who now, since they have got into position, seem to be actuated by a jealousy, lest they should encourage too much competition.

I have recently heard of the case of a young man who applied to a colored Presbyterian clergyman for counsel and aid to enable him to obtain an education for the ministry, and was advised to go and join a body where it would require less education to be a minister. The young man was a member of that minister's church, and that church is under the care of one of the wealthiest Presbyteries in the city of New York. Now, it is known that that colored minister is strongly under the influence of prominent men of the colonization school. Hence the tree is known by its fruit. It has been a part of the deep laid plan to divide the councils of colored men, and beset the government to unite colonization with emancipation. But God be thanked, that while emancipation is going on well, the unseemly colonization scheme which the President was induced to hitch on to his plan, has proved a failure. This fact should open the eyes of colored men who have been deluded by colonization emissaries.

About a year and a half ago, an official of the colonization society in New York remarked to me, with an appearance of satisfaction, that there was no doubt that the government would appropriate a large amount of money for colonization purposes. But as I said, thank God, it has failed. It is now evident that the country has no colored men to spare to people foreign countries; and no money to spare for expatriating them. The old colonization scheme has been buried so deep, that a century will not give it a resurrection.

SPIRIT OF PATRIOTISM—FAITH IN GOD

LASTLY, WE SHOULD REMEMBER that emancipation was resorted to, as a purely military necessity imposed upon this Government in the Providence of an alwise God. The President has no alternative but to fall into the powerful current of events which God had put in motion.

This view of the subject is essential to the cultivation of a true and lofty spirit of patriotism. A true patriot must always feel that he owns and contends for property which God gave him, whether it be life, or liberty, or the pursuit of happiness. His greatest strength will be in the firm conviction that God is transacting his business, so to speak; even though he be called to pass through bitter waters of adversity, he feels that God has not undertaken for him in vain.

When the hand of God is with us, we are strong, and when he shows us his will, in regard to our duties, we should be in earnest to do it.

A TERRIBLE CONTINGENCY

AN INTELLIGENT VIEW OF the history of God's providential dealings with slavery, leaves no room to doubt that its doom is sealed in this country; but let us not forget that there is yet a terrible contingency before us. We may have to face, in the field, an army of our own colored brethren of the South! Already it is known that the southern commanders have made use of slaves in battle. And already it is rumored that the Confederate Government thinks seriously of arming the slaves as a retaliative military necessity. It is admitted, that from 1,750,000 to 2,000,000 out of 4,000,000 of the slaves are yet in the possession of the rebels; of this number they can spare for arms at least 300,000 able bodied men. These men armed and so used, certainly cannot be expected to exercise any more liberty of choice than the poor white union men. So that if those men remain beyond our reach, and are armed and commanded by the Confederates to fight us, they will be obliged to do so. If we take them prisoners, I suppose they will have to be exchanged as others. If they desert and come to us, the case will be different. It is presumed they will do so, when the opportunity presents itself—but, how much mischief they may be compelled to do, in the meantime, it is impossible to foresee.

In my opinion, nothing is more likely to take place, under French influence, than this arming of the slaves by the rebels with the promise of freedom. It would be but a reproduction of the French plan in St. Domingo in 1794, to be followed by the same treachery by the Confederates, should they use the slaves successfully.

I have no doubt that Louis Napoleon is advising Jeff. Davis to this plan. Every weeks' delay in crushing out this rebellion increases the danger that the slaves may be brought into the field against us. I confess I am not of the number of those who covet such an event, with the expectation that the slaves would come to us *en masse*. It is not to be expected that, in the event of the rebels arming the slaves they would neglect also to present them with every possible allurement to fight hard; and at the same time, to surround them with every imaginable obstacle to their desertion. On our side, the only wise and safe course is to press rapidly into the heart of the slave country, and work out the problem of the Proclamation of freedom. We must prove to the slaves that we have both the will and the power to give effect to the proclamation, and that it is not a mere sound, reaching their ears, upon the wings of the wind. Here is where our danger lies. The President is right. The proclamation is the word of God's holy Providence, so to speak; but the great North is slow to repent of slavery. There is yet a great deal of wicked, angry, and unrighteous feeling in the heart of the Northern people. It may be that God intends to use the sword as a lance to bleed the whole nation, until she begins to faint, for very loss of blood, and then to swathe up the opened vein, and apply restoratives.

Let us, then, not flatter ourselves that we shall escape. Let us not be deceived by those who would persuade us that there is any destiny for us, as an integral part of this American nation, separate from the nation, as a whole. If the slaves are brought into the field by the Confederates, it will be a sad and awful day for us.

CONCLUSION

WE CONCLUDE, THEN, THAT those who, in the late riots undertook to expel by murder, fire, and persecution, the colored people for the accomplishment, either of sham democratic, or Roman Catholic pro[pa]gandism, have undertaken a heavy and dangerous task, a task in which all the plans and purposes of a just God are against them. And it now remains to be seen whether intelligent colored men among us who have suffered in the late riots will allow the history of that outrageous scheme to pass unrecorded. Shall a few thousand dollars of relief money, and a few words of good counsel, and consolation, be a sufficient inducement to neglect our own history? Remember, that one of the great tests of civilization, is that a people should be able to record their own annals, by the pens of their own historians.

How does this matter sum up? It sums up thus; for more than a year, the riot spirit had been culminating, before it burst forth. The police authorities were frequently applied to, by respectable colored persons, without being able to obtain any redress when assaulted and abused in the streets. We have sometimes pointed to the aggressors but no arrest have been made. We have appealed to them for protection and apprised them of the fact that we had good reason to believe that a general attack was about to be made upon us, under false pretenses. We have pointed to the street corners, and to the rowdies who stood at them, and in open day light assaulted colored persons, in passing. We have presented proof sufficient to indict houses where rioters assembled. We have named men who hired idle boys to throw stones at colored men, and offered to prove it. The hand of the ruffian has done its work, in sending to the bar of God, a number of swift witnesses against the perpetrators of the deeds of July, 1863. The better class of people of New York city would doubtless feel relief, could these departed spirits be called back to their earthly homes, and their testimony, now recorded on the book of God against the bloody city, be erased. But as now, no power can restore those valuable members of society, so the full history of the riot must stand in all its painful bearings.

The loss of life and property make only a small part of the damage. The breaking up of families; and business relations just beginning to prosper; the blasting of hopes just dawning; the loss of precious harvest time which will never again return; the feeling of insecurity engendered; the confidence destroyed; the reaction; and lastly, the gross insult offered to our character as a people, sum up a weight of injury which can only be realized by the most enlightened and sensitive minds among us.

The injury extends to our churches, schools, societies for mutual aid and improvement, as well as to the various branches of industry. And amidst the most honest, trustworthy, useful, laborious, pious, and respected, none have suffered more than the sisters of the laundry. These excellent women are the support of our churches, ministers, and the encouragement of our school teachers. In these worthy women, New York landlords have found their best tenants. Many of them are the only support of orphan children. Many of them, the wives of absent seamen, and some of coasting men, and others who are absent during the week, but spend their Sabbaths in the city. The nature of the business of these women is such, that they are entrusted by their customers with large quantities of valuable clothing, from Monday morning until Saturday evening, when they are expected to return them, to a piece, in perfect order. The attack made upon the houses of the colored people has had the effect to render it extra hazardous to have valuable articles in their houses in trust, as anything found in their houses by rioters would be looked upon as common plunder.

The pretense, therefore, that there was no intention, on the part of the rioters, to injure our women, is false. The severest blow was aimed at them.

There was not only an attempt to murder, *en masse*, their only male protectors, but it was the design of the rioters also to render their homes dangerous and insecure, both for life and business.

For all the purposes, therefore, of social, civil, and religious enjoyment, and right, we hold New York solemnly bound to insure us as citizens, permanent security in our homes. Relief, and damage money, is well enough. But it cannot atone, fully, for evils done by riots. It cannot bring back our murdered dead. It cannot remove the insults we feel; and finally, it gives us no proof that the people have really changed their minds for the better, towards us.

During the late riots, my wife, and other lone females in the same tenement house, were repeatedly annoyed and threatened with mob law and violence. When there was not a man about the house, by night or by day, the rioters prowled about, watching for the return of absent marked victims. Failing to secure those, the defenceless women were repeatedly ordered, or mobishly advised to leave the house, and told that they *"must not be seen to carry a parcel away in their hands!"* Such was the treatment which our families received at the hands of the New York mobites, in the absence of their male protectors, which leaves no manner of doubt that a part of the hellish scheme was to mob and otherwise maltreat our women. Read this, and judge of its design:

"The mob will come to this house soon. You nigger wenches must leave here, and you must not carry away a bundle, or anything, with you."

Such is a copy of a paper stuck under the door.

New York, *National Principia*, January 7, 14, 1864. Reproduced in *The Black Abolitionist Papers*, microfilm edition, reel 15:0192–0205.

---

1. The African Methodist Episcopal Church (AME Church) began when black parishioners withdrew from white-dominated Methodist churches in Baltimore and Philadelphia at the close of the eighteenth century. New churches, led by Richard Allen and Absalom Jones, joined with other re-

gional black churches in 1816 to establish the AME Church. It grew
steadily, and after the war it took a leading role in sending missionaries to
the newly freed slaves. The African Methodist Episcopal Zion Church
(AMEZ Church) also grew out of the withdrawal of black parishioners from
racist Methodist churches. From the 1790s to the 1830s, William Miller, a
free-born Maryland black, played a major role in organizing AMEZ
churches in New York and Washington, D.C. Both churches were slow to
take aggressive stands against slavery for fear of jeopardizing their Southern
brethren, although as individuals black Methodists aggressively fought slavery. The trauma of the 1850s brought both bodies completely into the antislavery movement. Ripley et al., *The Black Abolitionist Papers*, 2:81, 4:195,
197.

6

Black Soldiers and the War, Part I:
What We Can Do

"the time is not far distant"
William H. Johnson to the *Pine and Palm*
NOVEMBER 11, 1861

After Confederate guns opened up on Fort Sumter in April 1861, African Americans rushed to volunteer for the Union army. In states across the North and even in Canada, blacks organized whole units to march in defense of the country and to put down the slave-masters' rebellion. But whites in and out of the government spurned black patriotism, declaring that this would be a "white man's war." Repudiation of their offer to fight soured many blacks on the Union cause. Debates raged within the black community over what, if anything, African Americans owed to a racist government. The African Methodist Episcopal Church believed that blacks had no business fighting for a country that oppressed them. But the New York *Weekly Anglo-African* advised its brethren not to become disillusioned. Their primary responsibility as free blacks in the United States remained the slave, the newspaper maintained. They should denounce the government's repugnant policies, but they should also organize, drill, and stand ready "as Minute Men, to *respond when the slave calls.*"

From the beginning, William H. Johnson heard the slave's call. Freeborn in 1833 in Alexandria, Virginia, Johnson became one of New York State's most aggressive proponents of civil rights. After leaving Virginia, Johnson divided his time between Philadelphia and Albany, New York, where in 1851 he assisted the city's efficient, black-led Underground Railroad. In 1855 he moved to Philadelphia and became part of the city's

black literary and reform elite. He joined the important Banneker Institute circle, a literary, library, and debating society that produced
some of the city's leading black abolitionists. His participation in a fugitive slave rescue sent him fleeing Philadelphia for Norwich, Connecticut, just before outbreak of the war.

Johnson also had served as a correspondent for several newspapers,
including Frederick Douglass's *North Star,* James Redpath's *Pine and
Palm,* which printed several of Johnson's letters, and the AME Church's
Christian Recorder. During the 1890s Johnson continued his journalism
career by publishing his own papers, *The Calcium Light* and *The Albany
Capitol.* But as a civil rights advocate, he had few equals. Courageous
and determined, Johnson once refused to leave his seat in a New York-
bound, whites-only railroad car. The train's conductor attempted to
eject him, but Johnson refused to budge. When the conductor acquired
additional assistance to remove Johnson from his seat, the men found
themselves staring "into the muzzle of my 'six-shooter'."

Johnson took the same sense of righteousness and bravery to the
battlefield. Although the 2nd Connecticut Regiment would not muster
the determined black man, it did permit him to arm himself and accompany the regiment to the front. While stationed at Camp Mansfield
in Washington, D.C., the 2nd Connecticut and other Union regiments
unexpectedly became home to runaway slaves. In early June 1861 six
runaways from Elliot Mills, Maryland, turned up in the 2nd's camp, while
another six entered the camp of the 14th New York Regiment. Under
orders from General Joseph Mansfield, Washington, D.C.'s military
commander, the 14th New York turned over the six runaways to their
owners. Under Johnson's leadership, the 2nd Connecticut refused to
cooperate: "We flatly refused to obey." Johnson hid the fugitives, and
"backed by almost the entire regiment, I went to the colonel's headquarters, where I was at once confronted with the slave hunters, whom
I, in measured tones, denounced and defied." The slave hunters went
away empty-handed and Johnson received the congratulations of the
regiment's commander, Col. Alfred H. Terry. The 2nd Connecticut, a
three month's unit, took not only the six fugitives back home with
them, but nine others who had escaped from Virginia.

Unsatisfied with his success, Johnson joined up with the 8th Connecticut Regiment at the end of 1861 and went on the Union expedition
to New Bern, North Carolina. Armed with a pistol and rifle, but again
no formal title of "soldier," Johnson determined to see the "decaying

chain of despotism" broken. The ever-growing number of fugitive slaves that entered Union lines convinced him that the institution of slavery would soon die.

Illness brought an end to Johnson's military career in the summer of 1862. But not long after after he returned to Albany, he began recruiting activities for the new black regiments forming in 1863 in the North. In 1864 he attended the Black National Convention held in Syracuse, New York, and he helped organize the state's Equal Rights League. For the rest of his life, Johnson continued his fight for racial equality. In 1900 Gov. Theodore Roosevelt recognized Johnson's important career by giving him the pen he had used to sign Bill Number 492, which ended discrimination against black children in New York public schools. Clarence G. Walker, *Rock in a Weary Land: The African Methodist Episcopal Church During the Civil War and Reconstruction* (Baton Rouge, LA: Louisiana State University Press, 1982), 32–34; New York *Weekly Anglo-African,* April 20, 27, 1861; Edwin S. Redkey, ed., *A Grand Army of Black Men: Letters from African-American Soldiers in the Union Army, 1861–1865* (Cambridge, MA: Cambridge University Press, 1992), 10–22; William H. Johnson, *The Autobiography of Dr. William H. Johnson* (Albany, NY: Argis Co., 1900), 2–19, 21, 123–124, 162–165.

I AM AGAIN AT the seat of war, and again preparing for active service. Our regiment (the 8th C.V.)[1] is in General [Ambrose E.] Burnside's Division, and our destination is said to be South Carolina, and we shall in all probability reinforce General [Thomas W.] Sherman. Annapolis has been chosen as a place of rendezvous, because it is a first class shipping port; it is located on the banks of the Chesapeake Bay, and its facilities for camping purposes most complete. There are now at this port, and attached to this Division, the 21st, 25th, 27th Massachusetts, 51st New York, and the 8th and 10th Connecticut regiments, numbering about 6,000 men. There are to be six other regiments joined to the Division, which will augment the number to 12,000 or 13,000. We expect to sail from here about the 25th inst.

The election here last week, whilst it resulted in a Union victory, demonstrated the fact that Annapolis is not quite free from secesh yet, and the process of purging it must still go on.

The proscribed Americans, (and there are many), attached to this regiment have since their encampment here, formed themselves into a defensive association. They propose to cultivate a correct knowledge of the manual of arms and military evolutions, with a view to self-protection. The association is based upon the principles of military discipline, morality and literature; and they hope by a strict observance of the rules and regulations they have adopted, to do credit to their people, and honor to themselves. The name of the association is *Self-Defenders of Connecticut,* and their officers are:—Wm. H. Johnson, Norwich, Conn., first officer; Frederick C. Cross, Hartford, second officer; Prince Robinson, Norwalk, third officer.[2] In forming this association, we have been actuated by the conviction that the time is not far distant when the black man of this country will be summoned to show his hand in this struggle for liberty.

Boston *Pine and Palm*, November 23, 1861.

---

1. The 8th Connecticut Regiment, organized in Hartford in September 1861, stayed in Annapolis, Maryland, from its arrival in November until January 1862. While the regiment did in fact remain with Burnside's command, they went to Roanoke Island and then on to New Bern, North Carolina, not to the Department of the South. Adjutant General's Office, *Record of Service of Connecticut Men in the Army and Navy of the United States During the War of the Rebellion* (Hartford, CT: Case, Lockwood & Brainard, 1889), 327.
2. None of the individuals mentioned by Johnson formally belonged to the 8th Connecticut, although occasionally African Americans did serve in white units before 1863. The men mentioned here most likely accompanied the regiment as officers' servants or valets.

"the hand of Providence appears to move slowly but it moves"
John V. Givens to Thomas Hamilton
OCTOBER 12, 1861

The New York City black activist John V. Givens typified African Americans who sought to aid their race and the cause of freedom. They refused to be stymied by the government's refusal to muster them into the army. Givens was active in the city's Masonic Mount Olivet Lodge

and lectured for the Masons in Connecticut. He opposed the emigrationist schemes of the African Civilization Society, worked for the
state's Free Suffrage Association, and helped raise funds in New York
and Newark, New Jersey, for the accused in Philadelphia's Moses
Horner fugitive slave case. In 1863 he became a busy recruiter of black
soldiers and an officer in the city's Loyal League. After the war, he filled
the pulpit at the John Wesley African Methodist Episcopal Zion Church
in Washington, D.C.

He left New York for Washington, D.C., shortly after the beginning
of the war, deeply troubled over the Lincoln administration's fugitive
slave policy. For over a year, Union forces returned all fugitives to
"loyal" masters, with soldiers rounding up the slaves and returning
them to the custody of professional slave catchers or directly to the
masters. Outraged over the practice, Givens accompanied a New York
regiment into the field to do his part to impede or reverse these injustices. Likely as an officer's servant or as a teamster, Givens, like
William H. Johnson, used his position to assist any contraband or fugitive slave that he encountered. After his return to the North in 1863
he reported on his contraband rescues and military activities in Virginia
and Maryland to a meeting at New York's Shiloh Presbyterian Church,
then ministered by Henry Highland Garnet.

Givens, who wrote only occasionally to the New York Weekly Anglo-
African, also reported seeing fully uniformed African Americans in the
rebel army. Although the Confederacy officially rejected the idea of
arming blacks until the desperate last months of the war, early on local
commanders did compel some blacks to serve. Most Southern blacks,
both free and slave, worked either as laborers or as body servants.
Newspapers, however, sometimes reported seeing large numbers of
uniformed black rebel soldiers, and William H. Johnson claimed to have
seen them at the First Battle of Bull Run. These eyewitness accounts
cannot be dismissed, and they probably represent isolated instances of
local commanders using the armed troops sent to them. Most of the
rebel blacks escaped at their first opportunity. Unfortunately, these
African Americans received cold receptions from the white Yankees,
whom they mistakenly thought would be eager to recruit them. New
York Weekly Anglo-African, September 14, 1861, March 22, April 12,
1862; Douglass' Monthly, June 1863; Redkey, A Grand Army of Black Men,
11; Ervin L. Jordan, Jr., Black Confederates and Afro-Yankees in Civil War

Virginia (Charlottesville, VA: University Press of Virginia, 1995), 222–226; New York *Weekly Anglo-African,* December 10, 31, 1859, April 21, May 19, 26, 1860, March 19, 26, April 9, 1864; *Liberator,* May 4, 1860, May 29, 1863; *Douglass' Monthly,* June 1863; John W. Cromwell, "The First Negro Churches in the District of Columbia," *Journal of Negro History,* 7 (Jan. 1922): 85.

Headquarters of the 9th Regt., N.Y.S.M.

Gen. Bank's Division, Darnestown, Md.

Oct., 12th, 1861.

MR. EDITOR:

I need not tell you of our march through Maryland and into Virginia, nor of the devastation that met the eye at every point, nor of our long and tiresome marches of days and nights, of our surprises, skirmishes and so on, but that more directly concerns you and I, and our people everywhere.

After leaving Camp Cameron in Washington, on the 11th of June, we took up our line of march for the Potomac and Monocacy Junction. About every other house on our line of march we found deserted. But what struck me most was to see the singular conduct of the slaves towards us, they ran from us as though we were the plague—but I have since ascertained that their owners have instructed them that the Northerners came to take them, and sell them for their own benefit. And some of the slaves believed their masters; but there were others that did not, and those would follow the regiment until they got a birth as cook or officer's servant.

The colored churches on the whole line of our march were closed with the exception of Quin's Chapel, (Methodist,) in Frederick.[1] They had orders to discontinue their services, but as the Union troops occupy Frederick, they have not obeyed the orders but continue their services.

The colored people of Frederick have more advantages of education than they do in any part of Maryland, Baltimore not excepted. They have eight colored churches, Baptist, Methodist, Presbyterian and a great number of them belong to the Catholic church. But still slavery casts her dark and gloomy mantel over all of this.

After six weeks marching and camping we arrived at Sandy Hook, opposite Harpers Ferry, and there we lost our first men in a skirmish. The rebels had evacuated Harpers Ferry five days before we got there.

But they left a picket guard behind them, but they also left in double quick as they saw our troops advancing. We continued our line of march on the Maryland side of the Potomac to Williamsport, and from there, on the 14th of July we crossed the Potomac into Virginia. We were then under that rebel General [Robert] Patterson.[2] And let me remark here that the Wisconsin regiment was two miles in the advance of the New York Ninth, when they fell in with the rear guard of the rebels retreating towards Martinsburg. They had a fight at the falls—and with the rebel prisoners they took fourteen colored men in uniform, and armed to the teeth, fighting the Union troops, one they killed outright and three others were wounded. They were not slaves but free black men that were pressed into the rebel service; and before we got to Martinsburg we got forty colored men who had deserted from the rebel ranks and came over to us. Some were barbers, shoemakers, carpenters, and waiters, and were forced to leave their families and join the rebel ranks—many of them left at the first opportunity and come to us, but how disappointed they were when they found that they could not fight in our ranks against their oppressors!

When we entered the city of Martinsburg we saw that desolation had spread its broad hands over everything and everywhere—famine, pestilence and death walked boldly from house to house. The Union troops entered Martinsburg twenty-five thousand strong, and occupied the city for a week, we then took up our line of march for Bunker Hill, and there I commenced my work. We left Bunker Hill for Charleston, and whilst on our march the rebels passed us on a road running parallel with ours, but General Patterson would not let us give them battle. So, as you know, General [Gen. Joseph E.] Johnston passed us without either of us striking a blow. We entered Charleston and what a sight presented itself, hundreds of colored men and women in the streets with their children; some in their mother's arms, some of the men armed and shouting and thanking God that we had come at last to free them. Most of their masters had ran off at our approach and left all behind them. The slaves had helped themselves, and now stood ready with open arms and shouts to receive their deliverers, who they believed had come for the sole purpose of freeing them. But what pen can describe the revulsion of their feelings when they were told that we came "not to free the slaves, but to preserve the Union as it was, with its millions of suffering slaves!" why, Mr. Editor, when the slaves heard that they cursed the

Union troops in their hearts, and some with tears in their eyes begged us not go away for now they had committed themselves against their masters—and if we went away their masters would come again and do worse than kill them; I could not bear the sight of their disappointment, so left them and visited the Court House where that murderous crew tried the noble John Brown; I visited the prison that held the hero, and looked at the old gallows in the prison yard that was honored by having so illustrious a charter die upon it—and visited the very spot that the hero was hung upon. I thought the shade of that venerable hero stood beside me and said, "the hand of Providence appears to move slowly but it moves; so wait patiently, the clouds are lifting, the signs are standing forth in bold relief." Here let me add, that the land they hung him on belonged to an old colored man named John Welcome, and this same John Welcome owned the horses and the cart that the hero rode upon to that fatal tree; and I also add that this same John Welcome drove the horse and cart himself to the murdering. The only piece of cannon they had on that memorable day, is now in Philadelphia, in possession of the Pennsylvania Regiment of three months volunteers. They captured it the day we entered Charlestown and have since left and returned home bearing the cannon with them as a trophy. We left Charlestown after campaigning for a week and then entered Harpers Ferry, remained there two weeks and again crossed the Potomac and entered Sandy Hook. Nothing worthy of note occurred until I reached Buckiestown. There two slaveholders entered the 29th Regiment of Pennsylvania Volunteers and gave Sergeant Stark of Company G and Corporal Harry Millard, five dollars each to catch two slaves for them that were then in the camp cooking; they succeeded in doing so, when the colored men interfered, but were driven off with the swords and pistols of the captains.

I shall in my next letter, give the condition of our people here.

JOHN V. GIVENS

New York *Weekly Anglo-African*, November 2, 1861.

---

1. The circuit rider William Paul Quinn founded the Quinn AME Church in 1817. Quinn, of mixed African and Hindu parentage, was born in Calcutta, India, at the end of the eighteenth century. Beginning in 1816, he preached to many black groups in Maryland, and he was the first black circuit rider

in the state. The congregation erected its first building in 1829, and it has remained on its original site. According to the 1860 federal census, 4,957 free African Americans and 3,243 slaves lived in Frederick County. Nina Honemond Clarke, *History of the Nineteenth-Century Black Churches in Maryland and Washington, D.C.* (New York: Vantage Press, 1983), 22–24.

2. Givens is making light of General Patterson (1792–1881), who failed to prevent Johnston from joining General Beauregard at Manassas. Patterson's ineptitude helped the Confederates win their first major engagement, and the War Department quickly dismissed him from the service. Stewart Sifakis, *Who Was Who in the Civil War* (New York: Facts on File, 1988), 491.

"This is our golden opportunity"
Frederick Douglass
MARCH 2, 1863

At the beginning of 1863, Massachusetts governor John A. Andrew received permission from the War Department to raise a regiment of African American troops. Although South Carolina, Louisiana, and Kansas had earlier fielded black regiments, the move in Massachusetts set the nation's standard. All eyes looked to the Old Bay State to raise a regiment that would carry the hopes of the North's white abolitionist community and the dreams of Northern blacks for liberty and equality. "Every black man and woman" in the North, the New York *Weekly Anglo-African* announced, "feels a special interest in the success in this regiment." The men of the 54th believed that they "must prove ourselves men" or risk complete humiliation and the end of their quest for equality. Everything rested on the success of the regiment. "If we do not fight," one black abolitionist proclaimed, "we are traitors to our God, traitors to our country, traitors to our race, and traitors to ourselves."

Frederick Douglass was the leading African American in the North, and as such, what he said mattered. Although he had been critical of Republicans in the past, Douglass believed what the War Department and Governor Andrew had promised in regard to fair treatment and equal rights for black soldiers. Although spurned in the past, black men now could join the army on an equal footing with white soldiers. This in itself represented an important victory, and it would be affirmed by filling the ranks of the 54th. Although black soldiers still did not receive an officer's commission, Governor Andrew believed that in time even this important restriction would fall. The manner in which the 54th conducted itself on the field of battle would be the determining factor. For Douglass and all African Americans of the North, the time to fight for their freedom had at last come. Slavery and the rebellion could be buried in one common grave. Strike now, Douglass exclaimed; "NOW OR NEVER," his broadside shouted. "The iron gate of our prison stands half open. One gallant rush from the North will fling it wide open. . . ." Yacovone, *A Voice of Thunder,* 30–31.

MEN OF COLOR, TO ARMS!

WHEN FIRST THE REBEL cannon shattered the walls of Sumter and drove away its starving garrison, I predicted that the war then and there inaugurated would not be fought entirely by white men. Every month's experience during these dreary years has confirmed that opinion. A war undertaken and brazenly carried on for the perpetual enslavement of colored men calls logically and loudly for colored men to help suppress it. Only a moderate share of sagacity was needed to see that the arm of the slave was the best defense against the arm of the slaveholder. Hence, with every reverse to the national arms, with every exulting shout of victory raised by the slaveholding rebels, I have implored the imperiled nation to unchain against her foes her powerful black hand. Slowly and reluctantly that appeal is beginning to be heeded. Stop not now to complain that it was not heeded sooner. That it should not may or may not have been best. This is not the time to discuss that question. Leave it to the future. When the war is over, the country saved, peace established and the black man's rights are secured, as they will be, history with an impartial hand will dispose of that and sundry other questions. Action! action! not criticism, is the plain duty of this hour. Words are now useful only as they stimulate to blows. The office of speech now is only to point out when, where, and how to strike to the best advantage. There is no time to delay. The tide is at its flood that leads on to fortune. From East to West, from North to South, the sky is written all over, "NOW OR NEVER." Liberty won by white men would lose half its luster. "Who would be free themselves must strike the blow." "Better even die free, than to live slaves." This is the sentiment of every brave colored man amongst us. There are weak and cowardly men in all nations. We have them amongst us. They tell you this is the "white man's war"—that you "will be no better off after than before the war"—that the getting of you into the army is to "sacrifice you on the first opportunity." Believe them not; cowards themselves, they do not wish to have their cowardice shamed by your brave example. Leave them to their timidity, or to whatever motive may hold them back. I have not thought lightly of the words I am now addressing you. The counsel I give comes of close observation of the great struggle now in progress, and of the deep conviction that this is your hour and mine. In good earnest, then, and after the best deliberation, I now, for the first time during this war, feel at liberty to call and counsel you to arms. By every consideration which binds you to your enslaved fellow-country-men and to the peace and welfare of your country, by every aspiration which you cherish for the freedom and equality of yourselves and your children, by all the ties of blood and identity which make us one with the brave black men now fighting our battles in Louisiana and in South Carolina,[1] I urge you to fly to arms, and smite with death the power that would bury the government and your liberty in the same hopeless grave. I wish I could tell you that the State of New York calls you to this high honor. For the moment her constituted authorities are silent on the subject. They will speak by and by, and doubtless on the right side, but we are not compelled to wait for her. We can get at the throat of trea-son and slavery through the State of Massachusetts. She was the first in the War of Independence, first to break the chains of her slaves, first to make the black man equal before the law, first to admit colored chil-dren to her common schools, and she was first to answer with her blood the alarm-cry of the nation, when its capital was menaced by rebels. You know her patriotic governor, and you know Charles Sumner.[2] I need not add more.

Massachusetts now welcomes you to arms as soldiers. She has but a small colored population from which to recruit. She has full leave of the general government to send one regiment to the war, and she has un-dertaken to do it. Go quickly and help fill up the first colored regiment from the North. I am authorized to assure you that you will receive the same wages, the same rations, the same equipments, the same protec-

tion, the same treatment, and the same bounty, secured to white soldiers. You will be led by able and skillful officers, men who will take especial pride in your efficiency and success. They will be quick to accord
to you all the honor you shall merit by your valor, and to see that your
rights and feelings are respected by other soldiers. I have assured myself
on these points, and can speak with authority. More than twenty years
of unswerving devotion to our common cause may give me some humble claim to be trusted at this momentous crisis. I will not argue. To do
so implies hesitation and doubt, and you do not hesitate. You do not
doubt. The day dawns—the morning star is bright upon the horizon!
The iron gate of our prison stands half open. One gallant rush from the
North will fling it wide open, while four millions of our brothers and sisters shall march out into liberty. The chance is now given you to end
in a day the bondage of centuries, and to rise in one bound from social
degradation to the place of common equality with all other varieties of
men. Remember Denmark Vesey of Charleston; remember Nathaniel
Turner of Southampton; remember Shields Green and [John A.]
Copeland, who followed noble John Brown, and fell as glorious martyrs
for the cause of the slave.[3] Remember that in a contest with oppression,
the Almighty has no attribute which can take sides with oppressors.
The case is before you. This is our golden opportunity. Let us accept it,
and forever wipe out the dark reproaches unsparingly hurled against us
by our enemies. Let us win for ourselves the gratitude of our country,
and the best blessings of our posterity through all time. The nucleus of
this first regiment is now in camp at Readville, a short distance from
Boston. I will undertake to forward to Boston all persons adjudged fit to
be mustered into the regiment, who shall apply to me at any time within
the next two weeks.

ROCHESTER, MARCH 2, 1863

Douglass' Monthly, March 1863.

---

1. The Corps d' Afrique fought heroically at Port Hudson and Milliken's Bend,
   Louisiana, and the First South Carolina Volunteers fought along the South
   Carolina, Georgia, and Florida coasts under the Massachusetts abolitionist
   Col. Thomas Wentworth Higginson.
2. Douglass refers to John A. Andrew (1818–1866), Massachusetts's aboli-
   tionist governor, who convinced the War Department to allow him to raise

the 54th Massachusetts Regiment, and to Charles Sumner (1811–1874), Massachusetts senator, abolitionist, and supporter of black rights. Faust, *Historical Times Illustrated Encyclopedia of the Civil War*, 17, 732.

3. Douglass refers to the nineteenth century's deadliest antislavery insurrections: the June 1822 Denmark Vesey conspiracy in Charleston, South Carolina; the Nat Turner revolt in Northampton, Virginia, in August 1831; and the October 1859 raid on Harpers Ferry, Virginia.

"You owe it to yourself and your race"
Frederick Douglass
APRIL 1863

Although Douglass and others had lent their reputations to the national effort to raise the 54th Massachusetts Regiment, many blacks in the North remained skeptical. Douglass, William Wells Brown, Charles L. Remond, John S. Rock, Mary Ann Shadd Cary, and scores of other black leaders across the North helped Governor Andrew and the 54th's organizing committee to raise the unit. With too small a number of black men of military age within its borders, Massachusetts looked to Pennsylvania, Ohio, Michigan, Illinois, and all the other states and every black community in the North to send its best men to Camp Meigs at Readville, Massachusetts, just outside of Boston.

While the most committed arrived quickly, soon the numbers began to recede. Henry Highland Garnet wondered aloud, "What have black men to fight for in this war?" Would the government keep its promises? Massachusetts might very well be relied upon; its governor possessed a reputation as an uncompromising abolitionist. And, after all, wasn't this the state of Senator Charles Sumner? But others, accustomed to the promises of self-professed "friends," doubted that the federal government would keep its word. "This is a *white* nation," after all, one black leader reminded his brethren, and "white men are the engineers over its . . . destiny; every dollar spent, every drop of blood shed and every life lost, was a *willing* sacrifice for the furtherance and perpetuity of a white nationality." William Wells Brown, at first, was equally blunt: "Equality first, guns afterward." The fact that no black would be commissioned an officer in the unit seemed to affirm what the regiment's doubters had feared. Why, John S. Rock had asked, should blacks "offer themselves on the altar of our country"? In crisp prose, Douglass answered every question about why Northern backs should support the 54th Massachusetts. If blacks failed to rally to the 54th, he warned, the "whole North will be but another Detroit," where white rioters had incinerated most of the black community. Enlist, he argued, and see the "fast dropping tears of gratitude of your kith and kin marked out for destruction, and who are but now ready to perish." Their lives, their future, and the course of freedom depended on what black men would now do. The result of Douglass's appeal was swift. The 54th filled in short order, and the state of Massachusetts began to organize two more black regiments. Yacovone, *A Voice of Thunder,* 30–31.

WHY SHOULD A COLORED MAN ENLIST?

THIS QUESTION HAS BEEN repeatedly put to us while raising men for the 54th Massachusetts regiment during the past five weeks, and perhaps we cannot at present do a better service to the cause of our people or to the cause of the country than by giving a few of the many reasons why a colored man should enlist.

1st. You are a man, although a colored man. If you were only a horse or an ox, incapable of deciding whether the rebels are right or wrong, you would have no responsibility, and might like the horse or the ox go on eating your corn or grass, in total indifference, as to which side is victorious or vanquished in this conflict. You are however no horse, and no ox, but a man, and whatever concerns man should interest you. He who looks upon a conflict between right and wrong, and does not help the right against the wrong, despises and insults his own nature, and invites the contempt of mankind. As between the North and South, the North is clearly in the right and the South is flagrantly in the wrong. You should therefore, simply as a matter of right and wrong, give your utmost aid to the North. In presence of such a contest there is no neutrality for any man. You are either for the Government or against the Government. Manhood requires you to take sides, and you are mean or noble according to how you choose between action and inaction.— If you are sound in body and mind, there is nothing in your *color* to excuse you from enlisting in the services of the republic against its enemies. If *color* should not be a criterion of rights, neither should it be a standard of duty. The whole duty of a man, belongs alike to white and black.

"A MAN'S A MAN FOR A' THAT"[1]

2ND. YOU ARE HOWEVER, not only a man, but an American citizen, so declared by the highest legal adviser of the Government, and you have hitherto expressed in various ways, not only your willingness but your earnest desire to fulfill any and every obligation which the relation of citizenship imposes. Indeed, you have hitherto felt wronged and slighted, because while white men of all other nations have been freely enrolled to serve the country, you a native born citizen have been coldly denied the honor of aiding in defense of the land of your birth. The injustice thus done you is now repented of by the Government and you are welcomed to a place in the army of the nation. Should you refuse to enlist *now*, you will justify the past contempt of the Government towards you and lead it to regret having honored you with a call to take up arms in its defense. You cannot but see that here is a good reason why you should promptly enlist.

3rd. A third reason why a colored man should enlist is found in the fact that every negro hater and slavery-lover in the land regards the arming of negroes as a calamity and is doing his best to prevent it. Even now all the weapons of malice, in the shape of slander and ridicule are used to defeat the filling up of the 54th Massachusetts (colored) regiment. In nine cases out of ten, you will find it safe to do just what your enemy would gladly have you leave undone. What helps you hurts him. Find out what he does not want and give him a plenty of it.

4th. You should enlist to learn the use of arms, to become familiar with the means of securing, protecting and defending your own liberty. A day may come when men shall learn war no more, when justice shall be so clearly apprehended, so universally practiced, and humanity shall be so profoundly loved and respected, that war and bloodshed, shall be confined only to beasts of prey. Manifestly however, that time has not yet come, and while all men should labor to hasten its coming, by the cultivation of all the elements conducive to peace, it is plain that for the present no race of men can depend wholly upon moral means for the maintenance of their rights. Men must either be governed by love or by fear. They must love to do right or fear to do wrong. The only way open to any race to make their rights respected is to learn how to defend them. When it is seen that black men no more than white men can be enslaved with impunity, men will be less inclined to enslave and oppress them. Enlist therefore, that you may learn the art and assert the ability to defend yourself and your race.

5th. Your are a member of a long enslaved and despised race. Men have set down your submission to Slavery and insult, to a lack of manly courage. They point to this fact as demonstrating your fitness only to be a servile class. You should enlist and disprove the slander, and wipe out the reproach. When you shall be seen nobly defending the liberties of your own country against rebels and traitors—brass itself will blush to use such arguments imputing cowardice against you.

6th. Whether you are or are not, entitled to all the rights of citizenship in this country has long been a matter of dispute to your prejudice. By enlisting in the service of your country at this trial hour, and upholding the National Flag, you will stop the mouths of traducers and win applause even from the iron lips of ingratitude. Enlist and you make this your country in common with all other men born in the country or out of it.

7th. Enlist for your own sake. Decried and derided as you have been and still are you need an act of this kind by which to recover your self-respect. You have to some extent rated your value by the estimate of your enemies and hence have counted yourself less than you are. You owe it to yourself and your race to rise from your social debasement and take your place among the soldiers of your country, a man among men. Depend upon it, the subjective effect of this one act of enlisting will be immense and highly beneficial. You will stand more erect, walk more assured, feel more at ease, and be less liable to insult than you ever were before. He who fights the battles of America may claim America as his country—and have that claim respected. Thus in defending your country now against rebels and traitors you are defending your own Liberty, honor, manhood and self-respect.

8th. You should enlist because your doing so will be one of the most certain means of preventing the country from drifting back into the whirlpool of Pro-Slavery Compromise at the end of the war, which is now our greatest danger. He who shall witness another Compromise with Slavery in this country will see the free colored man of the North more than ever a victim of the pride, lust, scorn and violence of all classes of white-men. The whole North will be but another Detroit, where every white fiend may with impunity revel in unrestrained beast-liness towards people of color; they may burn their houses, insult their wives and daughters, and kill indiscriminately. If you mean to live in this country now is the time for you to do your full share in making it a country where you and your children after you can live in comparative safety. Prevent a compromise with the traitors, compel them to come back to the Union whipped and humbled into obedience and all will be well. But let them come back as masters and all their hate and hellish ingenuity will be exerted to stir up the ignorant masses of the North to hate, hinder and persecute the free colored people of the North. That most inhuman of all modern enactments, with its bribed judges, and summary process, the Fugitive Slave Law, with all its infernal train of canting divines, preaching the gospel of kidnapping, as twelve years ago, will be revived against the free colored people of the North. One or two black brigades will do much to prevent all this.

9th. You should enlist because the war for the Union, whether men so call it or not, is a war for Emancipation. The salvation of the coun-try, by the inexorable relation of cause and effect, can be secured only by the complete abolition of Slavery. The President has already pro-claimed emancipation to the Slaves in the rebel States which is tanta-mount to declaring Emancipation in all the States, for Slavery must ex-ist every where in the South in order to exist any where in the South. Can you ask for a more inviting, ennobling and soul enlarging work, than that of making one of the glorious Band who shall carry Liberty to your long enslaved people. Remember that identified with the Slave in color, you will have a power that white soldiers have not, to attract them to your lines and induce them to take up arms in a common cause. One black Brigade will, for this work, be worth more than two white ones. Enlist, therefore, enlist without delay, enlist now, and forever put an end to the human barter and butchery which have stained the whole South with the warm blood of your people, and loaded its air with their groans. Enlist, and deserve not only well of your country, and win for yourselves, a name and a place among men, but secure to yourself what is infinitely more precious, the fast dropping tears of gratitude of your kith and kin marked out for destruction, and who are but now ready to perish.

When time's ample curtain shall fall upon our national tragedy, and our hillsides and valleys shall neither redden with the blood nor whiten with the bones of kinsmen and country-men who have fallen in the sanguinary and wicked strife; when grim visaged war has smoothed his wrinkled front and our country shall have regained its normal condition as a leader of nations in the occupation and blessings of peace—and history shall record the names of heroes and martyrs—who bravely answered the call of patriotism and Liberty—against traitors theives and assassins—let it not be said that in the long list of glory, composed of men of all nations—there appears the name of no colored man.

Rochester (N.Y.) *Douglass' Monthly*, April 1863.

---

1. Robert Burns, "For A' That," (1795), *The Songs of Robert Burns, with Music* (Glasgow: D. Jack, 1859).

"If I die tonight I will not die a coward"
Sgt. Lewis H. Douglass to Frederick and Anna Murray Douglass
JULY 20, 1863

On July 18, 1863, the 54th Massachusetts Regiment fought its most important engagement. On the beach of Morris Island, at the mouth of Charleston Harbor in South Carolina, stood the palmetto log and sand parapets of Fort Wagner. Part of a defensive ring of forts and military emplacements around Charleston, Wagner had to fall if the Union expected to silence Fort Sumter and ultimately capture Charleston, the seat of secession. About a week earlier, a frontal assault on the fort by Union forces ended in disaster. Hoping to avoid more slaughter, Union army and naval commanders commenced the most furious bombardment of the war in an attempt to silence the fort's guns and, thus, assure the next assault's success. But it was not to be. The sand absorbed all the iron balls and explosives that the Union could throw at it, with hardly any loss of life and little damage to the fort. When the 54th led the assault on the evening of July 18, 1863, they met Wagner's full fury. The resulting losses decimated the 54th; about half of the regiment's attacking force of 600 men were killed, wounded, or captured. One thousand five hundred and fifteen Union soldiers, black and white, ultimately died in unsuccessful attempts to seize the Confederate fort. Nearly every officer in the 54th's attacking force had been wounded, and two were killed, as was the unit's young commanding officer, Col. Robert Gould Shaw.

Lewis Henry Douglass (1840–1908) had learned the printer's trade by working in his father's various newspaper officers. He also had accompanied his famous father on many of his antislavery lecture tours, and he married Amelia Loguen, the daughter of Syracuse, New York's famed black abolitionist minister, Jermaine Wesley Loguen. One of two Douglass sons to serve in Massachusetts regiments, Lewis Douglass stood on Wagner's parapet with Colonel Shaw. The highest ranking enlisted man in the unit, Lewis survived the assault and the war, although he left the army in May 1864, stricken with typhoid fever and unable to perform his duties. For the rest of his life, he promoted reform and defended black rights. His letter to his parents, written two days after the assault, captures the everyday heroism that was expected from the men in the 54th and which secured the rights of African Americans to serve in the army. Ultimately about 179,000 black men served in the Union army, representing about 10 percent of all Union troops. Emilio, *A Brave Black Regiment,* 67–104; Edwin S. Redkey, "Brave Black Volunteers: A Profile of the Fifty-fourth Massachusetts Regiment," in Martin H. Blatt, Thomas J. Brown, and Donald Yacovone, eds., *Hope & Glory: Essays on the Legacy of the 54th Massachusetts Regiment* (Amherst, MA: University of Massachusetts Press, 2001), 21–34; Ripley, et al., *The Black Abolitionist Papers,* 5:244–245.

MORRIS ISLAND,
S[outh] C[arolina]
July 20th, 1863

MY DEAR FATHER AND MOTHER:

Wednesday July 8th, our regiment left St. Helena Island for Folly Island, arriving there the next day, and were then ordered to land on James Island, which we did. On the upper end of James Island is a large rebel battery with 18 guns. After landing we threw out pickets to within two miles of the rebel fortification. We were permitted to do this in

peace until last Thursday, 16th inst., when at four o'clock in the morning the rebels made an attack on our pickets, who were about 200
strong. We were attacked by a force of about 900. Our men fought like
tigers; one sergeant killed five men by shooting and bayoneting.[1] The
rebels were held in check by our few men long enough to allow the 10th
Conn[ecticut]. to escape being surrounded and captured, for which we
received the highest praise from all parties who knew of it. This performance on our part earned for us the reputation of a fighting regiment.

Our loss in killed, wounded and missing was forty-five. That night we
took, according to our officers, one of the hardest marches on record,
through woods and marsh. The rebels we defeated and drove back in
the morning. They, however, were reinforced by 14,000 men, we having only half a dozen regiments. So it was necessary for us to escape.

I cannot write in full, expecting every moment to be called into another fight. Suffice it to say we are now on Morris Island. Saturday night
we made the most desperate charge of the war on Fort Wagner, losing
in killed, wounded and missing in the assault, three hundred of our men.
The splendid 54th is cut to pieces. All our officers, with the exception
of eight, were either killed or wounded. Col. [Robert Gould] Shaw is a
prisoner and wounded.[2] Major [Edward N.] Hallowell is wounded in
three places, Adj't [Garth W.] James in two places. Serg't [Robert J.]
Simmons is killed, Nat[haniel]. Hurley (from Rochester) is missing, and
a host of others.[3]

I had my sword sheath blown away while on the parapet of the Fort.
The grape and cannister, shell and minnies swept us down like chaff,
still our men went on and on, and if we had been properly supported,
we would have held the Fort, but the white troops could not be made
to come up. The consequence was we had to fall back, dodging shells
and other missiles.

If I have another opportunity, I will write more fully. Goodbye to all.
If I die tonight I will not die a coward. Goodbye.

LEWIS

Rochester (N.Y.) *Douglass' Monthly*, August 1863.

---

1. During the July 16 battle of James Island, Sgt. Joseph D. Wilson fought five
   Confederates, killing three, and then attacked several rebel cavalrymen before being killed. Emilio, *A Brave Black Regiment*, 58.

2. Immediately after the battle, many rumors circulated that Shaw survived the attack, but he was shot through the heart on the parapet of Wagner and was buried by the Confederates with others of his regiment.

3. Hallowell (1836–1871) and James (1845–1883) recovered from their wounds; Hallowell later assumed command of the 54th. Simmons (1839–1863) actually survived the assault, but later died in a Confederate prison after the amputation of an arm. Hurley (1846–1865) was also captured, and he died after two years as a prisoner. Emilio, *A Brave Black Regiment*, 93, 163–164, 190–191, 328, 333–334, 348, 361.

"this ungodly rebellion shall be put down"
Pvt. Samuel Cable to Leah Ward Cable
[1863]

The following two letters poignantly reveal what military service in the Civil War meant to the ordinary black man and the slave. Samuel Cable (1843–1906), who signed his pension papers with an 'X,' probably dictated his letter to a fellow soldier. Born in Brunswick, Missouri, the light-skinned Cable was working as a waiter in Keokuk, Iowa, at the time he enlisted in the 55th Massachusetts Regiment, the second black regiment raised in the state, in June 1863. He suffered a leg wound from a cannon shell explosion on Long Island, South Carolina, but remained with his regiment until the close of the war. He did not formally marry his wife until 1866, and he had one son. After discharge from the military, he lived in Colorado and spent his last years in declining health at the National Military Home in Leavenworth, Kansas. Octave Johnson, an illiterate Louisiana slave, dictated the story of his life to the American Freedman's Inquiry Commission. One is hard-pressed to read a more compelling explanation of why a slave wished to join the Union army. Samuel Cable pension file, RG 15, National Archives; [Charles B. Fox], *Record of the Service of the Fifty-fifth Regiment of Massachusetts Volunteer Infantry* (Cambridge, MA: John Wilson and Son, 1868), 133.

DEAR WIFE I HAVE enlisted in the army[.] i am now in the state of Massachussetts but before this letter reaches you i will be in north Carolina and though great is the present national dificulties yet i look foward to a brighter day When i shall have the opertunity of seeing you in the full enjoyment of fredom[.] i would like to no if you are still in slavery[?] if you are it will not be long before we shall have crushed the system that now opreses you for in the Course of three months you shall have your liberty[.] great is the outpouring of the colered people that is now rally-ing with the hearts of lions against that very curse that has seperated you an me[.] yet we shall meet again and oh what a happy time that will be when this ungodly rebellion shall be put down and the curses of our land is trampled under our feet[.] i am a soldier now and i shall use my utmost endeavers to strike at the rebellion and the heart of this system that so long has kept us in chains. Write to me just as soon as you git this letter[.] tell me if you are still living in the cabin where you use to live. tell eliza i send her my best respects and love[.] ike and sully lik-wise[.] i would send you some money but i now it is impossible for you to git it[.]

i would like to see little jenkins now but i no it is impossibl at pre-sent[.] se no more but remain your own afectionate husband until death

SAMUEL CABBLE

Samuel Cable pension file, RG 15, National Archives.

"in 1855 master sold my mother, and in 1861 he sold me"
Testimony of Cpl. Octave Johnson
[FEBRUARY?] 1864

[New Orleans. February? 1864]

Deposition of Octave Johnson, Corporal Co. C, 15th Regt. Corps d'Afrique.[1]

I WAS BORN IN New Orleans; I am 23 years of age; I was raised by Arthur Thiboux of New Orleans; I am by trade a cooper; I was treated pretty well at home; in 1855 master sold my mother, and in 1861 he sold me to S. Contrell of St. James Parish for $2,400; here I worked by task at my trade; one morning the bell was rung for us to got to work so early that I could not see, and I lay still, because I was working by task; for this the overseer was going to have me whipped, and I ran away to the woods, where I remained for a year and a half; I had to steal my food; took turkeys, chickens and pigs; before I left our number had increased to thirty, of whom ten were women; we were four miles in the rear of the plantation house; sometimes we would rope beef cattle and drag them out to our hiding place; we obtained matches from our friends on the plantation; we slept on logs and burned cypress leaves to make a smoke and keep away mosquitoes; Eugene Jardeau, master of hounds, hunted for us for three months; often those at work would betray those in the swamp, for fear of being implicated in their escape; we furnished meat to our fellow-servants in the field, who would return corn meal; one day twenty hounds came after me; I called the party to my assistance and we killed eight of the blood hounds; then we all jumped into Bayou Faupron; the dogs followed us and the alligators caught six of them; "the alligators preferred dog flesh to personal flesh;" we escaped and came to Camp Parapet,[2] where I was first employed in the Commissary's office, then as a servant to Col. Hanks; then I joined his regiment.

American Freedmen's Inquiry Commission papers, RG 94, Letters Received, ser. 12, O-328, National Archives. Reprinted in Berlin, et al., *Freedom: The Destruction of Slavery*, 1:217.

---

1. The 15th Corps d'Afrique was organized in New Orleans in August 1863. It became the 5th Regiment Engineers, and in April 1864 was redesignated the 99th USCT. It fought in one significant engagement at Natural Bridge, Florida. Wilson, *The Black Phalanx*, 476.
2. Camp Parapet, just north of New Orleans, was the site where Union forces under Gen. Benjamin F. Butler organized the Louisiana Native Guard. It remained a camp for black troops for the rest of the war. James G. Hollandsworth, Jr., *The Louisiana Native Guard: The Black Military Experience During the Civil War* (Baton Rouge, LA: Louisiana State University Press, 1995), 27.

"I propose, sir, an army of blacks"
Martin R. Delany meets with Abraham Lincoln
FEBRUARY 1865

Few African Americans attained the stature of Martin R. Delany (1812–1885). The nineteenth century's leading advocate of black nationalism, Delany became one of the most prominent black intellectuals in the North. Born free in Charlestown, Virginia, he saw firsthand the reality of slavery, and he heard tales of his African ancestors from his grandmother. His family fled to Pennsylvania after civil authorities in Virginia caught his mother attempting to educate her children. At age nineteen, Delany enrolled in Lewis Woodson's African Educational Society School in Pittsburgh. He learned fast and well and began training to be a physician. Harvard College accepted his application for enrollment, but student protests forced him to leave after one term. He returned to Pittsburgh, published a newspaper for several years, and in 1852 published his great treatise on black nationalism and emigration, *The Condition, Elevation, Emigration and Destiny of the Colored People of the United States.* Rejecting American racism and wishing to assert black worth, Delany left for Canada and in 1859 visited West Africa in anticipation of founding a free labor colony there. He remained in Europe, attempting to whip up support for his African venture, until 1863.

But the Emancipation Proclamation changed everything. Delany returned to the United States eager to help fill the ranks of the 54th Massachusetts Regiment and any units that the government might permit blacks to raise. He wrote directly to Secretary of War Edwin M. Stanton in 1863 (Stanton likely never read the letter or dismissed it immediately) asking for federal authority to recruit black troops in the South. Delany believed that African Americans like himself were best suited for this vital task. Despite Stanton's support for the recruitment of black soldiers, it would not be until February 1865, as Charleston was falling to Union troops and the war neared its conclusion, that Delany received a chance to put his proposal to raise a black army directly to the president. Lincoln liked what he heard and compelled the secretary of war to commission Delany as a major, the highest rank attained by a black during the Civil War. This achievement, in addition to gaining an audience with the president, made Delany a hero to many African Americans.

Frances Rollin Whipper wrote her biography of Delany in the fall and winter of 1867–1868. She published it under a pseudonym, Frank A. Rollin, perhaps because she believed that male authorship would lend credibility to the project, or because the publishers insisted on it. Frances Rollin Whipper wrote the book out of genuine admiration for Delany, believing that he embodied black manhood and would be an irresistible role model. She gained Delany's cooperation in the project, and the following interview with Lincoln that Whipper recorded in her book came directly from Delany. Ripley et al., *The Black Abolitionist Papers*, 4:128–130, 5:261–262; William L. Andrews, ed., *Two Biographies by African-American Women* (New York: Oxford University Press, 1991), xxxiii–xliii.

THE COUNCIL-CHAMBER.—PRESIDENT LINCOLN

WE GIVE IN MAJOR [Martin R.] Delany's own language his interview with President Lincoln.

He tells us, "On entering the executive chamber, and being introduced to his excellency, a generous grasp and sake of the hand brought me to a seat in front of him. No one could mistake the fact that an able and master spirit was before me. Serious without sadness, and pleasant withal, he was soon seated, placing himself at ease, the better to give me a patient audience. He opened the conversation first.

"'What can I do for you, sir?' he inquired.

"'Nothing, Mr. President,' I replied; 'but I've come to propose something to you, which I think will be beneficial to the nation in this critical hour of her peril.' I shall never forget the expression of his countenance and the inquiring look which he gave me when I answered him.

"'Go on, sir,' he said, as I paused through deference to him. I continued the conversation by reminding him of the full realization of arming the blacks of the South, and the ability of the blacks of the North to defeat it by complicity with those at the South, through the medium of the *Underground Railroad*—a measure known only to themselves.

"I next called his attention to the fact of the heart-less and almost relentless prejudice exhibited towards the blacks by the Union army, and that something ought to be done to check this growing feeling against the slave, else nothing that we could do would avail. And if such were not expedited, all might be lost. That the blacks, in every capacity in which they had been called to act, had done their part faithfully and well. To this Mr. Lincoln readily assented. I continued: 'I would call your attention to another fact of great consideration; that is, the position of confidence in which they have been placed, when your officers have been under obligations to them, and in many instances even the army in their power. As pickets, scouts, and guides, you have trusted them, and found them faithful to the duties assigned; and it follows that if you can find them of higher qualifications, they may, with equal credit, fill higher and more important trusts.'

"'*Certainly,*' replied the president, in his most emphatic manner. 'And what do you propose to do?' he inquired.

"I responded, 'I prose this, sir; but first permit me to say that, whatever I may desire for black men in the army, I know that there exists too much prejudice among the whites for the soldiers to serve under a black commander, or the officers to be willing to associate with him. These are facts which must be admitted, and, under the circumstances, must be regarded, as they cannot be ignored. And I propose, as a most effective remedy to prevent enrollment of the blacks in the rebel service, and induce them to run to, instead of from, the Union forces—the commissioning and promotion of black men now in the army, according to merit.'

"Looking at me for a moment, earnestly yet anxiously, he demanded, 'How will you remedy the great difficulty you have just now so justly described, about the objections of white soldiers to colored commanders, and officers to colored associates?'

"I replied, 'I have the remedy, Mr. President, which has not yet been stated; and it is the most important suggestion of my visit to you. And I think it is just what is required to complete the prestige of the Union army. I propose, sir, an army of blacks, commanded entirely by black officers, except such whites as may volunteer to serve; this army to penetrate through the heart of the South, and make conquests, with the banner of Emancipation unfurled, proclaiming freedom as they go, sustaining and protecting it by arming the emancipated, taking them as fresh troops, and leaving a few veterans among the new freedmen, when occasion requires, keeping this banner unfurled until every slave is free, according to the letter of your proclamation. I would also take from those already in the service all that are competent for commission officers, and establish at once in the South a camp of instructions. By this we could have in about three months an army of forty thousand blacks in motion, the presence of which anywhere would itself be a power irresistible. You should have an army of blacks, President Lincoln, commanded entirely by blacks, the sight of which is required to give confidence to the slaves, and retain them to the Union, stop foreign intervention, and speedily bring the war to a close.'

"'This,' replied the president, 'is the very thing I have been looking and hoping for; but nobody offered it. I have thought it over and over again. I have talked about it; I hoped and prayed for it; but till now it never has been proposed. White men couldn't do this, because they are doing all in that direction now that they can; but we find, for various reasons, it does not meet the case under consideration. The blacks should go to the interior, and the white be kept on the frontiers.'

"'Yes, sir,' I interposed; 'they would require but little, as they could subsist on the country as they went along.'

"'Certainly,' continued he; 'a few light artillery, with the cavalry, would comprise your principal advance, because all the siege work would be on the frontiers and waters, done by the white division of the army. Won't this be a grand thing?' he exclaimed, joyfully. He continued, 'When I issued my Emancipation Proclamation, I had this thing in contemplation. I then gave them a chance by prohibiting any interference on the part of the army; but they did not embrace it,' said he, rather sadly, accompanying the word with an empathic gesture.

"'But, Mr. President,' said I, 'these poor people could not read your proclamation, nor could they know anything about it, only, when they did hear, to know that they were free.'

"'But you of the North I expected to take advantage of it,' he replied.

"'Our policy, sir,' I answered, 'was directly opposite, supposing that it met your approbation. To this end I published a letter against embarrassing or compromising the government in any manner whatever; for us to remain passive, except in case of foreign intervention, then immediately to raise the slaves to insurrection.'

"'Ah, I remember the letter,' he said, 'and thought at the time that you mistook my designs. But the effect will be better as it is, by giving

character to the blacks, both North and South, as a peaceable, inoffen-
sive people.' Suddenly turning, he said, 'Will you take command?'

'If there be none better qualified than I am, sir, by that time I will.
While it is my desire to serve, as black men we shall have to prepare
ourselves, as we have had no opportunities of experience and practice
in the service as officers.'

'That matters but little, comparatively,' he replied; 'as some of the
finest officers we have never studied the tactics till they entered the
army as subordinates. And again,' said he, 'the tactics are easily learned,
especially among your people. It is the head that we now require most—
men of plans and executive ability.'

"'I thank you, Mr. President,' said I, 'for the—'

"'No—not at all,' he interrupted.

"'I will show you some letters of introduction, sir,' said I, putting my
hand in my pocket to get them.

"'Not now,' he interposed; 'I know all about you. I see nothing now
to be done but to give you a line of introduction to the secretary of war.'

"Just as he began writing, the cannon commenced booming.

"'Stanton is firing! listen! he is in his glory! noble man!' he exclaimed.

"'What is it, Mr. President?' I asked.

"'The firing!'

"'What is it about, sir,' I reiterated, ignorant of the cause.

"'Why, don't you know? Haven't you heard the news? Charleston is
ours!'[1] he answered, straightening up from the table on which he was
writing for an instant, and then resuming it. He soon handed me a card,
on which was written,—

'February [1]8, 1865.
'Hon. E. M. Stanton, *Secretary of War.*
'Do not fail to have an interview with this most extraordinary and in-
telligent black man.

'A. Lincoln .'

"This card showed he perfectly understood my views and feelings;
hence he was not content that my color should make its own impression, but he expressed it with emphasis, as though a point was gained.
The thing desired presented itself; not simply a man that was *black*, because these had previously presented themselves, in many delegations
and committees,—men of the highest intelligence,—for various ob-

jects; but that which he had wished and hoped for, their own proposed measures matured in the council-chamber had never been fully presented to them in the person of a black man."

This, then, was what was desired to complete the plans of the president and his splendid minister, the secretary of war. The "ponderous beam," being removed, to use his figurative expression, the passport was clear to every part of the mansion. He entered the war department for the purpose of seeing the minister. As he entered, a glance revealed to him the presiding genius of the situation, surrounded by his assistants. In the room was a pressing crowd of both sexes, representing nearly every condition of life, each in turn endeavoring to reach the centre of the room, where, at an elevated desk, stood one of the greatest men of the times, and the able director of the war department.

After he had sent forward his card, he was requested by the secretary in person, to whom he was not previously unknown, to call at the department again.

He had gained the interview with the president that he wished, and the indications were brighter than his most sanguine expectations had promised. The war minister's influence alone could effect the balance.

He sought Dr. William Elder, the distinguished biographer of Dr. [Elisha Kent] Kane, of Arctic memory, who was then chief of the bureau of statistics, and gave him an account of his mission to the president.

After explaining everything to the doctor, his face assuming an expression peculiar to himself, of a whole-souled satisfaction, he exclaimed, "I'll be hanged if I haven't got the thing! just the thing! Will you give me that in writing?" he asked; "I mean the points touched upon, that may be written in a letter to me."

On receiving it, in the afternoon of the same day, after he had read it, he turned to the future major, and said, "*You shall* have what you want," in like manner as he replied to a speech of Louis Kossuth,[2] when he told him if he went to war with Austria, *he shouldn't die*.

When Delany left Dr. Elder, he was thoroughly convinced, that if the secretary of war could be influenced by any man, in regard to his mission, in none abler could he depend than upon his true and earnest advocate of his race.

The next call at the war department was made the following Monday, the 12th inst. His reception there, being equally as cordial as the first, seemed already to indicate success to his measures.

"What do you propose to do, doctor?" asked the secretary, as Dr. Delany began to explain to him as he did to the president. "I understand the whole thing, and fully comprehend your design; I have frequently gone over the whole ground, in council with the president. What do you wish? What position?" He replied,—

"In any position or place whatever, in which I may be instrumental in promoting the measures proposed, and be of service to the country, so that I am not subject and subordinate to every man who holds a commission, and, with such, chooses to assume authority."

"Will you take the field?" asked the secretary.

"I should like to do so as soon as possible, but not until I have had sufficient discipline and practice in a camp of instruction, and a sufficient number of black officers to command each regiment," was the answer given.

"Of course," said the secretary, "you must establish your camp of instruction; and as you have a general knowledge of the qualified colored men of the country, I propose to commission you at once, and send you South to commence raising troops, to be commanded by black officers, on the principles you proposed, of which I most highly approve, to prevent all clashing or jealousy,—because of no contact to arouse prejudices. It is none of white men's business what rank a black man holds over his own people. I shall assign you to Charleston, with advices and instructions to Major General [Rufus] Saxton. Do you know him?" he asked. Being answered, he continued, "He is an unflinching friend of your race. You will impart to him, in detail, that which will not be written. The letter giving special instruction will be given to you—all further instructions to be obtained at the department."

Assistant Adjutant General of Volunteers Colonel C[harles]. W. Foster, at this juncture having been sent for, was instructed by the secretary of war to take him to his department, and make the necessary examination; there being no rejection, to prepare and fill out a parchment, with commission of *Major of Infantry*, the *regiment* to be left blank, to be filled by order of Major General Saxton, according to instructions to be given, and to report the next morning at eleven o'clock.

After the examination by the adjutant general, he remarked, "This is certainly an important and interesting feature of the war. And the secretary must expect much to be done by you, for he certainly holds you in high esteem."

"I hope, colonel," he replied, "that neither the honorable secretary of war nor the government will expect too much from an individual like myself. My only hope is, that I may be able to do my duty well and satisfactorily."

"I have no fears for your success," returned the colonel; "you have qualifications and ability, and must succeed, when your chances are such as they will now be. This is a great thing for you," he continued, "and you have now an opportunity of making yourself *anything that you please*, and doing for your race all that may be required at the hands of the government." He, attempting to thank the colonel for the encouraging as well as complimentary remarks, was stopped by him, saying, "I speak as I think and feel about it. The secretary has great confidence in you, and I simply wish to endorse it for your encouragement. There is nothing now to be done," he continued, " but to call tomorrow, and go with me to the war department to report finally to the secretary of war, and receive your commission from his hands." All arrangements being completed in the adjutant's department, he withdrew.

Frank A. Rollin [Frances E. Rollin Whipper], *Life and Public Services of Martin R. Delany* (Boston: Lee and Shepard, 1883), 166–175.

---

1. Confederate troops began evacuating Charleston on the evening of February 17. Elements of the 54th Massachusetts Regiment were the first Union troops to enter the city, which was fully occupied the following day. The 21st USCT, comprised of former South Carolina slaves, triumphantly paraded through the newly won city. Yacovone, *A Voice of Thunder*, 80–81.
2. Louis Kossuth (1802–1894), a Hungarian freedom fighter, toured the United States in support of Hungarian independence from the Austrian Empire.

7

Black Soldiers and the War, Part II: The Hate We Face

*"colored men have their rights that
white men are bound to respect"*
Alexander T. Augusta to the *National Republican*
MAY 15, 1863

An African American soldier with shoulder straps possessed immense symbolism. Although medical officers and recruiters held their commissions out of the regular army chain of command, they nevertheless represented the "willingness of the government to secure justice to the black man." To African Americans, a black officer symbolized racial progress, power, and recognition of black worth and ability. Perhaps men such as Dr. Alexander T. Augusta or a Dr. John V. DeGrass, the first black member of the Massachusetts Medical Society who served with the 35th USCT, were harbingers of commissions for worthy black combat troops. But to most whites in and out of the military, a uniformed African American assaulted white racial pride and their sense of manhood. The very idea of a black officer who might exercise authority over white men represented an intolerable threat, if not a perversion of nature. At the close of the war, when the 54th Massachusetts Regiment starting commissioning black soldiers, several of the white officers in the unit resigned their commissions rather than serve alongside a black officer. "Things are going to the devil fast," one white officer bitterly complained.

Alexander T. Augusta (1825–1890), a freeborn African American from Virginia, determined to become a physician and refused to allow

121

American racial prejudice to stop him. He received instruction informally from white doctors, and in 1856 he graduated from the Trinity
Medical College of the University of Toronto. After the war, he joined
the staff of Howard University's medical department. Despite his abilities, the white medical establishment refused to accept him or recognize his accomplishments.

While living in Toronto, Augusta wrote to President Lincoln and
Secretary of War Stanton in January 1863, volunteering to serve as a
doctor in a black regiment "where I can be of use to my race." Although
it originally turned down Augusta's request, the War Department reversed its decision three months later. The very next month, as Augusta traveled through Baltimore in full uniform, whites expressed their
feelings about officers' commissions for black soldiers. New York
Weekly Anglo-African, May 9, 1863; Yacovone, *A Voice of Thunder,* 90, 237;
Berlin et al., *Freedom: The Black Military Experience,* 310–312, 354–355;
Ripley et al., *The Black Abolitionist Papers,* 5:211.

Washington, [D.C.]

May 15, 1863

Sir:[1]

Inasmuch as many misstatements relative to the assault upon me in
Baltimore have been made, I deem it necessary, in justice to myself, as
well as to all parties concerned, to give to the public a true statement
of the facts as they occurred.

I started from my lodgings in Mulberry Street, near Pine, about a
quarter past nine o'clock, on the morning of 1st inst., in order to take
the 10 a.m. train for Philadelphia. I went down Mulberry Street to
Howard, Howard to Baltimore, Baltimore to Gay, Gay to Pratt, Pratt to
President, and thence to the depot. No one interfered with me during
the whole route. I obtained my ticket from the agent, without the usual
bond required of colored persons wishing to proceed North, and took
my seat in the car—little expecting anyone would make an attack upon
me then.

After remaining in my seat about five minutes, I heard someone conversing behind me, but paid no attention to what they were talking
about, when of a sudden a boy about fifteen years of age, who appeared
to be employed about the depot, came up behind me, and, swearing at
me, caught hold of my right shoulder-strap, and pulled it off. I jumped
up, and, turning towards him, found a man standing by his side who had

directed me which car to get in, and while I was remonstrating with the boy for what he had done, he pulled the other one off; while at the same time the boy threatened to strike me with a club he held in his hand. I then turned towards the door of the car where I was standing, and found I was surrounded by about eight or ten roughs; and knowing that should I touch one of them all the rest would pounce upon me, I thought it best to take my seat and await what further issue might take place.

Shortly after I had taken my seat, the parties who had assaulted me left the car, and a policeman came in and stood near me. A person standing by asked him if he intended to interfere. He answered by say-ing it depended upon circumstances. I then turned towards him, and said to him, "If you are a policeman, I claim your protection as a United States officer, who has been assaulted without a cause." Just about that time, I was informed that the provost guards were in the car, and that I had better apply to them for protection. I called to the guards and told them I was a United States officer; that I had been assaulted and my shoulder-straps torn off by employees of the road, and that I claimed their protection. Having satisfied them of my connection with the ser-vice, they assured me of their protection. I might have gone on in that train, but I was determined to stop back, so as to have the parties pun-ished, knowing full well that the same thing might occur again, unless a stop was put to it at once. I therefore went up to the provost marshal's office with one of the guard, and reported the facts to Lieut. Col. Fish, the provost marshal.

He examined my commission, and finding it was all right, said he did not care who it was, so he was a United States officer, and claimed his protection, he should have it to the fullest extent. He then deputed Lieut. Morris to accompany me to the depot and arrest the parties. The lieutenant told me I was as much authorized as an officer to arrest them as he was; and that I had better go ahead of him and the guard, fearing that if the parties saw them they would get out of the way. He directed me, at the same time, that when I saw any one of the parties to go up to him and place my hand upon his shoulder and claim him as my pris-oner, and he would be on hand to take him in charge. I knew this was as extraordinary step for me to take in Baltimore, but I told him I would do it. I accordingly went down to the depot, and when near it I recog-nized one of the parties crossing the street; I went up to him, and, while accusing him of taking off my straps, put my hand upon his shoulder and claimed him as my prisoner. I then ordered the guard to take him into custody, which he did. I then hunted around the depot for the boy, but could not find him.

The lieutenant having come up to me by this time, was started for the provost marshal's office, and then opposite Marsh market on Baltimore street, Lieut. Morris, the guard, and the prisoner, being on the opposite side of the street, a man, whom I learned afterwards to be named Hancock, emerged from the market and assaulted me. I called the guard across and had him taken into custody. We then proceeded to the office unmolested, where I remained until about half past twelve o'clock, when Lieut. Morris told me it was time to start for the depot, to take the one o'clock train. I got ready and we proceeded together, and every step we took after leaving the office, the crowd which was standing around the door increased. No one, however, interfered with me until we arrived at the corner of Pratt and President streets, when a man, whose name I since learned to be Dunn, was standing in our way, and as soon as I reached him, he dealt me a severe blow on the face, which stunned me for a moment and caused the blood to flow from my nose very freely. In an instant, Lieut. Morris seized him by the collar and held him fast; and I not knowing that there was anyone else in the crowd to protect me, made for the first door I saw open. When I reached it, a woman was standing there and pushed me back to prevent me from entering. In the meantime I looked back and saw a person with my cap and a revolver in his hand. He told me to stand still, that I was protected. I came down the steps, and proceeded between two guards with revolvers drawn until we reached the depot.

Upon our arrival, Lieut. Morris put the prisoner upon a settee, and placed a guard over him, with orders to shoot him if he dared to stir from the spot. A short time after we arrived, two other persons were identified as having been engaged in the last assault upon me, and were arrested. I washed the blood from my face and prepared to take my seat in the cars, when an officer, whom I subsequently learned to be Major Robertson,[2] of Maj. Gen. [Joseph] Hooker's staff, having learned the facts of the case from Lieut. Morris, came up to me and told me he was going to Philadelphia, and offered to protect me at the risk of his own life. The guard surrounded me with drawn revolvers, conducted me to the cars, and remained with me until the train started. During the same time we were waiting for the train to start, I learned from the guard that when I was struck by Dunn, they were in the crowd dressed in citizens' clothes, and were just about to shoot him when Lieut. Morris ordered them not to shoot, as he had the prisoner safe.

When the train was about to start, Lieut. Morris, in addition to Maj. Robertson, who had volunteered to protect me, sent on two armed cavalry to guard me to Philadelphia, or as long as I might want them. I, however, did not consider it necessary to detain them after we arrived, and accordingly discharged them from any further attendance upon me. Since my return to Washington, I have learned that some of the parties have been tried, and sent to Fort McHenry.[3]

These, Mr. Editor, are the facts of the case, and I deny, in toto, the profane language attributed to me by the Baltimore *Clipper*.

Now it seems that, in this transaction, I have been blamed by two classes of persons. The first say that I should not have passed through Baltimore in uniform, because, say they, the people of Baltimore are opposed to it, and even Union men do not wish to see colored men wearing the United States uniform.

Well, in answer to this class, I will say that the people of Baltimore were opposed to the Massachusetts troops passing through there two years ago, and mobbed them, but the Government of the United States was strong enough to put down that spirit then, and I apprehend it is strong enough now to protect colored troops under similar circumstances. And furthermore, while I have always known Baltimore as a place where it is considered a virtue to mob colored people, still, I had a right to expect a safe transit through there after the resolution passed only two weeks before at the National Union League,[4] on the anniversary of the attack upon the Massachusetts troops, calling on the President of the United States to place not only spades but muskets in the hands of black men to put down the rebellion. And more especially, as I had only volunteered to bind up the wounds of those colored men who should volunteer, as well as those rebels and Copperheads whom the fortune of war might throw into my hands. But, sir, I may take still higher grounds than these to justify my course. For I hold that my position as an officer of the United States entitles me to wear the insignia of my office, and if I am either afraid or ashamed to wear them anywhere, I am not fit to hold my commission, and should resign it at once.

The other class that blame me are those who say I acted wrongly in not shooting down anyone who dared to interfere with me. Well, in answer to this class, I can only say that while I am aware that I had the authority as an officer of the United States to defend myself to that extremity, I do not think, had I have done so, I would have accomplished so much for liberty as I did by allowing those whose special duty it was to protect me.

The question has no doubt been frequently asked, "What has been gained by this transaction?" I will answer. It has proved that even in *rowdy Baltimore* colored men have their rights that white men are bound to respect. For I was told by a gentleman since I returned, whom I saw in the crowd at Baltimore, that when Dunn was taken to the provost marshal's office, the marshal reprimanded the officer who had him in charge for not shooting him when he struck me, and told him if a case of the kind occurs again, and the officer in charge does not shoot the aggressor, his commission shall be broken.

In conclusion, Mr. Editor, I desired to return my sincere thanks to Lieut. Col. Fish for his prompt protection, to Lieut. Morris for the alacrity with which he carried out Col. Fish's orders, to Major Robertson for his kindness in volunteering his services, and the brave men of the guard for risking their lives in my defence. I remain, sir, Yours, very respectfully,

A. T. AUGUSTA
Bachelor of Medicine,
Surgeon U.S.V.

Philadelphia *Christian Recorder*, May 30, 1863. Reprinted in Ripley et al, *The Black Abolitionist Papers*, 5:205–210.

---

1. William J. Murtagh edited and published the Washington, D.C., *National Republican*. Augusta probably chose to publish his account of the incident in Murtagh's paper because it reached many white Republicans and usually reported favorably on the city's African Americans. Ripley et al., *The Black Abolitionist Papers*, 5:210.
2. Maj. George H. Roberts, Jr.
3. Fort McHenry, made famous during the War of 1812, became a prison for those charged with disloyalty during the Civil War.
4. In April 1863, the Union League of Maryland met to urge the Lincoln administration to employ all men, black and white, for the army to defeat the rebellion. Ripley, et al., *The Black Abolitionist Papers*, 5:210–211.

"Is there no justice in America?"
Sgt. George E. Stephens to Robert Hamilton
AUGUST 7, 1863

Although comparatively rare, letters from black soldiers survive in sufficient quantity for us to understand the men's motivations and preoc-
cupations. Like every other soldier, they worried over their fate, their
families, and the conditions of their service. But when they wrote
home, especially to the newspapers that eagerly carried their correspondence, they did not dwell on their combat experience or a narrow
escape from what seemed certain death. They wrote of their desire to
end the cursed institution of slavery and of their demands for racial justice. Regrettably, both the army and events on the home front gave
them many opportunities for expression.

No soldier wrote more often to the popular press or with more passion on the subject of justice for African Americans than Sgt. George
E. Stephens (1832–1888). A Philadelphia cabinet maker and a member
of the city's educated black elite, Stephens received a firsthand view of
the reality of slavery when he visited Charleston, South Carolina, before the war as crew member of a U.S. Coast Survey vessel. When war
erupted in 1861, Stephens traveled with the Army of the Potomac for
two years, regularly sending dispatches back to the New York *Weekly
Anglo-African* that described life on the front lines and the ugly reality of
slavery. In early 1863 he helped recruit for the 54th Massachusetts Regiment and then joined the unit himself to do his part to defeat slavery
and establish racial justice. As a member of the 54th Massachusetts, the
best-known of all the black Civil War regiments, he continued his popular correspondence for the *Weekly Anglo-African*. Stephens's views carried much authority, and his colleagues quickly recognized him as the
unofficial voice of the men in the regiment. Stephens joined the 54th
Massachusetts to end slavery and racial prejudice with the same musket. But the army proved no refuge from the racial prejudice that had
dogged him in his native Philadelphia, and the War Department refused
to honor its promise of equal pay. News of the white rioters in New
York City in July 1863 left him nearly bereft of hope. The rioters had

even attacked the families of some of the very men who had given up their lives for the Union and liberty at Fort Wagner. What more could African Americans do to prove their worthiness and their patriotism, Stephens asked? Edwin S. Redkey, ed., *A Grand Army of Black Men: Letters from African-American Soldiers in the Union Army, 1861–1865* (Cambridge, England: Cambridge University Press, 1992); Yacovone, *A Voice of Thunder,* 250–257.

In camp, Morris Island, S.C.,
Aug. 7, 1863

MR. EDITOR: Since I wrote my last letter the startling news of the mobs, riots, incendiarism, pillage and slaughter, recently so rife in the North, particularly in New York City, has reached here. You may judge what our thoughts and feelings were as we read bulletin after bulletin depicting to the life the scenes of violence and bloodshed which rivaled and even surpassed in their horrors, those which were perpetrated in Paris, during the bloody French Revolution, for we are yet to find an instance there where the orphan was ruthlessly assailed, or women and children murdered and maltreated without cause or provocation, simply for belonging to another race or class of people.

What cause or provocation have the New York rabble for disloyalty to their country, and for their bloody, atrocious assaults on my countrymen? Are we their enemies? Have we tyrannized over them? Have we maltreated them? Have we robbed them? Are we alien enemies? And are we traitors? Has not the unrequited labor of nearly four million of our brethren added to the country's wealth? Have we not been loyal to the country, in season and out of season, through good report and evil? And even while your mob-fiends upheld the assassin knife, and brandished the incendiary torch over the heads of our wives and children and to burn their homes, we were doing our utmost to sustain the honor of our country's flag, to perpetuate, if possible, those civil, social, and political liberties, they, who so malignantly hate us, have so fully enjoyed. Oh! how causeless, senseless, outrageous, brutal, and violative of every sentiment of manhood, courage and humanity these attacks on our defenseless brethren have been!

Fearful as these mobs have been, I trust they may prove to be lessons, though fearful ones, to guide the popular and loyal masses in the country, in all times of national emergency and peril, for when the services of every citizen or denizen of the country are imperatively required to defend it against powerful and determined foes, either foreign or domestic, and there can be found a strong minority ready and willing to subvert the government by popular violence and tumult or a base submission unworthy the meanest varlet of some monarchy; much less the boasted citizens of this great and magnificent country, it will bring still more forcibly to their minds the truism that "eternal vigilance is the price of liberty."[1]

These mobs are the stepping-stones upon which base traitors and demagogues hope to mount into arbitrary power, and to overawe and subvert liberty and law. They seek anarchy; and despotism, they think, must succeed. First anarchy, then despotism. They make the negro the catspaw or victim; but the loyalist and the friend of law and order cannot fail to see that every blow directed against the negro is directed against them. Our relation to the government is and has been that of unflinching, unswerving loyalty. Even when the government, by its every precept and practice, conserved the interests of slavery, and slaves were hunted down by United States soldiers and surrendered to traitorous slave-masters, the conduct of the negro was marked with distinguished loyalty. The instances are too numerous to cite of their braving the most fearful dangers to convey valuable information to the Union armies, and for this, the half yet untold, such has been our reward. Does not Milliken's Bend and Port Hudson furnish a chapter of valor and faithful loyalty? Is there no justice in America—or are we doomed to general massacre, as Mr. [Montgomery] Blair said we would be, in the event of the issue of the President's Emancipation proclamation? If this be our doom let us prepare for the worst.

The siege of Charleston has not yet commenced. The preparations of Gen. [Quincy A.] Gillmore are very ample. There is no doubt that this citadel of treason will fall. Every one is impatient at the delay; but the siege of a stronghold upon which all of the engineering skill of the rebel Confederacy has been lavished, cannot be planned and matured in a day. They harass our fatigue parties considerably with their shells, but they only succeed in killing and wounding one or two men a day. These shells are very disagreeable at first, but after one is under them a while he can learn to become accustomed to them. The men sing, dance, and play cards and sleep as carelessly within range of them as if they were no more harmful than so many soap bubbles.

This Morris Island is the most desolate heap of sand-hills I ever saw. It is so barren that you cannot find so much as a gypsum weed growing. Our situation is almost unbearable. During the day the sun is intensely hot, and this makes the sand hot; so we are sandwiched between the hot sun and the hot sand. Happily, the evenings are cool and bracing—so much so, that woolen blankets are not uncomfortable. The bathing is most delightful. I think Morris Island beach the most magnificent on the whole Atlantic coast. Had we in the North such a bathing shore, it would soon eclipse Newport, Atlantic City or Long Branch, and the other bathing resorts. The beach at some points is at least one-third of a mile in width, descending at an almost imperceptible angle into the more refreshing breakers.

There is quite a stir in the camp of the 54th just at this moment, created by an attempt on the part of the Paymaster and Col. [Milton S.] Littlefield of the 4th Connecticut volunteers[2] (who has been temporarily assigned to the command of our regiment since the death of Col. Shaw, our lamented commander) to pay us off with the paltry sum of $10 per month, the amount paid to contrabands. Col. Littlefield had the men drawn up in their company streets, and addressed them in a style something like this: "Gentlemen, I know that you are in want of money. Many of you have families who are dependent on you for support. The Paymaster refuses to pay any of the colored troops more than $10 per month. I have no doubt that Congress, when it meets next December, will pay you the balance of your pay. The government, in paying you this sum, only advances you this amount—it is not considered paying you off." Only one company consented to take this sum. The rest of the regiment are highly incensed at the idea that after they have been enlisted as Massachusetts soldiers, and been put into the active service of the United States government, they should be paid off as the drafted ex-slaves are. The non-commissioned officers are to be paid the same as the privates.

There is to be, according to the Colonel's and Paymaster's arrangement, no distinction. Our First Sergeants, Sergeant-Major, and other Sergeants are to be paid only $10 per month. Now, if this $10 per month is advanced by the Paymaster, and he is so confident or certain that the next Congress will vote us the pay that regularly enlisted soldiers, like the 54th, generally receive, why does he not advance the privates and non-commissioned officers their full pay? Or does he not fear that the next Congress may refuse to have anything to do with it, and conclude that if we could receive $10 and make out until then, we could make out with that amount to the end of our term? To offer our non-commissioned officers the same pay and reducing them to the level of privates, is, to say the least, insulting and degrading to them.

Then, again, if we are not placed on the same footing with other Massachusetts soldiers, we have been enlisted under false pretenses. Our enlistment itself is fraudulent. When Gov. Andrew addressed us at Readville[3] on the presentation of our colors, he claimed us as Massachusetts soldiers. Frederick Douglass, in his address to the colored people to recruit the 54th, and who penned it by the authority of Gov. Andrew, declares that we form part of the quota of troops furnished by the State of Massachusetts. If this be the case, why make this invidious distinction? We perform the same duties of other Massachusetts troops, and even now we have to perform fatigue duty night and day, and stand in line of battle from 3 to 5 a.m. with white soldiers, and for all this, not to say anything of the many perils we necessarily encounter, we are offered $10 per month or nothing until next December or January! Why, in the name of William H. Seward, are we treated thus? Does the refusal to pay us our due pander to the pro-slavery Cerberus? Negroes in the navy receive the same pay that the Irish, English, German, Spanish or Yankee race do, and take it as a matter of course. Why, sir, the State of Massachusetts has been rebuked and insulted through her colored soldiers, and she should protect us, as Gov. Andrew has pledged his word she would. Since our regiment has been in this department, an attempt has been made to substitute the dark for the light-blue pantaloons of the U. S. army. This was at St. Helena. Col. Shaw rejected them, and we continue to wear the uniform of the U.S. Infantry corps.

The ever-memorable anniversary of British West India Emancipation was observed by the non-commissioned officers of the 54th, by calling, on the 1st instant, a meeting, and passing a series of resolutions. This meeting was organized by the appointment of Sergeant-Major Douglass, Chairman, and Sergt. Fletcher, Co. A, Secretary. A long list of Vice-Presidents were appointed, representing nearly every State. Commissary-Sergeant Lee represented South Carolina; Sergt. Grey, Massachusetts; Sergt. Swails, Pennsylvania. A Committee, consisting of Sergts. Francis, Stephens, Barquet, Johnson and Gambier, presented the following resolutions, which were passed:[4]

1. Resolved, That we look with joy upon the example set by Great Britain twenty-nine years ago in liberating the slaves in her West India Islands, thereby making a long stride in the pathway of civilization, and eliciting the gratitude of enthralled millions everywhere—contributing largely to influence the people of this country to seek the overthrow of that system which has brought the nation to the verge of dissolution. We hail with more than gratification the determination of our government to follow her great and good example as evinced by that glorious instrument of January 1st, 1863, proclaiming freedom to slaves of rebels in Southern States—the desire to purchase those in loyal States—the decision of Attorney-General [Edward] Bates, and the calling to its aid the strong arms and loyal hearts of its black citizens.

2. Resolved, That we have another day added to our small family of holidays; we hail the 1st of January as twin-sister to the 1st of August; and as we have met together within six miles of the birthplace of secession to commemorate this day, we trust that on the 1st day of January next, by the blessing of God on our arms, the city of Charleston will ring with the voices of free men, women and children shouting, "Truly, the day of Jubilee has come."

3. Resolved, That while we look forward with sanguine hope for that day, and have the arms in our hands to help bring it about, we will use them, and put forth all our energies, and never cease until our ears shall hear the jubilant bell that rings the knell of slavery.

4. Resolved, That in our humble opinion the force of circumstances has compelled the loyal portion of this nation to acknowledge that man is physically the same, differing only in the circumstances under which he lives, and that action—true, manly action, only—is necessary to secure to us a full recognition of our rights as men by the controlling masses of this nation; and we see in the army, fighting for liberty and Union, the proper field for colored men, where they may win by their valor the esteem of all loyal men and women—believing that "Who would be free, themselves must strike the blow."

5. Resolved, That we recognize in the brilliant successes of the Union armies the proofs that Providence is on our side; that His attributes cannot take sides with the oppressor.

Private John Peer, Co. B, died at 6 o'clock p.m. this instant.

G. E. S.

New York, *Weekly Anglo-African*, August 22, 1863. Reprinted in Yacovone, *A Voice of Thunder*, 250–255.

---

1. Commonly associated with Thomas Jefferson, the phrase originated with John P. Curran (1750–1817) who in 1790 said, "The condition upon which God haith given liberty to man is eternal vigilance." *The Oxford Dictionary of Quotations*, 167.
2. Littlefield (1832–1899) actually commanded the 21st USCT. He was later court-marshaled for skimming bounty payments. Found innocent, he left the service in 1866. Yacovone, *A Voice of Thunder*, 255–256.
3. Readville, just outside of Boston, was the site of the largest army camp in the state and the training site for the 54th and 55th Massachusetts Regiments and the 5th Massachusetts Cavalry.
4. Stephens mentions Sgt. Maj. Lewis Douglass, Sgt. Francis H. Fletcher, a Salem, Mass., clerk, Sgt. Arthur B. Lee, a South Carolina harness maker, William H. W. Gray, a New Bedford, Mass., seaman, Sgt. Stephen A. Swails, an Elmira, New York boatman who became the first African American combat officer commissioned by the War Department, Sgt. Joseph H. Barquet, a mason born in Charleston, South Carolina, and Sgt. Frederick Johnson, a Boston hairdresser. Francis and Gambier are likely misspellings of two other unidentified individuals. Yacovone, *A Voice of Thunder*, 256–257.

"For what are we to be grateful?"
Sgt. George E. Stephens to Thomas Hamilton
OCTOBER 3, 1863

Perhaps nothing better symbolized the racial prejudice that black soldiers endured during the Civil War than the speech Col. James Montgomery gave to the men of the 54th Massachusetts Regiment in the fall of 1863. With the assault upon Fort Wagner and the government's recent offer of unequal pay fresh in their minds, the men gathered to hear the leader of the 2nd South Carolina Volunteers and their own former brigade commander address them. Montgomery, an early advocate of

black recruitment and an uncompromising enemy of secession and slavery, first won public notice for his role in the Kansas warfare of the
1850s. Montgomery justifiably enjoyed a reputation as a harsh disciplin-
arian, particularly for his willingness to execute his black soldiers for in-
fractions of military discipline. No one in the 54th Massachusetts, however, suspected that he was anything but an abolitionist and an ally in
the cause of black freedom. Thus, his attitudes toward the pay crisis fell
with crushing effect on the troops. Sgt. Stephens, who maintained his
regular column in the *Weekly Anglo-African* until the final settlement of
the pay crisis, composed the following letter to ensure that his Northern audience understood the true conditions facing the black Union
soldier. Yacovone, *A Voice of Thunder*, 39, 61, 242, 273–274, 277–279.

Morris Island, S. C.
Oct. 3, 1863

MR. THOMAS. HAMILTON—Dear Friend: It has been a long time since I
wrote you in my old-fashioned way. I have not sent you a line since my
advent as a soldier. I thank God that I am at last in a position to learn
to be a soldier. I believe that since the chieftains of the slavery party
have sought and obtained the arbitrament of the bullet in their question of control of power with the Freedom party, every man should become a soldier, ready to do and to die in defence of freedom. Every
Christian and enlightened man desires to see great principles and measures triumph through peaceful means, where reason rules her just sway,
and amenity, conciliation, and love, take the place of hatred, passion
and revenge.

The present century has been immortalized with the grandest re-
forms. From the abolition of the slave trade in 1808 down to the freeing of the Danish colonies, peaceful reform seems to have marched
steadily on. Science, art and invention, a noble sisterhood, sat in counsel and astonished the world with their achievements. The very elements seemed to pay homage to the genius and skill of man. No man
dare say what human ingenuity may not accomplish. The enlightened
statesmen have in America hoped to secure the annihilation of every
wrong and injustice through the agency of that power which [Charles
Maurice de] Talleyrand considered more irresistible than the proudest
and most powerful potentate, namely "public opinion." The slavery

party is arraigned at the bar of "public opinion." Its vile vision is tortured and haunted by the wild spirit of reform. This is a subtle spirit. The engines of warfare cannot impede its progress. It is deathless and omnipresent. It underlies all the pageantry and misery of this gigantic war. The slavery party aims to plunge the country into disorder and anarchy and to establish by force of arms their hell-born system. There is but one alternative left to the freedom party if it would avert terrorism, proscription, and humiliation: 'Tis steel for steel; bullet for bullet; life for life; man for man; blood for blood.

These are some of the notions that led me to join the 54th Mass. Volunteer Infantry. And again I thought that the true interests of all classes of men in our country depended on the success of our party. That they were the true representatives of the newest and best form of government ever established for the government of mankind and are the highest, noblest, and most progressive type of civilization. I can not see on what ground any man can discourage enlistments. Some urge that the treatment of colored citizens is exceptionable—that the guarantees of freedom vouchsafed to us by the government are tardy and doubtful—that some of our representative men, those who are considered the exponents of the principles of the freedom party are as bitter in their assaults on our race and as prejudiced as those of the slavery party. This is true, but these questions are only incidental in their character and cannot effect the general and fundamental principles and theories of the party: It must be remembered that the other class have suffered a slavery of the mind, just as brutalizing, just as debasing as that physical or social thraldom our class are suffering. It is prejudice and a disregard of the inalienable rights of their fellow men. Their notions of justice are so blinded they can without the least remorse rob their fellow-men of every sacred right. These men are to be elevated and their mental or moral condition must be ameliorated, just the same as the condition of those of our class who are debased by slavery should be ameliorated. They deserve the same pity and commiseration that the poor black slave does and we should "pass their imperfection by" just as willingly. Let us be charitable and contend only for the principles of liberty, government and civilization.

The siege of Charleston drags its slow length. Morris Island can never be retaken by the enemy. Fifty thousand men could be swept away in fifty minutes by our guns. Our fatigue parties are somewhat annoyed by the rebel shell, but our labor progresses. The casualties are very few, I had prepared for your satisfaction a complete list of them, but lost my notes. The health of our regiment is bad. We average one hundred and fifty sick per day, caused no doubt, by excessive fatigue duty.

You have also heard I suppose of this matter of pay, it has caused a great deal of trouble, and if it is not adjusted one of the best regiments that ever left Massachusetts will become utterly demoralized. The tribulations of our regiment have been many since we arrived in this department. The first business we were called on to participate in was the burning of Darien, Ga.[1] Our officers, Col. Shaw among the rest, disapproved of the wanton destruction of that town defenseless and unoccupied as it was by the enemy. The men of this regiment have a distaste for this sort of warfare—we want to enter the field honorably—to fight a legitimate warfare. After our return from this expedition, we were sent to St. Helena. While there a proposition was made to take our arms from us and give in their stead long pikes. Col. Shaw expressed his disapprobation of this scheme. Then there was an offer made to pay us ten dollars per month less three for clothing, in other words pay us seven dollars per month. The men were enlisted as a part of the Mass. State quota of troops and never dreamed that any other pay but that of other Massachusetts soldiers would be given them. We have been urged and urged again to accept seven dollars a month, all, sergeant-major down to the humblest private to get no more. There are respectable and well to do men in this regiment, who have accepted positions. It is insulting to them to offer them about half the pay of a poor white private.

To give you an idea of the feelings of some of the officers here with regard to us on this point, I will give you a short speech made Sept. 30th by Col. James Montgomery, 2d South Carolina Vols., of Kansas fame, and commander of the Brigade to which we have been recently joined.[2] Col. Montgomery was not in command of the brigade. He has been sick some time past. The paymaster was in Col. Littlefield's tent. Some ten or twelve officers of our own and other regiments were present. The men had not accepted their pay and the well men were on fatigue duty, at Battery Shaw and Wagner. Col. M. had those who were left in camp drawn up in line and addressed them as follows:

"I want to speak to you. You want plain talk and I shall give it to you. I am your friend. I made the first anti-slavery speech ever made in Kansas. I was the first man that employed negroes in the United States service. I fought six years in Kansas for nothing and I do not come here for pay. I can make $5,000 a year. I get only $2,200 here. I sacrifice my ease and comfort (for I enjoy myself at home). I have fought United States soldiers. There is a General now in the Rebel service whom I fought, killed his horse from under him and took him prisoner when in the United States service. I would have been hung long ago if I had held still. Old Jimmy Buchanan offered a reward for my head. It was a very mean one to be sure, and I was very indignant. He offered only a yearling nigger worth about two hundred and fifty dollars. If he had offered a full-grown nigger I would not have cared so much. You ought to be glad to pay for the privilege to fight, instead of squabbling about money. A great many of you are fugitive slaves, and can by law be returned to your masters. The government by its act in setting you free has paid you a thousand dollars bounty. I know what the trouble is: the noisy Abolitionists have been telling you you are better than anybody else. They are your worst enemies. You have two classes of friends: those who tell you what you are and those who sees in the Ethiopian a symbol of injured innocence. I have seen a hundred regiments but I never saw one so fully equipped as this. Look at your tents and cooking stoves. You want to be placed on the same footing as white soldiers. You must show yourselves as good soldiers as the white. For all anybody knows you did very well here. You must show it by bravery in battle. I should be glad to make you as good soldiers as the white. You are a race of slaves. A few years ago your fathers worshipped snakes and crocodiles in Africa. Your features partake of a beastly character. Your religious exercises in this camp is a mixture of barbarism and Christianity. I am disgusted with the mean, low habits you have learned from the low whites. I hear them say to you, 'bully boys, bully boys, don't take this pay.' What do they mean by this? Do you mean to bully the government out of your money or that you are stubborn as bulls? You would rather go out here and dig in the trenches than stay here in camp and be paid off. Gov. Andrew advises you to take this money and Frederick Douglass also. I have a letter here from Fred. He has been on a tour to Washington and had an interview with Sec. [Edwin M.] Stanton on the subject of enlistments. He advised that all that was needed was to treat the negro as a man. There are two classes of colored men: the indolent and careless; the industrious and ambitious. He (Douglass) called on Senator [Samuel Clarke] Pomeroy, but did not call on Jim Lane. He perhaps had found Lane out. There are two Senators from Kansas. Pomeroy is a pretty fair sort of man, but Jim Lane is at present a noisy Abolitionist. Some time ago he wanted to buy some lands, utensils and niggers, but not having any money had to do without the niggers. He will buy and sell a nigger as quick as anybody else, but since the majority are in favor of liberty, he is very loud-mouthed. Fred Douglass is far above the mass of his race; but he is not equal to the great men of this country, such as Wendell Phillips, Ralph Waldo Emerson, Sumner, and others. You can be improved by education. Irishmen come to this country and in a few years become the same as other white men. Education expands the brain and improves the features. Your features can be improved. Your beauty cannot recommend you. Your yellow faces are evidences of rascality. You should get rid of this bad blood. My advice to you is the lightest of you must marry the blackest woman. You owe your sutler nearly $2,000 and your refusing to take your pay show that you intend to cheat him out of his goods. You went to his agent after he had gone away, and because he would not trust you broke open his place and robbed him. The men that robbed him should be hung. He had no right to trust you and could be handled for it. It is mutiny to refuse to take your pay, and mutiny is punishable with death."

The Colonel spoke nearly an hour and I cannot stoop to give all the bad epithets directed to our regiment. We had not the remotest idea that he entertained such a spirit of hatred for our regiment. Had he scarcely left the bench on which he stood while addressing the men, when Col. Littlefield who was in command of the Brigade at the time, stood up and said: "Men, I cannot let this opportunity pass. The regiment has endeared itself to me. You have done your whole duty. You have written your names on the scroll of fame and any man who defames this regiment defames me. Such a man is my enemy and if I have any fighting to do I will defend you. I do not urge you to take this money, but I am willing to give you a pledge of my honor that you will get your full pay. I have made a promise of $1,000 to Gen. Saxton for a monument to Col. Shaw, and I would have you take this money and make up this sum to commemorate the name of your noble leader."

This instantly dispelled the bad effects of Col. Montgomery's remarks. I am astonished that some insubordinate demonstration was not made, but Col. M. is our superior officer and our boys respect their superior officers. The speech of Col. M. has fixed the determination in the

minds of the men to await calmly and patiently. If we thought that our
enemies would make this course on our part a ground of assault against
colored soldiers, I for one should go for taking $7 per month, nay $2
would be enough, but as the Colonel says, all the private soldiers here
are vehement in urging us to refuse this paltry pay. They say if we take
this money they will want to cut down their wages next. I have never
yet heard a man say that we have failed to perform our duty. We have
been complimented for our arduous labor in the trenches and whenever
paraded have cleaner clothes, cleaner arms, better polished equipments
than any other colored regiment on the Island. In truth there is no negro regiment compared to the 54th. In the last review the palm for martial bearing, accurate marching, and *cleanliness* is disputed with the 54th
by the 100th New York Volunteers. The crime that has unfortunately
incurred the displeasure of our General is that we do not sign the pay
rolls, and the pay-master will not give us money unless we sign and thus
give him receipt in full for pay up to the 1st of August. The words of
Col. Montgomery fell with crushing effect on the regiment. We did not
enlist for money but we feel that the men who enlisted us and those who
accepted our service never intended that we should be treated different
from other Massachusetts men. If the government had been too poor to
pay us we would have been willing to give our services for nothing. But
the government seems fully able to pay her soldiers, for just on the
threshold of this great war she increased their pay.

We are told that by law we are slaves and can be returned to our masters. This I deny. But a few years ago when the slavery party controlled
affairs, fugitives were hunted like so much wild game all over the country, and it was quite a paying business. A few years ago the same party,
so the speech shows, made him an outlaw and would have hung him.
Their power is broken and we are now United States soldiers and he a
responsible citizen and high official. It would be just as incorrect—just
as cruel, to call him an outlaw amenable to the law, as to call us fugitive slaves returnable to our masters by law. In truth there are necessarily some few fugitives here, but is the 54th made up of fugitive slaves?
No, there are hundreds that have been blessed with a New England education, and have learned their duty as freemen, and know their rights
and dare stand up for them, and if they cannot get their rights they can
have the manly satisfaction that they stood up for them. Col. Montgomery unfortunately has been accustomed to the negro as a slave or

freedman. It startles and astonishes him to see him stand erect with intelligence beaming in his countenance. He perhaps never saw a negro
approach a white man except with hat in hand and bowed head. He says
further, that he wishes to make us as good soldiers as the white. How
can this be done if every stimulant to heroic actions are denied? The
only hope of the negro soldiers as his status now appears, is half pay and
the name not the rank of sergeant. To urge us to be good soldiers without throwing around us the influences which alone make the soldier,
without which the noblest races will become varlet, is grossly absurd.
But there seems to be an intimation here that we are not as good soldiers as whites. Is there to be a new theory developed? Everybody, citizens, soldiers, and the rest of mankind say, "thus far the negro soldier
has done his whole duty." Does Col. M. deny this? Is his services in ratio of value as $7 is to $13. It is said that the Government supports the
worn-out and non-combatant slaves, but I understand that all of these
classes of slaves or freedmen are self-supporting—that the government
is now realizing an income from the Southern plantations. And does
the government not expend hundreds of thousands in subsistence to the
families of rebels in arms? Should those rebels return to their allegiance
and espouse the Union cause would Uncle Sam ask them to work and
fight for $7 a month?

Then again "we should be glad to pay for the privilege to fight." After we have endured a slavery of two hundred and fifty years we are to
pay for the privilege to fight and die to enable the North to conquer the
South—what an idea! to pay for the privilege to fight for that tardy and
at best doubtful freedom vouchsafed to us by the government. For what
are we to be grateful? Here the white man has grown rich on our unpaid
labor—has sold our children—insulted our wives—shut us out from the
light of education, and even kept the Bible from us, and the moment
he becomes convinced that these deeds of his are producing the desired
results to his country and people, he gets to work and attempts to restore some of those rights and to allow for some of those wrongs. I think
it a question of repentance on his part instead of gratitude on ours.
What do you think of him should he demand your services and life, for
a restoration of your rights and a release from his persecutions? If we are
taunted because the suicidal course of the government has been
changed, in the name of God, men of the freedom party, go back to your
old policy[.] [E]xclude every fugitive from the armies—invalidate the

President's Emancipation Proclamation, let your officers be slaves—spies and catchers for Southern rebels, for no negro who has two ideas, one to rub against another, is willing to rest under this new slavery his presumed friends are marking out for him, namely: to keep ever present to the memory that his are a race of slaves and have an eternal tribute to pay to their oppressors. I want to feel as if I had a right to liberty and life, and that if I enjoy it, do not wish it said, that I owe to this one or that one.

It cannot be gainsayed that there is a frightful amount of profanity said to have been learned from the "low whites." Now these "low whites" belong to that race which the Colonel presumes to be the superior race. In what constitutes its superiority if it has a deleterious influence on our actions and character? I think there can be found more instances of barbarism in the whites in this country than in the blacks. Look at the Lawrence massacre, the New York mobs, and the Port Hudson atrocities! The fair Southern belle adorns her person with trinkets made from the bones of slaughtered Yankees.[3] Is this not a "polished barbarism"? But the argument of this speech is not logical. It assumes the inferiority of our race, and denies its inferiority by declaring that all that is bad in us has been obtained from the whites which I think very true.

Profanity is a low mean vice, but it is universal in the army. Men are drawn into it almost unconsciously. Those who have been restrained by the associations at home when they get in the army seem to obtain a sort of immoral license. They contract habits and manners there from which they would shrink at home. Our regiment has been peculiarly unfortunate in this manner of spiritual instruction and advice. There have been but a half a dozen lectures delivered to the regiment since it left Readville, 28th last May. But this moral and spiritual void has been filled somewhat by instructive religious tracts and papers contributed by Christian and noble hearted friends in the North—yet while we have so much to regret, there are abundant evidences of a religious revival in our regiment. Are our prayer-meetings a mixture of paganism or barbarism and Christianity? I have witnessed camp-meetings of white Methodists and have seen just as much vehemence and excitement as our meetings are characterized with. It is a characteristic of Methodism in these later days to be exuberant, vehement, and boisterous; and Methodism is almost universal with the American negroes. There are more Methodists, I think statistics say, than every other sect among them unitedly.

The sutler was robbed of his goods by some five or six men in the regiment. The regiment did not rob the sutler. It is utterly impossible to get together any nine hundred or thousand men without some of them being bad enough to do almost anything. All soldiers regard sutlers as regimental Shylocks who demand their money or their lives. They have to pay them fifty cents per pound for rascally butter and twenty-five cents per pound for the blackest kind of sugar; and for everything else they pay equally exorbitant rates. There are few soldiers who think it highly penal to get the best of the sutler. Now this stealing for which the regiment is accused was perpetrated by men whose names are known, and whom Col. Littlefield intends to make pay for the small amount taken. Nor can this be called stealing but a sort of bushwacking raid.

The circumstances are as follows; Mr. [Mark R.] De Mortie told the men in the regiment some two or three weeks ago, before he left for his home, that if they would not take the money the paymaster offered them, he would trust them. He went home, and his partners or agents refused to trust the men. The soldiers of other regiments who had been paid off came and bought the sutler's stock out, and he replenished and sold out again, and any one of the 54th could with difficulty get accommodated. This incensed the men and five or six of the most violent tore down his tent. The sutler ran to the Colonel and he reported the circumstance and instantly sent the men off and put a guard over his tent. It was more a riot and a little spitefulness than robbery. The Colonel (Littlefield) had the whole affair quelled in less time than has been occupied in writing this account of it. How unjust to cast odium on the regiment for this act of half a dozen men. Raiding on sutlers is a most common thing in every camp. I have been the witness of many such catastrophes. I don't dispute that the sutler is a very nice man and as just as sutlers generally can be, but I do say this, if his treatment of the men had been more conciliatory this would not have happened. His agent seems to have forgotten that he is a sutler of the 54th and should be prepared to fully accommodate *their* wants, as well as to make his fortune. The sutler trusted the men to two dollar checks, and compelled them to take the entire two dollars worth or nothing. He had no checks of smaller denomination than two dollars thus taking away the chance to economize. Two dollars is enough to answer the wants of a soldier from one to two months. Are we to be denounced as thieves for this?

As to yellow faces I don't indulge in any controversy about color. I think " 'tis the mind that makes the man," not the color of his skin or any peculiarity of his hair. All I wish to know is the man just, is he humane and generous—noble-spirited—if yes, he is a man, if no, he is a slave to passion and iniquity.

I must not forget to tell you that Gov. Andrew has presented us with a new flag (State flag). In the charge on Fort Wagner, the old flag was torn asunder. In his speech to our regiment, Gov. A. told us that the State flag had never fallen into the hands of the enemy and urged if we could not save the flag, save the shreds—if we could not save the shreds save the staff, and his appeal has been heeded to the letter. When on the parapet of Fort Wagner, Corporal Peal, Co. F,[4] who has had the honor to bear the State colors, inadvertently let the flag lean over the crest of the work, a rebel seized it, then commenced a desperate struggle between the corporal and the rebel for its possession. Unfortunately the color parted from the staff and thus by accident the flag was lost. The corporal said, "Ah you dirty rascal you did not get the staff any way," and he brought the staff away with the spear. This flag is a facsimile of the old one, and when Col. Littlefield unfurled it the boys gave it three rousing cheers.

Trusting that health and prosperity are with you, I remain truly yours,

G. E. STEPHENS.

New York, *Weekly Anglo-African*, October 24, 1863. Reprinted in Yacovone, *A Voice of Thunder*, 275–284.

---

1. The destruction of Darien, Georgia, took place on June 11, 1863. Although the town was largely deserted, the 54th's brigade commander, Col. James Montgomery, ordered it burned. Shaw and others protested the move, but in the end few ordinary soldiers showed much concern for the loss of rebel property. Yacovone, *A Voice of Thunder*, 39, 241–242.
2. Col. James Montgomery (1814–1871) supported John Brown and the warfare in Kansas in the late 1850s. He commanded the 2nd South Carolina Volunteers, a regiment of former slaves organized in May 1863 that participated in various engagements in the southeast, including the Union defeat

at Honey Hill, South Carolina. It was redesignated the 34th USCT. Yacovone, *A Voice of Thunder*, 243.

3. Confederate soldiers executed captured black troops after the May 1863 battle at Port Hudson. Official Confederate policy throughout the war encouraged the mistreatment or killing of black Union prisoners. Yacovone, *A Voice of Thunder*, 287.

4. Cpl. Henry F. Peal (1837–1864), a shoemaker from Oberlin, Ohio, carried the state flag at Wagner and at the February 1864 Battle of Olustee, where he was killed. Peal was one of four members of the unit to receive the Gillmore Medal for bravery. Yacovone, *A Voice of Thunder*, 287–288.

Fort Pillow
Testimony of Jacob Thompson and Ransome Anderson
1864

"Remember Fort Pillow" became the rallying cry for black Union soldiers. Some even stitched those words on their uniforms. From the beginning of their combat experience, black troops entered battle believing that they might suffer summary execution or enslavement if captured. After April 12, 1864, however, black soldiers expected no quarter and increasingly refused to grant it. For black troops, the character of the war had changed, taking on a level of savagery that few white troops knew.

Led by the resourceful and ruthless Gen. Nathan Bedford Forrest, rebel troops struck north out of Mississippi in March 1864 and penetrated through western Tennessee into Kentucky, hoping to take the Union garrison at Paducah. Accustomed to success, Forrest's men were hurled back by the white and black defenders. Looking to inflict the same pain on Union forces, Forrest's men eyed the 13th Tennessee Cavalry (white) and the black troops of the 6th U.S. Colored Heavy Artillery Regiment and the 2nd U.S. Colored Light Artillery Regiment precariously perched on a bluff overlooking the Mississippi River. Fort Pillow contained approximately 582 Union soldiers and an unknown number of civilians, mostly black.

Precisely what happened on April 12, 1864, remains a subject of debate. But no one disputes that an inordinate number of Union soldiers

died during the attack, most after what appeared to be the fort's ca-
pitulation. Forrest's Confederate apologists heaped blame upon the defenders, especially the black troops, for bringing on their own fate. Most
of the troops, especially the black ones, one former rebel soldier argued, were "either insanely intoxicated" or, convinced they would be
killed, adamant in their refusal to surrender. They "determined to sell
their lives as dearly as possible" and continued to fight even after the
fort's surrender. Their deaths, therefore, were entirely justifiable. We
cannot know if Forrest and his men had planned the atrocities that took
place, or if this level of viciousness was unleashed in the heat of battle.
But we do know that about half the Union command was killed, 277 to
297 soldiers, and an unknown number of black civilians. A staggering 64
percent of the black troops lost their lives at Fort Pillow. As the testimony of survivors given before a Congressional committee makes
clear, a massacre most certainly occurred, and its racial character remains inescapable. John Allan Wyeth, *That Devil Forrest: Life of Nathan
Bedford Forrest* (orig., 1899; Baton Rouge, LA: Louisiana State University Press, 1989), 299–341; Trudeau, *Like Men of War*, 156–181.

"JACOB THOMPSON, (COLORED), sworn and examined. By Mr. [Daniel
W.] Gooch:

'Question. Were you a soldier at Fort Pillow? 'Answer. No, sir, I was
not a soldier; but I went up in the fort and fought with the rest. I was
shot in the hand and the head.

'Question. When were you shot? 'Answer. After I surrendered.

'Question. How many times were you shot? 'Answer. I was shot but
once; but I threw my hand up, and the shot went through my hand and
my head.

'Question. Who shot you? 'Answer. A private.

'Question. What did he say? 'Answer. He said, 'G——d d——n you,
I will shoot you, old friend.'

'Question. Did you see anybody else shot? 'Answer. Yes, sir; they just
called them out like dogs, and shot them down. I reckon they shot about
fifty, white and black, right there. They nailed some black sergeants to
the logs, and set the logs on fire.

'Question. When did you see that? 'Answer. When I went there in
the morning I saw them; they were burning all together.

'Question. Did they kill them before they burned them? 'Answer.

No, sir, they nailed them to the logs; drove the nails right through their hands.

'Question. How many did you see in that condition? 'Answer. Some four or five; I saw two white men burned.

'Question. Was there any one else there who saw that? 'Answer. I reckon there was; I could not tell who.

'Question. When was it that you saw them? 'Answer. I saw them in the morning after the fight; some of them were burned almost in two. I could tell they were white men, because they were whiter than the colored men.

'Question. Did you notice how they were nailed? 'Answer. I saw one nailed to the side of a house; he looked like he was nailed right through the wrist. I was trying then to get to the boat when I saw it.

'Question. Did you see them kill any white men? 'Answer. They killed some eight or nine there. I reckon they killed more than twenty after it was all over; called them out from under the hill, and shot them down. They would call out a white man and shoot him down, and call out a colored man and shoot him down; do it just as fast as they could make their guns go off.

'Question. Did you see any rebel officers about there when this was going on? 'Answer. Yes, sir; old Forrest was one.

'Question. Did you know Forrest? 'Answer. Yes, sir; he was a little bit of a man. I had seen him before at Jackson.

'Question. Are you sure he was there when this was going on? 'Answer. Yes, sir.

'Question. Did you see any other officers that you knew? 'Answer. I did not know any other but him. There were some two or three more officers came up there.

'Question. Did you see any buried there? 'Answer. Yes, sir; they buried right smart of them. They buried a great many secesh, and a great many of our folks. I think they buried more secesh than our folks.

'Question. How did they bury them? 'Answer. They buried the secesh over back of the fort, all except those on Fort hill; them they buried up on top of the hill where the gunboats shelled them.

'Question. Did they bury any alive? 'Answer. I heard the gunboat men say they dug two out who were alive.

'Question. You did not see them? 'Answer. No, sir.

'Question. What company did you fight with? 'Answer. I went right into the fort and fought there.

'Question. Were you a slave or a free man? 'Answer. I was a slave.

'Question. Where were you raised? 'Answer. In old Virginia.

'Question. Who was your master? 'Answer. Colonel Hardgrove.

'Question. Where did you live? 'Answer. I lived three miles the other side of Brown's mills.

'Question. How long since you lived with him? 'Answer. I went home once and staid with him a while, but he got to cutting up and I came away again.

'Question. What did you do before you went into the fight? 'Answer. I was cooking for Co. K, of Illinois cavalry; I cooked for that company for nearly two years.

'Question. What white officers did you know in our army? 'Answer. I knew Captain Meltop and Colonel Ransom; and I cooked at the hotel at Fort Pillow, and Mr. Nelson kept it. I and Johnny were cooking together. After they shot me through the hand and the head, they beat up all this part of my head (the side of his head) with the breach of their guns."

"RANSOME ANDERSON, (COLORED), Co. B., 6th United States heavy artillery,[1] sworn and examined. By Mr. Gooch:

'Question. Where were you raised? 'Answer. In Mississippi.

'Question. Were you as slave? 'Answer. Yes, sir.

'Question. Where did you enlist? 'Answer. At Corinth.

'Question. Were you in the fight at Fort Pillow? 'Answer. Yes, sir.

'Question. Describe what you saw done there. 'Answer. Most all the men that were killed on our side were killed after the fight was over. They called them out and shot them down. Then they put some in the houses and shut them up, and then burned the houses.

'Question. Did you see them burn? 'Answer. Yes, sir.

'Question. Were any of them alive? 'Answer. Yes, sir; they were wounded, and could not walk. They put them in the houses, and then burned the houses down.

'Question. Do you know they were in there? 'Answer. Yes, sir; I went and looked in there.

'Question. Do you know they were in there when the house was burned? 'Answer. Yes, sir; I heard them hallooing there when the houses were burning.

'Question. Are you sure they were wounded men, and not dead, when they were put in there?' 'Answer. Yes, sir; they told them they were going to have the doctor see them, and then put them in there and shut them up, and burned them.

'Question. Who set the house on fire?' 'Answer. I saw a rebel soldier take some grass and lay it by the door, and set it on fire. The door was pine plank, and it caught easily.

'Question. Was the door fastened up?' 'Answer. Yes, sir; it was barred with one of those wide bolts."

Congressional testimony, reprinted in Joseph T. Wilson, *The Black Phalanx: African American Soldiers in the War of Independence, the War of 1812 & the Civil War* (Hartford, CT: American Publishing Co., 1890), 331–333.

---

1. The 6th U.S. Colored Heavy Artillery Regiment (USCHA), organized in Natchez, Mississippi, in September 1863 as the 2nd Regiment, was redesignated the 6th USCHA just a week before the battle. Approximately 270 members of the unit, nearly all former slaves from the region, fought at Fort Pillow. Wilson, *The Black Phalanx*, 465; Trudeau, *Like Men of War*, 161.

From the Eighth U.S. Heavy Artillery
Isaac Van Loon to Robert Hamilton
August 1864

The first battalion of the 8th U.S. Colored Heavy Artillery Regiment arrived at the front in January 1864. After a brief but troubled stop along the Texas coast, the men moved to the oppressive humidity of the bayou north of New Orleans. Bad luck haunted the unit from the start. One man "of Moorish descent" had to be pinioned to shave his long knotted hair and eliminate the "vermin" nesting there. Another soldier, perhaps inconsolable over the conditions he faced, placed his rifle's muzzle in his mouth and blew out his brains. Dissention roiled the ranks from the start of the 8th USCHA's duty in the Department of the Gulf over the government's refusal to give them equal pay. The unit's commanding officer arrested many of the soldiers, including noncommissioned officers, and charged them with mutiny. One soldier was shot and killed for protesting his pay.

The experiences of the 8th USCHA also typified the hazards that all black soldiers faced when meeting the enemy. From the moment the Union fielded black troops, the Confederate government denounced the move and declared its refusal to treat them as anything other than slaves in rebellion. It promised to execute or sell into slavery any black caught in uniform. Wherever black soldiers faced rebel troops—Port Hudson, Olustee, Petersburg, or even Fort Wagner—enemy soldiers usually refused to take prisoners. African Americans came to expect such treatment and, in time, gave as good as they got. "Remember Fort Pillow" could be heard on more than one battlefield. When soldiers from the 11th USCHA, stationed with the 8th USCHA in Louisiana, were found butchered by their comrades, the commanding officer informed his Confederate opponents that when they killed surrendering black soldiers, an equal number of rebel troops would be put to the sword. Refusing to recognize the legitimacy of black Union soldiers, the rebels issued a counter warning: if Confederate soldiers or citizens were executed for "killing negroes under arms," an equal number of white Union troops would be killed. With such a standoff, the solution would be worked out on the battlefield. Isaac Van Loon, from Providence, Rhode Island, a musician in the 8th USCHA, joined the regiment on October 23, 1863, and remained with it until mustering out in October 1865. His letter recorded the risks black men took to bring freedom to their brethren in chains. Berlin et al., *Freedom: The Black Military Experience,* 395–397, 439; William H. Chenery, *The Fourteenth Regiment of Rhode Island Heavy Artillery. . .* (Providence, RI: Snow & Farnham, 1898), 20, 27–34, 42–43, 78–79, 212.

Camp Shaw, Plaquemine, La.,[1]
August, 1864

DEAR ANGLO: Having a few leisure moments, I thought I could do no better than to devote them to you; for we colored soldiers have not much time, I can assure you, to devote to much else than military duties.

Saturday, the 6th of August, is a day that will long be remembered by the 2d Battalion. We were aroused about 4 o'clock in the morning by the firing of musketry in the village and the old cry of "The Rebs!

the Rebs!" Such hurrying to and fro of armed and unarmed soldiers, being awakened as we were from a sound sleep, beggars description. But, nevertheless, we were quickly in line, and we double-quicked to the fort, ready and willing to offer up our lives at the shrine of Liberty; but our fighting qualities were not called into requisition; it proved to be only one of those rebel raids that frequently occur near small towns, where they dash in for provisions. Being driven to the last extremity for the necessities of life, they will often dash into the midst of Union troops, intent only on one object—something to eat; but here they were sadly disappointed. They rushed right into the midst of our Provost Guard, who caused them to beat a hasty retreat, carrying with them three of our advance pickets—Saml. O. Jefferson, of Troy; Saml. Mason and Anthony King, who are, I believe, Western boys, all of Co. I.[2] They were all good soldiers. They were taken by those fiends in human shape a short distance down the road and then inhumanly shot, being first stripped of all clothing, and then brutally murdered and left upon the road. Think of us, ye Northern men!—of the poor soldier who has forsaken home comforts—yes, everything! to aid in this civil sacrifice of life. But, dear ANGLO, I will not weary your patience any longer.

Nothing pleases the colored soldier better than to receive a copy of your heart-cheering paper. I hear from you often through my father, Dr. William Van Loon, who forwards me your paper, which has to go the grand rounds through our camp before I can get a chance to peruse it thoroughly myself. You will hear from me again.

ISAAC VAN LOON,
Co. C, 8th U.S. (formerly 14th R.I.) H.A.[3]

New York *Weekly Anglo-African*, September 3, 1864.

---

1. Camp Shaw at Plaquemine, Louisiana, lay about 160 miles north of New Orleans. The 2nd battalion of the 8th USCHA was stationed there, with about nine cannon. The 8th moved there from Camp Parapet in April 1864 to help complete construction of the fort. Chenery, *The Fourteenth Regiment, Rhode Island Heavy Artillery* . . . , 43, 51, 94; Adjutant General's Office, *Annual Report of the State of Rhode Island* (Providence, RI: Providence Press, 1866), 626.
2. The three soldiers Van Loon mentioned, Samuel O. Jefferson, Anthony King, and Samuel Mason, all came from Providence, Rhode Island. They

enlisted on November 4 and belonged to Company G, not I. Confederate guerrillas captured and executed the three on August 6, 1864, at Indian Village, Louisiana. *Annual Report of the State of Rhode Island*, 657–658.

3. The 8th USCHA, as the 14th Rhode Island, was one of the earliest black regiments raised in New England and the only African American one from Rhode Island. The unit was divided into three battalions, which were stationed at three different Union forts in Louisiana. The first battalion of the regiment was organized in August 1863 in Providence. Martin R. Delany helped recruit it. *Annual Report of the State of Rhode Island*, 625–630; Berlin et al., *Freedom: The Black Military Experience*, 75, 102, 366, 407.

8

Equal Pay and Equal Rights

"the Black man laid his life at the
Altar of the Nation"
James Henry Gooding to Abraham Lincoln
SEPTEMBER 28, 1863

To the black troops, the government's refusal to fulfill its promise of equal pay represented an act of injustice and racial bigotry as offensive as the Supreme Court's Dred Scott decision. Indeed, it fulfilled Chief Justice Roger B. Taney's dictum that black men had no rights that white men were bound to respect. As the soldiers made clear countless times, the dispute was not about money, but rights. Would the federal government recognize their rights as American citizens, or would it continue to follow Taney's opinion and reduce free men to servitude? The committee that had organized the 54th Massachusetts Regiment, and had repeated the government's promise of equal pay in its recruitment campaign, felt humiliated and used. The black soldiers had been betrayed, one committee member grumbled, and would not even be permitted "to die for their country on an equality with other soldiers." They must be made to "to feel that they still are only *niggars* not men." Black troops across the South protested the government's astonishing policy, at times verging on mutiny. To maintain order and discipline, the army executed several soldiers over the pay crisis. For eighteen months many of the troops, especially those from Massachusetts, refused all pay until the government reversed its position. Even when it did so in the late summer of 1864, equal pay was granted only to those men who had been free at time of their enlistment. Thus, the majority of black troops did not receive their full and proper pay until the end of the war, when the Lincoln administration finally relented. Many a black soldier went to his grave knowing that the government he fought to defend considered him to be worth only half the pay of a white private.

James Henry Gooding (1837–1864), a New Bedford, Massachusetts, seaman and sometime poet, originally from Troy, New York, enlisted in the 54th Massachusetts Regiment on Valentine's Day, 1863. He chronicled his experiences in a series of letters published in the white-owned *New Bedford Mercury*. He kept his community well informed about the regiment's activities and wrote letters to the president and to others about the injustices of unequal pay. No one he knew would take one penny short of what they deserved while the bleaching bones of their comrades lay on the beaches before Fort Wagner. The men would not, he assured his readers, "sell our manhood for ten dollars per month." He proved equally direct with President Lincoln. In his September 1863 letter, which Lincoln likely never read, Gooding advised the president that the black soldier ran the same risks and endured the same ordeal as white soldiers. Both groups dyed the ground red with their blood. Black soldiers deserved the same pay as "american SOLDIERS, not menial hierlings." Unfortunately, Gooding never received his equal pay. Rebel forces captured him at the Battle of Olustee, Florida, and he died at the Andersonville prison camp. Yacovone, *A Voice of Thunder*, 60; Virginia M. Adams, ed., *On the Altar of Freedom: A Black Soldier's Civil War Letters from the Front* (Amherst, MA: University of Massachusetts Press, 1991), 49; Emilio, *A Brave Black Regiment*, 350.

Morris Island [South Carolina]. Sept 28th 1863

YOUR EXCELENCY WILL PARDON the presumtion of an humble individual like myself, in addressing you. but the earnest Solicitation of my Comrades in Arms, besides the genuine interest felt by myself in the matter is my excuse, for placing before the Executive head of the Nation our Common Grievance: On the 6th of the last Month, the Paymaster of the department, informed us, that if we would decide to recieve the sum of $10 (ten dollars) per month, he would come and pay us that sum, but, that, on the sitting of Congress, the Regt would, in his opinion, be *allowed* the other 3 (three). He did not give us any guarantee that this would be, as he hoped, certainly *he* had no authority for making any such guarantee, and we can not supose him acting in any way interested. Now the main question is. Are we *Soldiers*, or are we LABOURERS. We are fully armed, and equipped, have done all the various Duties, pertaining to a Soldiers life, have conducted ourselves, to the complete satisfaction of General Officers, who, were if any, prejudiced *against* us, but who now accord us all the encouragement, and honour due us: have shared the perils, and Labour, of Reducing the first stronghold, that flaunted a Traitor Flag: and more, Mr President. To-day, the Anglo Saxon Mother, Wife, or Sister, are not alone, in tears for departed Sons, Husbands, and Brothers. The patient Trusting Decendants of Africs Clime, have dyed the ground with blood, in defense of the Union, and Democracy. Men too your Excellency, who know in a measure, the cruelties of the Iron heel of oppression, which in years gone by, the very Power, their blood is now being spilled to maintain, ever ground them to the dust. But When the war trumpet sounded o'er the land, when men knew not the Friend from the Traitor, the Black man laid his life at the Altar of the Nation, —and he was refused. When the arms of the Union, were beaten, in the first year of the War, And the Executive called more food. for its ravaging maw, again the black man begged, the privelege of Aiding his Country in her need, to be again refused, And now, he is in the War: and how has he conducted himself? Let their dusky forms, rise up, out the mires of James Island, and give the answer. Let the rich mould around Wagners parapets be upturned, and there wil be found an Eloquent answer. Obedient and patient, and Solid as a wall are they. all we lack, is a paler hue, and a better acquaintance with the Alphabet. Now Your Excellency, We have done a Soldiers Duty. Why cant we have a Soldiers pay? You caution the Rebel Chieftain, that the United States, knows no distinction, in her Soldiers: She insists on having all her Soldiers, of whatever, creed or Color, to be treated, according to the usages of War. Now if the United States exacts uniformity of treatment of her Soldiers, from the Insurgents, would it not be well, and consistent, to set the example herself, by paying all her *Soldiers* alike? We of this Regt. were not enlisted under any "contraband" act. But we do not wish to be understood, as rating our Service, of more Value to the Government, than the service of the exslave, Their Service is undoubtedly worth much to the Nation, but Congress made express, provision touching their case, as slaves freed by military necessity, and assuming the Government, to be their temporary Gaurdian:—Not so with us—Freemen by birth, and consequently, having the advantage of *thinking*, and acting for ourselves, so far as the Laws would allow us. We do not consider ourselves fit subjects for the Contraband act. We appeal to You, Sir: as the Executive of the Nation, to have us Justly Dealt with. The Regt, do pray, that they be assured their service will be fairly appreciated, by paying them as american SOLDIERS, not as menial hierlings. Black men You may well know, are poor, three dollars per month, for a year, will suply their needy Wives, and little ones, with fuel. If you, as chief Magistrate of the Nation, will assure us, of our whole pay. We are content, our Patriotism, our enthusiasm will have a new impetus, to exert our energy more and more to aid Our Country. Not that our hearts ever flagged, in Devotion, spite the evident apathy displayed in our behalf, but We feel as though, our Country spurned us, now we are sworn to serve her.

Please give this a moments attention

JAMES HENRY GOODING

H-133, 1863, Letters Received, ser. 360, Colored Troops Division, RG 94, National Archives. Reprinted in Berlin et al., *Freedom: The Black Military Experience*, 385–386, and Adams, *On the Altar of Freedom*, 118–120.

"under the guns of prejudice and hate"
"Bay State" to Robert Hamilton
APRIL 10, 1864

As the crisis over equal pay ground into 1864, the men of the black regiments became increasingly impatient with the government's broken promises and insults. Letters poured into Governor Andrew's office from the men and families of the state's regiments and from supporters around the country demanding equal pay. Andrew supported the soldiers's demands and did everything he could to insure that the crisis ended peacefully and that the men received everything due them. The Commonwealth of Massachusetts even offered to diffuse the crisis by paying the men the difference between the white and black pay rates. While the soldiers appreciated the gesture, they refused to compromise their principles. Honor, dignity, and the soldiers' postwar hopes for the vote and racial justice hinged on the federal government recognizing their rights as full citizens and men.

The 55th Massachusetts Regiment, which served alongside the 54th in the Department of the South, possessed a slightly higher percentage of men who had been slaves before the war. But like the 54th, it was primarily comprised of freeborn and well-educated Northern African Americans. Accustomed to asserting their rights, they would not abandon them in the face of the government's mulish intransigence. Many preferred to die before they would give up their central principles. As this anonymous soldier warned President Lincoln in his open letter to the New York *Weekly Anglo-African,* they would "settle it for ourselves before this war is over, *and settle it right too, or die in the attempt.*"

HEADQUARTERS 55TH REG. MASS. INFANTRY,[1]
Palatka, Fla., April 10th, 1864

MR. EDITOR: This Regiment was mustered into the United States service about the 18th or 20th of June, 1863, consequently we have been ten months working for Uncle Sam, not taking into account the time when some of us were sworn in.

The only thing that engrosses the mind now, is the old and troublesome subject of pay.

We have been promised that we would be paid, and a paymaster came (last November) to pay us. He offered us $7 per month. We enlisted for $13 per month, with the promise (and I wish the public to keep this fact before them, to see how these promises are being fulfilled) that we should be treated in all respects like white soldiers, our bounty, rations, and emoluments being the same. The same inducements were held out to us as to all Massachusetts volunteers.

You, sir, no doubt, have copies of the circulars that were distributed through the country to encourage enlistments. By whose authority this was done I cannot say; but I know that his Excellency, John A. Andrew, Governor of Massachusetts, name was on them.

Mr. Editor, we wish to be plain, and state the exact truth, and this we shall do regardless of whomsoever we may offend.

We do not look upon Massachusetts as being responsible for our sufferings; but upon the government of the United States, and how a government, with such a lofty reputation can so act, is beyond our conception or comprehension. We know, and the world knows that had we been white men the whole land would have been in a blaze of indignation in regard to the great injustice done us.

How the authorities expect our families to live without the means to buy bread, pay house rent, and meet the other incidental expenses of living in these terrible times, we know not; but if it does not exert its well known power it certainly will not be held guiltless in this matter.

Are our parents, wives, children, and sisters to suffer, while we, their natural protectors, are fighting the battles of the nation? We leave the government and Congress to answer.

That they *do* suffer we have abundant evidence.

I have seen a letter from a wife in Illinois to her husband, stating that she had been sick for six months, and begged him to send her the sum of *fifty cents*. Was it any wonder that the tears rolled in floods from that stout-hearted man's eyes.

How can it be expected that men will do their duty consistently with a soldier's training, under such circumstances?

Patience has an end, and with us will soon cease to be a virtue. We would be contented and happy could we but receive our pay.

I have been asked by officers, not connected with our Regiment, why we did not take our pay when we could get it. My answer was: that our pay has never been sent to us. True, money has been sent here, but it was not our pay. When the United States authorities shall send us $13 per month, which is our just due, we will take it, *and not until then, will we take one cent*.

We cannot accept pay from the Old Bay State while we are working for the United States; for we do not want two paymasters. One will answer, provided he be the right one.

We have waited long for our just dues, but many have waited and many will wait in vain.

The battle-field and grief are doing their work, and many a poor fellow will sleep his last sleep ere the adjusting time shall come. We begin to think that that time will never come *as long as we stay in the field*.

There is evidently something wrong about this business. The United States government says nothing about it, and Gov. Andrew never comes to see us! Does it not seem strange? The presence of Gov. Andrew here would inspire us with renewed confidence, and send a thrill of great joy through our victimized regiments.

Money has been sent to us through different channels which we have refused, and which we must continue to refuse. To accept our pay in this way would degrade us, and mark us as inferior soldiers, and would be a complete annihilation of every vestige of our manhood.

The United States knows our value as soldiers too well to suppose that we will sacrifice the position that we have gained by most arduous labor, and we, thoroughly comprehending our relation to the past glorious history of our race, and the verdict that must fall upon us in the future if we falter; will stand up for our rights, come what may.

As regard the question whether we are equal in value as soldiers to white troops, we have only to say that if Port Hudson, Milliken's Bend, Pocotaligo,[2] Fort Wagner, Olustee, and Fort Pillow, do not settle it in our favor, then it is because our enemies *will not* have it settled in that way.

But it is a matter of indifference to us now how they settle it; we, by God's help, will settle it for ourselves before this war is over, *and settle it right too, or die in the attempt.*

It is glorious to see how our noble fellows stand up under their trials. Pride has kept them where they are to-day, and they certainly deserve to be respected.

But you, sir, was not aware of the fact that we have passed into an Holy (holey) and hungry order—but it is true. The boys pantaloons are at this time flapping about their legs trying to whip them to death; while the "vacuum" within is calling for something to assuage the gnawing. Scarce rations have been our luck since we came to the department.

Our men, as a general thing, are obedient, and the detachment now at Yellow Bluff, Fla., under [Lt.] Col. [Charles B.] Fox, and which has been there since February 28, are the ones to whom I allude as being so ragged. Yet only one of these men has been punished for disobedience.

We have been silent in regard to our wrongs hitherto, but it will not do to be so any longer. Agitation and legislation must do what silence has failed to accomplish.

We have been tried in the fire both of affliction and of the rebels, and nothing remains but pure metal. We took our first lesson at Forts Wagner and Gregg,[3] and our last we are now taking in the field of want, and under the guns of prejudice and hate.

We should like to know whether we belong to Massachusetts or Uncle Sam; for we are tossed about from pillar to post, one saying come here, and another saying go there, and we come and go like dogs, and this has been the case ever since we went to Folly Island.

Promises have no weight with us now, until the past and present is fulfilled—future ones we will not heed.

Three years cannot pass in this way. Some change must come.

The words of cheer that we once received from our mothers, wives and sisters, are becoming fainter and fainter, and their cries of want stronger and stronger with each revolving day. In the picture of our desolate households, and the gaunt figures of our friends now suffering almost the pangs of starvation, to haunt us by day and night in our camp? Is this dread sight to hang between us and our starry flag upon the battlefield?

Oh God! most bitter is the cup presented to our lips; but that others may live we will drink it even to the dregs.

Our debasement is most compete. No chances for promotion, no money for our families, and we little better than an armed band of laborers with rusty muskets and bright spades, what is our incentive to duty? Yet God had put it into our hearts to believe that we will survive or perish with the liberty of our country. If she lives, we live; if she dies we will sleep with her, even as our brave comrades now sleep with Col. Shaw within the walls of Wagner.

More anon,
BAY STATE

New York *Weekly Anglo-African*, April 30, 1864.

---

1. The 55th Massachusetts Regiment began to take shape as the 54th was beginning its work in the spring of 1863. Like the 54th Massachusetts, it experienced enormous turmoil over the issue of unequal pay. One soldier was executed because of the pay crisis, causing outrage both in the regiment and among its supports back home. Governor Andrew personally protested to the War Department and the president. The 55th served in a variety of engagements in the Department of the South, particularly the Union defeat at Honey Hill. Several of its enlisted men became officers at the close of the war, including James Monroe Trotter, father of the radical Boston reformer William Monroe Trotter. [Charles Fox], *Record of the Service of the Fifty-fifth Regiment of Massachusetts Volunteer Infantry* (Cambridge, MA: J. Wilson and Son, 1868).

2. The November 1864 attack at Honey Hill was intended to deprive Confederate troops at Pocotaligo, South Carolina, access to the Charleston and
   Savannah Railroad. Because of poor planning and failed leadership, the
   Union forces suffered many casualties. The 55th Massachusetts alone lost
   137 men. Trudeau, *Like Men of War*, 313–331.
3. Fort Gregg lay behind Fort Wagner on Morris Island; both were abandoned
   by the Confederates in September 1863.

"we have never had our Just Rights"
Sgt. William J. Brown to Edwin M. Stanton
APRIL 27, 1864

Secretary of War Stanton was barraged with demands for equal pay.
From the men of the black regiments, like Sergeant Brown in Kentucky,
to Governor Andrew of Massachusetts, again and again Stanton heard
the same refrain: live up to your promises, treat these men with dignity, *pay* them equal wages. Charles Sumner, the great abolitionist senator from Massachusetts, argued with Stanton so often about the pay
issue that Stanton "'lost his temper'" and refused to see him again. Even
as late as June 1864 the government still argued that, because of the
1862 Militia Act, they could not legally pay the men at the same rate as
whites. The federal government's refusal to treat black soldiers equally
drove several units to the brink of mutiny and dramatically increased
the sufferings of the common soldier. At Columbus, Kentucky, many
families of black soldiers, as well as the contraband families who had taken
up residence at camps that were established on federally controlled
lands there, suffered terribly. By July 1863, fifty-four refugees at the
camp had died and dozens more lay sick. The Lincoln administration's
refusal to accord black soldiers the equality they had earned not only
represented an indignity and insult, it increased the sufferings of those
who had offered their lives for the Union. Yacovone, *A Voice of Thunder*, 77–78; Berlin et al., *Freedom: The Wartime Genesis of Free Labor: The
Upper South*, 626, 631, 654.

Fort Halleck Columbus—Ky.[1] Aprile 27th 1864

I SIR BY WAY OF Introduction was made 1st Sergeant of Co. C which was then denominated as 2nd *Tenn* Heavey Artillery now as 3d United States Heavey Artillery,[2] as I wish to state to you, the facts which can be Relied, upon as I am fuly able to prove if necessary I may say to you this *Reg.* is a *coloured* one of Southern Birth consequently have no Education, not so with my self I was Freeborn and Educated to some extent which makes me know we know that we have never had our Just Rights, by the Officers who command us, the white officers of other *Reg.* here persuaded me to Join when there were no *Reg.* of coloured here to Join so I consented and being the first to sign my name in this *Reg.* They promiced to pay us the same wages as was paid the whites & Rations & clothing the same they have given us clothing & Rations sufficient for the time but have not paid us our Money according to promice the white privates tell us we Should get the same pay as they do but none of us has yet we never have been paid more than Seven Dollars per Month they now say that is all we are allowed by the Govornment of the United States Many of these people have Families to support and no other means of doing it than what they get in this way. Such of those that are not able Bodied men are employed on Govornment work and are paid Ten Dollars per Month We who belong to this *Reg.* have done more work than they on Fatigue and other wise the very Labour that was appointed for them we have had to toil day and night when necessity demands it, I may say to you at the presant our Regimental officers are nearly played out they have been Turned out and their places have not been furished with other commanders now *Hon.* Secretary of war I wish to ask you not only for my own Satisfaction but at the Request of my *Reg.* is Seven Dollars per month all we Soldiers are to get or may we Expect in the final settlement to get our full Rights as was promiced us at the first

If we are to Recieve as much as White Soldiers or the Regular thirteen Dollars per Month then we Shall be Satisfied and on the field of Battle we will prove that we were worthy of what we claim for our Rights

With this Statement I may close by Requesting your Answer to this for the many Anxious and disappointed men of this *Reg.* I am Sir your obedient Servant

WM. J. BROWN

PS) Direct yours to me in care of Co. C 3ᵈ U States Heavey *Arty*.² Care of *Lieut*. Adams of Co. A 3ᵈ U. States Heavey *Arty*.

Berlin et al., *Freedom: The Black Military Experience*, 377–378.

———

1. Fort Halleck, at Columbus, Kentucky, lay on the Mississippi River and had been occupied by Union troops for most of the war. Although Kentucky never seceded from the Union and slavery there remained legal, hundreds of contraband and runaways fled to the camps established in Columbus. In order to placate local slave owners, at one point federal authorities removed the slaves and their families to Island 10 in the middle of the Mississippi River. Berlin et al., *Freedom: The Wartime Genesis of Free Labor: The Upper South*, 43, 626.

2. The 3rd USCHA, organized at Memphis and Fort Pickering, Tennessee, had been designated the 1st and then the 2nd Tennessee Heavy Artillery before becoming the 3rd in April 1864, the same month that the War Department mustered the unit out of service. Wilson, *The Black Phalanx*, 464–465.

"we came to fight For Liberty justice & Equality"
Soldiers of the 55th Massachusetts Regiment
to Abraham Lincoln
JULY 16, 1864

Lincoln was aware of the crisis over equal pay, but he refused to participate in the debates, leaving it to the War Department and Congress to settle the matter. The president never understood the depth of the problem, the principles at stake, or its significance to African Americans. When he and Frederick Douglass discussed the issue in the White House, Lincoln explained that blacks should see military service as a great benefit and be "willing to enter the service under any condition." He told Douglass that unequal pay represented a reasonable concession to the prejudices of white soldiers who did not want blacks in the army at all. The president's unwillingness to settle the pay crisis jeopardized the lives of his soldiers and increased the misery of their families. Governor Andrew was fully justified in laying blame for the severity of the crisis "at the door of the executive."

Outraged at the government's refusal to treat them with dignity and respect, seventy-three men of Company D, of the 55th Massachusetts Regiment went beyond what "Bay State" had earlier threatened. Disgusted with the indignities that poured over them, relegated largely to grinding fatigue duty, and forced to endure the taunts of racist white officers, they wrote directly to President Lincoln threatening "more stringent measures" if justice did not come to them soon. Yacovone, *A Voice of Thunder,* 77; Donald Yacovone, "The Fifty-fourth Massachusetts Regiment, the Pay Crisis, and the Lincoln Despotism," in Martin H. Blatt, Thomas J. Brown, and Donald Yacovone, eds. *Hope & Glory: Essays on the Legacy of the 54th Massachusetts Regiment* (Amherst, MA: University of Massachusetts Press, 2001), 45.

Folly island   South Carolina July 16th 18.64

Sir We The Members of Co D of the 55th Massechusetts vols Call the attention of your Excellency to our case

1st First We wase enlisted under the act of Congress of July 18.61 Placing the officers non Commissioned officers & Privates of the volunteer forces in all Respects as to Pay on the footing of Similar Corps of the Regular Army   2nd We Have Been in the Field now thirteen months & a Great many yet longer We Have Recieved no Pay & Have Been offered only seven Dollars Pr month Which the Paymaster Has said was all He Had ever Been authorized to Pay Colored Troops   this was not acording to our enlistment   Consequently We refused the Money   the Commonwealth of Massechusetts then Passed an act to make up all Deficienceys which the general Government Refused To Pay But this We Could not Recieve as The Troops in the general service are not Paid Partly By Government & Partly By State   3rd that to us money is not object we came to fight For Liberty justice & Equality. These are gifts we Prise more Highly than Gold For these We Left our Homes our Famileys Friends & Relatives most Dear to take as it ware our Lives in our Hands To Do Battle for God & Liberty

4th after the elaps of over thirteen months spent cheerfully & willingly Doing our Duty most faithfully in the Trenches Fatiegue Duty in

camp and conspicious valor & endurence in Battle as our Past History
will Show

P 5th therefore we Deem these sufficient Reasons for Demanding our
pay from the Date of our inlistment & our imediate Discharge Having
Been enlisted under False Pretence as the Past History of the Company
will Prove

6th Be it further Resolved that if imediate steps are not taken to Relieve us we will Resort to more stringent mesures

We have the Honor to Remin your Obedint Servants

The members of Co D
[Sergt. John F. Shorter and 73 other signatures]

L-211, 1864, Letters Received, ser. 360, Colored Troops Division, RG
94, National Archives. Reprinted in Berlin et al., *Freedom: The Black
Military Experience*, 401–402.

"because I am black, they tamper with my rights"
Sgt. George E. Stephens to the *Weekly Anglo-African*
AUGUST 1, 1864

At the beginning of 1864, no one believed that the pay crisis would be
satisfactorily resolved. Many of the black regiments, especially those from
Massachusetts, boiled over with anger and mutinous resistance. At times
the men stacked their weapons and refused to do guard duty. Anonymous letters mysteriously appeared in officers' tents threatening death if
the men went into battle without a full and proper settlement of the pay
crisis. The execution of Sgt. William Walker of the 21st USCT and Pvt.
Wallace Baker of the 55th Massachusetts Regiment only inflamed the soldiers and did nothing to restore discipline. In the first of the following
two letters, Sgt. George E. Stephens of the 54th Massachusetts Regiment
expressed the historical claims of the men and advised his readers back
home that whatever the government might do, he and his comrades
would not "tamely submit like spaniels to every indignity." The "Lincoln
despotism" would not, Stephens assured them, be permitted to degrade
the black soldier. Pvt. George G. Freeman of the 102nd USCT, also in

the Department of the South, joined his regiment in Detroit, Michigan. At the time of his letter, he lay in a hospital because, as his commander wrote, he suffered from a "verry lothsome type of Syphilis." The pay crisis drove him to write to the chief justice of the United States Supreme Court, the abolitionist-minded Salmon P. Chase. His appeal revealed the terrible toll the crisis was taking on the soldiers' families.

The resolution of the pay crisis late in 1864 represented a victory that, historically, meant as much to the black soldiers as the 54th Massachusetts's heroism at Fort Wagner. In July, Attorney General Edward Bates reversed his previous ruling that black soldiers had been enrolled under the discriminatory 1862 Militia Act that mandated that blacks be paid only $10 a month, minus $3 for clothing. While the empowering legislation meandered through Congress, black soldiers remained unpaid; most would not get their pay until the end of September and the beginning of October, and the regiments comprised of soldiers who had been slaves prior to their enlistment would not get their full pay until 1865. Yacovone, *A Voice of Thunder*, 70–74, 78–79; Berlin et al., *Freedom: The Black Military Experience*, 380–381.

Morris Island, S.C.
Aug. 1, 1964

Mʀ Eᴅɪᴛᴏʀ: Two or three months ago, it was announced that Congress had passed a law equalizing the pay of colored troops. This was at the closing period of the session. The colored troops which had been enlisted under the law of 1862, were unpaid. This was known, of course, at Washington. The noble Major [George L.] Stearns was compelled to resign, because the pledges he had been authorized by Sec. [Edwin M.] Stanton to make to the colored man, were broken by the War Department, who refused to pay soldiers who had black skins more than seven dollars per month.

Thus free men were reduced to servitude. No matter what services he might render—no matter how nobly he might acquit himself—he must carry with him the degradation of not being considered a man, but a thing. The foreigner, the alien of whatever color, or race, or country, are enrolled and paid like native Americans; but the latest refinement of cruelty has been brought to bear on us.

In the Revolutionary War, and in the War of 1812, colored men fought, and were enrolled, and paid, the same as the whites; and not only this, were drilled and enlisted indiscriminately in the same companies and regiments. Little did our forefathers think that they were forging chains for the limbs of their own race. Look how nobly Forten, Bowers, and Cassey,[1] and those colored patriots of the last war, rallied to the defence of Philadelphia; yet how were the colored people repaid? By stripping them in '36 of their right of franchise. Now the plan is to inveigle the black man into the service by false pretences, and then make him take half pay. If he don't take half pay and behave himself, as a vender of religious tracts down here said, "Shoot 'em." Why, sir, the rebels have not reached the daring extreme of reducing free men to slaves. Does the Lincoln despotism think it can succeed? There are those who say, you should not talk so—"you hurt yourself." Let me say to those men, we cannot be injured more. There is no insult—there is no cruelty—there is no wrong, which we have not suffered. Torture, massacre, mobs and slavery. Do you think that we will tamely submit like spaniels to every indignity?

I shall speak hereafter my wrongs, and nothing shall prevent me but double irons or a pistol-ball that shall take me out of the hell I am now suffering: Nearly eighteen months of service—of labor—of humiliation—of danger, and not one dollar. An estimable wife reduced to beggary, and dependent upon another man—what can wipe out the wrong and insult this Lincoln despotism has put upon us? Loyal men everywhere hurl it from power—dismember it—grind it to atoms? Who would have believed that all the newspaper talk of the pay of colored soldiers having been settled by Congress was a base falsehood. There is not the least sign of pay, and there are hints from those in authority that we will not get paid, and will be held to service by the terrors of our own bullets. Seventeen months and upwards! Suppose we had been white? Massachusetts would have inaugurated a rebellion in the East, and we would have been paid. But—Oh, how insulting!—because I am black, they tamper with my rights. How dare I be offered half the pay of any man, be he white or red.

This matter of pay seems to some of those having slaveholding tendencies a small thing, but it belongs to that system which has stripped the country of the flower of its youth. It has rendered every hamlet and fireside in this wide country desolate, and brought the country itself to bankruptcy and shame. It is a concomitant of the system. Like as the foaming waves point the mariner to the hidden rocks on which his storm-driven ship will soon be lost, this gross injustice reveals to us the hidden insidious principles on which the best hopes of the true patriot will be dashed.

G. E. S.

New York *Weekly Anglo-African*, August 27, 1864. Reprinted in Yacovone, *A Voice of Thunder*, 319–321.

---

1. Stephens refers to James Forten, Jr. (1766–1839), John C. Bowers, Sr., and Joseph Cassey (1789–1848), who assisted in assembling 360 black Philadelphians in 1814 to help construct bulwarks in anticipation of a British attack. All three became prominent black abolitionist leaders. Yacovone, *A Voice of Thunder*, 321.

"I was foold in the first place"
Pvt. George G. Freeman to Chief Justice of the United States
JUNE 25, 1865

General Hospitle Beaufort S[outh] C[arolina] June 25th 1865.

DEAR, SIR, I AM under the painfull necesity of writing you a few lines for Redresse I hav been in The Sirvice of the united states since Nov fifth one thousand eight hundred and sixty four and hav never recieve pay but twice once in June sixty four and then in, August What you paid me in June was seven doll. Per months I hav not recieved my Back pay From the government yet I am a man of faimley a Wife and two small children I was foold in the first place my famley Recieves no Relief from my state as was Promesed me For I was stolen from my town of Enrollment and creaded to the city of Detroit, state of Michigan by H. Barnes the one that got up the Regiment for the state of Michigan I could tell you Of a great deal of rascality that has Ben a going on in the Regtment that I belong if it was nesicary but I only want obliging my self as you are one of the head of our great governent I write you for assistance I want them to Give me my discharge and let me go and worke and suporte my Familey for they are nearly starved and hav not

suitabal cloathing to hide thair neckedness   my familey depends upon
my daily labor for their suporte   when I enterd the service i felt it my
Duty to go   I meryed along all to my duty untill about the last two
months   I hav ben in the Hospitle   I went with out Pay nearly all of
the time I hav ben out   now the ware is over I think that it is no moore
than wright that I should Have my Discharge as I was sick and in the
hospitle before the order was Ishued to discharge men in hospitle Some
of the officers have eaven taken the mens Discharge papers away from
them in the 32nd USC Troops[1]   Is that right   some officers will not
send the mens discriptive list to them   that is the case with me   If I
hav don wrong in writing to my superior i pray Pardon me For so doing
But I should like to Recieve some money from the governent and go
and see after my fanliey   Nomore From your moste humble Servent
and Solgier

GEORGE G FREEMAN

I am a colord man one that has no advantage

F-155, 1865, Letters Received, ser. 360, Colored Troops Division, RG 94,
National Archives. Reprinted in Berlin et al., *Freedom: The Black Military
Experience*, 379.

---

1. The 32nd USCT, organized at Camp William Penn near Philadelphia in
   February 1864, served alongside the 54th and 55th Regiments in the Department of the South and, as Freeman's letter reveals, also suffered much
   dissension over unequal pay. Wilson, *The Black Phalanx*, 469; Trudeau, *Like
   Men of War*, 253, 256, 354.

9

The Black Sailor

The USS Kearsarge and the CSS Alabama
Charles B. Fisher
1863–1864

"[N]o other course. . . could be adopted without violating every principle of humanity," declared crusty old Secretary of the Navy Gideon Welles in July 1861. He advised the commander of the Union's Atlantic blocking squadron that "you will do well to employ" black sailors, particularly escaped slaves. The navy's surprising support for the recruitment of African Americans did not stop there. "If employed they are entitled to compensation," Secretary Welles wrote "—not mere compensation," but equal pay. These extraordinary statements came from the same administration that in 1861 barred *all* African Americans from the army. When the government began general black recruitment in 1863, it refused to pay them at the same rates as whites. The reason for the difference in policy rested on one simple fact: chronically short of men, the navy could not operate without the talent and experience of black sailors.

African American service in the maritime industry goes back to the colonial period and grew along with the new republic. Whether in the coastal trades or in the whaling industry, African Americans (and many others of non-European backgrounds) played central roles. Not only did they have the experience required by the navy, but Southern African Americans also had the knowledge of local conditions and rebel dispositions that proved essential to the Union navy. From the war's outset, the navy happily employed escaped slaves and benefited from their unique knowledge. When the slave Robert Smalls escaped from

Charleston Harbor in May 1862 with the rebel vessel *Planter,* he was hailed in the North as a hero and grand evidence of the value of African Americans to the Union cause. But he proved far more valuable than the vessel he had "liberated." As a trained pilot, his knowledge of local waterways proved of great use to the navy, and he continued to command his own vessel for the remainder of the war.

African Americans also played important roles in the blue-water vessels of the navy, and the extraordinary diary of Charles Fisher reflects the treatment that most blacks received. While discrimination certainly existed—blacks would never rise very high in the ranks or become officers—they otherwise received the same treatment and benefits as all other naval personnel. Fisher, born about 1840 in Alexandria, Virginia, became a bookbinder, served honorably during the Civil War, and afterward commanded the first black militia in Washington, D.C. We know little more about Fisher, except that prior to enlisting in the navy in 1862 at age twenty-six in Boston, he had served on a steamship that plied the Mississippi River.

We do not know exactly how many men like Fisher served in the navy. Unlike the army, the navy did not record enlistments by race. Estimates of the number of blacks in the navy range from 10,000 to 18,000—perhaps 16 percent of the navy's forces, not counting the thousands that worked in naval shipyards. The documentary record of black sailors is also disappointingly thin. Until recently, Fisher's was the only published diary of a black sailor, and few if any letters from black sailors have been found. Contemporary newspapers, white and African American, published scores of letters from black soldiers at the front. But they largely ignored black sailors, despite the many literate Northern African Americans who served in the navy during the war and who undoubtedly wrote to newspapers back home. This makes Fisher's diary all the more valuable.

This diary is also important as a record of the only major engagement between Union and Confederate war vessels on the high seas during the war. Capture or destruction of the English-made rebel ship *Alabama* was one of the navy's highest priorities. The *Alabama* systematically preyed on Union ships, sending thousands of tons to the bottom or into Confederate hands. Fisher's account of life on his vessel, the *Kearsarge,* is the only sailor's-eye view of the days leading up to the famous engagement and the combat that took place on June 19, 1864, near Cherbourg, France. Paul E. Sluby, Sr., and Stanton L. Wormley, eds., *Diary of Charles B. Fisher* (Washington, DC: Columbian Harmony Society, 1983); Steven J. Ramold, *Slaves, Sailors, Citizens: African Americans in the Union Navy* (Dekalb, IL: Northern Illinois University Press, 2002); William Marvel, *The* Alabama *and the* Kearsarge*: The Sailor's Civil War* (Chapel Hill, NC: University of North Carolina Press, 1996).

AUGUST 19TH: AT SEA "All Hands to Bury the Dead"
This is the saddest day that we have ever had in the ship this cruise. Death is in our midst and a ship mate has gone to his last account. At eight o'clock this morning Mark W. Emory of Bucksport, Maine breathed his last. Al night he was calling on his mother and imagined everyone of us that stood around him was her—he would say "If I could only get my money and see my mother I would get well." he died of Fever and was 21 years old only. His mess mates performed the last rites for him and laid him out in his hammock. At ten the sail makers mates and after putting three shots in the foot of his hammock, he sewed him up, and wrapped the American Union Jack around the corpse. He was then taken aft to the Quarter Deck and at three the Boatswain's shrill call was heard and immediately after his mates sang out "All hands bury the Dead"—it was a solemn sound and went to the hearts of all those that heard it—We all go aft in the port gangway where the Captain [John A. Winslow] and officers are assembled. All stand uncovered and as the words of the Funeral Service for seamen fall upon the air, stony men who have followed the sea many years and battled with death in all his worst forms and have never shrunk back from the thunder and lightning of the worst storm, now stand like children and weep! For there is one less in the mess and there . . .

AUGUST 19 1863: BURIAL AT SEA
. . . is a vacant place in the muster roll.[1] When the Captain come to the part "we commit this body to the Deep" his mess mates who acted as Pallbearers, raised his head and placed the foot of the board out of the gangway and tilted it over the side of the ship. A dull splash in the water and all shudder for we know he has gone to his home in the deep, deep sea. Mark was very much beloved by the Ships company and his death is felt and mourned by us all. It is a very impressive scene, a burial at sea and one that leaves an impression never to be forgotten while

life lasts. We all return to our several avocations sadder, wiser if not better men. The wind is encreasing and appearances indicate a gale tonight. The land at 4 o'ck is plainly to be seen on the port bow and the ship is flying before the wind 12 × 2. Come to under the lee of Flores at six o'ck and sent a boat ashore. It is now blowing a gale and our boat will have a hard time of it landing tonight through the surf. At ten o'ck our boat returned and in hauling her up to the Davits the Falls gave away and the boats crew and all the marketing all went over into the sea—Everything was lost including chickens and livestock and we came near losing two of the crew—William Gowan and Chas. Moore but both being excellent swimmers, saved themselves.

FEB 13TH [1864]: CADIZ [Spain]
The usual monotonous routine of duty to perform varied with occasional visits to the city and its gaities and I cannot complain of the pleasures I have for this is truly a Land of Beauty and all the love tales and romances of boyhood are more than realized in this fair walled White City—in imagination one can see in passing through these narrow streets at night Old Mustapha in the Arabian nights walking blindfold an putting his chalk mark upon the door post of certain houses. And not only these flights of fancy are warranted but one is brought to realize the beautiful at every turn. The women of this land are certainly lovely to look upon—such a majestic walk—such beautiful black eyes—small feet and round well turned ancles are not to be seen anywhere in [the] world but here where you meet the pure Castilian beauty in all her most perfect charms. But sometimes you are disappointed here as elsewhere for I caught sight of a lady today sailing majestically along and eager to catch a glimpse at the lovely charmers face I hauled close on a wind and thought I'd just come athwart her house. My manouvers were successful and just as I come up in the winds eye—Oh Lord the ugliest black gal Africa ever produced—there are plenty here.

FEB 14TH [1864]: UP ANCHOR
We go to sea today bound for Brest to have our fight with the Confeds, but I'm afraid they will play out before we get up there and act as they always have—show the White feather. I am very sorry to leive here indeed. I dont know when I was ever so Loth to go to sea. Purchased sea

stores and up anchor. Stood out the harbor at 9½ ock and shaped our course with fail wind a beam. 15th: Passed Burling lights at two ock— General Quarters at nine—to a long shoreman this scene in Man O War life would be startling. General Quarters means every man to his fighting station and here every man and boy must fight. The drum taps quick and lively Tram, Tram and up and over we go running, tumbling, jumping and quick away to be first to your station. The guns are cast loose and provided for the men arm themselves—armship ports, ports and pivot the port or starboard battery as the command may be. The magazines are open—the Firemen stand ready with their scalding hot water to warm anybody who may attempt to board us & the mastmen stand ready with axes to cut away the masts and rigging when it is necessary. We go through all the manouvers of an action and then secure the batteries and the retreat is sounded.

Feb 19th [1864]: Arrive at Brest [France]

Fifteenth to nineteenth at sea the same as our homeward trip. It is clear and cold—had to go to market—it snowing like the devil and the sea running high—the wind pierces through a fellow like a knife after being down in summer weather so long. The Florida has gone to Davy Jones or some other old codger and I hope we will never hear from her again. She sneaked out the slush channel while we were away and went to sea in a storm for fear we might be waiting some where around to catch her so all our 4 months blockade duty goes for nothing at all.

May 3rd [1864]: Blockading from Dover [England] to Calaise [France]

Holy stones and sand make beautiful music this clear and cold morning but their song does not rival the notes of the nightingale. The Georgia is in Liverpool. Received the news of the Capture and massacre of the garrison at Fort Pillow. I little thought in '62 in May when I was bringing guns to Randolph [Tennessee] that our color would man that fort and lose their lives in its defence. But times have changed since I was on the "Fanny Bullitt."[2] 4th: More mails from home but no letters for me. There is one consolation and a very poor one too, that if I do not get any letters I'll have not postage to pay and more time to write my log. A 4 oclock the carpet was hoisted at the fore and a gun fired for all officers and men to be on board ship immediately. As we proceed to sea Dame

Rumor or Mrs. Busybody says we are going to Flushing Holland. It is strange how an old sailor will tell lies and yarns. Some of them aboard this remind me of old Betty Herbert and those old tattlers I left at Washington. They find out everything before it happens and keep lies cut and dried and use them up as occasion requires. It makes one mad to hear them up chaffing—we pass Deal and Ramsgate and are now on our course standing for the North Sea. I hope we are not going up to Dutchland again. I hate the devilish sour Krout eating Lager bloated boors.

MAY 5TH [1864]: COAST OF BELGIUM. Flushing on the Scheldt
The fields and meadows of the old world look lovely this spring morning and as we steam swiftly along the coast the scene is varied and panoramic—ever changing and always presenting something more interesting than the last. Ancient villages, church spires, farm houses and country residences are seen situated on verdant hill and in pleasant valley. At seven the Flushing pilot came on board and at eleven we entered the Scheldt. It is a majestic stream some two miles wide at the mouth and as we approached the Flushing Roadstead there is a strong five knot current setting us faster on way. Flushing is on the left bank of the Scheldt as you go up toward Antwerp. Come to anchor in the roadstead and made preparations to dock ship. Ashore at three oclock. Made the acquaintance of Mr. Fagg who was kind enough to show me the town and such objects of interest as the place contains for the stranger which are not many—but this is the cleanest place I was ever in. All the principal work is done by the women (A good idea. Keeps them out of mischief) and every morning early the sidewalks are all scrubbed and washed down—besides washing windows. Cleaning, paint & c makes this altogether a sweet pleasant place. The city of Middleburg is four miles distant from Flushing and the road leading to Middleburg is the most lovely the eye could rest upon. The fields and meadows are all alive with the song of birds and perfume of lilacs and spring flowers. The only road I have ever seen to compare with this is the Bayou Road at New Orleans.

MAY 30TH [1864]: FLUSHING—All hands to Muster
We came up the coast of Belgium last night and anchored here at 10— Got out the swinging boom and prepared to paint ship. Capt.— Doctor—purser have gone to the [unknown]. Dutch are very glad to see us and kind as ever. We will remain here probably some time. June 1st

to 2nd: Nothing of interest. Same routine of duty to perform. The First Lieutenant returned as our Captain was coming off in his gig. The people who thronged the pier gave him three cheers. This appeared strange to us and we did not know what to make of it. As soon as the Captain came on board he gave the order to get underweigh immediately. We were soon steaming down the Scheldt. As soon as we were out of the Roads all hands were "piper to muster." We all went to the Quarter Deck in a flurry to know what was up. As soon as we were silent the Captain stepped forward. "My lads," said he, "I am happy to congratulate you that the Alabama[3] has arrived at Cherbourg and your duty will here after be off that port. She is a ship that is noted for her speed and cleverness in eluding our cruisers—and if we take her it will be rendering our country great service. She has a great reputation in England. Pipe down sir!" But pipe down it wasn't for our boys were wild in a minute. Some jumped on the Pivot Gun & some on the hatch and gave three cheers for the Kearsarge[4] and three for Capt. [John A.] Winslow. The old man was much pleased to see us manifest our love for him in this way. 13th: Touched at Dover. 14th: We arrived at Cherburg this evening and sure enough here she is lying inside the mole.

June 15th '64: Blockading the Alabama
Stood in close to the break water this morning and had a good sight of the celebrated crusier and allowed her a chance to see the ship that has come to take her. The U.S. Consular Agent communicated with us. When we again hauled off the port mant bets are offered and taken that she will not come out to fight us. 16th: We have news this morning that [Capt. Raphael] Semmes in a letter to the Confed. Agent here said that if the Kearsarge would wait a day or two he would come out and fight her. 17th: "All hands to muster" this morning and the Captain addressed us. "My Lads. Captain Semmes says he will come out and fight us if we will wait one or two days for him. I have no intention of going away. He is a man of his word and will do as he says he will. I knew him in Mexico and he is a brave man." We all retired from the Quarter Deck confident that we would have to fight her—and the boys were in high glee at the prospect. 18th: Fire Quarters. "All hands repel boarders." We are all up and off at the sound of the bell. Everything in readiness in one minute and a half. This is the quickest time we have ever made at General Quarters. There is every indication of a battle before we are 24 hours older. Still no man is down hearted. All

the boys are in high glee. Some dancing. Some singing their Saturday songs and some spinning cuffers as usual. All seem to have forgotten the existence of the Alabama.

JUNE 19TH: 1864: BATTLE

Off the land twelve miles. The morning is thick and hazy. The shore is scarcely distinguishable. There is all the preparations being made for our Sabbath Day devotions. Inspection at quarters at ten oclock after which we are all waiting to hear the Church bell toll. At ten minutes after ten the fore top man at the mast head sang out—Steamer under the land! Standing out! That's the Alabama, said the quarter master. We all were anxious to catch a glimpse of her before going into battle. The bell sounded fire quarters and the boys were to be seen tumbling down the forecastle ladders—fore rigging Jacobs Ladders & c trying who could be first at their quarters. She was coming straight out for us and we were all ready for the conflict in just three minutes. Decks sanded down. Batteries cast loose and manned. Magazines opened & all reported ready. Go ahead fast, said the Captain. The Alabama was now about two miles distant and coming on fast. Lay down! Every man, said the Captain, and down we all lay flat on the deck. And now as I lay down not knowing how soon I might be killed or maimed for life I thought of home and how I had been neglected by those who should have been all in all to me. My thoughts were bitter, bitter scenes long since forgotten came back to my memory as vividly as if they were being enacted now. Friends and those who wee dear to me came before me and I wondered if any of them could know my situation now. Would they feel my sorrow or think kindly of me after I was no more. These and many other thoughts went through my mind swift as lightning. I also thought of Bud and prayed that he might not get hurt in any way. But no time was now given for thoughts or feelings. The Alabama had now opened fire with her starboard battery. Distance one thousand yards. The shell were flying screaming through our rigging and bursting far astern of us. She fired seven times. We keeping head on to her and going full speed. At the seventh shot the 30 pound rifle parrott on our forecastle paid our compliments to her and down came her flag. The gaff was shot away—we still going ahead—she broadside too. She fired five more shot. None of her shot had as yet struck us. We were not quite near her and our helm was put hard a starboard and our noble ship came up beautifully and showed her an awful battery with no men but the Marines on the forecastle. "Ready." "Fire," and our two eleven inch three broadside & rifle pivot sent death and destruction aboard her. We kept around in a circle and it seemed strange how cooly our men now faced her fire amidst the groans of the dying and the cusses of the wounded. Around went the Kearsarge—the Alabama keeping up a hot fire upon us. We could see the shell and solid shot coming and some of them would pass so close that the hot wind from them would puff in our faces. Still nobody hurt aboard of us. One shot had now struck our rudder post and another went through our smoke stack. To those who have never head the whistle of a shell there is something unearthly and terrible in the sound. One is led to imagine that all the devils in hell are let loose to play around ones ears. The conflict hand [had] now lasted half an hour and our boys had commenced to warm to their work. Everytime the Alabama fired a broadside we could see the shot and shell coming at us and everyone of us would drop flat on the deck seeking the protection of the water ways. In this way a good many lives were saved from the passing balls. A soon as her shot passed our boys were up in minute and had our guns loaded & fired before she could again bring her guns to bear. We were steaming fast around her in a circle all the time and they fired two shots to our one, but our boys were cool and took deliberate aim and then fired and we could see the shell pass clean through her and burst on the other side. Our second broadside. Every shell done its work—we could see the splinters and coal dust fly in every direction. The battle had now lasted three quarters of an hour and she commenced to set sail and try to escape to the French coast—seeing which our boys sent up a cheer after cheer which made the ship fairly shake—and the battle raged fiercer than ever. One of her shell now struck our engine house and explodings wounded three men two severely and one not. The Chief Engineer Mr. [William H.] Cushman also had a narrow escape at this time. The Captain also narrowly escaped but was pushed down by Clem Johnson who pushed him down out of the way. A shell from our forward pivot 11 inch now exploded right in her stern carrying away the stern—breaking her fan and killing the men at the wheel also wounding Capt. Semmes and a great number more. She now became perfectly unmanageable and we came around on her port side and pound in a murderous fire of shot and shell and the sight was awful and sublime. The execution was terrible. We came up

again intending to rake her decks fore & aft which would have killed or
wounded every soul on her. But she fired three <u>Sea Guns</u> and haul down
her flag. The order passed <u>Cease Firing</u>. The battle had been fought and
won in one hour and ten minutes. Her boat was not coming toward us
but we noticed her settling down and made all haste to lower our boats
to save the wounded and survivors. But before our boats could get to her
she gave a wild leap forward, threw her bow high in the air and went
down stern first. It was painful to see her men as they jumped into the
sea to meet a watery grave or threw their arms wildly above their heads
to cry for help.

We who one moment before would have cut them down to a man,
now strained every nerve and made every effort to save them. A perfect
sea of heads could now be seen floating on the surface, some clinging to
the pieces of wreck or such frail support as they could find. Our boats—
that is two of them were picking them up as fast as they could, but numbers of the wounded were sinking fast. The English Yacht <u>Deerhound</u>
now came up and assisted us in picking up the drowning men, but she
did not pick up many. She got Semmes and steamed away to Southampton. We did not follow her but continued to pick up the men. Several
French pilots now came up and saved eight men all together. The
French iron clad "Corunne" did not lend any assistance. The sight was
pitiful to see them dragging half drowned on board the ship with no
clothing on and all with the "shivers" from being so long in the water.
We gave them dry clothes and rubbed them in blankets to bring them
too, and the wounded were carried below and received the same attention from our surgeon that our own did. Her surgeon was killed and her
assistant was brought on board us and assisted our surgeon to care for
the wounded. We picked up 42 not wounded and eleven wounded and
three dead. One of the latter was the carpenter [William] Robinson of
New Orleans. Of her crew of one hundred and fifty—only eighty were
saved all told. The rest went down with their ship. On our side John W.
Dempsey, quarter gunner, lost his right arm. William Gowan, seaman,
leg broken in two places. James Macbeth, seaman, wounded in the calf
of his leg.[5] None were killed on our ship and except a splitting head
ache I was neither frightened nor hurt. We now broke our three flags at
the mast heads in token of the great victory we had won. We commenced fighting at the same time people at home were going to church
and ended as the minister completed his sermon. We are all too busy

now to think of our success but we know the weight of the service we have now rendered our country and will impatiently await the news from home. At two oclock we stood away for the port of Cherbourg and left the Alabama down—down 200 fathoms in her watery home beneath the waves. We came to anchor in the harbor at 3½ oc and sent the wounded ashore to the French hospital. The Kearsarge was struck twenty eight times in her hull and rigging and received no damage but what can be repaired in a few hours. The shore is lined with anxious people and boats are coming off to see us. The French admiral has sent two launches to help convey the wounded men ashore and they are now alongside. The blood from the wounded Pirates covers our berth deck and their groans are awful to hear as they lay dying on our deck. Scarcely five hours have elapsed since they left this port in their noble cruiser hoping to capture the U.S. Sloop Kearsarge and murder her crew. As they said before going into action they would show us no quarter, but the Lord protected us and their fate was sealed.

JUNE 20TH [1864]: CHERBOURG. After the Battle
Up this morning bright and early to remove the blood from our decks and put the ship to rights again. After Holy stones and sand and plenty of fresh water was freely used at 8 ock every vestage of the conflict was removed except the gap in our smoke stack and the dead on the quarter deck. We all feel the effect of the heavy fireing being very sore and stiff and head ache. While the battle waged fiercest our little dog <u>Mose</u> would run out from under the Forecastle and pick up the splinters in his mouth and run in again. It was evidently good fun for him. The other dogs run away and hid when the firing commenced.

Another incident of the fight but more terrible was when our second shell busted aboard of her. It was just in the midst of her rifle guns crew and out of a crew of ten men it killed eight dead. A[s] quick as a flash another rifle shell from us struck a man on her Knight head taking out all of his stomach. He run to the starboard gangway and there fell down on a pile of the wounded and dead. The same shell cut two other men completely in two and exploded beyond her. They all say our firing was just as accurate as target practise and did terrible execution and that we may be glad we did not see her decks before she went down as the sight was sickening in the extreme. She was perfectly riddled fore and aft. One shot passed clean through her.

JUNE 21ST [1864]: AFTER THE BATTLE

Just after she went down Tom Holloway and myself pulled one poor fellow out of the boat that was very nearly gone. We carried him down below and after rubbing him with towels & blankets brought him too. The
first thing he said was. Oh! Boys you showed us no quarter. They told
us you would not and you didn't. We did fire into five times after her
flag was first struck, but they continued firing after the flag was struck—
and as we had shot it away three times and it had been put up again,
when the flag was hauled down we did not know it. One thing we knew
if we fell into their hands not one of us would have been left to tell the
tale as they had sworn to show us no quarter and the hatred between us
previous to the battle was very bitter. But now we have nothing against
them and our kindness have quite won their esteem. While our boats
were picking them up in our boats three or four jumped out and swam
to the Deerhound. They were terror stricken and many would rather
have drowned than come on board our ship—to me as they thought a
worse fate. One little messenger boy came over the gangway bitterly and
it was some time before the 1st Lieut. could pacify him. The other was
saucy and defiant and didn't care whether he lived or died. Many other
incidents occured during the fight.

JUNE 22ND [1864]: CHERBOURG

Ashore at five oclock and almost imagined myself back again in Brest.
This place is so much like that. The streets are the same—scenes the
same—shops the same. I do not like the appearance of things here at
all. Nothing but Man-O-Wars, men and soldiers. The harbor is better
and more formidable and has near three thousand guns to defend it. Returned to breakfast. After a good nap I went on deck to see the last of
the Confederate dead. They are to be buried ashore in the Protestant
Burial Ground. Our boys in the hospital are doing very well we hear and
we have hopes Gowan will live although he is very down hearted.
Evening we are an object of curiosity to everyone and crowds in the
boats are going around u[s] and looking at the "Black Spirit"—as if she
was something evil indeed. We have always been in all the places we
have visited quite the rage and the people have admired our ship and
company very much. Now we will be the Lyon of the Day—and can
now blow a living stream of Gass to the Juicers on the other side of the
Channel. Evening all the boys are engaged writing home to let their

people know that none of us are killed. I sent a letter to mother, Rosa, John and Miss M.L. and I hope they will go safe to their destination. I am tired and sore and so stiff that I can scarcely move one foot before the other. Turned in at eight oclock.

Sluby and Wormley, *Diary of Charles B. Fisher*, 46–47, 60–61, 76–77, 82–92.

---

1. Ellipsis appears in the Sluby-Wormley edition of the Fisher diary. The original manuscript remains in private hands.
2. For a brief time in 1860, Fisher worked as a steward on the Mississippi side-wheel steamer *Fanny Bullitt* and helped deliver ordnance to the bluffs that later became Fort Pillow. The 438-ton vessel, built in 1854, sank on March 15, 1864. Marvel, *The* Alabama *& the* Kearsarge, 239, 295; Ramold, *Slaves, Sailors, Citizens*, 168. William M. Lytle and Forrest R. Holdcamper, comps., *Merchant Steam Vessels of the United States, 1790–1868* (Staten Island: Steamship Historical Society of America, 1975), supplement #1.
3. The CSS *Alabama* had been constructed in the Liverpool shipyards in 1862 for the Confederacy. Before its encounter with the *Kearsarge*, the *Alabama* had accumulated a deadly record against Union shipping, taking sixty-four ships worth $6.5 million. Most of its career was spent plying the Atlantic Ocean, and the vessel never docked at a Southern port. Faust, *Historical Times Illustrated Encyclopedia of the Civil War*, 3–4.
4. The USS *Kearsarge*, launched in 1862, cruised off the western European coast, from Gibraltar to England in search of Confederate vessels. Its excellent crew and weaponry, especially its two 11-inch pivot guns, proved far superior to those of other wooden vessels. Although decommissioned at the close of 1864, the vessel continued to sail until 1894. Faust, *Historical Times Illustrated Encyclopedia of the Civil War*, 409.
5. Robinson, a Massachusetts native who had moved to Louisiana, soon died of his wounds. John W. Dempsey, a troublesome Boston Irishman, announced to the dismay of his black fellow crewmen that he opposed emancipation. His right arm had been shredded below the bicep and removed by the ship's surgeon at the shoulder. He later fell ill from dysentery, never regained his health, and died at home in 1869. William Gowan performed with Fisher and other sailors in a musical troupe and habitually broke regulations. His leg had been shattered in two places during the engagement, with bones protruding through the skin. After its amputation, Gowan lingered and died on June 27. Marvel, *The* Alabama *& the* Kearsarge, 43, 47, 60, 90, 257, 259, 260, 267.

10

Black Women and the War

"Reminiscences of My Life in Camp"
Susie King Taylor
1863–1864

In the story of the Civil War, little space has been devoted to discussions about the role of women, and historians have all but ignored the participation of African American women. Military service offered black men a direct way to destroy the institution of slavery and lay the basis for their postwar claims for citizenship, but black women never benefited from their experience in the war as much as men. Nevertheless, as spies, scouts, nurses, teachers, workers, and by courageous acts of compassion and selflessness, black women were important participants. If a woman was a married slave, the military service of her husband might become a fatal act for both, as outraged Union slave masters took revenge on the wives of their "property" who volunteered for the army. Often anonymous in official records or seen as indistinct, shadowy figures at the periphery of photographs, black women nevertheless had a ubiquitous presence in the war. That presence was, at times, an important factor in weakening the chains of slavery.

When they entered Union lines to escape marauding rebel forces or to secure their freedom, black women brought vital information concerning the disposition of rebel troops to Union commanders. They also informed on white Confederate sympathizers who provided aid and comfort to rebel soldiers. Behind rebel lines, they worked with Union spies, such as Richmond's Elizabeth Van Lew, to carry correspondence and maps to Union forces. One slave, Mary Elizabeth Bowser, worked as a maid in Jefferson Davis's official residence and passed on whatever useful information she could find to Van Lew and her network. Black women were also more directly involved in the war: Harriet Tubman served as a spy and a scout for Maj. Gen. David Hunter in the Department of the South. Hundreds of others risked their lives to help Union soldiers avoid capture or escape from rebel prisons. Susie King Taylor knew of many black women who were punished for taking food to starving Union prisoners, an act that could lead to a savage beating or even death.

Yet the only personal account we have of a black woman's role in the Civil War remains Taylor's brief but extraordinary 1902 recollections. Born on August 6, 1848, the oldest of six slave children in a family outside of Savannah, Georgia, Taylor fled from slavery as Union forces captured nearby Fort Pulaski in April 1862. That October, at age fourteen, she became the regimental laundress for the 1st South Carolina Volunteers (33rd USCT). Having learned to read and write despite being a slave, she eagerly began teaching the soldiers in her new husband's company. As a laundress, cook, seamstress, and nurse—one that could shoulder a musket—she won the respect and admiration of everyone in the regiment.

Taylor taught in Savannah, Georgia, after the war and witnessed the suppression of her brethren by the Klan and other enemies of black freedom. She moved to Boston in 1874, where she continued to work for black uplift and helped organize the Boston branch of the Women's Relief Corps, an auxiliary of the Grand Army of the Republic. Although she found comparative freedom in Boston, the postwar years offered unending hardship for most African Americans. "Was the war in vain?" she asked. "Has it brought freedom, in the full sense of the word, or has it not made our condition more hopeless? In this 'land of the free' we are burned, tortured, and denied a fair trial, murdered for any imaginary wrong conceived in the brain of the negro-hating white man." Taylor's recollections of her service in the war are invaluable, and her assessment of conditions after the war stand as an indictment. Berlin et al., *Freedom: The Black Military Experience*, 30, 240–241, 244, 247, 268–269; Elizabeth D. Leonard, *All the Daring of a Soldier: Women of the Civil War Armies* (New York: Penguin, 2001), 53–55. 70, 83, 152–153; Susie King Taylor, *Reminiscences of My Life in Camp with the 33rd United States Colored Troops Late 1st S. C. Volunteers* (Boston: by the author, 1902).

[CHAPTER] V
MILITARY EXPEDITIONS, AND LIFE IN CAMP

IN THE LATTER PART OF 1862 the regiment made an expedition into Darien, Georgia, and up the Ridge, and on January 23, 1863, another up St. Mary's River, capturing a number of stores for the government; then on to Fernandina, Florida. They were gone ten or twelve days, at the end of which time they returned to camp.

March 10, 1863, we were ordered to Jacksonville, Florida. Leaving Camp Saxton[1] between four and five o'clock, we arrived at Jacksonville about eight o'clock next morning, accompanied by three or four gunboats. When the rebels saw these boats, they ran out of the city, leaving the women behind, and we found out afterwards that they thought we had a much larger fleet than we really had. Our regiment was kept out of sight until we made fast at the wharf where it landed, and while the gunboats were shelling up the river and as far inland as possible, the regiment landed and marched up the street, where they spied the rebels who had fled from the city. They were hiding behind a house about a mile or so away, their faces blackened to disguise themselves as negroes, and our boys, as they advanced toward them, halted a second, saying, "They are black men! Let them come to us, or we will make them know who we are." With this, the firing was opened and several of our men were wounded and killed. The rebels had a number wounded and killed. It was through this way the discovery was made that they were white men. Our men drove them some distance in retreat and then threw out their pickets.

While the fighting was on, a friend, Lizzie Lancaster, and I stopped at several of the rebel homes, and after talking with some of the women and children we asked them if they had any food. They claimed to have only some hard-tack, and evidently did not care to give us anything to eat, but this was not surprising. They were bitterly against our people and had no mercy or sympathy for us.

The second day, our boys were reinforced by a regiment of white soldiers, a Maine regiment, and by cavalry, and had quite a fight. On the third day, Edward Herron, who was a fine gunner on the steamer John Adams,[2] came on shore, bringing a small cannon, which the men pulled along for more than five miles. This cannon was the only piece for shelling. On coming upon the enemy, all secured their places, and they had a lively fight, which lasted several hours, and our boys were nearly captured by the Confederates; but the Union boys carried out all their plans that day, and succeeded in driving the enemy back. After this skirmish, every afternoon between four and five o'clock the Confederate General [Joseph] Finegan would send a flag of truce to Colonel [Thomas Wentworth] Higginson, warning him to send all women and children out of the city, and threatening to bombard it if this was not done. Our colonel allowed all to go who wished, at first, but as General Finegan grew more hostile and kept sending these communications for nearly a week, Colonel Higginson thought it not best or necessary to send any more out of the city, and so informed General Finegan. This angered the general, for that night the rebels shelled directly toward Colonel Higginson's headquarters. The shelling was so heavy that the colonel told my captain to have me taken up into the town to a hotel, which was used as a hospital. As my quarters were just in the rear of the colonel's, he was compelled to leave his also before the night was over. I expected every moment to be killed by a shell, but on arriving at the hospital I knew I was safe, for the shells could not reach us there. It was plainly to be seen now, the ruse of the flag of truce coming so often to see us. The bearer was evidently a spy getting the location of the headquarters, etc., for the shells were sent too accurately to be at random.

Next morning Colonel Higginson took the cavalry and a regiment on another tramp after the rebels. They were gone several days and had the hardest fight they had had, for they wanted to go as far as a station which was some distance from the city. The gunboats were of little assistance to them, yet notwithstanding this drawback our boys returned with only a few killed and wounded, and after this we were not troubled with General Finegan.

We remained here a few weeks longer, when, about April first, the regiment was ordered back to Camp Saxton, where it stayed a week, when the order came to go to Port Royal Ferry on picket duty. It was a gay day for the boys. By seven o'clock all the tents were down, and each company, with a commissary wagon, marched up the shell road, which is a beautiful avenue ten or twelve miles out of Beaufort. We arrived at Seabrooke at about four o'clock, where our tents were pitched and the men put on duty. We were here a few weeks, when Company E was ordered to Barnwell plantation for picket duty.

Some mornings I would go along the picket line, and I could see the rebels on the opposite side of the river. Sometimes as they were changing pickets they would call over to our men and ask for something to eat, or for tobacco, and our men would tell them to come over. Sometimes one or two would desert to us, saying, they "had no negroes to fight for." Others would shoot across at our picket, but as the river was so wide there was never any damage done, and the Confederates never attempted to shell us while we were there.

I learned to handle a musket very well while in the regiment, and could shoot straight and often hit the target. I assisted in cleaning the guns and used to fire them off, to see if the cartridges were dry, before cleaning and reloading, each day. I thought this great fun. I was also able to take a gun all apart, and put it together again.

Between Barnwell and the mainland was Hall Island. I went over there several times with Sergeant [Edward] King and his comrades.[3] One night there was a stir in camp when it was found that the rebels were trying to cross, and next morning Lieutenant Parker told me he thought they were on Hall Island; so after that I did not go over again.

While planning for the expedition up the Edisto River, Colonel Higginson was a whole night in the water, trying to locate the rebels and where their picket lines were situated. About July the boys went up the Edisto to destroy a bridge on the Charleston and Savannah road. This expedition was twenty or more miles into the mainland. Colonel Higginson was wounded in this fight and the regiment nearly captured. The steamboat John Adams always assisted us, carrying soldiers, provisions, etc. She carried several guns and a good gunner, Edward Herron. Henry Batchlott, a relative of mine, was a steward on this boat. There were two smaller boats, Governor Milton and the Enoch Dean, in the fleet, as these could go up the river better than the larger ones could. I often went aboard the John Adams. It went with us into Jacksonville, to Cole and Folly Island, and Gunner Herron was always ready to send a shell at the enemy.

One night, Companies K and E, on their way to Pocotaligo to destroy a battery that was situated down the river, captured several prisoners. The rebels nearly captured Sergeant King, who, as he sprang and caught a "reb," fell over an embankment. In falling he did not release his hold on his prisoner. Although his hip was severely injured, he held fast until some of his comrades came to his aid and pulled them up. These expeditions were very dangerous. Sometimes the men had to go five or ten miles during the night over on the rebel side and capture or destroy whatever they could find.

While at Camp Shaw,[4] there was a deserter who came into Beaufort. He was allowed his freedom about the city and was not molested. He remained about the place a little while and returned to the rebels again. On his return to Beaufort a second time, he was held as a spy, tried, and sentenced to death, for he was a traitor. The day he was shot, he was placed on a hearse with his coffin inside, a guard was placed either side of the hearse, and he was driven through the town. All the soldiers and people in town were out, as this was to be a warning to the soldiers. Our regiment was in line on dress parade. They drove with him to the rear of our camp, where he was shot. I shall never forget this scene.

While at Camp Shaw, Chaplain [James H.] Fowler, Robert Defoe, and several of our boys were captured while tapping some telegraph wires. Robert Defoe was confined in the jail at Walterborough, S. C., for about twenty months. When [Gen. William T.] Sherman's army reached Pocotaligo he made his escape and joined his company (Company G). He had not been paid, as he had refused the reduced pay offered by the government. Before we got to camp, where the pay-rolls could be made out, he sickened and died of small-pox, and was buried at Savannah, never having been paid one cent for nearly three years of service. He left no heirs and his account was never settled.

In winter, when it was very cold, I would take a mess-pan, put a little earth in the bottom, and go to the cook-shed and fill it nearly full of coals, carry it back to my tent and put another pan over it; so when the provost guard went through camp after taps, they would not see the light, as it was against the rules to have a light after taps. In this way I was heated and kept very warm.

A mess-pan is made of sheet iron, something like our roasting pans, only they are nearly as large round as a peck measure, but not so deep. We had fresh beef once in a while, and we would have soup, and the vegetables they put in this soup were dried and pressed. They looked like hops. Salt beef was our stand-by. Sometimes the men would have what we called slap-jacks. This was flour, made into bread and spread thin on the bottom of the mess-pan to cook. Each man had one of them, with a pint of tea, for his supper, or a pint of tea and five or six hard-tack. I often got my own meals, and would fix some dishes for the non-commissioned officers also.

Mrs. Chamberlain, our quartermaster's wife, was with us here.[5] She was a beautiful woman; I can see her pleasant face before me now, as she, with Captain [Charles T.] Trowbridge, would sit and converse with me in my tent two or three hours at a time. She was also with me on Cole Island, and I think we were the only women with the regiment while there. I remember well how, when she first came into camp, Captain Trowbridge brought her to my tent and introduced her to me. I found her then, as she remained after, a lovely person, and I always admired her cordial and friendly ways.

Our boys would say to me sometimes, "Mrs. King, why is it you are so kind to us? you treat us just as you do the boys in your own company." I replied, "Well, you know, all the boys in other companies are the same to me as those in my Company E; you are all doing the same duty, and I will do just the same for you." "Yes," they would say, "we know that, because you were the first woman we saw when we came into camp, and you took an interest in us boys ever since we have been here, and we are very grateful for all you do for us."

When at Camp Shaw, I visited the hospital in Beaufort, where I met Clara Barton.[6] There were a number of sick and wounded soldiers there, and I went often to see the comrades. Miss Barton was always very cordial toward me, and I honored her for her devotion and care of those men.

There was a man, John Johnson, who with his family was taken by our regiment at Edisto. This man afterwards worked in the hospital and was well known to Miss Barton. I have been told since that when she went South, in 1883, she tried to look this man up, but learned he was dead. His son is living in Edisto, Rev. J. J. Johnson,[7] and is the president of an industrial school on that island and a very intelligent man. He was a small child when his father and family were captured by our regiment at Edisto.

[CHAPTER] VI
ON MORRIS AND OTHER ISLANDS

FORT WAGNER being only a mile from our camp, I went there two or three times a week, and would go up on the ramparts to watch the gunners send their shells into Charleston (which they did every fifteen minutes), and had a full view of the city from that point. Outside of the fort were many skulls lying about; I have often moved them one side out of the path. The comrades and I would have quite a debate as to which side the men fought on. Some thought they were the skulls of our boys; others thought they were the enemy's; but as there was no definite way to know, it was never decided which could lay claim to them. They were a gruesome sight, those fleshless heads and grinning jaws, but by this time I had become accustomed to worse things and did not feel as I might have earlier in my camp life.

It seems strange how our aversion to seeing suffering is overcome in war,—how we are able to see the most sickening sights, such as men with their limbs blown off and mangled by the deadly shells, without a shudder; and instead of turning away, how we hurry to assist in alleviating their pain, bind up their wounds, and press the cool water to their parched lips, with feelings only of sympathy and pity.

About the first of June, 1864, the regiment was ordered to Folly Island, staying there until the latter part of the month, when it was ordered to Morris Island. We landed on Morris Island between June and July, 1864. This island was a narrow strip of sandy soil, nothing growing on it but a few bushes and shrubs. The camp was one mile from the boat landing, called Pawnell Landing, and the landing one mile from Fort Wagner.

Colonel Higginson had left us in May of this year, on account of wounds received at Edisto. All the men were sorry to lose him. They did not want him to go, they loved him so. He was kind and devoted to his men, thoughtful for their comfort, and we missed his genial presence from the camp.

The regiment under Colonel Trowbridge did garrison duty, but they had troublesome times from Fort Gregg, on James Island,[8] for the rebels would throw a shell over on our island every now and then. Finally orders were received for the boys to prepare to take Fort Gregg, each man to take 150 rounds of cartridges, canteens of water, hard-tack, and salt beef. This order was sent three days prior to starting, to allow them to be in readiness. I helped as many as I could to pack haversacks and cartridge boxes.

The fourth day, about five o'clock in the afternoon, the call was sounded, and I heard the first sergeant say, "Fall in, boys, fall in," and they were not long obeying the command. Each company marched out of its street, in front of their colonel's headquarters, where they rested for half an hour, as it was not dark enough, and they did not want the enemy to have a chance to spy their movements. At the end of this time the line was formed with the 103d New York (white) in the rear, and off they started, eager to get to work. It was quite dark by the time they reached Pawnell Landing. I have never forgotten the good-bys of that day, as they left camp. Colonel Trowbridge said to me as he left, "Good-by, Mrs. King, take care of yourself if you don't see us again." I went with them as far as the landing, and watched them until they got out of sight, and then returned to the camp. There was no one at camp but those left on picket and a few disabled soldiers, and one woman, a friend of mine, Mary Shaw, and it was lonesome and sad, now that the boys were gone, some never to return.

Mary Shaw shared my tent that night, and we went to bed, but not to sleep, for the fleas nearly ate us alive. We caught a few, but it did seem, now that the men were gone, that every flea in camp had located my tent, and caused us to vacate. Sleep being out of the question, we sat up the remainder of the night.

About four o'clock, July 2, the charge was made. The firing could be plainly heard in camp. I hastened down to the landing and remained there until eight o'clock that morning. When the wounded arrived, or rather began to arrive, the first one brought in was Samuel Anderson of our company. He was badly wounded. Then others of our boys, some with their legs off, arm gone, foot off, and wounds of all kinds imaginable. They had to wade through creeks and marshes, as they were discovered by the enemy and shelled very badly. A number of the men were lost, some got fastened in the mud and had to cut off the legs of their pants, to free themselves. The 103d New York suffered the most, as their men were very badly wounded.

My work now began. I gave my assistance to try and alleviate their sufferings. I asked the doctor at the hospital what I could get for them to eat. They wanted soup, but that I could not get; but I had a few cans of condensed milk and some turtle eggs, so I thought I would try to make some custard. I had doubts as to my success, for cooking with turtle eggs was something new to me, but the adage has it, "Nothing ventured, nothing done," so I made a venture and the result was a very delicious custard. This I carried to the men, who enjoyed it very much. My services were given at all times for the comfort of these men. I was on hand to assist whenever needed. I was enrolled as company laundress, but I did very little of it, because I was always busy doing other things through the camp, and was employed all the time doing something for the officers and comrades.

After this fight, the regiment did not return to the camp for one month. They were ordered to Cole Island in September, where they remained until October. About November 1, 1864, six companies were detailed to go to Gregg Landing, Port Royal Ferry, and the rebels in some way found out some of our forces had been removed and gave our boys in camp a hard time of it, for several nights. In fact, one night it was thought the boys would have to retreat. The colonel told me to go down to the landing, and if they were obliged to retreat, I could go aboard one of our gunboats. One of the gunboats got in the rear, and began to shell General [P. G. T.] Beauregard's force, which helped our boys retain their possession.

About November 15, I received a letter from Sergeant King, saying the boys were still lying three miles from Gregg Landing and had not had a fight yet; that the rebels were waiting on them and they on the rebels, and each were holding their own; also that General [William T.] Sherman had taken Fort McAllister, eight miles from Savannah. After receiving this letter I wanted to get to Beaufort, so I could be near to them and so be able to get news from my husband. November 23 I got a pass for Beaufort. I arrived at Hilton Head about three o'clock next day, but there had been a battle, and a steamer arrived with a number of wounded men; so I could not get a transfer to Beaufort. The doctor wished me to remain over until Monday. I did not want to stay. I was anxious to get off, as I knew no one at Hilton Head.

I must mention a pet pig we had on Cole Island. Colonel Trowbridge brought into camp, one day, a poor, thin little pig, which a German soldier brought back with him on his return from a furlough. His regiment, the 74th Pennsylvania, was just embarking for the North, while it was ordered to join the 10th corps, and he could not take the pig back with him, so he gave it to our colonel. That pig grew to be the pet of the camp, and was the special care of the drummer boys, who taught him many tricks; and so well did they train him that every day at practice and dress parade, his pigship would march out with them, keeping perfect time with their music. The drummers would often disturb the devotions by riding this pig into the midst of evening praise meeting, and many were the complaints made to the colonel, but he was always very lenient towards the boys, for he knew they only did this for mischief. I shall never forget the fun we had in camp with "Piggie."

Susie King Taylor, *Reminiscences of My Life in Camp with the 33rd United States Colored Troops Late 1st S. C. Volunteers* (Boston: Published by the Author, 1902), 22–36.

----

1. At Beaufort on Port Royal Island, the headquarters of General Rufus Saxton.
2. The *John Adams*, an armed troop transport, remained in the Sea Islands and was later used by the 54th Massachusetts on its first military mission. Emilio, *A Brave Black Regiment*, 40.
3. Sgt. Edward King, the author's husband, who died shortly after the end of the war. The couple was married in 1862 and both remained in the army until February 1866.
4. On Morris Island, near the mouth of Charleston Harbor.
5. Mrs. Chamberlain, wife of Lieut. G. M. Chamberlain, arrived in the Sea Islands with a new baby. The pipe-smoking Susie King Taylor was taken on as a nursemaid. Thomas Wentwork Higginson, *Army Life in a Black Regiment* (1870, reprint Boston: Beacon Press, 1962), 185–186, 270.
6. Clara H. Barton (1821–1912) worked under the surgeon general and assisted the wounded as a nurse in the Department of the South for most of 1863. Faust, *Historical Times Illustrated Encyclopedia of the Civil War*, 43.
7. Rev. J. J. Johnson established the Edisto Island Industrial School in 1897. George Brown Tindall, *South Carolina Negroes, 1877–1900* (Columbia, SC: University of South Carolina Press, 1966), 226.
8. It is not clear which Confederate fortification on James Island the 33rd USCT prepared to attack. This should not be confused with Fort Gregg, located on the tip of Morris Island, which had been captured by Union forces in September 1863.

11

Emancipation

"It is now, or never: now, if ever"
Robert Hamilton
JANUARY 17, 1863

Despite its considerable shortcomings, the Emancipation Proclamation changed the character of the war. Until January 1, 1863, however, the Union defended slavery and the Lincoln administration reversed the decisions of army commanders who attempted to free all slaves within their grasp. Secretary of State William H. Seward proclaimed to the world that "however the war for the Union might terminate, no change would be made in the relation of master and slave." As Frederick Douglass wrote in his memoir, "We fought the rebellion but not its cause. The key to the situation was the four millions of slaves; yet the slave, who loved us, was hated, and the slaveholder, who hated us was loved." Given the horrors inflicted on the country by the rebellion, free blacks could not understand the timidity of the government on the issue of slavery: "our honest but incompetent President adopts a halfway measure, which purports to give freedom to the bulk of the slave population beyond the reach of our arms, while it ignores or defies justice, by clinching the rivets of the chain which binds those whom alone we have present power to redeem. The proclamation," the San Francisco *Pacific Appeal* exclaimed, "should have been made to include every bondsman on the soil of America."

Nevertheless, there was cause for joy. January 1, 1863, saw meetings and rallies break out across the North to praise what everyone hoped would be a new day. Douglass presided over a mass meeting in

Boston, declaring that he now saw a bright light where before there
had been only darkness. If he did not exactly see the end of the world's
worst curse, "he thought he saw the beginning of the end." For the soldiers of Col. Thomas Wentworth Higginson's 1st South Carolina Volunteers in the South Carolina Sea Islands, a new era had commenced.
During a ceremony to celebrate the proclamation, Higginson's men, all
one thousand former slaves, formed by company in a striking pose with
their blue coats and red trousers. After the presentation of a new flag
to the regiment, a lone, elderly black male voice began to sing. Soon the
voices of two women joined in, spontaneously singing "My country 'tis
of thee/ Sweet land of Liberty." The three sang on, sending "verse after verse" out onto the light seacoast breezes. "I never saw anything
so electric," Higginson wrote in his journal, "it made all other words
cheap, it seemed the choked voice of a race, at last unloosened."

Celebrations notwithstanding, the editor of the New York *Weekly
Anglo-African* reminded his brethren that the time for hard work had arrived. The responsibility for bringing four million slaves into the light of
day, to educate them, to give them school books and Bibles lay with
those black men and women in the North who have had the good fortune to enjoy a small measure of freedom. "It is our work, and always
has been," he explained. Frederick Douglass, *Life and Times of Frederick
Douglass* (1892, New York: Collier Books, 1962), 351–352; C. Peter
Ripley et al., eds., *Witness for Freedom: African American Voices on Race,
Slavery, and Emancipation* (Chapel Hill, NC: University of North Carolina Press, 1993), 221–222; John W. Blassingame, et al., eds., *The Frederick Douglass Papers* (New Haven, CT: Yale University Press, 1985),
3:546–547; Christopher Looby, ed., *The Complete Civil War Journal and
Selected Letters of Thomas Wentworth Higginson* (Chicago: University of
Chicago Press, 2000), 76–77.

THE PRESENT—AND ITS DUTIES

AFTER THE FEAST, comes the reckoning. The good things served up to
and by our people in the way of hearty and spontaneous rejoicing over
the PROCLAMATION OF FREEDOM should be immediately followed by
such practical results as will show that the rejoicing was not a mere out-
burst of feeling. Let us therefore endeavor to see our relations and duties in regard to this great event.

It is well known that in the great battle of Waterloo, Wellington held in reserve until late in the afternoon the bravest and most effective of his British troops, and when the final moment came to turn the doubtful fortunes of the day, he exclaimed to them, "*Up Guards, and at them!*" We long ago took ground, that, in our present war, the black man is the "reserve guard," and the hour has come when our Commander-in-chief has exclaimed to them, "up blacks, and at them!"

What, therefore, the hour demands of us is action, immediate, pressing action! And the kind of action required is well described in one of the outbursts of Mr. [Henry Highland] Garnet's eloquent speech at the Cooper Institute—"We must fight! fight! fight!"[1] It is a fight for freedom and we are bound to go in. Let us organize one regiment in every large northern city, and send our offer of services directly to the President or the Secretary of War. We have been pronounced citizens by the highest legal authority, why should we not share in the perils of citizenship? What better field to claim our rights than in the field of battle? Where will prejudice be so speedily overcome? Where will brotherhood be so quickly and firmly cemented? It is now, or never: now, if ever. A century may elapse before another opportunity shall be afforded for reclaiming and holding our withheld rights. If freedmen are accepted as soldiers to man the forts in the Mississippi and the Southern coast, why shall not free men be also accepted? If freedmen are accepted to man the fleets of the United States, why shall not free men also be received?

Let us at this moment get rid of one great difficulty in our way; let us understand thoroughly that we have got to do our own work. It is no time to stop, with Professor Wilson,[2] and cast about in search of the duties of Abolitionists in the matter of our advancement; we must depend on no one under God for our elevation. It is our own work, and always has been. All we wanted was OPPORTUNITY, and that, blessed be GOD, has come! Freedom is ours. And its fruit, equality, hangs temptingly on the tree, beckoning our own brave arms to rise and clutch it. If we rise in tens of thousands, and say to the President, "here we are, take us!" we will secure to our children and children's children all that our fathers have labored and suffered and bled for! But if we tamely suffer this hour to pass, then will we sink, in the public estimation, lower down than the vilest slanders of our foes could carry us. We know that there are partial military organizations in most of our large cities, let those having them in charge bestir themselves, assured that this time they will work for something.

There are other labors also which we must undertake. The process of transforming three millions of slaves into citizens requires the aid of intelligent colored men and women. We are, and can be, nearer to them than any other class of persons; we can enter into their feelings and attract their sympathies better than any others can. We can more patiently help and teach, and more jealously defend them, than any others can. We are manifestly destined for this work of mercy. It is for this trial God has given us the partial freedom, and such education, and the irrepressible desire for equality which consumes our souls. This labor of love and humanity His Providence has assigned to us; and we will be false to our destiny if we fail to do it. Our brethren are strangers, and naked, and hungered and athirst, and woe be unto us if we fail to minister to their wants. We are bound to be foremost in this good work; not pushing others aside, nor suffering others to push us aside, but straining every nerve to do our whole duty. We know that some of us are now engaged in this good work; what we claim is that *all* should be engaged in like manner.

And as no work can be carried on efficiently without organization, so all these separate efforts should be combined under one great national organization, which shall have power and authority to do the work thoroughly. Our leading men and women should, by correspondence, or convention, immediately get up this organization. We feel jealous of this good work, jealous that our people shall do it, and thereby assert before the world the high character which is really ours. We have started so many good organizations, and suffered the other class to enjoy the fruits of them, that this effort should be guarded at all points. No nobler work could engage the labors of men or angels. Among the objects which should engage the attention of this organization should be,

1. The furnishing of clothing to the freedmen.
2. The furnishing and supporting teachers among them.
3. The furnishing and supporting physicians among them.
4. The furnishing and supporting of instructors in household labors, economics and industries.

An organization for these and kindred purposes, got up and managed by colored persons, would command the sympathies, support and pecuniary aid of the benevolent throughout this land and all christendom.

Especially would it have a claim on the great Avery fund[3] which has hitherto laid dormant so far as its American legatees are concerned.

New York *Weekly Anglo-African*, January 17, 1863.

---

1. New York's Cooper Institute (Union), founded in 1857, maintained a library and offered working citizens a free education. Its auditorium had been the scene of many important public addresses, including Lincoln's 1860 speech outlining the Republican Party's stand on slavery. On January 5, 1863, Garnet spoke at the Cooper Institute to celebrate the Emancipation Proclamation. Yacovone, *A Voice of Thunder*, 313; Ripley et al., *The Black Abolitionist Papers*, 5:177.
2. William J. Wilson (1818–?), who usually wrote under the pseudonym "Ethiop," was a New York black abolitionist and teacher who promoted education for African Americans. Beginning in 1863, he devoted himself to freedmen's education. Ripley et al., *The Black Abolitionist Papers*, 4:144–145.
3. Founded by Charles Avery in 1858, the fund supported Christian missions in Africa and black education in the United States. In 1878 the fund established Charleston's Avery Normal Institute for African American students. Ripley et al., *The Black Abolitionist Papers*, 5:178.

Fulfilling Their Duty
Harriet and Louisa M. Jacobs to Lydia Maria Child
MARCH 26, 1864

"I am a poor Slave Mother," Harriet Jacobs wrote in 1857. But she was much more than that. The author of the most important female slave narrative, Harriet Ann Jacobs (1813?–1897) spoke for all women in chains. Her *Incidents in the Life of a Slave Girl: Written by Herself* (1861) published under the pseudonym Linda Brent, revealed a horrid tale of sexual exploitation and a seven-year ordeal in the crawl space above a storeroom in the home of her free grandmother. She escaped from slavery in 1842 and eventually was reunited with her children. From 1863 to 1866, Harriet and her daughter Louisa Matilda Jacobs (1833–?) worked among the freedmen in northern Virginia and Washington,

D.C. From 1866 to 1868 they lived in Savannah, Georgia, and assisted the newly emancipated slaves there. In 1868 Harriet Jacobs traveled to Great Britain to raise additional funds for the former slaves and to found a home for the aged in Savannah. In 1885 both women moved to Washington, D.C., where Louisa helped organize meetings of the National Association of Colored Women.

Harriet Jacobs often wrote to the antislavery and reform press to inform the public about her activities and to increase the amount of money and supplies available to promote her work. She and hundreds of other African Americans, freeborn and former slaves, traveled south to help the slaves in their transition to freedom. Harriet A. Jacobs, *Incidents in the Life of a Slave Girl, Written by Herself,* ed. Jean Fagan Yellin, (Cambridge, MA, Harvard University Press, 1987).

ALEXANDRIA, March 26, 1864.

DEAR MRS. CHILD:[1] When I went to the North, last Fall, the Freedmen here were building a school-house, and I expected it would have been finished by the time I returned. But when we arrived, we found it uncompleted. Their funds had got exhausted, and the work was at a standstill for several weeks. This was a disappointment; but the time did not hang idle on our hands, I assure you. We went round visiting the new homes of the Freedmen, which now dot the landscape, built with their first earnings as free laborers. Within the last eight months seven hundred little cabins have been built, containing from two to four rooms. The average cost from one hundred to two hundred and fifty dollars. In building school-houses or shelters for the old and decrepid, they have received but little assistance. They have had to struggle along and help themselves as they could. But though this has been discouraging, at times, it teaches them self-reliance; and that is good for them, as it is for everybody. We have over seven thousand colored refugees in this place, and, including the hospitals, less than four hundred rations are given out. This shows that they are wiling to earn their own way, and generally capable of it. Indeed, when I look back on the condition in which I first found them, and compare it with their condition now, I am convinced they are not so far behind other races as some people represent them. The two rooms we occupy were given to me by the Military Governor, to be appropriated to the use of decrepid women, when we leave them.

When we went round visiting the homes of these people, we found much to commend them for. Many of them showed marks of industry, neatness, and natural refinement. In others, chaos reigned supreme. There was nothing about them to indicate the presence of a wifely wife, or a motherly mother. They bore abundant marks of the half-barbarous, miserable condition of Slavery, from which the inmates had lately come. It made me sad to see their shiftlessness and discomfort; but I was hopeful for the future. The consciousness of working for themselves, and of having a character to gain, will inspire them with energy and enterprise, and a higher civilization will gradually come.

Children abounded in these cabins. They peeped out from every nook and corner. Many of them were extremely pretty and bright-looking. Some had features and complexions purely Anglo-Saxon; showing plainly enough the slaveholder's horror of amalgamation. Some smiled upon us, and were very ready to be friends. Others regarded us with shy, suspicious looks, as is apt to be the case with children who have had a cramped childhood. But they all wanted to accept our invitation to go to school, and so did all the parents for them.

In the course of our rounds, we visited a settlement which had received no name. We suggested to the settlers that it would be proper to name it for some champion of Liberty. We told them of the Hon. Chas. Sumner, whose large heart and great mind had for years been devoted to the cause of the poor slaves. We told how violent and cruel slaveholders had nearly murdered him for standing up so manfully in defence of Freedom. His claim to their gratitude was at once recognized, and the settlement was called Sumnerville.

Before we came here, a white lady, from Chelsea, Mass., was laboring as a missionary among the Refugees; and a white teacher, sent by the Educational Commission of Boston, accompanied us.[2] One of the freedmen, whose cabin consisted of two rooms, gave it up to us for our school. We soon found that the clamor of little voices begging for admittance far exceeded the narrow limits of this establishment.

Friends at the North had given us some articles left from one of the Fairs. To these we added what we could, and got up a little Fair here, to help them in the completion of the school-house. By this means we raised one hundred and fifty dollars, and they were much gratified by the result. With the completion of the school-house our field of labor widened, and we were joyful over the prospect of extended usefulness.

But some difficulties occurred, as there always do in the settlement of such affairs. A question arose whether the white teachers or the colored teachers should be superintendents. The freedmen had built the school-house for their children, and were Trustees of the school. So, after some discussion, it was decided that it would be best for them to hold a meeting, and settle the question for themselves. I wish you could have been at that meeting. Most of the people were slaves, until quite recently, but they talked sensibly, and I assure you that they put the question to vote in quite parliamentary style. The result was a decision that the colored teachers should have charge of the school. We were gratified by this result, because our sympathies are closely linked with our oppressed race. These people, born and bred in slavery, had always been so accustomed to look upon the white race as their natural superiors and masters, that we had some doubts whether they could easily throw off the habit; and the fact of their giving preference to colored teachers, as managers of the establishment, seemed to us to indicate that even their brief possession of freedom had begun to inspire them with respect for their race.

On the 11th of January we opened school in the new school-house, with seventy-five scholars. Now, we have two-hundred and twenty-five. Slavery had not crushed out the animal spirits of these children. Fun lurks in the corners of their eyes, dimples their mouths, tingles at their fingers' ends, and is, like a torpedo,[3] ready to explode at the slightest touch. The war-spirit has a powerful hold upon them. No one turns the other cheek for a second blow. But they evince a generous nature. They never allow an older and stronger scholar to impose upon a younger and weaker one; and when they happen to have any little delicacies, they are very ready to share them with others. The task of regulating them is by no means an easy one; but we put heart, mind, and strength freely into the work, and only regret that we have not more physical strength. Their ardent desire to learn is very encouraging, and the improvement they make consoles us for many trials. You would be astonished at the progress many of them have made in this short time. Many who less than three months ago scarcely knew the A. B. C. are now reading and spelling in words of two or three syllables. When I look at these bright little boys, I often wonder whether there is not some Frederick Douglass among them, destined to do honor to his race in the future. No one can predict, now-a-days, how rapidly the wheels of progress will move on.

There is also an evening-school here, chiefly consisting of adults and largely attended; but with that I am not connected.

On the 10th of this month, there was considerable excitement here. The bells were rung in honor of the vote to abolish slavery in Virginia.[4] Many did not know what was the cause of such a demonstration. Some thought it was an alarm of fire; others supposed the rebels had made a raid, and were marching down King St. We were, at first, inclined to the latter opinion; for, looking up that street we saw a company of the most woe-begone looking horsemen. It was raining hard, and some of them had dismounted, leading their poor jaded skeletons of horses. We soon learned that they were a portion of [Gen. Judson] Kilpatrick's cavalry, on their way to Culpepper. Poor fellows! they had had a weary tramp, and must still tramp on, through mud and rain, till they reached their journey's end. What hopeless despondency would take possession of our hearts, if we looked only on the suffering occasioned by this war, and not on the good already accomplished, and the still grander results shadowed forth in the future. The slowly-moving ambulance often passes by, with low beat of the drum, as the soldiers convey some comrade to his last resting-place. Buried on strange soil, far away from mother, wife, and children! Poor fellows! But they die the death of brave men in a noble cause. The Soldier's Burying Ground here is well cared for, and is a beautiful place.

How nobly are the colored soldiers fighting and dying in the cause of Freedom! Our hearts are proud of the manhood they evince, in spite of the indignities heaped upon them. They are kept constantly on fatigue duty, digging trenches, and unloading vessels. Look at the Massachusetts Fifty-Fourth! Every man of them a hero! marching so boldly and steadily to victory or death, for the freedom of their race, and the salvation of their country! *Their* country! It makes my blood run warm to think how that country treats her colored sons, even the bravest and the best. If merit deserves reward, surely the 54th regiment is worthy of shoulder-straps. I have lately heard, from a friend in Boston, that the rank of second-lieutenant has been conferred.[5] I am thankful there is a beginning. I am full of hope for the future. A Power mightier than man is guiding this revolution; and though justice moves slowly, it will come at last. The American people will outlive this mean prejudice against complexion. Sooner or later, they will learn that "a man's a man for a' that."

We went to the wharf last Tuesday, to welcome the emigrants returned from Hayti. It was a bitter cold day, the snow was falling, and they were barefooted and bareheaded, with scarcely rags enough to cover them. They were put in wagons and carried to Green Heights. We did what we could for them. I went to see them next day, and found that three had died during the night. I was grieved for their hard lot; but I comforted my-self with the idea that this would put an end to colonization projects. They are eight miles from here, but I shall go to see them again to-morrow. I hope to obtain among them some recruits for the [5th] Massa-chusetts Cavalry. I am trying to help Mr. [George T.] Downing[6] and Mr. [Charles L.] Remond; not for money, but because I want to do all I can to strengthen the hands of those who are battling for Freedom.

Thank you for your letter. I wish you could have seen the happy group of faces round me, at out little Fair, while I read it to them. The memory of the grateful hearts I have found among these freed men and women, will cheer me all my life.

Yours truly,
H. Jacobs and L. Jacobs

New York *National Anti-Slavery Standard*, April 16, 1864.

----

1. Lydia Maria Child (1802–1880), abolitionist, reformer, and popular author, edited and helped publish Jacobs's *Incidents in the Life of a Slave Girl* (1861). Harriet Jacobs, *Incidents in the Life of a Slave Girl: Written by Herself*, Ed. Jean Fagan Yellin, (Cambridge, MA: Harvard University Press, 1987).

2. The Boston Education Commission soon changed its name to the New Eng-land Freedman's Aid Society. By 1866 it was sending 180 teachers to the freedmen. In March 1865 the largest Northern freedmen's aid and educa-tion societies combined to form the American Freedmen's Aid Union. Willie Lee Rose, *Rehearsal for Reconstruction: The Port Royal Experiment* (New York: Vintage Books, 1964), 333–336.

3. Torpedoes, or mines, were used on land or in water and exploded on con-tact with their detonators.

4. In February 1864 a constitutional convention of loyal Virginians met in Alexandria to adopt a new constitution that abolished slavery, disfran-chised most Confederates, reduced prohibitive requirements for voting and office holding, and established the state's first system of free public educa-tion. This progressive and democratic constitution became the fundamen-tal law of the state until it was overthrown during the Reconstruction.

Richard Lowe, *Republicans and Reconstruction in Virginia, 1856–70* (Charlottesville, VA: University Press of Virginia, 1991), 22.

5. Jacobs refers to Stephen A. Swails (1832–1900), who became a second lieutenant in March 1864, although the War Department did not recognize the promotion until January 1865. This represented the first instance of a black soldier rising through the ranks to receive a combat commission, although blacks briefly had been officers in the Corps d'Afrique units, and others, such as surgeons and recruiters, had commissions out of the regular chain of command. Swails's hard-fought promotion seemed a harbinger of greater levels of equality achieved by blacks. But only a handful of black soldiers won such promotions, and most of them were awarded after Lee's surrender. Emilio, *A Brave Black Regiment*, 336; Yacovone, *A Voice of Thunder*, 257.

6. The 5th Massachusetts Cavalry, organized at Readville in May 1864, took part in action around Petersburg and guarded Confederate prisoners at Lookout Point, Maryland. Frederick Douglass's second son, Charles R. Douglass, served in the regiment. George T. Downing (1819–1903), one of the country's wealthiest African Americans, lived in New York and Rhode Island and became one of the most articulate advocates of school desegregation. He recruited men for Massachusetts's black regiments and helped in the fight for equal pay. Ripley et al., *The Black Abolitionist Papers*, 4:317–318; Wilson, *The Black Phalanx*, 464.

"Forever free! forever free!"
Charlotte Forten Grimké
MAY–JUNE 1864

The South beckoned black leaders to leave their homes and employ their education and abilities in an historic effort to transform a land and a people. With much justification, free African Americans of the North believed that the fate of the freedmen and the destiny of the race rested on their shoulders. Failure to act, and act decisively, would ensure another hundred years of servitude. As "a Coloured man," one freeborn black abolitionist announced, "I feel it my duty [to go south] and take up my cross there among my people." Their identification with the former slaves rested on the belief that white racism gave them a common purpose and a common enemy.

Most black abolitionists who went South proudly carried Northern middle-class values in their carpetbags. Their air of superiority, their attempt to remake the freedmen in their own image, revealed the profound cultural chasm that separated Northern blacks from their Southern brethren. Black abolitionists made heroic efforts to aid, educate, and uplift the freedmen, but they could not suppress their disapproval of Southern cultural ways, and they tended to view the former slaves as exotics—at best. They treated them as "untutored children," which caused much jealousy and resentment. Their tireless inculcation of the bourgeois principles of work, self-reliance, economy, "the accumulation of wealth," and the "acquisition of knowledge and virtue" grew wearisome. According to black abolitionists, freedmen utterly lacked the elements of Christian civilization, and "the principles of domestic economy," and they required strict tutoring in the "saving of time and money, the laws of health, and the training of children." The former slave Harriet Jacobs considered many of her former brethren to be "shiftless," and other black abolitionists admonished the freedmen that freedom did not mean license or "exemption from honest labor."

Northern black efforts to reform slave religion may have caused the greatest friction between Northern and Southern blacks. African American missionaries, agents of Northern evangelical Protestantism, rejected the African elements of slave religion as uncivilized, and they considered its practitioners "ignorant and fanatical." The former sergeant of the 54th Massachusetts Regiment, George E. Stephens, went to Virginia after the war and established two freedmen's schools. But he could not accept Southern black religion, which he condemned as "spurious" and "grotesque." Although he had committed himself and all his resources to the education of the former slaves, he censured them as "infidels." Missionaries who refused to adapt to local conditions failed, and some were threatened with beatings. In one case, twenty women led by an "Emperor Williams" denounced an overbearing AME Church clergyman in his pulpit. Rev. Amos G. Beman learned through hard experience that Southern blacks wanted their clergymen to be "of them 'bone of their bone flesh of their flesh'."

Charlotte Forten Grimké (1837–1914), who married Rev. Francis Grimké after the war, typified the hundreds of Northern blacks who traveled South during Reconstruction to help in the slave's transition to freedom. Daughter of the Philadelphia black elite and granddaughter of the famed businessman and abolitionist James Forten (1766–1842), Grimké received an excellent education in private schools in Philadelphia and in Salem, Massachusetts, where in 1853 she lived in the home of the popular abolitionist speaker Charles L. Remond. She then completed a course of study at the State Normal School in Salem and became the first African American in the city to teach a grammar-school class of white students.

In August 1862 the poet John Greenleaf Whittier suggested to Grimké that she take up duties in the South teaching the freedmen. The suggestion stuck, and in October she traveled to Port Royal, South Carolina, to participate in what became a model Reconstruction program. She taught reading, writing, spelling, history, and math, hoping to bring Northern middle-class values to a people systematically denied them by the institution of slavery. She believed that her work was essential to the freedmen's ability to live in what she expected to be a racially integrated future. Clearly, the experience proved thrilling, and she met a fascinating array of characters, black and white. But as so many of her Northern colleagues discovered, the culture of Southern blacks proved alien, and Grimké never got over the feeling that she was observing a bizarre and exotic people. Northern blacks had always proclaimed that they, no matter how free, felt solidarity with those in chains. The reality, however, proved not so simple. Nevertheless, Grimké produced one of the most important accounts of a free black's Reconstruction experience available to us. Her two 1864 articles for the *Atlantic Monthly* have an astonishing immediacy: they allow us to feel the heat of the day, hear the buzz of the vexing black flies, and see the gray-green Spanish moss cascading from the trees. Most important, they give us a rare window into Sea Island black culture on the eve of freedom. New York *Weekly Anglo-African,* January 3, 1863; January 30, April 16, November 19, December 24, 1864; March 18, December 23, 1865; Joe M. Richardson, *Christian Reconstruction: The American Missionary Association and Southern Blacks, 1861–1890* (Athens, GA: University of Georgia Press, 1986), 143–145, 156–159, 190–192, 199; Eric Foner, *Reconstruction: America's Unfinished Revolution, 1863–1877* (New York: Harper & Row, 1988), 100–102, 113; Clarence G. Walker, *Rock in a Weary Land: The African Methodist Episcopal Church During the Civil War and Recon-*

struction (Baton Rouge, LA: Louisiana State University Press, 1982), 47, 64–65, 75–76; Richard Blackett, *Beating Against the Barriers: The Lives of Six Nineteenth-Century Afro-Americans* (Baton Rouge, LA: Louisiana State University Press, 1986), 18–19; Yacovone, *A Voice of Thunder*, 106; Brenda Stevenson, "Introduction," *The Journals of Charlotte Forten Grimké* (New York: Oxford University Press, 1988).

LIFE ON THE SEA ISLANDS
PART I

IT WAS ON THE afternoon of a warm, murky day late in October that our steamer, the United States,[1] touched the landing at Hilton Head. A motley assemblage had collected on the wharf,—officers, soldiers, and "contrabands" of every size and hue: black was, however, the prevailing color. The first view of Hilton Head is desolate enough,—a long, low, sandy point, stretching out into the sea, with no visible dwellings upon it, except the rows of small white-roofed houses which have lately been built for the freed people.

After signing a paper wherein we declared ourselves loyal to the Government, and wherein, also, were set forth fearful penalties, should we ever be found guilty of treason, we were allowed to land, and immediately took General [Rufus] Saxton's boat, the Flora, for Beaufort. The General was on board, and we were presented to him. He is handsome, courteous, and affable, and looks—as he is—the gentleman and the soldier.

From Hilton Head to Beaufort the same long, low line of sandy coast, bordered by trees; formidable gunboats in the distance, and the gray ruins of an old fort, said to have been built by the Huguenots more than two hundred years ago. Arrived at Beaufort, we found that we had not yet reached our journey's end. While waiting for the boat which was to take us to our island of St. Helena, we had a little time to observe the ancient town. The houses in the main street, which fronts the "Bay," are large and handsome, built of wood, in the usual Southern style, with spacious piazzas, and surrounded by fine trees. We noticed in one yard a magnolia, as high as some of our largest shade-maples, with rich, dark, shining foliage. A large building which was once the Public Library is now a shelter for the freed people from Fernandina [Florida]. Did the Rebels know it, they would doubtless upturn their aristocratic noses, and exclaim in disgust, "To what bases uses," etc. We confess that it was highly satisfactory to us to see how the tables are turned, now that "the whirligig of time has brought about its revenges." We saw the market-place, in which slaves were sometimes sold; but we were told that the buying and selling at auction were usually done in Charleston. The arsenal, a large stone structure, was guarded by cannon and sentinels. The houses in the smaller streets had, mostly, a dismantled, desolate look. We saw no one in the streets but soldiers and freed people. There were indications that already Northern improvements had reached this Southern town. Among them was a wharf, a convenience that one wonders how the Southerners could so long have existed without. The more we know of their mode of life, the more are we inclined to marvel at its utter shiftlessness.

Little colored children of every hue were playing about the streets, looking as merry and happy as children ought to look,—now that the evil shadow of Slavery no longer hangs over them. Some of the officers we met did not impress us favorably. They talked flippantly, and sneeringly of the negroes, whom they found we had come down to teach, using an epithet more offensive than gentlemanly. They assured us that there was great danger of Rebel attacks, that the yellow fever prevailed to an alarming extent, and that, indeed, the manufacture of coffins was the only business that was at all flourishing at present. Although by no means daunted by these alarming stories, we were glad when the announcement of our boat relieved us from their edifying conversation.

We rowed across to Ladies Island, which adjoins St. Helena, through the splendors of a grand Southern sunset. The gorgeous clouds of crimson and gold were reflected as in a mirror in the smooth, clear waters below. As we glided along, the rich tones of the negro boatmen broke upon the evening stillness,—sweet, strange, and solemn:—

"Jesus make de blind to see,
Jesus make de cripple walk,
Jesus make de deaf to hear.
Walk in, kind Jesus!
No man can hender me."

It was nearly dark when we reached the island, and then we had a three-miles' drive through the lonely roads to the house of the superintendent. We thought how easy it would be for a band of guerrillas, had

they chanced that way, to seize and hang us; but we were in that excited, jubilant state of mind which makes fear impossible, and sang
"John Brown" with a will, as we drove through the pines and palmettos. Oh, it was good to sing that song in the very heart of Rebeldom!
Harry, our driver, amused us much. He was surprised to find that we had
not heard of him before. "Why, I thought eberybody at de Nort had
heard o' me!" he said, very innocently. We learned afterward that Mrs.
[Austa] F[rench]., who made the tour of the islands last summer, had
publicly mentioned Harry. Some one had told him of it, and he of
course imagined that he had become quite famous. Notwithstanding
this little touch of vanity, Harry is one of the best and smartest men on
the island.

Gates occurred, I seemed to us, at every few yards' distance, made in
the oddest fashion,—opening in the middle, like folding-doors, for the
accommodation of horsemen. The little boy who accompanied us as
gate-opener answered to the name of Cupid. Arrived at the headquarters of the general superintendent, Mr. [Richard] S[oule]., we were
kindly received by him and the ladies, and shown into a large parlor,
where a cheerful wood-fire glowed in the grate. It had a home-like look;
but still there was a sense of unreality about everything, and I felt that
nothing less than a vigorous "shaking-up," such as Grandfather Small-
weed[2] daily experienced, would arouse me thoroughly to the fact that I
was in South Carolina.

The Next morning L[izzie, Elizabeth Hunn]. and I were awakened by
the cheerful voices of men and women, children and chickens, in the
yard below. We ran to the window, and looked out. Women in bright-
colored handkerchiefs, some carrying pails on their heads, were crossing the yard, busy with their morning work; children were playing and
tumbling around them. On every face there was a look of serenity and
cheerfulness. My heart gave a great throb of happiness as I looked at
them, and thought, "They are free! so long down-trodden, so long
crushed to the earth, but now in their old homes, forever free!" And I
thanked God that I had lived to see this day.

After breakfast Miss [Laura] T[owne]. drove us to Oaklands, our future home. The road leading to the house was nearly choked with
weeds. The house itself was in a dilapidated condition, and the yard and
garden had a sadly neglected look. But there were roses in bloom; we
plucked handfuls of feathery, fragrant acacia-blossoms; ivy crept along

the ground and under the house. The freed people on the place seemed glad to see us. After talking with them, and giving some directions for cleaning the house, we drove to the school, in which I was to teach. It is kept in the Baptist Church,—a brick building, beautifully situated in a grove of live-oaks. These trees are the first objects that attract one's attention here: not that they are finer than our Northern oaks, but because of the singular gray moss with which every branch is heavily draped. This hanging moss grows on nearly all the trees, but on none so luxuriantly as on the live-oak. The pendants are often four or five feet long, very graceful and beautiful, but giving the trees a solemn, almost funeral look. The school was opened in September. Many of the children had, however, received instruction during the summer. It was evident that they had made very rapid improvement, and we noticed with pleasure how bright and eager to learn many of them seemed. They sang in rich, sweet tones, and with a peculiar swaying motion of the body, which made their singing the more effective. They sang "Marching Along," with great spirit, and then one of their own hymns, the air of which is beautiful and touching:—

"My sister, you want to git religion,
   Go down in de Lonesome Valley;
My brudder, you want to git religion,
   Go down in de Lonesome Valley.
            CHORUS.
"Go down in de Lonesome Valley,
Go down in de Lonesome Valley, my Lord,
Go down in de Lonesome Valley,
   To meet my Jesus dere!
"Oh, feed on milk and honey,
Oh, feed on milk and honey, my Lord,
Oh, feed on milk and honey,
   Meet my Jesus dere!
"Oh, John he brought a letter,
Oh, John he brought a letter, my Lord,
Oh, Mary and Marta read 'em,
   Meet my Jesus dere!
            CHORUS.
"Go down in de Lonesome Valley," etc.

They repeat their hymns several times, and while singing keep perfect time with their hands and feet.

On our way homeward we noticed that a few of the trees were beginning to turn, but we looked in vain for the glowing autumnal hues of our Northern forests. Some brilliant scarlet berries—the cassena—were growing along the roadside, and on every hand we saw the live-oak with its moss-drapery. The palmettos disappointed me; stiff and ungraceful, they have a bristling, defiant look, suggestive of Rebels starting up and defying everybody. The land is low and level,—not the slightest approach to a hill, not a rock, nor even a stone to be seen. It would have a desolate look, were it not for the trees, and the hanging moss and numberless vines which festoon them. These vines overrun the hedges, form graceful arches between the trees, encircle their trunks, and sometimes climb to the topmost branches. In February they begin to bloom, and then throughout the spring and summer we have a succession of beautiful flowers. First comes the yellow jessamine, with its perfect, gold-colored, and deliciously fragrant blossoms. It lights up the hedges, and completely canopies some of the trees. Of all the wild-flowers this seems to me the most beautiful and fragrant. Then we have the snow-white, but scentless Cherokee rose, with its lovely, shining leaves. Later in the season come the brilliant trumpet-flower, the passion-flower, and the innumerable others.

The Sunday after our arrival we attended service at the Baptist Church. The people came in slowly; for they have no way of knowing the hour, except by the sun. By eleven they had all assembled, and the church was well filled. They were neatly dressed in their Sunday attire, the women mostly wearing clean, dark frocks, with white aprons and bright-colored head-handkerchiefs. Some had attained to the dignity of straw hats with gay feathers, but these were not nearly as becoming nor as picturesque as the handkerchiefs. The day was warm, and the windows were thrown open as if it were summer, although it was the second day of November. It was very pleasant to listen to the beautiful hymns, and look from the crowd of dark, earnest faces within, upon the grove of noble oaks without. The people sang, "Roll, Jordan, roll," the grandest of all their hymns. There is a great, rolling wave of sound through it all.

> "Mr. Fuller settin' on de Tree ob Life,
> Fur to hear de ven Jordan roll.
> Oh, roll, Jordan! roll, Jordan! roll, Jordan roll!

CHORUS.
"Oh, roll, Jordan, roll! oh, roll, Jordan, roll!
My soul arise in heab'n, Lord,
Fur to hear de ven Jordan roll!
"Little chil'en, learn to fear de Lord,
And let your days be long.
Oh, roll, Jordan! roll, Jordan! roll, Jordan, roll!
CHORUS.
"Oh, march, de angel, march! oh, march, de
    angel, march!
My soul arise in heab'n, Lord,
Fur to hear de ven Jordan roll!"

The "Mr. [Richard] Fuller" referred to was their former minister, to whom they seem to have been much attached. He is a Southerner, but loyal, and is now, I believe, living in Baltimore. After the sermon the minister called upon one of the elders, a gray-headed old man, to pray. His manner was very fervent and impressive, but his language was so broken that to our unaccustomed ears it was quite unintelligible. After the services the people gathered in groups outside, talking among themselves, and exchanging kindly greetings with the superintendents and teachers. In their bright handkerchiefs and white aprons they made a striking picture under the gray-mossed trees. We drove afterward a mile farther, to the Episcopal Church, in which the aristocracy of the island used to worship. It is a small white building, situated in a fine grove of live-oaks, at the juncture of several roads. On one of the tombstones in the yard is the touching inscription in memory of two children,— "Blessed little lambs, and *art thou* gathered into the fold of the only true shepherd? Sweet *lillies* of the valley, and *art thou* removed to a more congenial soil?" The floor of the church is of stone, the pews of polished oak. It has an organ, which is not so entirely out of tune as are the pianos on the island. One of the ladies played, while the gentlemen sang,—old-fashioned New-England church-music, which it was pleasant to hear, but it did not thrill us as the singing of the people had done.

During the week we moved to Oaklands, our future home. The house was of one story, with a low-roofed piazza running the whole length. The interior had been throughly scrubbed and white washed; the exterior was guiltless of whitewash or paint. There were five rooms, all quite small, and several dark little entries, in one of which we found shelves lined with old medicine-bottles. These were a part of the possessions of the former owner, a Rebel physician, Dr. [Melvin M.] Sams by name. Some of them were still filled with his nostrums. Our furniture consisted of a bedstead, two bureaus, three small pine tables, and two chairs, one of which had a broken back. These were lent to us by the people. The masters, in their hasty flight from the islands, left nearly all their furniture; but much of it was destroyed or taken by the soldiers who came first, and what they left was removed by the people to their own houses. Certainly, they have the best right to it. We had made up our minds to dispense with all luxuries and even many conveniences; but it was rather distressing to have no fire, and nothing to eat. Mr. [John] H[unn]. had already appropriated a room for the store which he was going to open for the benefit of the freed people, and was superintending the removal of his goods. So L[izzie]. and I were left to our own resources. But Cupid the elder came to the rescue,—Cupid, who, we were told, was to be our right-hand man, and who very graciously informed us that he would take care of us; which he at once proceeded to do by bringing in some wood, and busying himself in making a fire in the open fireplace. While he is thus engaged, I will try to describe him. A small, wiry figure, stockingless, shoeless, out at the knees and elbows, and wearing the remnant of an old straw hat, which looked as if it might have done good service in scaring the crows from a cornfield. The face nearly black, very ugly, but with the shrewdest expression I ever saw, and the brightest, most humorous twinkle in the eyes. One glance at Cupid's face showed that he was not a person to be imposed upon, and that he was abundantly able to take care of himself, as well as of us. The chimney obstinately refused to draw, in spite of the original and very uncomplimentary epithets which Cupid heaped upon it,—while we stood by, listening to him in amusement, although nearly suffocated by the smoke. At last, perseverance conquered, and the fire began to burn cheerily. Then Amaretta, our cook,—a neat-looking black woman, adorned with the gayest of head-handkerchiefs,—made her appearance with some eggs and hominy, after partaking of which we proceeded to arrange our scanty furniture, which was soon done. In a few days we began to look civilized, having made a table-cover of some red and yellow handkerchiefs which we found among the store-goods,—a carpet of red and black woolen plaid, originally intended for frocks and shirts,—a cushion, stuffed with corn-husks and covered with calico, for a lounge, which Ben, the carpenter, had made for us of pine boards,—and lastly some corn-husk beds, which were an unspeakable luxury, after having endured agonies for several nights, sleeping on the slats of a bedstead. It is true, the said slats were covered with blankets, but these might as well have been sheets of paper for all the good they did us. What a resting-place it was! Compared to it, the gridiron of St. Lawrence—fire excepted—was a bed of roses.[3]

The first day at school was rather trying. Most of my children were very small, and consequently restless. Some were too young to learn the alphabet. These little ones were brought to school because the older children—in whose care the parents leave them while at work—could not come without them. We were therefore willing to have them come, although they seemed to have discovered the secret of perpetual motion, and tried one's patience sadly. But after some days of positive, though not severe treatment, order was brought out of chaos, and I found but little difficulty in managing and quieting the tiniest and most restless spirits. I never before saw children so eager to learn, although I had had several years' experience in New-England schools. Coming to school is a constant delight and recreation to them. They come here as other children go to play. The older ones, during the summer, work in the fields from early morning until eleven or twelve o'clock, and then come into school, after hard toil in the hot sun, as bright and as anxious to learn as ever.

Of course there are some stupid ones, but these are the minority. The majority learn with wonderful rapidity. Many of the grown people are desirous of learning to read. It is wonderful how a people who have been so long crushed to the earth, so imbruted as these have been,—and they are said to be among the most degraded negroes of the South,—can have so great a desire for knowledge, and such a capacity for attaining it. One cannot believe that the haughty Anglo-Saxon race, after centuries of such an experience as these people have had, would be very much superior to them. And one's indignation increases against those who, North as well as South, taunt the colored race with inferiority while they themselves use every means in their power to crush and degrade them, denying them every right and privilege, closing against them every avenue of elevation and improvement. Were they, under such circumstances, intellectual and refined, they would certainly be vastly superior to any other race that ever existed.

After the lessons, we used to talk freely to the children, often giving them slight sketches of some of the great and good men. Before teaching them the "John Brown" song, which they learned to sing with great spirit, Miss T[owne]. told them the story of the brave old man who had died for them. I told them about Toussaint,[4] thinking it well they should know what one of their own color had done for his race. They listened attentively, and seemed to understand. We found it rather hard to keep their attention in school. It is not strange, as they have been so entirely unused to intellectual concentration. It is necessary to interest them every moment, in order to keep their thoughts from wandering. Teaching here is consequently far more fatiguing that at the North. In the church, we had of course but one room in which to hear all the children; and to make one's self heard, when there were often as many as a hundred and forty reciting at once, it was necessary to tax the lungs very severely.

My walk to school, of about a mile, was part of the way through a road lined with trees,—on one side stately pines, on the other noble live-oaks, hung with moss and canopied with vines. The ground was carpeted with brown, fragrant pine-leaves; and as I passed through in the morning, the woods were enlivened by the delicious songs of mocking-birds, which abound here, making one realize the truthful felicity of the description in "Evangeline,"—

> The mocking-bird, wildest of singers,
> Shook from his little throat such floods of delirious music
> That the whole air and the woods and the waves seemed silent to
> listen.

The hedges were all aglow with the brilliant scarlet berries of the cassena, and on some of the oaks we observed the mistletoe, laden with its pure white, pearl-like berries. Out of the woods the roads are generally bad, and we found it hard work plodding through the deep sand.

Mr. H[unn]'s store was usually crowded, and Cupid was his most valuable assistant. Gay handkerchiefs for turbans, pots and kettles, and molasses, were principally in demand, especially the last. It was necessary to keep the molasses-barrel in the yard, where Cupid presided over it, and harangued and scolded the eager, noisy crowd, collected around, to his heart's content; while up the road leading to the house came constantly processions of men, women, and children, carrying on their heads cans, jugs, pitchers, and even bottles,—anything, indeed, that was capable of containing molasses. It is wonderful with what ease they carry all sorts of things on their heads,—heavy bundles of wood, hoes and rakes, everything, heavy or light, that can be carried in the hands; and I have seen a woman, with a bucketful of water on her head, stoop down and take up another in her hand, without spilling a drop from either.

We noticed that the people had much better taste in selecting materials for dresses than we had supposed. They do not generally like gaudy colors, but prefer neat, quiet patterns. They are, however, very fond of all kinds of jewelry. I once asked the children in school what their ears were for. "To put ring in," promptly replied one of the little girls.

These people are exceedingly polite in their manner towards each other, each new arrival bowing, scraping his feet, and shaking hands with the others, while there are constant greetings, such as, "Huddy? How's your lady?" ("How d' ye do? How's your wife?") The hand-shaking is performed with the greatest possible solemnity. There is never the faintest shadow of a smile on anybody's face during this performance. The children, too, are taught to be very polite to their elders, and it is the rarest thing to hear a disrespectful word from a child to his parent, or to any grown person. They have really what the New-Englanders call "beautiful manners."

We made daily visits to the "quarters," which were a few rods from the house. The negro-houses, on this as on most of the other plantations, were miserable little huts, with nothing comfortable or home-like about them, consisting generally of but two very small rooms,—the only way of lighting them, no matter what the state of the weather, being to leave the doors and windows open. The windows, of course, have no glass in them. In such a place, a father and mother with a large family of children are often obliged to live. It is almost impossible to teach them habits of neatness and order, when they are so crowded. We look forward anxiously to the day when better houses shall increase their comfort and pride of appearance.

Oaklands is a very small plantation. There were not more than eight or nine families living on it. Some of the people interested us much. Celia, one of the best, is a cripple. Her master, she told us, was too mean to give his slaves clothes enough to protect them, and her feet and legs were so badly frozen that they required amputation. She has a lovely face,—well-featured and singularly gentle. In every household where there was illness or trouble, Celia's kind, sympathizing face was the first to be seen, and her services were always the most acceptable.

Harry, the foreman on the plantation, a man of a good deal of natural intelligence, was most desirous of learning to read. He came in at night to be taught, and learned very rapidly. I never saw any one more determined to learn. We enjoyed hearing him talk about the "gunshoot,"—so the people call the capture of Bay Point and Hilton Head. They never weary of telling you "how Massa run when he hear de fust gun."

"Why didn't you go with him, Harry?" I asked.

"Oh, Miss, 't wasn't cause Massa didn't try to 'suade me. He tell we dat de Yankees would shoot we, or would sell we to Cuba, an' do all de wust tings to we, when dey come. 'Bery well, Sar,' says I. 'If I go wid you, I be good as dead. If I stay here, I can't be no wust; so if I got to dead, I might's well dead here as anywhere. So, I'll stay here an' wait for de "dam Yankees." Lor', Miss, I know he wasn't tellin' de truth all de time."

"But why didn't you believe him, Harry?"

"Dunno, Miss; somehow we hear de Yankees was our friends, an' dat we'd be free when dey come, an' pears like we believe *dat*."

I found this to be true of nearly all the people I talked with, and I thought it strange they should have had so much faith in the Northerners. Truly, for years past, they had had but little cause to think them very friendly. Cupid told us that his master was so daring as to come back, after he had fled from the island, at the risk of being taken prisoner by our soldiers; and that he ordered the people to get all the furniture together and take it to a plantation on the opposite side of the creek, and to stay on that side themselves. "So," said Cupid, "dey could jus' sweep us all up in a heap, an' put us in de boat. An' he telled me to take Patience—dat's my wife—an' de chil'en down to a certain pint, an' den I could come back, if I choose. Jus' as if I was gwine to be sich a goat!" added he, with a look and gesture of ineffable contempt. He and the rest of the people, instead of obeying their master, left the place and hid themselves in the woods; and when he came to look for them, not one of all his "faithful servants" was to be found. A few, principally house-servants, had previously been carried away.

In the evenings, the children frequently came in to sing and shout for us. These "shouts" are very strange,—in truth, almost indescribable.[5]

It is necessary to hear and see in order to have any clear idea of them. The children form a ring, and move around in a kind of shuffling dance, singing all the time. Four or five stand apart, and sing very energetically, clapping their hands, stamping their feet, and rocking their bodies to and fro. These are the musicians, to whose performance the shouters keep perfect time. The grown people on this plantation did not shout, but they do on some of the other plantations. It is very comical to see little children, not more than three or four years old, entering into the performance with all their might. But the shouting of the grown people is rather solemn and impressive than otherwise. We cannot determine whether it has a religious character or not. Some of the people tell us that it has, others that it has not. But as the shouts of the grown people are always in connection with their religious meetings, it is probable that they are the barbarous expression of religion, handed down to them from their African ancestors, and destined to pass away under the influence of Christian teachings. The people on this island have no songs. They sing only hymns, and most of these are sad. Prince, a large black boy from a neighboring plantation, was the principal shouter among the children. It seemed impossible for him to keep still for a moment. His performances were most amusing specimens of Ethiopian gymnastics. Amaretta the younger, a cunning, kittenish little creature of only six years old, had a remarkably sweet voice. Her favorite hymn, which we used to hear her singing to herself as she walked through the yard, is one of the oddest we have heard:—

"What makes ole Satan follow me?
Satan got nuttin' 't all fur to do wid me.
    CHORUS.
"Tiddy Rosa, hold your light!
Brudder Tony, hold your light!
All de member, hold bright light
   On Cannan's shore!"

This is one of the most spirited shouting-tunes. "Tiddy" is their word for sister.

A very queer-looking old man came in to the store one day. He was dressed in a complete suit of brilliant Brussels carpeting. Probably it had been taken from his master's house after the "gun-shoot"; but he looked so very dignified that we did not like to question him about it. The people called him Doctor Crofts,—which was, I believe, his master's name, his own being Scipio. He was very jubilant over the new state of things, and said to Mr. H[unn].,—"Don't hab me feelins hurt now. Used to hab me feelins hurt all de time. But don't hab 'em hurt now no more. " Poor old soul! We rejoiced with him that he and his brethren no longer have their "feelins" hurt, as in the old time.

On the Sunday before Thanksgiving, General Saxton's noble Proclamation was read at church.[6] We could not listen to it without emotion. The people listened with the deepest attention, and seemed to understand and appreciate it. Whittier has said of it and its writer,—"It is the most beautiful and touching official document I ever read. God bless him! 'The bravest are the tenderest.'"

General Saxton is truly worthy of the gratitude and admiration with which the people regard him. His unfailing kindness and consideration for them—so different from the treatment they have sometimes received at the hands of other officers—have caused them to have unbounded confidence in General "Saxby," as they call him.

After the service, there were six couples married. Some of the dresses were unique. One was particularly fine,—doubtless a cast-off dress of the bride's former mistress. The silk and lace, ribbons, feathers and flowers, were in a rather faded and decayed condition. But, comical as the costumes were, we were not disposed to laugh at them. We were too glad to see the poor creatures trying to lead right and virtuous lives. The legal ceremony, which was formerly scarcely known among them, is now everywhere consecrated. The constant and earnest advice of the minister and teachers has not been given in vain; nearly every Sunday there are several couples married in church. Some of them are people who have grown old together.

Thanksgiving-Day was observed as a general holiday. According to General Saxton's orders, an ox had been killed on each plantation, that the people might that day have fresh meat, which was a great luxury to them, and, indeed, to all of us. In the morning, a large number—superintendents, teachers, and freed people—assembled in the Baptist Church. It was a sight not soon to be forgotten,—that crowd of eager, happy black faces, from which the shadow of Slavery had forever passed. "Forever free! forever free!" those magical words of the Proclamation were constantly singing themselves in my soul. After an appropriate prayer and sermon by Mr. [Samuel] P[hillips]., and singing by the people, General Saxton made a short, but spirited speech, urging the young men to enlist in the regiment then forming under Colonel Higginson. Mrs. [Frances D.] Gage told the people how the slaves in Santa Cruz had secured their liberty. It was something entirely new and strange to them to hear a woman speak in public; but they listened with great attention, and seemed much interested. Before dispersing, they sang "Marching Along," which is an especial favorite with them. It was a very happy Thanksgiving-Day for all of us. The weather was delightful; oranges and figs were hanging on the trees; roses, oleanders, and japonicas were blooming out-of-doors; the sun was warm and bright; and over all shone gloriously the blessed light of Freedom,—Freedom forevermore!

One night, L[izzie]. and I were roused from our slumbers by what seemed to us loud and most distressing shrieks, proceeding from the direction of the negro-houses. Having heard of one or two attempts which the Rebels had recently made to land on the island, our first thought was, naturally, that they had forced a landing, and were trying to carry off some of the people. Every moment we expected to hear them at our doors; and knowing that they had sworn vengeance against all the superintendents and teachers, we prepared ourselves for the worst. After a little reflection, we persuaded ourselves that it could not be the Rebels; for the people had always assured us, that, in case of a Rebel attack, they would come to us at once,—evidently thinking that we should be able to protect them. But what could the shrieks mean? They ceased; then, a few moments afterwards, began again, louder, more fearful than before; then again they ceased, and all was silent. I am ashamed to confess that we had not he courage to go out and inquire into the cause of the alarm. Mr. H[unn].'s room was in another part of the house, too far for him to give us any aid. We hailed the dawn of day gladly enough, and eagerly sought Cupid,—who was sure to know everything,—to obtain from him a solution of the mystery. "Why, you was n't scared at *dat*?" he exclaimed, in great amusement; "'t wasn't nuttin' but de black sogers dat comed up to see der folks on t'oder side ob de creek. Dar was n't no boat fur 'em on dis side, so dey jus' blowed de whistle dey had, so de folks might bring one ober fur 'em. Dat was all 't was." And Cupid laughed so heartily that we felt not a little ashamed of our fears. Nevertheless, we both maintained that *we* had never seen a whistle from which could be produced sounds so startling, so distressing, so perfectly like the shrieks of a human being.

Another night, while staying at a house some miles distant from ours, I was awakened by hearing, as I thought, some one trying to open the door from without. The door was locked; I lay perfectly still, and listened intently. A few moments elapsed, and the sound was repeated; whereupon I rose, and woke Miss [Harriet] W[are]., who slept in the adjoining room. We lighted a candle, took our revolvers, and seated ourselves on the bed, keeping our weapons, so formidable in practised male hands, steadily pointed towards the door, and uttering dire threats against the intruders,—presumed to be Rebels, of course. Having maintained this tragical position for some time, and hearing no further noise, we began to grow sleepy, and extinguished our candle, returned to bed, and slept soundly till morning. But that mystery remained unexplained. I was sure that the door had been tried,—there could be no mistaking it. There was not the least probability that any of the people had entered the house, burglars are unknown on these islands, and there is nobody to be feared but the Rebels.

The last and greatest alarm we had was after we had removed from Oaklands to another plantation. I woke about two o'clock in the morning, hearing the tramp of many feet in the yard below,—the steady tramp of soldiers' feet. "The Rebels! they have come at last! all is over with us now!" I thought at once, with a desperate kind of resignation. And I lay still, waiting and listening. Soon I heard footsteps on the piazza; then the hall-door was opened, and steps were heard distinctly in the hall beneath; finally, I heard some one coming up the stairs. Then I grasped my revolver, rose, and woke the other ladies.

"There are soldiers in the yard! Somebody has opened the hall-door, and is coming up-stairs!"

Poor L[izzie]., but half awakened, stared at me in speechless terror. The same thought filled our minds. But Mrs. B., after listening for a moment, exclaimed,—

"Why, that is my husband! I know his footsteps. He is coming up-stairs to call me."

And so it proved. Her husband, who was a lieutenant in Colonel [James] Montgomery's regiment, had come up from camp with some of his men to look after deserters. The door had been unfastened by a servant who on that night happened to sleep in the house. I shall never forget the delightful sensation of relief that came over me when the whole matter was explained. It was almost overpowering; for, although I had made up my mind to bear the worst, and bear it bravely, the thought of falling into the hands of the Rebels was horrible in the extreme. A year of intense mental suffering seemed to have been compressed into those few moments.

PART II
[June 1864]

A FEW DAYS BEFORE Christmas, we were delighted at receiving a beautiful Christmas Hymn from [John Greenleaf] Whittier, written by request, especially for our children. They learned it very easily, and enjoyed singing it. We showed them the writer's picture, and told them he was a very good friend of theirs, who felt the deepest interest in them, and had written this hymn expressly for them to sing,—which made them very proud and happy. Early Christmas morning, we were wakened by the people knocking at the doors and windows, and shouting, "Merry Christmas!" After distributing some little presents among them, we went to the church, which had been decorated with holly, pine, cassena, mistletoe, and the hanging moss, and had a very Christmas-like look. The children of our school assembled there, and we gave them the nice, comfortable clothing, and the picture-books, which had been kindly sent by some Philadelphia ladies. There were at least a hundred and fifty children present. It was very pleasant to see their happy, expectant little faces. To them, it was a wonderful Christmas-Day,— such as they had never dreamed of before. There was cheerful sunshine without, lighting up the beautiful moss-drapery of the oaks, and looking in joyously through the open windows; and there were bright faces and glad hearts within. The long, dark night of the Past, with all its sorrows and its fears, was forgotten; and for the Future,—the eyes of these freed children see no clouds in it. It is full of sunlight, they think, and they trust in it, perfectly.

After the distribution of the gifts, the children were addressed by some of the gentlemen present. They then sang Whittier's Hymn, the "John Brown" song, and several of their own hymns, among them a very singular one, commencing,—

"I wonder where my mudder gone;
    Sing, O graveyard!
Graveyard ought to know me;
    Ring, Jerusalem!
Grass grow in de graveyard;
    Sing, O graveyard!
Graveyard ought to know me;
    Ring, Jerusalem!"

They improvise many more words as they sing. It is one of the strangest, most mournful things I ever heard. It is impossible to give any idea of the deep pathos of the refrain,—

"Sing, O graveyard!"

In this, and many other hymns, the words seem to have but little meaning; but the tones,—a whole lifetime of despairing sadness is concentrated in them. They sing, also, "Jehovyah, Hallelujah," which we like particularly:—

"Da foxes hab holes,
An' de birdies hab nes',
But de Son ob Man he hab not where
To lay de weary head.
CHORUS.
"Jehovyah, Hallelujah! De Lord He will purvide!
Jehovayh, Hallelujah! De Lord He will purvide!"

They repeat the words many times. "De foxes hab holes," and the succeeding lines, are sung in the most touching, mournful tones; and then the chorus—"Jehovyah, Hallelujah"—swells forth triumphantly, in glad contrast.

Christmas night, the children came in and had several grand shouts. They were too happy to keep still.

"Oh, Miss, all I want to do is to sing and shout!" said our little pet, Amaretta. And sing and shout she did, to her heart's content.

She read nicely, and was very fond of books. The tiniest children are delighted to get a book in their hands. Many of them already know their letters. The parents are eager to have them learn. They sometimes said to me,—

"Do, Miss, let de chil'en learn ebery-ting dey can. We nebber hab no chance to learn nuttin', but we wants de chil'en to learn."

They are willing to make many sacrifices that their children may attend school. One old women, who had a large family of children and grandchildren, came regularly to school in the winter, and took her seat among the little ones. She was at least sixty years old. Another woman—who had one of the best faces I ever saw—came daily, and brought her baby in her arms. It happened to be one of the best babies in the world, a perfect little "model of deportment," and allowed its mother to pursue her studies without interruption.

While taking charge of the store, one day, one of the men who came in told me a story which interested me much. He was a carpenter, living on this island, and just before the capture of Port Royal had been taken by his master to the mainland,—"the Main," as the people call it,—to assist in building some houses which were to shelter the families of the Rebels in case the "Yankees" should come. The master afterward sent him back to the island, providing him with a pass, to bring away a boat and some of the people. On his arrival he found that the Union troops were in possession, and determined to remain here with his family instead of returning to his master. Some of his fellow-servants, who had been left on "the Main," hearing that the Federal troops had come, resolved to make their escape to the islands. They found a boat of their master's, out of which a piece six feet square had been cut. In the night they went to the boat, which had been sunk in a creek near the house, measured the hole, and, after several nights' work in the woods, made a piece large enough to fit in. They then mended and sank it again, as they had found it. The next night five of them embarked. They had a perilous journey, often passing quite near the enemy's boats. They travelled at night, and in the day ran close up to the shore out of sight. Sometimes they could hear the hounds, which had been sent in pursuit of them, baying in the woods. Their provisions gave out, and they were nearly exhausted. At last they succeeded in passing all the enemy's boats, and reached one of our gun-boats in safety. They were taken on board and kindly cared for, and then sent to this island, where their families, who had no hope of ever seeing them again, welcomed them with great rejoicing.

We were also told the story of two girls, one about ten, the other fifteen, who, having been taken by their master up into the country, on
the mainland, at the time of the capture of the islands, determined to
try and escape to their parents, who had been left on the island. They
stole away at night, and travelled through the woods and swamps for
two days, without eating. Sometimes their strength gave out, and they
would sink down, thinking they could go no further; but they had brave
little hearts, and got up again and struggled on, till at last they reached
Port-Royal Ferry, in a state of utter exhaustion. They were seen there
by a boat-load of people who were also making their escape. The boat
was too full to take them in; but the people, on reaching this island, told
the children's father of their whereabouts, and he immediately took a
boat, and hastened to the ferry. The poor little creatures were almost
wild with joy when they saw him. When they were brought to their
mother, she fell down, "jes' as if she was dead,"—so our informant expressed it,—overpowered with joy on beholding the "lost who were
found."

New-Year's-Day—Emancipation-Day—was a glorious one to us.
The morning was quite cold, the coldest we had experienced; but we
were determined to go to the celebration at Camp Saxton,—the camp
of the First Regiment South Carolina Volunteers,—whither the General [Saxton] and Colonel [Thomas Wentworth] Higginson had bidden
us, on this, "the greatest day in the nation's history." We enjoyed perfectly the exciting scene on board the Flora. There was an eager, wondering crowd of the freed people in their holiday-attire, with the gayest
of head-handkerchiefs, the whitest of aprons, and the happiest of faces.
The band was playing, the flags streaming, everybody talking merrily
and feeling strangely happy. The sun shone brightly, the very waves
seemed to partake of the universal gayety, and danced and sparkled
more joyously than ever before. Long before we reached Camp Saxton
we could see the beautiful grove, and the ruins of the old Huguenot fort
near it. Some companies of the First Regiment [33rd USCT] were
drawn up in line under the trees, near the landing, to receive us. A fine,
soldierly-looking set of men; their brilliant dress against the trees (they
were then wearing red pantaloons) invested them with a semi-barbaric
splendor. It was my good fortune to find among the officers an old
friend,—and what it was to meet a friend from the North, in our iso-

lated Southern life, no one can imagine who has not experienced the pleasure. Letters were an unspeakable luxury,—we hungered for them, we could never get enough; but to meet old friends,—that was "too much, too much," as the people here say, when they are very much in earnest. Our friend took us over the camp, and showed us all the arrangements. Everything looked clean and comfortable, much neater, we were told, than in most of the white camps. An officer told us that he had never seen a regiment in which the men were so honest. "In many other camps," he said, "the colonel and the rest of us would find it necessary to place a guard before our tents. We never do it here. They are left entirely unguarded. Yet nothing has ever been touched." We were glad to know that. It is a remarkable fact, when we consider that these men have all their lives been *slaves;* and we know what the teachings of Slavery are.

The celebration took place in the beautiful grove of live-oaks adjoining the camp. It was the largest grove we had seen. I wish it were possible to describe fitly the scene which met our eyes as we sat upon the stand, and looked down on the crowd before us. There were black soldiers in their blue coats and scarlet pantaloons, the officers of this and other regiments in their handsome uniforms, and crowds of lookers-on,—men, women, and the children, of every complexion, grouped in various attitudes under the moss-hung trees. The faces of all wore a happy, interested look. The exercises commenced with a prayer by the chaplain of the regiment. An ode, written for the occasion by Professor [John] Zachos, was read by him, and then sung. Colonel Higginson then introduced Dr. [William H.] Brisbane, who read the President's Proclamation, which was enthusiastically cheered. Rev. Mr. [Mansfield] French presented to the Colonel two very elegant flags, a gift to the regiment from the Church of the Puritans,[7] accompanying them by an appropriate and enthusiastic speech. At its conclusion, before Colonel Higginson could reply, and while he still stood holding the flags in his hand, some of the colored people, of their own accord, commenced singing, "My Country, 't is of thee." It was a touching and beautiful incident, and sent a thrill through our hearts. The Colonel was deeply moved by it. He said that that reply was far more effective than any speech he could make. But he did make one of those stirring speeches which are "half battles." All hearts swelled with emotion as we listened to his glorious words,—"stirring the soul like the sound of a trumpet."

His soldiers are warmly attached to him, and he evidently feels towards them all as if they were his children. The people speak of him as "the officer who never leaves his regiment for pleasure," but devotes himself, with all his rich gifts of mind and heart, to their interests. It is not strange that his judicious kindness, ready sympathy, and rare fascination of manner should attach them to him strongly. He is one's ideal of an officer. There is in him much of the grand, knightly spirit of the olden time,—scorn of all that is mean and ignoble, pity for the weak, chivalrous devotion to the cause of the oppressed.

General Saxton spoke also, and was received with great enthusiasm. Throughout the morning, repeated cheers were given for him by the regiment, and joined in heartily by all the people. They know him to be one of the best and noblest men in the world. His Proclamation for Emancipation-Day we thought, if possible, even more beautiful than the Thanksgiving Proclamation.

At the close of Colonel Higginson's speech he presented the flags to the color-bearers, Sergeant [Prince] Rivers and Sergeant [Robert] Sutton,[8] with an earnest charge, to which they made appropriate replies. We were particularly pleased with Robert Sutton, who is a man of great natural intelligence, and whose remarks were simple, eloquent, and forcible.

Mrs. Gage also uttered some earnest words; and then the regiment sang "John Brown" with much spirit. After the meeting we saw the dress-parade, a brilliant and beautiful sight. An officer told us that the men went through the drill remarkably well,—that the ease and rapidity with which they learned the movements were wonderful. To us it seemed strange as a miracle,—this black regiment, the first mustered into the service of the United States, doing itself honor in the sight of the officers of other regiments, many of whom, doubtless, "came to scoff." The men afterwards had a great feast, ten oxen having been roasted whole for their especial benefit.

We went to the landing, intending to take the next boat for Beaufort; but finding it very much crowded, waited for another. It was the softest, loveliest moonlight; we seated ourselves on the ruined wall of the old fort; and when the boat had got a short distance from the shore the band in it commenced playing "Sweet Home." The moonlight on the water, the perfect stillness around, the wildness and solitude of the ruins, all seemed to give new pathos to that ever dear and beautiful old song. It came very near to all of us,—strangers in that strange Southern land. After a while we retired to one of the tents,—for the night-air, as usual, grew dangerously damp,—and, sitting around the bright wood-fire, enjoyed the brilliant and entertaining conversation. Very unwilling were we to go home; for, besides the attractive society, we knew that the soldiers were to have grand shouts and a general jubilee that night. But the Flora was coming, and we were obliged to say a reluctant farewell to Camp Saxton and the hospitable dwellers there in, and hasten to the landing. We promenaded the deck of the steamer, sang patriotic songs, and agreed that moonlight and water had never looked so beautiful as on that night. At Beaufort we took the row-boat for St. Helena; and the boatmen, as they rowed, sang some of the sweetest, wildest hymns. It was a fitting close to such a day. Our hearts were filled with an exceeding great gladness; for, although the Government had left much undone, we knew that Freedom was surely born in our land that day. It seemed too glorious a good to realize,—this beginning of the great work we had so longed and prayed for.

L[izzie]. and I had one day an interesting visit to a plantation about six miles from ours. The house is beautifully situated in the midst of noble pine-trees, on the banks of a large creek. The place was owned by a very wealthy Rebel family, and is one of the pleasantest and healthiest on the island. The vicinity of the pines makes it quite healthy. There were a hundred and fifty people on it,—one hundred of whom had come from Edisto Island at the time of its evacuation by our troops. There were not houses enough to accommodate them, and they had to take shelter in barns, out-houses, or any other place they could find. They afterwards built rude dwellings for themselves, which did not, however, afford them much protection in bad weather. The superintendent told us that they were well-behaved and industrious. One old woman interested us greatly. Her name was Daphne; she was probably more than a hundred years old; had had fifty grandchildren, sixty-five great-grandchildren, and three great-great-grandchildren. Entirely blind, she yet seemed very cheerful and happy. She told us that she was brought with her parents from Africa at the time of the Revolution. A bright, happy old face was hers, and she retained her faculties remarkably well. Fifteen of the people had escaped from the mainland in the previous spring. They were pursued, and one of them was overtaken by his master in the swamps. A fierce grapple ensued,—the master on horseback, the man on foot. The former drew a pistol and shot his slave through the arm, shattering it dreadfully. Still, the heroic man fought desperately, and at last succeeded in unhorsing his master, and beating him until he was senseless. He then made his escape, and joined the rest of his party.

One of the most interesting sights we saw was a baptism among the people. On one Sunday there were a hundred and fifty baptized in the creek near the church. They looked very picturesque in their white aprons and bright frocks and handkerchiefs. As they marched in pro-cession down to the river's edge, and during the ceremony, the specta-tors, with whom the banks were crowded, sang glad, triumphant songs. The freed people on this island are all Baptists.

We were much disappointed in the Southern climate. We found it much colder than we expected,—quite cold enough for as thick winter clothing as one would wear at the North. The houses, heated only by open fires, were never comfortably warm. In the floor of our sitting-room there was a large crack through which we could see the ground beneath; and through this and the crevices of the numerous doors and windows the wind came chillingly. The church in which we taught school was particularly damp and cold. There was no chimney, and we could have no fire at all. Near the close of the winter a stove came for us, but it could not be made to draw; we were nearly suffocated with smoke, and gave it up in despair. We got so thoroughly chilled and be-numbed within, that for several days we had school out-of-doors, where it was much warmer. Our school-room was a pleasant one,—for ceiling the blue sky above, for walls the grand old oaks with their beautiful moss-drapery,—but the dampness of the ground made it unsafe for us to continue the experiment.

At a later period, during a few days' visit to some friends living on the Milne Plantation, then the head-quarters of the First South-Carolina, which was on picket-duty at Port-Royal Ferry, we had an op-portunity of seeing something of Port-Royal Island. We had pleasant rides through the pine barrens. Indeed, riding on horseback was our chief recreation at the South, and we enjoyed it thoroughly. The "Se-cesh" horses, though small, poor, and mean-looking, when compared with ours, are generally excellent for the saddle, well-trained and very easy. I remember particularly one ride that we had while on Port-Royal Island. We visited the Barnwell Plantation, one of the finest places on the island. It is situated on Broad River. The grounds are extensive, and are filled with magnificent live-oaks, magnolias, and other trees. We saw one noble old oak, said to be the largest on these islands. Some of the branches have been cut off, but the remaining ones cover an area more than a hundred feet in circumference. We rode to a point whence the Rebels on the opposite side of the river are sometimes to be seen. But they were not visible that day; and we were disappointed in our long-cherished hope of seeing a "real live Rebel." On leaving the plantation, we rode through a long avenue of oaks,—the moss-hung branches forming a perfect arch over our heads,—and then for miles through the pine barrens. There was an Italian softness in the April air. Only a low, faint murmur—hardly "the slow song of the sea"—could be heard among the pines. The ground was thickly carpeted with ferns of a vivid green. We found large violets, purple and white, and azaleas of a deeper pink and heavier fragrance than ours. It was leaving Paradise, to emerge from the beautiful woods upon the public road,—the shell-road which runs from Beaufort to the Ferry. Then we entered a by-way leading to the plantation, where we found the Cherokee rose in all its glory. The hedges were white with it; it canopied the trees, and hung from their branches its long sprays of snowy blossoms and dark, shining leaves, forming perfect arches, and bowers which seemed fitting places for fairies to dwell in. How it gladdened our eyes and hearts! It was as if all the dark shadows that have so long hung over this Southern land had flitted away, and, in this garment of purest white, it shone forth transfigured, beautiful, forever-more.

On returning to the house, we were met by the exciting news that the Rebels were bringing up pontoon-bridges, and were expected to attempt crossing over near the Ferry, which was only two or three miles from us. Couriers came in every few moments with various reports. A superintendent whose plantation was very near the Ferry had been watching through his glass the movements on the opposite side, and reported that the Rebels were gathering in large force, and evidently preparing for some kind of demonstration. A messenger was despatched to Beaufort for reinforcements, and for some time we were in a state of expectancy, not entirely without excitement, but entirely without fear. The officers evidently enjoyed the prospect of a fight. One of them assured me that I should have the pleasure of seeing a Rebel shell during the afternoon. It was proposed that the women should be sent into

Beaufort in an ambulance; against which ignoble treatment we indignantly protested, and declared our intention of remaining at out post,
if the Colonel would consent; and finally, to our great joy, the best of
colonels did consent that we should remain, as he considered it quite
safe for us to do so. Soon a light battery arrived, and during the evening
a brisk firing was kept up. We could hear the explosion of the shells. It
was quite like being in the war; and as the firing was principally on our
side, and the enemy was getting the worst of it, we rather enjoyed it. For
a little while the Colonel read to us, in his spirited way, some of the stirring "Lays of the Old Cavaliers."[9] It was just the time to appreciate them
thoroughly, and he was of all men the fittest person to read them. But
soon came a courier, "in hot haste," to make report of the doings without, and the reading was at an end. In the midst of the firing, Mrs. [G.
W.] D[ewhurst]. and I went to bed, and slept soundly until morning. We
learned afterward that the Rebels had not intended to cross over, but
were attempting to take the guns off one of our boats, which they had
sunk a few days previous. The timely arrival of the battery from Beaufort prevented them from accomplishing their purpose.

In April we left Oaklands, which had always been considered a particularly unhealthy place during the summer, and came to "Seaside," a
plantation on another and healthier part of the island. The place contains nearly a hundred people. The house is large and comparatively
comfortable. Notwithstanding the name, we have not even a distant
glimpse of the sea, although we can sometimes hear its roar. At low tide
there is not a drop of water to be seen,—only dreary stretches of marsh-
land, reminding us of the sad outlook of Mariana in the Moated
Grange,—

"The level waste and rounding gray."[10]

But at night we have generally a good sea-breeze, and during the
hottest weather the air is purer and more invigorating than in many
parts of the island.

On this, as on several other large plantations, there is a "Praise-
House," which is the special property of the people. Even in the old days
of Slavery, they were allowed to hold meetings here; and they still keep
up the custom. They assemble on several nights of the week, and on

Sunday afternoons. First, they hold what is called the "Praise-Meeting," which consists of singing, praying, and preaching. We have heard some of the old negro preachers make prayers that were really beautiful and touching. In these meetings they sing only the church-hymns which the Northern ministers have taught them, and which are far less suited to their voices than their own. At the close of the Praise-Meeting they all shake hands with each other in the most solemn manner. Afterward, as a kind of appendix, they have a grand "shout," during which they sing their own hymns. Maurice, an old blind man, leads the singing. He has a remarkable voice, and sings with the greatest enthusiasm. The first shout that we witnessed in the Praise-House impressed us very much. The large, gloomy room, with its blackened walls,—the wild, whirling dance of the shouters,—the crowd of dark, eager faces gathered around,—the figure of the old blind man, whose excitement could hardly be controlled, and whose attitude and gestures while singing were very fine,—and over all, the red glare of the burning pine-knot, which shed a circle of light around it, but only seemed to deepen and darken the shadows in the other parts of the room,—these all formed a wild, strange, and deeply impressive picture, not soon to be forgotten.

Maurice's especial favorite is one of the grandest hymns that we have yet heard:—

"De tallest tree in Paradise
De Christian calls de Tree ob Life,
An' I hope dat trumpet blow me home
To my New Jerusalem.
            Chorus.
"Blow, Gabriel! trumpet, blow louder, louder!
An' I hope dat trumpet blow me home
To my New Jerusalem!
"Paul and Silas jail-bound
Sing God's praise both night and day,
An' I hope sat trumpet blow me home
To my New Jerusalem.
            Chorus.
"Blow, Gabriel! trumpet, blow louder, louder!
An' I hope dat trumpet blow me home
To my New Jerusalem!"

The chorus has a glad, triumphal sound, and in singing it the voice of old Maurice rings out in wonderfully clear, trumpet-like tones. His blindness was caused by a blow on the head from a loaded whip. He was struck by his master in a fit of anger. "I feel great distress when I become blind," said Maurice; "but den I went to seek de Lord; and eber since I know I see in de next world, I always hab great satisfaction." We are told that the master was not a "hard man" except when in a passion, and then he seems to have been very cruel.

One of the women on the place, Old Bess, bears on her limbs many marks of the whip. Some of the scars are three and four inches long. She was used principally as a house-servant. She says, "Ebery time I lay de table I put cow-skin on one end, an' I git beatin' and thumpin' all de time. Hab all kinds o' work to do, and sich a gang {of children} to look after! One person couldn't git along wid so much work, so it go wrong, and den I git beatin'."

But the cruelty of Bess's master sinks into insignificance, when compared with the far-famed wickedness of another slave-holder, known all over the island as "Old Joe Eddings." There seem to have been no bounds to his cruelty and licentiousness; and the people tell tales of him which make one shudder. We were once asking some questions about him of an old, half-witted woman, a former slave of his. The look of horror and loathing which overspread her face was perfectly indescribable, as, with upraised hands, she exclaimed, "What! Old Joe Eddings? Lord, Missus, he second to none in de world but de Debil!" She had, indeed, good cause to detest him; for, some years before, her daughter, a young black girl, maddened by his persecutions, had thrown herself into the creek and been drowned, after having been severely beaten for refusing to degrade herself. Outraged, despised, and black, she yet preferred death to dishonor. But theses are things too heart-sickening to dwell upon. God alone knows how many hundreds of plantations, all over the South, might furnish a similar record.

Early in June, before the summer heat had become unbearable, we made a pleasant excursion to Edisto Island. We left St. Helena village in the morning, dined on one of the gun-boats stationed near our island, and in the afternoon proceeded to Edisto in two row-boats. There were six of us, besides an officer and the boats' crews, who were armed with guns and cutlasses. There was no actual danger; but as we were going into the enemy's country, we thought it wisest to guard against surprises. After a delightful row, we reached the island near sunset, landing at a place called Eddingsville, which was a favorite summer resort with the aristocracy of Edisto. It has a fine beach several miles in length. Along the beach there is a row of houses, which must once have been very desirable dwellings, but have now a desolate, dismantled look. The sailors explored the beach for some distance, and returned, reporting "all quiet, and nobody to be seen"; so we walked on, feeling quite safe, stopping here and there to gather the beautiful tiny shells which were buried deep in the sands.

We took supper in a room of one of the deserted houses, using for seats some old bureau-draws turned edgewise. Afterward we sat on the piazza, watching the lightning playing from a low, black cloud over a sky flushed with sunset, and listening to the merry songs of the sailors who occupied the next house. They had built a large fire, the cheerful glow of which shone through the windows, and we could see them dancing, evidently in great glee. Later, we had another walk on the beach, in the lovely moonlight. It was very quiet then. The deep stillness was broken only by the low, musical murmur of the waves. The moon shone bright and clear over the deserted houses and gardens, and gave them a still wilder and more desolate look.

We went within-doors for the night very unwillingly. Having, of course, no beds, we made ourselves as comfortable as we could on the floor, with boat-cushions, blankets, and shawls. No fear of Rebels disturbed us. There was but one road by which they could get to us, and on that a watch was kept, and in case of their approach, we knew we should have ample time to get to the boats and make our escape. So, despite the mosquitoes, we had a sound night's sleep.

The next morning we took the boats again, and followed the course of the most winding of little creeks. In and out, in and out, the boats went. Sometimes it seemed as if we were going into the very heart of the woods; and through the deep silence we half expected to hear the sound of a Rebel rifle. The banks were over-hung with a thick tangle of shrubs and bushes, which threatened to catch our boats, as we passed close beneath their branches. In some places the stream was so narrow that we ran aground, and then the men had to get out, and drag and pull with all their might before we could be got clear again. After a row full of excitement and pleasure, we reached our place of destination,—the Ed-

dings Plantation, whither some of the freedmen had preceded us in their
search for corn. It must once have been a beautiful place. The grounds
were laid out with great taste, and filled with fine trees, among which we
noticed particularly the oleander, laden with deep rose-hued and deliciously fragrant flowers, and the magnolia, with its wonderful, large blossoms, which shone dazzlingly white among the dark leaves. We explored
the house,—after it had first been examined by our guard, to see that no
foes lurked there,—but found nothing but heaps of rubbish, an old bedstead, and a bathing-tub, of which we afterward made good use. When
we returned to the shore, we found that the tide had gone out, and between us and the boats lay a tract of marsh-land, which it would have
been impossible to cross without a wetting. The gentlemen determined
on wading. But what were we to do? In this dilemma somebody suggested
the bathing-tub, a suggestion which was eagerly seized upon. We were
placed in it, one at a time, borne aloft in triumph on the shoulders of four
stout sailors, and safely deposited in the boat. But, through a mistake, the
tub was not sent back for two of the ladies, and they were brought over
on the crossed hands of two of the sailors, in the "carry-a-lady-to-
London" style. Again we rowed through the windings of the creek, then
out into the open sea, among the white, exhilarating breakers,—reached
the gun-boat, dined again with its hospitable officers, and then returned
to our island, which we reached after nightfall, feeling thoroughly tired,
but well pleased with our excursion.

From what we saw of Edisto, however, we did not like it better than
our own island,—except, of course, the beach; but we are told that farther in the interior it is much more beautiful. The freed people, who left
it at the time of its evacuation, think it the loveliest place in the world,
and long to return. When we were going, Miss T[owne].—the much-
loved and untiring friend and physician of the people—asked some
whom we met if we should give their love to Edisto. "Oh, yes, yes, Miss!"
they said. "Ah, Edisto a beautiful city!" And when we came back, they
inquired, eagerly,—"How you like Edisto? How Edisto stan'?" Only the
fear of again falling into the hands of the "Secesh" prevents them from
returning to their much-loved home.

As the summer advanced, the heat became intense. We found it almost overpowering, driving to school near the middle of the day, as we
were obliged to do. I gave up riding, and mounted a sulky, such as a sin-

gle gentleman drives in at the North. It was exceedingly high, and I found it no small task to mount up into it. Its already very comical appearance was enhanced by the addition of a cover of black India-rubber cloth, with which a friend kindly provided me. Thus adorned, it looked like the skeleton of some strange creature surmounted by a huge bonnet, and afforded endless amusement to the soldiers we chanced to meet, who hailed its appearance with shouts of laughter, and cries of "Here comes the Calithumpian!" This unique vehicle, with several others on our island, kindred, but not quite equal to it, would create a decided sensation in the streets of a Northern city.

No description of life on these islands would be complete without a word concerning the fleas. They appeared at the opening of spring, and kept constantly "risin'," as the people said, until they reached a height the possibility of which we had never conceived. We had heard and read of fleas. We had never *realized* them before. Words utterly fail to describe the tortures we endured for months from these horrible little tyrants. Remembering our sufferings "through weary day and weary *night*," we warn everybody not gifted with extraordinary powers of endurance to beware of a summer on the Sea Islands.

Notwithstanding the heat, we determined to celebrate the Fourth of July as worthily as we could. The freed people and the children of the different schools assembled in the grove near the Baptist Church. The flag was hung across the road, between two magnificent live-oaks, and the children, being grouped under it, sang "The Star-Spangled Banner" with much spirit. Our good General could not come, but addresses were made by Mr. [Edward] P[hilbrick].,—the noble-hearted founder of the movement for the benefit of the people here, and from first to last their stanch and much-loved friend,—by Mr. [James] L[ynch].,[11] a young colored minister, and others. Then the people sang some of their own hymns; and the woods resounded with the grand notes of "Roll, Jordan, roll." They all afterward partook of refreshments, consisting of molasses and water,—a very great luxury to them,—and hard-tack.

Among the visitors present was the noble young Colonel [Robert Gould] Shaw, whose regiment was then stationed on the island. We had met him a few nights before, when he came to our house to witness one of the people's shouts. We looked upon him with the deepest interest. There was something in his face finer, more exquisite, than one often sees in a man's face, yet it was full of courage and decision. The rare and

singular charm of his manner drew all hearts to him. He was deeply interested in the singing and appearance of the people. A few days afterwards we saw his regiment on dress-parade, and admired its remarkably
fine and manly appearance. After taking supper with the Colonel we sat
outside the tent, while some of his men entertained us with excellent
singing. Every moment we became more and more charmed with him.
How full of life and hope and lofty aspirations he was that night! How
eagerly he expressed his wish that they might soon be ordered to
Charleston! "I do hope they will give *us* a chance," he said. It was the
desire of his soul that his men should do themselves honor,—that they
should prove themselves to an unbelieving world as brave soldiers as
though their skins were white. And for himself, he was like the Cheva-
lier of old, "without reproach or fear." After we had mounted our horses
and rode away, we seemed still to feel the kind of clasp of his hand,—to
hear the pleasant, genial tones of his voice, as he bade us good-bye, and
hoped that we might meet again. We never saw him afterward. In two
short weeks came the terrible massacre at Fort Wagner, and the beautiful head of the young hero and martyr was laid low in the dust. Never
shall we forget the heart-sickness with which we heard of his death. We
could not realize it at first,—we, who had seen him so lately in all the
strength and glory of his young manhood. For days we clung to a vain
hope; then it fell away from us, and we knew that he was gone. We knew
that he died gloriously, but still it seemed very hard. Our hearts bled for
the mother whom he so loved,—for the young wife, left desolate. And
then we said, as we say now,—"God comfort them! He only can." During a few of the sad days which followed the attack on Fort Wagner, I
was in one of the hospitals of Beaufort, occupied with the wounded soldiers of the Fifty-fourth Massachusetts. The first morning was spent in
mending the bullet-holes and rents in their clothing. What a story they
told! Some of the jackets of the poor fellows were literally cut in pieces.
It was pleasant to see the brave, cheerful spirit among them. Some of
them were severely wounded, but they uttered no complaint; and in
their letters which they dictated to their absent friends there was no
word of regret, but the same cheerful tone throughout. They expressed
an eager desire to get well, that they might "go at it again." Their at-
tachment to their young colonel was beautiful to see. They felt his death
deeply. One and all united in the warmest and most enthusiastic praise
of him. He was, indeed, exactly the person to inspire the most loyal de-

votion in the hearts of his men. And with everything to live for, he had given up his life for them. Heaven's best gifts had been showered upon him, but for them he had laid them all down. I think they truly appreciated the greatness of the sacrifice. May they ever prove worthy of such a leader! Already, they, and the regiments of freedmen here, as well, have shown that true manhood has no limitations of color.

Daily the long-oppressed people of these islands are demonstrating their capacity for improvement in learning and labor. What they have accomplished in one short year exceeds our utmost expectations. Still the sky is dark; but through the darkness we can discern a brighter future. We cannot but feel that the day of final and entire deliverance, so long and often so hopelessly prayed for, has at length begun to dawn upon this much-enduring race. An old freedman said to me one day, "De Lord make me suffer long time, Miss. 'Peared like we nebber was gwine to git troo. But now we's free. He bring us all out right at las'." In their darkest hours they have clung to Him, and we know He will not forsake them.

> "The poor among men shall rejoice,
> For the terrible one is brought to nought."

While writing these pages I am once more nearing Port Royal. The Fortunate Isles of Freedom are before me. I shall again tread the flower-skirted wood-paths of St. Helena, and the sombre pines and beaded oaks shall whisper in the sea-wind their grave welcome. I shall dwell again among "mine own people." I shall gather my scholars about me, and see smiles of greeting break over their dusk faces. My heart sings a song of thanksgiving, at the thought that even I am permitted to do something for a long-abused race, and aid in promoting a higher, holier, and happier life on the Sea Islands.

"Life in the Sea Islands" parts I & II, *Atlantic Monthly* 13 (May–June 1864): 587–596, 666–676.

---

1. Forten arrived at Hilton Head on the steamer *United States* on the evening of October 28, 1862. Brenda Stevenson, ed., *The Journals of Charlotte Forten Grimké* (New York: Oxford University Press, 1988), 388.

2. An emaciated and unappealing character in Charles Dickens's *Bleak House* (New York: Harper and Bros., 1852–1853), first American edition.

3. According to legend, Saint Lawrence was martyred in 258 C.E. by roasting on a gridiron. When he had spent sufficient time on one side he allegedly said to his executioner "Let my body be turned; one side is broiled enough." Michael Walsh, ed., *Butler's Lives of the Saints* (San Francisco, CA: Harper-Collins, 1991), 245.

4. Toussaint L'Ouverture (1748–1803), the slave-born Haitian revolutionary who became a great symbol of liberty and power to African Americans. A representative sketch of L'Ouverture is in William Wells Brown's *The Black Man: His Antecedents, His Genius, and His Achievements* (New York: Thomas Hamilton, 1863); Yacovone, *A Voice of Thunder*, 225, 226.

5. A shout, or ring shout, a characteristic African ceremony found particularly in Dahomey, is a counterclockwise dance-and-song ceremony directed at ancestors and African gods. In some areas of the South, shouts were performed by individuals and in groups, and some took on great complexity, nevertheless, the ceremony helped to culturally bind blacks of differing regional and tribal backgrounds. Because of the high percentage of African Americans in the Sea Islands, the persistence of the slave trade, and the regions' relative isolation, ring shouts and other African cultural practices remained strong, especially in combination with elements of Christianity. Sterling Stucky, *Slave Culture: Nationalist Theory and the Foundations of Black America* (New York: Oxford University Press, 1987), 12, 24, 36, 43, 57.

6. Saxton issued a proclamation declaring November 27, 1862, a day of thanksgiving and prayer to celebrate Union victories and the freedom of slaves on the Sea Islands. Stevenson, *The Journals of Charlotte Forten Grimké*, 592.

7. Church of Rev. George B. Cheever in New York City. Cheever (1807–1890) was an ardent abolitionist and a prolific author. Louis Ruchames and Walter Merrill, eds., *The Letters of William Lloyd Garrison*, 6 vols. (Cambridge, MA: Harvard University Press, 1971–1981), 4:626.

8. Both men belonged to Higginson's regiment. Prince Rivers had been a "crack coachman" in Beaufort for P. G. T. Beauregard before the Civil War and had petitioned the governor of South Carolina on behalf of a group of slaves. Confederate authorities offered a $2,000 reward for his capture. Smart, strong, tall, and with the gait of a panther, Rivers cut a striking figure, and his authority in the regiment was unmatched. In 1868 he lived in violence-prone Edgefield County and served in the state legislature and as a delegate to the 1868 constitutional convention. "If Sergeant Rivers was a natural king among my dusky soldiers, Corporal

Robert Sutton was the natural prime-minister." Sutton, a skilled river pilot upon whom Higginson depended, received a promotion to sergeant in 1863. Higginson, *Army Life in a Black Regiment*, 57–58, 62–63, 83, 94–95; Alrutheus A. Taylor, *The Negro in South Carolina During the Reconstruction* (Washington, DC: Association for the Study of Negro Life and History, 1924), 127; Thomas Holt, *Black Over White: Negro Political Leadership in South Carolina During Reconstruction* (Urbana, IL: University of Illinois Press, 1979), 47, 62, 78, 79, 80.

9. Grimké slightly misstated the title of an extremely popular book by William E. Aytour, *Lays of the Scottish Cavaliers* (Edinburgh: William Blackwood & Sons, 1849).

10. A rendering of: "The level waste, the rounding gray," from Alfred Lord Tennyson's "Mariana in the Moated Grange," *Poems, Chiefly Lyrical* (London: E. Wilson, 1830).

11. James Lynch, a Baltimore black abolitionist who had attended Dartmouth College, briefly served as chaplain of the 54th Massachusetts Regiment. On July 5 he conducted one of his first sermons for the regiment. After the war, Lynch organized the AME Church in Charleston. Yacovone, *A Voice of Thunder*, 272; Taylor, *The Negro in South Carolina During the Reconstruction*, 113.

12

Conditions in Dixie

"I am about thirteen years old"
Jim Heiskell
MARCH 30, 1864

The following three brief documents graphically and poignantly illustrate the conditions suffered by African American civilians and slaves during the Civil War. While we might expect that slaves would endure much brutality by their owners in the Confederacy, the slaves and free blacks in these narratives lived in areas occupied by Union troops. The provisions of the Emancipation Proclamation allowed loyal slave owners, or those who professed to be, to retain both their slaves and their full rights to retrieve them under provisions of the hated Fugitive Slave Law. They also, as described in the narrative of the unfortunate Jim Heiskell, could discipline their "property" with all the brutality they chose to employ. While Congress specifically barred Union soldiers from participating in the recapture of runaway slaves, many flouted the law or found indirect ways to assist slave owners. Others, such as the Union officers who took the following depositions, sought to assist blacks who lodged complaints at their offices. But the army proved an inefficient guardian of civilians, especially when legal bondage, guaranteed by Congress and the Emancipation Proclamation, enormously complicated the legal terrain. In cities, towns, and in the camps set up reluctantly by Union forces, slaves arrived in increasing numbers as the war dragged on, placing unprecedented burdens on an ill-prepared and largely insensitive Union army.

[Knoxville, Tennessee. March 30, 1864]

STATEMENT OF "JIM" HEISKELL

MY NAME IS JIM; I have been living on Bull run, with a man by the name of Pierce; they call him Cromwell Pierce. I run off from him nearly two months ago, because he treated me so mean: he half starved and whipped me. I was whipped three or four times a week, sometimes with a cowhide, and sometimes with a hickory. He put so much work on me, I could not do it; chopping & hauling wood and lumber logs. I am about thirteen years old. I got a pretty good meal at dinner, but he only gave us a half pint of milk for breakfast and supper, with cornbread. I ran away to town; I had a brother "Bob" living in Knoxville, and other boys I knew. I would have staid on the plantation if I had been well used. I wanted also to see some pleasure in town. I hired myself to Capt. Smith as a servant, and went to work as a waiter in Quarter Master Winslow's office as a waiter for the mess. After Capt. Winslow went home, I went to live with Bob, helping him.

Last Friday just after dinner, I saw Pierce Mr. Heiskell's overseer. He caught me on Gay street, he ran after me, and carried me down Cumberland street to Mr. Heiskell's house. Mr. Heiskell, his wife and two sons, and a daughter were in the house. Mr. Heiskell asked me what made me run away; he grabbed me by the back of the ears, and jerked me down on the floor on my face; Mr. Pierce held me & Mr. Heiskell put irons on my legs. Mr. Heiskell took me by the hair of my head, and Mr. Pierce took me around my body, they carried me upstairs, and then Mr. Heiskell d[r]agged me into the room by my hair. They made me stand up, and then they laid me down on my belly & pulled off my breeches as far as they could, and turned my shirt and jacket up over my head. (I heard Mr[.] Heskell ask for the cowhide before he started with me upstairs.) Mr. Pierce held my legs, and Mr. Heiskell got a straddle of me, and whipped me with the rawhide on my back & legs. Mr. Pierce is a large man, and very strong. Mr. Heiskell rested two or three times, and begun again. I hollowed—"O, Lord" all the time. They whipped me, it seemed to me, half an hour. They then told me to get up and dress, and said if I didn't behave myself up there they would come up again and whip me again at night. The irons were left on my legs. Mr. Heiskell came up at dark and asked me what that "yellow nigger was talking to me about". He meant my brother Bob, who had been talking to me opposite the house. I was standing up and when he (Mr. Heiskell) asked me about the "yaller nigger", he kicked me with his right foot on my hip and knocked me over on the floor, as the irons were on my feet, I could not catch myself. I knew my brother Bob was around the house trying to get me out. About one hour by sun two soldiers came to the house, one staid & the other went away. I saw them through the window. They had sabres. I thought they had come to guard me to keep Bob from getting me. I heard Bob whis[t]ling, and I went to the window and looked through the curtain. Bob told me to hoist the window, put something under it & swing out of the window. I did as my brother told me, and hung by my hands. Bob said "Drop," but I said I was afraid I would hurt myself. Bob said "Wait a minute and I will get a ladder". He brought a ladder and put it against the house, under the window. I got halfway down before they hoisted the window; I fell & Bob caught me and run off with me in his arms. I saw Mr. Pierce sitting at the window, he had a double-barreled gun in his hands. By the time I could count three I heard a gun fired two or three times, quick, I heard Mr. Pierce call "Jim" "Jim" and the guards hollered "halt; halt!" I had no hat or shoes on. We both hid, and laid flat on the ground. I saw the guard, running around there hunting for us. After lying there until the guards had gone away, we got up and Bob carried me to a friend's house. I had the irons on my legs. I got some supper and staid there until next day. My irons were taken off by a colored man, who carried me to the hospital. I am now employed working in the hospital N° I.

his

–signed– JIM X HEISKELL–

mark

Records of the General Agent, RG 366, National Archives. Reprinted in Berlin et al., eds., *Freedom: The Destruction of Slavery*, 1:320–322.

"I was in a miserable-destitute condition"
Mrs. Amey Carrington
August 10, 1865

Memphis Tenn August 10th1865.

PERSONALLY APPEARED BEFORE ME Edward R[.] Beach Ist Lieutenant and Acting Adjutant 88th USC Infy.1 Mrs Amey Carrington (colored) who after being duly qualified according to law testified as follows.

On or about the 27th day of June 1863, I was driven from home at Germantown Tenn by my master Mr Larodes—without provication. I immediately went to Memphis Tenn where my husband was living at the time. I was in a miserable-destitute condition with hardly enough clothing to cover my nakedness. and have received no mony or clothing from my master since December 1860. I left my children (four in number) with my master who hired them out. and has received compensation for their services since July 1863. I had made several efforts since I was driven from home to get posession of my children but failed in every instance until the 23rd day of July 1865, when I succeeded in finding them and with the assistance of Lieut Col Wedelstandt2 Asst. Topl Engineer D.W.T. brought them to Memphis Tenn My children were in a destitute condition with hardly any clothing on them and had ben treated in a brutal manner. My children nor my self have not received mony or clothing as compensation for their services.

Memphis, Tennessee, Provost Marshal of Freedmen, Affidavits & Statements, RG 105, National Archives. Reprinted in Berlin et al., eds., *Freedom: The Destruction of Slavery*, 1:307–308.

---

1. The 88th USCT, organized in Memphis, Tennessee, was consolidated with the 3rd U.S. Colored Heavy Artillery in December 1865. Wilson, *The Black Phalanax*, 475.
2. Carrington refers to Lt. Col. Charles Wedelstaedt of the 88th USCT.

Defying the Fugitive Slave Law
Dola Ann Jones to Col. Jonathan Eaton, Jr.
AUGUST 16, 1865

Washington, Aug, 16, 1865.

COLONEL: I HAVE THE HONOR to state that in Nov. 1863, my husband, Jno. Jones, and Richard Coats, & Caleb Day—(Colored men) were arrested & tried at Port Tobacco, Md, and sentenced to be confined in the Penitentiary at Baltimore, for the term of eleven years & eleven months, for assisting three colored women, & four children, to escape from slavery.

Richard Coats was the slave of Geo. Wm. Carpenter, of Harris Cove, (opposite Acquia Creek); Said Carpenter has several times, been confined in the "Old Capitol" for smuggling goods to the rebels.

Before turning my husband, Jno. Jones—& Richard Coats over to the authorities—Carpenter whipped them so severely with a stave—in which he had bored auger holes, that they suffered severely for over two months.— Caleb Day & my husband—Jno. Jones were free men.

I would earnestly, and respectfully request that you use your influence to procure for the parties named full pardon—& release from imprisonment.— Very Respectfully Your Obt. Servant,

her

DOLA ANN   X   JONES

mark

Unregistered Letters Received, series 457 RG 105, National Archives. Reprinted in Berlin et al., eds., *Freedom: The Destruction of Slavery*, 1:376–377.

"The Story of Mattie J. Jackson"
Mattie J. Jackson
1866

Mattie Jackson's narrative, reproduced in its entirety here, pays tribute to the heroic actions of her mother, Ellen Turner, to keep her slave family together under harrowing conditions. The beatings, separations, and constant cruelty represent an indictment of the institution of slavery and a complete repudiation of the racist notion of the contented slave. Her narrative is not, however, intended to wrench sympathy from the reader, but to assert the African American call for justice and racial equality. It also represents a rare assertion of female slave heroism in a genre dominated by black male voices.

It is unusual that Jackson knew so much about her family and its past, and even more unusual that her mother could read. Ellen Turner's literacy inspired anger in her owners, and when they found a picture of Abraham Lincoln on her wall, she was beaten and confined to a slave trader's yard for a month. Her father, Westly Jackson, was sold away to a neighboring Missouri plantation and eventually ran away to Chicago. Her mother also attempted to flee with her children; they reached Illinois before they were recaptured and sold to the Lewis family. The Lewis's barbarism knew few bounds. In one particularly cruel act, they confined Jackson's brother in a box for his entire brief life. Her mother later "remarried," only to have Lewis humiliate her second husband, who retaliated by fleeing to Canada, again leaving Turner alone to care for her family.

The Civil War brought no relief. An especially savage beating sent Jackson to Union troops, who apparently boarded her so she would not have to return to her master. But she did eventually return and she, as had her mother before her, spent weeks in a slave trader's yard as punishment. Lewis's action violated instructions he had received from a Union commander, and in an unusual move, he was made to pay for his cruelty with 100 lashes and a $3,000 fine. The punishment only fired Lewis's anger. He then sold Jackson and her family and smuggled them to Kentucky, where they were resold to separate masters. For two additional years her family remained in chains, but sometime in late 1864 Jackson made her escape on a steamer and reached Indianapolis and freedom. After the war, Jackson and her mother returned to Missouri, where they met the Lewises in a memorable encounter. The eventual reunification of the Jackson's family in Massachusetts represented an astonishing achievement.

The Story of Mattie J. Jackson appeared in 1866, as the South began to resist Reconstruction and President Andrew Johnson sought to quickly reestablish national reunification based on white rule. It represented a timely reminder, if one was needed, of what had caused the war and the direction that postwar politics should take. Jackson's amanuensis, "Dr. L. S. Thompson," clearly wished *The Story of Mattie J. Jackson* to influence the course of Reconstruction and gain support for a people "who have been bound down by a dominant race in circumstances over which they had no control." It sought to smash lingering racial stereotypes and, through Jackson and her mother, sympathetically illuminate black worth and character.

A mysterious figure, Thompson revealed on the book's title page that she was the former "Mrs. Schuyler," and in the foreword she identified herself as a black woman. It is likely that she was the new wife of George Brown, Jackson's stepfather who had earlier fled from the Lewis family's cruelty. There is, however, sufficient ambiguity in the story to provide some anonymity for those involved. Thompson also admitted to being only twenty years old, and she explained that she published Jackson's narrative to help defray the costs of her own education.

Based on the tradition of the antebellum slave narratives, this text customarily would have included a foreword by a prominent abolitionist or a letter from a witness (usually white) to events in the book to establish credibility for a presumably white audience. Here, however, the call for racial equality and justice relies entirely on the credibility of black women's voices. William L. Andrews, "Introduction," *Six Women's Slave Narratives* (New York: Oxford University Press, 1988).

MATTIE'S STORY

MY ANCESTORS WERE transported from Africa to America at the time the slave trade flourished in the Eastern States. I cannot give dates, as my progenitors, being slaves, had no means of keeping them. By all accounts my great grandfather was captured and brought from Africa. His original name I never learned. His master's name was Jackson, and he resided in the State of New York. My grandfather was born in the same State, and also remained a slave for some length of time, when he was emancipated, his master presenting him with quite an amount of property. He was true, honest and responsible, and this present was given him as a reward. He was much encouraged by the cheering prospect of better days. A better condition of things now presented itself. As he possessed a large share of confidence, he came to the conclusion, as he was free, that he was capable of selecting his own residence and manage his own affairs with prudence and economy. But, alas, his hopes were soon blighted. More heart rending sorrow and degradation awaited him. He was earnestly invited by a white decoyer to relinquish his former design and accompany him to Missouri and join him in speculation and become wealthy. As partners, they embarked on board a schooner for St. Charles, Mo. On the passage, my grandfather was seized with a fever, and for a while was totally unconscious. When he regained his reason he found himself, near his journey's end, divested of his free papers and all others. On his arrival at St. Charles he was seized by a huge, surly looking slaveholder who claimed him as his property. The contract had previously been concluded by his Judas-like friend, who had received the bounty. Oh, what a sad disappointment. After serving for thirty years to be thrust again into bondage where a deeper degradation and sorrow and hopeless toil were to be his portion for the remaining years of his existence. In deep despair and overwhelmed with grief, he made his escape to the woods, determined to put an end to his sorrows by perishing with cold and hunger. His master immediately pursued him, and in twenty-four hours found him with hands and feet frost-bitten, in consequence of which he lost the use of his fingers and toes, and was thenceforth of little use to his new master. He remained with him, however, and married a woman in the same station in life. They lived as happily as their circumstances would permit. As Providence allotted, they only had one son, which was my father, Westly Jackson. He had a deep affection for his family, which the slave ever cherishes for his dear ones. He had no other link to fasten him to the human family but his fervent love for those who were bound to him by love and sympathy in their wrongs and sufferings. My grandfather remained in the same family until his death. My father, Westly Jackson, married, at the age of twenty-two, a girl owned by James Harris, named Ellen Turner. Nothing of importance occurred until three years after their marriage, when her master, Harris failed through the extravagance and mismanagement of his wife, who was a great spendthrift and a dreaded terror to the poor slaves and all others with whom she associated in common circumstances, consequently the entire stock was sold by the sheriff to a trader residing in Virginia. On account of the good reputation my mother sustained as a worthy servant and excellent cook, a tyrannical and much dreaded slaveholder watched for an opportunity to purchase her, but fortunately arrived a few moments too late, and she was bid off in too poor a condition of health to remain long a subject of banter and speculation. Her husband was allowed to carefully lift her down from the block and accompany her to her new master's, Charles Canory, who treated her very kindly while she remained in his family. Mr. Canory resided in St. Charles County for five years after he purchased my mother. During that time my father and mother were in the same neighborhood, but a short distance from each other. But another trial awaited them. Her master removed twenty miles away to a village called Bremen, near St. Louis, Mo. My father, thereafter, visited my mother once a week, walking the distance every Saturday evening and returning on Sunday evening. But through all her trials and deprivations her trust and confidence was in Him who rescued his faithful followers from the fiery furnace and the lion's den, and led Moses through the Red Sea. Her trust and confidence was in Jesus. She relied on His precious promises, kind ever found Him a present help in every time of need. Two years after this separation my father was sold and separated from us, but previous to his delivery to his new master he made his escape to a free State. My mother was then left with two children. She had three during the time they were permitted to remain together, and buried one. Their names were Sarah Ann, Mattie Jane and Esther J. When my father left I was about three years of age, yet I can well remember the little kindnesses my father used to bestow upon us, and the deep affection and fondness he manifested for us. I shall never forget the bitter anguish of my parents' hearts, the sighs they uttered or the profusion of tears which coursed down their sable checks. O, what a horrid scene, but he was not her's, for cruel hands had separated them.

The strongest tie of earthly joy that bound the aching heart—
His love was e'er a joyous light that O'er the pathway shone—

A fountain gushing ever new amid life's desert wild—
His slightest word was a sweet tone of music round her heart—
Their lives a streamlet blent in one. O, Father, must they part?
They tore him from her circling arms, her last and fond embrace—
O never again can her sad eyes gaze upon his mournful face.
It is not strange these bitter sighs are constant bursting forth.
Amid mirth and glee and revelry she never took a part,
She was a mother left alone with sorrow in her heart.

But my mother was conscious some time previous of the change that was to take place with my father, and if he was sold in the immediate vicinity he would be likely to be sold again at their will, and she concluded to assist him to make his escape from bondage. Though the parting was painful, it afforded her solace in the contemplation of her husband becoming a free man, and cherishing a hope that her little family, through the aid of some angel of mercy, might be enabled to make their escape also, and meet to part no more on earth. My father came to spend the night with us, according to his usual custom. It was the last time, and sadness brooded upon his brow. It was the only opportunity he had to make his escape without suspicion and detection, as he was immediately to fall into the hands of a new master. He had never been sold from the place of his birth before, and was determined never to be sold again if God would verify his promise. My father was not educated, but was a preacher, and administered the Word of God according to the dictation and revelation of the spirit. His former master had allowed him the privilege of holding meetings in the village within the limits of his pass on the Sundays when he visited my mother. But on this Saturday evening he arrived and gave us all his farewell kiss and hurried away. My mother's people were aware of my father's intention, but rather than spare my mother, and for fear she might be detected, they secreted his escape. His master called a number of times and enquired for him and strongly pressed my mother to give him an account of my father, but she never gave it. We waited patiently, hoping to learn if he succeeded in gaining his freedom. Many anxious weeks and months passed before we could get any tidings from him, until at length my mother heard that he was in Chicago, a free man and preaching the Gospel. He made every effort to get his family, but all in vain. The spirit of slavery so strongly existed that letters could not reach her; they were all destroyed.

My parents had never learned the rescuing scheme of the underground railroad which had borne so many thousands to the standard of freedom and victories. They knew no other resource than to depend upon their own chance in running away and secreting themselves. If caught they were in a worse condition than before.

THEIR ATTEMPT TO MAKE THEIR ESCAPE

TWO YEARS AFTER MY father's departure, my mother, with her two children, my sister and myself, attempted to make her escape. After traveling two days we reached Illinois. We slept in the woods at night. I believe my mother had food to supply us but fasted herself. But the advertisement had reached there before us, and loafers were already in search of us, and as soon as we were discovered on the brink of the river one of the spies made enquiries respecting her suspicious appearance. She was aware that she was arrested, consequently she gave a true account of herself—that she was in search of her husband. We were then destitute of any articles of clothing excepting our wearing apparel. Mother had become so weary that she was compelled to leave our package of clothing on the way. We were taken back to St. Louis and committed to prison and remained there one week, after which they put us in Linch's trader's yard, where we remained about four weeks. We were then sold to William Lewis. Mr. Lewis was a very severe master, and inflicted such punishment upon us as he thought proper. However, I only remember one severe contest Mr. Lewis had with my mother. For some slight offence Mrs. Lewis became offended and was tartly and loudly reprimanding her, when Mr. L. came in and rashly felled her to the floor with his fist. But his wife was constantly pulling our ears, snapping us with her thimble, rapping us on the head and the sides of it. It appeared impossible to please her. When we first went to Mr. L.'s they had a cowhide which she used to inflict on a little slave girl she previously owned, nearly every night. This was done to learn the little girl to wake early to wait on her children. But my mother was a cook, as I before stated, and was in the habit of roasting meats and toasting bread. As they stinted us for food my mother roasted the cowhide. It was rather poor picking, but it was the last cowhide my mother ever had an opportunity to cook while we remained in his family. Mr. L. soon moved about six miles from the city, and entered in partnership with his brother-in-law. The servants were then divided and distributed in both families. It unfortunately fell to my lot to live with Mrs. Larry, my mistress' sister, which rendered my condition worse than the first. My master even disapproved of my ill treatment and took me to another place; the place my mother resided before my father's escape. After a short time Mr. Lewis again returned to the city. My mother still remained as cook in his family. After six years' absence of my father my mother married again a man by the name of George Brown, and lived with her second husband about four years, and had two children, when he was sold for requesting a different kind and enough food. His master considered it a great insult, and declared he would sell him. But previous to this insult, as he called it, my step-father was foreman in Mr. L.'s tobacco factory. He was trusty and of good moral habits, and was calculated to bring the highest price in the human market; therefore the excuse to sell him for the above offence was only a plot. The morning this offence occurred, Mr. L. bid my father to remain in the kitchen till he had taken his breakfast. After pulling his ears and slapping his face bade him come to the factory; but instead of going to the factory he went to Canada. Thus my poor mother was again left alone with two more children added to her misery and sorrow to toil on her weary pilgrimage.

Racked with agony and pain she was left alone again,
With a purpose nought could move
And the zeal of woman's love,
Down she knelt in agony
To ask the Lord to clear the way.

True she said O gracious Lord,
True and faithful is thy word;
But the humblest, poorest, may
Eat the crumbs they cast away.

Though nine long years had passed
Without one glimmering light of day
She never did forget to pray
And has not yet though whips and chains are castaway.

For thus said the blessed Lord,
I will verify my word;

By the faith that has not failed,
Thou hast asked and shall prevail.

We remained but a short time at the same residence when Mr. Lewis moved again to the country. Soon after, my little brother was taken sick in consequence of being confined in a box in which my mother was obliged to keep him. If permitted to creep around the floor her mistress thought it would take too much time to attend to him. He was two years old and never walked. His limbs were perfectly paralyzed for want of exercise. We now saw him gradually failing, but was not allowed to render him due attention. Even the morning he died she was compelled to attend to her usual work. She watched over him for three months by night and attended to her domestic affairs by day. The night previous to his death we were aware he could not survive through the approaching day, but it made no impression on my mistress until she came into the kitchen and saw his life fast ebbing away, then she put on a sad countenance for fear of being exposed, and told my mother to take the child to her room, where he only lived one hour. When she found he was dead she ordered grave clothes to be brought and gave my mother time to bury him. O that morning, that solemn morning. It appears to me that when that little spirit departed as though all heaven rejoiced and angels veiled their faces.

My mother too in concert joined —
Her mingled praise with them combined.
Her little saint had gone to God
Who saved him with his precious blood.
Who said "Suffer little children to come unto me and forbid
    them not."

THE SOLDIERS, AND OUR TREATMENT
DURING THE WAR

SOON AFTER THE WAR commenced the rebel soldiers encamped near Mr. Lewis' residence, and remained there one week. They were then ordered by General [Nathaniel] Lyons to surrender, but they refused. There were seven thousand Union and seven hundred rebel soldiers. The Union soldiers surrounded the camp and took them and exhibited them through the city and then confined them in prison. I told my mistress that the Union soldiers were coming to take the camp. She replied that it was false, that it was General [John H.] Kelly coming to re-enforce Gen. [Daniel Marsh] Frost. In a few moments the alarm was heard. I told Mrs. L[ewis]. the Unionists had fired upon the rebels. She replied it was only the salute of Gen. Kelley. At night her husband came home with the news that Camp Jackson was taken and all the soldiers prisoners. Mrs. Lewis asked how the Union soldiers could take seven hundred men when they only numbered the same. Mr. L[ewis]. replied they had seven thousand. She was much astonished, and cast her eye around to us for fear we might hear her. Her suspicion was correct; there was not a word passed that escaped our listening ears. My mother and myself could read enough to make out the news in the papers. The Union soldiers took much delight in tossing a paper over the fence to us. It aggravated my mistress very much. My mother used to sit up nights and read to keep posted about the war. In a few days my mistress came down to the kitchen again with another bitter complaint that it was a sad affair that the Unionists had taken their delicate citizens who had enlisted and made prisoners of them—that they were babes. My mother reminded her of taking Fort Sumter and Major [Robert] Anderson and serving them the same and that turn about was fair play. She then hastened to her room with the speed of a deer, nearly unhinging every door in her flight, replying as she went that the Niggers and Yankees were seeking to take the country. One day, after she had visited the kitchen to superintend some domestic affairs, as she pretended, she became very angry without a word being passed, and said—"I think it has come to a pretty pass, that old Lincoln, with his long legs, an old rail splitter, wishes to put the Niggers on an equality with the whites; that her children should never be on an equal footing with a Nigger. She had rather see them dead." As my mother made no reply to her remarks, she stopped talking, and commenced venting her spite on my companion servant. On one occasion Mr. Lewis searched my mother's room and found a picture of President Lincoln, cut from a newspaper, hanging in her room. He asked her what she was doing with old Lincoln's picture. She replied it was there because she liked it. He then knocked her down three times, and sent her to the trader's yard for a month as punishment. My mistress indulged some hopes till the victory of New Orleans, when she heard the famous Union song sang to the tune of Yankee Doodle:

The rebels swore that New Orleans never should be taken,
But if the Yankees came so near they should not save their bacon.
That's the way they blustered when they thought they were so
    handy,
But [Adm. David G.] Farragut steamed up one day and gave them
    Doodle Dandy

Ben. Butler then was ordered down to regulate the city;
He made the rebels walk a chalk, and was not that a pity?
That's the way to serve them out—that's the way to treat them,
They must not go and put on airs after we have beat them.

He made the rebel banks shell out and pay the loyal people,
He made them keep the city clean from pig's sty to church steeple.

That's the way Columbia speaks, let all men believe her;
That's the way Columbia speaks instead of yellow fever.

He sent the saucy women up and made them treat us well
He helped the poor and snubbed the rich; they thought he was the
    devil.

Bully for Ben. Butler, then, they thought he was so handy;
Bully for Ben Butler then,—Yankee Doodle Dandy.

The days of sadness for mistress were days of joy for us. We shouted
and laughed to the top of our voices. My mistress was more enraged than
ever—nothing pleased her. One evening, after I had attended to my
usual duties, and I supposed all was complete, she, in a terrible rage, declared I should be punished that night. I did not know the cause, neither did she. She went immediately and selected a switch. She placed
it in the corner of the room to await the return of her husband at night
for him to whip me. As I was not pleased with the idea of a whipping I
bent the switch in the shape of W, which was the first letter of his name,
and after I had attended to the dining room my fellow servant and myself walked away and stopped with an aunt of mine during the night. In
the morning we made our way to the Arsenal, but could gain no admission. While we were wandering about seeking protection, the girl's

father overtook us and persuaded us to return home. We finally complied. All was quiet. Not a word was spoken respecting our sudden departure. All went on as usual. I was permitted to attend to my work without interruption until three weeks after. One morning I entered Mrs. Lewis' room, and she was in a room adjoining, complaining of something I had neglected. Mr. L. then enquired if I had done my work. I told him I had. She then flew into a rage and told him I was saucy, and to strike me, and he immediately gave me a severe blow with a stick of wood, which inflicted a deep wound upon my head. The blood ran over my clothing, which gave me a frightful appearance. Mr. Lewis then ordered me to change my clothing immediately. As I did not obey he became more enraged, and pulled me into another room and threw me on the floor, placed his knee on my stomach, slapped me on the face and beat me with his fist, and would have punished me more had not my mother interfered. He then told her to go away or he would compel her to, but she remained until he left me. I struggled mightily, and stood him a good test for a while, but he was fast conquering me when my mother came. He was aware my mother could usually defend herself against one man, and both of us would overpower him, so after giving his wife strict orders to take me up stairs and keep me there, he took his carriage and drove away. But she forgot it, as usual. She was highly gratified with my appropriate treatment, as she called it, and retired to her room, leaving me to myself. I then went to my mother and told her I was going away. She bid me go, and added "May the Lord help you." I started for the Arsenal again and succeeded in gaining admittance and seeing the Adjutant. He ordered me to go to another tent, where there was a woman in similar circumstances, cooking. When the General found I was there he sent me to the boarding house. I remained there three weeks, and when I went I wore the same stained clothing as when I was so severely punished, which has left a mark on my head which will ever remind me of my treatment while in slavery. Thanks be to God, though tortured by wrong and goaded by oppression, the hearts that would madden with misery have broken the iron yoke.

MR. LEWIS CALLS AT THE BOARDING HOUSE

AT THE EXPIRATION OF three weeks Mr. Lewis called at my boarding house, accompanied by his brother-in-law, and enquired for me, and

the General informed him where I was. He then told me my mother was
very anxious for me to come home, and I returned. The General had ordered Mr. Lewis to call at headquarters, when he told him if he had
treated me right I would not have been compelled to seek protection of
him; that my first appearance was sufficient proof of his cruelty. Mr. L.
promised to take me home and treat me kindly. Instead of fulfilling his
promise he carried me to the trader's yard, where, to my great surprise,
I found my mother. She had been there during my absence, where she
was kept for fear she would find me and take my brother and sister and
make her escape. There was so much excitement at that time, (1861),
by the Union soldiers rendering the fugitives shelter and protection, he
was aware that if she applied to them, as he did not fulfill his promise
in my case, he would stand a poor chance. If my mother made application to them for protection they would learn that he did not return me
home and immediately detect the intrigue. After I was safely secured in
the trader's yard, Mr. L. took my mother home. I remained in the yard
three months. Near the termination of the time of my confinement I
was passing by the office when the cook of the Arsenal saw and recognized me and informed the General that Mr. L. had disobeyed his orders, and had put me in the trader's yard instead of taking me home.
The General immediately arrested Mr. L and gave him one hundred
lashes with the cow-hide, so that they might identify him by a scarred
back, as well as his slaves. My mother had the pleasure of washing his
stained clothes, otherwise it would not have been known. My master
was compelled to pay three thousand dollars and let me out. He then
put me to service, where I remained seven months, after which he came
in great haste and took me into the city and put me into the trader's
yard again. After he received the punishment he treated my mother and
the children worse than ever, which caused her to take her children and
secrete themselves in the city, and would have remained undetected
had it not been for a traitor who pledged himself to keep the secret. But
King Whiskey fired up his brain one evening, and out popped the secret. My mother and sister were consequently taken and committed to
the trader's yard. My little brother was then eight years of age, my sister sixteen, and myself eighteen. We remained there two weeks, when
a rough looking man, called Capt. Tirrell, came to the yard and enquired for our family. After he had examined us he remarked that we
were a fine looking family, and bid us retire. In about two hours he re-

turned, at the edge of the evening, with a covered wagon, and took my mother and brother and sister and left me. My mother refused to go without me, and told him she would raise an alarm. He advised her to remain as quiet as possible. At length she was compelled to go. When she entered the wagon there was a man standing behind with his hands on each side of the wagon to prevent her from making her escape. She sprang to her feet and gave this man a desperate blow, and leaping to the ground she made an alarm. The watchmen came to her assistance immediately, and there was quite a number of Union policemen guarding the city at that time, who rendered her due justice as far as possible. This was before the emancipation proclamation was issued. After she leaped from the wagon they drove on, taking her children to the boat. The police questioned my mother. She told them that Capt. Tirrell had put her children on board the boat, and was going to take them to Memphis and sell them into hard slavery. They accompanied her to the boat, and arrived just as they were casting off. The police ordered them to stop and immediately deliver up the children, who had been secreted in the Captain's private apartment. They were brought forth and returned. Slave speculation was forbidden in St. Louis at that time. The Union soldiers had possession of the city, but their power was limited to the suppression of the selling of slaves to go out of the city. Considerable smuggling was done, however, by pretending Unionism, which was the case with our family.

RELEASED FROM THE TRADER'S YARD
AND TAKEN TO HER NEW MASTER

IMMEDIATELY AFTER DINNER MY mother called for me to accompany her to our new home, the residence of the Captain, together with my brother and sister. We fared very well while we were there. Mrs. Tirrell was insane, and my mother had charge of the house. We remained there four months. The Captain came home only once a week, and he never troubled us for fear we might desert him. His intention was to smuggle us away before the State became free. That was the understanding when he bought us of Mr. Lewis, as it was not much of an object to purchase slaves while the proclamation was pending, and they likely to lose all their property; but they would, for a trifle purchase a whole family of four or five persons to send out of the State. Kentucky paid as much, or more than ever, for slaves. As they pretended to take no part in the rebellion they supposed they would be allowed to keep them without interference. Consequently the Captain's intention was to keep as quiet as possible till the excitement concerning us was over, and he could get us off without detection. Mr. Lewis would rather have disposed of us for nothing than have seen us free. He hated my mother in consequence of her desire for freedom, and her endeavors to teach her children the right way as far as her ability would allow. He also held a charge against her for reading the papers and understanding political affairs. When he found he was to lose his slaves he could not bear the idea of her being free. He thought it too hard, as she had raised so many tempests for him, to see her free and under her own control. He had tantalized her in every possible way to humiliate and annoy her; yet while he could demand her services he appreciated and placed perfect confidence in mother and family. None but a fiendish slaveholder could have rended an honest Christian heart in such a manner as this.

> Though it was her sad and weary lot to toil in slavery
> But one thing cheered her weary soul
> When almost in despair
> That she could gain a sure relief in attitude of prayer

CAPT. TIRRELL REMOVES THE FAMILY— ANOTHER STRATEGY

ONE DAY THE CAPTAIN commenced complaining of the expense of so large a family, and proposed to my mother that we should work out and he take part of the pay. My mother told him she would need what she earned for my little brother's support. Finally the Captain consented, and I was the first to be disposed of. The Captain took me in his buggy and carried me to the Depot, and I was put into a Union family, where I remained five months. Previous to my leaving, however, my mother and the Captain entered into a contract—he agreeing not to sell us, and mother agreeing not to make her escape. While she was carrying out her promise in good faith, he was plotting to separate us. We were all divided except mother and my little brother, who remained together. My sister remained with one of the rebels, but was tolerably treated. We all fared very well; but it was only the calm before the rending tornado. Captain T. was Captain of the boat to Memphis, from which the Union soldiers had rescued us. He commenced as a deck hand on the boat, then attained a higher position, and continued to advance until he became her Captain. At length he came in possession of slaves. Then his accomplishments were complete. He was a very severe slave master. Those mushroon slaveholders are much dreaded, as their severity knows no bounds.

Bondage and torture, scourges and chains
Placed on our backs indelible stains.

I stated previously, in relating a sketch of my mother's history, that she was married twice, and both husbands were to be sold and made their escape. They both gained their freedom. One was living,—the other died before the war. Both made every effort to find us, but to no purpose. It was some years before we got a correct account of her second husband, and he had no account of her, except once he heard that mother and children had perished in the woods while endeavoring to make their escape. In a few years after his arrival in the free States he married again.

When about sixteen years of age, while residing with her original master, my mother became acquainted with a young man, Mr. Adams, residing in a neighboring family, whom she much respected; but he was soon sold, and she lost trace of him entirely, as was the common occurrence with friends and companions though united by the nearest ties. When my mother arrived at Captain Tirrell's, after leaving the boat, in her excitement she scarce observed anything except her little group so miraculously saved from perhaps a final separation in this world. She at length observed that the servant who was waiting to take her to the Captain's residence in the country was the same man with whom she formed the acquaintance when sixteen years old, and they again renewed their acquaintance. He had been married and buried his wife. It appeared that his wife had been in Captain Tirrell's family many years, and he also, for some time. They had a number of children, and Capt. Tirrell had sold them down South. This cruel blow, assisted by severe flogging and other ill treatment, rendered the mother insane, and finally caused her death.

In agony close to her bosom she pressed,
The life of her heart, the child of her breast—
Oh love from its tenderness gathering might
Had strength[en]ed her soul for declining age.

But she is free. Yes, she has gone from the land of the slave;
The hand of oppression must rest in the grave.
The blood hounds have missed the scent of her way,
The hunter is rifled and foiled of his prey.

After my mother had left the Captain to take care of herself and
child, according to agreement with the Captain, she became engaged
to Mr. Adams. He had bought himself previously for a large price. After they became acquainted, the Captain had an excellent opportunity
of carrying out his stratagem. He commenced bestowing charity upon
Mr. Adams. As he had purchased himself, and Capt. T. had agreed not
to sell my mother, they had decided to marry at an early day. They hired
a house in the city and were to commence housekeeping immediately.
The Captain made him a number of presents and seemed much pleased
with the arrangement. The day previous to the one set for the marriage,
while they were setting their house in order, a man called and enquired
for a nurse, pretending he wanted one of us. Mother was absent; he said
he would call again, but he never came. On Wednesday evening we attended a protracted meeting. After we had returned home and retired,
a loud rap was heard at the door. My Aunt enquired who was there. The
reply was, "Open the door or I will break it down." In a moment in
rushed seven men, four watchmen and three traders, and ordered
mother to take my brother and me and follow them, which she hastened
to do as fast as possible, but we were not allowed time to put on our usual
attire. They thrust us into a close carriage. For fear of my mother alarming the citizens they threw her to the ground and choked her until she
was nearly strangled, then pushed her into a coach. The night was dark
and dreary; the stars refused to shine, the moon to shed her light.

'Tis not strange the heavenly orbs
In silence blushed 'neath Nature's sable garb
When woman's gagged and rashly torn away
Without blemish and without crime.

Unheeded by God's holy word:—
Unloose the fetters, break the chain,
And make my people free again,
And let them breath pure freedom's air
And her rich bounty freely share.
Let Eutopia stretch her bleeding hands abroad;
Her cry [o]f anguish finds redress from God.

We were hurried along the streets. The inhabitants heard our cries and rushed to their doors, but our carriage being perfectly tight and the alarm so sudden, that we were at the jail before they could give us any relief. There were strong Union men and officers in the city, and if they could have been informed of the human smuggling they would have released us. But oh, that horrid, dilapidated prison, with its dim lights and dingy walls, again presented itself to our view. My sister was there first, and we were thrust in and remained there until three o'clock the following afternoon. Could we have notified the police we should have been released, but, no opportunity was given us. It appears that this kidnaping had been in contemplation from the time we were before taken and returned; and Captain Tirrell's kindness to mother,—his benevolence towards Mr. Adams in assisting him to furnish his house,—his generosity in letting us work for ourselves,—his approbation in regard to the contemplated marriage was only a trap. Thus instead of a wedding Thursday evening, we were hurled across the ferry to Albany Court House and to Kentucky through the rain and without our outer garments. My mother had lost her bonnet and shawl in the struggle while being thrust in the coach, consequently she had no protection from the storm, and the rest of us were in similar circumstances. I believe we passed through Springfield. I think it was the first stopping place after we left East St. Louis, and we were put on board the cars and secreted in the gentlemen's smoking car, in which there were only a few rebels. We arrived in Springfield about twelve o'clock at night. When we took the cars it was dark, bleak and cold. It was the 18th of March, and as we were without bonnets and clothing to shield us from the sleet and wind, we suffered intensely. The old trader, for fear that mother might make her escape, carried my brother, nine years of age, from one train to the other. We then took the cars for Albany, and arrived at eight o'clock in the morning. We were then carried on the ferry in a wagon. There was another family in the wagon, in the same condition. We landed at Portland, from thence to Louisville, and were put into John Clark's trader's yard, and sold out separately, except my mother and little brother, who were sold together. Mother remained in the trader's yard two weeks, my sister six, myself four.

THE FARE AT THEIR NEW HOMES

MOTHER WAS SOLD TO Captain Plasio, my sister to Benj Board, and myself to Capt Ephraim Frisbee. The man who bought my mother was [a] Spaniard. After she had been there a short time he tried to have my mother let my brother stop at his saloon, a very dissipated place; to wait upon his miserable crew, but my mother objected. In spite of her objections he took him down to try him, but some Union soldiers called at the saloon, and noticing that he vas very small, they questioned him, and my brother, child like, divulged the whole matter. The Captain, fearful of being betrayed and losing his property, let him continue with my mother. The Captain paid eight hundred dollars for my mother and brother. We were all sold for extravagant prices. My sister, aged sixteen, was sold for eight hundred and fifty dollars; I was sold for nine hundred dollars. This was in 1863. My mother was cook and fared very well. My sister was sold to a single gentleman, whose intended took charge of her until they were married, after which they took her to her home. She was her waiter, and fared as well as could be expected. I fared worse than either of the family. I was not allowed enough to eat, exposed to the cold, and not allowed through the cold winter to thoroughly warm myself once a month. The house was very large, and I could gain no access to the fire. I was kept constantly at work of the heaviest kind,—compelled to move heavy trunks and boxes,—many times to wash till ten and twelve o'clock at night. There were three deaths in the family while I remained there, and the entire burden was put upon me. I often felt to exclaim as the Children of Israel did: "O Lord, my burden is greater than I can bear." I was then seventeen years of age. My health has been impaired from that time to the present. I have a severe pain in my side by the slightest over exertion. In the Winter I suffer intensely with cold, and cannot get warm unless in a room heated to eighty degrees. I am infirm and burdened with the influence of slavery, whose impress will ever remain on my mind and body. For six months I tried to make my escape.

I used to rise at four o'clock in the morning to find some one to assist me, and at last I succeeded. I was allowed two hours once in two weeks to go and return three miles. I could contrive no other way than to improve one of those opportunities, in which I was finally successful. I became acquainted with some persons who assisted slaves to escape by the underground railroad. They were colored people. I was to pretend going to church, and the man who was to assist and introduce me to the proper parties was to linger on the street opposite the house, and I was to follow at a short distance. On Sunday evening I begged leave to attend church, which was reluctantly granted if I completed all my work, which was no easy task. It appeared as if my mistress used every possible exertion to delay me from church, and I concluded that her old cloven-footed companion had impressed his intentions on her mind. Finally, when I was ready to start, my mistress took a notion to go out to ride, and desired me to dress her little boy, and then get ready for church. Extensive hoops were then worn, and as I had attached my whole wardrobe under mine by a cord around my waist, it required considerable dexterity and no small amount of maneuvering to hide the fact from my mistress. While attending to the child I had managed to stand in one corner of the room, for fear she might come in contact with me, and thus discover that my hoops were not so elastic as they usually are. I endeavored to conceal my excitement by backing and edging very genteelly out of the door. I had nine pieces of clothing thus concealed on my person, and as the string which fastened them was small it caused me considerable discomfort. To my great satisfaction I at last passed into the street, and my master and mistress drove down the street in great haste and were soon out of sight. I saw my guide patiently awaiting me. I followed him at a distance until we arrived at the church, and there met two young ladies, one of whom handed me a pass and told me to follow them at a square's distance. It was now twilight. There was a company of soldiers about to take passage across the ferry, and I followed. I showed my pass, and proceeded up the stairs on the boat. While thus ascending the stairs, the cord which held my bundle of clothing broke, and my feet became entangled in my wardrobe, but by proceeding, the first step released one foot and the next the other. This was observed only by a few soldiers, who were too deeply engaged in their own affairs to interfere with mine. I seated myself in a remote corner of the boat, and in a few moments I landed on free soil for the first time in my life, except when hurled through Albany and Springfield at the time of our capture. I was now under my own control. The cars were waiting in Jefferson City for the passengers for Indianapolis, where we arrived about nine o'clock.

MATTIE IN INDIANAPOLIS.—THE GLORY OF FREEDOM.— PRESIDENT LINCOLN'S REMAINS EXHIBITED

MY FIRST BUSINESS AFTER my arrival at Indianapolis was to find a boarding place in which I at once succeeded, and in a few hours thereafter was at a place of service of my own choice. I had always been under the yoke of oppression, compelled to submit to its laws, and not allowed to advance a rod from the house, or even out of call, without a severe punishment. Now this constant fear and restless yearning was over. It appeared as though I had emerged into a new world, or had never lived in the old one before. The people I lived with were Unionists, and became immediately interested in teaching and encouraging me in my literary advancement and all other important improvements, which precisely met the natural desires for which my soul had ever yearned since my earliest recollection. I could read a little, but was not allowed to learn in slavery. I was obliged to pay twenty-five cents for every letter written for me. I now began to feel that as I was free I could learn to write, as well as others; consequently Mrs. Harris, the lady with whom I lived, volunteered to assist me. I was soon enabled to write quite a legible hand, which I find a great convenience. I would advise all, young, middle aged or old, in a free country, to learn to read and write. If this little book should fall into the hands of one deficient of the important knowledge of writing I hope they will remember the old maxim:— "Never to[o] old to learn." Manage your own secrets, and divulge them by the silent language of your own pen. Had our blessed President considered it too humiliating to learn in advanced years, our race would yet have remained under the galling yoke of oppression. After I had been with Mrs. Harris seven months, the joyful news came of the surrender of Lee's army and the capture of Richmond.

Whilst the country's hearts were throbbing,
Filled with joy for victories won;

Whilst the stars and stripes were waving
O'er each cottage, ship and dome,
Came upon like winged lightning
Words that turned each joy to dread,
Froze with horror as we listened:
Our beloved chieftain, Lincoln's dead.

War's dark clouds has long held o'er us,
They have rolled their gloomy fold's away,
And all the world is anxious, waiting
For that promised peaceful day.
But that fearful blow inflicted,
Fell on his devoted head,
And from every town and hamlet
Came the cry our Chieftain's dead.

Weep, weep, O bleeding nation
For the patriot spirit fled,
All untold our century's future—
Buried with the silent dead.
God of battles, God of nations to our country send relief
Turn each lamentation into joy whilst we mourn our murdered chief.

On the Saturday after the assassination of the President there was a meeting held on the Common, and a vote taken to have the President's body brought through Indianapolis, for the people to see his dear dead face. The vote was taken by raising the hands, and when the question was put in favor of it a thousand black hands were extended in the air, seemingly higher and more visible than all the rest. Nor were their hands alone raised, for in their deep sorrow and gloom they raised their hearts to God, for well they knew that He, through martyred blood, had made them free. It was some time before the remains reached Indianapolis, as it was near the last of the route. The body was placed in the centre of the hall of the State House, and we marched in by fours, and divided into twos on each side of the casket, and passed directly through the Hall. It was very rainy,—nothing but umbrellas were to be seen in any direction. The multitude were passing in and out from eight o'clock in the morning till four o'clock in the afternoon. His body remained un-

til twelve o'clock in the evening, many distinguished persons visiting
it, when amid the booming of cannon, it moved on its way to Springfield, its final resting-place. The death of the President was like an electric shock to my soul. I could not feel convinced of his death until I
gazed upon his remains, and heard the last roll of the muffled drum and
the farewell boom of the cannon. I was then convinced that though we
were left to the tender mercies of God, we were without a leader.

> Gone, gone is our chieftain,
> The tried and the true;
> The grief of our nation the world never knew.
> We mourn as a nation has never yet mourned;
> The foe to our freedom more deeply has scorned.
> In the height of his glory in manhood's full prime,
> Our country's preserver through darkest of time;
> Amerciful being, whose kindness all shared
> Shown mercy to others. Why was he not spared?
>
> The lover of Justice, the friend of the slave,
> He struck at oppression and made it a grave;
> He spoke for our bond-men, and chain's from them fell,
> By making them soldiers they served our land well.
>
> Because he had spoken from sea unto sea
> Glad tidings go heavenward, our country is free,
> And angels I'm thinking looked down from above,
> With sweet smiles approving his great works of love.
>
> His name with the honor forever will live,
> And time to his laurels new lustre will give;
> He lived so unselfish, so loyal and true,
> That his deeds will shine brighter at every view.
>
> Then honor and cherish the name of the brave,
> The champion of freedom, the friend to the slave,
> The far-sighted statesman who saw a fair end,
> When north land and south land one flag shall defend.

Rest, rest, fallen chieftain, thy labors are o'er,
For thee mourns a nation as never before;
Farewell honored chieftain whom millions adore,
Farewell gentle spirit, whom heaven has won.

SISTER LOST—MOTHER'S ESCAPE

IN TWO OR THREE weeks after the body of the President was carried through, my sister made her escape, but by some means we entirely lost trace of her. We heard she was in a free State. In three months my mother also escaped. She rose quite early in the morning, took my little brother, and arrived at my place of service in the afternoon. I was much surprised, and asked my mother how she came there. She could scarcely tell me for weeping, but I soon found out the mystery. After so many long years and so many attempts, for this was her seventh, she at last succeeded, and we were now all free. My mother had been a slave for more than forty-three years, and liberty was very sweet to her. The sound of freedom was music in our ears; the air was pure and fragrant; the genial rays of the glorious sun burst forth with a new lustre upon us, and all creation resounded in responses of praise to the author and creator of him who proclaimed life and freedom to the slave. I was overjoyed with my personal freedom, but the joy at my mother's escape was greater than anything I had ever known. It was a joy that reaches beyond the tide and anchors in the harbor of eternal rest. While in oppression, this eternal life-preserver had continually wafted her toward the land of freedom, which she was confident of gaining, whatever might betide. Our joy that we were permitted to mingle together our earthly bliss in glorious strains of freedom was indescribable. My mother responded with the children of Israel,—"The Lord is my strength and my song. The Lord is a man of war, and the Lord is his name." We left Indianapolis the day after my mother arrived, and took the cars at eleven o'clock the following evening for St. Louis, my native State. We were then free, and instead of being hurried along, bare headed and half naked, through cars and boats, by a brutal master with a bill of sale in his pocket, we were our own, comfortably clothed, and having the true emblems of freedom.

MOTHER'S MARRIAGE

IT APPEARED TO ME that the city presented an entirely new aspect. The reader will remember that my mother was engaged to be married on the evening after we were kidnapped, and that Mr. Adams, her intended, had prepared the house for the occasion. We now went in search of him. He had moved about five miles into the country. He had carefully preserved his furniture and was patiently awaiting our return. We were gone two years and four months. The clothing and furniture which we had collected were all destroyed. It was over a year after we left St. Louis before we heard from there. We went immediately from the cars to my aunt's, and from there went to Mr. Adams' residence and took him by surprise. They were married in a week after our return. My mother is comfortably situated on a small farm with a kind and affectionate companion, with whom she had formed an early acquaintance, and from whom she had been severed by the ruthless hand of Wrong; but by the divine hand of Justice they were now reunited forever.

MATTIE MEETS HER OLD MASTER.—GOES TO SERVICE.—IS SENT FOR BY HER STEP-FATHER IN LAWRENCE, MASS.

IN A SHORT TIME I had selected a place of service, and was improving my studies in a small way. The place I engaged was in the family where I was born, where my mother lived when my father Jackson made his escape. Although Mr. Canory's family were always kind to us, I felt a great difference between freedom and slavery. After I had been there a short time my step-father sent for me and my half brother to come to Lawrence. He had been waiting ever since the State was free, hoping to get some account of us. He had been informed, previously, that mother, in trying to make her escape, had perished by the way, and the children also, but he was never satisfied. He was aware that my aunt was permanently in St. Louis, as her master had given her family their freedom twenty years previous. She was formerly owned by Major Howe, harness and leather dealer, yet residing in St. Louis. And long may he live and his good works follow him and his posterity forever. My father well knew the deception of the rebels, and was determined to persevere until he had obtained a satisfactory account of his family. A gentleman moved directly from

Lawrence to St. Louis, who made particular enquiries for us, and even called at my aunt's. We then heard directly from my father, and commenced correspondence. He had not heard directly from us since he made his escape, which was nine years. He had never heard of his little son who my mother was compelled by Mrs. Lewis to confine in a box. He was born eight months after he left. As soon as possible after my mother consented to let my little brother go to his father he sent means to assist us to make preparations for our journey to the North. At first he only sent for his little son. My mother was anxious about sending him alone. He was only eleven years old, and perfectly unused to traveling and had never been away from his mother. Finally my father came to the conclusion that, as my mother had endured such extreme hardships and sufferings during the nine years he was not permitted to participate or render her any assistance that it would afford him much pleasure in sending for us both, bearing our expenses and making us as comfortable as his means would allow. Money was sent us, and our kind friend, Mr. Howe, obtained our tickets and voluntarily assisted us in starting. We left for the North on Monday, April 9th, and arrived, safe and sound, on the 11th. We found my step-father's residence about six o'clock in the evening. He was not expecting us till the next day. Our meeting is better imagined than told. I cannot describe it. His little son was only two years old when he left, and I was eleven, and we never expected to meet him again this side of eternity. It was Freedom that brought us together. My father was comfortably situated in a nice white cottage, containing some eight rooms, all well furnished, and attached to it was a fine garden. His wife, who is a physician, was absent, but returned on the following day. The people were kind and friendly. They informed me there was no other colored family in the city, but my step-mother was continually crowded with friends and customers without distinction. My step-mother had buried her only son, who returned from the war in a decline. The white friends were all in deep sympathy with them. I felt immediately at home among such kind and friendly people, and have never felt homesick, except when I think of my poor mother's farewell embrace when she accompanied us to the cars. As soon as my step-mother had arrived, and our excitement was over, they commenced calculating upon placing me in the Sabbath school at the church where my mother belonged. On the next Sabbath I accompanied her and joined the Sabbath school, she occupying a side seat about middle way up the house. I was not reminded of my color except by an occasional loafer or the Irish, usually the colored man's enemy. I was never permitted to attend a white church before, or ride in any public conveyance without being placed in a car for the especial purpose; and in the street cars we were not permitted to ride at all, either South or West. Here I ride where I please, without the slightest remark, except from the ignorant. Many ask me if I am contented. They can imagine by the above contrast. My brother and myself entered the public school, and found a host of interested friends and formed many dear acquaintances whom I shall never forget. After attending school a month the term closed. I advanced in my studies as fast as could be expected. I never attended school but one month before. I needed more attention than my kind teacher could possibly bestow upon me, encumbered as she was by so many small children. Mother then proposed my entering some select school and placing myself entirely under its discipline and influence. I was much pleased with the idea, but as they had already been to so much expense for me, I could not wish to place them under any heavier contribution. I had previously told my step-mother my story, and how often my own mother had wished she could have it published. I did not imagine she could find time to write and arrange it, but she immediately proposed writing and publishing the entire story, by the sale of which I might obtain the aid towards completing my studies. I am glad I came to the old Bay State, the people of which the rebels hate with an extreme hatred. I found it just such a place as I had imagined by the appearance of the soldiers and the kindness they manifested.

New England, that blessed land,
All in a happy Union band;
They with the needy share their bread
And teach the weak the Word of God.

We never heard from my sister Hester, who made her escape from Kentucky, except when she was on the cars, though we have no doubt she succeeded in gaining her freedom.

SUMMARY

ON MY RETURN TO St. Louis I met my old master, Lewis, who strove so hard to sell us away that he might avoid seeing us free, on the street.

He was so surprised that before he was aware of it he dropped a bow. My mother met Mrs. Lewis, her old mistress, with a large basket on her arm, trudging to market. It appeared she had lived to see the day when her children had to wait upon themselves, and she likewise. The Yankees had taken possession, and her posterity were on an equality with the black man. Mr. Lewis despised the Irish, and often declared he would board at the hotel before he would employ Irish help, but he now has a dissipated Irish cook. When I was his slave I was obliged to keep away every fly from the table, and not allow one to light on a person. They are now compelled to brush their own flies and dress themselves and children. Mr. Lewis' brother Benjamin was a more severe slave master than the one who owned me. He was a tobacconist and very wealthy. As soon as the war commenced he turned Unionist to save his property. He was very severe in his punishments. He used to extend his victim, fastened to a beam, with hands and feet tied, and inflict from fifty to three hundred lashes, laying their flesh entirely open, then bathe their quivering wounds with brine, and, through his nose, in a slow rebel tone he would tell them "You'd better walk a fair chalk line or else I'll give yer twice as much." His former friends, the guerrillas, were aware he only turned Union to save his cash, and they gave those persons he had abused a large share of his luxury. They then, in the presence of his wife and another distinguished lady, tortured him in a most inhuman manner. For pretending Unionism they placed him on a table and threatened to dissect him alive if he did not tell them where he kept his gold. He immediately informed them. They then stood him against the house and fired over his head. From that, they changed his position by turning him upside down, and raising him two feet from the floor, letting him dash his head against the floor until his skull was fractured, after which he lingered awhile and finally died. There was a long piece published in the paper respecting his repentance, benevolence, &c. All the slaves who ever lived in his family admit the Lord is able to save to the uttermost. He saved the thief on the cross, and perhaps he saved him.

When I made my escape from slavery I was in a query how I was to raise funds to bear my expenses. I finally came to the conclusion that as the laborer was worthy of his hire, I thought my wages should come from my master's pocket. Accordingly I took twenty-five dollars. After I was safe and had learned to write, I sent him a nice letter, thanking him for the kindness his pocket bestowed to me in time of need. I have never received any answer to it.

When I complete my education, if my life is spared, I shall endeavor to publish further details of our history in another volume from my own pen.

CHRISTIANITY

CHRISTIANITY IS A SYSTEM claiming God for its author, and the welfare of man for its object. It is a system so uniform, exalted and pure, that the loftiest intellects have acknowledged its influence, and acquiesced in the justness of its claims. Genius has bent from his erratic course to gather fire from her altars, and pathos from the agony of Gethsemane and the sufferings of Calvary. Philosophy and science have paused amid their speculative researches and wondrous revelations, to gain wisdom from her teachings and knowledge from her precepts. Poetry has culled her fairest flowers and wreathed her softest, to bind her Author's "bleeding brow." Music has strung her sweetest lyres and breathed her noblest strains to celebrate His fame; whilst Learning has bent from her lofty heights to bow at the lowly cross. The constant friend of man, she has stood by him in his hour of greatest need. She has cheered the prisoner in his cell, and strengthened the martyr at the stake. She has nerved the frail and sinking heart of woman for high and holy deeds. The worn and weary have rested their fainting heads upon her bosom, and gathered strength from her words and courage from her counsels. She has been the staff of decrepit age, and the joy of manhood in its strength. She has bent over the form of lovely childhood, and suffered it to have a place in the Redeemer's arms. She has stood by the bed of the dying, and unveiled the glories of eternal life; gilding the darkness of the tomb with the glory of the resurrection.

Christianity has changed the moral aspect of nations. Idolatrous temples have crumbled at her touch, and guilt owned its deformity in her presence. The darkest habitations of earth have been irradiated with heavenly light, and the death shriek of immolated victims changed for ascriptions of praise to God and th[e] Lamb. Envy and Malice have been rebuked by her contented look, and fretful Impatience by her gentle and resigned manner.

At her approach, fetters have been broken, and men have risen redeemed from dust, and freed from chains. Manhood has learned its dignity and worth, its kindred with angels, and alliance to God.

To man, guilty, fallen and degraded man, she shows a fountain drawn from the Redeemer's veins; there she bids him wash and be clean. She points him to "Mount Zion, the city of the living God, to an innumerable company of angels, to the spirits of just men made perfect, and to Jesus the Mediator of the new Covenant," and urges him to rise from the degradation of sin, renew his nature and join with them. She shows a pattern so spotless and holy, so elevated and pure, that he might shrink from it discouraged, did she not bring with her a promise from the lips of Jehovah, that he would give power to the faint, and might to those who have no strength. Learning may bring her ample pages and her ponderous records, rich with the spoils of every age, gathered from every land, and gleaned from every source. Philosophy and science may bring their abstruse researches and wondrous revelations—Literature her elegance, with the toils of the pen, and the labors of the pencil—but they are idle tales compared to the truths of Christianity. They may cultivate the intellect, enlighten the understanding, give scope to the imagination, and refine the sensibilities; but they open not to our dim eyes and longing vision, the land of crystal founts and deathless flowers. Philosophy searches earth; Religion opens heaven. Philosophy doubts and trembles at the portals of eternity; Religion lifts the veil, and shows us golden streets, lit by the Redeemer's countenance, and irradiated by his smile. Philosophy strives to reconcile us to death; Religion triumphs over it. Philosophy treads amid the pathway of stars, and stands a delighted listener to the music of the spheres; but Religion gazes on the glorious palaces of God, while the harpings of the blood-washed, and the songs of the redeemed, fall upon her ravished ear. Philosophy has her place; Religion her important sphere; one is of importance here, the other of infinite and vital importance both here and hereafter.

Amid ancient lore the Word of God stands unique and preeminent. Wonderful in its construction, admirable in its adaptation, it contains truths that a child may comprehend, and mysteries into which angels desire to look. It is in harmony with that adaptation of means to ends which pervades creation, from the polypus tribes, elaborating their coral homes, to man, the wondrous work of God. It forms the brightest link of that glorious chain which unites the humblest work of creation with the throne of the infinite and eternal Jehovah. As light, with its infinite particles and curiously blended colors, is suited to an eye pre-pared for the alterations of day; as air, with its subtle and invisible essence; is fitted for the delicate organs of respiration; and, in a word, as this material world is adapted to man's physical nature; so the word of eternal truth is adapted to his moral nature and mental constitution. It finds him wounded, sick and suffering, and points him to the balm of Gilead and the Physician of souls. It finds him stained by transgressions and defiled with guilt, and directs him to the "blood that cleanseth from all unrighteousness and sin." It finds him athirst and faint, pining amid the deserts of life, and shows him the wells of salvation and the rivers of life. It addresses itself to his moral and spiritual nature, makes provi-sion for his wants and weaknesses, and meets his yearnings and aspira-tions. It is adapted to his mind in its earliest stages of progression, and its highest state of intellectuality. It provides light for his darkness, joy for his anguish, a solace for his woes, balm for his wounds, and heaven for his hopes. It unveils the unseen world, and reveals him who is the light of creation, and the joy of the universe, reconciled through the death of His Son. It promises the faithful a blessed re-union in a land undimmed with tears, undarkened by sorrow. It affords a truth for the living and a refuge for the dying. Aided by the Holy Spirit, it guides us through life, points out the shoals, the quicksands and hidden rocks which endanger our path, and at last leaves us with the Eternal God for our refuge, and his everlasting arms for our protection.

Dr. L. S. Thompson, ed., *The Story of Mattie J. Jackson; Her Parentage—Ex-perience of Eighteen Years in Slavery—Incidents During the War—Her Escape from Slavery. A True Story. . . As Given by Mattie* (Lawrence, Massachu-setts, Sentinel Office, 1866).

13

War's End

Occupying the Other "Hall of Congress"
Rollin [T. Morris Chester] to the Philadelphia *Press*
APRIL 4 AND 6, 1865

Every African American, and certainly every soldier in the Union army, waited anxiously for the day that the stars and stripes would again fly over Richmond, Virginia. President Lincoln spoke for most of the North when he told Adm. David Dixon Porter the day that Jefferson Davis evacuated the city, "Thank God I have lived to see this. It seems to me that I have been dreaming a horrid dream for four years, and now the nightmare is gone." Porter took Lincoln to the former seat of the Confederacy. As the president walked the streets that had only hours before been held by the rebels, an "impenetrable cordon" of African Americans surrounded him, shouting "Glory, Hallelujah." The "great Messiah" had come "to free his children from bondage." One black man fell to his knees before Lincoln, overcome with happiness and thanks. "Don't kneel to me," Lincoln remarked. "That is not right. You must kneel to God only, and thank Him for the liberty you will enjoy hereafter."

T. Morris Chester (1834–1892), the thirty-year-old black correspondent for the Philadelphia *Press,* had tramped with the Army of the James since August 1864, and felt more kinship with the soldiers, black and white, who had made this day possible. The son of a runaway slave and a free black father from Harrisburg, Pennsylvania, Chester had many spent years in Liberia. During the early years of the war, he traveled to England on a speaking tour to counteract Confederate influence there. As the only black reporter for a major daily newspaper, Chester

275

represented both a unique career path and a singular voice. He covered the war while traveling with the Army of the James and made sure that his readers knew about the exploits and heroism of the black soldier. Chester condemned the racial attitudes and repulsive conduct of white officers who aimed to increase the misery of the African Americans they encountered.

As Chester sat in the chair of the Speaker of the Confederate House of Representatives, he took delight in advising his readers about Lincoln's visit and in describing the remnants of rebel rule. As he sat writing out the following two dispatches, a recently paroled Confederate officer entered the room and demanded that Chester immediately leave. The *Press* reporter momentarily lifted his eyes and then returned to his pen. Enraged, the rebel rushed at Chester. A well-placed blow sent the attacker sprawling to the floor. He picked himself up and demanded the sword of a nearby Union officer, who had been watching the encounter. The Union soldier denied the request, but expressed his willingness to clear out a space in the hall so that the two could have a fair fight. At that, the affair ended and Chester resumed his work, dryly commenting, "I thought I would exercise my rights as a belligerent."

Chester went on to an important postwar career, spent three years in London earning a law degree, and became the first black admitted to the English bar. He traveled to Russia, dined with the Czar and his family, and during the 1870s became prominent in Louisiana politics. The violence that continually erupted in New Orleans nearly killed Chester in 1872 when, in what was most likely a failed assassination attempt, he was shot in the head. The next year, he became the first black admitted to the Louisiana bar and brigadier general of the state militia. Democratic victories in 1876 and 1877 sent Chester packing, and he briefly served as special assistant to the U.S. attorney for the eastern district of Texas. He married in 1879 and for the remainder of his life traveled between Harrisburg, Pennsylvania, and New Orleans, keeping up his private practice and various business ventures. His final years saw him completely withdraw from politics and activism, and at age fifty-eight he died in his mother's home in 1892. For a man who had fought racial discrimination all his life, his burial in a segregated Harrisburg cemetery represented a final bitter irony. McPherson, *Battle Cry of Freedom*, 846–847; R. J. M. Blackett, ed., *Thomas Morris Chester, Black Civil War*

Correspondent: His Dispatches from the Virginia Front (Baton Rouge, LA: Louisiana State University Press, 1989), 3–91.

HALL OF CONGRESS

Richmond, April 4, 1865.

SEATED IN THE SPEAKER'S CHAIR, so long dedicated to treason, but in the future to be consecrated to loyalty, I hasten to give a rapid sketch of the incidents which have occurred since my last despatch.

To Major General Godfrey Weitzel was assigned the duty of capturing Richmond. Last evening he had determined upon storming the rebel works in front of Fort Burnham. The proper dispositions were all made, and the knowing ones retired with dim visions of this stronghold of treason floating before them. Nothing occurred in the first part of the evening to awaken suspicion, though for the past few days it has been known to the authorities that the rebels, as I informed you, were evacuating the city. After midnight explosions began to occur so frequently as to confirm the evidence already in possession of the General-in-chief, that the last acts of an out-generalled army were in course of progress. The immense flames curling up throughout the rebel camps indicated that they were destroying all that could not be taken away.

The soldiers along the line gathered upon the breastworks to witness the scene and exchange congratulations. While thus silently gazing upon the columns of fire one of the monster rams was exploded, which made the very earth tremble. If there was any doubt about the evacuation of Richmond that report banished them all. In a very few moments, though still dark, the Army of the James, or rather that part of it under General Weitzel, was put in motion.

It did not require much time to get the men in light-marching order. Every regiment tried to be first. All cheerfully moved off with accelerated speed. The pickets which were on the line during the night were in the advance.

Brevet Brigadier General [Alonzo G.] Draper's brigade of colored troops, Brevet Major General [August Valentine] Kautz's division, were the first infantry to enter Richmond. The gallant 36th U.S. Colored Troops, under Lieutenant Colonel B. F. Pratt, has the honor of being the first regiment.[1] Captain Bicnnef's company has the pride of leading the advance.

The column having passed through Fort Burnham, over the rebel works, where they were moving heavy and light pieces of artillery, which the enemy in his haste was obliged to leave behind, moved into the Osborn road, which leads directly into the city.

In passing over the rebel works, we moved very cautiously in single file, for fear of exploding the innumerable torpedoes which were planted in front. So far as I can learn none has been exploded, and no one has been injured by those infernal machines. The soldiers were soon, under engineers, carefully digging them up and making the passage way beyond the fear of casualties.

Along the road which the troops marched, or rather double quicked, batches of negroes were gathered together testifying by unmistakable signs their delight at our coming. Rebel soldiers who had hid themselves when their army moved came out of the bushes, and gave themselves up as disgusted with the service. The haste of the rebels was evident in guns, camp equipage, telegraph wires, and other army property which they did not have time to burn.

When the column was about two miles from Richmond General Weitzel and staff passed by at a rapid speed, and was hailed by loud cheering. He soon reached the city, which was surrendered to him informally at the State House by Mr. Joseph Mayo, the mayor. The General and staff rode up Main street amid the hearty congratulations of a very large crowd of colored persons and poor whites, who were gathered together upon the sidewalks manifesting every demonstration of joy.

There were many persons in the better-class houses who were peeping out of the windows, and whose movements indicated that they would need watching in the future. There was no mistaking the curl of their lips and the flash of their eyes. The new military Governor of Richmond will, no doubt, prove equal to such emergencies.

When General Draper's brigade entered the outskirts of the city it was halted, and a brigade of [Gen. Charles] Devens's[2] division, 24th Corps, passed in to constitute the provost guard. A scene was here witnessed which was not only grand, but sublime. Officers rushed into each other's arms, congratulating them upon the peaceful occupation of this citadel. Tears of joy ran down the faces of the more aged. The soldiers cheered lustily, which were mingled with every kind of expression of delight. The citizens stood gaping in wonder at the splendidly-equipped army marching along under the graceful folds of the old flag. Some waved their hats and women their hands in token of gladness. The pious old negroes, male and female, indulged in such expressions: "You've come at last"; "We've been looking for you these many days"; "Jesus has opened the way"; "God bless you"; "I've not seen that old flag for four years"; "It does my eyes good"; "Have you come to stay?"; "Thank God", and similar expressions of exultation. The soldiers, black and white, received these assurances of loyalty as evidences of the latent patriotism of an oppressed people, which a military despotism has not been able to crush.

Riding up to a group of fine looking men, whose appearance indicated that they would hardly have influence enough to keep them out of the army, I inquired how it was they were not taken away with the force of Lee. They replied that they had hid themselves when the rebel army had evacuated the city, and that many more had done likewise, who would soon appear when assured that there was no longer any danger of falling into the power of the traitorous army.

These scenes all occurred at the terminus of Osborn road, which connects with the streets of the city, and is within the municipal limits. There General Draper's brigade, with the gallant 36th U.S.C.T.'s drum corps, played "Yankee Doodle" and "Shouting the Battle Cry of Freedom," amid the cheers of the boys and the white soldiers who filed by them. It ought to be stated that the officers of the white troops were anxious to be the first to enter the city with their organizations, and so far succeeded as to procure an order when about three miles, distant, that General Draper's brigade should take the left of the road, in order to allow those of the 24th Corps, under General Devens, to pass by. General Draper obeyed the order, and took the left of the road in order to let the troops of Devens go by, but at the same time ordered his brigade on a double-quick, well knowing that his men would not likely be over taken on the road by any soldiers in the army. For marching or fighting Draper's 1st Brigade, 1st Division, 25th Corps, is not to be surpassed in the service, and the General honors it with a pride and a consciousness which inspire him to undertake cheerfully whatever may be committed to his execution. It was his brigade that nipped the flower of the Southern army, the Texas brigade, under [Gen. Martin Witherspoon] Gary, which never before last September knew defeat. There may be others who may claim the distinction of being the first to enter the city, but as I was ahead of every part of the force but the cavalry, which of necessity must lead the advance, I know whereof I affirm when I announce that General Draper's brigade was the first organization to enter the city limits. According to custom, it should constitute the provost guard of Richmond.

Kautz's division, consisting of Draper's and [Col. Edward Augustus] Wild's brigades, with troops of the 24th Corps, were placed in the trenches around the city, and [Gen. Henry G.] Thomas' brigade was assigned to garrison Manchester. Proper dispositions have been made of the force to give security, and, soldier-like, placed the defences of the city beyond the possibility of a surprise.

As we entered all the Government buildings were in flames, having been fired by order of the rebel General [Richard S.] Ewell. The flames soon communicated themselves to the business part of the city; and continued to rage furiously throughout the day. All efforts to arrest this destructive element seemed for the best part of the day of no avail. The fire department of Richmond rendered every aid, and to them and co-operate labors of our soldiers belongs the credit of having saved Richmond from the devastating flames. As it is, all that part of the city lying between Ninth and Fourteenth streets, between Main street and the river inclusive, is in ruins. Among the most prominent buildings destroyed are the rebel War Department, Quartermaster General's Department, all the buildings with commissary stores, Shockoe's and Dibbrel's warehouses, well stored with tobacco, *Dispatch* and *Enquirer* newspaper buildings, the court house, (Guy) House, Farmers' Bank, Bank of Virginia, Exchange Bank, Tracers' bank, American and Columbia hotels, and the Mayo bridge which unites Richmond with Manchester. The buildings of the largest merchants are among those which have been reduced to ashes.

The flames, in spreading, soon communicated to poor and rich houses alike. All classes were soon rushing, into the streets with their goods, to save them. They hardly laid them down before they were picked up by those who openly were plundering everyplace where anything of value was to be obtained. It was retributive justice upon the aiders and abettors of treason to see their property fired by the rebel chiefs and plundered by the people whom they meant to forever enslave. As soon as the torch was applied to the rebel storehouses, the negroes and poor whites began to appropriate all property, without respect to locks or bolts. About the time our advance entered the city the tide of this inadmissable confiscation was at its highest ebb. Men would rush to the principal stores, break open the doors, and carry off the contents by the armful.

The leader of this system of public plundering was a colored man who carried upon his shoulder an iron crow-bar, and as a mark of distinguishment had a red piece of goods around his waist which reached down to his knees. The mob, for it could not with propriety be called anything else, followed him as their leader; moved on when he advanced, and rushed into every passage which was made by the leader with his crow-bar. Goods of every description were seized under these circumstances and personally appropriated by the supporters of an equal distribution of property. Cotton goods in abundance, tobacco in untold quantities, shoes, rebel military clothing, and goods and furniture generally were carried away by the people as long as any thing of value was to be obtained. As soon as Gen. [Edward Hastings] Ripley was assigned to provost duty, all plundering immediately ceased, the flames were arrested, and an appearance of recognized authority fully sustained. Order once more reigns in Richmond. The streets were as quiet last night as they possibly could be. An effective patrolling and provost guard keeps everything as quiet as can be expected.

The F.F.V.'s[3] have not ventured out of their houses yet, except in a few cases, to apply for a guard to protect their property. In some cases negroes have been sent to protect the interests of these would-be man sellers. It is pleasant to witness the measured pace of some dark sentinel before the houses of persons who, without doubt, were out-spoken rebels until the Union army entered the city, owing the security which they feel to the vigilance of the negro guard.

When the army occupied the city there were innumerable inquiries for Jeff Davis, but to all of which the answer was made that he went off in great haste night before last, with all the bag and baggage which he could carry. The future capital of the Confederacy will probably be in a wagon for the facilities which it affords to travel. Jeff's mansion, where he lived in state, is now the headquarters of Gen. Weitzel.

Brigadier General [George Foster] Shepley has been appointed Governor of Richmond, and has entered upon the arduous duties of the office. A better selection could not have been made.

It is due to Major [Atherton H.] Stevens, of the 4th Massachusetts Cavalry, provost marshal, on the staff of Gen. Weitzel, to give him credit for raising the first colors over the State House. He hoisted a couple of guidons, in the absence of a flag, which excited prolonged cheering. Soon after General Shepley's A. D. C. raised the first storm flag over the Capitol. It is the acme standard which General Shepley laid a wager would wave over the St. Charles Hotel in the beginning of the rebellion, and he also laid another that it would be hoisted over Richmond, both of which he has had the satisfaction of winning.

During the early part of the day a number of rebel officers were captured at the Spottswood House, where they were drinking freely. They belonged to the navy, the last of which disappeared in smoke, excepting a few straggling officers and men. These fellows, when arrested, did not wish to walk through the street under guard, but solicited the favor of being permitted to go to the provost marshal in a carriage. Their impudence was received as it deserved, with suppressed contempt.

On Sunday evening, strange to say, the jails in this place were thrown open, and all runaway negroes, those for sale and those for safe keeping were told to hop out and enjoy their freedom. You may rely upon it that they did not need a second invitation. Many of these persons will have no difficulty in convincing themselves that they were always on the side of the Union and the freedom of the slave. Great events have a wonderful influence upon the minds of guilty, trembling wretches.

When the rebels blew up the magazine in the vicinity of French Garden Hill, the people were not informed of the fact. Some of them knew it, but the great body of those in the vicinity were ignorant of what was taking place. The result was that quite a number were killed. Nearly if not quite all the paupers in the poor house—the numbers not being large—which was very near the magazine, were instantly killed also.

The fire is still burning, but not to much damage.

Philadelphia *Press*, April 6, 1865.

------

1. The 36th USCT, previously the 2nd North Carolina, was organized in February 1864 and performed heroically at the Battle of New Market Heights. Which unit actually entered Richmond first is difficult to determine. Elements of the 36th USCT or the 5th Massachusetts Cavalry may have been the first; whatever the case, black troops likely comprised the first Union soldiers in the city. Major Stevens of the 4th Massachusetts Cavalry, whom

Chester mentions, claimed that he and Companies E and H of the 4th first entered Richmond. Stevens did enter the capitol building and seized the Confederate flag. Trudeau, *Like Men of War*, 292–293, 421–422; *Massachusetts Soldiers, Sailors, and Marines in the Civil War*. 9 vols. (Norwood, MA: Norwood Press, 1933), 6:421–422.
2. Chester originally had written Devin, but the similarity of two Union generals' names must have been a source of confusion.
3. With derision, the First Families of Virginia.

HALL OF CONGRESS

Richmond, April 6, 1865

THE EXULTATION OF THE loyal people of this city, who, amid the infamy by which they have been surrounded, and the foul misrepresentations to allure them from their allegiance, have remained true to the old flag, is still being expressed by the most extravagant demonstrations of joy. The Union element in this city consists of negroes and poor whites, including all that have deserted from the army, or have survived the terrible exigencies which brought starvation to so many homes. As to the negroes, one thing is certain, that amid every disaster to our arms, amid the wrongs which they daily suffered for their known love for the Union, and amid the scourging which they received for trying to reach our army and enlist under our flag, they have ever prayed for the right cause, and testified their devotion to it in ten thousand instances, and especially in aiding our escaped prisoners to find our lines when to do so placed their own lives in peril.

The great event after the capture of the city was the arrival of President Lincoln in it. He came up to Rocket's wharf in one of Admiral [David Dixon] Porter's vessels of war, and, with a file of sailors for a guard of honor, he walked up to Jeff Davis' house, the headquarters of General Weitzel. As soon as he landed the news sped, as if upon the wings of lightning, that "Old Abe," for it was treason in this city to give him a more respectful address, had come. Some of the negroes, feeling themselves free to act like men, shouted that the President had arrived.

This name having always been applied to Jeff, the inhabitants, coupling it with the prevailing rumor that he had been captured, reported that the arch-traitor was being brought into the city. As the people pressed near they cried "Hang him!" "Hang him!" "Show him no quarter!" and other similar expressions, which indicated their sentiments as to what should be his fate. But when they learned that it was President Lincoln their joy knew no bounds. By the time he reached General Weitzel's headquarters, thousands of persons had followed him to catch a sight of the Chief Magistrate of the United States. When he ascended the steps he faced the crowd and bowed his thanks for the prolonged exultation which was going up from that great concourse. The people seemed inspired by this acknowledgment, and with renewed vigor shouted louder and louder, until it seemed as if the echoes would reach the abode of those patriot spirits who had died without witnessing the sight.

General Weitzel received the President upon the pavement, and conducted him up the steps. General Shepley, after a good deal of trouble, got the crowd quiet and introduced Admiral Porter, who bowed his acknowledgments for the cheering with which his name was greeted. The President and party entered the mansion, where they remained for half an hour, the crowd still accumulating around it, when a headquarters' carriage was brought in front, drawn by four horses, and Mr. Lincoln, with his youngest son, Admiral Porter, General Kautz, and General Devens entered. The carriage drove through the principal streets, followed by General Weitzel and staff on horseback, and a cavalry guard. There is no describing the scene along the route. The colored population was wild with enthusiasm. Old men thanked God in a very boisterous manner, and old women shouted upon the pavement as high as they had ever done at a religious revival. But when the President passed through the Capitol yard it was filled with people. Washington's monument and the Capitol steps were one mass of humanity to catch a glimpse of him.

It should be recorded that the Malvern, Admiral Porter's flag-ship, upon which the President came; the Bat, Monticello, Frolic, and the Symbol,[1] the torpedo-boat which led the advance and exploded these infernal machines, were the first vessels to arrive in Richmond.

Nothing can exceed the courtesy and politeness which the whites everywhere manifest to the negroes. Not even the familiarity peculiar to Americans is indulged in, calling the blacks by their first or Christ-

ian names, but even masters are addressing their slaves as "Mr. Johnson," "Mrs. Brown," and "Miss Smith." A cordial shake of the hand and
a gentle inclination of the body, approaching to respectful consideration, are evident in the greetings which now take place between the oppressed and the oppressor.

Masters are looking through the camps of our colored troops to find
some of their former slaves to give them a good character. The first
night our troops quartered in the city this scene was enacted in Gen.
Draper's brigade limits, his being the first organization to enter the city.
His troops now hold the inner lines of works. The rapid occupation of
the city cut off the retreat of many rebels, who are daily being picked
up by the provost guard.

Every one declares that Richmond never before presented such a
spectacle of jubilee. It must be confessed that those who participated in
this informal reception of the President were mainly negroes. There
were many whites in the crowd, but they were lost in the great concourse of American citizens of African descent. Those who lived in the
finest houses either stood motionless upon their steps or merely peeped
through the window-blinds, with a very few exceptions. The Secesh-
inhabitants still have some hope for their tumbling cause.

The scenes at the Capitol during the day are of a very exciting character. The offices of General Shepley, the Military Governor, and
Colonel Morning, the Provost Marshal General, are besieged by
crowds, mostly poor people, with a small sprinkling of respectability,
upon every kind of pretext. They want protection papers, a guard over
their property, to assure the authorities of their allegiance, to take the
oath, to announce that they are paroled prisoners and never have been
exchanged, and don't desire to be, and innumerable other circumstances to insure the protection of the military authorities.

The people of Richmond, white and black, had been led to believe
that when the Yankee army came its mission was one of plunder. But
the orderly manner in which the soldiers have acted has undeceived
them. The excitement is great, but nothing could be more orderly and
decorous than the united crowds of soldiers and citizens.

The Capitol building all day yesterday from the moment we took possession was surrounded by a crowd of hungry men and women clamoring for something to eat. The earnestness of their entreaties and looks
showed that they were in a destitute condition. It was deemed necessary

to station a special guard at the bottom of the steps to keep them from filling the building. These suffering people will probably be attended to in a day or so in that bountiful manner which had marked the advance of the Union armies.

I visited yesterday (Tuesday) several of the slave jails, where men, women, and children were confined, or herded, for the examination of purchasers. The jailors were in all cases slaves, and had been left in undisputed possession of the buildings. The owners, as soon as they were aware that we were coming, opened wide the doors and told the confined inmates they were free. The poor souls could not realize it until they saw the Union army. Even then they thought it must be a pleasant dream, but when they saw Abraham Lincoln they were satisfied that their freedom was perpetual. One enthusiastic old negro woman exclaimed: "I know that I am free, for I have seen Father Abraham and felt him."

When the President returned to the flag-ship of Admiral Porter, in the evening, he was taken from the wharf in a cutter. Just as he pushed off, amid the cheering of the crowd, another good old colored female shouted out, "Don't drown, Massa Abe, for God's sake!"

The fire, which was nearly extinguished when I closed my last despatch, is entirely so now. Thousands of persons are gazing hourly with indignation upon the ruins. Gen. Lee ordered the evacuation of the city at an hour known to the remaining leaders of the rebellion, when Gens. Ewell and [John Cabell] Breckinridge, and others, absconded, leaving orders with menials, robbers, and plunderers, kept together during the war by the "cohesive power of public plunder," to apply the torch to the different tobacco warehouses, public buildings, arsenals, stores, flour mills, powder magazines, and every important place of deposit. A south wind prevailed, and the flames spread with devastating effect. The offices of the newspapers, whose columns have been charged with the foulest vituperation against our Government, were on fire; two of them have been reduced to ashes, another one injured beyond repair, while the remaining two are not much damaged. Every bank which had emitted the spurious notes of the rebels was consumed to ruins. Churches no longer gave audience to empty prayers, but burst forth in furious flames. Magazines exploded, killing the poor inhabitants. In short, Secession was burnt out, and the city purified as far as fire could accomplish it.

As I informed you in a previous despatch, the Union soldiers united with the citizens to stay the progress of the fire, and at last succeeded, but not until all the business part of the town was destroyed.

About three o'clock on Monday morning the political prisoners who were confined in Castle Thunder, and the Union prisoners who were in Libby, were marched out and driven off.[2] Some of our officers escaped and were kindly cared for by the good Union folks of this city. The rebels also gathered together as many colored persons as possible, and were forcing them ahead with drawn sabres, but before they were out of the city [Col. Samuel Perkins] Spear's cavalry came down upon them, rescued the negroes, and captured seventeen of the Johnnies, with their horses.

Yesterday afternoon I strolled through Castle Thunder, where so many Union men have suffered every species of meanness and tyranny which the rebels could invent. The only thing that attracted especial attention was the large number of manacles which were for the benefit of the prisoners. This place has been so often described, that it would be unnecessary to weary the reader again. The Castle is empty at present, and is in charge of Capt. [Lucius V. S.] Mattison, 81st New York Volunteers, who, by the way, is a very accommodating officer. The Hotel de Libby is now doing a rushing business in the way of accommodating a class of persons who have not heretofore patronized that establishment. It is being rapidly filled with rebel soldiers, detectives, spies, robbers, and every grade of infamy in the calendar of crime. The stars and stripes now wave gracefully over it, and traitors look through the same bars behind which loyal men were so long confined.

Quite a large number of rebels were brought into the city last night. I did not for a certainty learn whether they were captured, or deserted from a bad cause—most probably the latter.

Lieut. Gen. [U. S.] Grant will arrive in this city tomorrow, and will doubtless receive an ovation equal to President Lincoln's.

Philadephia *Press*, April 11, 1865. Reprinted in R. J. M. Blackett, ed., *Thomas Morris Chester, Black Civil War Correspondent: His Dispatches from the Front* (Baton Rouge, LA: Louisiana State University Press, 1989), 288–299.

---

1. The *Malvern*, a sidewheel steamer of 1,477 tons, was built in October 1860. The vessel had been a blockade runner before its capture in November 1863

and became the flagship of the North Atlantic Blockading Squadron. The *Bat*, a 750-ton sidewheel steamer that was commissioned by the navy in December 1864, could reach 16 knots. The *Monticello*, a 655-ton steamer that was constructed in 1859, had a crew of 137 men, and could reach 11.5 knots. The *Frolic*, an unarmed 296-ton steamer, was built in 1860 in Wheeling, Virginia. The *Symbol* is unidentified. Paul Silverstone, *Warships of the Civil War Navies* (Annapolis, MD: Naval Institute Press, 1989), 70, 75, 93; William M. Lytle and Forrest R. Holdcamper, comps., *Merchant Steam Vessels of the United States, 1790–1868* (Staten Island, NY: Steamship Historical Society of America, 1975), 77.

2. The Confederacy maintained two prisons named Castle Thunder. The one in Richmond, a former tobacco warehouse, housed political prisoners, spies, and criminals. As soon as Union forces occupied Richmond, Castle Thunder held Confederates accused of war crimes. Libby prison, also in Richmond, was reserved for captured Union officers. Its three floors were horribly crowded, and prisoners were forced to sleep in shifts. On the night of February 9, 1864, 109 officers escaped through a tunnel, but about half were recaptured. Faust, *Historical Times Illustrated Encyclopedia of the Civil War*, 120, 437–438.

The Second Inauguration
Elizabeth Keckley
1868

"My life has been an eventful one. I was born a slave—was the child of slave parents—therefore I came upon the earth free in God-like thought, but fettered in action." So began the memoir of Elizabeth Keckley (1818?–1907), perhaps the most famous black woman to emerge out of the Civil War. The personal seamstress of Mary Todd Lincoln, she also sewed for wives of members of the Lincoln cabinet and, before the war, for Varina Howell Davis, wife of Jefferson Davis. As a confidante and travel companion of Mrs. Lincoln and a frequent visitor to the White House, she enjoyed a relationship with the Lincoln family that few others, black or white, knew. Although it was ghostwritten, the book nevertheless accurately expresses Keckley's views about the Lincolns and her earlier life as a slave. It is an astonishing tale of personal fortitude and persistence. As an inside look at the Lincoln family, it is as unique as it is gracious and understanding.

But such was not the perception of readers when the book appeared in 1868. Mrs. Lincoln found it deeply offensive, primarily because of the segment that revealed how she was compelled to sell her clothes to pay her debts, and never again spoke to Keckley. Many African Americans in the Washington area considered Keckley a traitor to the Lincoln family and refused all contact with her. Her dressmaking business declined. She briefly taught at Wilberforce University, and she founded the Home for Destitute Women and Children, but Keckley spent the bulk of her postwar years living quietly and obscurely, surviving off the pension she received as the mother of a Union soldier. Her only son, George, had been killed in 1861 at Wilson's Creek, Missouri.

During the Civil War, Keckley spent much time with the Lincoln family and, along with 40 area black women, helped found the Contraband Relief Association of Washington, D.C. Organized in 1862, the association collected money and supplies from black churches and women's groups from Baltimore to Boston and distributed them to the thousands of needy freedmen who found their way to the nation's capital. Mrs. Lincoln gave the group $200 and fifteen boxes of clothing, and one black church in Boston sent twelve barrels of clothes. In 1864 the organization began assisting the families of black soldiers and changed its name to the Ladies' Freedmen and Soldiers' Relief Association.

In the chapter below, Keckley reveals the trepidation that Lincoln felt during the 1864 election, and she describes the Lincoln visit to Richmond from the perspective of an entourage member. One wonders if Keckley and T. Morris Chester exchanged glances as they both watched Lincoln walk through the city, and if they witnessed the same Richmond blacks hail the president as their liberator. Edward T. James, Janet Wilson James, Paul S. Boyer, eds., *Notable American Women,* 3 vols. (Cambridge, MA: Belknap Press of Harvard University Press, 1971), 2:310–311; Elizabeth Keckley, *Behind the Scenes, Or, Thirty Years a Slave and Four Years in the White House* (New York: Oxford University Press, 1988); Ripley et al., *The Black Abolitionist Papers,* 5:248–252.

MRS. LINCOLN came to my apartments one day towards the close of the summer of 1864, to consult me in relation to a dress. And here let me remark, I never approved of ladies, attached to the Presidential household, coming to my rooms. I always thought that it would be more consistent with their dignity to send for me, and let me come to them, instead of their coming to me. I may have peculiar notions about some things, and this may be regarded as one of them. No matter, I have recorded my opinion. I cannot forget the associations of my early life. Well, Mrs. Lincoln came to my rooms, and, as usual, she had much to say about the Presidential election.

After some conversation, she asked: "Lizzie, where do you think I will be this time next summer?"

"Why, in the White House, of course."

"I cannot believe so. I have no hope of the re-election of Mr. Lincoln. The canvass is a heated one, the people begin to murmur at the war, and every vile charge is brought against my husband."

"No matter," I replied, "Mr. Lincoln will be re-elected. I am so confident of it, that I am tempted to ask a favor of you."

"A favor! Well, if we remain in the White House I shall be able to do you many favors. What is the special favor?"

"Simply this, Mrs. Lincoln—I should like for you to make me a present of the right-hand glove that the President wears at the first public reception after his second inaugural."

"You shall have it in welcome. It will be so filthy when he pulls it off, I shall be tempted to take the tongs and put it in the fire. I cannot imagine, Lizabeth, what you want with such a glove."

"I shall cherish it as a precious memento of the second inauguration of the man who has done so much for my race. He has been a Jehovah to my people—has lifted them out of bondage, and directed their footsteps from darkness into light. I shall keep the glove, and hand it down to posterity."

"You have some strange ideas, Lizabeth. Never mind, you shall have the glove; that is, if Mr. Lincoln continues President after the 4th of March next."

I held Mrs. Lincoln to her promise. That glove is now in my possession, bearing the marks of the thousands of hands that grasped the honest hand of Mr. Lincoln on that eventful night. Alas! it has become a prouder, sadder memento than I ever dreamed—prior to making the request—it would be.

In due time the election came off, and all of my predictions were verified. The loyal States decided that Mr. Lincoln should continue at the nation's helm. Autumn faded, winter dragged slowly by, and still the country resounded with the clash of arms. The South was suffering, yet suffering was borne with heroic determination, and the army continued to present a bold, defiant front. With the first early breath of spring, thousands of people gathered in Washington to witness the second inauguration of Abraham Lincoln as President of the United States. It was a stirring day in the National Capital, and one that will never fade from the memory of those who witnessed the imposing ceremonies. The morning was dark and gloomy; clouds hung like a pall in the sky, as if portending some great disaster. But when the President stepped forward to receive the oath of office, the clouds parted, and a ray of sunshine streamed from the heavens to fall upon and gild his face. It is also said that a brilliant star was seen at noon-day. It was the noon-day of life with Mr. Lincoln, and the star, as viewed in the light of subsequent events, was emblematic of a summons from on high. This was Saturday, and on Monday evening I went to the White House to dress Mrs. Lincoln for the first grand levee. While arranging Mrs. L.'s hair, the President came in. It was the first time I had seen him since the inauguration, and I went up to him, proffering my hand with words of congratulation.

He grasped my outstretched hand warmly, and held it while he spoke: "Thank you. Well, Madame Elizabeth"—he always called me Madam Elizabeth—"I don't know whether I should feel thankful or not. The position brings with it many trials. We do not know what we are destined to pass through. But God will be with us all. I put my trust in God." He dropped my hand, and with solemn face walked across the room and took his seat on the sofa. Prior to this I had congratulated Mrs. Lincoln, and she had answered with a sigh, "Thank you, Elizabeth; but now that we have won the position, I almost wish it were otherwise. Poor Mr. Lincoln is looking so broken-hearted, so completely worn out, I fear he will not get through the next four years." Was it a presentiment that made her take a sad view of the future? News from the front was never more cheering. On every side the Confederates were losing ground, and the lines of blue were advancing in triumph. As I would look out my window almost every day, I could see the artillery going past on its way to the open space of ground, to fire a salute in honor of some new victory. From every point came glorious news of the success of the soldiers that fought for the Union. And yet, in their private chamber, away from the curious eyes of the world, the President and his wife wore sad, anxious faces.

I finished dressing Mrs. Lincoln, and she took the President's arm and went below. It was one of the largest receptions ever held in Washington. Thousands crowded the halls and rooms of the White House, eager to shake Mr. Lincoln by his hand, and receive a gracious smile from his wife. The jam was terrible, and the enthusiasm great. The President's hand was well shaken, and the next day, on visiting Mrs. Lincoln, I received the soiled glove that Mr. Lincoln had worn on his right hand that night.

Many colored people were in Washington, and large numbers had desired to attend the levee, but orders were issued not to admit them. A gentleman, a member of Congress, on his way to the White House, recognized Mr. Frederick Douglass, the eloquent colored orator, on the outskirts of the crowd.

"How do you do, Mr. Douglass? A fearful jam to-night. You are going in, of course?"

"No—that is, no to your last question."

"Not going in to shake the President by the hand! Why, pray?"

"The best reason in the world. Strict orders have been issued not to admit people of color."

"It is a shame, Mr. Douglass, that you should thus be placed under ban. Never mind; wait here, and I will see what can be done."

The gentleman entered the White House, and working his way to the President, asked permission to introduce Mr. Douglass to him.

"Certainly," said Mr. Lincoln. "Bring Mr. Douglass in, by all means. I shall be glad to meet him."

The gentleman returned, and soon Mr. Douglass stood face to face with the President. Mr. Lincoln pressed his hand warmly, saying: "Mr. Douglass, I am glad to meet you. I have long admired your course, and I value your opinions highly."

Mr. Douglass was very proud of the manner in which Mr. Lincoln received him. On leaving the White House he came to a friend's house where a reception was being held, and he related the incident with great pleasure to myself and others.

On the Monday following the reception at the White House, everybody was busy preparing for the grand inaugural ball to come off that night. I was in Mrs. Lincoln's room the greater portion of the day. While dressing her that night, the President came in, and I remarked to him

how much Mr. Douglass had been pleased on the night he was presented to Mr. Lincoln. Mrs. L. at once turned to her husband with the
inquiry, "Father, why was not Mr. Douglass introduced to me?"

"I do not know. I thought he was presented."

"But he was not."

"It must have been an oversight then, mother; I am sorry you did not
meet him."

I finished dressing her for the ball, and accompanied her to the door.
She was dressed magnificently, and entered the ball-room leaning on
the arm of Senator [Charles] Sumner, a gentleman that she very much
admired. Mr. Lincoln walked into the ball-room accompanied by two
gentlemen. This ball closed the season. It was the last time that the
President and his wife ever appeared in public.

Some days after, Mrs. Lincoln, with a party of friends, went to City
Point on a visit.

Mrs. Lincoln had returned to Washington prior to the 2nd of April.
On Monday, April 3d, Mrs. Secretary [James] Harlan came into my room
with material for a dress. While conversing with her, I saw artillery pass
the window; and as it was on its way to fire a salute, I inferred that good
news had been received at the War Department. My reception-room
was on one side of the street, and my work-room on the other side.
Inquiring the cause of the demonstration, we were told that Richmond
had fallen. Mrs. Harlan took one of my hands in each of her own, and
we rejoiced together. I ran across to my work-room, and on entering it,
discovered that the girls in my employ also had heard the good news.
They were particularly elated, as it was reported that the rebel capital
had surrendered to colored troops. I had promised my employees a
holiday when Richmond should fall; and now that Richmond had
fallen, they reminded me of my promise.

I recrossed to my reception-room, and Mrs. Harlan told me that the
good news was enough for her—she could afford to wait for her dress,
and to give the girls a holiday and a treat, by all means. She returned to
her house, and I joined my girls in the joy of the long-promised holiday.
We wandered about the streets of the city with happy faces, and hearts
overflowing with joy. The clerks in the various departments also enjoyed a holiday, and they improved it by getting gloriously fuddled. Towards evening I saw S., and many other usually clear-headed men, in
the street, in a confused, uncertain state of mind.

Mrs. Lincoln had invited me to accompany her to City Point. I went to the White House, and told her that if she intended to return, I would regard it as a privilege to go with her, as City Point was near Petersburg, my old home. Mrs. L. said she deigned returning, and would be delighted to take me with her; so it was arranged that I should accompany her.

A few days after we were on board the steamer, *en route* for City Point. Mrs. Lincoln was joined by Mrs. Secretary Harlan and daughter, Senator Sumner, and several other gentle men.

Prior to this, Mr. Lincoln had started for City Point, and before we reached our destination he had visited Richmond, Petersburg, and other points. We arrived on Friday, and Mrs. Lincoln was much disappointed when she learned that the President had visited the late Confederate capital, as she had greatly desired to be with him when he entered the conquered stronghold. It was immediately arranged that the entire party on board the River Queen[1] should visit Richmond, and other points, with the President. The next morning, after the arrangement was perfected, we were steaming up James River—the river that so long had been impassable, even to our gunboats. The air was balmy, and the banks of the river were beautiful, and fragrant with the first sweet blossoms of spring. For hours I stood on deck, breathing the pure air, and viewing the landscape on either side of the majestically flowing river. Here stretched fair fields, emblematic of peace—and here deserted camps and frowning forts, speaking of the stern vicissitudes of war. Alas! how many changes had taken place since my eye had wandered over the classic fields of dear old Virginia! A birth-place is always dear, not matter under what circumstances you were born, since it revives in memory the golden hours of childhood, free from philosophy, and the warm kiss of a mother. I wondered if I should catch a glimpse of a familiar face; I wondered what had become of those I once knew; had they fallen in battle, been scattered by the relentless tide of war, or were they still living as they lived when last I saw them? I wondered, now that Richmond had fallen, and Virginia been restored to the clustering stars of the Union, if the people would come together in the bonds of peace; and as I gazed and wondered, the River Queen rapidly carried us to our destination.

The Presidential party were all curiosity on entering Richmond. They drove about the streets of the city, and examined every object of interest. The Capitol presented a desolate appearance—desks broken, and papers scattered promiscuously in the hurried flight of the Confederate Congress. I picked up a number of papers, and, by curious coincidence, the resolution prohibiting all free colored people from entering the State of Virginia. In the Senate chamber I sat in the chair that Jefferson Davis sometimes occupied; also in the chair of the Vice-President, Alexander H. Stephens. We paid a visit to the mansion occupied by Mr. Davis and family during the war, and the ladies who were in charge of it scowled darkly upon our party as we passed through and inspected the different rooms. After a delightful visit we returned to City Point.

That night, in the cabin of the River Queen, smiling faces gathered around the dinner-table. One of the guests was a young officer attached to the Sanitary Commission. He was seated near Mrs. Lincoln, and, by way of pleasantry, remarked: "Mrs. Lincoln, you should have seen the President the other day, on his triumphal entry into Richmond. He was the cynosure of all eyes. The ladies kissed their hands to him, and greeted him with the waving of handkerchiefs. He is quite a hero when surrounded by pretty young ladies."

The young officer suddenly paused with a look of embarrassment. Mrs. Lincoln turned to him with flashing eyes, with the remark that his familiarity was offensive to her. Quite a scene followed, and I do not think the Captain who incurred Mrs. Lincoln's displeasure will ever forget that memorable evening in the cabin of the River Queen, at City Point.

Saturday morning the whole party decided to visit Petersburg, and I was only too eager to accompany them.

When we arrived at the city, numbers crowded around the train, and a little ragged negro boy ventured timidly into the car occupied by Mr. Lincoln and immediate friends, and in replying to numerous questions, used the word "tote."

"Tote," remarked Mr. Lincoln; "what do you mean by tote?"

"Why, massa, to tote um on your back."

"Very definite, my son; I presume when you tote a thing, you carry it. By the way, Sumner," turning to the Senator, "what is the origin of tote?"

"Its origin is said to be African. The Latin word *totum*, from *totus*, means all—an entire body—the whole."

"But my young friend here did not mean an entire body, or anything of the kind, when he said he would tote my things for me," interrupted the President.

"Very true," continued the Senator. "He used the word tote in the African sense, to carry, to bear. Tote in this sense is defined in our standard dictionaries as a colloquial word of the Southern States, used especially by the negroes."

"Then you regard the word as a good one?"

"Not elegant, certainly. For myself, I should prefer a better word; but since it has been established by usage, I cannot refuse to recognize it."

Thus the conversation proceeded in pleasant style.

Getting out of the car, the President and those with him went to visit the forts and other scenes, while I wandered off by myself in search of those whom I had known in other days. War, grim-visaged war, I soon discovered had brought many changes to the city so well known to me in the days of my youth. I found a number of old friends, but the greater portion of the population were strange to me. The scenes suggested painful memories, and I was not sorry to turn my back again upon the city. A large, peculiarly shaped oak tree, I well remember, attracted the particular attention of the President; it grew upon the outskirts of Petersburg, and as he had discovered it on his first visit, a few days previous to the second, he insisted that the party should go with him to take a look at the isolated and magnificent specimen of the stately grandeur of the forest. Every member of the party was only too willing to accede to the President's request, and the visit to the oak was made, and much enjoyed.

On our return to City Point from Petersburg the train moved slowly, and the President, observing a terrapin basking in the warm sunshine on the wayside, had the conductor stop the train, and one of the brakemen bring the terrapin in to him. The movements of the ungainly little animal seemed to delight him, and he amused himself with it until we reached James River, where our steamer lay. Tad stood near, and joined in the happy laugh with his father.

For a week the River Queen remained in James River, anchored the greater portion of the time at City Point, and a pleasant and memorable week was it to all on board. During the whole of this time a yacht lay in the stream about a quarter of a mile distant, and its peculiar movements attracted the attention of all on board. General Grant and Mrs. Grant were on our steamer several times, and many distinguished officers of the army also were entertained by the President and his party.

Mr. Lincoln, when not off on an excursion of any kind, lounged about the boat, talking familiarly with every one that approached him.

The day before we started on our journey back to Washington, Mr. Lincoln was engaged in reviewing the troops in camp. He returned to the boat in the evening, with a tired, weary look.

"Mother," he said to his wife, "I have shaken so many hands to-day that my arms ache to-night. I almost wish that I could go to bed now."

As the twilight shadows deepened the lamps were lighted, and the boat was brilliantly illuminated; as it lay in the river, decked with many-colored lights, it looked like an enchanted floating palace. A military band was on board, and as the hours lengthened into night it discoursed sweet music. Many officers came on board to say good-by, and the scene was a brilliant one indeed. About 10 o'clock Mr. Lincoln was called upon to make a speech. Rising to his feet, he said:

"You must excuse me, ladies and gentlemen. I am too tired to speak to-night. On next Tuesday night I make a speech in Washington, at which time you will learn all I have to say. And now, by way of parting from the brave soldiers of our gallant army, I call upon the band to play Dixie. It has always been a favorite of mine, and since we have captured it, we have a perfect right to enjoy it." On taking his seat the band at once struck up with Dixie, that sweet, inspiring air; and when the music died away, there were clapping of hands and other manifestations of applause.

At 11 o'clock the last good-by was spoken, the lights were taken down, the River Queen rounded out into the water and we were on our way back to Washington. We arrived at the Capital at 6 o'clock on Sunday evening, where the party separated, each going to his or her own home. This was one of the most delightful trips of my life, and I always revert to it with feelings of genuine pleasure.

Elizabeth Keckley, *Behind the Scenes. Or, Thirty Years a Slave, and Four Years in the White House* (New York: G. W. Carleton & Co., 1868), 152–173.

---

1. The 536-ton unarmed sidewheel steamer *River Queen* was built in 1864 in Keyport, New Jersey. William M. Lytle and Forrest R. Holdcamper, comps., *Merchant Steam Vessels of the United States, 1790–1868* (Staten Island, NY: Steamship Historical Society of America, 1975), 185.

14

Lincoln's Death and the Future

"From one we may learn all"
Robert Hamilton
APRIL 22, 1865

Our understanding of the relationship between Northern blacks and Lincoln has been clouded by the response to the president's assassination and by subsequent political history. Given the unexpected pro-Southern policies of his successor Andrew Johnson and the widespread resistance to Reconstruction, Lincoln quickly became an appealing symbolic figure. Abolitionists and most Republicans turned Lincoln into the hero of emancipation and the savior of the Union, despite their previous dissatisfaction with his presidency. Lincoln suddenly became a rallying point for those who saw a "higher purpose" in the war, uniting emancipation with nationalism and the romance of reunion.

But this did not reflect the ways African Americans, abolitionists, and many Republicans viewed Lincoln *prior* to the assassination. Indeed, during his rise to national prominence, Lincoln proved a largely unappealing figure to Northern blacks. His opposition to equal rights, support of the nation's infamous "black laws" and the loathsome Fugitive Slave Law, his rejection of immediate emancipation, and his support of colonization repudiated every goal that black leaders had sought since the beginning of the organized antislavery movement. African Americans in the North rightly worried that Republicans, led by Lincoln, guaranteed to preserve slavery "where it is, and endorse[d] a policy which looks to the expulsion of the free black American from his native land." All the major parties appeared "barren and unfruitful." Lincoln's victory in the 1860 election saddened black leaders, and they turned away from

298

it "with a heavier heart and with a more dead despair of our future here." To many, Lincoln only represented "the fag end of a series of pro-slavery administrations." Viewed from the perspective of 1860, with the legacy of the Dred Scott decision fresh in their minds, African Americans had every reason to conclude that Lincoln embodied the "Godless will of a criminal nation."

Even one of Lincoln's greatest achievements, the Emancipation Proclamation, at best proved an ambiguous act during the war. At rallies across the North on January 1, 1863, African Americans thanked God, not Lincoln, for the change in policy; Lincoln was only God's "bell-ringer." Many black leaders criticized Lincoln for doing the very least, rather than the very most, that he could have done against slavery. African Americans North and South certainly welcomed the act, and from the perspective of the slave it heralded slavery's ultimate demise. But it left bondage quite alive in the border states, causing endless misery, and did not represent the moral condemnation of the institution that African Americans needed and deserved. They took Lincoln at his word that he issued the proclamation as an unavoidable war measure, not a moral statement. It was "no more humanitarian than a hundred pounder rifled cannon." The New York *Weekly Anglo-African* spoke for most Northern blacks when it charged that the Emancipation Proclamation was brought forth "by timid and heaven-doubting mid-wives" which "proved an incompetent and abominable abortion." Sgt. George E. Stephens, in the trenches with the 54th Massachusetts Regiment, had seen the workings of the proclamation and considered the document a strange "creature—an abortion wrung from the Executive womb by necessity." Slave owners still benefited from the Fugitive Slave Law, and they still possessed more rights than loyal blacks; most disappointing of all, the document freed no slaves in areas that the Union controlled. Coupled with the discrimination that black soldiers suffered, and which Lincoln refused to address, one could not help but conclude that the apparent change in war aims had little real foundation.

Lincoln rightly saw his chances for reelection in 1864 as slim at best. Prominent members of his own party, Salmon P. Chase and John C. Frémont, challenged his renomination, and many abolitionists, led by Wendell Phillips, supported the "Path Finder" over the "Rail-Splitter." The great black orator and author William Wells Brown spoke for many when he declared that the "colored people of the country rejoice in what Mr. Lincoln has done for them, but they all wish that Gen. Fremont had be[e]n in his place." As the *Weekly Anglo-African's* editor Robert Hamilton pointed out, what blacks knew about Lincoln's Reconstruction policies, as they worked out in Louisiana, stood as an ominous warning.

The following two editorials reflect the ambiguous place Lincoln held in African American history. On one hand, he stood in the way of racial progress, but on the other, he proved a martyr to freedom and democracy. The first, written by the *Weekly Anglo-African's* Robert Hamilton, concluded that Lincoln's time had come and gone, and that a new man committed to true democracy and civil rights needed to take the reins of power. The second, published shortly after Lincoln's assassination, was written by the former slave and editor of the New Orleans *Black Republican*, Rev. Stephen Walter Rogers (1839–1872). Rogers, emancipated by his owner's will in 1852, represented a rare case of a slave gaining literacy while in bondage. Not only did Rogers forge an editorial career, he also compiled a fifty-page book of hymns, titled *Roger's Compositions*. His editorial shows how quickly the Lincoln mythology settled into public consciousness. New York *Weekly Anglo-African*, August 27, 1859, December 22, 1860, March 16, 1861; *Liberator*, July 13, 1860; James M. McPherson, *The Struggle for Equality* (Princeton, NJ: Princeton University Press, 1964), 260–86; Yacovone, *A Voice of Thunder*, 13,18–19; C. Peter Ripley, *Slaves and Freedmen in Civil War Louisiana* (Baton Rouge, LA: Louisiana State University Press, 1976); Ripley et al., *The Black Abolitionist Papers*, 5:315; Howard N. Rabinowitz, ed., *Southern Black Leaders of the Reconstruction Era* (Urbana, IL: University of Illinois Press, 1982), 157, 167; *Ouachita Telegraph*, July 22, 1872.

"THY WILL BE DONE"

SINCE THAT COLD NIGHT in December nearly seventy years ago, when a grief-stricken rider rushed from Mount Vernon laden with the sad news of the death of Washington, no event has shed so profound a grief over the land as the murder of Abraham Lincoln. Then the nation all told, was a little over three million, now, it mounts up thirty millions of souls: spaces over which the news travelled, then in days and weeks, it reaches now in minutes and hours, so that the sudden news and extent of the shock, is, in the latter event tenfold the greater. Washington's career, moreover, to mortal eyes had run its course, and he was cut off rather from the comforts and delights of a well-earned retirement than arrested in the midst of his usefulness to mankind. With Abraham Lincoln it was different. He was still in the midst, and apparently an indispensable part of great events daily transpiring, and was really leaned upon by the best hopes of an immense majority of the people. Within a week of his death, a newspaper (*The N.Y. Express*) which has most bitterly opposed him, his party and his policy, uttered the remark that it *"had learned to pray for the preservation of his life."* Men had learned to trust the future of the nation to his keeping. So calmly had he met, so quietly and wisely had he overcome all past difficulties that we all regarded him as more than equal to any coming emergencies, and in the joy of our hearts were forgetting past afflictions, in the joyous sunlight of a golden peace in which he figured as the great central peacemaker. No matter what course he had chosen, we would have cheerfully acquiesced in it—sure that his wise instincts had led to what was best.

It was at this stage of his career that Abraham Lincoln was suddenly removed from our midst, and the nation aroused from that almost dreary confidence wherewith it had shifted to one poor mortal brain the responsibilities which really rested upon the intelligent millions. In the darkest hours of the rebellion when the yelling hosts of the insurgents pressed triumphantly on the soil of a free State, the people came to the rescue, and above and beyond the free devotion of their means, their time and their lives to the common safety, they helped him *think* the way out of danger. But now, that the immediate dangers and horrors of war have passed away, and there is only peace to be negotiated, the masses have suddenly stopped their helpful thinking and left the conditions of peace or reconstruction to the unaided judgment and discretion of one man, to whom, if Providence had not kindly removed him, the gigantic task would have been an impossible duty; who would have gone down under a more dismal fate than the assassin's bullet.

The lesson for the day therefore, is, that the people shall take up for themselves, and think out this problem of peace, or rather the principle on which alone peace can safely rest. There should not be any hurry in welcoming back to our outstretched hands and fervent breasts, the wolves, serpents and savage barbarians who yet constitute the head and front of the Southern people, and whose hearts are now dancing the scalp dance over the remains of our murdered President. HON. DANIEL

S. DICKINSON, [1] who, from long associations, must be thoroughly acquainted with this class, says, "the only safety of the country is in hunting them like wild beasts until they are all killed or driven out."

We are of the belief that loyal whites in the Southern States will require protection, if the slaveholding are allowed to remain under slacks of "oaths of allegiance." In the first place, they have no regard for such oaths; and in the next place, they must have a class to lord it over. The blacks will no longer be that class. They know the slaveocrats too well, have measured strength with them and will no longer submit. And, what will add to their resistance, is a consciousness that the Northern people are their friends. But the poor whites who are not learning to read, who are the political serfs of the dominant class will be kept in a condition of abject ignorance and poverty little if any removed from slavery. If the franchise be withheld from the freedmen, then the old slaveholding class, will, as before, fill all the offices and return to Congress as before in one compact body. Such will be the result of the reconstruction on the principles which seemed uppermost in the mind of our late deeply lamented President.

We think there is now an end to this policy. In a way which could have been compassed by no less a sacrifice, the North has been awakened to the danger into which it was drifting. The dreams of early peace[,] easy reconstruction, and grand material prosperity have been rudely broken by one dreadful reality. A "new born Cain" more reckless than his prototype flourishes his blood stained weapon in the face of the whole nation and boastfully recounts his horrible deed. From one we may learn all.

If the slaveholding class be awarded a milder punishment than banishment, then let it be entire disfranchisement during their natural lives. And not only the officers, but all the soldiers engaged in the rebellion should be disfranchised, the first as having forfeited the right by their own acts, and the last as showing utter incapacity for exercising the same. On these conditions, and these alone, there will be some hope of peace with the South. The franchise, the framing and the conduct of the government would be left to loyal hands and loyal hearts. The present generation of slaveholders would live and die in the presence of a gladder sight than they deserve to see—their country free, happy and prosperous—and their children, growing up under better auspices, might become partakers in the common weal.

In view, then, that this terrible awakening was required by this great nation in order to change its course of conduct, in view of the real peace, and sounder, if slower prosperity which will follow this change of policy, we can only, with uncovered heads and reverent hearts, and in the GREAT PRESENCE exclaim, THY WILL BE DONE.

New York *Weekly Anglo-African*, April 22, 1865.

---

1. Daniel S. Dickinson (1800–1866), former U.S. senator and unreconstructed Jacksonian Democrat, had been elected attorney general of New York in 1861. He aggressively supported the war effort and black recruitment. But he was no friend of African Americans, and he believed that a Union victory would help rid the North of its black population. *Biographical Directory of the American Congress, 1774–1949* (Washington, DC: Government Printing Office, 1950), 1083–1084; Allan Nevins, *The War for the Union*, 4 vols. (New York: Charles Scribner's Sons, 1959–1971) 3:168; Phyllis Field, *The Politics of Race in New York: The Struggle for Black Suffrage in the Civil War Era* (Ithaca, NY: Cornell University Press, 1982), 151–152.

"'Abraham, the Martyr'"
S. W. Rogers
APRIL 22, 1865

ASSASSINATION OF PRESIDENT LINCOLN

THE 13TH OF APRIL will be a day forever memorable in history by an act of atrocity that has no parallel in the annals of men. On the evening of that day, the President of the United States of America, while sitting quietly in his box at the theater—almost his only relaxation—in the capital of the country, in the company of his wife, in the very midst of his friends, at the zenith of his power, was shot to death by an assassin, who, after the deed of blood, leaped from the box to the stage, and exclaimed: "Now the South is avenged—be it so to all tyrants," and succeeded in escaping. At the same hour, the Hon. William H. Seward, Secretary of State, while lying hopelessly ill in his bed, in his own house, in the same city, is assaulted by a desperate accomplice of the murderer of Mr. Lincoln, and cut nearly to death, in the midst of his family and attendants, several of whom were seriously if not fatally wounded.

In the face of crimes so appalling, men are stunned. "Who next?" is the whispered inquiry.

These dreadful deeds are a fitting finale of this brutal and bloody rebellion. They are the natural results of it. By the rebellion, these men were instigated to the perpetuation of crimes that are but the *great* crime compressed into individual acts. They are the fell spirit of slavery breaking from the knife of the assassin—slavery, that for two hundred years has educated whole generations in cruelty and the spirit of murder; that, in the end, drove half a nation to a rebellion to destroy liberty, now whets the knife of the assassin to murder, in cold blood, the most illustrious exemplar of freedom.

Rebels may condemn these horrible acts; they may seek to run down the responsibility to some individual insanity, but they can never clear the skirts of the rebellion of the responsibility for the madness of the murderers. The assassins are the natural outcrop of that vast stratum of cruelty and of crime which slavery has been so long depositing below the surface of society. The greatest earthly friend of the colored race has fallen by the same spirit that has so long oppressed and destroyed us. In giving us our liberty, he has lost his own life. Following the rule of the great and glorious in the world, he has paid the penalty of Apostleship. He has sealed with his blood his Divine commission to be the liberator of a people. Hereafter, through all time, wherever the Black Race may be known in the world; whenever and wherever it shall lay the foundations of its power; build its cities and rear its temples, it will sacredly preserve if not deify the name of "*Abraham, the Martyr*."

New Orleans *The Black Republican*, April 22, 1865. Reprinted in Ripley et al., *The Black Abolitionist Papers*, 5:315–316.

"We ask for our rights,
upon the principle of our loyalty"
Rev. John J. Moore
OCTOBER 27, 1865

African Americans had organized state and national conventions since the 1830s. Such meetings proved important debate forums for African American leaders to hammer out national policies, strategies, and tactics. Every important subject in the history of the black abolitionist movement, from moral reform and education to emigration and slave violence, found a voice at these conventions. The national convention movement, understandably, proved a more difficult enterprise to sustain. While unanimity existed on the broadest subjects, little agreement could be established over strategy and tactics, and national conventions met infrequently and often inconclusively. But the state conventions proved more enduring, showed a greater degree of cooperation and agreement on goals and tactics, and better focused their energies.

California blacks staged four state conventions before 1865, beginning in 1855, with the largest held in October 1865 and dedicated to achieving black suffrage. Despite having won other rights, and the North's victory in the war, most blacks across the nation remained disfranchised. African Americans had justified their participation in the war on the basis that military service would be the foundation for their postwar claims for full citizenship. At state conventions across the nation and at soldiers and sailors conventions, the demand for the right to vote could be heard as loud as a volley of Enfield rifles. Blacks announced that "the bloody plains of Fort Pillow" cried out for justice. The South, they warned, may be defeated, but it was not vanquished. They "have not yet relinquished the purposes they sought to accomplish upon the field of battle; they are determined again to be in power, to curb the despised Yankees in all their isms, and grind deeper down in despair the unprotected Negro." From the Sea Islands of South Carolina to San Francisco, California, black soldiers, former slaves, and free blacks unanimously asserted that "traitors shall not dictate or prescribe to us the terms or conditions of our citizenship." The vote meant everything, and it represented the key to a future of full rights and justice.

To blacks such as the popular San Francisco abolitionist and AMEZ Church clergyman John Jamison Moore (1804–1893), African Americans had proven their right to the vote on every battlefield in American history, from "Bunker Hill to Richmond, where black American warriors now sleep in their bloody winding sheets, in thousands. No race on American soil, has given such proof of patriotism as the black race." Moore, a former Virginia slave, escaped with his parents to Pennsylvania and later settled in Baltimore and Boston. He moved to California in 1852, founded the first AMEZ Church in San Francisco, and played a leading role in all the California state conventions, serving as the conventions' official chaplain. Committed to the cause of freedom, he left the comforts of San Francisco in 1868 to labor among the former slaves, and he organized many churches in North Carolina, Georgia, and in the Bahama Islands. Philip S. Foner and George E. Walker, eds., *Proceedings of the Black State Conventions, 1840–1865,* 2 vols. (Philadelphia: Temple University Press, 1980), 2: 113, 134–135, 186; Eric Foner, *Reconstruction: American's Unfinished Revolution, 1863–1877* (New York: Harper & Row, 1988), 110–111; Quintard Taylor, *In Search of the Racial Frontier: African Americans in the American West, 1528–1990* (New York: W.W. Norton, 1998), 87, 103; Ripley et al., *The Black Abolitionist Papers,* 2: 404–405.

MR. PRESIDENT:[1]—On rising to address this Convention upon the momentous subject (political franchise), the first great right of an American citizen, which we are deprived of in this State by a Constitutional prohibition, I am aware, sir, that for me to attempt to supercede the able speech of the gentleman who has just taken his seat—whose masterly oratory, stirring pathos, and thundering eloquence, has captured every thought in the house—such an attempt by me would be the vainest act of my life. Yet, sir, I cannot let this great question of our right to the political franchise pass, without adding a word in behalf of our claim to that right.

I wish, sir, to make a few remarks upon the ground of our appeal to the State Legislature for the concession of our right of suffrage, by an amendment to the State Constitution, so as to secure to us this God given right. The Chairman of the Committee on Franchise, in his very profound remarks on presenting the able report, made a brilliant allusion to the unequalled bravery of the American Negro as a soldier—as tested in the bloody strife of the rebellion just past, where the nation's existence was staked upon the battle-field, in a chance at war. From this point he presented a masterly appeal as a basis of our claim. Now, sir to this category of argument in favor of our sacred cause, we wish to contribute. Sir, in the outset we appeal to the Legislature of a Christian people for our right of suffrage, upon the broad principle of human justice, as taught by the great rule, "Do unto others as you would they should do unto you." Ask them, if, in our stead, they would be willing to consent to such injustice as we suffer by them. Would they like such treatment at our hands? If honest in their answer, they will tell us no. Ask them if it was wrong for England to impose upon their forefathers "taxation without representation?" They must answer yes, or condemn their revolutionary fathers. Ask them if taxation without representation was any greater injustice imposed upon their forefathers, by England, than as imposed upon us by the law of this State? If candid, they will answer no. Why, then, will a Christian people commit such a flagrant wrong, which they so loudly condemn in others? Why will they perpetrate a knowing wrong upon a people because they know that they have not power to vindicate by force their just rights?

We appeal to them upon the principle of man's natural equal rights, as vindicated and set forth in the "Declaration of American Independence"—upon which rests the foundation of the Republic. That declaration sets forth that "All men are created equal" in human rights, or have the same natural rights, which man cannot justly invade or take away; and that to secure these rights equally to all men, "Governments are established among men, deriving their just powers from the consent of the governed." This is the doctrine of the Declaration of Independence; if this sentiment is wrong, why do not the American people blot it from their political creed? If it is right, then we appeal for our natural right to "Equality before the Law," as it sets forth. We appeal to them as friends of their own Republican principles, which they violate when they refuse us the right of suffrage.

We ask for our rights, upon the principle of our loyalty; we have never sworn falsely to the Government; we have never taken up arms against it,—we have never attempted to betray it into the hands of foreign powers. This is what no other race of men can truthfully assert in

America. We have prayed for it—fought for it—bled for it, and perished by thousands in its defence.

We make our appeal upon the principle of our patriotism. We have consecrated every battle-field of the country with our blood, to maintain its existence, from our love to the country, while it thrusts us with a cold heart and villainous hand from all its political rights and immunities. We rallied around its only standard of hope and fought in, deadly battle, the country's worst foes, foreign and domestic. He who doubts this, let him read the history of the death warrants of the battle grounds from Bunker Hill to Richmond, where black American warriors now sleep in their bloody winding sheets, in thousands. No race on American soil, has given such proof of patriotism as the black race; without boasting, we challenge a refutation of this position. We ask history, has any other nation on earth, under the light of Christianity, (but America), disfranchised its most loyal and patriotic citizens; preferring to grant [the] franchise to those that have desired and aimed to destroy the Government? We ask our Government to be as Republican as England, though pronounced a tyrannical monarchy. She gives her *black* and her *white* citizens alike privileges in political franchise; while in Republican America, white citizens only have the universal privilege of suffrage. We ask for our right to "Equality before the Law" upon the principle, that, it does not degrade the white man to fight along side of the Negro on the battle-field to save the country, or save the lives of white American citizens, it will not degrade white men, to vote side by side with Negroes, to preserve a Republican form of Government, and preserve the country from another war, which it does not require inspiration to predict, if the claims of justice are not meted out in Government affairs. We claim our rights of suffrage upon the ground that the opponents of our right to "Equality before the Law," have never adduced a single sound argument to prove what they raise as a objection to our right of suffrage; that is, that it will degrade the white man, deteriorate the Saxon race, amalgamate the two races, and take the country out of white men's hands. We can prove by calling the history of the country to our support that the spirit that opposes the black man's right to "Equality before the Law," has been baptized by the very institution of the country, (slavery), that has been fostering for two and a half centuries, the very evils of which our enemies pretend to fear.

The thirteen original States, at one period of their history, (all but South Carolina), allowed their colored citizens to vote; and history does not place a single fact upon record, showing that granting the Negroes the right of suffrage in any of those States engendered amalgamation of the black and white races, or that it caused a deterioration of the Saxon race, nor was the Government ever threatened with black sovereignty. No! this was not the fear of political power in the black man's hand; it was slavery looking out for its own interest, feared the free Negro in political power; because he was of the enslaved race, and in stronger sympathy with the slave; it took its stand-point in South Carolina, and swept from the Negro's hand the ballot box in every State it could influence politically; and it is the spirit of slavery that now opposes Negro suffrage throughout the land.

We hurl back with scorn and contempt the frequent intimation of scurrilous newspapers that granting us "Equality before the Law," would induce us to thrust ourselves into the society of the whites. Notwithstanding they, through their beloved institution of slavery, have thrust their race upon us,—we want it to be particularly understood, we never have had and are not likely to have, any particular fondness for the Saxon race above our own. Whatever isolated cases of amalgamation of the two races have occurred in any part of the country, on marriage principles, on the part of the whites it has been mostly the Irish, who pretend to be the most violent enemies of Negro rights; and what is a remarkable truth, that where such conjugal unity takes place, while the party of the Celtic race retains his caste or social standing, the party of the African race looses his caste or social standing generally among his sable brethren, of the higher order of society. We appeal to every true American whose voice shall respond in the proud capital over which the glorious stars and stripes shall float, to give us our rights in the name and spirit of the murdered and immortal Lincoln, who sealed our rights with his hallowed blood, who said this people, (the colored), ought to have "Equality before the Law."

Upon these logical principles we make our simple, unsophisticated and earnest appeal to every friend of justice and humanity—every Republican, true Union man and Christian, in the Legislature, in the State and in the country. In vindication of our holy cause, we appeal to every true Union journal in the State and on the Pacific coast, while we shall also supplicate with Christian fervor, the Great Sovereign of all men, and of all nations of men, and the absolute defender of human rights, and all great principles in his moral government; to Him also will we appeal for an interposing hand in the defence of our glorious cause, while there is a sable American son to plead for justice in his race. This is our land where we have had our birth, for it we have fought and bled, here we will remain, as a race, until eternities thunders shake us from this soil.

Proceedings of the California State Convention of the Colored Citizens, Held in Sacramento on the 25th, 26th, 27th and 28th of October 1865 (San Francisco: Office of the Elevator, 1865). Reprinted in Philip S. Foner and George E. Walker, eds., *Proceedings of the Black State Conventions, 1840–1865*, 2 vols. (Philadelphia: Temple University Press, 1980), 2:189–190.

---

1. Frederick G. Barbadoes, a San Francisco black abolitionist, served as president of the convention. He had moved to California in the 1850s and attended several black state and national conventions. After the Civil War, he returned to Massachusetts and continued to fight for black rights. Philip S. Foner and George E. Walker, eds., *Proceedings of the Black National Conventions, 1865–1900* (Philadelphia: Temple University Press, 1986), 341, 344.

PART II

Memory's Battlefield

15

The Context of Black Service

"The Negro as a Soldier"
Christian A. Fleetwood
1895

The struggle to reforge national unity, founded upon the political compromise of 1877, also included a social compromise between the North and the South. Southern whites, abetted by the connivance or indifference of most Northerners, won a free hand to maintain order and racial dominance. The legacy of black military heroism could occupy no place in supremacist schemes that depicted the Old South as a golden age of chivalry and its slaves as either happy and loyal or vicious beasts eager to insult true white womanhood. This "Lost Cause" mythology, popularized in the North, suffocated white social thought on the question of race and placed an appealing cover over the systematic murder and suppression of African Americans.

In every war since the Civil War, white Americans raised the issue of racial inferiority to crush black aspirations and denigrate their achievements. In a war that would erupt three years after publication of Christian A. Fleetwood's (1840–1914) history of black military service, the best that whites could muster to recognize the black soldier's service in Cuba was "God bless the nigger!" The Spanish-American War, despite the black heroism displayed in it, only further spurred Civil War white reunionist sentiment and allowed the South to harden its apartheid system. Little public awareness of black participation in the Civil War survived; its legacy remained alive primarily among aging members of the Grand Army of the Republic and among the even older reformers of Boston and its vicinity.

313

A few surviving black soldiers, however, fought this national amnesia by publishing memoirs of their service or, as in the case of Fleetwood, by placing the African American role in the Civil War in its historical context. One cannot overestimate the importance of Fleetwood's pamphlet, reproduced in full here. At a time when whites sought to expunge the role of blacks from the nation's military history, *The Negro as a Soldier,* presented at the 1895 Negro Congress and International Exposition in Atlanta, Georgia, defiantly traced black service and heroism from the beginning of the nation's history.

Born of free parents in Baltimore and educated under the auspices of the Maryland Colonization Society, Fleetwood lived briefly in Liberia and Sierra Leone. He returned to the United States to attend the Ashmund Institute (later renamed Lincoln University) and, after his graduation in 1860, he published the *Lyceum Observer* in Baltimore. He joined the 4th USCT on August 14, 1863, fought in North Carolina and Georgia, and won the Medal of Honor for heroism in the battle of Chaflin's Farm, Virginia, on September 29, 1864. Every white officer in his regiment recommended Fleetwood for an officer's commission, but the War Department rejected the promotion on account of Fleetwood's race. After the war, Fleetwood organized black militia and cadet corps in Washington, D.C., and became renowned for his singing talents, receiving the support of the wives of Presidents Hayes and Cleveland. Adele Logan Alexander, *Homelands and Waterways: The American Journey of the Bond Family, 1846–1926* (New York: Vintage, 1999), 251; David W. Blight, *Race and Reunion: The Civil War in American Memory* (Cambridge, MA: Harvard University Press, 2001), 348–353; Rayford W. Logan and Michael R. Winston, eds., *Dictionary of American Negro Biography* (New York: W.W. Norton, 1982), 223–224.

IN THE WAR OF THE REVOLUTION

FOR SIXTEEN HUNDRED YEARS prior to the war between Great Britain and the Colonies, the pages of history bear no record of the Negro as a soldier. Tracing his separate history in the Revolutionary War, is a task of much difficulty, for the reason that while individual instances of valor and patriotism abound there were so few separate bodies of Negro troops, that no separate record appears to have been made. The simple fact is that the fathers as a rule enlisted men both for the Army and the

Navy, just as now, is only continued by the Navy, that is to say, they were assigned wherever needed, without regard to race or color. Varner's[1] Rhode Island Battalion appears to have been the only large aggregation of Negroes in this war, though Connecticut, New York, and New Hampshire each furnished one separate company in addition to individuals scattered through their other organizations, so that ere the close of the war, there were very few brigades, regiments, or companies in which the Negro was not in evidence.

The free Negro appears to have gone in from the beginning without attracting or calling out special comment. Later, as men grew scarcer and necessity more pressing, slaves were taken in also, and then the trouble began. Those who held slaves did not care to lose them in this way. Others who had not, did not think it just the thing in a war for avowed freedom to place an actual slave in the ranks to fight. Some did not want the Negro, bond or free, to take part as a soldier in the struggle. So that in May, 1775, the Massachusetts Committee of Safety voted that thereafter only free men should be enlisted. In July, Gen. [Horatio] Gates issued an order prohibiting further enlistments of Negroes, but saying nothing of those already in the service.

In October, a council of war, presided over by Gen. [George] Washington, comprising three Major Generals and six Brigadier Generals, voted unanimously against the enlistment of slaves, and by a decided majority against further enlistments of Negroes. Ten days later in a conference held at Cambridge, Mass., participated in by Gen. Washington, Benj. Franklin, Benj. Harrison, Thos. Lynch, and the deputy governors of Connecticut and Rhode Island, the same action was taken.

On the 7th November, 1775, Earl Dunmore, commanding the forces of His Majesty the King, issued a proclamation offering freedom and equal pay to all slaves who would join his armies as soldiers.[2] It did not take the colonists long to find out their mistake, although Gen. Washington, in accordance with the expressed will of his officers and of the Committee of Safety, did on the 17th Nov., 1775, issue a proclamation forbidding the further enlistment of Negroes. Less than two months later, that is to say on the 30th Dec., 1775, he issued a second proclamation again authorizing the enlistment of free Negroes. He advised Congress of his action, and stated that he would recall it if so directed. But he was not. The splendid service rendered by the Negro and the great and pressing need of men were such, that although the opposition continued from some sections, it was not thereafter strong enough to get recognition. So the Negroes went and came much as did other men.

In all the events of the war, from Bunker Hill to Yorktown, they bore an honorable part. The history of the doings of the armies is their history, as in everything they took part and did their share. Their total enlistment was about 3,000 men. A very fair percentage for the then population. I might instance the killing of Major [John] Pitcairn, at Bunker Hill, by Peter Salem, and of Major [William] Montgomery at Fort Griswold [Groton, Connecticut] by Jordan Freeman. The part they took in the capture of Major-General [Richard] Prescott at Newport; their gallant defense of Colonel [Christopher] Greene, their beloved commander, when he was surprised and murdered at Croton River [Battle of Red Bank], May 13, 1781, when it was only after the last of his faithful guards had been shot and cut down that he was reached; or at the battle of Rhode Island, when a battalion of 400 Negroes withstood three separate and distinct charges from 1,500 Hessians under Count [Carl Emil Kurt von] Donop, and beat them back with such tremendous loss that Count Donop at once applied for an exchange, fearing that his men would kill him if he went into battle with them again, for having exposed them to such slaughter; and many other instances that are of record. The letter following, written Dec. 5, 1775, explains itself;

To the Honorable General Court of the Massachusetts Bay.

The subscribers beg leave to report to your Honorable House which we do in justice to the character of so brave a man, that under our own observation we declare that a Negro Man named Salem Poor, of Col. [Joseph] Frye's Regiment, Cap. [John] Ames' Company, in the late battle at Charleston, behaved like an experienced officer as well as an excellent soldier. To set forth particulars of his conduct would be tedious. We would only beg to say, in the person of this Negro centers a brave and gallant soldier. The reward due to so great and distinguished a character, we submit to Congress.

JONA. BREWER, Col.	WM. PRESCOTT, Col.
THOMAS NIXON, Lt. Col.	EPHM. COREY, Lieut.
JOSEPH BAKER, Lieut.	JOSHUA ROW, Lieut.
JONAS RICHARDSON, Capt.	ELIPHALETT BODWELL, Sergt.
EBENEZER VARNUM, 2 Lt.	WM. HUDSON BALLARD, Capt.
WILLIAM SMITH, Capt.	JOHN MORTON, Sergt.
RICHARD WELSH, Lieut.	

This is a splendid and well attested tribute to a gallant and worthy Negro. There were many such, but, beyond receiving and reading no action was taken thereon by Congress. There is no lack of incidents and the temptation to quote many of them is great, but the time allotted me is too brief for extended mention and I must bring this branch of my subject to a close. It is in evidence that while so many Negroes were offering their lives a willing sacrifice for the country, in some sections the officers of the Continental Forces received their bounty and pay in Negroes, "grown" and "small," instead of "dollars" and "cents." Fighting for *Liberty* and taking pay in *Slaves!*

When the war was over the free men returned to meet their same difficulties; the slaves were caught when possible and reenslaved by their former masters. In Boston a few years later we find a party of black patriots of the Revolution mobbed on Boston Common while celebrating the anniversary of the abolition of the slave trade.[3]

The captain of a vessel trading along the coast tells of a Negro who had fought in the war and been distinguished for bravery and soldiery conduct. He was reclaimed and reenslaved by his master after the war, and served him faithfully until old age rendered him useless. The master then brought the poor old slave to this captain and asked him to take him along on his trip and try to sell him. The captain hated to sell a man who had fought for his country, but finally agreed, took the poor old man to Mobile, and sold him for $100 to a man who put him to attending a chicken coop. His former master continued to draw the old slave's pension as a soldier in the Revolution, until he died.

THE WAR OF 1812

THE WAR OF 1812 was mainly fought upon the water, and in the American navy at that time the Negro stood in the ratio of about one to six. We find record of complaint by Commodore [Oliver Hazzard] Perry at the beginning because of the large number of Negroes sent him, but later the highest tribute to their bravery and efficiency. Capt. Shaler, of the armed brig General Thompson, writing of an engagement between his vessel and a British frigate, says:

"The name of one of my poor fellows, who was killed, ought to be registered in the book of fame, and remembered as long as bravery is a virtue. He was a black man, by the name John Johnson. A twenty-four pound shot struck him in the hip, and took away all the lower part of his body. In this state the poor brave fellow lay on the deck, and several times exclaimed to his shipmates: 'Fire away, my boys; no haul a color down!' Another black man, by the name of John Davis, who was struck in much the same manner, repeatedly requested to be thrown overboard, saying that he was only in the way of others."

I know of nothing finer in history than these.

As before, the Negro was not universally welcomed to the ranks of the American army; but later continued reverses and a lack of enthusiasm in enlistments made it necessary to seek his aid, and from Mobile, Ala., on September 21, 1814, General [Andrew] Jackson issued a stirring call to the free colored people of Louisiana for aid. It began thus:

"Through a mistaken policy you have heretofore been deprived of a participation in the glorious struggle for national rights in which our country is engaged. This no longer shall exist."

In a remarkably short period, two battalions were raised, under Majors LaCaste and Savary, which did splendid service in the battle of New Orleans. New York enrolled two battalions, and sent them to Sacketts Harbor. Pennsylvania enrolled twenty-four hundred, and sent them to Gray's Ferry at the capture of Washington, to prepare for the invading column. Another battalion also was raised, armed, equipped and ready to start to the front, when peace was declared.

Let us hear the testimony of that original democrat, General Jackson. Under the date of Dec. 18, 1814, he writes as follows:

"To the men of color, soldiers: From the shores of Mobile I called you to arms. I invited you to share in the perils and to divide the glory of your white countrymen. I expected much from you; for I was not uninformed of those qualities which must render you so formidable to an invading foe. I knew you could endure hunger and thirst, and all the hardships of war. I knew that you loved the land of your nativity, and that, like ourselves, you had to defend all that is most dear to man. But you surpass my hopes. I have found in you, united to those qualities, that noble enthusiasm that impels to great deeds.

"Soldiers: The President of the United States shall be informed of your conduct on the present occasion, and the voice of the representatives of the American nation shall applaud your valor, as your general now praises your ardor. The enemy is near. His sails cover the lakes, but the brave are united, and if he finds us contending among ourselves, it will be for the prize of valor, and fame its noblest reward."

In one of the actions of this war, a charging column of the American army was repulsed and thrown into great disorder. A Negro private, seeing the disaster, sprang upon a horse, and by heroic effort rallied the troops, led them back upon a second charge, and completely routed the enemy. He was rewarded by General Jackson with the honorary title of Major. Under the laws he could not commission him.

When the war was over, this gallant man returned to his home in Nashville, Tenn., where he lived for years afterward, highly respected by its citizens of all races.

At the age of seventy years, this black hero was obliged, *in self-defense*, to strike a white ruffian, who had assaulted him. Under the laws of the State he was arrested and given nine and thirty lashes on his bare back. It broke his heart, and Major Jeffreys died.[4]

THE WAR FOR THE UNION

IT SEEMS A LITTLE singular that in the tremendous struggle between the States in 1861–1865, the south should have been the first to take steps toward the enlistment of Negroes. Yet such is the fact. Two weeks after the fall of Fort Sumter, the "Charleston Mercury" records the passing through Augusta of several companies of the 3rd and 4th Georgia Regt., and of sixteen well-drilled companies *and one Negro company* from Nashville, Tenn.

"The Memphis Avalanche" and "The Memphis Appeal" of May 9, 10, and 11, 1861, give notice of the appointment by the "Committee of Safety" of a committee of three persons "to organize a volunteer company composed of our patriotic freeman of color of the city of Memphis, for the service of our common defense."

A telegram from New Orleans dated November 23, 1861, notes the review by Gov. [Thomas Overton] Moore of over 28,000 troops, and that one regiment comprised "*1,400 colored men.*" "The New Orleans Picayune," referring to a review held February 9, 1862, says: "We must also pay a deserved compliment to the companies of free colored men, all very well drilled and comfortably equipped."

It is a little odd, too, that in the evacuation of New Orleans a little later, in April, 1862, all of the troops succeeded in getting away except the Negroes. They "got left."

It is not in the line of this paper to speculate upon what would have been the result of the war had the South kept up this policy, enlisted the freemen, and emancipated the enlisting slaves and their families.

The immense addition to their fighting force, the quick recognition of them by Great Britain, to which slavery was the greatest bar, and the fact that the heart of the Negro was with the South but for slavery, and the case stands clear. But the primary successes of the South closed its eyes to its only chance of salvation, while at the same time the eyes of the North were opened.

In 1865, the South saw, and endeavored to remedy its error. On March 9, 1865, the Confederate Congress passed a bill, recommended by Gen. Lee, authorizing the enlistment of 200,000 Negroes; but it was then too late.

The North came slowly and reluctantly to recognize the Negro as a factor for good in the war. "This is a white man's war," met the Negroes at every step of their first efforts to gain admission to the armies of the Union.

To General David Hunter more than to any other one man, is due the credit for the successful entry upon the stage of the Negro as a soldier in this war.

In the spring of 1862, he raised and equipped a regiment of Negroes in South Carolina, and when the fact became known in Washington and throughout the country, such a storm was raised about the ears of the administration that they gracefully stood aside and left the brave general to fight his enemies in the front and rear as best he might. He was quite capable to do both, as it proved.

On the 9th of June, 1862, Mr. [Charles A.] Wickcliffe, of Kentucky, introduced a resolution in the House of Representatives, which was passed, calling upon the Secretary of War for information as to the fact of these enlistments and by what authority this matter was done.

The Secretary of War replied under date June 14, 1862, disavowing any official knowledge of such a regiment and denying that any authority had been given therefor. He referred the resolution to Gen. Hunter. His reply is one of the best things of the war. I quote it entire.

Headquarters, Department of the South,
Port Royal, S.C. , June 23, 1862.

Hon. Edwin M. Stanton, Secretary of War,
Washington.

SIR: I have the honor to acknowledge the receipt of a communication from the Adjutant-General of the Army, dated June 16, 1862, requesting me to furnish you with the information necessary to answer certain resolutions introduced in the House of Representatives June 9, 1862, on motion of the Hon. Mr. Wickcliffe, of Kentucky, their substance being to inquire: First, whether I had organized, or was organizing, a regiment of fugitive slaves in this department; Second, whether any authority had been given to me from the War Department for such organization; and Third, whether I had been furnished by order of the War Department with clothing, uniforms, arms, equipments, etc., for such a force.

Only having received the letter conveying the inquiries at a late hour on Saturday night, I urge forward my answer in time for the steamer sailing to-day (Monday), this haste preventing me from entering as minutely as I could wish upon many points of detail, such as the paramount importance of the subject calls for. But in view of the near termination of the present session of Congress, and the widespread interest which must have been awakened by Mr. Wickliffe's resolution, I prefer sending even this imperfect answer to waiting the period necessary for the collection of fuller and more comprehensive data.

To the first question, therefore, I reply that no regiment of "fugitive slaves" has been or is organized in this department. There is, however, a fine regiment of persons whose late masters are "fugitive rebels," men who everywhere fly before the appearance of the national flag, leaving their servants behind them to shift as best they can for themselves. So far, indeed, are the loyal persons composing this regiment from seeking to avoid the presence of their late owners that they are now, one and all, working with remarkable industry to place themselves in a position to go in full and effective pursuit of their fugacious and traitorous proprietors.

To the second question, I have the honor to answer, that the instructions given to Brig. General W. T. Sherman by the Hon. Simon Cameron, late Secretary of War, and turned over to me by succession for my guidance, do distinctly authorize me to employ all loyal persons offering their services in defense of the Union and for the suppression of this rebellion in any manner I might see fit, or that the circumstances might call for. There is no restriction as to the character or color of the persons who might be employed, or the nature of the employment; whether civil or military, in which their services could be used. I conclude, therefore, that I have been authorized to enlist "fugitive slaves" as soldiers, could any be found in this department.

No such characters have, however, yet appeared within our most advanced pickets, the loyal slaves everywhere remaining on their plantations to welcome us, and supply us with food, labor and information. It is the masters who have, in every instance, been the "fugitives"—running away from loyal slaves as well as loyal soldiers, and whom we have only partially been able to see—chiefly their heads over ramparts, or, rifle in hand, dodging behind trees, in the extreme distance. In the absence of any "fugitive master" law, the deserted slaves would be wholly without remedy, had not the crime of treason given them the right to pursue, capture, and bring back those persons of whose protection they have been thus suddenly bereft.

To the third interrogatory, it is my painful duty to reply, that I have never received any specific authority for issuing clothing, uniforms, arms, equipments, etc., to the troops in question. My general instructions from Mr. Cameron, to employ them in any manner I might find necessary, and the military exigencies of the department and the country being my only, but, in my judgement, sufficient justification. Neither have I had any specific authority for supplying these persons with shovels, spades and pickaxes when employing them as laborers, nor with boats and oars when using them as lightermen; but these are not points included in Mr. Wickcliffe's resolution. To me it seemed that liberty to employ men in any particular capacity implied with it liberty also to supply them with the necessary tools; and acting under this faith I have clothed, equipped and armed the only loyal regiment yet raised in South Carolina.

I must say in vindication of my conduct that had it not been for the many other diversified and imperative claims on my time, a much more satisfactory result might have ben hoped for; and that, in place of only one, as at present, at least five or six well-drilled, brave, and thoroughly acclimated regiments should by this time have been added to the loyal forces of the Union.

The experiment of arming the blacks, so far as I have made it, has been a compete and even marvellous success. They are sober, docile, attentive, and enthusiastic, displaying great natural capacities for acquiring the duties of a soldier. They are eager beyond all things to take the field and be led into action; and it is the unanimous opinion of the officers who have had charge of them, that in the peculiarities of this climate and country, they will prove invaluable auxiliaries, fully equal to the similar regiments so long and successfully used by the British authorities in the West Indies.

In conclusion I would say it is my hope, there appearing to be no possibility of other reinforcements owing to the exigencies of the campaign in the peninsular, to have organized by the end of next fall and to be able to present to the Government from forty-eight to fifty thousand of these hardy and devoted soldiers.

Trusting that this letter may form part of your answer to Mr. Wickliffe's resolution.

I have the honor to be, most respectfully, your obedient servant,

D. HUNTER,
Major General Commanding.

The reading of this famous document in the House brought out such a storm of laughter, from both friends and foes that further action was impossible. The Hon. Sunset Cox speaking of the matter some years later said: "I tell you that letter from Hunter spoiled the prettiest speech I had ever thought of making. I had been delighted with Wickliffe's motion, and thought the reply to it would furnish us with the first-rate democratic thunder for the next election. I made up my mind to sail in on Hunter's answer no matter what it was—the moment it came, and to be even more humorously successful in its delivery and reception than I was in my speech against war-horse [John A.] Gurley of Ohio. Well you see, man proposes, but Providence orders otherwise. When the clerk announced the receipt of the letter, and that he was about to read it, I caught the Speaker's eye, and was booked for the first speech against your Negro experiment. The first sentence being formal and official was very well; but at the second the House began to grin, and at the third, there was not a man on the floor, except Father Wickliffe, of Kentucky, perhaps, who was not convulsed with laughter. Even my own risibles I found to be affected, and before the document was concluded, I motioned to the Speaker that he might give the floor to whom he pleased, as my desire to distinguish myself in that particular tilt was over."

The beginning of 1863, saw the opening of the doors to the Negro in every direction. General Lorenzo Thomas went in person to the valley of the Mississippi to supervise it there. Massachusetts was authorized to fill its quota with Negroes. The States of Maryland, Missouri, Delaware and Tennessee were thrown open by order of the War Department, and all slaves enlisting therefrom declared free. Ohio, Connecticut, Pennsylvania and New York joined the band and sent the stalwart black boy

in blue to the front singing, "Give us a flag, all free, without a slave."
For two years the fierce and determined opposition had kept them out,
but now the bars were down and they came pouring in. Some one said
he cared not who made the laws of a people if he could make their songs.
A better exemplification of this would be difficult to find than is the
song written by "Miles O'Reily" (Col. [Charles G.] Halpine), of the old
10th Army Corps. I cannot resist the temptation to quote it here. With
General Hunter's letter and this song to quote from, the episode was
closed:

> Some say it is a burning shame to make Naygurs fight,
>   An' that the trade o' being kilt belongs to the white:
> But as for me, upon me sowl, so liberal are we here,
>   I'll let Sambo be murthered, in place of meself, on every day of the
>   year.
> On every day of the year, boys, and every hour in the day,
>   The right to be kilt I'll divide wid him, and divil a word I'll say.

> In battles wild commotion I shouldn't at all object,
>   If Sambo's body should stop a ball that was coming for me direct,
> An' the prod of a southern bayonet, so liberal are we here,
>   I'll resign and let Sambo take it, on every day in the year,
> On every day in the year, boys, an' wid none of your nasty pride,
>   All right in a southern bagnet prod, wid Sambo I'll divide.

> The men who object to Sambo, should take his place and fight,
>   An' it is betther to have a Naygur's hue, than a liver that's weak
>   an' white,
> Though Sambo's black as the ace of spades, his finger a thryger can
>   pull,
>   An' his eye runs straight on the barrel sight from under its thatch
>   of wool,
> So hear me all, boys, darlin, don't think I'm tipping you chaff,
>   The right to be kilt, I'll divide with him, an' give him the largest
>   half.

It took three years of war to place the enlisted Negro upon the same
ground as the enlisted white man as to pay and emoluments; *perhaps* six

years of war might have given him shoulder-straps, but the war ended without authorization of law for that step. At first they were received, under an act of Congress that allowed each one, without regard to rank, ten dollars per month, three dollars thereof to be retained for clothing and equipments. I think it was in May, '64, when the act was passed equalizing the pay, but not opening the doors to promotion.[5]

Under an act of the Confederate Congress, making it a crime punishable with death for any white person to train any Negro or mulatto to arms, or aid them in any military enterprise, and devoting the Negro caught under arms to the tender mercies of the "present or future laws of the State" in which caught, a large number of *promotions* were made by the way of a rope and a tree along the first year of the Negro's service (I can even recall one instance as late as April 1865, though it had been long before then generally discontinued).

What the Negro did, how he did it, and where, it would take volumes to properly record, I can however give but briefest mention to a few of the many evidences of his fitness for the duties of the war, and his aid to the cause of the Union.

The first fighting done by organized Negro troops appears to have been done by Company A, First South Carolina Negro Regiment, at St. Helena Island, November 3–10, 1862, while participating in an expedition along the cost of Georgia and Florida under Lt.-Col. O. T. Beard, of the Forty-eighth New York Infantry, who says in his report:—

"The colored men fought with astonishing coolness and bravery. I found them all I could desire, more than I had hoped. They behaved gloriously, and deserve all praise."

The testimony thus inaugurated runs like a cord of gold through the web and woof of the history of the Negro as a soldier from that date to their final charge, the last made at Clover Hill, Va., April 9, 1865.

Necessarily the first actions in which the Negro bore a part commanded most attention. Friends and enemies were looking eagerly to see how they would acquit themselves, and so it comes to pass that the names of Fort Wagner, Olustee, Millikens Bend, Port Hudson and Fort Pillow are as familiar as Bull Run, Antietam, Shiloh and Gettysburg, and while those first experiences were mostly severe reverses, they were by that very fact splendid exemplifiers of the truth that the Negroes could be relied upon to fight under the most adverse circumstances, against any odds, and could not be discouraged.

Let us glance for a moment at Port Hudson, La., in May, 1863, assaulted by General [Nathaniel P.] Banks with a force of which the First and Second Regiments, Louisiana Native Guards, formed a part. When starting upon their desperate mission, Colonel [Spencer H.] Stafford of the First Regiment[6] in turning over the regimental colors to the color guard, made a brief and patriotic address, closing in the words:

"Color Guard: Protect, defend, die for, but do not surrender these colors." The gallant flag-sergeant, [Anselmas] Planciancois,[7] taking them replied: "Colonel: I will bring back these colors to you in honor, or report to God the reason why."

Six times with desperate valor they charged over ground where success was hopeless, a deep bayou between them and the works of the enemy at the point of attack rendered it impossible to reach them, yet strange to say, six times they were ordered forward and six times they went to useless death, until swept back by the blazing breath of shot and shell before which nothing living could stand. Here fell the gallant Captain [Andre] Cailloux,[8] black as the ace of spades; refusing to leave the field though his arm had been shattered by a bullet he returned to the charge until killed by a shell.

A soldier limping painfully to the front was halted and asked where he was going, he replied: "I am shot bad in de leg, and dey want me to go to de hospital, but I guess I can give 'em a little more yet."

The colors came back but crimsoned with the blood of the gallant Planciancois, who reported to God from that bloody field.

Shall we glance from this to Millikens Bend, La., in January, 1863, garrisoned by the Ninth and Eleventh Louisiana and the First Mississippi,[9] all Negroes, and about one hundred and sixty of the twenty-third Iowa (white), about eleven hundred fighting men in all. Attacked by a force of six Confederate regiments, crushed out of their works by sheer weight of numbers, borne down toward the levee, fighting every step of the way, hand to hand, clubbed musket, bayonets and swords, from three a. m. to twelve, noon, when a Union gun-boat came to the rescue and shelled the desperate foe back to the woods, with a total loss to the defenders of 437 men, two-fifths of their strength.

Shall we turn with sadness to Fort Wagner, S. C., in July, 1863, when the Fifty-fourth Mass. won its deathless fame, and its grand young commander, Col. Robert Gould Shaw, passed into the temple of immortality. After a march of all day, under a burning sun, and all night through a tempest of wind and rain, drenched, exhausted, hungry, they wheel into line, without a murmur for that awful charge, that dance of death, the struggle against hopeless odds, and the shattered remnants were hurled back as from the mouth of hell, leaving the dead bodies of their young commander and his noble followers to be buried in a common grave. Its total loss was about one-third of its strength.

Here it was that the gallant Flag-sergeant [William H.] Carney,[10] though grievously wounded, bore back his flag to safety, and fell faint-ing and exhausted with loss of blood, saying "Boys, the old flag never touched the ground!" Or another glance, at ill-starred Olustee, where the gallant 8th U. S. C. T. lost 87 killed of its effective fighting force, the largest loss in any one colored regiment in any one action of the war. And so on, by Fort Pillow, which let us pass in merciful silence, and to Honey Hill, S. C., perhaps the last desperate fight in the far south, in which the 32nd, 35th and 102nd U. S. C. T. and the 54th and 55th Mass. Inf. won fresh and fadeless laurels for splendid fighting against hopeless odds and insurmountable difficulties, and then to Nashville, Tennessee, with its recorded loss of 84 killed in the effectives of the 13th U. S. C. T.[11]

These were all brilliant actions, and they covered the actors with and reflected upon the race a blaze of glory. But it was in the armies of the James and of the Potomac that the true metal of the Negro as a soldier rang out its clearest notes amid the tremendous diapasons that rolled back and forth between the embattled hosts. Here was war indeed, upon its grandest scale, and in all its infinite variety. The tireless march un-der burning sun, chilling frosts and driven tempests, the lonely vigil of the picket under starless skies, the rush and roar of countless "hosts to battle driven" in the mad charge and the victorious shout that pursued the fleeing foe; the grim determination that held its line of defenses with set teeth, blood-shot eye and strained muscle beating back charge after charge of the foe; the patient labor in trench and mine, on hill and in valley, swamp and jungle, with disease adding its horrors to the dec-imation of shot and shell.

Here the Negro stood in the full glare of the greatest search light, part and parcel of the grandest armies ever mustered upon this continent, competing side by side with the best and bravest of the Union army against the flower of the Confederacy, the best and bravest of Lee's army, and losing nothing in the contrast. Never again while time lasts will the doubt arise as in 1861, "Will the Negro fight?" As a problem, it has been solved, as a question it has been answered, and as a fact it is as established as the eternal hills. It was they who rang up the curtain upon the last act of the bloody tragedy at Petersburg, Va., June 15, 1864, and they who rang it down at Clover Hill, Va., April 9, 1865. They were one of the strong fingers upon the mighty hand that grasped the giant's throat at Petersburg and never flexed until the breath went out at Appomattox. In this period it would take page on page to recount their deeds of valor and their glorious victories.

See them on the 15th of June, 1864, carrying the outpost at Baylor's field in early morning, and all that long, hot, summer day advancing, a few yards at a time, then lying down to escape the fire from the works, but still gradually creeping nearer and nearer, until, just as the sun went down, they swept like a tornado over the works and started upon a race for the city, close at the heels of the flying foe, until mistakenly ordered back. Of this day's experience Gen. [Adam] Badeau writes: "No worse strain on the nerves of troops is possible, for it is harder to remain quiet under cannon fire, even though comparatively harmless, than to advance against a storm of musketry." General W. F. "Baldy" Smith, speaking of their conduct, says: "No nobler effort has been put forth today, and no greater success achieved than that of the colored troops."

In his order of the day he says:

"To the colored troops comprising the Division of General [Edward W.] Hinks, the general commanding would call the attention of his command. With the veterans of the Eighteenth corps, they have stormed the works of the enemy and carried them, taking guns and prisoners, and in the whole affair they have displayed all the qualities of good soldiers."

Or, again, at the terrible mine explosion of July 30, 1864, on the Petersburg line, and at the fearful slaughter of September 29, 1864, at New Market Heights and Fort Harrison. On this last date in the Fourth U.S. Col. Troops, out of a color-guard of twelve men, but one came off the field on his own feet.[12] The gallant Flag-sergeant [Alfred B.] Hilton, the last to fall, cried out as he went down, "Boys, save the colors;" and they were saved.

After the magnificent fighting of this last date, under date of Oct. 11, 1864, Maj.-General B. F. Butler issued an order, a portion of which I quote, as follows:

"Of the colored soldiers of the third divisions of the 18th and 10th Corps and the officers who led them, the general commanding desires to make special mention. In the charge on the enemy's works by the colored division of the 18th Corps at New Market, better men were never better led, better officers never led better men. A few more such gallant charges and to command colored troops will be the post of honor in the American armies. The colored soldiers, by coolness, steadiness, determined courage and dash, have silenced every cavil of the doubters of their soldiery capacity, and drawn tokens of admiration from their enemies, have brought their late masters even to the consideration of the question whether they will not employ as soldiers the hitherto despised race."

Some ten or more years later, in Congress, in the midst of a speech advocating the giving of civil rights to the Negro, Gen. Butler said, referring to this incident:

"There, in a space not wider than the clerk's desk, and three hundred yards long, lay the dead bodies of 543 of my colored comrades, slain in the defense of their country, who had laid down their lives to uphold its flag and its honor, as a willing sacrifice. And as I rode along, guiding my horse this way and that, lest he should profane with his hoofs what seemed to me the sacred dead, and as I looked at their bronzed faces upturned in the shining sun, as if in mute appeal against the wrongs of the country for which they had given their lives, and whose flag had been to them a flag of stripes, in which no star of glory had ever shone for them—feeling I had wronged them in the past, and believing what was the future duty of my country to them—I swore to myself a solemn oath: 'May my right hand forget its cunning, and my tongue cleave to the roof of my mouth, if ever I fail to defend the rights of the men who have given their blood for me and my country this day and for their race forever.' And, God helping me, I will keep that oath."

Or another instance: when under Butler first and [Gen. Alfred Howe] Terry later, driven by storms and tempestous seas to powerful Fort Fisher, cooperating with our gallant Navy in its capture, and thence starting on the long march that led through Wilmington, and on to Goldsboro, N. C., where [Gen. Joseph E.] Johnson's army, the last large force of the Confederacy in the field, was caught between the forces under Terry and the forces under [Gen. Oliver O.] Howard; and the war as such was ended with his surrender, April 26, 1865.

A little of statistics, and I will close.

The total number of colored soldiers in this last war was 178,975, and the number of deaths 36,847.

Of enlistments the United States made 96,337, and the several States 79,638.

Enlistments were divided as follows:

Alabama	2,969	Mississippi	17,869
Louisiana	24,052	Maine	104
New Hampshire	125	Vermont	120
Massachusetts	3,966	Rhode Island	1,837
Connecticut	1,764	New York	4,125
New Jersey	1,185	Pennsylvania	8,612
Delaware	954	Maryland	8,718
Dist. of Columbia	3,269	Virginia	5,723
North Carolina	5,035	West Virginia	196
South Carolina	5,462	Georgia	3,486
Florida	1,044	Arkansas	5,526
Tennessee	20,133	Kentucky	23,703
Michigan	1,387	Ohio	5,092
Indiana	1,537	Illinois	1,811
Missouri	8,344	Minnesota	104
Iowa	440	Wisconsin	165
Kansas	2,080	Texas	47
Colorado Ter.	95	Miscellaneous	5,896

The completed organizations were as follows:

138 regiments of infantry.
6   ”   ” cavalry.
14   ”   ” heavy artillery.
1   ”   ” light artillery.

On 449 occasions their blood was spilled.

These are a few of the regiments having the largest number of men killed in any one engagement.

The	8th	U. S. C. T.,	at Olustee,	87	killed.
”	13th	”	Nashville,	84	”
”	23rd	”	Petersburg,	81	”
”	7th	”	Fort Gilmore,	68	”
”	5th	”	Chaffin's Farm	63	”
”	6th	”	” ”	61	”
”	54th	Mass. Inf.	Fort Wagner,	58	”

The regiments having more than fifty men killed during their period of service are as follows:

Seventy-ninth	U. S. C. T.	Total killed,	183
Eighth	”	”	115
Fourth	”	”	102
Thirteenth	”	”	86
Seventh	”	”	84
Twenty-third	”	”	82
Sixth	”	”	79
Fifth	”	”	77
Twenty-second	”	”	70
First	”	”	67
Forty-ninth	”	”	59

Sometimes a comparison will illustrate better than figures alone. I give a single instance: Every one has heard of the charge of the Light Brigade, at Balaklava. I will put beside it a Black Brigade of about the same number of men.

Here they are:

Duncan's brigade, comprising the Fourth and Sixth regiments at

New Market Heights,		Had	683	Lost	365	Percent	53.7
Light Brigade, Balaklava,	”		673	”	247	”	36.7
Excess in Duncan's Brigade,	”		10	”	118	”	17

Sanford B. Hunt, M. D., late surgeon of U. S. Volunteers, made an exhaustive research into the capacity of the negro as a soldier. As to his—

1. Aptitude for drill.
2. Capacity for marching.
3. Endurance of fatigue and hunger.
4. Powers of digestion and assimilation.
5. Immunity from or liability to disabling diseases.

All of which points are treated with great detail, and summed up as follows:

"For the purposes of the soldier he has all the physical characteristics required, his temperament adapts him to camp life, and his morale conduces to discipline. He is also brave and steady in action. In all subsequent wars the country will rely largely upon its Negro population as a part of its military power."

Under the act of Congress passed July 12, 1862, the President of the United States was authorized to have prepared, with suitable emblematic devices, Medals of Honor to be presented in the name of the Congress to such soldiers as should most distinguish themselves by their gallantry in action and other soldierly qualities. So chary has the Government been in their issue that the award has not reached two thousand among the three millions of volunteers and regulars in the Army and Navy. So that these medals are more rare than the "Victoria Cross" of England, the "Iron Cross" of Germany, or the "Cross of the Legion of Honor" of France.

I copy the list of those issued to Negro soldiers as they stand upon the records, that is, in the numerical order of the regiments to which the recipients belonged. It will be therefore understood that this order does not indicate priority of time or degree of excellence.

Christian A. Fleetwood,	Sergeant Major,	Fourth	U. S. C. T.
Alfred B. Hilton,	Color Sergeant,	"	"
Charles Veal,	Corporal,	"	"
Milton M. Holland,	Sergeant Major,	Fifth	"
James Brownson,	First Sergeant,	"	"
Powhatan Beatty,	First Sergeant,	"	"
Robert Pinn,	First Sergeant,	"	"
Thomas R. Hawkins,	Sergeant Major,	Sixth	"
Alexander Kelly,	First Sergeant,	"	"
Samuel Gilchrist,	Sergeant,	Thirty-sixth	"
William Davis,	Sergeant,	"	"
Miles James,	Corporal,	"	"
James Gardner,	Private,	"	"
Edward Ratcliffe,	First Sergeant,	Thirty-eighth	"
James Harris,	Sergeant,	"	"
William Barnes,	Private,	"	"
Decatur Dorsey,	Sergeant,	Thirty-ninth	"[13]

After each war, of 1776, of 1812, and of 1861, history repeats itself in the absolute effacement of remembrance of the gallant deeds done for the country by its brave black defenders and in their relegation to outer darkness.

History further repeats itself in the fact that in every war so far known to this country, the first blood, and this in some cases, the last also, has been shed by the faithful Negro, and in spite of all the years of bondage and oppression, and of wrongs unspeakable. Under the sun there has nothing been known in the history of any people more marvellous than these facts!

Oh, to the living few,
Comrades, be just, be true.
Hail them as heroes tried,
Fight with them side by side;
Never in field or tent,
Scorn the Black Regiment.

It is but a little thing to ask, they could ask no less: *be just*; but, oh, the shame of it for those who need be asked!

There is no need for panegyric, for sounding phrases or rounded periods. The simple story is eloquent with all that is necessary to make the heart swell with pride. In the hour allotted to me to fill, it is possible only to indicate in skeleton the worth of the Negro as a soldier. If this brief sketch should awaken even a few to interest in his achievements, and one be found willing and fitted to write the history that is their due, that writer shall achieve immortality.

Christian A. Fleetwood, *The Negro as a Soldier* (Washington, DC: George Wm Cook, 1895).

---

1. Fleetwood mistakenly referred to Gen. James Mitchell Varnum, a good officer and a well-connected Rhode Island lawyer. In January 1778 Varnum urged Washington to permit Rhode Island to end its chronic shortage of troops by recruiting a battalion of African Americans. In February the General Assembly adopted legislation permitting the recruitment of slaves, with compensation to their owners, free blacks, and Indians. Eventually about 300 blacks served in Varnum's regiment, and they fully justified his confidence in them. Paul. F. Dearden, *The Rhode Island Campaign of 1778: Inauspicious Dawn of Alliance* (Providence, RI: Rhode Island Publications Society, 1980), 23–24, 37.
2. On November 7, 1775, John Murray, Lord Dunmore issued a proclamation in Virginia that announced "I do hereby further declare all indentured servants, Negroes, or others, (appertaining to Rebels,) free, that are able and willing to bear arms, they joining His Majesty's Troops, as soon as may be, for the more speedily reducing the Colony to a proper sense of their duty, to His Majesty's crown and dignity." Benjamin Quarles, *The Negro in the American Revolution* (orig., 1961, Chapel Hill: University of North Carolina Press, 1996), 19.

3. After 1808, Boston blacks annually celebrated the legal end of the slave trade. According to the abolitionist Lydia Maria Child, at some point white boys began harassing the celebrations. One year, the white rioters drove city blacks off Boston Common with clubs and stones, chasing them through the streets. Colonel Middleton, a black veteran of the Revolution who had been given a flag for his service by John Hancock, stepped from his door and, with a loaded musket at the ready, "shrieked death to the first white who should approach." A Captain Winslow Lewis came to the aid of the black victims and struggled with the white leaders to end the riot. William C. Nell, *Colored Patriots of the American Revolution* (Boston: Robert F. Wallcut, 1855), 26–27.

4. Fleetwood probably repeated the story concerning "Major Jeffrey" from William C. Nell's earlier work, which duplicates the information about the unfortunate black veteran of the war of 1812. Nell, *Colored Patriots of the American Revolution,* 188.

5. Congress's legislation equalizing pay rates for those soldiers who were free at the start of the war passed on June 15, 1864. Soldiers who had been slaves at the start of the war, however, still received unequal pay. The outrageous ruling continued to cause dissension, and it was not corrected until March 1865. Congress did not, however, legislate on the issue of commissions for black soldiers. Berlin, Reidy, Rowland, *Freedom: The Black Military Experience,* 367–368.

6. The 1st Louisiana Native Guard, organized in September 1862 in New Orleans, became the 1st Corps d'Afrique and in 1864 was redesignated the 73rd USCT. After the war it merged with the 96th USCT. The 2nd Louisiana Native Guard, formed in New Orleans in October 1862, became the 2nd Corps d'Afrique in April 1864, and was later redesignated the 74th USCT. Wilson, *The Black Phalanx,* 473.

7. Anselmas Planciancois, of the 1st Louisiana Native Guard, carried the regiment's colors when he was killed at Port Hudson. Trudeau, *Like Men of War,* 41.

8. Capt. Andre Cailloux, also of the 1st Louisiana Native Guard, had been a slave but attained prominence in New Orleans society, spoke English and French, and possessed a reputation for horsemanship and boxing. He acted with enormous bravery at Port Hudson: although seriously wounded, he repeatedly attacked until he was killed. He received an elaborate funeral in New Orleans and his fame spread quickly, making him a hero to black soldiers. Trudeau, *Like Men of War,* 27, 38, 41–43, 45.

9. The 9th Corps d'Afrique, formed in September 1863 at Port Hudson, was redesignated the 81st USCT in April 1864. The 11th Corps d'Afrique, formed at Port Hudson in August 1863, became the 83rd USCT in April

1864. Both remained in service until 1866. The 1st Mississippi, organized at Milliken's Bend and at Vicksburg, Mississippi, in May 1863, became the 51st USCT in March 1864. Wilson, *The Black Phalanx*, 471, 474.

10. William H. Carney (1841–1908), a seaman and postman from New Bedford, Massachusetts, later received the Medal of Honor for his gallantry at Fort Wagner. Emilio, *A Brave Black Regiment*, 349.

11. The 8th USCT, organized at Camp William Penn outside of Philadelphia in September 1863, was inexperienced when it was thrown into the February 1864, Battle of Olustee, Florida. Its commanding officer was killed and the regiment suffered many casualties. Organized at Nashville, Tennessee, in November 1863, the 13th USCT fought its first engagement at the Battle of Nashville. The 33rd USCT, organized at Camp William Penn in February 1864, fought at the Battle of Honey Hill, South Carolina. The 35th USCT, originally the 1st North Carolina, became the 35th in February 1864 and was commanded by James C. Beecher, a brother of Harriet Beecher Stowe. The 102nd was formed in Detroit, Michigan, in February 1864 as the 1st Michigan; it became the 102nd in May 1864. It also fought at Honey Hill. Emilio, *A Brave Black Regiment*, 149; Wilson, *The Black Phalanx*, 467, 468, 469, 476; Trudeau, *Like Men of War*, 340–350.

12. The 4th USCT, organized in Baltimore, Maryland, in July 1863, fought in the Petersburg campaign and mustered out of service in 1866. It and the 29th Connecticut fought at Fort Harrison (also known as Fort Burnham) in Virginia, as well as in the Fort Fisher, Petersburg, and New Market Heights campaigns. Wilson, *The Black Phalanx*, 467; Trudeau, *Like Men of War*, 202, 220–227, 286–300, 359–364, 420.

13. Since William H. Carney did not receive his medal until 1900, he was not included in Fleetwood's list.

"Public Opinion"
Joseph T. Wilson
1890

No nineteenth-century book on the Civil War took on the issue of racial prejudice like Joseph T. Wilson's *The Black Phalanx* (1890). His 528-page history covered the same time period as Fleetwood's pamphlet, but fleshed out the role of blacks in the nation's wars from the Revolution to the Civil War in enormous detail. For a generation or more, Wilson's book stood as the most comprehensive study of African American military service available.

Wilson (1836–1891), born in Norfolk, Virginia—perhaps as a slave—shrewdly read his Alexis de Tocqueville. He marshaled the Frenchman's famous analysis of American democracy and democratic culture to explain the hurdles that African Americans had to overcome just to become soldiers and risk their lives for a nation mired in racial hatred. While Northerners liked to think of themselves as immune from the influence of slavery, Tocqueville reminded them that while they may have disliked the institution of slavery, they hated its victims even more. Much to Tocqueville's surprise, he found that those areas of the nation that had ended slavery manifested a higher level of race hatred than areas that still retained the peculiar institution: "' . . . the prejudice of the race appears to be stronger in those States which have abolished slavery, than in those where it still exists.'" Because of this race hate, when the war began in 1861 "a Chinese wall only more impregnable, encircled the negro, and formed a barrier betwixt him and the army." Despite this prejudice, Wilson advised his readers, the black man waited and then did his duty.

Wilson was among the first to offer his services to the nation. As he revealed in a footnote to his book, as soon as his whaling vessel docked in Valparaiso, Chile, and he learned of the war (he had been on a three-year cruise), he rushed to New York to volunteer. Although the army accepted his two Spanish companions, who could not speak English, it removed Wilson from the service when it discovered that he was black. Determined to get into the fight, he went to New Orleans, Louisiana, looking for his father who had been sold there, and then enlisted into the 2nd Louisiana Native Guards on September 30, 1862. He fought at Port Hudson and then returned to New Bedford, Massachusetts, where he had begun his whaling career. He joined Company C of the 54th Massachusetts Regiment, was wounded at the Battle of Olustee, Florida, in February 1864, and was discharged from the army on May 8, 1864. He worked for the secret service attached to the Army of the James until the end of the war.

Wilson's postwar career proved equally fascinating. In 1865 he briefly took a position in a government supply store in his native Norfolk, Virginia, and then became editor of the *True Southerner,* a paper designed to promote black suffrage. The next year a white mob destroyed his press and Wilson fled to Petersburg, where he became active in the Republican Party. In 1867 he established the *Union Republican* in which he advocated the confiscation of rebel property and redistribution of it to the former slaves. For a few years he worked as a gauger for the Internal Revenue Service, won election to the Norfolk city council in 1870, and became the aide-de-camp for the commander of the Grand Army of the Republic. In 1876 he unsuccessfully ran for Congress and then returned to Petersburg, where in the 1880s he published two more papers, the *American Sentinel* and the *Right Way.* He ended his days in Richmond, Virginia, as a businessman, but also managed to publish three other books besides his study of blacks in the Civil War: *Emancipation: Its Course from 1481 to 1875* (1881), *Voice of a New Race* (1882), and *Twenty-two Years of Freedom* (1882). George H. Tucker, *Norfolk's Highlights, 1584–1881,* www.norfolkhistorical.org; Dudley Taylor Cornish, foreword to *The Black Phalanx: African American Soldiers in the War of Independence, the War of 1812 & the Civil War* (New York: Da Capo, 1994); Eric Foner, *Freedom's Lawmakers: A Directory of Black Officeholders During Reconstruction* (Baton Rouge, LA: Louisiana State University Press, 1996), 233–234.

It seems proper, before attempting to record the achievements of the negro soldiers in the war of the Rebellion, that we should consider the state of public opinion regarding the negroes at the outbreak of the war; also, in connection therewith, to note the rapid change that took place during the early part of the struggle.

For some cause, unexplained in a general sense, the white people in the Colonies and in the States, came to entertain against the colored races therein a prejudice, that showed itself in a hostility to the latter's enjoying equal civil and political rights with themselves. Various reasons are alleged for it, but the difficulty of really solving the problem lies in the fact that the early settlers in this country came without prejudice against color. The Negro, Egyptian, Arab, and other colored races known to them, lived in European countries, where no prejudice, on account of color existed. How very strange then, that a feeling antagonistic to the negroes should become a prominent feature in the character of the European emigrants to these shores and their descendants. It has been held by some writers that the American prejudice against the negroes was occasioned by their docility and unresenting spirit. Surely no one acquainted with the Indian will agree that he is docile or wanting in spirit, yet occasionally there is manifested a prejudice against him; the recruiting officers in Massachusetts refused to enlist Indians, as well as negroes, in regiments and companies made up of white citizens, though members of both races, could sometimes be found in white regiments. During the rebellion of 1861–5, some Western regiments had one or two negroes and Indians in them, but there was no general enlistment of either race in white regiments.[i] The objection was on account of color, or, as some writers claim, by the fact of the races—negro and Indian[ii]—having been enslaved. Be the cause what it may, a prejudice, strong, unrelenting, barred the two races from enjoying with the white race equal civil and political rights in the United States. So very strong had that prejudice grown since the Revolution, enhanced it may be by slavery and docility, that when the rebellion of 1861 burst forth, a feeling stronger than law, like a Chinese wall only more impregnable, encircled the negro, and formed a barrier betwixt him and the army. Doubtless peace—a long peace—lent it aid materially to this state of affairs. Wealth, chiefly, was the dream of the American from 1815 to 1860, nearly half a century; a period in which the negro was friendless, save in a few strong-minded, iron-hearted men like John Brown in Kansas, Wendell Phillips in New England, Charles Sumner

---

[i] I arrived in New York in August, 1862, from Valpariso, Chile, on the steamship "Bio-Bio," of Boston, and in company with two Spaniards, neither of whom could speak English, enlisted in a New York regiment. We were sent to the rendezvous on one of the islands in the harbor. The third day after we arrived at the barracks, I was sent with one of my companions to carry water to the cook, an aged negro, who immediately recognized me, and in such a way as to attract the attention of the corporal, who reported the matter to the commanding officer, and before I could give the cook the hint, he was examined by the officer of the day. At noon I was accompanied by a guard of honor to the launch, which landed me in New York. I was a negro, that was all; how it was accounted for on the rolls I cannot say. I was honorably discharged, however, without receiving a certificate to that effect.

[ii] The Indians referred to are many of those civilized and living as citizens in the several States of the Union.

in the United States Senate, Horace Greeley in New York and a few others, who dared, in the face of strong public sentiment, to plead his cause, even from a humane platform. In many places he could not ride in a street car that was not inscribed, "*Colored persons ride in this car.*" The deck of a steamboat, the box cars of the railroad, the pit of the theatre and the gallery of the church, were locations accorded him. The church lent its influence to the rancor and bitterness of a prejudice as deadly as the sap of the Upas.

To describe public opinion respecting the negro a half century ago, is no easy task. It was just budding into maturity when [Alexis] De Tocqueville visited the United States, and, as a result of that visit, he wrote, from observation, a pointed criticism upon the manners and customs, and the laws of the people of the United States. For fear that I might be thought over-doing—heightening—giving too much coloring to the strength, and extent and power of the prejudice against the negro I quote from that distinguished writer, as he clearly expressed himself under the heading, "*Present and Future condition of the three races inhabiting the United States.*"[1] He said of the negro:

I see that in a certain portion of the United States at the present day, the legal barrier which separates the two races is tending to fall away, but not that which exists in the manners of the country. Slavery recedes, but the prejudice to which it has given birth remains stationary. Whosoever has inhabited the United States, must have perceived, that in those parts of the United States, in which the negroes are no longer slaves, they have in nowise drawn nearer the whites; on the contrary, the prejudice of the race appears to be stronger in those States which have abolished slavery, than in those where it still exists. And, nowhere is it so intolerant as in the states where servitude has never been known. It is true, that in the North of the Union, marriages may be legally contracted between negroes and whites, but public opinion would stigmatize a man, who should content himself with a negress, as infamous. If oppressed, they may bring an action at law, but they will find none but whites among their judges, and although they may legally serve as jurors, prejudice repulses them for that office. In theatres gold cannot procure a seat for the servile race beside their former masters, in hospitals they lie apart. They *are* allowed to invoke the same divinity as the whites.

The gates of heaven are not closed against those unhappy beings; but their inferiority is continued to the very confines of the other world. The negro is free, but he can share, neither the rights, nor the labor, nor the afflictions of him, whose equal he has been declared to be, and he cannot meet him upon fair terms in life or death.

De Tocqueville, as is seen, wrote with much bitterness and sarcasm, and, it is but fair to state, makes no allusion to any exceptions to the various conditions of affairs that he mentions. In all cases matters might not have been exactly as bad as he pictures them, but as far as the deep-seated prejudice against the negroes, and indifference to their rights and elevation are concerned, the facts will freely sustain the views so forcibly presented.

The negro had no remembrance of the country of his ancestry, Africa, and he abjured their religion. In the South he had no family; women were merely the temporary sharer of his pleasures; his master's cabins were the homes of his children during their childhood. While the Indian perished in the struggle for the preservation of his home, his hunting grounds and his freedom, the negro entered into slavery as soon as he was born, in fact was often purchased in the womb, and was born to know, first, that he was a slave. If one became free, he found freedom harder to bear than slavery; half civilized, deprived of nearly all rights, in contact with his superiors in wealth and knowledge, exposed to the rigor of a tyrannical prejudice moulded into laws, he contented himself to be allowed to live.

The Negro race, however, it must be remembered, is the only race that has ever come in contact with the European race, and been able to withstand its atrocities and oppression; all others, like the Indian, whom they could not make subservient to their use, they have destroyed. The Negro race, like the Israelites, multiplied so rapidly in bondage, that the oppressor became alarmed, and began discussing methods of safety to himself. The only people able to cope with the Anglo-American or Saxon, with any show of success, must be of *patient fortitude, progressive intelligence, brave in resentment and earnest in endeavor.*

In spite of his surroundings and state of public opinion the African lived, and gave birth, largely through amalgamation with the representatives of the different races that inhabited the United States, to a new race,—the *American Negro.* Professor [John P.] Sampson[2] in his mixed races says:

"The Negro is a new race, and is not the direct descent of any people that have ever flourished. The glory of the negro race is yet to come."

As evidence of its capacity to acquire glory, the record made in the late struggle furnishes abundant proof. At the sound of the tocsin at the North, negro waiter, cook, barber, boot-black, groom, porter and laborer stood ready at the enlisting office; and though the recruiting officer refused to list his name, he waited like the "patient ox" for the partition—*prejudice*—to be removed. He waited two years before even the door of the partition was opened; then he did not hesitate, but walked in, and with what effect the world knows.

The war cloud of 1860 still more aroused the bitter prejudice against the negro at both the North and South; but he was safer in South Carolina than in New York, in Richmond than in Boston.

It is a natural consequence, when war is waged between two nations, for those on either side to forget local feuds and untie against the common enemy, as was done in the Revolutionary war. How different was the situation now when the threatened war not one between nations, but between states of the same nation. The feeling of hostility toward the negro was not put aside and forgotten as other troublesome matters were, but the bitterness became intensified and more marked.

The Confederate Government though organized for the perpetual enslavement of the negro, fostered the idea that the docility of the negroes would allow them to be used for any purpose, without their having the least idea of becoming freemen. Some idea may be formed of public opinion at the South at the beginning of the war by what Mr. Pollard, in his history,[3] gives as the feeling at the South at the close of the second year of the struggle:

Indeed, the war had shown the system of slavery in the South to the world in some new and striking aspects, and had removed much of that could of prejudice, defamation, falsehood, romance and perverse sentimentalism through which our peculiar institution had been formerly known to Europe. It had given a better vindication of our system of slavery than all the books that could be written in a generation. It had shown that slavery was an element of strength to us; that it had assisted us in our struggle; that no servile insurrections had taken place in the South, in spite of the allurements of our enemy;

that the slave had tilled the soil while his master had fought; that in large districts, unprotected by our troops, and with a white population, consisting almost exclusively of women and children, the slave had continued his work, quiet, faithful, and cheerful; and that, as a conservative element in our social system, the institution of slavery had withstood the shocks of war, and been a faithful ally of our army, although instigated to revolution by every art of the enemy, and prompted to the work of assassination and pillage by the most brutal examples of the Yankee soldiers.

With this view, the whole slave population was brought to the assistance of the Confederate Government, and thereby caught the very first hope of freedom. An innate reasoning taught the negro that slaves could not be relied upon to fight for their own enslavement. To get to the breastworks was but to get a chance to run to the Yankees; and thousands of those whose elastic step kept time with the martial strains of the drum and fife, as they marched on through city and town, enroute to the front, were not elated with the hope of Southern success, but were buoyant with the prospects of reaching the North. The Confederates found it no easy task to watch the negroes and the Yankees too; their attention could be given to but one at a time; as the slave expressed it, "when marsa watch the Yankee, nigger go; when marsa watch the nigger, Yankee come." But the Yankees did not always receive him kindly during the first year of the war.

In his inaugural, Mr. Lincoln declared "that the property, peace and security of no section are to be in anywise endangered by the new incoming administration." The Union generals, except [John C.] Frémont and [John W.] Phelps and a few subordinates, accepted this as public opinion, and as their guide in dealing with the slavery question. That opinion is better expressed in the doggerel, sung in after months by the negro troops as they marched along through Dixie:

"McClellan went to Richmond with two hundred thousand braves,
He said, 'keep back the niggers and the Union he would save.'
Little Mac, he had his way, still the Union is in tears,
And they call for the help of the colored volunteers."[4]

The first two lines expressed the sentiment at the time , not only of the Army of the Potomac, but the army commanders everywhere, with the exceptions named. The administration winked at the enforcement of the fugitive slave bill by the soldiers engaged in capturing and returning the negroes coming into the Union lines. Undoubtedly, it was the idea of the Government to turn the course of the war from its rightful channel, or in other words,—in the restoration of the Union,—to eliminate the anti-slavery sentiment, which demanded the freedom of the slaves.

Hon. Elisha R. Potter, of Rhode Island,—"who may," said Mr. [Horace] Greeley, "be fairly styled the hereditary chief of the Democratic party of that State,"—made a speech on the war in the State Senate, on the 10th of August 1861, in which he remarked:

I have said that the war may assume another aspect, and be a short and bloody one. And to such a war—*an anti-slavery war*—it seems to me we are *inevitably* drifting. It seems to me hardly in the power of human wisdom to prevent it. We may commence the war without meaning to interfere with slavery; but let us have one or two battles, and get our blood excited, and we shall not only not restore any more slaves, but shall proclaim freedom wherever we go. And it seems to me almost judicial blindness on the part of the South that they do not see that this must be the inevitable result, if the contest is prolonged.

This sentiment became bolder daily as the thinking Union men viewed the army turning aside from its legitimate purposes, to catch runaway negroes, and return them. Party lines were also giving away; men in the army began to realize the worth of the negroes as they sallied up to the rebel breastworks that were often impregnable. They began to complain, finding the negro with his pick and spade, a greater hindrance to their progress than the cannon balls of the enemy; and more than one said to the Confederates, when the pickets of the two armies picnicked together in the battle's lull, as frequently they did: "We can whip you, if you keep your negroes out of your army."

Quite a different course was pursued in the navy. Negroes were readily accepted all along the coast on board the war vessels, it being no departure from the regular and established practice in the service. The view with which loyal friends of the Union, began to look at the negro and the rebellion, was aptly illustrated in an article in the Montgomery (Ala.) *Advertiser* in 1861, which said:

THE SLAVES AS A MILITARY ELEMENT IN THE SOUTH.—The total white population of the eleven States now comprising the Confederacy is 6,000,000, and, therefore, to fill up the ranks of the proposed army (600,000) about ten percent of the entire white population will be required. In an other country than our own such a draft could not be met, but the Southern States can furnish that number of men, and still not leave the material interests of the country in a suffering condition. Those who are incapacitated for bearing arms can oversee the plantations, and the negroes can go on undisturbed in their usual labors. In the North the case is different; the men who join the army of subjugation are the laborers, the producers, and the factory operatives. Nearly ever man from that section, especially those from the rural districts, leave some branch of industry to suffer during their absence. The institution of slavery in the South alone enables her to place in the field a force much larger in proportion to her white population than the North, or indeed any country which is dependent entirely on free labor. The institution is a tower of strength to the South, particularly at the present crisis, and our enemies will be likely to find that the 'moral cancer' about which their orators are so fond of prating, is really one of the most effective weapons employed against the Union by the South. Whatever number of men may be needed for this war, we are confident our people stand ready to furnish. We are all enlisted for the war, and there must be no holding back until the independence of the South is fully acknowledged.

The facts already noted became apparent to the nation very soon, and then came a change of procedure, and the was began to be prosecuted upon quite a different policy. Gen. [George B.] McClellan, whose loyalty to the new policy was doubted, was removed from the command of the Army of the Potomac, and slave catching ceased. The XXXVII Congress convened in Dec. 1861, in its second session, and passed the following additional article of war:

All officers are prohibited from employing any of the forces under their respective commands for the purpose of returning fugitives from service or labor who may have escaped from any person to whom such service or labor is claimed to be due. Any officer who shall be found guilty by court-martial of violating this article shall be dismissed from the service.

This was the initiatory measure of the new policy, which progressed to its fulfillment rapidly. And then what Mr. [Simon] Cameron, Secretary of War, had recommended in December 1861, and to which the President objected, very soon developed, through a series of enactments, in the arming of the negro; in which the loyal people of the whole country acquiesced, save the border states people, who fiercely opposed it as is shown in the conduct of Mr. [Charles A.] Wickcliffe of Kentucky; [Sen. Willard] Salisbury, of Delaware, and others in Congress.

Public opinion was now changed, Congress had prohibited the surrender of the negroes to the rebels, the President issued his Emancipation Proclamation, and more than 150,000 negroes were fighting for the Union. The Republican party met in convention in Chicago, and nominated Mr. Lincoln for the second term as President of the United States; the course of his first administration was now to be approved or rejected by the people. In the resolutions adopted, the fifth one of them related to Emancipation and the negro soldiers. It was endorsed by a very large majority of the voters. A writer in one of the magazines, prior to the election, thus reviews the resolutions:

The fifth resolution commit us to the approval of two measures that have aroused the most various and strenuous opposition, the Proclamation of Emancipation and the use of negro troops. In reference to the first, it is to be remembered that it is a war measure. The express language of it is: 'By virtue of the power in me vested as commander-in-chief of the army and navy of the United States in time a actual armed rebellion against the authority and Government of the United States, and as a *fit and necessary war measure for suppressing said rebellion.*' Considered thus, the Proclamation is not merely defensible, but it is more; it is a proper and efficient means of weakening the rebellion which every person desiring its speedy overthrow must zealously and perforce uphold. Whether it is of any legal effect beyond the actual limits of our military lines, is a question that need not agitate us. In due time the supreme tribunal of the nation will be called to determine that, and to its decision the country will yield with all respect and loyalty. But in the meantime let the Proclamation go wherever the army goes, let it go wherever the navy secures a foothold on the outer border of the rebel territory, and let it summon to our aid the negroes who are truer to the Union than their disloyal masters; and when they have come to us and put their lives in our keeping, let us protect and defend them with the whole power of the nation. Is there anything unconstitutional in that? Thank God, there is not. And he who is willing to give back to slavery a single person who has heard the summons and come within our lines to obtain his freedom, he who would give up a single man, woman, or child, once thus actually freed, is not worthy the name of American. He may call himself Confederate, if he will.

Let it be remembered, also that the Proclamation has had a very important bearing upon on foreign relations. It evoked in behalf of our country that sympathy on the part of the people in Europe, whose is the only sympathy we can ever expect in our struggle to perpetuate free institutions. Possessing that sympathy, moreover, we have had an element in our favor which has kept the rulers of Europe in wholesome dread of interference. The Proclamation relieved us from the false position before attributed to us of fighting simply for national power. It placed us right in the eyes of the world, and transformed men's sympathies from a confederacy fighting for independence as a means of establishing slavery, to a nation whose institutions mean constitutional liberty, and, when fairly wrought out, must end in universal freedom.

The change of policy and of public opinion was so strongly endorsed that it affected the rebels, who shortly passed a Congressional measure for arming 200,000 negroes themselves. What a reversal of things; what a change of sentiment, in less than twenty-four months![iii] Mr. Lincoln, in justifying the change, is reported to have said to Judge [Joseph T.] Mills, of Wisconsin:

[iii]"Those who have declaimed loudest against the employment of negro troops have shown a lamentable amount of ignorance, and an equally lamentable lack of common sense. They know as little of the military history and martial qualities of the African race as they do of their own duties as commanders.

"All distinguished generals of modern times who have had opportunity to use negro soldiers, have uniformly applauded their subordination, bravery, and powers of endurance. Washington solicited the military services of negroes in the revolution, and rewarded them. Jackson did the same in the war of 1812. Under both those great captains, the negro troops fought so well that they received unstinted praise."—*Charles Sumner*.

The slightest knowledge of arithmetic will prove to any man that the rebel armies cannot be destroyed with Democratic strategy. It would sacrifice all the white men of the North to do it. There are now in the service of the United States near two hundred thousand able-bodied colored men, most of them under arms, defending and acquiring Union territory. The Democratic strategy demands that the forces be disbanded, and that the masters be conciliated by restoring them to slavery. The black men who now assist Union prisoners to escape, they are to be converted into our enemies in the vain hope of gaining the good will of their masters. We shall have to fight two nations instead of one. You cannot conciliate the South if you guarantee to them ultimate success; and the experience of the present war proves their success is inevitable if you fling the compulsory labor of millions of black men into their side of the scale. Will you give our enemies such military advantages as insure success, and then depend on coaxing, flattery, and concession to get them back into the Union? Abandon all the posts now garrisoned by black men; take two hundred thousand men from our side and put them in the battlefield or cornfield against us, and we would be compelled to abandon the war in three weeks. We have to hold territory in inclement and sickly places; where are the Democrats to do this? It was a free fight, and the field was open to the war Democrats to put down this rebellion by fighting against both master and slave, long before the present policy was inaugurated. There have been men base enough to propose to me to return to slavery the black warriors of Port Hudson and Olustee, and thus win the respect of the masters they fought. Should I do so, I should deserve to be damned in time and eternity. Come what will, I will keep my faith with friend and foe. My enemies pretend I am now carrying on this war for the sole purpose of abolition. So long as I am President, it shall be carried on for the sole purpose of restoring the Union. But no human power can subdue this rebellion without the use of the emancipation policy, and every other policy calculated to weaken the moral and physical forces of the rebellion. Freedom had given us two hundred thousand men raised on southern soil. It will give us more yet. Just so much it has subtracted from the enemy; and instead of alienating the South, there are now evidences of a fraternal feeling growing up between our men and the rank and file of the rebel soldiers. Let my enemies prove to the country that the destruction of slavery is not necessary to the restoration of the Union. I will abide the issue.[5]

But the change of policy did not change the opinion of the Southerners, who, notwithstanding the use which the Confederate Government was making of the negro, still regard him, in the *United States* uniform, as a vicious brute, to be shot at sight. I prefer, in closing this chapter, to give the Southern opinion of the negro, in the words of a distinguished native of that section. Mr. George W. Cable, in his "Silent South,"[6] thus gives it:

> He was brought to our shores a naked, brutish, unclean, captive, pagan savage, to be and remain a kind of connecting link between man and the beasts of burden. The great changes to result from his contact with a superb race of masters were not taken into account. As a social factor he was intended to be as purely zero as the brute at the other end of his plow line. The occasional mingling of his blood with that of the white man worked no change in the sentiment; one, two, four, eight, multiplied upon or divided in to zero, still gave zero for the result. Generations of American nativity made no difference; his children and childrens' children were born in sight of our door, yet the old notion held fast. He increased to vast numbers, but it never wavered. He accepted our dress, language, religion, all the fundamentals of our civilization, and became forever expatriated from his own land; still he remained, to us, an alien. Our sentiment went blind. It did not see that gradually, here by force and there by choice, he was fulfilling a host of conditions that earned at last a solemn moral right to that naturalization which no one at first had dreamed of giving him. Frequently he even bought back the freedom of which he had been robbed, became a tax-payer, and at times an educator of his children at his own expense; but the old idea of alienism passed laws to banish him, his wife, and children by thousands from the States, and threw him into loathsome jails as a common felon for returning to his native land. It will be wise to remember that these were the acts of an enlightened, God fearing people.

Joseph T. Wilson, *The Black Phalanx* (Hartford, CT: American Publishing Company, 1890), 93–110.

1. Wilson refers to chapter 10 in volume 1 of *Democracy in America:* "Some Considerations Concerning the Present State and Probable Future of the Three Races that Inhabit the Territory of the United States." Alexis de Tocqueville, *Democracy in America,* J. P. Mayer, ed. (Garden City, NY: Anchor Books, 1969), 316–407.
2. John Patterson Sampson, *Mixed Races: Their Environment, Temperament, Heredity and Phrenology* (Hampton, VA: Normal School Press, 1881).
3. Edward A. Pollard, *The Second Year of the War* (New York: C. B. Richardson, 1866).
4. The lyrics of this song were written by an anonymous soldier in Co. A of the 54th Massachusetts Regiment and first appeared in the Boston *Transcript* on June 2, 1863.
5. The New York *Tribune,* September 10, 1864, published a version of this that was probably based on Mills's diary. See: Roy P. Basler, ed., *The Collected Works of Abraham Lincoln,* 8 vols. (New Brunswick, NJ: Rutgers University Press, 1953): 7:506–508.
6. George W. Cable, *The Silent South: Together with the Freedmen's Case in Equity and the Convict Lease System* (New York: Charles Scribner's Sons, 1889). The book was first serialized in the New Orleans *Democrat* (1881–1882).

16

Glory

"The Massachusetts Fifty-Fourth"
Frances Ellen Watkins Harper
OCTOBER 10, 1863

Harper (1825–1911) was the most successful African American poet prior to the Harlem Renaissance. Americans of all colors read her poems, which resonate with defiance, compassion, and faith. Freeborn in Baltimore, she grew up in a dedicated antislavery family amid one of the centers of early abolitionism. During the 1850s she moved to Pennsylvania and eventually to Philadelphia, where she lived in a building that also housed William Still's famed Underground Railroad operations. But it was an 1853 encounter with the fragility of black life in the border states—a free Maryland black sold into Georgia slavery—that moved her to speak out. "Upon that grave," she exclaimed, "I pledged myself to the anti-Slavery cause." She became a well-known antislavery lecturer, exponent of women's rights, and, after the Civil War, a popular novelist who explored the themes of race and slavery. But her poetry, especially her often reprinted "Bury Me in a Free Land," remains her most enduring voice.

The recently rediscovered poem, "The Massachusetts Fifty-Fourth," was first published in the New York *Weekly Anglo-African* a few months after the ill-fated attack on Fort Wagner. It is the only known contemporary poem about the 54th Massachusetts Regiment and its heroic action in South Carolina by an African American. The 54th Massachusetts has retained so much of our attention over the years because it served a unique role in the war. Despite the many Southern black regiments

350

that the Union fielded before the 54th, the future of black recruitment and, perhaps, the course of the war, depended upon this regiment's conduct in the field. All the nation's eyes looked toward the 54th to see if its men could withstand the test of battle. Had they failed, had the men of the 54th not acted heroically—and nothing less than heroism was expected of them—Northern enemies of black rights would have put an end to the "experiment" of black recruitment. African Americans would not have been allowed to *again* prove their right to full citizenship by serving in the army, thus destroying their hopes for the postwar world. Equally important, without black troops it is unlikely that the North would have defeated the South, and slavery may well have endured into the twentieth century.

Harper fully understood what the men of the 54th Massachusetts had accomplished at Fort Wagner. Despite their failure to seize the fortification, their heroism served a far higher purpose. After the events at Fort Wagner, no one could legitimately deny black worth, African Americans' right to serve in the army, or their sacrifices to rescue the nation from destruction and perpetual slavery. They had indeed "poured out a balm/ To heal the wounded nation's life," and in Harper's poem they did so without white mediation. Much of the prose and poetry written after the war focused on Col. Robert Gould Shaw, but Harper never mentioned him. She focused on what African Americans had accomplished, and with James Monroe Trotter's poem that follows, she sought to rivet their importance in the nation's imagination. Reading these two poems in tandem permits us to appreciate how Trotter, who had served in the 54th's sister regiment, the 55th Massachusetts, responded to the political imperatives of the 1880s by linking black service to white sacrifice. Donald Yacovone, "Sacred Land Regained: Francis Ellen Watkins Harper and 'The Massachusetts Fifty-Fourth,' a Lost Poem," *Pennsylvania History* 62 (Winter 1995): 90–110; Maryemma Graham, ed., *Complete Poems of Frances E. W. Harper* (New York: Oxford University Press, 1988); James Smethurst, "'Those Noble Sons of Ham': Poetry, Soldiers, and Citizens at the End of Reconstruction," in Martin H. Blatt, Thomas J. Brown, and Donald Yacovone, eds., *Hope & Glory: Essays on the Legacy of the 54th Massachusetts Regiment* (Amherst, MA: University of Massachusetts Press, 2001), 168–187.

THE MASSACHUSETTS FIFTY-FOURTH

WHERE STORMS OF DEATH were sweeping,
    Wildly through the darkened sky,
Stood the bold but fated column,
    Brave to do, to dare, and die.

With cheeks that knew no blanching,
    And brows that would not pale;
Where the bloody rain fell thickest,
    Mingled with the fiery hail.

Bearers of a high commission
    To break each brother's chain;
With hearts aglow for freedom,
    They bore the toil and pain.

And onward pressed though shot and shell
    Swept fiercely round their path;
While batteries hissed with tongues of flame,
    And bayonets flashed with wrath.

Oh! not in vain those heros fell,
    Amid those hours of fearful strife;
Each dying heart poured out a balm
    To heal the wounded nation's life.

And from the soil drenched with their blood,
    The fairest flowers of peace shall bloom;
And history cull rich laurels there,
    To deck each martyr hero's tomb.

And ages yet uncrossed with life,
    As sacred urns, do hold each mound
Where sleep the loyal, true, and brave
    In freedom's consecrated ground.

New York *Weekly Anglo-African*, October 10, 1863.

"The Fifty-Fourth at Wagner"
James Monroe Trotter
December 8, 1883

The legacy of the 54th Massachusetts Regiment carried enormous meaning for a man like Trotter. Indeed, history seemed to stalk Trotter's heels. Born in 1842, the son of a Mississippi slave, Trotter and his mother escaped to Cincinnati, Ohio, in the 1850s. In nearby Hamilton, Ohio, he received a solid education in a private academy and then went on to teach school. During the war he joined the 55th Massachusetts Regiment, serving alongside the famed 54th in South Carolina and becoming one of the few African Americans to win an officer's commission. In 1868 he returned to Ohio to marry Virginia Isaacs, the daughter of a slave at Jefferson's Monticello. James Trotter, whose son William would become the renowned advocate of civil rights in Boston and a successful publisher, also turned to the world of print and published *Music and Some Highly Musical People* (1878), a tribute to black musical accomplishments.

Like Harper's, Trotter's poem about the 54th Massachusetts sought to remind Americans of the accomplishments of the country's black Civil War soldiers whose sacrifices helped secure freedom and preserve the Union. With no granite monuments erected anywhere to commemorate black soldiers' contributions, poems such as Trotter's served, to borrow from Frederick Douglass, as "monuments of the mind." At a time of increasing racial strife and a growing "spirit of secession" after the end of the Reconstruction, Trotter urgently wished to keep the African American role in establishing freedom before an increasingly intolerant and forgetful public. Black soldiers, Trotter reminded his readers, carried within them the same love of liberty that had moved the Founding Fathers to secure independence. His work invoked the truth that all, regardless of race, were one, and that the men of the 54th had given "proof that, in contest with the country's common foe/ The spirit of liberty fills all men souls." As he equated white with black, he also diminished the distinctions so many had drawn between the martyred Shaw and the men he led. Black men too had died, he wrote, and their sacrifice meant as much as Shaw's. As whites could look back upon a history of great heroes, so too could African Americans: "Attucks, Salem, Hannibal, O grand Toussaint." In the Civil War, William H. Carney saved the national flag at Fort Wagner and belatedly received the Medal of Honor for his heroism long after Trotter's death: a race's honor, the commonwealth's free banner, all "saved in glorious manner!"

Trotter, along with many other soldiers in the commonwealth's black Civil War regiments, had waged a heroic eighteen-month campaign for equal pay. The discrimination he endured then followed him throughout his life, and at about the time he composed this poem it cost him a lucrative job in Washington, D.C. He died in 1892, perhaps believing that better times awaited his talented, activist son. Stephen R. Fox, *The Guardian of Boston: William Monroe Trotter* (New York: Atheneum, 1970), 3–10, 16; David W. Blight, "The Shaw Memorial in the Landscape of Civil War Memory," in Blatt, Brown, and Yacovone, *Hope & Glory,* 79–93.

THE FIFTY-FOURTH AT WAGNER

WITH TIME'S SURE MARCH came the day at last
   when slavery's strength
Defiance spoke, seemed all-potential, through
   the country's length;
In God's own time came the day at last, long
   much desired,
When black men, armed, themselves and friends
   with longing fired
To strike the monster wrong avenging deadliest
   blow;
To give the proof that, in contest with the country's
   common foe,
The spirit of liberty fills all men's souls, and in
   them burns alike,
While with it all may win when for it all in
   heart and hand unite.
"To arms! to arms!" with unpent souls, their
   valorous leaders cried;

"Now call they for help who erst so long, so
    bitterly denied;
Strike, strike ye for freedom! rush quickly to
    the fore!
Thy great wrongs now forgot, but be slaves
    nevermore!"
And so, with gladdened eagerness, in hosts they
    bravely came
From North, from East, from West, and many,
    too, from Southern cane,
These dusky warriors, with life in hand, with
    purpose great,
To swell our ranks, to charge the foe, and
    honor give a race and state.
Night had her mantle thrown o'er Charleston's
    warlike isle;
Silent, grim was Wagner; Sumter, erst thunder-
    tongued, rested, while
All seemed peace, yet two armies, prepared for
    devastating fray.
Still, eager vigil kept far more than if 'twere
    open day.
"To front of column, Massachusetts fifty-
    fourth!" Thus the order came.
"'Tis what we wish!" their gallant Shaw exultingly
    did quick exclaim;
"With most at stake, my men undaunted now
    do claim this hour
To glorious victory gain, at least to show no
    fear of slavery's power."
Momentous hour! A race on trial, which oft in
    this and other lands
Had filled the deadly breach, had helped to
    burst foul slavery's bands!
O shades of Attucks, Salem, Hannibal, O grand
    Toussaint,
Thy valor's lost, thy fame is nough, if these
    now prove faint!

And so most valiant men, and so heroic leaders
    went
To meet the enemy's vantage fire behind strong
    entrenchment;
On, on they charge, who do not fall, [none] falter
    as they reach the walls,
'Midst deadly rain of cannister,' midst piercing
    rifle-balls!
Not till many scaled the parapet, or waited
    soldiers' graves,
Though thinned their ranks, their colonel
    sleeping with his braves,
Paused these black heroes whose standard-bearer's
    crown
Came in glory, as he cried, "The old flag never
    touched the ground!"[1]
Alas! that valor, unmindful of wounds or even
    death's sad blight,
Brought not victory to our worthy arms that
    fateful night!
Brought not victory? O dull the sight that cannot
    see
Triumph on a field of glory long held 'gainst
    odds for liberty!
Ay, noble men, dead and living, O "famous 54,"
In change through deadly field, o'er firey ramparts
    then you bore
A race's honor, its friends' deep hopes, a state's
    free banner—
These, in thy keeping, were not lost, but saved
    in glorious manner!

Boston *Commonwealth*, December 8, 1883.

———

1. The words of William H. Carney, who, despite several wounds, carried the
national flag back from the failed assault on Fort Wagner.

17

Out of the Briars

"My War Record and Sketch of the Twenty-ninth Regiment"
Alexander H. Newton
1910

Alexander H. Newton (originally Newtown) joined the 29th Connecticut Regiment on December 18, 1863, became commissary sergeant on October 31, 1864, and received his discharge on October 24, 1865. But this tells us nothing about why Newton joined the army or why he wrote his memoir. Born in November 1837 in New Bern, North Carolina, of a free black mother and a slave father, Newton grew up with the horrors of slavery. The steel shackles, the whipping post, and the auction block, upon which the cries of divided families still rang in his ears, remained in his very bones. As a free African American in the South, Newton lived only one step away from enslavement, and while working as an apprentice he suffered a terrible whipping for disobeying his employer. The crimes he both saw and endured made him dream of "playing the part of a Moses in behalf of my people," and he found ways to help slaves escape north. On July 4, 1857, he ran away to join his mother, who had earlier fled North Carolina for New York to earn enough money to buy her husband out of slavery. Newton continued to work on Underground Railroad activities and became acquainted with some of the city's leading abolitionists, Henry Ward Beecher, Henry Highland Garnet, and the publisher Robert Hamilton, whose daughter, Olivia A. Hamilton, Newton later married. His story is one of courage and persistence.

Organized in New Haven between August 1863 and January 1864, the 29th Connecticut, in which Newton served, was comprised entirely of black men who lived in the state. This distinguished the unit from the three, better-known, Massachusetts black regiments that drew upon all sections of the country to fill its ranks. After a ceremony in March 1864, in which the unit received a flag made by black women of New Haven, the 29th left for Annapolis, Maryland, and the war. The regiment served almost entirely in Virginia, particularly in the Petersburg campaign, as Newton describes. The unit ended its days, as did many other black regiments, roasting on the Texas–Mexico border where the last fighting of the war transpired. The regiment's wartime casualties testified to the ordeal that Newton and his brethren experienced: 226 dead, 139 wounded, and 103 discharged for disabilities.

After his discharge from the army, Newton became an AME Church minister and filled pulpits in Arkansas, Tennessee, North Carolina, and New Jersey. Each state offered him abundant evidence that the war he had recently helped win had done nothing to improve the condition of American blacks. In the North, talented and skilled black men were shut out of trade unions: "He cannot work because he is not allowed to work." The economic conditions of African Americans steadily declined because white men, even those who had fought side by side with black soldiers, "do not want to work by the side of the black man." In the South, the reign of terror inflicted on African Americans by the Klan and similar terrorist organizations made Newton recoil in horror. He saw one black man beaten to death by a mob simply for allowing his horse to be watered at the same public watering place as a white man. One of Newton's parishioners was gunned down on his own doorstep in front of his horror-struck family. Such "fearful atrocities," Newton wrote, "are not easily forgotten."

By the time Newton published his autobiography in 1910, Americans had largely forgotten about the Civil War service of African Americans. If they gave a moment's notice to American blacks, it was to ponder the nation's chronic and mislabeled "negro problem." With the nation in the grips of historical amnesia, Newton sought to preserve the record of Connecticut's black regiment and his own efforts to "uplift" his race. Adjutant General's Office, *Record of Service of Connecticut Men in the Army and Navy of the United States During the War of the Rebellion* (Hartford, CT: Case, Lockwood & Brainard, 1889), 859–861, 881;

Alexander H. Newton, *Out of the Briars: An Autobiography and Sketch of the Twenty-ninth Regiment Connecticut Volunteers* (orig., 1910; Miami, FL: Mnemosyne Publishing, 1969), 19–28, 103, 106, 167–168.

IN 1861 WHEN PRESIDENT Lincoln issued a call for 75,000 troops I engaged myself for the great Civil War, the War of the Rebellion. I went into the company of the Thirteenth Regiment, of Brooklyn. I went to the front, as the United States was not taking Negro troops. In 186[3] there was a riot in New York City. The colored people were being dreadfully treated, being stoned, killed, and shown how despised they were even in the North. An orphan asylum (colored) was burned, having at that time three hundred children in it. I returned to Brooklyn under the command of General B. F. Butler, who had been ordered to put down the riot. While engaged in this mission I got into the very midst of the rioters. Soon they were after me. I ran through the streets of New York like a wild steer, while the rioters cried out, "Head the Nigger Off!" At length, I reached the New Haven boat which brought us safely to New Haven, Conn. While there I engaged at my trade with Mr. W. Clark. On the 18th of December, 1863, I enlisted in the Twenty-ninth regiment, of the Connecticut Volunteers, as a private. On March 8, 1864, the regiment broke camp and left New Haven for Annapolis, Md., with Colonel W[illiam]. B. Wooster in command. On the next Sabbath after we reached Annapolis, I attended the Methodist Church and listened to a powerful sermon by Rev. I. J. Hill,[1] he being an orderly to Colonel Wooster.

While in the camp at New Haven, Conn., we employed our idle time in discussing the great problems that confronted the country at that time. Lieutenant Seymour, Uncle Fred Moore,[2] Horace Louden, Rev. I. J. Hill and myself were the participants in these discussions. The new party, the Republican, was then formed, the prime purpose of which was the freedom of the slaves. We were most frequently surmising and prophesying as to what would be the final outcome and the ultimate benefits to the Negro race. There were vital questions at stake then. The spirit of patriotism and the desire to lift oppression, were afire in every breast of every true American. It would be well for the many young Afro-Americans of today to remember that the supreme purpose of the Republican party when it was organized, was not only to prohibit the further extension of slavery, but to exterminate it as a system of barter and traffic. On the other hand, the Democratic party at that time was in favor of the infernal system of slavery, and in our day, it is in sympathy with any movement that looks to keeping the Negro race in some kind of shackles. They are still in favor of keeping the Afro-American in slavery in some form. And they are succeeding reasonably well. For at last, we are forced to conclude that no man is really free unless he holds in his bosom the right of franchise and has received the liberty to exercise that right. Have the ten millions of Afro-Americans in the United States that right to-day? The answer comes from many States, NO!

Inspired with the thought of Shakespeare, who said, "He who would be free, let him first strike the blow himself," my bosom burned with the fire of patriotism for the salvation of my country and the freedom of my people. I was rejoiced when the Hon. Abraham Lincoln was elected President of these United States, and when it was my fortune to see him emancipate the millions of members of the downtrodden race. I shall never forget when I saw him riding through the streets of New York, with throngs of humanity on either side of him. He was on his way then to the inauguration at Washington, D. C., to assume control of the terror-stricken country and to take the reigns of government in his own hands. While it became necessary that blood should flow freely, I was reminded, that no sin is ever wiped out without the spilling of blood. This seems to be a decree of High Heaven, even among the affairs of men. And God has made no exception to this decree, in the salvation of men from their personal sins. I was indeed willing to unite with the party, the Republican party and the abolition movement for their high and holy purposes, and to be associated with such men as Rev. Henry Ward Beecher, Rev. Henry Highland Garnett, Theodore Tilden, Lewis Tappan, William Still,[3] of Philadelphia; Charles Sumner, Thaddeus Stevens and many other such men, whose platform was justice and right and freedom extended to all without regard to color or previous condition of servitude, and to enforce these rights and privileges even at the point of the bayonet.

At New Haven we had been promised $15 bounty on our enlistment, but this had not been allowed, no effort, it seems had been made to pay us this money, but we did not shirk our duty because we had not received our just dues. We had long been accustomed to such impositions; but we said that we would honor Old Glory, obey God, and contend for our prize, Liberty, and will contend in this conflict until the sound of clanking slave chains shall be heard no more in the length and breadth of this fair and goodly land. When kings, princes and nobles shall have been swept into merited oblivion and the Civil War forgotten, posterity will catch the glowing theme of Liberty and enroll with rapture the names of those heroes who bought this boon with blood on the battlefield.

The regiment paraded the streets while multitudes looked with wonder, some laughing, others cheering, mothers with their babies in their arms, crying and holding on to their husbands, as they marched away to do battle for the noblest of causes. It was a scene never to be forgotten. We marched from Chapel street, where we embarked on a Government transport. As I went on board the vessel, mother, father, wife and children, ladies and gentlemen, of my friends, both white and black, were bidding me goodbye and expressing the hope that I might have a safe return. I cannot express the sobbing emotions of my heart, when I ungrasped the hands of these loved ones and friends and turned my face away from them, knowing that I might be going to my death and never again see them in this world.

When we reached Annapolis, Md., we were encamped three miles out of town. Here for the first time we put up our tents. It was cold and damp. We dug holes about two feet wide extending from within [to] outside the tent, and placed sheet iron over these and in these small trenches started our fires. In this way we were able to have heat within and force the smoke outside.

The colored people in this place were afraid to speak to us. Their masters looked on us with contempt. On Sunday a reverend gentleman came into camp to preach to us and we listened to a very interesting sermon. After remaining here for eight or ten days, we received orders to strike tents. We left for Hilton Head, S. C., arriving at this place April 16, 1864. We marched through the main street and went into camp with the Twenty-sixth, of New York. On May 25 the paymaster arrived at Beaufort, S. C., where the Twenty-ninth Regiment was at this time stationed, and our spirits were greatly lifted up when we saw him, for as yet we had received no pay for our services. But when we were told by him that we could receive only $7 per month each, for our services our spirits fell. So I, together with the rest of my comrades, was really disgusted with this failure on the part of the Government to give us a decent compensation for our work as soldiers. The officers advised us to take it and assured us that at the next payment we should receive our full compensation. We decided to follow their advice. We quieted our passions and went to work like good soldiers. My great desire was to get into contact with the Southern forces that we might be working out the decision of this great problem. I had no ill feeling for the Southern white people, some of them had been my best friends; but this was not a personal matter, but a question of national issue, involving the welfare of millions, and my soul was on fire for the question, Slavery or No Slavery, to be forever settled and that too as soon as possible.

While the troops were at Bermuda Hundred [Virginia] having disembarked from the transport Alabama, I recalled an incident. When my father and mother were sitting at the table of my father's owner, master Park Custis, a son of Mr. and Mrs. Custis, saw a piece of pie on the table and started to help himself, without any formalities, my mother objected to his uncouthness, caught hold of him and would have handled him quite roughly, but my father caught hold of her and held her until the youngster got away with his prize. He was very insolent and insulting. It all came over me and I thought how I would like to find him at that time and administer the very flogging which my dear mother started to give him. I was indeed in a proper mood to have done it, if I had came across him. This is but a little illustration of hundreds of incidents that came into my mind when the army was in the South, and as I felt then, that I was duly protected, I confess that I had a burning desire to eke out some vengeance which for years had been pent up in my nature. But, of course, from the Christian standpoint, this was all wrong. I was all wrong. I was then on a much higher mission than trying to get personal vengeance on those who had mistreated me and mine, I was fighting for the liberty of my people and the righting of many wrongs that belonged to their social and religious welfare. While I had not learned much of the laws of commerce and politics, I knew only a little of the arts and sciences, which I had picked up here and there, by an attentive mind, in mixing with the educated people of the South; I knew nothing of military science, but I had been watching the Southerners drill for several years seemingly getting ready for some unexpected conflict; but I did not know that the time was fast approaching when a great problem would have to be settled by bloodshed, when I would be called on to make my life a personal sacrifice on the altar of my country and for the sake of my people. I knew that slavery and its inhuman machinery must be put out of existence and that the simple principles of liberty of thought and action in politics, society and religion must prevail. And, at this time, I was in the full realization of what it meant to be again in the South, not a cringing black man, but a proud American soldier with the Union and Old Glory behind, before, over and under me. I had heard, in the fifties, from the Southerners, that there would be a war and that if any of the colored people aided the North in it, they would catch them and cut out their tongues and make them drink their mothers' blood. Well, at this time, I was in the South to have my tongue cut out and to drink my mother's blood if it had been necessary. But thank God, I helped to save my own tongue and my mother's blood and my race! This is enough glory for me!

All the soldiers of the Twenty-ninth Regiment, although dark-skinned, felt the full responsibility of their mission. They were in the South to do, to dare, and to die. And while they had not been trained in military tactics at West Point and were backward in their movements, they had been to the armory of God and had received weapons of the heart, that made them daring and dangerous foes—men to be really reckoned with. And I am proud to say, that the history of the colored man in warfare has been an enviable one. He has always showed his patriotism by action, by deeds of sacrifice, by death itself. We had the same muscle, the same strength, the same heart, the same conscience, the same cause, the same right, the same liberty as the white man. We were fighting under the same flag and the same God. I remember the words of General [Rufus] Saxton, "Boys, if you want to make good soldiers you must look a white man straight in the face and let him know that you are a man." This gave us fresh courage to press forward as soldiers to certain victory.

On the 14th of August, 1864, a time long to be remembered with us, an oppressively hot day, we marched into Virginia. We were worn out, weary, thirsty, hungry, and completely exhausted. We were compelled to carry our blankets, knapsack, musket, and sixty pounds of cartridges. About 4 P. M. we reached the headquarters of General [David B.] Birney, in the woods and encamped. I was so overcome with the heat that I fell to the ground and was soon asleep. We had no feather beds to lie upon, only the bare ground—but this bed always supplied by Mother earth, was delightful this time for rest. We had for our dinner, breakfast and supper, half-done salt pork, which was placed on a stick and held over a blaze to warm it; hard tack, on which one could hardly make an impression with the teeth, and sometimes coffee, if it could be gotten. These were some of the hardships of the soldier and these were enough; but when you add to these the mental condition of many, such as myself, almost afraid of my own shadow, ready to shoot at anything that made a threatening noise,—I remember that I shot at the limb of a tree floating down the river, thinking that it was a rebel skiff with spies—it was a sore and trying ordeal. Every soldier was in constant expectation of surprises from the Johnnies, or rebels. Lee's and Johnston's army was near Buzzard's Roost, in face of a rocky-faced ridge, to pass him meant suffering and death. We were surrounded by Dutch Gap Canal, James River, over which we had to cross on a pontoon bridge, and Fort Hell to be captured and taken. But knowing that Generals [Godfrey] Weitzel, [William T.] Sherman, [Ulysses] Doubleday and [Benjamin F.] Butler had 35,200 men under them, we went bravely forward, determined that Old Glory should not trail in the dust.

We crossed the pontoon bridge near Deep Bottom and marching about two miles, halted in a corn field. Here we rested, but in momentary readiness for a call to action as the rebels were very near us. We were soon aroused and called to the fort at Malvern Hill. Here we entered into an engagement with the rebels and many were wounded, killed and taken prisoners. I had a very narrow escape and thought several times that "my time" had come. I remember a twenty-pound cannon ball coming towards me, I could see it distinctly through the smoke. It looked like it had been sent especially for me. I said quickly, "Lord, you promised that a thousand should fall at my side, but that it should not come nigh me." It was quick praying, quick thinking, quick coming; but when the ball was within about three feet of me it struck the ground and bounded over my head. So I was saved. God's promise was fulfilled in my case.

On the 16th we joined the Third Division, Tenth Army Corps, General Birney's Brigade, composed of the Twenty-second, Seventh, Eight, Ninth and Twenty-ninth, United States Cavalry Troops, numbering 5000 men.[4] We took up our march for Jones' Landing, recrossed the pontoon bridge under very disagreeable circumstances, rain, mud and slush, but we were thankful and cheerful; glad that we had not been killed, or wounded or taken prisoners, in the encounter just passed through. Again we camped in an open field and raised our tents, prepared our bacon and coffee and hard tack. We were soon ready to take a good night's sleep. I remembered my loved ones and wondered how they were faring and my privations, but I found myself willing to undergo all this for the cause of liberty.

On the 17th we arose early and received word to advance. In a short time we were in a fierce battle. Our lieutenant colonel was wounded in the engagement. Again, I thought that my time had come. By some awkward movement, I was thrown into the line of the enemy. The Johnnies were very much excited and did their best to capture me, but I succeeded in getting back into the Union lines. I knew then that the prayers of my good old mother were being heard; for surely the Lord delivered me from the snare of the fowler and from the noisome pestilence. Our lieutenant colonel had his horse shot from under him and Orderly I. J Hill was wounded.

I prayed in this battle whenever I had opportunity to look towards Heaven, for grape and canister and bullets of all shapes and sizes were falling thick and fast about me. We were in close quarters with the enemy and our ranks were being thinned by reason of the wounded and dead lying on the battlefield. Although I came out of this battle pretty well shaken up, excepting for a few scratches, my life was on the altar for my country and my people, and I was not especially concerned as to the outcome regarding my own life; but I was determined to do all that I could to bring our cause to a victorious end. The Union forces moved back and remained all day about twelve miles from Richmond.

On the 18th, the Twenty-ninth Regiment, of which I was commissary sergeant, and the Third Division, moved down the valley, halting in the open fields for two hours. We were opposite the pontoon bridge which crossed the Chickahominy, and remained until the bridge was put in repair. While here I gave out hard tack and pork to the soldiers as best I could. For myself, I built a little fire and roasted a bit of pork over the fire, which together with water from the river, formed my meal. On the 20th we marched for the forts on the right of Point Rock Hospital, near Petersburg. On the 21st we were almost flanked by the rebels and retreated to Malvern Hill and repaired the breastworks. Here we had another skirmish. Some lost their lives and others were wounded, but we were successful in capturing seventy-five prisoners.

On the 23d we crossed the James River on the pontoon bridge, passing the heights where the New Jersey Battery was stationed. They greeted us with shouts and "Hurrah boys! we are here to stay!" Such a round of cheers you never heard. You would not have thought that they were on their way to battle, and some to death and the Judgment Throne. Uncle Freddie Moore and Orderly I. J. Hill were the only preachers we had with us, excepting the chaplain. They used to say to us, "boys get ready, for if there ever were a time when you should be ready, it is now; for you do not know when you may be called to go, you are continually in death's jaws."

We were soon in front of Petersburg, Va., looking upon the doomed city. We were greeted by a shell from the rebels, or Grey Backs, as we sometimes called them. It fell near the colonel, who was sitting on his horse at the right of the brigade. We countermarched and fell back to the woods, where we remained until 5 o'clock, when orders were received from the general to fall back to the fort and protect the pontoon bridge. On our way we met a lot of troopers making their way to the front, who wanted to know our reason for returning. We told them that the rebels were after us. It was very amusing to see them falling into line. Some of them could march faster than we. We reached the fort, but when we found that the Johnnies were not coming after us, we became anxious to see them and meet the issue. We found quite a number of our associates from New Haven and Hartford, Conn., and Woodbury, N. J. We were all delighted that our lives had been spared to see each other again in the flesh and chatted freely about our friends at home, our wives, mothers and children. I had often heard of the horrors of war, but now I began to experience what it meant, in the joy of meeting friends whom I never expected to see again on the earth, or at least some of them. There was a sense in which I had a new understanding of that marvelous passage of Scripture, regarding death, "Oh death, where is thy sting; Oh, grave, where is thy victory." We had not yet felt the sting of death and we had not experienced the victory of the grave, yet we had been in the very midst of both.

Once again we marched in front of the horrible pit, Petersburg. Some of the whites said, see they are taking those colored soldiers to the slaughter pen. Truly, they had said so, for I never saw such a scene the first night. Shot and shell were raining fast around us. Henry Migs, a native of Africa, was killed.[5] He died as a soldier, true to his adopted country, but a stranger to God. I thought that every bullet was sent for me and was doing some real praying. We do not know what prayer is, until we are reduced to our extremity. Then we realize with a new experience, that our extremity is God's opportunity. I told the Lord that He had promised to "Rescue the perishing and care for the dying," and that I wanted Him to keep the promise of that song, so far as I was concerned. Well, praise His name, He did so. Thank God to-day that I am still living and permitted to write this bit of fearful experience, so others may know what it is to trust in God.

On the 24th, Private Sam Bertim, of Company E, was killed, having been shot through the head. Private George Porter was also killed.[6] Colonel Wooster was taken sick and was carried from the rifle pits to the rear. The rebels captured one of our officers, while changing those on picket duty. Two men from the Twenty-ninth were slaughtered, they were members of Company A. The colored troops did some good fighting in this engagement. We were told by the enemy that if we were captured our tongues would be cut out, or we would be starved to death; that there would be no exchange of prisoners in our case. So this was a rather fearful inspiration, but it served its purpose, of causing us to fight to the best of our ability; for we really feared that in case we were captured that such barbarities might be administered to us.

On the 1st of September we were ordered to strike tents and to move on, we knew not whither we were going. We did not care either, for now we were thoroughly enthused with the issues of war. We had tasted of the dangers of battle, and this taste brought out the desire that we should fight to the finish. Some of our dear friends had laid down their lives already, and we reasoned that if it should be necessary for them to give such a sacrifice, that we were no better than they. So in our judgement, we were becoming calm, and in our determination, we were becoming more and more fixed.

With President Lincoln and our great generals and loyal soldiers, we felt that the issue was assured. Of course we did not forget the divine side of the question, that God was on His throne and that right and justice and mercy would at last prevail. While it had always been said that this was a white man's country, we were determined that the black man should share in this honor of ownership. And the best way that this ownership could be established was through the loyalty of the black man on the battlefield. For surely it will be conceded that when a man has bought his adopted country by his blood, it is his own. While, as a race, the Negro race, this is our adopted land, yet as individuals, it is our native land, our fatherland.

The colored troops numbered at this time about 75,000. The Twenty-ninth Regiment, which was my own, formed the center. We were in line of march toward the city but were turned in our course and crossed the pontoon bridge, which landed us near the city of Petersburg. When daylight came we were on the Old Market Road and headed for Richmond, Va. We were very much exhausted and were hoping for a rest, when we heard the music of the bugle, which told us that our rest had come.

At this time it was dangerous for live things to get in out way, we were hungry for something besides hard tack, bad coffee and salt pork. We wanted fresh meat and plenty of it. So it was a bad time for chickens and terrapin, for when we could find these living edibles, we generally appropriated them without any thought of the criminality of the act or of the danger of being detected or arrested. Our hunger gave us license to satisfy it in the quickest and best way available.

On the 2d of September we were once again in front of the enemy and ready to do battle. We entered the engagement with enthusiasm and rapidly drove the enemy before us. We were assisted by a large Mogul, which we called the Petersburgh Express and one or two gunboats on the James River, which fired balls half as big as a common sized water bucket.[7] Soon victory was perched on our banners and with flying colors, we advanced by a right flank and entered the rebel lines after a bad fought battle of six hours, leaving many dead and wounded on the battlefield. My brother, William Henry Newton, was in the same regiment with me, not as a soldier but as a valet, he attended Captain [Charles] Griswold. We charged two of the rebel forts, the left of the line was charged by the Eight United States Troops, supported by the Twenty-ninth; the center was charged by the Ninth Maryland, supported by the Seventh United States Troops.[8] In the history of my war record, I shall never forget this day's experience. The rebels fought hard and nobly, but the colored troops defeated them and gained another victory in favor of the Union army. Our loss was very heavy and the true story of the suffering and heartaches will never be known until the Judgment Day.

Captain [Edwin A.] Thorp and Lieutenant [Louis R.] McDonough were wounded. I came on my rounds, bringing refreshments and stopped where the surgeons were at work. I shall never forget the fearful sight that met my eyes. It was indeed sickening. There were arms and legs piled up like hogs' feet in a butcher shop. The dead and the dying were strewn over the battlefield for five miles. Drum Major John D. Cowes,[9] of New Haven, with his corps, were busy carrying the wounded off the battlefield. I said to myself, war is a terrible way to adjust differences, when it might be done by the implements of peace. But I remembered that it is much easier to wield the sword than to use the pen; much easier to give a command which will send hundreds to their death, than to be a master of assemblies and speak the word which gives peace and happiness to millions. We lay all night in front of the rebel works and in the morning we were warmly saluted by fierce bombarding. So we were again in the midst of battle which waged hotly. The enemy carried their dead and wounded out of their trenches as lively as they were able. They did this so as to keep from trampling on them and to have room for the soldiers who were doing the work of death. In this engagement several were wounded but not many killed. Our colonel was not able to do duty and our lieutenant colonel was sick at Fortress Monroe.[10]

On the morning of the 4th, we advanced to the left of the line, planting our flag under the rebel fire of grape and canister, bombshell and musketry. The dead were lying in every direction and the wounded were falling everywhere, cared for by the rear guard. On the 5th and 6th, we had to endure the hardships and exposure of the rifle pits, with advance pickets stationed in front of the rebel garrison. It was the fighting of a duel, so to speak, between two armies, although quite a distance apart. After [a]while the Twenty-ninth was ordered to headquarters, but did not get far on its way, when a fire broke out in our midst, we were shifted into a double-quick and returned to the breastworks where we held our position until the 8th, when we moved on the right to support the Forty-fifth,[11] on Lookout Mountain. We were worn out and had hoped that we would be allowed to rest; but we received orders to take position on the front to support the Eighth United States Cavalry troops, who had charge of the breastworks. Six days of hard fighting, fatigue and exposure, was our experience here. Under orders of the general we scouted and explored the territory and drove the enemy from the woods. We were able to take charge of the situation, much to our pride; still holding the rebels at bay and driving them further, to hunt new quarters.

On the 14th we abandoned the breastworks, General Birney leading the Third Division, Tenth Army Corps, numbering 75,000 colored troops. We were not formed into a fighting position at this time, perhaps for the reason that the enemy were too strong for us. So we were brought to the rear of the breastworks. For a long while the rain had been pouring in torrents and there was not a dry place to be found nor a dry thread on our bodies, we were covered with dirt and mud from head to foot, and not only felt to be in a terrible plight, but must have looked worse. The troops were ordered to prepare two days' rations and to get ready for light marching. I had opportunity now to be in the company of commissioned officers for a few hours at a time, when we halted for rest. We would spread our meals on the wet ground, not a very inviting table, but the best that we could find. I somehow had the feeling that something was going on, or was going to happen, that would require one to be wise and cunning. The officers had a queer expression on their faces, and in fact all the field officers seemed to be uneasy. Three o'clock one morning, my surmises were justified, for the long roll was sounded and soon we were in line for work. We engaged in a bloody struggle. We moved to the right and some one began to sing,

> "Sure, I must fight if I would win,
>   Increase my courage Lord;
> I'll bear the toil, endure the pain,
>   Supported by Thy Word."

We thus cheered ourselves by the singing of songs while we fought and while we marched through the Virginia mud, such songs as "Tramp, Tramp, the Boys are Marching," "Beneath the Starry Flag." The rebel lines were fortified, but under our noble leaders, we marched on to certain victory and the old Twenty-ninth was ready for any fray. The rising sun would seem to say to us, after he had broken thorough the darkness and the clouds, "Cheer up boys, don't be despondent, but vigilant, strong, courageous, protecting the flag, the country, women and children, rights and liberty, and all things will come out right." Thus it will be seen, how often God speaks to us through nature, how often we are cheered and helped by a bright day. How dependent we are upon our surroundings, for support. I do not say that this should be so, for a soldier should be strong, regardless of such things, but nevertheless they have their effect.

We were on the extreme right of the front and within three miles of Richmond, where our white troops were repulsed. The colored troops were commanded to halt and line up for action in front of the woods. Again the thought came to me, although this is called the white man's country, they need us in war as in peace, to make and to keep the country. And why is not this fact fully realized by the white people? We are more than ten million strong and are ready at any time to lay down our lives for the nation and to give our lives in service, in times of peace, in all lines of activity. This we are doing. The progress which the Negro race has made since the war is an enviable one. No people or race would be ashamed of it. We have made this progress as honest, industrious citizens. We have shown our manhood in both times of war and peace, and our record has been written. Then why are we not accorded the place that we have rightly merited? In the sentiment of the white people there lurks a deep-rooted prejudice against us, and in their course of action discrimination is made against the Negro. We do not understand why this should be, unless there is a feeling on the part of the white people, that there is danger that we should become too prosperous and too many—the feeling which the ancient Egyptians had against the Hebrews—hence, they took steps to check the Hebrews. These may be the steps taken by the white man to check our progress. But the same God who overruled the destinies of the Hebrew slaves and brought them to their Promised Land, will take care of us and, we too, one day, shall enter our Promised Land, of equal rights and liberty.

On the 29th, there [w]as a fierce encounter. The battle was indeed a slaughter pen. The enemy fought like tigers. The battle became general along the entire line. Adjutant [J. Lewis] Spaulding was wounded. Corporal George Burr, Company L; Corporal Sidney, of Company E, and many others were killed. Private George E. Peters, Sergeant George Halstead, James Evans and many others were wounded.[12] I, myself, feared, shook, and thought that my time had come. I was full of thoughts of my loved ones at home. I knew that they were praying that I should be delivered from the jaws of death. This thought cheered and comforted me; and yet I saw friends falling around me, whose loved ones and friends, were also praying for their protection. Their prayers were not being answered and why? Why should I think that the prayers offered for me were more availing than those offered for them? Why should I have any special reason for encouragement? These thoughts come to one when he is in the midst of circumstances which seems to upset many of our principles of religious faith. They come to us not only in war but in work. They must be reckoned with. The only answer that I could find as to why the prayers offered for me were availing up to this time, was that my time had not come, and that it had not come because God had not ordered it, and God had not ordered it because He had something for me to do. Of course, He had heard the prayers which had been offered for me and they entered into His decree regarding my life. The only answer we can find to many perplexing questions which come in life is, "It is God's way, His will."

I was very busy in supplying the regiment with food, vinegar and water, and such edibles as I could get together. The doctors were busy sawing off legs and arms, and binding up wounds, and giving medicines to the wounded and sick. The women were busy in preparing bandages, lint, and doing what they could in the alleviation of human suffering. God bless the dear women who had the faith and the courage to breast the trials and hardships of soldier life. These scenes would have made your heart sore. Dear reader, the wounded and dying scattered over the battlefield thick, the hurrying to and fro of the physicians and the nurses; the prayers and groans and cries of the wounded, the explosion of bombs, the whizzing of bullets, the cracking of rifles; you would have thought that the very forces of hell had been let loose. And, indeed, it was hell, the horrors of which no one could ever forget.

We finally retreated under the cover of the cavalry. The colored troops were the first to enter the field and the last to fall back. We thereby demonstrated to our President, Abraham Lincoln, and our General, U. S. Grant, that we were among their best supporters. The white man had no record to make. He was known as a fighter for centuries, our record was to be made and we were making it. The flag of our regiment could be seen floating among the pines. We were glad that Old Glory was above us with her folds pierced with many bullet holes. We returned to camp and took our former position in front of Richmond, where we remained for a while.

We were again in battle array, having been marched up to the rifle pits. Our field officers being absent, we were under the command of Captain [Frederick E.] Camp, of Company D, our own colonel, W. B. Wooster, was at home on sick furlough. Lieutenant Colonel W. L. Ward, who had been promoted to the rank of colonel, was in charge of the Forty-first United States Cavalry Troop. The lieutenant colonel said to us, "Boys, we must fight to-day, let me have your best. Duty demands it. I will stand by you until the last. Watch, keep in line, and obey orders." He brought us up double-quick to the rifle pits and the bugle sounded charge. We charged, firing, yelling, using our bayonets and our arms in the most cruel manner, but still in accordance with the tactics of warfare. We were there to kill in every manner possible. We held the pits for twenty-four hours, brought the rebels to their knees, brought down their flag and unfurled the Stars and Stripes to the breezes.

This was a disastrous battle, probably the most disastrous I had ever witnessed. I should probably make exception of the Fort Pillow Massacre, in which my brother, Steven Newton, was killed. He was a member of the Fourteenth, Rhode Island Battery.[13] Charles Beman, [son of] Rev. Amos G. Beman[14] and Corporal W. W. Wilkins were with him to the end and were able to make the report of his death to me. We lost in this battle over one hundred, i. e., I am counting only the loss of the Twenty-ninth Regiment. This regiment fought most bravely, gaining great praise, and receiving many compliments from the officers high up in rank. When the battle was over, we fell back and camped in front of Richmond. While there we attended the funeral of Private Charles Bently, who was killed early in the engagement. He died a champion for liberty and an earnest Christian. Jones Spriggs and thirteen others were buried at this time.[15]

Many of the veterans went out on foraging expeditions. While resting we would engage in religious and patriotic songs. One of our favorites was, "Tenting on the Old Camp Ground." About this time, the Third Division, Tenth Army Corps, Twenty-ninth Regiment, and General Birney, were surprised with the presentation of the United States national colors, which greatly pleased the boys. The flag was presented by the Forty-fifth United States Cavalry Troops to our lieutenant colonel, in a most pleasing manner. He spoke of the great bravery of the soldiers in battle. Colonel Ward replied that he had 672 guns which would speak whenever occasion demanded it. He also said that his boys were filled with as noble sentiments as any that had ever filled the breasts of the boys before the guns.

While on dress parade we received the sad announcement from our lieutenant colonel that he would leave the regiment, as he had been promoted to the rank of colonel. This was indeed sad news to us. He had been with us in many hard-fought battles. We had learned to love him and had great confidence in his ability. He knew what course to pursue in order to avert many of the tricks of the Johnnies, not only being well up in military science, but well acquainted with many little games that are often played in war.

We remained in front of Richmond five days. While there we were quiet and enjoyed the much needed sleep that we had. We were greatly annoyed here as well as in other places with what the soldiers called greybacks, not the rebels, however; they were genuine creepers. They molested us no little. Whenever I could get off I would go to the creek and disrobe myself and pick them out of my clothes, then wash my clothes and hang them on the bushes to dry. Then I would dress myself and feel like a king, because once again I was clean and free from these unearthly vermin.

From the first to the eighth of November, 1864, we were at Malvern Hill. I was Commissary Sergeant and was careful to keep as near the regiment as possible with my department. Sergeant Quartermaster D. L. Lathrop[16] had charge of the ammunition, knapsacks, etc., under the command of our regimental quartermaster, there was always detailed a guard to protect us. We always followed the army with our train. I remember once that I got into the line of the Johnnies and I ran as if the hounds of hell were after me. I heard the whizzing of a bullet over my head, but it missed me. So I said, well they did not get me that time and Libby Prison has been robbed of an expected treasure.

While here the Twenty-ninth Regiment had charge of the fort until the third of December.

It was whispered about that Generals Lee, Johnston and others were in a position to watch our movements and that we might expect an attack at any time. But we were not worried over this report with such Generals as U. S. Grant, Sherman, [Oliver O.] Howard, Weitzel and others. We knew that they would be able to flank any movement that they might make.

On Monday the fifth, we took up our line of march to a destination unknown to us, there were all kinds of rumors as to where we would stop, but at last we found ourselves to the left of Fort Harrison on the left of the line. Here we camped under orders. We engaged in the usual preparations for a stay, putting up our tents, building huts and making things convenient for all concerned. But the next day the Colored troops were ordered to prepare two days' rations and to advance. Then our countenances changed. We did not know but that another fierce battle was in store for us; and we had had quite enough fighting to satisfy us for a long while. On Wednesday, we were in front of the Johnnies, with our breastworks thrown up ready for fight.

The Colored regiments were consolidated in the Second Division, Third Brigade, Twenty-Fifth Army Corps. A number of detached men were taken from the regiments. Orderly I. J. Hill was Brigade Postmaster. I was with the commissary department. All things were quiet along the lines excepting the laughing and yelling of the Johnnies. Once in a while they would throw a shell into our camp. At this time we would hear their cheers and laughter.

On January the first, we were in front of Richmond, Va. Here we engaged in battle with the Rebels, which was terrific. The anxiety, suffering, slashing, shooting, were beyond description. Many lay dead on the battlefield, baking in the sun. There were dead animals which had been exposed for two weeks, the stench was unbearable. These are some of the indescribable tortures of war.

The rebels soon retired from their position, for they would not have been able to withstand the Union Army. They were in constant expectation of the coming of Sherman who at the time was in the vicinity of Atlanta, Ga. We were under marching orders until the thirteenth. Colonel Wooster received orders to place his headquarters near our own regiment. I was determined that I would keep up my enthusiasm and do all in my power to supply the boys with something to eat.

On the twenty-third the rebel fleet moved down the James River towards the Dutch Gap Canal and opened fire on Fort Bradley keeping it up all night. The following morning the whole line was drawn up for action, at long range with reinforcements in the rear. The shelling was terrific all day. I was in the basement of a house, when a shell came through the window, burst and tore its way through the building. This house was used for headquarters. Fortunately none of us were hurt. Only the everlasting arm of God protected us, for all our friends who witnessed the shell and its devastations, supposed that we were all killed. The Quartermaster having received a wound in the knee, the Quartermaster sergeant and I had to do all the work. At this time Orderly I. J. Hill and others were let off on parole and went home for twenty days. The Confederates made another dash to retake their lost territory and to make sure of the permanent establishment of the Slave Traffic which had been the curse of every nation or people who has adopted it. Their plan was to out-flank us and to effect a great slaughter and capture many of our men and guns and ammunition. And it seemed to us that they were after the Colored troops. But our leaders were too shrewd for them and they were repulsed and their depot, magazines and machine shops at Beaufort, N. C., were blown up and also at New Berne. A great battle was fought about Fort Fisher and the Rebels were overcome. Hundreds were killed and wounded in this battle.

The Colored troops in front of Richmond were moved from the breastworks on the left at Fort Harrison, to the hill in the center, where we built up a fine elevation overlooking the Rebel works in Richmond. Here we remained several days under heavy cannonading. We held the enemy so that they were unable to make any gains on us for four weeks. They made several attempts to storm and to cut off our supply, but they signally failed. But our men understood how to construct railroads and we would frequently hear the whistle of a locomotive in some direction bringing in our supplies. Our forces were well guarded on every hand by squads which were experts in caring for the welfare and needs of an army. We could hear the result of our bombarding in such cities as Petersburg, etc., and knew that our forces were gradually gaining and that the Rebels were gradually losing in their strongest holds.

On the twenty-seventh of March we struck our tents and moved on to Richmond. We were soon formed in line of battle in front of this city. The Rebels blew up three gunboats and evacuated their works immediately in front of us. There was heavy cannonading from the gunboats in the James River, the Monitor and other boats.

At this time there were many refugees coming to us by the hundreds. This was in past the result of Sherman's march to the sea. He left in his wake many monuments of this famous march. There were deserted villages, chimneys standing without the houses about them, and troops of stragglers following the army.

Colonel Wooster ordered the 29th Regiment to advance and to do some daring work in the digging up of buried torpedoes which had been planted to impede the march of the Union Army. We were however equal to the task. We captured five hundred pieces of artillery, six thousand small arms, and the prisoners I did not count, but when we looked on them in the prison pen, the number seemed to be enormous.

We were present in Richmond when President Lincoln made his triumphal entry into the city. It was a sight never to be forgotten. He passed through the main street. There were multitudes of Colored people to greet him on every hand. They received him with many demonstrations that came from the heart, thanking God that they had seen the day of their salvation, that freedom was theirs, that now they could live in this country, like men and women, and go on their way rejoicing. Orderly I. J. Hill said that he saw a colored woman trying to get a look at the president, at last he came along and Orderly Hill said to her: "Madame, there is the man that made you free." She shouted, "Is that President Lincoln? Glory to God, give Him praise for His goodness." The President, with his son, and Admiral Porter, together with others walked over a mile to the headquarters of General Weitzel, at the mansion of Jeff Davis. A colored man acted as the guide. There were six Union soldiers as advance guard, then came President Lincoln, his son, and Admiral Porter, while on his right and his left were other officers. He was followed by six sailors with their carbines. This march created the wildest enthusiasm of the Colored people. They had lived to see the day of their liberty drawing. I was reminded of what had been done for the ancient Hebrews by Moses when he led them out of the land of their bondage, into the land of their promised liberty. Lincoln was indeed our Moses. He led us forth. He gave us our freedom. I noticed one white lady in a window, who turned away from the whole scene as if in utter disgust. There were still two sides to the question, then and there are two sides to it today. How long will these two sides remain, is the question. As the President looked out upon the poor Colored people and remembered how many lives had been lost in working out their salvation, he was not able to keep the tears from his eyes. There were tears of gladness and sorrow, of regret and delight; but the tears of my own people were the tears of the greatest joy.

The President went to the state capitol where he made a short address in which he said: "Now you Colored people are free, as free as I am. God has made you free and if those who are your superiors are not able to recognize that you are free, we will have to take the sword and musket and again teach them that you are free. You are as free as I am, having the same rights of liberty, life and the pursuit of happiness."

While at Richmond, we engaged in many foraging expeditions. We found such things as eggs, chickens, butter, bread, fruit, tobacco. There were bales of tobacco in the street free for every one who enjoyed the weed. And I must sat that many were delighted with their free smokes.

There were plenty of Confederate money too, which was often blown about by the wind as so much worthless waste paper. Well it was waste paper. With the passing of the Confederacy, the money value passed away on all such currency.

On April 16th, 1865, we were painfully shocked to hear of the death of President Lincoln, at the hands of an assassin. No one can measure the consternation which struck our hearts. This great and wonderful man who had guided the Ship of State through four years of such perilous waves and winds, that he should thus pass away and in such an infamous manner, was more than we could stand. But it was so. Our faith was almost staggered, that faith which had sustained us in so many battles, was now staggering under a blow which was severer than any battles, the death of our Immortal leader. Thus in four years from the first shot fired on Fort Sumter, four years from the very day of the first shot, the shot was fired from the hand of Booth, that removed one of the greatest men the world ever knew, from the scenes of human actions. He was removed too at a time when he was most needed. Yes, he was more needed, than when the nation was in the midst of a bloody conflict. He was now needed to set up the battlements of peace, which is a more difficult work than the forts of warfare.

On the twenty-fourth, we moved from the camp near Petersburg, to Camp Lincoln where we enjoyed our camp life for awhile. We had lost many of our numbers through death on the battlefield and disease in the camp, but losses were now being recruited by volunteers coming to us. I was kept busy filling our regimental papers, ordering and issuing rations. Some of our men had become so rum thirsty that they would offer me ten dollars for a canteen full of whisky. But I was not allowed to sell it, and to give it out only on the orders of the Quartermaster.

We were not here long. We embarked on the Demolay for Norfolk, Va. General Russel[17] and staff came on board to tell us goodbye. I had two barrels of supposed corn beef, the boys called it salt-horse, which I suppose was nearer the truth. I had also a barrel of sugar. These I could not ship, so I left them on the ground, for some poor fellows that could use them. Colonel Wooster came also and saw us off. We left many friends, some of them with tears in their eyes. They had become very dear to us. We had shared together the hardships of camp-life and of the battlefield. Human suffering makes men very near akin. As we glided swiftly down the James River, for a while we could hear their

cheers and when sound was out of touch, we could see their salutes of
hats and handkerchiefs. We enjoyed the day as soldiers on board the
vessel. I was astonished at the behavior of the soldiers. They gave
themselves over to all kinds of sports and jestings, which disgusted me
most thoroughly. Many were unruly, even threatening the lives of
those who favored going to Texas whither we had been ordered for garrison duty. Some of the gang were arrested for their insubordination.
My heart was made to shudder at the degrading and shameful life
which was manifested on board the ship. Their swearing, drinking,
gambling, dancing, etc., was heartsickening. It was indeed a revelation
and shows what men will do when not under the eye of authority. Human nature is indeed most sinful, and were it not for the restrictions
which are thrown about us, none of us know what might come to pass.
We arrived at Norfolk and anchored for the night. With having witnessed the debauchery on board the vessel and at the same time
wrought with anxiety for my wife and two babies, my father and
mother at home, I confess I was in a most depressed condition of mind
and heart. "Be strong and of good courage," came to me like a flash and
I was strong and buoyant in a little while. How grand is the truth of
God, when we find it such a rock of refuge in times of trouble; I was
thus greatly consoled and went to bed looking up at the shining stars,
as if they were so many angels, sent by God, to guard me.

There was quite an excitement on board when it was whispered
about that the officers had covenanted together to take the soldiers on
board, to Cuba, and sell them as slaves. There was quite an indignation
against I. J. Hill, for it was thought that he was in some manner party
to this arrangement. The men were suspicious also of Sam Brown, a
clerk. I, together with others, had the good fortune to escape any insults
or indignities. While at Norfolk, we went to church and saw quite a
number of well-to-do Colored people. Rev. J. M. Brown,[18] of the A. M.
E. Church, I think was pastor. He treated us very cordially indeed. We
were introduced to many of the congregation. The church had a Sunday School of six or seven hundred members. It was an inspiring sight
to see them nicely dressed and to hear them sing so sweetly, many beautiful Sunday school songs. But the time had come when we had to leave
the many dead of our comrades. We had done all that we could for them
in the last sad rites of death and now their bodies were resting under the
cold sods of the South, awaiting the Resurrection Day, when we will all

meet again and hear our record of the deeds done in the body and the judgment based on these deeds. The memories of war are one of the saddest features thereof. These memories can never be blotted out; for as we grow older they seem to become more vivid.

We took shipping on the transport, Blackstone, for Texas. We were about fifteen days on the waters, the ocean was calm. There were six or seven hundred on board. It was no little job to take care of the hungry stomachs of these men. But we had a most pleasant trip and enjoyed the ocean waves and breezes. The officers spent most of their time in fishing. Once in awhile a fish six or seven feet long would be hauled in. For two days we were out of sight of land and only one small schooner passed us. There was much complaint on board on account of the army food which I was compelled to give them salt pork or hard tack and bad coffee. They thought that being on board of ship warranted better food, but I told them that I had to give them what I had. And so we fought the battle of the stomach. There were many however who were afflicted with sea-sickness and had no concern for something to eat. We had a burial at sea. The poor soldier was sewed up in a blanket and consigned to a grave in the bottom of the deep. The funeral service was very impressive to many of us, for it was the first burial at sea we had witnessed. I must confess that there was a grandeur about it that inspired one—as the boundless ocean received the body of our comrade, eternity had received his soul. I thought of his loved ones and that in all probability they would never hear of him. Then I wondered if that grand song could not be an interpretation of this burial,

"Rock in the cradle of the deep,
I lay me down in peace to sleep,
In ocean cave still safe with Thee,
The germ of Immortality."[19]

At this time I was not a member of the church. But my father had taught me to pray. And as I have frequently related, I often prayed in battle when I thought that my time had come. I had a sense of guilt of sin and of the need of confession of my sins. So I had also, the sense of peace which comes from a man's justification through Jesus Christ. My case I am sure is but an illustration of the cases of many men and women who have not connected themselves with the church. They are real

Christians as I was, having the ordinary experience of the Christian, but not having made any outward profession. We are therefore unable to know who are the children of God, for certainly there are believers outside of the church. Our judgment therefore must always be a charitable one. Yet I do not want the impression to be made that I, in any sense, approve of believers remaining outside of the church. An outward profession of faith in our blessed Lord, Jesus Christ, is an open badge of our religion which men can see. We should not hide our light under a bushel, but put it on a candle stick that all about us may see what we are by what we live. When we rounded the Florida reefs, the boys' hearts were gladdened, because thay had seen the land once again and their thought was that they were nearing the end of the voyage. We had some sickness on board, such diseases as yellow jaundice, malaria, chills and fever. We were huddled together like a lot of wild ducks and the sanitary conditions were against our health. When about seven days on our trip, our drinking water failed us. We were on the water, yet we had no water to drink; but we did the best we could under the circumstances.

We were glad when we came into the harbor at Mobile, Ala. Here we found many transports lying in the harbor. Fort Gaines was to our right and Fort Morgan to our left. The boys were all delighted, because they were wild to get to land again, and especially to get a drink of good water. How dependent we are on mother earth after all for our lives. After passing the forts a short distance the anchor was dropped. The surroundings were grand. There were gunboats lying in the stream, with their artillery of death-dealing cannon looking forth from the decks and thoroughly manned with the smaller-implements of naval warfare. But our hopes were not fulfilled, for a command came that we were to sail immediately to New Orleans. The men were bitter in their disappointment, but such is the experience of war. Men are not free, they are the parts of the gigantic machine of death, so many cogs in the wheels, or so many wheels in the machine, or so many parts of the machine. They soon became reconciled however. We had plenty of hard tack and salt horse left us, and with this we could not starve to the death. Our voyage was an uneventful one, save for the good weather and the fine ocean. We were soon in the channel for New Orleans. When we reached the forts Jackson and Phillips, a signal stopped us for inspection. We were told that we could not go to New Orleans, that none of the men or officers could go any further without an order from General

Grant. The officers telegraphed to Washington to General Grant. We were in rather a dilapidated condition, about out of coal and in need of better fuel for the stomach, with the men completely worn out with the voyage.

We were however permitted to go on land at Fort Jackson. This was a magnificent fort with its seventy guns overlooking the water inlet. There were many alligators in this place and we amused ourselves by killing them, which of course was a greatly desired thing. I had plenty of hard tack and this seemed to attract the reptiles. I remember one fellow over seven feet long I killed.

At this place the Colored troops had been shamefully and barbarously treated. As I thought of the outrages which they had suffered only about one month before our arrival, I felt that if I could, I would like a little revenge on their account. But there was no opportunity for such outlet of wicked feeling. At last we received an order from General Grant to take the transport to New Orleans, to get a supply of coal and oil, and to have the transport repaired. But to our dismay, only the officers were permitted to go. We were left at Fort Phillips.

I managed however, to get to New Orleans, in that I had charge of the commissary department. We were already beginning to forget the hardships of the battlefield. Our minds were turning to the ordinary life which we live, and looking forward to the pleasures connected with home and with business. And I assure you, my dear readers, that it was a happy release. We had the constant joy in our hearts that our beloved people had their freedom, bought with the blood of those who now slept the last sleep on many battlefields; but we did not believe that the price paid for this boon of liberty was too dear. The price of human liberty can never be estimated. This is especially true of those who knew what slavery meant. And the Colored Race has an endless debt to pay their White friends who bought their liberty with their own blood. While it is true that the White people brought our forefathers here and sold them into slavery, which of course they had no right to do, this does not diminish the price which this same race had to pay in order to buy us out of the slavery into which they had sold us. And it does not in the least diminish the debt of gratitude which we shall owe them as long as time exists.

I had a short but very pleasant stay in New Orleans. On Sunday we went to the A. M. E. Church, of which the Rev. William A. Dove was pastor.[20] This was the St. James A. M. E. Church. We were most cordially received by the pastor and members. They were kind enough to take care of us while in the city. We learned from the members that while we were on the battlefield, they were at home fasting and praying that our grand cause might be victorious. "Fight and pray" is sure to win the day for any just cause. The services were very pleasing and profitable. The pastor preached in the morning and our orderly I. J. Hill, at night. I and others, were much lifted up and realized anew what it was to draw water from the wells of salvation. We spent much of our time in seeing the sights of the unique city of the South. Our friends were more than kind to us during our stay. We lacked nothing for good beds and good food and good society; and we were in good shape to appreciate these things, because of the privations, losses, suffering, and fears through which we had passed.

Our transport having been repaired and furnished with needed coal and oil and food, we were soon on our way back to the fort. We had not gone far on our course until there was an alarm of fire. This created quite a panic, but the blaze was soon put out and we were enjoying our trip down the "Father of Waters."

We arrived at Fort Phillips with more soldiers for the Twenty-ninth Regiment, they having been brought in from other quarters.

We were soon off for Texas. With the transport loaded with human freight, we started for Brazos De Santiago, Texas. We found the gulf quite rough on our entering it. This produced sea sickness with a great many. I remember one fellow who was very sea sick. I was unable to do anything with him. He was continually calling out, "New York, New York." "There goes my liver," he cried, having spit up some blood. Our great trouble on this voyage was the lack of water. They had a condenser on board which reduced the amount of salt a few degrees, but we could easily taste the saline property of the water. We found Brazos a most undesirable place, there were plenty of fleas and mosquitoes and sand burrs. We had our headquarters at this place which was knee deep in water. Our Colored troops were nearly perishing for water. The suffering was most intense. It was heart-rending. I cried out to God to send us some help. We had but little water and that was quite brackish. Our means of condensing the water gave us only about five thousand gallons when we were in need of not less than ten thousand gallons. We paid ten cents a canteen for water and would have been willing to have paid fifty cents, or any price.

After a while we met some Mexicans who had brought water from the Rio Grande and sold it for ten cents a canteen. Colonel Sadrick was very indignant over this hardship. When he saw our scars and realized how much these good soldiers had suffered and the privations through which they had already passed, he saw General Wietzel and requested that the troops should be taken from Brazos. He met with success and we took our line of march for White ranch on the Rio Grande River about ten miles south of Brazos. The march was one of great trial. We were in mud knee deep and in some places the water was waist deep. When we reached the Ranch, the soldiers were well nigh famished. They made a mad rush for the river and while many of them were on the bank, it gave way, and several of them were drowned. We were all greatly saddened over this misfortune. It seemed enough that men should have given up their lives on the battlefield, this was matter of course; but when men who had stemmed the tide of death which swept the battlefield were drowned, it seemed more than we could stand to see them cut off from their loved ones by a mere accident. But it was the Lord's way to take some more of them home.

It was not a hard matter for us to sleep the first night. We spread our rubber blankets on the bare ground and enjoyed our rest as much as if our beds had been made of feathers. The next morning we saw the body of a man floating down the muddy river. He too had evidently met with some accident, or had been killed and thrown into the river. It was not our duty to make any investigation.

I prepared the best breakfast possible for the boys. Our fuel was gathered from the woods and rail fences. I said woods, but unfortunately there was not a tree in the whole country, so we had to do the best we could. But we had coffee, rice, sweet potatoes and our regular rations. We put up our tents here and soon had the camp under military discipline. Then we left for Brownsville, Texas, a distance of twenty miles. The march was a trying one on account of the bad roads. We were not able to keep our stores with us on this account and left a detail of soldiers to guard them. Many a soldier sickened and had to be taken to White Ranch to be cared for by Orderly Hill. Some of the men died on the way and were buried under the Texas sod with no stone to identify them. One boat was on its way to Brownsville with rations. I remember my homesickness at this time. After the battles had been fought, I was anxious to return to my loved ones. I felt that my duty had been done towards my country and that now I must take up my duty to my dear ones. We were soon joined by Orderly Hill. He said that he had gotten tired of waiting for the boat and had come on to be with us. He threw a few chunks together and started a fire and lighted his pipe. After a few moments reflection, he said: "These light afflictions are but for a moment, for they work for us a far more and exceeding weight of glory." We met a drove of hungry wolves which made two or three attempts to come to us, but about fifteen shots from out guns were enough to satisfy them they had no more need of us than we had of them. In time we reached Brownsville. We saw strange things there. The houses were little huts; the people dressed in their shirts and drawers; the women dressed in a long shirt with their breast exposed, seemingly caring nothing for decency or modesty. It did not look to me that the people here had ever known what it was to know or to serve the true and living God. They were certainly far from any such practical knowledge, judging from their daily lives. I thought "If the righteous scarcely be saved where then shall the sinner and the ungodly appear?" The next morning I was not feeling well. I went to one of the streams and bathed. There were plenty of lizards, frogs and horned toads about. The horns of the toad reminded one of the horns of a goat. It was a place of trials. Some of the men swore and cursed, others were kept too busy scratching, while others were praying. It was a time of sore trials. One of our officers, Captain [Clarence M.] Clarke ought to have been with the Greys instead of the Blues, he had so little use for the Colored troops. So he marched them almost to death on this march. Colonel Wooster, a man of tender feeling and of a proper sense of right and justice and without prejudice against the Colored people, saw the outrage perpetrated against us and put Clark under arrest. He was kept there until Colonel Wooster resigned. After he left, we were again under the command of Captain Clark. Orderly Hill was very sick and was ordered to the General Hospital. As I looked upon him I said to myself, Hill you are a very sick man and your warfare is about ended. There we about seven hundred in the hospital sick. They were treated as if they had been brutes, doctors and nurses being without any feeling. They were dying at the rate of ten a day. The stewards would search the dead, take their valuables, then report them dead. What a contrast between our camp on the banks of the James River and the camp in this far off, God-for-saken town of Brownsville, Texas.

And now after all our hard fought battles, our fears and foreboding, our privations and losses, we received the news form the War Department that the Twenty-ninth Regiment was ordered home. It is needless to say, that the home-fever spread more rapidly than any fever that had ever prevailed in our ranks. We looked for and patiently awaited the day when we would be ordered out. On the fourteenth day of October, 1865, at nine o'clock a. m., the recruiting officer was on the ground, at which time Company K. was mustered out. We were escorted through Brownsville by the Ninth U. S. C. T., Colonel [Thomas] Bayley being in command. We marched to an open field where the two regiments bid each other goodbye. It was an impressive scene, for these regiments had shared each others fortunes and misfortunes through the war. They had become inseparable, but now the best of friends must part. How happy we were that we should be permitted to breathe fresh air again and to tramp through the country as free men. Yet I had the feeling that the Civil War was the mighty struggle of the White Race and that the struggle of the Colored Race was yet in the future. There is such a thing as a man having to work out of his own salvation, and this is also true of a race. Our salvation had been bought for us by the nation, but it is ours now to work out this salvation. As we marched out through the grand country and these thoughts came to me, I cried out to God, "Can these dry bones live? Will this country give the Colored man an equal chance in the marts of trade, in industrial fields, and in the professions? He is yet untried in the ranks of an aggressive civilization, for he has been a slave. Can these dry bones live?" These were the prayer-thoughts that were filling my mind and heart. Our march was a trying one on account of the bad condition of the roads, but we were going home. No one but the soldier who has ben honorably discharged after an issue has been settled, knows the joys that well-up in the heart as he turns his face homeward. The feeling is indescribable. There were several boys sick, but their spirits were revived on account of homegoing. We soon reached Brazos where we spent the night. I was very glad to say goodbye to my Texas friends and experience. They could live on the sandy plains of Brownsville, as long as they pleased; they could eat the strips of dried goat meat until they were satisfied; they could drink and relish the muddy water of the Rio Grande considering it the best water in the world; but as for me, I would choose other quarters. Now that the Confederacy had surrendered, now that the Palmetto Flag had been lowered forever and Old Glory floated in its stead, now that millions of people were made free and could live and think as real men and women, I was more than happy to say goodbye to all these things and begin life anew.

We embarked on the transport Alabama, for New Orleans. Our voyage on the gulf was a rough one on account of a heavy storm. We were forced to cast anchor. We passed Galveston and were much pleased with the place. We found the citizens much more sociable than we had expected, for we knew that they were Secessionists and Rebels and that they had about as much use for Negro soldiers as the Devil has for Holy Water. Nevertheless, we went through the town and made the acquaintance of some of our brethren. We met an old lady who had been a slave. When she saw us and realized that the victorious end had come, she cried at the top of her voice, "The Lord, the Mighty One has conquered and we are all free! Glory to God!" We took on wood and I regulated my rations for we were four hundred and fifty miles from New Orleans. We were again on board the transport for New Orleans, but we were unable to leave the harbor on account of a fearful gale that swept the gulf. We made an attempt, but were forced back again into the harbor. The soldiers became quite unruly owing to their impatience and also, I suppose the feeling that they could do as they pleased. After a hard voyage we landed safely in New Orleans. We found an open lot in the south side of the city and put up our tents and made ready for a good night's sleep. We felt that we could sleep now. That we had taken part in a mighty conflict and had shared in the victories of the war, it was now our right to rest. It was the sleep of the just man.

We had a quiet Sunday in New Orleans. Our chaplain preached for us. Great crowds came out to visit us and to give us their most hearty congratulations. They gave us coffee, sandwiches, fruits, etc., in token of the appreciation of our services in their behalf. We saw strange things in New Orleans. We found the mixture of French and Negro, called Creole, speaking a dialect of the French. We found the Octoroon and that some of these unions had from one to seven children. We found that marriage among them was rather an uncommon thing and that a man could establish almost any relationship that pleased him and enter into the Creole life and be received and welcomed as one of them. We found that they drank more claret, champagne, whisky, beer, etc., than they did water. They of course had no sense of their obligation to

God and I suppose that many of them really had no conception of the real and True God. Their lives gave no evidence of such a knowledge.

The first annual conference of the A. M. E. Church was being held by Bishop J. P. Campbell.[21] We enjoyed the services very much being in the spirit of our Lord Jesus Christ. We were in New Orleans two weeks. At the end of this time one of the men was shot. This created quite an excitement among us. We broke camp soon and marched through the streets to the wharf where we took ship. We were enthusiastically greeted on every hand, receiving god-speeds and congratulations and blessings. I shall never forget the musical voices of the people as they sang. The music sounded like a thousand silver harps, so soft and delicate and stirring it was! We went on board the steamer Champion.[22] We said good-bye to the old city of New Orleans and to many of the new friends which we had made. We had a heavy sea. The storms were terrific. Our clothes were almost continuously wet owing to the rocking of the vessel, for days it was impossible to find a place to sleep. The voyage was quite rough all the way to New York. At last we arrived at New York City. It was morning. We remained on board until about two p.m., when we left the boat and marched through the principle streets, receiving cheers and salutes. We had not forgotten our former experiences here however. And we were inwardly revolving the thought that as Black men we had done our part in bringing about a change of sentiment that would make a new city out of New York and every other city in the Union. And we felt that it was but just that we should receive some of the plaudits of praise and reward. When we passed down Broadway in front of the St. Nicholas Hotel, the flags of the Nation and of the state were suddenly hoisted by a Colored man and we gave three lusty cheers for the flag and country and home. At last the orders came to fall into line for our final trip. We marched to pier twenty eight East River where the steamer, Granite State,[23] was waiting to carry us to Hartford, Conn. The distance was about one hundred and fifty miles. We were cheered by every town and village that we passed. We arrived at Hartford and were escorted to the camp grounds and tendered a fine reception by the citizens, a most pleasing welcome.

At eight o'clock one morning we were paid off, all but one hundred dollars bounty which was to be paid at some future date. Some went to their homes, others remained in Hartford, until they had spent all their money and were locked up in the prisons by the police officers. After having cleared up my commissary department and turning over my books and papers to the proper custodian, and having said farewell to my comrades, I took a midnight train for my home in New Haven.

The occasion of my sudden departure from Hartford is very interesting. One of our soldiers was passing a Jew store. He was begged to go in and buy a suit. He got the suit of clothes and walked out without paying for it. The soldier came into camp and soon the Jew followed. I would not allow him to enter the camp and arrest[ed] the soldier. Not long afterward, I went down town and the Jew had me arrested and locked up. I was in jail until about midnight when some of my friends liberated me. Immediately I made my way to the station and left Hartford. I do not know that the Jew got his money and I was not much concerned.

I arrived at home at seven o'clock in the morning and found my wife and children, my father and mother, ready to give me the most hearty welcome and greeting which I received with a glad heart. I was not seen out of my house for about three weeks. I simply wanted to rest and to drink in the joys that were awaiting me. Then I went to Brooklyn, my wife's home, and registered as a citizen of the United States. I again thanked God that the war was over and that slavery was dead. "Now unto Him that hath loved us amd washed us from our sins in His blood, to Him be glory and dominion and power, now and forevermore. Amen!"

Alexander H. Newton, *Out of the Briars: An Autobiography and Sketch of the Twenty-ninth Regiment Connecticut Volunteers* (Philadelphia: A.M.E. Book Concern, 1910), 31–89.

---

1. Isaac J. Hill, from Stonington, Connecticut, was the 29th Connecticut's orderly and brigade postmaster and an AME Church minister. He joined the regiment on January 6, 1864, and mustered out on October 24, 1865. Immediately after the war he filled a pulpit in the Baltimore conference and in Virginia, and in the 1870s he was transferred to New York. He wrote a memoir of his war service in the 29th, *A Sketch of the 29th Regiment of Connecticut Colored Troops* (Baltimore, MD: Daugherty, Maguire & Co., 1867). Israel L. Butt, *History of African Methodism in Virginia* (Hampton, VA: Hampton Institute Press, 1908), 35, 37, 51; *Record of the Service of Connecticut Men in the Army and Navy . . .*, 868.
2. Newton may be referring to Frederick S. Moore, from New Haven, Connecticut, who joined the 29th Connecticut on January 4, 1864, and

mustered out on October 24, 1865. *Record of the Service of Connecticut Men in the Army and Navy . . .* , 874.

3. William Still (1821–1901), the famed leader of the Philadelphia branch of the Underground Railroad, was self-taught and worked his way up the ranks to become chairman of the General Vigilance Committee of Philadelphia. His efficient managerial and organizational skills helped hundreds of fugitives reach safety in the North and in Canada. Although sometimes dismissed by historians, his book *The Underground Railroad* (1872) is an invaluable first-person account of the central African American role in the legendary resistance network. Ripley et al., *The Black Abolitionist Papers*, 4:59–60.

4. The 1st Brigade, Third Division, of the Tenth Army Corps included the 7th, 9th, and 16th USCT units and the 29th Connecticut, under the command of Col. James Shaw, Jr. The 2nd Brigade under Col. Ulysses Doubleday included the 8th, 41st, 45th, and 127th USCT units. Wilson, *The Black Phalanx*, 479.

5. A misprint; no Henry Migs served in the regiment.

6. Another misprint; no Sam Bertim served in Company E of the 29th. George T. Porter, from Greenwich, Connecticut, served in Company D (not E). He enlisted on December 15, 1863, and died on October 24, 1865. *Record of the Service of Connecticut Men in the Army and Navy . . .*, 868.

7. Newton is probably referring to the large mortars that the Union forces employed in their seige of the Petersburg works.

8. The 9th USCT was formed at Camp Staunton, Maryland, in November 1863. It fought exclusively in Virginia in the Petersburg campaign and was mustered out in November 1866. The 7th USCT, organized in Baltimore in September 1863, fought in many battles during the Petersburg campaign and remained active until October 1866. Wilson, *The Black Phalanx*, 467.

9. John D. Cowes, from New Haven, Connecticut, the unit's principle musician, enlisted on November 18, 1863, and mustered out on October 24, 1865. *Record of the Service of Connecticut Men in the Army and Navy . . .*, 861.

10. Fortress Monroe, situated near the mouth of the James River in Virginia, became the center for escaping slaves seeking safety behind Union lines. Within a few months of the start of the war, the American Missionary Society began relief and evangelical services for the escaped slaves that Gen. Benjamin F. Butler had labeled "contraband" of war. Ripley et al., *The Black Abolitionist Papers*, 5:133.

11. The 45th USCT, formed in Philadelphia in June 1864, fought in the Petersburg campaign, especially at Hatcher's Run, and mustered out of the service in November 1865. Wilson, *The Black Phalanx*, 470.

12. George W. Burr, of Company I—there are no L companies in Civil War regiments—was from Glastonbury, Connecticut. He joined the regiment on January 5, 1864, and was killed on October 13, 1864, at Darbytown Road, Virginia. Cpl. William Sidney, from Berlin, Connecticut, enlisted on January 2, 1864, and was killed at Richmond on October 13, 1864. George E. Peters, from Hebron, Connecticut, joined the regiment on December 15, 1863, was wounded at Darbytown Road, Virginia, and died on October 30, 1864. Cpl. George Halstead, from Danbury, Connecticut, enlisted on December 21, 1863, and despite his wounds remained in the unit until the end of the war. Sgt. James Evans, from Newtown, Connecticut, enlisted on December 31, 1863, became a sergeant in September 1864, was wounded on October 13, 1864, at Darbytown Road, Virginia, and died on November 19, 1864. *Record of the Service of Connecticut Men in the Army and Navy* . . ., 869, 870, 875, 877.

13. Newton is in error about his brother's regiment. The 14th Rhode Island Heavy Artillery did not serve at Fort Pillow; only the 6th USCHA and the 2nd USCLA had been stationed there.

14. Amos G. Beman (1812–1874), a congregational minister and black abolitionist leader, had lived in New Haven until the death of his wife and two of his four children, in 1856 and 1857, from typhoid fever. He remarried in 1858 and moved to a congregation in Portland, Maine. Beginning in 1859, he worked for the American Missionary Association and traveled extensively in the South before returning to Connecticut. Ripley et al., *The Black Abolitionist Papers*, 4:11–12.

15. Pvt. Charles Bentley, from New Haven, Connecticut, joined the 29th Connecticut on December 10, 1863, and was killed on October 27, 1864, at Kell House, Virginia. James B. Spriggs, from New Haven, Connecticut, enlisted on November 27, 1863, and was killed at Kell House on October 27, 1964. *Record of the Service of Connecticut Men in the Army and Navy* . . ., 862.

16. Quartermaster Sgt. Daniel S. Lathrop, from New Haven, Connecticut, enlisted on November 18, 1863, and mustered out on October 24, 1865. *Record of the Service of Connecticut Men in the Army and Navy* . . ., 861.

17. The *Demolay*, a 1,295-ton steamer, built in 1863 in Medford, Massachusetts, operated out of Boston and was the vessel that first brought the 54th Massachusetts Regiment to South Carolina. After the war, the vessel was renamed the *Cortez*. The identity of the officer is unknown; no Union General Russel or Russell was alive at this time. Perhaps Newton incorrectly recalled the officer's rank. William M. Lytle and Forrest R. Holdcamper, comp., *Merchant Steam Vessels of the United States, 1790–1868* (Staten Island, NY: Steamship Historical Society of America, 1975), 53.

18. Newton may be referring to Pvt. Samuel R. Brown, from Meridan, Connecticut, who enlisted on December 17, 1863, and mustered out with the regiment on October 24, 1865. The Rev. John M. Brown, AME Church minister in Norfolk, had filled a pulpit in Columbus, Ohio, during the 1830s. In 1858 he took over the Bethel AME Church in Baltimore, and in 1863 he was assigned to the Norfolk congregation by Bishop Daniel A. Payne. He left Norfolk in 1866 to serve in Charleston, South Carolina, and in 1868 became the AME Church Bishop of South Carolina. *Record of the Service of Connecticut Men in the Army and Navy . . .*, 870. [Daniel A. Payne], *Biography of Rev. David Smith of the A.M.E. Church. . .* (Xenia, OH: Gazette Office, 1881), 77; Alexander W. Wayman, *My Recollections of African M.E. Ministers, or Forty Years' Experience in the African Methodist Episcopal Church* (Philadelphia: A.M.E. Book Room, 1881), 69, 93, 120–121, 132, 157.

19. "Cradle of the Deep," a popular hymn by Emma C. Willard, who first published the words in Henry Ward Beecher's *Plymouth Collection of Hymns for the Use of Christian Congregations* (New York: A.S. Barnes, 1855).

20. William A. Dove began his AME Church career in 1852 at the Indiana Conference, became a full member in 1855, and earned a reputation as a "great itinerant." He served on the church standing committee on slavery and was a traveling elder for the church when Newton met him in New Orleans. After the war, Dove filled pulpits in Missouri. Charles Spencer Smith, *A History of the African Methodist Episcopal Church: Being a Volume Supplement to A History of the African Methodist Episcopal Church, by Daniel A. Payne. . .* (Philadelphia: Book Concern of the AME Church, 1922), 26, 28, 98, 436, 525, 540.

21. Bishop Jabez P. Campbell (1815–1892) of the AME Church was born to free parents in Delaware. Fearing enslavement, he ran away to Pennsylvania. In 1838 he began preaching for the church, and from 1839 to 1854 he filled several pulpits in New England. From 1864, when he became bishop, to 1867, Campbell traveled 40,000 miles in his service as an AME Church bishop in Indiana, Missouri, California, and New Orleans, Louisiana. Benjamin T. Tanner, *An Apology for African Methodism* (Baltimore, MD: n.p., 1867), 158–173; Butt, *History of African Methodism in Virginia*, 138.

22. The *Champion*, a 115-ton stern wheel steamer, was constructed in 1860. Paul H. Silverstone, *Warships of the Civil War Navies* (Annapolis, MD: Naval Institute Press, 1989), 170.

23. The *Granite State*, an unarmed 887-ton steamer built in 1853 in Greenport, New York, operated out of New Haven, Connecticut. William M. Lytle and Forrest R. Holdcamper, comps., *Merchant Steam Vessels of the United States, 1790–1868* (Staten Island, NY: Steamship Historical Society of America, 1975), 89.

18

Remembering Slavery and the Civil War in Missouri

"The New Man. Twenty-Nine Years a Slave.
Twenty-Nine Years a Free Man."
Henry Clay Bruce
1895

Not every male slave joined the Union Army, but each had a story of survival in resisting the bonds of servitude. Henry Clay Bruce proudly boasted that, unlike most slaves, he knew his birthday—March 3, 1836. Born in Virginia, he was moved often by his owners and for most of his twenty-nine years in slavery was hired out for his labor, mostly in tobacco work and brickmaking. Although his father died when he was a boy, his mother and his many siblings remained together or in close proximity despite their many moves. Bruce and his family, generally well-treated by their owners, sometimes felt the lash from employers. His minimal learning and pride made him an object for discipline with the whip throughout his childhood, and at age eighteen he received an especially harsh punishment for fighting. He ran away often, usually to escape what was expected to be a brutal beating, but always returned to his owners, usually expecting to be saved by them from punishment by an employer.

When the contentious 1860 election broke in Missouri, white voters spoke heatedly about the candidates, sometimes in earshot of slaves. Bruce's memoir reveals how any scrap of information gained by such eavesdropping, or gathered more directly by the few slaves who could read the newspapers, would be shared among the slaves. They met clandestinely, passing on their interpretations of what Lincoln and the Republicans had declared. When war broke out, many believed that Lincoln and the Union ultimately meant freedom.

Although little official military action took place in Missouri, the state still suffered intensely from guerrilla warfare that had its origins in the Kansas wars of the 1850s. Chariton County, in the north-central part of the state, near the Missouri River where Bruce lived, was as divided as any section of the state, "splintered into contentious factions of outright secessionists, rebel sympathizers, fence-sitters, and unionists of every stripe." While whites usually adopted any position that would save their lives and protect their property, most whites stood united in opposing unrestricted black freedom. The state's 115,000 slaves and 3,600 free blacks experienced the Civil War never knowing security or freedom. The military enforced the Fugitive Slave Law, and the government fully compensated every loyal slave owner who gave up his "property" to the army. Any African American who thought they could escape "stood in constant danger of reenslavement" or seizure by Union press gangs looking to fill a quota. Never giving a thought to enlisting in the army (although two-fifths of Missouri's service-eligible black males did enlist), Bruce gathered up the female slave, from another plantation, that he intended to marry and ran away to Leavenworth, Kansas. For many years, Bruce worked successfully as a businessman in Kansas, proud that a semiliterate slave could educate himself and succeed despite the many hucksters waiting to fleece an unsuspecting and inexperienced newly emancipated black man. He ran for the state senate in 1880, but lost, and then a series of fires and bad luck left him and his growing family nearly destitute. Political friends bailed him out, new positions came his way, and his now-famous younger brother, U.S. Senator Blanche K. Bruce, obtained jobs for him in Washington, D.C., in the post office and the pension office. But, as the following part of his memoir reveals, hard work and responsible living offered no protection from the Klan and race hatred. Henry Clay Bruce, *The New Man. Twenty-Nine Years a Slave. Twenty-Nine Years a Free Man.* (York, PA: P. Anstadt & Sons, 1895), 1–26, 29–30, 66, 100–102; Berlin et al., *Freedom: The Wartime Genesis of Free Labor: The Upper South,* 551, 552, 554, 557.

CHAPTER VIII

EARLY IN THE SPRING of 1856, our master had bought the Mann Plantation, located about seven miles east of Brunswick, and had made all arrangements to move to it, taking mother and four of her children, including myself. I did not want to go, but my desires in that respect were not considered, and I went without entering even a mild protest. Having lived in the city so long, I had lost all love for farm life. I had no knowledge of farming, especially that kind carried on in that part of the state, and personal experience taught me that my master possessed but little more than I did, because he ordered so many things done that were a loss of time and money. In his experimenting, for such it was, he would give an order one day, and change it the next, causing the loss of many days of labor. But it was my duty to obey him, right or wrong, and I did it right along.

After I had gained some practical knowledge, by experience, of the system of farming in that county, I ventured to suggest to him when I saw a better plan, or the uselessness of the order given. Of course he would not take the course I had suggested at the time, and in its entirety, but after thinking it over, he would change his orders as nearly to my plans as possible, without adopting them. But, oh, how I would catch it if he found flaws in them afterwards.

He worked the first year on that plantation almost as steadily as any of us, but that was his last year of work while he was my owner. He was a man who never talked much to his slaves at any time, as I have worked with him without a word being said, aside from my duty, between us many days, and I rather preferred it, because if he said anything, it would usually be scolding. I have a very clear recollection of the amount of scolding I got the first Spring on that farm, when laying off corn and tobacco rows. It was my first effort, and in nearly every row there would be one or more crooks, for which he would scold, then take my horse and plow, straighten the row, and give them back; pretty soon I would have it as crooked as before. The result of all this was that I soon learned to lay off a row nearly as straight as he could, and I will state that he could and did lay off the straightest row I had ever seen. He insisted that corn grew better in straight rows than in crooked ones, and I became convinced of the truth of his statements and took pride in having every row as straight as if laid off by line, and have been complimented on account of it.

At this plantation we had some neighbors whom I did not like, men who came from Kentucky and other southern states, and who tried to keep up the customs in vogue in those states of curtailing the liberties of their slaves, liberties which slaves in other parts of Missouri enjoyed; but even then the life of a slave in that part of Missouri was far better than in some of the older slave states.

Being a green hand at farming, I made many mistakes, which caused the boss to scold, but as that was all the punishment he inflicted, I soon became used to that, and went ahead doing the best I could. My boss really delighted in scolding; he could quarrel, make more noise, and do less whipping than any man in that county. He was not mean, in the sense that some of his neighbors were, and I have always believed that he tried to appear to his neighbors what he was not, a hard master. The reason why I entertained this belief is that in the presence of a neighbor he always scolded more, acted more crabbed, and was harder to please than when alone with us, for as soon as the neighbor left, we could get along with him very well. We were well fed, had such vegetables as were raised on the farm, and save biscuit and coffee, we had such food as was prepared for him.

Farming in Missouri consisted in raising tobacco, corn, wheat and stock, but tobacco was the principal product for sale. With five hands we usually raised about twenty thousand pounds, which at that time sold in Brunswick for about eight cents per pound. Each man was allowed one acre of ground to raise his own little crop, which, if well cultivated, would produce about nine hundred pounds of tobacco. We used his horse and plow, and worked our crop as well as we did his in the daytime, and when ready for market, he sold our crop with his, giving each one his share. This was our money, to be spent for whatever we wanted aside from that given by him. He gave two suits of summer and one of winter clothes, hats and boots, blankets and underwear. Our cash was spent for Sunday clothes, sugar, coffee and flour, for we would have biscuits at least once a week, and coffee every day.

The practice of allowing slaves ground to raise a little crop obtained generally among slave owners, but most of them had to work their crop of tobacco after sundown, and without plowing. The master got the benefit of this money after all, because the slave spent it for his own pleasure and comfort, which was a direct advantage to his master.

There were several slave owners around us at this farm, some were called mean and some considered fair, but the meanest man near us was a Yankee teacher, preacher and farmer, S. J. M. Bebee, who owned or hired four or five slaves, and treated them very meanly. This man came to that county from the East, and by teaching and preaching saved up money enough to buy a farm, and was considered by the Colored people meaner than the original slave-holders. I lived on a farm within two miles of Mr. Bebee's farm, and had good opportunities to know the truth of what I state.

There lived near our home an old gentleman named Ashby, usually called "Father Ashby," who was a good man, much beloved by white and black, and who dropped dead in the pulpit at the close of one of his sermons. Previous to his death I used to visit his place, and sometimes we exchanged work. He owned three or four slaves and treated them kindly. Pending the campaign of 1856, when [John C.] Frémont was the Republican nominee for President, I had a talk with "Father Ashby." He then said that he believed slavery to be wrong, but it was handed down to him from his father, and although he held and owned slaves, he had never bought or sold one, and had always treated them well.

I had learned to read, and could understand enough of the political situation at that date to be a "Frémont man," but a very silent one. I am safe in saying that Frémont did not receive one vote in Chariton County at that election. Certainly there was not an outspoken Republican in the county. Slave holders never talked politics in the presence of slaves, but by some means they learned the news, kept posted as to what was going on, and expected to be set free if Frémont was elected. A Colored man who could read was a very important fellow, for they would come miles and bring stolen papers for him to read to them at night or on Sunday, and I have known them to go to town and buy them from Dr. Blue, an old slave-holder, and bring them to some slave who could read.

Our owner did not like the farm he owned, and early in 1857 sold it, and bought uncultivated land adjoining his brother-in-law, W. B. Bruce. Here I had to open a place in the brush for a home, and for our own quarters, assist in putting up buildings, make the rails necessary to fence eighty acres of land, break it up and put in a crop, all of which was accomplished in one year. I had got used then to farm life, and rather enjoyed it.

This farm was only one-half a mile from W. B. Bruce's, and the families were now practically together. Our master and his son, Willie, spent a great deal of their time at Bruce's, and so did the Colored families.

I was then a full fledged foreman with four younger brothers, who constituted my force, but as a matter of fact, I got more scolding than any one of them, for the reason that I was held responsible for everything, as our owner seldom went over any part of the farm, and left me to manage it entirely, reporting to him every morning. I really had full control of the place, but he did not want me to think so, and acted rather queer quite often. He had a habit of calling me to his door every morning after breakfast, to report what was done the previous day, and what I thought should be done that day. I would state my opinion, and he would be certain to make light of it, get angry, tell me I had no sense, etc., make some suggestions, then cool down and tell me to go ahead and do just the work I had suggested. He, I believe, enjoyed that kind of acting, and I had got used to it and took it quietly, for that was the extent of my punishment.

We had but one neighbor who was called a hard master, Charles Cabel, for whom I had previously worked. Cabel had rather a lazy set of slaves, with one exception, a young man named Samuel Savage, and this, I suppose, made him appear meaner than he really was. His farm joined ours, and therefore I could hear and see much that was done. I am not an apologist for Mr. Cabel simply because he treated me nicely, not only when I was hired to him, but often afterwards on our farm. He saw what fine crops we raised every year, more and better tobacco, which sold for more money than his, while we worked but five hands, and he had ten or twelve.

There was no whipping on our place at any time, while on his some one was whipped nearly every week. Mr. Cabel used to come over on our land and talk with me quite often, and insisted that his Negroes made him appear mean, that if he had such Negroes as we were, he would never hit one. He said this to me many times; yet his slaves called him the meanest man in the county. I am safe in stating, that I had more talk with Mr. Cabel during the five or six years we lived as neighbors than with any slave owner during my service as a slave. Often he would come where I was at work and entertain me for an hour, he evidently enjoyed my company, and I confess a liking for him.

I recall an instance where he whipped four of his men within calling or hearing distance of me. I went to the timber to make some rails. Our timber land which was four miles away, joined Mr. Cabel's, and he sent four of his men to make rails, and we all went on Monday. With the aid of a brother about sixteen years old, I had cut and split four hundred rails by two o'clock, or thereabouts, on Wednesday, not quite three days. Mr. Cabel came to me and asked when I commenced, and on being told, proceeded to count my rails, and when through, went over to where his men were. I don't think he found them at work; at any rate, in a short time, I heard the lash and the men begging for mercy. Pretty soon he came back to me, and said his men had made only two hundred and sixty rails, and then asked if I blamed him for punishing them. What could I say under the circumstances, knowing that there were four of them as against two of us, and one a mere boy?

My opinion is that Mr. Cabel as well as his slaves were to be blamed for the condition that existed on that farm, based upon the following reasons: The master who treated his slaves humanely had less trouble with them, got better service from them, and could depend upon their doing his work faithfully, even in his absence, having his interest in view always. Maltreated slaves and ill-treated beasts of burden are much alike; if trained to be punished, whether deservedly or not, they take no interest in their service, and go no further than the lash forces them, because they receive no encouragement even when they perform their duty well.

I recall a case in point, and as the parties mentioned are living I call upon them to set me right if I misrepresent the facts in the case. My master bought three yoke of oxen to break up this new land heretofore mentioned, much of which was covered with hazel brush about four feet high, and to haul rails and firewood from the timber land four miles away. I had the sole management of this team, in fact had to break them in. I took pride in that team, trained my oxen to obey without the use of the whip, fed and watered them well under all circumstances, and they looked sleek, fat and cheerful, if I may use the term for an ox. I was the master in this case and almost loved my oxen, and believe they loved me. When I said "Go," they went, regardless of the load, and the question was whether the wagon would bear it up.

W. B. Bruce, before mentioned, owned three yoke of oxen and a driver named Bob or Robert Bruce, who had no love or mercy for his team, took no pride or interest in his oxen, not even enough to feed and water them regularly. He used a rawhide whip, and I have seen him break their hides and bring out the blood when using the lash. I have said he did not feed them well, and the reasons why I say it are these: His master, W. B. Bruce, always raised plenty of corn and other kinds of stock feed and allowed his dumb creatures enough, and there existed no sufficient reasons why Bob's team should not look as fat and as sleek, and draw as heavy a load as mine; but they did not, and the reasons are very plain. I cared for mine, and by so doing won their confidence and love and obedience, without the use of the lash, while Bob used the lash in the place of kind treatment and kind words.

In 1857, the county had become pretty thickly settled with pro-slavery men from the South, mostly from Virginia and Kentucky, with a few Eastern men and Germans. Of course the men from the East, as soon as they landed, proclaimed themselves in favor of slavery and often hired slaves, and in such cases treated them meaner than the slave owner. They, it seemed, regarded the slave as a machine which required no rest, and they gave him none; they would drive the slave in all kinds of weather without mercy, so much so that slaves who belonged to estates or others who were for hire, would beg to be hired to some southern man, who had a knowledge of slave labor and the slave.

The Germans were quite different; they never hired slaves, and I can recall the name of only one who owned a slave. His name was Goss and he lived about six miles North of our place. He treated his slaves as he did his children; he owned four or five.

There was a lot of poor white trash scattered over that county, as there was in other southern states, and they answered the same purpose, as servants to their masters. But few of them could get a job as overseer, for the reason that there were but few large slave owners in that county; I mean that there were not a dozen men in the county owning over forty, and most of them owned less; they did their own over-seeing. But I must say that the poor whites, as a general thing, in that county at least, worked hard for a living, and I can mention several who, by dint of hard labor and economy, attained to a fair standing in their community.

After the landing at Brunswick, of the first installment of Germans, and as they obtained homes and money they sent for relatives and

friends in Germany, so that there was a steady stream of German immigrants to that county each year up to 1864. But from 1853 to 1864,
they had to submit to many indignities from ultra pro-slavery men. I
have seen them kicked off the principal street without resistance by
Col. Pugh Price, a brother, I think, of Gen. Sterling Price. But still they
came, and soon some of them had opened business places such as cooper
and shoe shops, cake and candy stands, and finally a brewery. It was
wonderful to see how rapidly the people learned to drink lager beer
made by a German, John Stroebe.

There was a large tract of land five or six miles below Brunswick,
called Bowling Green, which lay quite low and was sometimes overflowed by the Missouri River. It was considered unhealthy in that locality and on that account the land sold cheap. The Germans bought
the greater part of it and formed quite a settlement. This land was
known as the richest in the county and retains that reputation to-day,
and is thickly settled and about as healthful as any other part of the
county, is more valuable and is still owned by Germans whom we considered quite prosperous farmers.

There was a feeling created against these people about 1859 and
1860, caused by some suspicious pro-slavery men charging them with
talking to slaves, and I cannot say they were not guilty[.] They were opposed to slavery and when they had an opportunity to tell a slave so,
without his master's knowledge, they often did it, especially if they had
confidence in the slave. Slaves never betrayed a friend; they would
stand severer punishment rather than give away a white friend who favored freedom for all.

There was a white man, Dan Kellogg by name, in Brunswick, who
was a peculiar fellow and one I could never understand, and who I think
was a northerner. For two or three years before the war he was known
as a friend of freedom, among the slaves at least. He had told some of
them so, and my impression is that as early as 1856, he told me that he
was opposed to the institution of slavery, but of course this was *sub rosa;*
but when the war broke out he had changed his mind and was classed
with bushwhackers in that county, too much of a coward to join the
Confederate Army and stand up in the open field to shoot and be shot
at; but he hid in dense forests and shot at Union citizens and soldiers as
they passed. I have been told that he was captured by one Captain Tru-
man, commanding a squad of the Fourth Missouri Volunteer Infantry,

and ordered to be hanged by the neck until dead, but was begged off by friends. I have not heard from Mr. Kellogg for many years and do not know whether he is dead or alive, but if he is alive and should read this statement he will, I think admit its truthfulness, May 20, 1893.

Since the above was written I have been reliably informed that Mr. Kellogg's death occurred about two years ago, and that he removed to Keytesville, the county seat of Chariton County, Mo., where he lived since the war, and had accumulated quite a little fortune and was up to the date of his death a staunch friend to the colored people, who greatly lamented his taking off.

He held the position of county treasurer for one or more terms, and regardless of politics, received almost the unanimous colored vote, he being a democrat.

CHAPTER IX

THE NATIONAL ELECTION OF 1860, created more excitement probably than any that had preceded it, not excepting the "Hard Cider Campaign" of 1840, because greater questions and issues had to be met and settled. The North was opposed to the extension, of slavery, in fact there was a strong sentiment against its existence, while the South wanted more territory for its extension; then there was a spirit of disunion existing North and South. The abolitionists of the North had declared the National Constitution to be a league with hell, while the extreme southern men such as Bob Toombs of Georgia, wanted to extend slavery to every State in the Union, and he declared in a speech delivered early in 1861, that he wanted to call the roll of his slaves on Bunker Hill, and would do so if the South was successful.

The campaign opened early in July that year, and kept red hot until the ballots were in the box. There was speaking once or twice a week at Brunswick, and several barbecues in different parts of the county. I remember attending one held five miles north of town, which appeared to be a joint affair, because there were speeches made in the interest of all the tickets except the Republican. My young master made his maiden effort for [John] Bell and [Edward] Everett, as I now remember.

The political excitement began in Missouri, especially in Chariton County, when the National Democratic Convention met at Charleston, S. C., April 23, 1860, and after spending ten days wrangling over the adoption of the platform, adjourned to meet at Baltimore, Md., June 18, 1860, without making a nomination for President. I might state that the main fight was upon the second section of the majority report of the Committee on Resolutions. The report reads as follows: Second, "Resolved; That it is the Duty of the Federal Government, in all its departments, to protect when necessary the rights of persons and property in the territories, and wherever else its constitutional authority extends." The minority report which was substituted for the majority by a vote of 165 to 138, reads as follows: "Inasmuch as difference of opinion exists in the Democratic party, as to the nature and extent of the powers of a territorial legislature, and as to the powers and duties of Congress, under the Constitution of the United States, over the institution of slavery within the Territories," Second, "Resolved, that the Democratic party will abide by the questions of constitutional law." After that vote many of the southern delegates withdrew from the Convention. Missouri stood solid in the [Stephen A.] Douglas column, refusing to secede with the other southern States, and cast her vote the following November for him for President and [Herschel V.] Johnson for Vice President.

If we stop to consider a moment, the fact that the Democratic party had the Supreme Court by a large majority at that time, we must arrive at the conclusion, that there existed no valid cause for the split in its national convention, thus dividing its strength and making it possible for the Republicans to elect their candidate; for it is generally believed that if there had been no split, Stephen A. Douglas would have been elected President and served his party as a good Democrat, for he owned a large plantation in the South, and the interest of the South would have been his as well. But it has always seemed to me that there was a higher power shaping matters and things at that time, which was irresistible. Hatred existed among Democrats North and South to such an extent, that southern Democrats denounced their northern brothers as "doughfaces" and cowards, which had the effect of driving many of them to vote the Republican ticket at the ensuing presidential election.

The extreme southern delegates who seceded from the National Convention, met and nominated John C. Breckinridge of Kentucky, for President, and Joseph Lane of Oregon, for Vice-President. From the day the campaign opened in the State of Missouri, especially in Chariton County, the two factions of the Democratic party were very bitter towards each other, and this condition of things existed up to and including the day of election, but when it was known later on that Lincoln was elected, all differences were healed and the factions came together, declaring for secession. They were joined by a large portion of the old line Whigs, who had voted for Bell and Everett at the last election; but there were a few who remained loyal to the Union. It is a wonder to me, even now, that they did so, when I recall the bulldozing, the taunts, jeers and epithets hurled against them. They were intensely hated and abused, more than the loyal Germans and northern men who had settled in that county, but they stood it out through trials and tribulations, remaining loyal to the close of the war.

There was another class of men who suffered severely during the war, known as "Neutrals," assisting neither side, but who were accused of aiding both and therefore hated by both.

During the years of 1860 and 1861, the slaves had to keep very mum and always on their masters' land, because patrols were put out in every township with authority to punish slaves with the lash, if found off their masters' premises after dark without a written pass from them. Patrol duty was always performed by the poor whites, who took great pride in the whipping of a slave, just as they do now in lynching a Negro. They whipped some slaves so unmercifully that their masters' attention was called to it, so that they met and issued an order to patrols, that in punishing a slave captured no skin should be broken nor blood brought out by the lash. There being no positive law of patrolling, it having existed as a custom to please a few mean slave holders, many men whose names I can give, would not submit to it, and threatened to punish any man or set of men interfering in any way with their slaves, although found off their lands. Of course the patrols carefully avoided such men's slaves wherever seen.

I have heard of many jokes played on these patrols by slaves, tending to show how easy it was to fool them, because they were as a rule illiterate, and of course could not read writing. The slaves knowing this would take a portion of a letter picked up and palm it off on them as a pass when arrested. The captain would take it, look it over wisely, then hand it telling the slave to go. Others would secure a pass from their master, get some one who could read writing to erase the day and month, then use it indefinitely, while others would get their young master or mistress to write them a pass whenever they wanted to go out, signing their father's name.

In order that the reader may clearly understand why slaves had to resort to so many tricks to get a pass. I will state that masters objected to giving passes often, upon the ground that they wanted the slave to stay at home and take his rest which he could not get if out often after dark.

In the fall of 1859 there was a dance given at Col. Ewing's farm, to which several young men and girls were invited and attended; most of them had passes except four girls, who had failed to secure them. The patrols came about twelve o'clock that night and surrounded the house, allowing those having passes to go free, and were preparing to whip the four girls who had none, right there in the presence of their beaux, who were powerless to protect them, when a young fellow, whose name was Lindsay Watts, came up and said, "Lor, masses, it am a great pity to whip dese sweet angels, 'deed 'tis; if you will let dem go, I will take the whippin' for dem all." His proposition was accepted, and the girls turned loose made rapid steps to their homes. The patrols took Lindsay outside of the yard, and stripped him naked, preparatory to giving him four times nine and thirty lashes, but being naked and hard to hold or grab, he escaped and ran home to his master in that condition, followed closely by the patrols. But his master protected him. The girls who barely escaped a lashing reached home safely and thankfully.

I remember another ball given at Day's Mill, near Brunswick, early in 1861, which I attended, and left about eleven o'clock that night. Later, a man named Price, without law or authority, as he lived in the city and was not an officer thereof, gathered a squad of roughs and went to the Mill and surrounded the ballroom. They ordered all who had passes to come forward, and they were allowed to go free. There were five men and one girl without a pass left in the room. The white men stood in the doorway, intending to whip each Negro and pass him out. They had given the order for each one to take off his shirt. There was a fellow whose name, for prudential reasons, I will call John Smith, who got a shovel and threw fire coals, one shovelful after another, at the patrols. The lights had been extinguished; some of them got burnt in the face and neck badly, while others got clothing burnt. This cleared the way, and the Negroes, even the woman, escaped. They never found the man who threw the fire. I remember that they offered a reward to other slaves to betray the one who threw it.

About the winter of 1858, the Colored people gave a dance, to which many of the young people were invited and attended, and were enjoying themselves to their hearts' content, when, about twelve o'clock, a squad of patrols appeared and surrounded the ballroom. Those having passes were not disturbed, but those without were arrested and taken out for punishment, which numbered five, and of these only two were whipped; the other three resisted, and in the scuffle got loose and ran.

There was at that time a poor white man at the head of the city patrols, named Brawner, whose jurisdiction covered the city limits only, and he had no legal rights as patrol outside of it. But the desire of this poor white man to whip a slave was so great, that he left his post of duty, gathered secretly a squad of men of his ilk, went two miles into the country, and that, too, without the knowledge or consent of the city officers, for they knew nothing of it until next day. Now comes the worst part of it; when they had finished their hellishness, they returned to the city to find it on fire in several places, and as a result, several frame buildings in different portions of the city were destroyed by fire. Many efforts were made to detect the incendiary, but in vain, and the blame for the fire fell upon the Chief of Patrolmen, Brawner, who was, I think, promptly dismissed. I write of this matter without the fear of contradiction, because I am sure that there are men now living, white and black, who will corroborate my statement.

Slaves were much truer to one another in those days than they have been since made free, and I am unable to assign any reason for it, yet it is a fact, nevertheless, and as further proof of it, I will state, that they would listen carefully to what they heard their owners say while talking to each other on political matters, or about the fault of another slave, and as soon as opportunity would admit, go to the quarters and warn the slave of his danger, and tell what they had heard the master say about the politics of the country.

The Colored people could meet and talk over what they had heard about the latest battle, and what Mr. Lincoln had said, and the chances of their freedom, for they understood the war to be for their freedom solely, and prayed earnestly and often for the success of the Union cause. When the news came that a battle was fought and won by Union troops, they rejoiced, and were correspondingly depressed when they saw their masters rejoicing, for they knew the cause thereof. As I have stated before, slaves who could read and could buy newspapers, thereby obtained the latest news and kept their friends posted, and from mouth to ear the news was carried from farm to farm, without the knowledge of masters. There were no Judases among them during those exciting times.

After the war had commenced, about the spring of 1862, and troops of both sides were often passing through that county, it was not safe for patrols to be out hunting Negroes, and the system came to an end, never to be revived. The regular confederate troops raised in that and adjoining counties went South as fast as recruited, so that only bushwhackers remained, and they were a source of annoyance to Union men and Union troops of that county up to the fall and winter of 1864, when they were effectually cleaned out. Many of these men claimed to be loyal, especially so in public and at their homes in the day time, in order to be protected, while at heart they were disloyal, aiding bushwhackers not only with ammunition, rations, and information as to when and where Union troops would pass, but with their presence at night on the roadside, shooting at Union citizens and soldiers while passing. They would select some safe spot where a returned fire would not reach them.

The spirit of secession was almost as strong in that county in 1861, as it was in South Carolina, and when Fort Sumter was fired upon, Col. Pugh Price, of Brunswick, hung out the confederate flag, and called for volunteers. There were two companies raised who went South, one of which was commanded by Capt. J. W. Price. That county furnished its full share to the confederate army, composed largely of the best blood, men who were willing to shoot and be shot at in the open field of battle.

There was a man named James Long, a plasterer by trade, who was a noisy fellow, and who cast the only vote Lincoln received in that county. When called upon to give his reasons for so doing, he stated that he did it for fun; he then and there cursed Lincoln in language quite strong, and said that he ought to be assassinated. A year later, a loyal man had to be appointed postmaster at Brunswick, and then this man Long came forward as the only original Lincoln man, stating that his vote represented his sentiments, and that his former denial was caused by intimidation. He got the appointment, and in a year or two was arrested, tried, convicted and sentenced to the penitentiary for misappropriation of government money. But the secessionists l[o]st a friend in him, because it was believed by Union men that he was not of them, and it was charged that he aided the rebels in every way possible, even to rifling Union men's letters, and giving their contents to rebels.

But this man's downfall was a blessing to some extent, to the Colored people who received mail through that office, for he would not give them their mail, but held it and delivered it to their masters[.] Our family had no trouble in this respect, for our master would bring our letters unopened and deliver them without question. I remember getting one from my brother, B[lanche]. K. Bruce,[1] who was in Lawrence, Kan., at the time of the [William C.] Quantrill raid, in 1863, which he brought from town, and waited to hear how B. K. Bruce escaped being killed in the Lawrence massacre.

From 1862 to the close of the war, slave property in the state of Missouri was almost a dead weight to the owner; he could not sell because there were no buyers. The business of the Negro trader was at an end, due to the want of a market. He could not get through the Union lines South with his property, that being his market. There was a man named White, usually called "Negro-trader White," who travelled over the state, buying Negroes like mules for the southern market, and when he had secured a hundred or more, he would take them, handcuffed together, to the South. He or his agents attended all sales where Negroes were to be sold without conditions. The sentiment against selling Negroes to traders was quite strong and there were many who would not sell at all, unless forced by circumstances over which they had no control, and would cry with the Negroes at parting. A Negro sold to a trader would bring from one to three hundred dollars more money.

I recall a case where a master was on a note as surety, and had the same, which was a large sum, to pay at maturity, and to do so he was forced to sell a young girl to raise the cash. He sent for Negro-trader White, and the sale was made in the city without his wife's knowledge, but when he attempted to deliver her, his wife and children clung to the girl and would not let her go. When White saw he could not get his Negro, he demanded a return of his money, which the seller had applied on the note and could not get back. The matter was finally settled in some way; at any rate the girl was not sold, and was in that county until 1864.

The Negro trader usually bought all Negroes who had committed murder or other crimes, for which public whipping was not considered sufficient punishment. Slaves usually got scared when it became known that Negro-trader White was in the community. The owners used White's name as a threat to scare the Negroes when they had violated some rule. "I'll sell you to the Negro trader, if you don't do better" was often as good or better punishment than the lash, for the slave dreaded being sold South, worse than the Russians do banishment to Siberia.

Excitement, such as I had never seen, existed not alone with the white people, but with the slaves as well. Work, such as had usually been performed, almost ceased; slaves worked as they pleased, and their masters were powerless to force them, due largely to the fact that the white people were divided in sentiment. Those who remained loyal advised the slaves who belonged to those called disloyal, not to work for men who had gone or sent their sons South, to fight against the government. Slaves believed, [d]eep down in their souls, that the government was fighting for their freedom, and it was useless for masters to tell them differently. They would leave home in search of work, and usually found it, with small pay, with some Union man and often without pay for weeks at a time, but his master had to clothe him as he had always done, and in some cases pay his own slave for his work.

Near the close of 1863, the Union men were on top, and the disloyal or southern sympathizer had to submit to everything. The lower class of so-called Union men almost openly robbed rebel sympathizers by going to their farms, dressed and armed as soldiers, taking such stock as they wanted, which the owner was powerless to prevent; in fact he would have been killed had he attempted it. The period had been reached when the master found his slave to be his best and truest friend, because it often happened that he was forced for self-protection to hide his valuables from these prowlers, and knowing that their quarters would not be invaded, he placed his precious property in their hands for safe keeping.

I remained on our farm, managing it as I had done in past years, but I saw that the time had about come when I could do so no longer. I saw men, whose names I could state, take from our farm hogs, cattle, and horses without permission and without paying for them, under the presence that it was a military necessity. Of course no such necessity existed, and the government received no benefit therefrom.

I remember that W. B Bruce owned a fine lot of horses and cattle in 1862, but by March, 1864, they had all or nearly all been taken, without his consent, and often without his knowledge. I speak of only two cases of this kind, because I have personal knowledge of them. After the war, many of these men who had lost their property, other than slaves, presented claims against the government for property supposed to have been confiscated or appropriated to the use of Uncle Sam, and these claiments were honest in their belief that their property was so taken, when, as a matter of fact, it was taken by thieves, dressed in uniform for the purpose of deception, men who were not in the Union army, and the stolen property was used for their own personal benefit. W. B. Bruce is now living and can, if he will, testify to the truthfulness of what I state here.

The Germans were all Union men, and on that account had suffered severely at the hands of the bushwhackers from the beginning of the war to January, 1864, after which time they [w]ere as secure as any other class, and finally became the leaders on the Union side. W. B. Bruce and my owner joined their fortunes with the men of the South, and lost all they had contributed. Agents stole through the lines from the South, authorized to recruit men and receive money donations. They told wonderful stories about the confederacy, its success, what it would do, etc; that they needed money and men, and in a very short time the war would be over, and the South would be on top.

I remember a young man named Kennedy, raised in Brunswick, and enlisted as a private in 1861, who went South in a Missouri rebel regiment. He came back in the fall of 1863 with the rank of Colonel, authorized to raise men and money for the southern confederacy. He was hiding around Brunswick and vicinity for a long time, and left without the Unionists knowing he had been there. Many southern sympathizers contributed money to the cause, which they have had dire need for since, and I believe my master and W. B. Bruce were among the victims.

I had several talks with my young master, W. E. Perkinson, in 1862, on the subject of loyalty. He wanted to join Col. Moberly's company of State militia, and if left to his choice, would have done so, but he was so bitterly opposed by his father and uncle, that he finally went South and served to the day of surrender, came home penniless, and with health gone. I am satisfied that he has sincerely regretted his action ever since, because he found young men, who were not his equals in ability and standing, but who had taken the Union side, occupying important positions in the city, county and state, while he was disfranchised and did not get his disabilities removed for many years. He had been reared in the lap of luxury, graduated from college, then had studied law, and never earned a dollar to defray expenses; and he returned to find his father dead, his Negroes freed, and stock stolen, but the land was there, and that alone constituted his earthly possession. I was his playmate and nurse in childhood, though but a few years older, and always liked him; we never had any harsh words at any time, even after he had become a man. I have been informed that he has succeeded as a lawyer and judge on the bench.

There were a few poor whites who failed to identify themselves with either side, and of course did not enlist in either army; they were anything to suit present company. Near the close of the winter of 1863–4 the Union side seemed to be getting on top, had a company of soldiers stationed at Brunswick, had rid the county of bushwhackers and rebel soldiers, and these fellows who had been on the fence for two years now openly declared for the Union.

CHAPTER X

THE ENLISTMENT OF COLORED MEN for the army commenced in Chariton County, Missouri, early in December, 1863, and any slave man who desired to be a soldier and fight for freedom, had an opportunity to do so. Certain men said to be recruiting officers from Iowa, came to Brunswick, to enlist Colored men for the United States Army, who were to be accredited not to Missouri, but to certain townships in Iowa, in order to avoid a draft there. I am unable to state the number of Colored men who enlisted in that county during the period from December, 1863, until the close of enlistments in the spring of 1865, but I am sure it was large. I had some trouble with these enlisted men, which was as follows: Being in the United States service themselves, they thought it no more than right to press in every young man they could find. Being secretly aided by these white officers, who, I learned afterwards, received a certain sum of money for each recruit raised and accredited as above described. These Colored men scoured the county in search of young men for soldiers, causing me to sleep out of nights and hide from them in the daytime. I was afraid to go to town while they were there, and greatly relieved when a company was filled out and left for some point in Iowa.

Our owner did not want us to leave him and used every persuasive means possible to prevent it. He gave every grown person a free pass, and agreed to give me fifteen dollars per month, with board and clothing, if I would remain with him on the farm, an offer which I had accepted to take effect January 1, 1864. But by March of that year I saw that it could not be carried out, and concluded to go to Kansas. I might have remained and induced others to do so and made the crop, which would have been of little benefit to him, as it would have been spirited away. I made the agreement in good faith, but when I saw that it could not be fulfilled had not the courage to tell him that I was going to leave him.

I was engaged to marry a girl belonging to a man named Allen Farmer, who was opposed to it on the ground, as I was afterwards informed, that he did not want a Negro to visit his farm who could read, because he would spoil his slaves. After it was known that I was courting the girl, he would not allow me to visit his farm nor any of his slaves to visit ours, but they did visit notwithstanding this order, nearly every Sunday. The girl's aunt was our mutual friend and made all arrangements for our meetings. At one of our secret meetings we decided to elope and fixed March 30, 1864, at nine o'clock, P. M., sharp, as the date for starting.

She met me at the appointed time and place with her entire worldly effects tied up in a handkerchief, and I took her up on the horse behind me. Then in great haste we started for Laclede, about thirty miles north of Brunswick, and the nearest point reached by the Hannibal and St. Joe Railroad. This town was occupied by a squad of Union Troops. Having traveled over that country so often, I had acquired an almost perfect knowledge of it, even of the by-paths. We avoided the main road, and made the entire trip without touching the traveled road at any point and without meeting any one and reached Laclede in safety, where we took the train for St. Joe, thence to Weston, where we crossed the Missouri River on a ferry boat to Fort Leavenworth, Kansas. I then felt myself a free man.

I learned soon afterwards that Jesse Boram, Allen Farmer and as many other men as could be hastily gotten together started in pursuit of us, following every road we were supposed to take, and went within six miles of Laclede, hoping to overtake us. Of course they would have ended my earthly career then and there, could they have found me that night. But I had carefully weighed the cost before starting, had nerved myself for action and would have sold my life very dearly had they overtaken us in our flight. How could I have done otherwise in the presence of the girl I loved, one who had forsaken mother, sister and brothers, and had placed herself entirely under my care and protection.

I am satisfied, even now, that I was braver that night than I have ever been since. I was a good shot and knew it, and intended to commence shooting as soon as my pursuers showed up; but it was a Godsend to all concerned, and especially to myself and bride, soon to be, that we were not overtaken; for I was determined to fight it out on that line, as surrender meant death to me. I had buckled around my waist a pair of Colt's revolvers and plenty of ammunition, but I feel now that I could not have held out long before a crowd of such men, and while I might have hit one or two of them, they would in the end have killed me.

My bravery, if that was what affected me, was not of the kind that will not shun danger, for I resorted to every scheme possible to avoid it. We had the start of our pursuers about an hour, or in other words the girl was missed from her room in that time; then it took probably another hour to get the men together. But they stood a very poor show to capture us on the main road, for we left it after the first half mile and took to the brush and by-paths. They expected to overtake us on the main road, where they would have killed me, taken the girl back and given her a severe flogging, but they were badly fooled, for we traveled east, nearly on a straight line for six miles, then turned north, the correct course of our destination.

I had heard it whispered among his Colored people, that Mr. Farmer's house was a kind of rendezvous for the bushwhackers in that part of the country, a place to meet to secure rations, ammunition and information, and that, occasionally, he went out with them at night. If it be true that he acted with bushwhackers, then I assert that he went out with them just once too often, for he was killed as such, during the Summer of 1864, while on the run after being halted.

As already stated in a preceding chapter, I had learned to read, but could not write. Prior to leaving home I printed with pen and ink a note, which was pinned to the bridle, telling a friend of my master, who lived within four miles of Laclede, and in whose front yard I tied the horse about daybreak, to whom it belonged, and requesting him to send it home or notify its owner to come for it. I learned afterwards that the horse, "Old Fiddler," was sent home the next day. I did not want to be called a horse thief, and ever afterwards be afraid to visit my old home, friends and relatives.

In January, 1865, I visited my old master and found him greatly disheartened and hard pressed. He told me that he wished I had kept the horse for he would have been better satisfied, as it had been taken from him by the thieves, dressed for self-protection in the uniform of Uncle Sam. He had but one horse on the farm at the time of my visit, and offered that to me as a gift, knowing that it was only a matter of time, when it, too, would be stolen. I did not accept the gift and was sorry that I did not, for I was informed by letter that three armed men appeared a few days afterward and took, not only the horse, but a wagon load of corn to feed it.

CHAPTER XI

ON MARCH 31, 1864, I landed at Leavenworth, Kansas, with my intended wife, without a change of clothing and with only five dollars in cash, two of which I gave Rev. John Turner,[2] Pastor of the A.M.E. Church, who united us in marriage in his parlor that day. I knew a friend in that city, who came from Brunswick, Paul Jones, and upon inquiry soon found and secured room and board with him. The next day I was out hunting for work, which I obtained with a brick contractor, at two dollars and seventy-five cents per day, to carry a mud-hod, which I had done before; so that the work was not entirely new, nor the contractor a stranger to me. His name was Amos Fenn; he had worked for a contractor named Hawkins, who built a row of brick buildings at Brunswick, Mo., in the Fall of 1854, where I worked a few weeks, and when we met I remembered him and he gave me a job.

For the first few weeks I was well pleased with the pay I received, and thought I would soon have plenty of money, but now I had a new problem to solve, which was to support and clothe myself and a wife and pay doctors' bills, which was something new to me. I had never been trained in the school of economy, where I could learn the art of self-support, as my master had always attended to that little matter from my earliest recollections. Now I had expenses to meet of every kind. The necessaries of life were all very high, including house rent, and by the time I paid up my bills on Saturday night, I found my week's earnings well nigh gone; this was the case right along. I also found that I had to make my own bargains for whatever necessaries we needed, and to provide for a rainy day, all of which experiences were new to me, yes, very new, and were a source of annoyance for a long time, because it taxed my mind each day to provide the necessaries for the next week and from week to week. I had lived to be twenty-eight years old, and had never been placed in a position where I had occasion to give this matter a single thought, for the reason that my master had it to attend to, as before stated.

I found myself almost as helpless as a child, so far as managing and providing for personal welfare and the future was concerned, and although I had been trained to work from a child and had acquired almost a perfect knowledge of it, together with a will and ability to perform hard manual labor, yet I had not learned the art of spending my earnings to the best advantage. I had a very limited knowledge of the value of any article, and often paid the price demanded without question, and ofttimes bought articles which were useless to me. My wife and I had good health and worked steadily every day, and by so doing managed to save up money enough in a short time to rent and fit up a small two-room house.

Continuing to enjoy good health and obtaining steady work, we had saved enough money within two years to buy the house and lot, having nearly two-thirds cash therefor. I felt proud, being then for the first time in my life a land-owner, but it was of short duration. I had relied upon the word of a white man, and had paid him the amount agreed upon, and had received what I had supposed to be a clear title to the land, but it turned out soon afterwards, that the man owned only the house, and the land upon which it stood was the property of another, who notified me to pay rent for the land or move my house away.

I found the white men of Kansas quite different from those of Missouri, in their dealings with Colored people or ex-slaves. They would talk and act nicely and politely, and in such a way as to win my confidence; always referring to my former condition and abusing pro-slavery men, pretending great friendship for me, and by so doing they ingratiated themselves into my confidence to such an extent, that I would follow their advice in the purchase of what they had to sell. Of course I believed what they told me and was often cheated out of my hard earnings.

I had been reared where it was a crime for me to dispute a white man's word, and that idea was so well and thoroughly grounded in me that it took time and great effort to eradicate it. It took me a long time to learn that a white man would lie as quickly as a black one, and there are thousands of illiterate ex-slaves now living who have not entirely dismissed that idea, that a white man can not lie, drilled into them from early childhood, for I have found this true in dealing with them.

Let any ex-slave, uneducated, wanting information come to an educated colored man for it, and obtain it, he will not be really satisfied until he lays the matter before some white man, and if approved, then it is allright, but if condemned then the white man's opinion is accepted and the other rejected; this holds good to-day, and in my opinion is one of the results of slavery, which I can only explain by stating that slaveholders considered it very low to lie to a slave, and would not do it under any circumstances, and had great contempt for another one who would purposely do so. I have known them to refuse to answer questions rather than tell a lie, when they could not afford to tell the truth. Many times the slave has wished that his master would lie, when he has told him that at a certain hour or upon a certain day he would punish him; for he knew he would get the promised flogging almost as surely as the day came. Sometimes he would be told, "I am doing this only to keep my word." My own personal experience is, that in dealing with slaves they master was perfectly honorable and truthful, and would not cheat or practice deception in any way with them, and the slave knew that the master would not lie and therefore believed what he said.

I found by sad experience that the white men in a free state, especially in business transactions, were not as truthful as the slave-holders of Missouri, in dealing with colored people, a fact to which many colored men in Leavenworth and Atchison, Kansas, can testify, men like myself who have been deceived into buying a lot, and who, in installments had paid the entire price agreed upon. After having built a house thereon, in a few years they found that the land was owned by some one else.

I could give the names of several colored men in the cities named above, who lost their property in that way, and who were forced to vacate or pay a higher price for the land than at first. Men from the South tell me that that class of white men in that section, who were almost the soul of honor, in dealing with the colored people, is fast dying out, and the young men taking their places will lie to and cheat the ex-slave of his earnings right along, and do not display the honor of their fathers in such dealings.

I am unable to vouch for the truthfulness of this statement, not having lived in the South and therefore having no personal knowledge on that point. If it be true that the young men of the South, who have taken their fathers' places, are less honorable, less reliable in dealings with their fathers' ex-slaves, cheating and by deception, defrauding them of their earnings, then I assert that it is a sad reflection upon the once boasted chivalry and honor of the southern gentlemen, the men of the old school. But I am of the opinion that the class of men in the South, who are cheating and lying to colored people, are the newcomers and oldtime slave drivers or their offspring, who were always the enemies of the slave, and to day are jealous of him as a free man, and will take the lead in any matter that will militate against the colored man.

In thus describing my own experience upon being emancipated from slavery, I only show that of over four million others. History does not record where four millions of people had been held in slavery so long, that they had lost all knowledge of the way to provide for their own support, to expend their earnings to advantage, to use economy in purchasing necessaries of life and to lay up for another day.

This was the condition of the Colored people at the close of the war. They were set free without a dollar, without a foot of land, and without the wherewithal to get the next meal even, and this too by a great Christian Nation, whose domain is dotted over with religious institutions and whose missionaries in heathen lands, are seeking to convert the heathen to belief in their Christian religion and their Christian morality.

These slaves had been trained to do hard manual labor from the time that they were large enough to perform it, to the end of their lives, right along, and received no education or instruction in the way of economy. They had no care as to the way they were to get the next meal, the next pair of shoes or suit of clothes. This being the duty of the master, they looked to him for these necessaries, just as a child looks to its mother or the horse to its master for its daily sustenance.

The history of this country, especially that portion of it south of Mason and Dixon's line, shows that the labor of these people had for two hundred years made the country tenable for the white man, had cleared away the dense forests and produced crops that brought millions of money annually to that section, which not only benefitted the South, but the North as well. It does seem to me, that a Christian Nation, which had received such wealth from the labor of a subjugated people, upon setting them free would, at least, have given them a square meal.

Justice seems to demand one year's support, forty acres of land and a mule each.

Did they get that or any portion of it? Not a cent. Four million people turned loose without a dollar and told to "Root hog or die!" Now, whose duty was it to feed them? Was it the former masters' or that of the general governments which had conquered the masters, and in order to make that victory complete freed their slaves? My opinion is that the government should have done it.

The master had been conquered, after four years' hard fighting, and largely by the aid of the two hundred thousand Colored volunteers, mustered in the United States Army, and told to fight for the freedom of their race. The history of that conflict says they did it loyally and bravely.

General Lee had surrendered. The South had staked its all upon that contest and had been conquered and laid waste, as it were; its business gone, its crops confiscated by both armies, and its slaves set free, but it had to feed these homeless and penniless people or see them starve. No one will say the masters did not feed the freedmen until a crop was made, and, too, at a time when they had no money in cash and no credit at the North.

When we take into consideration the penniless condition of these four million people at the close of the war, and the fact that they were destitute of education and turned loose in the midst of a people educated in science, art, literature and economy, a people owning the land and chattels of every kind, with money to do the business of the country and with the experience and training of a thousand years, the fact that the freed-men did succeed under these adverse conditions in obtaining a living, and in many cases in getting little homes for themselves and families, instead of becoming a public charge, is greatly to their credit.

Many white people who were friendly to them had great mis-givings and doubts as to whether these freed-men could succeed in making themselves self-supporting in the race of life, with so many obstacles to meet and overcome. They were illiterate, without money and confronted with a prejudice due in part to their former condition and in part to the fact of their being candidates for the labor work, which, up to that period, had been performed by the poor whites, especially foreigners, in the North, East and West.

The freeing of the American slaves and their partial migration to these states, seeking employment, excited the enmity of the white laborers, particularly the Irish, because at that time they constituted fully seventy-five per cent of the laboring class, and who imagined that the influx of Negro laborers from the South, would divide the labor monopoly which they held, and of course they became opposed to the Colored people and so much so, that they would have done almost anything calculated to extirpate them. They were always ready to incite a riot and take the lead in it, and had not the business men, capitalists and ministers frowned upon their course, would have succeeded in doing serious harm.

I remember the bitter feeling existing between the Irish and the Colored laborers in Leavenworth, Kansas, which had its beginning about the close of the war. They had several little conflicts, and on one occasion the civil authorities interfered to prevent bloodshed.

I recall an instance when the Colored people had been informed that the Irish were intent on surrounding the Baptist Church, corner Third and Kiowa streets, to "clane the nagurs out," on Sunday night. The Colored people prepared to meet them, by selecting Fenton Burrell as captain, and secreting nearly fifty armed men in a vacant lot in the rear of the church, to await the appearance of the Irish. Soon a squad of them came up Third street to within a hundred yards of the church, but after halting a few minutes marched back and dispersed. I learned afterwards that Col. D. R. Anthony, a recognized friend of both races, went in person to the leaders and informed them of the reception they would receive if they proceeded further, and advised them to disperse and go home, which they did.

The Negro has committed no offense against the Irish; the two races had never lived together at any time to engender hatred, and as I understand it, there is no valid reason why the Irish should have been so bitter against the Negro, except the fact that they were both seekers after the unskilled labor of this country. I have stated that it was the labor question that excited the enmity of the Irish against the Colored people, and the reason why I say this is, that the past history of the two races since the conquest of Ireland, by England is much alike; both had been in bondage a long time. While the Irish had not been in slavery, pure and simple, they had been held in a state of subjugation and servitude, nearly approaching to it, and enjoyed but few more liberties than the American slave. They had a country only in name and no voice in the government thereof or ownership in the land on which they lived, any more than the slaves in the United States. They were not free men until they reached the United States. With such a similarity in past history and present condition, it would seem that these two races should have been friends instead of foes, and in my opinion they would have been, had they not been seekers for the same kind of employment, and thus becoming competitors. So that the scramble for that employment has caused the Irish to resort to means, which have aided largely in kindling the feeling of prejudice against the Colored people. They were aided in thus accomplishing this object by the native poor white, and the further fact that they were white men, because whenever that question or issue is raised, it will catch the illiterate whites en masse, and in many cases the thoughtless aristocratic class, who will join a mob to lynch a Colored man without giving the matter a second thought, as to whether he is guilty or not. In many cases the charge is cooked up for a sinister purpose, to get rid of him, or in order to obtain a lucrative position held by him.

I have stated before that it is the labor question, more than any other, which causes the Colored people to suffer greater indignities than any other class of Americans in this country, and I believe it is not on account of their color, so much as it is the desire of white laborers to do the work and to receive pay which might go to him[.] It is an admitted fact that these same laborers or mechanics in search of a job, will go South, where the Colored men have charge of such work, or nearly so, and will not only work with them, but hire to them and be bossed by them. Foreigners, seeking employment, have gone to the South in large numbers during the last five years, and finding there the typical poor whites, who are the ancient enemies of the Colored people and ever ready to do them harm, have united with them on the color line and raised that old familiar cry that "this is a white man's country, that white men must and shall rule it; no Negro domination over white men." When that feeling has grown sufficiently strong to cover the real designs of the vicious elements, and to deceive the better class, then it is that the charges against some harmless, helpless Colored man are trumped up, and they lynch him. So rapid is the mob in forming and blood-thirsty in its murderous howls, that the better class is powerless to assist the helpless victim while alive, and when dead the charges which were pr[of]ferred by a poor white man or a foreigner, for a mere trifle or sinister purpose, are magnified until it would appear that the victim was a savage brute and deserved the punishment inflicted. So brutal are these charges made to appear after the death of the victim, that the better class of southern white people, allow these lynchers to escape punishment, upon the ground, I suppose, that they had rid the community of a bad character.

The lynching of the Colored people is always the work of the poor white laboring class, and as a striking incident tending to show the facts, I call attention to the list of the killed and wounded at Roanoke, Va., in September, 1893, when the State militia, in upholding the dignity of the law of the State, fired into a mob, killing and wounding thirty men, twenty-four of whom were laborers, track-walkers, section hands, and employees in the machine shops of that city. I take these figures from the published report made at the time of the occurrence; and to my mind one thing is made plain by this incident, which is this, that it was not the aristocracy that was doing the lynching at the South, or any other part of the country, though they are held morally responsible in the eyes of the nation.[3]

But the aristocracy of the South is getting its eyes open to this growing evil, and I am of the opinion, that its eyes will not have been opened any too soon, for this is only another form of anarchy, which is feeding itself upon the Colored people, and will ere long turn upon the aristocrat and the capitalist, and serve them even worse than the Colored people have been.

The better class at the South will soon see the error of their past conduct, if they have not already done so, in taking the poor whites into their confidence and social circle, which, I suppose, was for political purposes, for they now feel themselves the equals of their former lords, and will not down at their bidding. They drove out the Republican government at the South by brutal force, and they had the acquiescence of their former lords, who enjoyed a benefit for a time, but this element of roughs, augmented by the influx of foreigners, is beginning to show its disloyalty to the old aristocratic element by leaving them at home, and when possible, sending one of its ilk as a representative to the legislative halls, State and National.

But as to lynching, I think I see among the better class evidence of a change of public sentiment taking place at the South, a return to law and order, as indicated by a few extracts from leading newspapers in that section. The first is from the *Indianapolis World*[4] (Colored), issue of September 19, 1893, as follows: "It looks as if light were breaking into the hitherto darkened condition of the South. The carnival of crime in which the depraved and merciless element of that section has reveled unchecked for many months, is at last arousing the dormant spirit of justice and fair play, inherent in the American bosom, and the fabric upon which our Constitution rests. Just as the insolent and exorbitant ambition of the slave power laid the train, which resulted in the downfall of the unfavorite institution, the repeated cruelties, tortures, and human outrages of southern brutes has awakened the conscience of the better classes, whose love for the fair name of their country outweighs all fear of Negro domination. The 'vaulting ambition' of the stake-burners and lynchers overstepped itself, and we verily believe the reign of misrule is reaching the beginning of the end."

A few months ago, scarcely a southern newspaper dared to lift up a voice against the inhuman practices of the mobs. They either gave open encouragement to their so-called "best citizens," or silently acquiesced. To-day, however, the leading journals of Virginia, South Carolina, Georgia, Tennessee and Louisiana, perceiving the change of the tide, and that the southern craft is dashing dangerously near the breakers of anarchy, are pleading for a cessation of horrors, and the re-establishment of law and order. The *Memphis Commercial* has been at all times one of the most arrogant and ungenerous enemies of the Negro throughout the South, but it is a revelation of a highly creditable character to hear it give birth to such sentiments as these:

> Even when outraged virtue and all the ties of nature and humanity call for the death of criminals, the demoralization of violence and the contagion of cruelty accompany these things. There is no passion which so thrives from gratification as the lust of cruelty. The English Parliament declared that public executions were debauching the whole British people. Mercy was drowned in blood during the reign of terror, and the whole future of French civilization is stained and poisoned by the memory of the guillotine. So it is with lynching in the South. The horror has spread, and a people, originally the gentlest, bravest, noblest in the world, are actually threatened with a generation of cruel and violent men. Every boy, who witnesses a

lynching loses something of his humanity. Every groan of the dying wretch kills part of his native tenderness, and every drop of blood congeals the mercy and gentleness of his heart. It were better that a young man should cut off his right hand than to see the torture of one man. It is better that he should be struck with deafness than to hear the death shriek of one dying ravisher.

Such scenes have made the Murats and Robespierres of history. Such things done in America will curse the future of civilization and darken the glory of coming years. Hence, we deem that swift and summary justice should be meted by law to all who practice these horrors, unless the flagrancy of the offence justify lawlessness by the higher law of necessary punishment. In Louisiana, a few day ago, a mob of brutal whites most cruelly lynched three innocent Negroes, and have sent word to the agents of the State's laws that they intend to burn another one in broad daylight. This constitutes treason, and we hold that the Governor of Louisiana should stamp it out at once, if it must be done with the bayonet of armed authority. It is the glory of the South, up to this time, in spite of all that may be said to the contrary, that she has been considerate, generous and kind in the face of the most difficult class of conditions that ever confronted a people. Let us not lose so fair a fame by any delays of laws or fears of prejudice.

These sentiments are their own comment, and indicate that if the appeals of the Negro for justice for justice's sake are ignored, the southern leaders are learning that they cannot escape the consequences of natural laws and are moved to action through the law of self-protection. The strong stand taken against mob violence by Governor [Frank] Brown of Maryland, Governor [Philip Watkins]McKinney of Virginia, and the ringing words of brave Mayor [H. L.] Trout of Roanoke, are all encouraging cases in point, which evidence the change of front by the intelligent, thrifty and liberty-loving people below the Mason and Dixon line.

We must not lose our head, or fly into an impotent rage when contemplating our wrongs. Let us recognize fully the seriousness of our condition, study the temper of the southern mind, analyze the cause of every action against us, and set about applying a sensible remedy, based upon the state of the case as shown by the symptoms. A condition which is the natural outgrowth of slavery will improve as the evils of that period diminish. Therefore let us grow in education, in wealth, in respectability, in morals, and in political generosity, and we will rise to our rightful place in the esteem and confidence of the nation. This will take time, and time is an essential element in the solution of all chronic complaints and in all great problems.

Before closing this chapter, I feel that an explanation should be made as to what I really mean in using the term "poor white" people, for I do not want to be understood as meaning that all poor white people are alike, and therefore are opposed to the Colored people's enjoying the rights and immunities conferred upon others by the law of the country, for such is far from my intention or desire. There are thousands of aristocratic white people who are poor, financially speaking, due to accident or misfortune, but they still retain in their veins the blood of aristocracy, that will not and cannot be concealed by the change of position. This class, as a result of the war, is more largely found in the South, but wherever found, as a rule, they always are the friends of the oppressed, and the Colored people regard them as their friends.

Blood and education will tell; even the children of that class of men are infinitely superior to those of the typical poor whites, whose offspring seldom rise above the positions held by their fathers' in life, and when we find one who has, we regard him as the exception, and not the rule. He may acquire wealth, and, on account of it, command respect, but will have all the failings and prejudices of his kind or line of consanguinity.

Now as to the Irish, I do not want it understood from what I have said concerning the position they have occupied toward the Colored people, that they are all enemies to the ex-slave, for such is not the case, because there are thousands of them in this country as friendly to the Colored people as any other class of American citizens, and just as ready to give them a fair show as any other.

But I will state, that my experience has been that this class of Irish Americans are the refined, educated class always, and not the common laborer, or the illiterate class. But I think I see a gre[a]t change for the better taking place.

The Irish who have been in this country long enough, and are educated, and have accumulated money, are giving up the labor work, and engaging in the various kinds of business, leaving the labor work to be performed by others, and in such cases they cease to be prejudiced. The Germans have never sought the labor work of the country, and therefore have always been friendly with the Colored people, and retain their friendship and confidence in return.

Henry Clay Bruce, *The New Man. Twenty-Nine Years a Slave. Twenty-Nine Years a Free Man.* (York, PA: P. Anstadt & Sons, 1895), 82–127.

---

1. Blanche K. Bruce (1841–1898), slave-born in Virginia, became the first African American to serve in the U.S. Senate. He was taken to Missouri in 1850 and received a education from his master's tutor. As H. C. Bruce indicated, Blanche escaped to Kansas in 1861 and returned to Missouri in 1864 to open the state's first school for African Americans. After the war he moved to Mississippi, served in a variety of local positions, and in 1874 was elected by the legislature to the Senate. A political moderate, he made friends among white planters in Mississippi and accumulated a small fortune through investments in land, stocks, and bonds. Eric Foner, *Freedom's Lawmakers: A Directory of Black Officeholders During Reconstruction* (Baton Rouge, LA: Louisiana State University Press, 1996), 29–30.

2. John Turner filled pulpits for the AME Church in Indiana during the 1850s. In 1861 he organized the AME Church in Leavenworth, Kansas, and after the Civil War ministered to St. Paul's Methodist Episcopal Church in St. Louis, one of the oldest black churches in the city. Alexander W. Wayman, *My Recollections of African M.E. Ministers, or Forty Years' Experience in the African Methodist Episcopal Church* (Philadelphia: A.M.E. Book Rooms, 1881), 56; http://stpaulstl.com/history.htm.

3. On September 20, 1893, whites in Roanoke, Virginia, accused an African American named Thomas Smith of attacking a Mrs. Sallie A. Bishop, robbing her, and smashing her head with a brickbat. Authorities quickly apprehended Smith and brought him to Mrs. Bishop—who had survived the beating—for identification. With impaired vision, she could not absolutely confirm Smith as the attacker. Nevertheless, authorities confined Smith to the jail, after a brief escape attempt by the prisoner and recapture. On the evening of the 20th, a crowd of 1,000 to 2,000 enraged whites appeared at the jail to remove Smith. Mayor H. L. Trout bravely admonished the crowd to disperse and assured them that if the prisoner indeed was the attacker, he would be punished. Fearing a riot, Mayor Trout called out the militia. At 7:30 P.M., the mob attempted to seize Smith, but were driven off at bayonet point. When the rioters rushed the jail at 8:00 P.M. the militia, under Trout's orders, fired into the mob, killing ten outright and wounding

many more. Trout and several African Americans had also been shot in the melee, indicating that some rioters came armed.

As sheriffs tried to remove the prisoner to another town for his safety, other rioters ambushed the party and seized Smith. They promptly hung him from a nearby tree and pumped several bullets into his body. As the corpse hung, someone attached a sign to Smith's back that read, "Mayor Trout's Friend." Rioters later cut down the body and incinerated it. A hastily convened jury determined that Smith had died "at the hands of parties unknown." As Bruce's comments indicate, the case came to symbolize the injustices African Americans endured. Unfortunately, rather than the close of a reign of terror, a horrid wave of lynching had just begun and would endure for another twenty-five years or more. Trout proved one of the few white Southerners who sought to uphold the law and resist lynching. Ronaoke *Daily Record*, September 21, 1893; Richmond *Daily Planet*, September 30, 1893; W. Fitzhugh Brundage, *Lynching in the New South: Georgia and Virginia, 1880–1930* (Urbana, IL: University of Illinois Press, 1993). For information on lynchings in the North, see Dennis B. Downey and Raymond M. Hyser, *No Crooked Death: Coatsville, Pennsylvania, and the Lynching of Zachariah Walker* (Urbana, IL: University of Illinois Press, 1991).

4. The Indianapolis *World* began publication in 1882 as *The Colored World*. Levi Christy, and several other African Americans, served as the paper's editor. The *World* became extremely successful, giving voice to many important black leaders including Ida B. Wells. It reported on the activities of African Americans around the country as well as in Indianapolis. In 1893 R. W. Thompson, a Democratic politician, took over as editor, although Christy remained as publisher. The paper returned to its more militant African American focus when Alexander E. Manning, an AME Church minister, and W. Allison Sweeny took over the paper until its demise in 1924. Emma Lou Thornbrough, *The Negro in Indiana Before 1900* (Bloomington, IN: Indiana University Press, 1993), 384–385, 388.

19

Remembering Slavery and the Civil War in Tennessee

"Slavery and the War of the Rebellion. Beginning of the War."
Louis Hughes
1897

At the time of the Civil War, 25 percent of Tennessee's population lived in chains. Most whites owned fewer than four slaves, and only 8 percent of the state's slave owners, such as Louis Hughes's masters, owned twenty or more. The overwhelming number of slaves lived in the middle and western part of the state, where Hughes spent most of his life as the property of the McGee family. The cruelty exhibited by Tennessee masters typified the experience slaves suffered throughout the South; the breakup of families, the beatings, the demeaning and dispiriting conditions that Hughes endured, and the occasional sincere attachments that whites and blacks formed characterized the institution of bondage. The destruction of black families perhaps represented slavery's worst crime. "This separation was common," Hughes recorded, "and many died heartbroken, by reason of it." Born in Virginia in 1832, Hughes was sold away from his mother at the tender age of six and eventually ended up in the hands of Edward McGee, who compelled Hughes and fifty-nine other slaves to walk from Richmond to Atlanta, Georgia. His owner moved him about, eventually settling him on a vast plantation outside of Memphis, where Hughes endured the best and worst conditions that slavery could offer. Hughes's willingness to risk his life again and again by running away and suffering savage beatings is stark testimony to the inhumanity visited upon African Americans by whites. His memoir represents one of the most intimate recreations of the nineteenth-century slave experience available to us, and it stands as a monument to human courage.

As elsewhere in the South, African Americans suffered terribly during the war. At first spurned by Union troops and hunted down by slave catchers and rebel soldiers, slaves who considered a dash for freedom risked their lives. Even after Congress authorized the army to retain "contraband," Union lines did not necessarily offer safe conditions. Blacks were moved about in accordance with the army's labor needs, and Confederate raiders represented real threats. Even ignoring the likely possibility of recapture, health conditions in Tennessee contraband camps proved lethal. In the winter of 1862–1863, for instance, 1,400 former slaves died in Nashville, and 1,200 in Memphis.

Hughes did not successfully escape slavery until late in 1865, long after the end of the war and Tennessee's ratification of the Thirteenth Amendment to the Constitution. His experience reflected slavery's slow death in the state. Despite a Union occupying force, whites resisted slavery's end and persisted in maintaining all aspects of the old regime, enforcing the slave code with the whip. Vigilantes roamed the state, avoiding Union soldiers in the countryside and terrorizing blacks. Former slaves like Hughes, who fled the state at the first opportunity after the war for the relative safety of Canada, proved a very fortunate few. Hughes bravely rescued his family and several relatives, taking them with him to Canada. He later resettled in Wisconsin, established a successful laundry business, and, through a series of fortunate circumstances, was reunited with the brother he had not seen since childhood. While the majority of former slaves did not experience Hughes's good fortune in the postwar years, they certainly shared his desire to reestablish their families and to continually remind fellow Americans of slavery's damaging injustices. John Cimprich, *Slavery's End in Tennessee, 1861–1865* (Tuscaloosa, AL: University of Alabama Press, 1985), 7–13, 39–45, 57, 118–121.

CHAPTER III
SLAVERY AND THE WAR OF REBELLION.
BEGINNING OF THE WAR.

I REMEMBER WELL WHEN Abraham Lincoln was elected. Boss and the madam had been reading the papers, when he broke out with the exclamation: "The very idea of electing an old rail splitter to the presidency of the United States! Well he'll never take his seat." When Lincoln was inaugurated, Boss, old Master Jack and a great company of men met at our house to discuss the matter, and they were wild with excitement. Was not this excitement an admission that their confidence in their ability to whip the Yankees, five or six to one, was not so strong as they pretended?

The war had been talked of for some time, but at last it came. When the rebels fired upon Fort Sumter, then great excitement arose. The next day when I drove Boss to town, he went into the store of one Williams, a merchant, and when he came out, he stepped to the carriage, and said: "What do you think? Old Abraham Lincoln has called for four hundred thousand men to come to Washington immediately. Well, let them come; we will make a breakfast of them. I can whip a half dozen Yankees with my pocket knife." This was the chief topic everywhere. Soon after this Boss bought himself a six-shooter. I had to mould the bullets for him, and every afternoon he would go out to practice. By his direction, I fixed a large piece of white paper on the back fence, and in the center of it put a large black dot. At this mark he would fire away, expecting to hit it; but he did not succeed well. He would sometimes miss the fence entirely, the ball going out into the woods beyond. Each time he would shoot I would have to run down to the fence to see how near he came to the mark. When he came very near to it—within an inch or so, he would say laughingly: Ah! I would have got him that time." (Meaning a Yankee soldier.) There was something very ludicrous in this pistol practice of a man who boasted that he could whip half a dozen Yankees with a jackknife. Every day for a month this business, so tiresome to me, went on. Boss was very brave until it came time for him to go to war, when his courage oozed out, and he sent a substitute; he remaining at home as a "home guard." One day when I came back with the papers from the city, the house was soon ringing with cries of victory. Boss said: "Why, that was a great battle at Bull Run. If our men had only known, at first, what they afterwards found out, they would have wiped all the Yankees out, and succeeded in taking Washington."

PETTY DISRESPECT TO THE EMBLEM OF THE UNION.

RIGHT AFTER THE BOMBARDMENT of Fort Sumter, they brought to Memphis the Union flag that floated over the fort. There was a great jubilee in celebration of this. Portions of the flag, no larger than a half dollar in paper money, were given out to the wealthy people, and these evidences of their treason were long preserved as precious treasures. Boss had one of these pieces which he kept a long time; but, as the rebel cause waned these reminders of its beginning were less and less seen, and if any of them are now in existence, it is not likely that their possessors will take any pride in exposing them to view.

As the war continued we would, now and then, hear of some slave of our neighborhood running away to the Yankees. It was common when the message of a Union victory came to see the slaves whispering to each other: "We will be free." I tried to catch everything I could about the war, I was so eager for the success of the Union cause. These things went on until

THE BATTLE OF SHILOH, APRIL 9, 1862.

BOSS CAME HURRYING IN one morning, right after breakfast, calling to me: "Lou, Lou, come; we have a great victory! I want to go up and carry the boys something to eat. I want you and Matilda to get something ready as quickly as you can." A barrel of flour was rolled into the kitchen, and my wife and I "pitched in" to work. Biscuit, bread, hoecake, ham, tongue—all kinds of meat and bread were rapidly cooked; and, though the task was a heavy one for my wife and me, we worked steadily; and, about five o'clock in the afternoon the things were ready. One of the large baskets used to hold cotton was packed full [of] these provisions. Our limbs ached from the strain of the work, for we had little help. One reason for the anxiety of the Boss for the preparation of this provision for the soldiers was that he knew so many in one of the companies, which was known as the "Como Avengers," and he had a son, a nephew and a brother of his wife connected with it; the latter a major on Gen. [William T.] Martin's staff. On the following morning I got up early, and hurried with my work to get through, as I had to go to the post office. Madam hurried me off, as she expected a letter from her husband, who had promised to write, at the earliest moment, of their friends and relatives. I rushed into the city, at full speed, got some letters and a morning paper, and, returning as rapidly as possible, gave them to her. She grasped them eagerly, and commenced reading the paper. In a short time I heard her calling me to come to her. I went in, and she said, in great excitement: "Louis, we want to have you drive us into town, to see the Yankee prisoners, who are coming through, at noon, from Shiloh." I went and told Madison to hitch up, as soon as he could. In the meantime I got myself ready, and it was not long before we were off for the city. The madam was accompanied by a friend of hers, a Mrs. Oliver. We were at the station in plenty of time. About twelve o'clock the train from Shiloh drew into the station; but the prisoners that were reported to be on board were missing—it proved to be a false report. While they were looking for the prisoners, Mrs. Oliver saw Jack, a servant of Edward McGee, brother of madam. "Oh! Look," said Mrs. Oliver, "there is Edward's Jack. Lou, run and call him." In a minute I was off the carriage, leaving the reins in madam's hands. Jack came up to the carriage, and the women began to question him: "Where is your Master, Ed," asked both of them. "He is in the car, Missis—he is shot in the ankle," said Jack. In a minute the women were crying. "I was going to get a hack," said Jack, "to—" "No, No!" said both of them. "Go, Lou, and help Jack to bring him to our carriage. You can drive him more steadily than the hackman." Jack and I went to the car, and helped him out, and after some effort, got him into our carriage. Then I went and got a livery hack to take the women and his baggage home. When we reached home, we found there old Mrs. Jack McGee, mother of the madam, Mrs. Charles Dandridge, Mrs. Farrington, sisters of madam, and Fanny, a colored woman, Edward's housekeeper and mistress—a wife in all but name. All of these had come to hear the news of the great battle, for all had near relatives in it. Mrs. Jack McGee and Mrs. Dr. Charles Dandridge had each a son in the terrible conflict.

MOURNING IN MASTER'S FAMILY.

IN THE AFTERNOON, WHEN all were seated in the library reading, and I was in the dining room, finishing up my work, I happened to look out of the window, and saw a messenger coming up the graveled walk. I went out to meet him. "Telegram for Mrs. McGee," he said. I took it to her; and, reading it without a word, she passed it to the next member of the family, and so it was passed around until all had read it except Mrs. Dandridge. When it was handed to her, I saw, at a glance, that it contained for her the most sorrowful tidings. As she read she became livid, and when she had finished she covered her face with her handkerchief, giving a great, heavy sob. By this time the whole family was crying and screaming: "Oh! our Mack is killed." "Mars, Mack is killed," was echoed by the servants, in tones of heart-felt sorrow, for he was an exceptional young man. Every one loved him—both whites and blacks. The affection of the slaves for him bordered on reverence, and this was true not alone of his father's slaves, but of all those who knew him. This telegram was from Boss, and announced that he would be home the next day with the remains. Mrs. Farrington at once wrote to old Master Jack and to Dr. Dandridge, telling them of Mack's death and to come at once. After I mailed those letters nothing unusual happened during the afternoon, and the house was wrapped in silence and gloom. On the following morning I went for the mail as usual, but there was nothing new. At noon, the remains of the much loved young man arrived at our station, accompanied by Boss and Dr. Henry Dandridge, brother of the father of the deceased, who was a surgeon in the rebel army. I went to the station with another servant, to assist in bringing the body to the house. We carried it into the back parlor, and, after all had been made ready, we proceeded to wash and dress it. He had lain on the battlefield two days before he was found, and his face was black as a piece of coal; but Dr. Henry Dandridge, with his ready tact, suggested the idea of painting it. I was there to assist in whatever way they needed me. After the body was all dressed, and the face painted, cheeks tinted with a rosy hue, to appear as he always did in life, the look was natural and handsome. We were all the afternoon employed in this sad work, and it was not until late in the evening that his father and mother came down to view the body for the first time. I remember, as they came down the broad stairs together, the sorrow-stricken yet calm look of those two people. Mrs. Dandridge was very calm—her grief was too great for her to scream as the others did when they went in. She stood and looked at her Mack; then turning to Boss, she said: "Cousin Eddie, how brave he was! He died for his country." Poor, sorrowing, misguided woman! It was not for his country he died, but for the perpetuation of the cruel, the infamous system of human slavery. All the servants were allowed to come in and view the body. Many sad tears were shed by them. Some of the older slaves clasped their hands, as if in mute prayer, and exclaimed, as they passed by the coffin: "He was a lovin' boy." It seems that all his company but five or six were killed. At an early hour next morning the funeral party started for the home in Panola, where the body of the lamented young man, sacrificed to an unholy cause, was buried, at the close of the same day.

Edward stayed at our house some six weeks, his ankle was so slow in getting well. At the end of that time, he could walk with the aid of crutches, and he took Fanny and went home.

ALARM OF THE MEMPHIS REBELS.

NOT LONG AFTER THIS the people were very much worked up over the military situation. The Yankees had taken Nashville, and had begun to bombard Fort Pillow. The officials of the Memphis and Ohio railroad company became alarmed at the condition of things, fearing for the safety of their stock. The officers, therefore, set about devising some plan by which they might get the cars down on the Memphis and Jackson road, where they imagine their property would be safe from the now terrible Yankees. The railroad officials at once set to work to buy the right of way through Main Street, to give them the connection with the southern road named. At first it was refused by the city authorities, but finally the right of way was granted. When, however, the railroad men began to lay the ties and rails, the people grew furious. Some fled at once, for they imagined that this act of the railroad officials indicated that the Yankees must be coming pretty near. Boss became so excited, at this time, that he almost felt like going away too. The family grew more and more uneasy; and it was the continual talk: "We must get away from Memphis. The companies are already moving their rolling stock, fearing the Yankees may come at any time and destroy everything; we must get away," said Boss, speaking to the madam.

THE FAMILY FLEE FROM MEMPHIS.

THINGS CONTINUED IN THIS way until about June, 1862. The Union troops had taken Fort Pillow. We had heard the firing of cannon, and did not know what it meant. One morning I was in the city after the mail, and I learned that a transient boat had just come down the river, which had lost a part of her wheelhouse. She was fired on from Fort Pillow, sustaining this serious damage from the shot. This increased the excitement among the people; and our folks became alarmed right away, and commenced talking of moving and running the servants away from the Yankees, to a place of safety. McGee was trying for some time to get some one to take the house, that is, to live in and care for it until after the war, while the family were gone. They never thought that slavery would be abolished, and so hoped to come back again. After some search, they found a widow, a Mrs. Hancock. She was to have full charge of the house and continue keeping boarders, as she had been doing in Memphis. The vaunted courage of this man seems to have early disappeared, and his thought was chiefly devoted to getting his family and his slaves into some obscure place, as far away as possible from the Yankees, that were to be so easily whipped. We were about two weeks getting ready to leave, stowing away some of the things they did not want to move. The Boss and his family, my wife and I, and all the house servants were to go to Panola, to his father's. The family went by rail, but I had to drive through in a wagon.

I AM TAKEN TO BOLIVAR FARM.

SOON AFTER THE FAMILY all reached Master Jack's, Boss took me to his own farm in Bolivar county. This separated me for a time from my wife, for she remained with the family. I had to look after the house at the farm, attend the dining room, and, between meals, sew every day, making clothes for the hands. I could run on the machine eighteen to twenty pairs of pants a day, but two women made the button holes and did the basting for me, getting the goods all ready for the machine.

CAPTURE OF A UNION TRADING BOAT.

THE YANKEES HAD MADE a raid through Bolivar, before I came, and the excitement had not abated, as they were spreading themselves all through the state. There was a Union trading boat, the Lake City, that had been successful in exchanging her goods for cotton that came from Memphis. She usually stopped at Helena, Fryer's Point and other small towns; but on a trip at this time she came about fifty miles farther down the river, to Carson's Landing, right at Boss' farm. She was loaded with all kinds of merchandise—sugar, tobacco, liquor, etc. She had a crew of about forty men, but they were not well prepared for a vigorous defense. The rebel soldiers stationed in the vicinity saw her as she dropped her anchor near the landing, and they determined to make an effort for her capture. They put out pickets just above our farm, and allowed no one to pass, or stop to communicate with the boat. Every one that sought to pass was held prisoner, and every precaution taken to prevent those on the boat from learning of the purposes of the rebels, knowing that the boat would land in the morning, if not informed of the danger, and then it was anticipated that they could easily make her a prize. There was a small ferry boat behind the steamer, and as the latter dropped down stream, and then steamed up to the landing, the former stood off for a few moments. As the steamer touched shore, the rebels charged on her, and captured her without a struggle. In the meantime the ferry boat, seeing what had happened, sped away up stream, the soldiers firing at her, but doing little damage, except the breaking of the glass in the pilot house. The rebels, seeing that the ferry boat had escaped them, turned their attention to the unloading of the steamer. They sent out for help in this work, and the summons was answered by the neighbors far and near. Wagons were brought, two of which were from our farm, and loaded with goods, which were taken to Deer Creek, forty miles from Carson Landing. What goods they found themselves unable to carry away were packed in the warehouse. The steamer was then burned. McGee was present, and the rebel captain gave him a written statement of the affair to the effect that the residents were not responsible for it, and that this should be a protection for them against the Union forces. The officers and crew of the steamer to the number of forty were made prisoners, and taken to Deer Creek, the rebel headquarters of that region, and put in the jail there. The ferry boat that escaped went to Helena, Arkansas, and carried the news of the affair to the Union forces there.

BOSS TAKEN PRISONER.

I WAS TOLD BY Boss to take my stand on our veranda, and keep watch on the river, and if I saw any boat coming down to let him know at once. I kept a close watch the next morning until about eight o'clock, when I saw a boat, but she had almost gone past our house before I discovered her. I ran into the house and told Boss. He ordered me to get his horse at once, which I did; and he mounted and went down to the landing as fast as he could. Upon reaching there, he was taken prisoner by the Union soldiers, who had just landed from the boat. All who came near were captured. The Union soldiers went to work and transferred all the goods which the rebels had put into the warehouse from the boat which they had captured, then setting fire to the warehouse and the post office, they pushed off yelling and shouting with glee. Among those captured by the Union soldiers were three other rich planters besides Boss, all of whom were taken to Helena. After they had been there about a week, the planters offered to secure the release of the Unionists captured on the boat which the rebels had burned at Carson Landing, and who had been sent to the rebel jail at Deer Creek, if they were guaranteed their own release in exchange. They offered to bear the expense of a messenger to the rebel officer, at Deer Creek, with this proposition. The Union officer at Helena accepted the proposition, and the messenger was sent off. It was arranged that he should stop over at our house, both on his way down and back. Upon his return, he stopped over night, and the next morning proceeded on his way. When he had gone about five miles, he saw a flatboat at a landing, on which were people drinking and having a merry time. He stopped, and went aboard; and, in joining the carousal, he soon became so intoxicated that he was unable to go on with his journey. Among those present was one Gilcrease, a cousin of the McGees, who recognized the man as the messenger in this important business, went to him and asked him for the letters he carried. The fellow refusing to give them up, Gilcrease took them from him, and at once sent to our overseer for a reliable man by whom to forward them to the commandant at Helena. The overseer called me up from the cabin to his room, and told me that I was to go to Helena to carry some important papers, and to come to him for them in the morning, and make an early start. I left him and went back to my cabin.

MY THIRD EFFORT FOR FREEDOM.

I MADE UP MY MIND that this would be a good chance for me to run away. I got my clothes, and put them in an old pair of saddlebags—two bags made of leather, connected with a strip of leather, and used when traveling horseback for the same purpose as a satchel is used in traveling in the cars. I took these bags, carried them about a half mile up the road, and hid them in a fence corner, where I could get them in the morning when I had started on my trip. Fryer's Point, the place to which I was to go, was about fifty miles from the farm. I started early in the morning, and, after I had gone twenty-five miles, I came to the farm of William McGee, a brother of the madam, and stopped to change horses. I found that William McGee was going, in the morning, down to old Master Jack's; so I took one of their horses, leaving mine to use in its place, went right to Fryer's Point, delivered the letters to a man there to carry to Helena, and got back to William McGee's farm that night. I made up my mind to go with William down to Panola, where madam was, to tell her about Boss being captured. The next morning, he started, and Gibson, his overseer and myself accompanied him. He questioned me about the capture of Boss, what the soldiers had done, etc., and I told him all I knew of the matter. "Well, Lou," he said, "why did you not bring us some whisky?" "I did bring a little with me," I said. He laughed, saying: "Oh, well, when we come to some clear water we will stop and have a drink." Then I said: "Mr. Smith will look for me tonight, but he won't see me. I am going to tell the madam that Boss is captured." "Hey, ho!" he said, "then you are running away." I replied: "Well I know Miss Sarah don't know Boss is in prison." We traveled on, all three of us, stopping at intervals to be refreshed. After two days, we arrived at Panola. Our journey was a tedious one. The streams were so swollen in places that we could hardly pass. The Tallehatchie we had to swim, and one of the men came near losing his horse and his life. The horses became tangled in a grape vine, as we were nearing the shore at which we aimed, and, the current being very swift, we were carried below the landing place; but, finally, we got safely ashore, McGee landing, and we following. Reaching Panola, wet and weary, I conveyed to madam the story of her husband's capture and imprisonment, a rumor of which had already reached her. The next morning was Christmas, and a number of the family had come to spend it together. They had heard that McGee was captured and in prison; but, now, as I told them every feature of the affair in detail, they grew excited and talked wildly about it. Among those who came were Dr. Dandridge and his wife, Blanton McGee and his wife, Tim Oliver and his wife. All these women were daughters of old Master Jack McGee, and sisters to the madam. Mrs. Farrington and old lady McGee were already there. These reunions on Christmas were a long established custom with them, but the pleasure of this one was sadly marred by the vicissitudes and calamities of the war. A shadow hung over all the family group. They asked me many questions about Boss, and, of course, I related all I knew.

After I had been there three days, they started me back with letters for Boss. When I left it was near night, and I was to stop over at Master Jack's farm fifteen miles away. It was expected that I would reach Fryer's Point on the third morning, thus allowing me three days to go sixty miles; but I could not make much headway, as the roads were so heavy. The understanding was that I was to deliver the letters to the same gentleman, at Fryer's, to whom I delivered the others, for forwarding to Boss at Helena. I was then to go straight to the farm at Boliver, and report to Smith, the overseer. But after I had got about four miles away, I concluded that I would not go back to the farm, but try to get to the Yankees. I knew I had disobeyed Smith by going down to the madam's to tell her about Boss, because he told me not to go when I spoke to him about it. And now if I went back I feared he would kill me; for I knew there would be no escape for me from being run into the bull ring, and that torture I could not think of enduring. I, therefore, stopped, and, taking the bridle and saddle from the horse, hid them in the corner of a fence in a cornfield. Then I went into the woods. The papers which I had were in the saddlebag safe. The place where I stayed in the daytime was in a large shuck-pen—a pen built in the field to feed stock from, in the winter time. This pen was on Dr. Dandridge's farm; and the second night I worked my way up near the house. Knowing all the servants, I was watching a chance to send word to the coachman, Alfred Dandridge, that I wanted him to tell my wife that I was not gone. I went down to his cabin, in the quarters; and, after a short time he came. I was badly scared, and my heart was heavy and sore; but he spoke comfortingly to me, and I was cheered, somewhat, especially when he promised to see Matilda, and tell her of my whereabouts. He gave me some food, and hid me away for the night in his house. I kept close all the next day; and, at night, when all was still, Alfred and I crept out, and went to old Master Jack's. The distance was not great, and we soon covered it. Alfred went in and told my wife that I was outside and wanted to see her. She came out, and was so frightened and nervous that she commenced sobbing and crying, and almost fainted when I told her, in low tones, that I was going to try to get to Memphis, and that Alfred was helping to plan a way to this end. The rebels occupied both roads leading to Memphis, and I was puzzled to know how to reach the city without coming in contact with them. Two days after I had talked with my wife, the rebel troops who were camped on the Holly Springs road left for some other point. My friend Alfred found this out, and came and told me the encouraging news. The following night I went to old Master Jack's and told my wife that the way now seemed clear, and that I was going at once. I was bent on freedom, and would try for it again. I urged my wife not to grieve, and endeavored to encourage her by saying that I would return for her, as soon as possible, should I succeed in getting to a land freedom. After many tears and blessings, we parted, and I left, Uncle Alfred going with me some three miles, as I was not acquainted with the road. When he left me I went on alone with gloomy forebodings, but resolved to do my best in this hazardous undertaking, whatever might happen. The road passed over hills and through swamps, and I found the traveling very wearisome. I had traveled some hours, and thought I was doing well; when, about one o'clock in the night, I came up out of a long swamp, and, reaching the top of a hill, I stopped for a moment's rest, raising myself to an erect position from that of walking, inclined by reason of weariness and the weight of the saddle-bags thrown across my shoulders. The weather was bad, a heavy mist had come up, and it was so dark that I could hardly see my way. As I started on, a soldier yelled at me from the mist: "Halt! advance and give the countersign." I stopped immediately, almost scared out of my wits. "Come right up here," said the soldier, "or I'll blow you into eternity." I saw at once he was a rebel soldier. I knew not what to do. This place where I was halted was Nelson's farm, and the house was held as head-quarters for a company of rebel soldiers, known as bushwhackers. While they belonged to the rebel army, they were, in a measure, independent of its regulations and discipline, kept back in the woods, ready for any depredation upon the property of unionists—any outrage upon their persons. The soldier who had halted me took me up to the house, and all began to question me. I told them that I had been sent on an errand, and that I had lost my way. The next morning I was taken about a mile away down in the swamp, over hills and through winding paths, till at last we came to the regular rebel camp. I was in great fear and thought my end had come. Here they began to question me again—the captain taking the lead; but I still stuck to my story that I had been sent on an errand, and had lost my way. I knew that this was my only chance. They tried to make me say that I had come from the Yankees, as they were in camp near Holly Springs. They thought the Yankees had sent me out as a spy; but I said the same as at first—that I had lost my way. A soldier

standing by said: "Oh! we will make you talk better than that;" and step-
ping back to his horse, he took a sea grass halter, and said: "I'll hang
you." There was a law or regulation of the rebel government directing
or authorizing the hanging of any slave caught running away; and this
fellow was going to carry it out to the letter. I talked and pleaded for my
life. My feelings were indescribable. God only knows what they were.
Dr. Carter, one of the soldiers, who knew me and the entire McGee
family, spoke up and said: "You had better let me go and tell Mr. Jack
McGee about him." The captain agreed to this, and the doctor went.
The following day, Old Jack came, and steadily refused to consent to
my being hung. He said: "I know Edmund would not have him hung-
ung. He is too valuable-aluable. No, no! we will put him in jail and feed
him on bread and water—too valuable a nigger to be hung-ung."

They tried again to make me say that I was with the Yankees. They
whipped me a while, then questioned me again. The dog-wood switches
that they used stung me terribly. They were commonly used in Mississippi for flogging slaves—one of the refinements of the cruelty of the institution of slavery. I refused to say anything different from what I had
said; but when they had finished whipping me I was so sore I could
hardly move. They made up their minds to put me in jail at Panola,
twenty-two miles away, to be fed on bread and water. The next day was
Sunday, and all arrangements having been made for taking me to the
place appointed for those whose crime was a too great love for personal
freedom, they started with me, passing on the way Old Master Jack's,
where they halted to let him know that his advice respecting me was to
be carried out. The old man called to my wife: "Come out and see
Louis." Some one had told her that they were going to hang me; and I
shall never forget her looks as she came out in the road to bid me good-
by. One of the soldiers was softened by her agony, and whispered to her:
"Don't cry, aunty, we are not going to hang him—we will only put him
in jail." I saw this changed my wife's looks in a minute. I said a few words
to her, and, with a prayer for God's blessing on us both, we parted, and
they moved on. After we had gone about seven miles, we met two soldiers, who belonged to the regiment at Nelson. They said: "Hello!
where you going with that [n]igger?" The two men in charge of me
replied: "We are going to take [h]im to Panola jail." "Why," said one of
the soldiers, "there is no jail there; the Yanks passed through and pulled
down the doors and windows of the jail, and let all the prisoners out."

This caused a stop; and a council of war was held in the fence corner, the result of which was a decision to take me back to old Jack McGee's. After we had gotten back there, they took me and gave me another flogging to satisfy the madam. I was never so lacerated before. I could hardly walk, so sore and weak was I. The law was given me that if ever I was caught out in the public road again, by any soldier, I was to be shot. Monday morning I was sent to the field to plow; and, though I was very stiff and my flesh seemed sore to the bone, my skin drawn and shriveled as if dead, I had, at least, to make the attempt to work. To have said: "Master, I am too sore to work," would only have gotten me another whipping. So I obeyed without a word.

REBELS BURN THEIR COTTON.

THE CAPTURE OF MEMPHIS by the Union troops closed the principal cotton market of the country, and there was, as a consequence, an immense accumulation of the product in the hands of the farmers of that region. They were, therefore, compelled to resort to temporary expedients for its protection from the elements. Old Master Jack had his piled up in a long rick, and shelters built over it. Other farmers did the same. As cotton was almost the only source of revenue for the farmers, and as there was now no opportunity of getting it to market, there was such a dearth of money as had seldom, if ever, been known, and a corresponding dearth of those necessaries of life which money was the only means of procuring. The accumulations of our family in this product were very great. While the rebel farmers were waiting for a time when they could turn their stores of this valuable article into money, proclamation was issued by the rebel government that all the owners of cotton that had it stored on their farms must prepare to have it burned. Hundreds of rebel soldiers marched to every section of Mississippi that they could reach, and applied the torch to these cotton ricks. The destruction was enormous. This was to prevent the cotton from falling into the hands of the Unionists. Jeff Davis said to his deluded followers that it was better for them to destroy this property than to risk its coming into the possession of their enemies, since that would equally impoverish themselves, while it might result to the pecuniary advantage of those with whom they were at war. I know that it was a terrible sight when our cotton was burned. Hundreds of bales were consumed, and it seemed like a wholly unnecessary destruction of property, and, therefore, unwise as a war measure. Many were sorry that they had acquiesced in the policy, as it cost them thousands of dollars, and made many poor. They thought that possibly their farms might have escaped the visits of the Union soldiers, and the property, so much needed, been saved in whole or in part. They reasoned, and reasoned correctly, that their condition would in no sense have been worse if their cotton had not been burned by their own soldiers, but might have been much better in many cases, without any real detriment to the rebel cause. The sacrifice of the property of their own people by the rebel authorities, was evidence of the desperation of the condition of the rebellion, and was so regarded by not a few at that time. Those were terrible days. One could see anxiety written on every face among the whites. The slaves even looked worried at times, though the war meant so much to them, as they were always looking forward to freedom, at its close, if the Union troops were successful.

MY FOURTH RUNAWAY TRIP.

AFTER I HAD BEEN working on the farm about two months, and had thoroughly talked the matter over with Alfred Dandridge, we planned to make a careful and persistent effort to escape from the land of bondage. We thought that as others, here and there, all through the neighborhood, were going, we would make trial of it. My wife and I were at old Master Jacks; and, after we had consulted with Alfred and Lydia, his wife, we all concluded to go at once. Alfred had been a teamster for Dandridge for many years, and was familiar with the road, as he had hauled cotton into Memphis for his master for so long a time he could hardly tell when he began. Matt Dandridge was a fellow servant, belonging to the same man, and both had, as was not unusual, taken their master's name, or, rather, were known by it. Matt had learned of our purpose to run away, and concluded to join our party. So one night, when all was still, we started. Uncle Alfred, as I always called him, was to be our leader. He was older than any of the rest of us, and had had a good deal of experience; we, therefore, all looked to him—in fact, we relied entirely upon him. After we had traveled about twelve miles, we came to a swamp, called Hicke-Halley. Here we stopped, as day was dawning, and settled down for the day, as we could travel only in the night, lest we should be seen and caught. We were wet—our clothes soaked through from the heavy dew. We had to travel through corn fields, cotton patches, oat fields and underbrush, not daring to take the main road. This is why we were so wet. Uncle Alfred traveled wholly by the stars—they were his guide. He knew by looking at them the four cardinal points of the compass. Many old slaves were guided in this way when traveling in the night, and some could tell the time of night by the position of the stars. We stayed in Hicke-Halley all day, and in the evening, when it was dark enough, we started on again, Uncle Alfred offering up a prayer to God to guide us safely through. Cold Water was our next stopping place, and here a difficulty rose before us that made us fearful. We had nothing to wear but what we had on, and not much of that, so had small space for carrying anything, and, therefore, had brought with us only a little bite to eat. As we had lived on this small provision for a day, there was now but little left for our increasing wants; and the difficulty of securing anything from the houses without danger of detection was almost insurmountable. But we felt encouraged as we thought of what we were striving for, and sped on our way. But the way was hard, for sometimes we got completely stuck in brier patches, and had to turn and go back, in order to find a way out. Old logs and drift-wood, that had been piled up year after year, were other obstacles in our way; and one can imagine how hard it was to make our way through such a mass of brush and forest by the dim light of the stars as they struggled through the dense branches of the trees. We stumbled on, however, as best we could, each fearful, yet silently praying for guidance and help. When within four or five miles of Cold Water, Uncle Alfred stopped [and] cautioned us not to speak above a whisper, as the rebel troops were camped on both sides of us. We were in a swamp between the two roads, gradually working our way through to the river, as we could not go on either of the roads for fear of detection. At the bridges, where these roads crossed the river, there were rebel camps, and it was useless for us to think of crossing either. We, therefore, worked our way carefully through the thicket that we were in until we came within sight of the river. Then Uncle Alfred went ahead, creeping a few steps, then stopping to see if the river was clear of soldiers. From this point it was some two and a half miles to the bridges, each way; and it was our idea that if we could cross here without being seen by the soldiers, we would be all right. Uncle Alfred came back to us and told us that he thought the way was clear. "I can not hear a sound," said he, "so let us go on."

We followed the river down until we came to a place where we could cross. Here we found some driftwood—an old tree had been blown down, nearly across the river, leaving a space of about twenty feet. Over this natural bridge we crept to the open space which we waded, the water being up to our knees; but we did not mind this. There was no talking above a whisper, for fear of being heard by the soldiers. Daylight had begun to dawn, and we felt good that we had succeeded thus far. We went on quietly until we got entirely out of the swamp and reached some hills. The woods were on each side of us and still thick; so we stopped here, on the side of a hill, where the sun shone brightly on us, expecting to rest for the day. Our clothes had already become quite dry from the sunshine; and, so far, we felt all right. Alfred and I had made a turn around the place, listening to see if we could hear any noise, or see any trace of soldiers; but we discovered no trace of them, and went back to our stopping place. I had been asleep and some of the others were still asleep, when suddenly I heard the yelp of bloodhounds in the distance. It seemed quite far away at first, but the sound came nearer and nearer, and then we heard men yelling. We knew now that they were on our trail, and became so frightened that we all leaped to our feet, and were about to run, when Uncle Alfred said: "Stop children, let me oil you feet." He had with him a bottle of ointment made of turpentine and onions, a preparation used to throw hounds off a trail. All stopped; and the women, having their feet anointed first, started off, Uncle Alfred telling them to run in different directions. He and I were the last to start. Alfred said: "Don't let the bushes touch you;" at the same time he ran through the bushes with such a rattling noise one could have heard him a great distance. He wore one of those old fashioned oil cloth coats made in Virginia; and, as he ran, the bushes, striking against the coat, made a noise like the beating of a tin board with sticks. The funny part of it was that, having cautioned us to be careful about noise, he made more than all of us. By this time the woods were resounding with the yelping of the hounds and the cries of their masters. The hounds numbered some fourteen. The men howled and cheered in concert with the brutes, for they knew that they were on the right trail, and it would be but a short time before they caught us all. I had gotten further away than any of them. Having run about a mile, I came to a farm, and started across an open field, hoping to reach a wood beyond, where I might conceal myself. Before I was half way across the field, on looking back, I saw the dogs coming over the fence, and knowing there was no chance of my getting to the woods, I turned around, and ran back to a persimmon tree, and just had time to run up one of the branches when the dogs came upon the ground. I looked and saw the men, Williams the nigger-catcher, and Dr. Henry and Charles Dandridge. As soon as Williams rode up, he told me to come down, but I was so frightened I began to cry, yet came down trembling. The dogs laid hold of me at once, tearing my clothes and biting my flesh. Dr. Dandridge was just riding up, and seeing what was happening, yelled out to Williams: "I thought your dogs didn't bite." "Oh! well," said Williams, 'he ain't hurt—we've got to let 'em bite a little."

They took us all back to the fence where I crossed over, all the others having been caught. Our hearts were filled with dismay. All looked as if they were condemned to be hung. We knew not what was to be done with us. The women were pitiful to see, crying and moaning—all courage utterly gone. They started back with us to Old Master Jack's, at Panola, and we stopped for the night at a small farm house. The old woman who kept it said, tauntingly: "You niggers going to the Yankees? You all ought to be killed." We started on the following morning, and got back home at one o'clock in the afternoon. All of us were whipped. All the members of the family were very angry. Old Lady Jack McGee was so enraged that she said to my wife: "I thought you were a Christian. You'll never see your God." She seemed to think that because Matilda had sought freedom she had committed a great sin.

INCIDENTS.

EVER SINCE THE BEGINNING of the war, and the slaves had heard that possibly they might some time be free, they seemed unspeakably happy. They were afraid to let the masters know that they ever thought of such a thing, and they never dreamed of speaking about it except among themselves. They were a happy race, poor souls! notwithstanding their downtrodden condition. They would laugh and chat about freedom in their cabins; and many a little rhyme about it originated among them, and was softly sung over their work. I remember a song that Aunt Kitty, the cook at Master Jack's, used to sing. It ran something like this:

There'll be no more talk about Monday, by and by,
But every day will be Sunday, by and by.

The old woman was singing, or rather humming, it one day, and old lady McGee heard her. She was busy getting her dinner, and I suppose never realized she was singing such an incendiary piece, when old Mrs. McGee broke in upon her: "Don't think you are going to be free; you darkies were made by God and ordained to wait upon us." Those passages of Scripture which refer to master and servants were always cited to us when we heard the Word preached; and they were interpreted as meaning that the relation of master and slave was right and proper— that they were rightly the masters and we the slaves.

I remember, not long after Jeff Davis had been elected president of the Confederacy, that I happened to hear old Master Jack talking to some of the members of the family about the war, etc. All at once the old man broke out: "And what do you think! that rascal, Abraham Lincoln, has called for 300,000 more men. What is Jeff Davis doin'-doin'?" He talked on, and seemed so angry that he gave no one a chance to answer: "Jeff Davis is a grand rascal-rascal," said he, "he ought to go into the field himself." At first all the Southerners were jubilant over Davis; but as they were losing so, and the Unionists gaining, they grew angry and denounced him oftentimes in unsparing terms.

UNION RAID AT MASTER'S FARM.

DURING THE TIME THE Union headquarters were at Helena, a Union gun-boat came down the river as far as Boliva, and stopped at Miles McGee's. The soldiers made a raid through the farm, taking chickens, turkeys, meat and everything that they could lay hands on. During this raid Miles McGee came out of the house with a gun, and shot the commanding officer of the party. He became alarmed over what he had done, and hid in the cabin of one of the servants. He never came near the house. The Union soldiers came three different times to catch him, but never succeeded. The last time they came, he made for the canebrake, and hid himself there until they were gone. But though he had escaped their righteous vengeance, he became so nervous that he left his hiding place in the canebraker, and went to Atlanta, Ga., and staid there among friends until things became more quiet. At last wearying of this, he determined to return to old Master Jack's, but not to his own home. Word had been received of his coming, and great preparations were made for his reception. After he had started on his return, he was taken ill on the train, and was left at a small town called Jackson, where he soon died.

I drove the family to the depot upon the day of his expected arrival, and as the train came in, the women waved their handkerchiefs; and, when the conductor stepped off, they asked him if Mr. McGee was aboard. He said no—"I have his remains." The scene that followed, I can not describe—such wailing and screaming! I could not but feel sad, even though they had treated me so meanly, causing the death of my children, and separating me from my wife. Their grief was indeed great. The sad news was conveyed to his mother, old Mrs. Jack McGee, at the house by an advance messenger, and we soon followed with the body. He was the favorite son of his mother, and her grief was very great. But for his wanton shooting of the Union officer, he would probably not have met his death as he did.

UNION SOLDIERS PASS THE PANOLA HOME.

ONE WINTER NIGHT, WHILE I was at old Master Jack's, I was awakened by a rumbling noise like that of heavy wagons, which continued steadily and so long a time that I finally concluded it must be an army passing, and such I found to be the case, upon getting up and venturing out, the rumbling which had awakened me being caused by the passing artillery.

I was afraid to go out straight to the soldiers, but would take a few steps at a time, then stop and listen behind a tree or the shrubbery. All seemed quiet—there was no talking. I had listened about twenty minutes when there seemed to be a halt at the creek, some distance from the house. Soon afterwards I heard the command given: "Forward!" I at once made up my mind that they were Yankee soldiers. I got on my knees and crawled to the fence, not daring to go openly, fearing that they might hear or see me and shoot, supposing me to be a spy. I went back into the house and told my wife that they were Yankees who had just passed. "Uncle George," said I, "this would be a good time for us to go." "Oh, no," said he, "we are not quite ready." Uncle George's cabin was where my wife and I stayed while at old Master Jack's. In the morning I was to carry a parcel to Como, a place not far from home, to Mr. James McGee, who was in the rebel army. It was not quite daylight when I made ready to go on my trip, for I was anxious to find out more about the soldiers. Going to the stable and saddling my horse, I mounted and rode out to the big gate leading to the main road, just as day was dawning. As I dismounted to open the gate, some soldiers were passing and an officer sung out to me, "Hello! which way are you going." I said "to Como, to carry this parcel of clothing to my young master in the war." "You have a fine horse," said the officer, "I guess I will exchange horses with you." He took my package of clothing and some letters which I had to mail and my horse, leaving me his, which was a very poor animal. I was badly scared at this performance, fearing that I would be severely whipped for the loss of the horse and package. Yet how could I help it? We knew nothing but to serve a white man, no matter what he asked or commanded. As a matter of course, I did not go to Como, as I had nothing to take—the officer had everything, but went back to the cabin. I supposed that the soldiers had all passed; but in about half an hour Aunt Kitty, on looking out of her cabin window, exclaimed: "My God! just look at the soldiers!" The yard was covered with the blue coats. Another venerable slave said: "My Lord! de year of jubilee am come." During the excitement I ran to the big house, and told the madam that the Yankees were there, and had taken my horse and everything I had. Old Master Jack had heard the news, but was not able to come out. He had arisen, but, when he knew of the presence of the Yankees, he went back to bed, calling for Kitty to get him a mush poultice. "Tell Kitty-ity-ity to get me a mush poultice-oltice." It was customary, after the beginning of the war, for him to take sick, and call for a poultice to be put upon his stomach whenever he heard of the Yankees being near. He and many like him were especially valorous only when the blue coats were far away. The soldiers went into the dairy and drank all the milk, helped themselves to butter, cheese, meat, bread and everything in sight which they wanted. Nothing was said to them by the white folks, but the slaves were glad, and whispered to each other: "Ah! we's goin' to be free." Old Master Jack, lying on his couch would ask every little while: "Where are they? Are they gone?" After they had all left the premises, he said: "My God! I can't stand it. Them devils-evils are just goin' through the country destroyin' everything." I was sent down to get Uncle Peter for old master, and when Peter came up the old man asked: "Well, did any of the servants go away? And, sir, them devils took Louis' horse and the clothes he had for his young master."

HIDING VALUABLES FROM THE YANKEES.

RIGHT AFTER THIS THE McGees commenced planning to put away their valuables, to keep them from the Union soldiers. All the servants had to fill up their bed-ticks with fine gin cotton—the lint part—for safekeeping. Great boxes and barrels were packed full of their best things, and put into the cellar, under the house. It was not exactly a cellar, but a large shallow excavation, which held a great deal. We put all the solid silver ware, such as cake baskets, trays, spoons, forks, dishes, etc., in boxes, and buried them under the hen house. Great packages of the finest clothing I had to make up, and these were given in charge of certain servants whose duty it was to run into the big house and get them, whenever they heard that the Yankees were coming, and take them to their cabins. This was a shrewd arrangement, for the soldiers never went into the cabins to get anything. When the soldiers had passed, these packages were taken back to the house. It speaks well for the honesty and faithfulness of the slaves that such trusts could be devolved upon them, notwithstanding all the cruelties inflicted upon them by their masters.

DEATH TO RUNAWAY SLAVES.

IT WAS ABOUT THIS time, that the law or regulation of the rebel government was promulgated, authorizing or directing the shooting or hanging of any slave caught trying to get away to the Union army. This barbarous law was carried out in many cases, for every little while we would hear of some slave who was caught running away, and hung or shot. A slave belonging to Boss, ran away, and got safely within the Union lines; but he returned to get his sister. They both got away from the house, but had gone only a few miles, when William McGee overtook them, and shot the man dead. William boasted of this, but told Uncle Peter, the foreman, that he never wanted it mentioned.

SLAVES HUNG AND LEFT TO ROT AS A WARNING.

TWO SLAVES BELONGING TO one Wallace, one of our nearest neighbors, had tried to escape to the Union soldiers, but were caught, brought back and hung. All of our servants were called up, told every detail of the runaway and capture of the poor creatures and their shocking murder, and then compelled to go and see them where they hung. I never shall forget the horror of the scene—it was sickening.

The bodies hung at the roadside, where the execution took place, until the blue flies literally swarmed around them, and the stench was fearful. This barbarous spectacle was for the purpose of showing the passing slaves what would be the fate of those caught in the attempt to escape, and to secure the circulation of the details of the awful affair among them, throughout all the neighborhood. It is difficult at this day for those not familiar with the atrocities of the institution of slavery to believe that such scenes could ever have been witnessed in this or any other civilized land, as a result simply of a human being's effort to reach a portion of the country, where the freedom of which it was said to be the home, could be enjoyed without molestation. Yet such was the horrible truth in not one case alone, but in many, as I know only too well.

RUNAWAY SLAVE CAUGHT AND WHIPPED.

ONE DAY WHILE I WAS waiting at dinner, some of the children from the slave quarters came running into the house, and said to old Master Jack: "Uncle John is going away—he is down to the creek." He had been put in the carpenter shop, fastened in the stocks, but by some means he had gotten the stocks off his feet, and got lose. All in the house immediately got up and ran out. Old master told me to run and catch the runaway. I did not like to do it, but had to obey. Old master and I ran in pursuit, and soon overtook him. He could not run, as the stocks were still on his arms and neck. We brought him back, and he was "staked out"—that is, four stakes were driven into the ground, the arms tied to two and the legs to the other two. He was then paddled with the whipping paddle upon the bottom of his feet, by old Master Jack, until blood blisters arose, when he took his knife and opened them. I was then sent for salt and water, and the bruises of the suffering chattel were washed as usual in the stinging brine.

A HOME GUARD ACCIDENTALLY SHOOTS HIMSELF.

AFTER THE CAPTURE OF Memphis by the Union forces, the soldiers were in the habit of making raids into the surrounding country. These were a source of alarm and anxiety among the people, and they were constantly on the watch to defend their property and themselves, as best they could. One day Dr. Charles Dandridge went over to one of our neighbors, Mr. Bobor's, to practice shooting, and to see if he had heard anything new about the war. It was the custom of the home guards to meet weekly, and practice with their fire-arms, in order to be the better prepared, as they pretended, for any sudden incursion of the now dreaded Yankee. Mr. Bobor had gotten a Yankee pistol from some friend, who was in the army, and Dr. Charles wanted to see and try it. It was shown him, and its workings explained. He took it and began shooting, and in showing the other men how quickly he could shoot a Yankee, and mount his horse, he accidentally shot himself under the short rib near his heart, and fell to the ground. All the men came running to him, picked him up and carried him into the house, immediately sending word to Mrs. Dandridge and Master Jack McGee, his father-in-law. The boys came hurrying in, and told us what had happened. I hitched up and drove Boss over to Mr. Bobor's. We found the wounded man rapidly sinking; and when, a little later, his wife came, he could not speak—only clasped her hand. He died that night, and we carried his body to the home, which so short a time before, he had left in health and high spirits.

No casket was to be had—everything of that kind had been consumed or shut out by the war. Accordingly two slaves were ordered to make a coffin, which they did, using plain boards. It was then covered with black alpaca from a dress of the madam, and lined with the cloth from Mrs. Dandridge's opera cloak. The regular material used for these purposes was not to be had. By the time the coffin was ready, the body was so bloated, that it could not be got into it. Resort was then had to a plain box, and in this the body of another of the stricken family group was laid away. At the suggestion of old Master Jack, the coffin was put up in the carriage house, for safe keeping, he saying it would do for him to be buried in. Sorrow had come to this family with such crushing force, that their former pride and boastful spirit had given place to utter dejection.

SUBSTITUTES FOR COFFEE.

DURING THE WAR EVERYTHING was scarce and dear, and substitutes were devised for many of those things which had formerly been regarded as the necessaries of life. Sweet potatoes were peeled, then cut in small pieces and put out in the sun to dry. They were then used as a substitute for coffee, when that article became so scarce, toward the close of the war. Great quantities of this preparation were used. Okra was another substitute for coffee. It was dried in the pod, then the seeds shelled out, and these were dried again and prepared something as the coffee is. This made a delicious drink when served with cream, being very rich and pleasant to the taste. Quinine was a medicine that had been of almost universal use in the south; yet it became so scarce that it was sold at seven dollars a bottle, and could not often be had at that price. Lemon leaves were used as a substitute in cases of chills and fever. The leaves were made into a tea, and given to the patient hot, to produce perspiration. During an attack of chills, I was treated in this manner to some advantage. At any rate I got well, which cannot always be said of all methods of treatment.

CHAPTER IV.
REBELLION WEAKENING—SLAVES' HOPES STRENGTHENING.
M'GEES SLAVES TAKEN TO ALABAMA.

WHILE I WAS ABSENT on my last runaway trip, the Yankees had made a raid through Panola; and our people had become greatly frightened. As soon as they had got back with me and my fellow runaways, they assembled a gang of slaves for the purpose of taking them to Atlanta, Ga., to get them out of the reach of the Union soldiers. Among the slaves selected for the transfer were myself, my wife Matilda, and the seamstress. The others all belonged to Dr. Dandridge and Blanton McGee. Both the Drs. Dandridge went with us to Atlanta. We traveled across the country until we came to Demopolis, Alabama, where we found Boss camped on the bank of the Tombigbee River with all the farm slaves from Bolivar county. This was the first time I had seen Boss since he was captured and taken to Helena. As my wife and I were the only ones in the gang who belonged to Boss, we left those with whom we had come and joined his gang. We all then went aboard a boat and were taken to the salt works, situated on the Tombigbee, ninety miles from Mobile. These salt works belonged to the rebel government. The first president of the works was Mr. Woolsey, of Salem, Alabama. During Mr. Woolsey's term, the first part of 1864, when we had been there some time, he wrote to Boss asking if he would sell myself and wife, and offering $3,000 for both of us. Boss was indignant at this and curtly refused. My wife acted as cook at the salt works, in the headquarters for the president, managers and clerks. Mr. Woolsey was delighted with her cooking; her bread and rolls, he said, could not be surpassed.

M'GEE'S GREAT SCHEME.

WHEN THE ELECTION OF officers of the works came off in the fall, Mr. Gallatin McGee was chosen president. Boss then hired us all, about 100 in number, to labor in these works, but he, of course, received all the revenue. The work assigned me was that of butler at headquarters, and my wife was cook. Both women and children, as well as men, were employed in these works. After some months labor here, soon after Gallatin McGee became president, Matilda and I were removed to the Montgomery headquarters, where we remained until nearly Christmas. A few days before that time, Boss came to Montgomery and arranged for us to meet him in Mobile. We started at the appointed time, reached the city in the morning and I went directly to the hotel where he told me he would be. I found him at once, and he informed me all about his plans for the future, and what he expected to accomplish. He had purchased an island in the bay, a little way from Mobile, where he had decided to establish salt works of his own. All the brick and lumber for the buildings had been carried there, and work upon them was to be commenced immediately after Christmas. He intended to make a home for the family on the island; and, as soon as he could complete the works, to remove all his hands from the government works to his own. He was very enthusiastic over this scheme, claiming that he would make far more money by it than he was then receiving from hiring out his slaves. He told me that he would remain in Mobile two or three days and would go to Panola to spend the holidays, after which he intended to bring all the family to Mobile, and remain there until the island was in readiness to be occupied. There was to be a general break up of the old home, and the beginning of a new manner of life. I stayed in his room at the hotel all the forenoon, listening to his plans; then I went back where my wife was stopping. As I left his room, he said: "Lou," as he always called me, "I will see you and Matilda at the boat this evening." We went to the boat at the appointed time and saw the Boss, but he did not come near us. As the boat was about to put off, I looked and saw him walking up and down the levee, apparently much excited, running his hands nervously through his hair—a habit common to him when he was worried. He seemed greatly distressed. The military situation troubled him, for the Union army had conquered nearly everything; and the fact now stared him in the face that he would soon lose his slaves. He never dreamed in the beginning of the war that the Unionists would conquer, and that the slaves would be freed; but now he saw that not only all his wealth in the bodies and souls of men was slipping away from him, but that much, if not all of the gain which these chattels had brought him was likely to "take wings and fly away."

M'GEE'S DEATH.

WE RETURNED TO THE salt works the morning after leaving Mobile. Boss remained two days in Mobile, and then started for Panola, the home of his father-in-law; but, on his way, he was taken sick, having contracted a heavy cold which ran into pneumonia, and he lasted only a short time, dying on New Year's day. He had taken cold in bringing the slaves from Bolivar over the river on barges. The river was overflowed about fifty miles out, and the only way he could get the slaves across was by using large barges made of logs. They were several days floating down in this way, before he could get out to the railroad at Jackson, Miss., where he transferred them to the cars. This was too much of an exposure and it killed him.

After Boss died all the plans were changed. Col. Hunting, son-in-law of old Master Jack, came down to the salt works and hired us all out there for another year. This was the beginning of the year 1865. Of master's plans concerning the island and his proposed salt works the family knew little, for they questioned me closely as to what he told me of the matter. What he spent on the island in lumber, brick, etc., was lost as they knew nothing of the particulars of the expenditure. The madam remained at her fathers, and the slaves at the works.

I MAKE SOME MONEY.

AS I WAS HERE for another year, acting as butler, thought I would try and see if I could not make some money for myself. I asked Mr. Brooks, the manager of the works, if he could get me some tobacco by sending to Mobile for it. He said he could; and on the fourth day thereafter, in the evening, it came. I was anxious to get it the same evening, but Mr. Brooks said: "Oh! I guess you had better wait until morning, then when you finish your work come down to the office and get it—you will then have more time to see the boys in the works." In the morning I was up early, and after doing my morning work I was off to Brooks' office. When I went in he said: "There it is under the table." The package was so small I felt disappointed—a hundred dollars worth ought to be more, said I to myself; but I took it, and went out among the men. I thought I would try to sell it at five dollars a plug, and if I could not sell it at that I would take four dollars. I must make something, for I had borrowed the money to buy it with; and I saw that to clear anything on it, I must at least get four dollars a plug. The money which I had borrowed was from three fellow servants, who had been fortunate in earning some little time and had saved their money. The first man I met in the works bought two plugs, at five dollars each; and after I had been there about an hour all was sold. So I went back with a light heart. Mr. Brooks said to me at dinner: "Well, how did you get along with your tobacco?" "I did very well," I said, "the only trouble was I did not have enough. I sold it for $180." "Well," said he, "if you did, you made more clear money than the works here. How much a plug did you sell it for?" at the same time drawing out his pencil and commencing to figure it up. "I had thirty-six plugs," said I, "and I sold them for five dollars a plug." Nothing more was said just then, but after dinner Brooks and two of the clerks went out on the veranda to smoke. When they were in a good way smoking, Brooks slipped into the dining room, and said: "Well, that was fine; you got five dollars a plug for the tobacco?" "Oh, yes!" I said, "tobacco is scarce, and they were hungry for it; it went like hot cakes— the price was not questioned, I sold at once." "What is the prospect for selling more?" he asked. "Will you sell it for half the profit if I furnish the tobacco?" I said "yes." So he sent the same day for a box of tobacco—about five hundred plugs. When the tobacco came the box was sawed in two and one-half sent up to my room. I put some fellows out as agents to sell for me—Uncle Hudson, who took care of the horses and mules at the works; John at the hospital; William, head chopper, among the 100 men in the woods. Each brought in from $40.00 to $50.00 every two or three days, and took another supply.

Sometimes, when I had finished my work in the afternoon, I would get an old pony and go around through the neighborhood and sell four or five plugs. It was a mystery to the servants how I got the tobacco; but I did not let on that Brooks was backing me. In two weeks we had taken in $1,600.00, and I was happy as I could be. Brooks was a fine fellow— a Northerner by birth, and did just what he said he would. I received one-half of the money. Of course this was all rebel money, but I was sharp, and bought up all the silver I could find. Just as we got on the other half of the box, Brooks received word that the Yankees were coming, and to send all the hands to their masters. I was glad that I had made some money, knowing that I would need it if I gained my freedom, which I now knew was quite probable, as the Union forces were gaining ground everywhere. But the message ended my moneymaking, and I prepared to go home to Panola.

GOING BACK TO PANOLA.

Mr. Brooks fixed the return papers so that my wife and I could leave the party of slaves at Demopolis, and go on thence to Panola by rail, to convey the news to madam that all hands were coming home; that the Yankees were expected to capture the salt works within a short time. At Jackson, some seven miles from the salt works, we were delayed over night by reason of lack of facilities for crossing the Tombigbee River. The report that the Yankees were coming through had created a panic among the white people; and hundreds, fleeing from their homes, had gathered at the river, waiting and clamoring for an opportunity to cross. Though slaves were property, and valuable on that account, the whites seemed to think that their own lives were in danger, and to be protected first. They therefore took precedence of us. In the morning about seven o'clock a steamer was seen coming at a distance; but it could not be discovered at once just what the character of it was. The whites became alarmed. Some said: "The Yankees are coming." Other said: "It is a gun boat—they will surely fire on us." But as the boat drew near the people saw that there was nothing to fear—it was only the regular passenger boat. Besides the hundreds of people, there were scores of wagons, filled with household goods to go over, and the passage was slow and tedious. We finally got across and traveled as far as Demopolis, where Matilda and I left the other slaves, and took a train and went on to Panola. I delivered the papers to the madam from Brooks, which told her all the particulars concerning the break up at the salt works. She sent wagons right away after the other slaves who were coming back on foot. They were not brought back to Panola; but were hired out to different farmers along the road home—some in Jackson, some in Granda and others in Panola town. These were all small towns in Mississippi. My wife and I went to work at old Master Jack's, I on the farm and my wife at her old duties in the house. We longed for freedom, but were content for the time with hoping and praying for the coming of the day when it should be realized. It was sad to see the changes that had come to the white folks. Sorrow had left its impress upon all and we felt it, notwithstanding all that we had suffered at their hands. Boss had willed the homestead in Memphis to Mrs Farrington, and she was getting ready to take possession. He had borrowed a great amount of money from her when he bought the island at Mobile; and the rapid coming on of the end of the rebellion destroyed all prospect of the success of his salt works scheme, even before his death, and really rendered him bankrupt. Hence the transfer of the Memphis property to her was the only way he could make good what he owed her. The madam now had no home, but was compelled to stay with her father, old Master Jack. She was sadly changed—did not appear like the same person. Her troubles and sorrows had crushed her former cruel and haughty spirit. Her mother had died a few months before, and then her husband had followed, dying suddenly and away from home. Then much of her property had been lost, and social pleasures and distinction were gone forever. Who shall say that the wrongs done her poor, helpless slaves were not avenged in this life? The last I knew of her she was still at her father's.

INCIDENTS.

A SERVANT WHO BELONGED to Dr. Dandridge ran away and got to Memphis just after it was captured by the Union soldiers. He was put into the army and was stationed at one of the entrances to the city. He was to halt all persons passing to or from the city, no difference who they were, and learn their names and their business. Young William McGee and his sister, Miss Cherry, one day went up to Memphis and, to their surprise, were halted by this former servant of their uncle. When they came home they were speaking of it to their father, and old Master Jack said:

"And you halted, did you?" "Why, yes," replied William, "we had to do it." "Well," said the old man, "I would have died-died before I would have done it. To think that a servant should have halted you, and one who has belonged to the family like Anderson!" This old man, notwithstanding all his boasting in the absence of immediate danger, was the verriest coward when danger was present; and if he had been in the place of young William, he would have halted with the greatest alacrity.

While at the salt works I had a little experience at nursing. A fellow slave was taken ill, and I was called on to care for him at night. I always liked this work; it was a pleasure to me to be in the sick room. Typhoid fever was a new case to me, but I remembered what instructions Boss had given me about it. I "pitched in" to do what I could; but the fever was so great he lasted only a few days.

MY FIFTH STRIKE FOR FREEDOM IS A SUCCESS.

WE HAD REMAINED AT old Jack's until June, 1865, and had tried to be content. The Union soldiers were still raiding all through that section. Every day some town would be taken, and the slaves would secretly rejoice. After we came back from Alabama we were held with a tighter rein than ever. We were not allowed to go outside of the premises. George Washington, a fellow servant, and Kitty, his wife, and I had talked considerably about the Yankees, and how we might get away. We knew it was our right to be free, for the proclamation had long been issued—yet they still held us. I did not talk much to my wife about going away, as she was always so afraid I would be killed, and did not want me to try any more to escape. But George, his wife and I continued to discuss the matter, whenever we had a chance. We knew that Memphis was headquarters for the Union troops, but how to reach it was the great question.

It was Sunday, and I had driven one portion of the family to church, and George the other. The family was now very large, as the madam and her family were there, in addition to Old Master Jack's, and all could not go in one carriage. On the way back, young William McGee came up through the farm, on horseback, a nearer way home from church, and encountered several servants belonging to some of the neighbors. He asked them what they were doing there, and if they had passes. To this last question all answered no. "Well," said he, "never come here again without having passes, all of you." At this they all quickly disappeared.

When Old Jack came home, Will told him what had passed; and he immediately called for George and Uncle Peter, the foreman, and told them that no one not belonging there was to come into the quarters without a pass; and any servant with a pass should be brought to the house, that the pass might be inspected. They thought, or feared, that if the servants were permitted to come together freely they might plan ways of escape, and communicate to each other what they knew about the war and the Yankees. George came out, and finding me, told me what they had said. "No slave from outside is to be allowed on the place," said he. I replied: "If we listen to them we shall be here until Christmas comes again." "What do you mean?" asked George. "I mean that now, today, is the time to make a start." So, late in the afternoon, during the servants' prayer meeting, of which I have heretofore spoken, we thought would be a good time to get away, as no one would be likely to see us. We talked with John Smith, another servant, and told him all about our plan, asking him not to say a word about our being gone until he was through feeding the stock. This would give us another hour to advance on our journey, as the feeding usually took about that time—from six o'-clock until seven. Our fear was that we might be overtaken by the blood-hounds; and, therefore, we wished to get as far away as possible before the white people knew we were gone. It was Sunday afternoon, June 26th, 1865, when George and I, having made ready for the start for the Union lines, went to bid our wives good-bye. I told my wife to cheer up, as I was coming again to get her. I said to Kitty, George's wife: "We are going, but look for us again. It will not be with us as with so many others, who have gone away, leaving their families and never returning for them. We will be here again." She looked up at me, smiling, and with a look of resolution, said: "I'll be ready." She was of a firm, daring nature—I did not fear to tell her all my plans. As my wife was so timid, I said as little as possible to her. George and I hurriedly said our farewells to our wives. The parting was heart-rending, for we knew the dangers were great, and the chances were almost even that we should not meet again. I could hardly leave my wife, her agitation and grief were so great. But we were off in a few moments. We crept through the orchard, passing through farm after farm until we struck the railroad, about seven miles from home. We followed this road until we reached Senatobia, about half past seven in the evening. We felt good, and, stopping all night, we started the next morning for Hernando, Miss., another small town, and reached there at two o'clock in the afternoon. The most of the bridges had been burned, by the troops, and there were no regular railroad trains. Fortunately, however, flat cars, drawn by horses were run over the road; and on a train of this kind we took passage. On several occasions, the passengers had to get out, and push the car over a bridge, as it was not made so horses could cross on it, the horses meantime being driven or led through the stream, and then hitched to the car again. After we had gone through this process repeatedly, we at last reached Memphis, arriving about seven o'clock Monday evening. The city was filled with slaves, from all over the south, who cheered and gave us a welcome. I could scarcely recognize Memphis, things were so changed. We met numbers of our fellow servants who had run away before us, when the war began. Tuesday and Wednesday we spent in making inquiries; and I visited our old home at McGee's station. But how different it was from what it had been when the McGees were there. All was changed. Thursday we went to see Col. Walker, a Union officer, who looked after the colored folks, and saw that they had their rights. When we reached his office we found it so filled with people, waiting to see him, that we were delayed about two hours, before we had an opportunity of speaking with him. When our turn came, we went in, and told him that we were citizens of Memphis until the fall of Fort Pillow and Donelson, when our master had run us off, with a hundred other slaves, into Mississippi, and thence to the salt works in Alabama. He questioned us as to where we lived in Memphis. I answered: "What is now headquarters of the Union forces was the home of master, Mr. Edmund McGee, who is now dead." After a few minutes, I said: "Colonel, we want protection to go back to Mississippi after our wives, who are still held as slaves." He replied: "You are both free men to go and come as you please." "Why," said I, "Colonel, if we go back to Mississippi they will shoot the gizzards out of us." "Well," said he, "I can not grant your request. I would be overrun with similar applications; but I will tell you what you can do. There are hundreds of just such men as you want, who would be glad of such a scout." We thanked him and left.

GOING BACK FOR OUR WIVES.

AFTER CAREFULLY CONSIDERING THE matter, we concluded to go back to Senatobia and see the captain of the Union troops there. The next day, Friday, we hired a two-horse wagon, and made preparations to start on our perilous undertaking Saturday morning. It was our hope to find some one at Senatobia to go with us to Panola, and protect us in the effort to bring away our wives. So, early in the morning, we set out. Our first stop was at Big Springs camping ground, where we made preparations for refreshing ourselves and spending the night. Just as we had finished building a fire, for cooking and keeping off the mosquitoes, two soldiers came riding up to the spring. "Hello," said one, "which way are you traveling?" "We are just from Memphis," said George. "Have you any whisky?" asked one of them. We replied "yes." "Will you give a fellow a horn?" We answered the question by handing them the bottle. While they were drinking, George and I stepped aside, and, after a few moments talk, we decided to put the question to them of going with us to get our wives. I asked: "Where are you from?" "Senatobia," replied one. We at once laid our cause before them, telling them what Col. Walker had said regarding our getting some one to go with us on our enterprise. They listened attentively, and when we had finished, one of them asked: "How much whisky have you?" George answered: "Two bottles." "What do you intend to do when you see the captain at Senatobia?" "Lay our complaint before him," said I. "Now my friend," said one of the soldiers, "I am afraid if you go to the captain you will be defeated. But I'll tell you what I'll do. Give my comrade and me one of your bottles of whisky, and we will put you on a straight track. The reason why I say this is that our captain has been sweetened by the rebel farmers. He is invited out to tea by them every evening. I know he will put you off. But I will write a note to some comrades of mine who, I know, will bring you out safe." We agreed at once to this proposition, and gave them the whisky. He wrote the note, and gave it to us, telling us to go to the last tent on the line in the camp, where we would find two boys to whom we should give it. "They are brave," said he, "and the only two I know of that can help you. If they are not there don't give the note to any one else, but wait till they come back, on Tuesday night. I feel satisfied that they will go and help you out." With these words, they rode off. George and I felt good over our prospects.

A HAZARDOUS TRIP.

THE NEXT MORNING WAS Sunday, and we started on, reaching Senatobia about eleven o'clock. We went into the camp, following the directions given us, to go to the last tent in the line; but, when we reached there, the soldiers were out. We lingered around the grounds a short time, then went back, and found them there. We gave them the note; and, after reading it, they simply asked us where we had stopped our wagon. I told them outside the village. "Go there," said one of them, "and remain until we come out to see you." Shortly they came out; and, after we had told them what we wanted, the distance to McGee's, which was about nineteen miles from Senatobia, and had given them such other information as they desired, they concluded that they would go. "We want to be back," said I, "before daylight Monday morning, be-cause we must not be seen on the road; for we are well known in that section, and, if discovered, would be captured and killed." "Well," said one of the soldiers, "we will have to go back to camp, and arrange to be excused from roll call this evening, before we can make the trip." They went back to camp; and, in about ten minutes they came out again say-ing: "All is right; we will go." We gave them each ten dollars; and promised, if they brought us out safely, to give each ten dollars more. It was now about half-past eleven o'clock. They had to go to camp, and slip their horses out cautiously, so as not to be seen by the captain. In half an hour we were on our way; and, after we had ridden some two miles, we were overtaken by the two soldiers. It was Sunday afternoon; and our having a wagon attracted much attention from the farmers as we passed along. They looked at us so sharply that George and I felt de-cidedly uneasy; yet we kept up courage and pressed steadily on. After a long and weary ride we reached old Master Jack's a little after sundown. The soldiers rode into the yard ahead of us, and the first person they met was a servant (Frank) at the woodpile. They said to him: "Go in and tell your master, Mr. McGee, to come out, we want to see him," at the same time asking for Louis' and George's wives. Young William McGee came out and the soldiers said to him: "We want feed for seventy-five head of horses." McGee said: "We have not got it." Just then George and I were coming up. We drove in at the gate, through the grove, and passed the woodpile where McGee and the soldiers were talking. McGee had just replied: "We have not got that much feed to spare—we are almost out." "Well," said the soldiers, "we must have it," and they followed on right after the wagons. As we drove past them, young McGee went running into the house, saying to his mother: "It is Louis and George, and I'll kill one of them to-night." This raised quite an alarm, and the members of the family told him not to do that, as it would ruin them. As soon as

George and I drove up to the first cabin, which was my wife's and Kitty's, we ran in. Kitty met us at the door and said: "I am all ready." She was looking for us. We commenced loading our wagon with our few things. Meanwhile the soldiers had ridden around a few rods and came upon old Master Jack and the minister of the parish, who were watching as guards to keep the slaves from running away to the Yankees. Just think of the outrage upon those poor creatures in forcibly retaining them in slavery long after the proclamation making them free had gone into effect beyond all question! As the soldiers rode up to the two men they said: "Hello! what are you doing here? Why have you not told these two men, Louis and George, that they are free men—that they can go and come as they like?" By this time all the family were aroused, and great excitement prevailed. The soldier's presence drew all the servants near. George and I hurried to fill up our wagon, telling our wives to get in, as there was no time to lose—we must go at once. In twenty minutes we were all loaded. My wife, Aunt Kitty and nine other servants followed the wagon. I waited for a few moments for Mary Ellen, sister of my wife; and as she came running out of the white folks' house, she said to her mistress, Mrs. Farrington: "Good-bye; I wish you good luck." "I wish you all the bad luck," said she in a rage. But Mary did not stop to notice her mistress further; and, joining me, we were soon on the road following the wagon.

TWO BRAVE MEN.

THOSE SOLDIERS WERE BRAVE indeed. Think of the courage and daring involved in this scheme—only two soldiers going into a country of which they knew nothing except that every white man living in it was their enemy. The demand which they made for food for seventy-five horses was a clever ruse, invented by them to alarm the McGees, and make them think that there was a troop of horses near by, and that it would not be safe for them to offer any resistance to our going away with our wives. Had they thought that there were but two soldiers, it is certain that they would have endeavored to prevent us getting away again, and one or more of us would undoubtedly have been killed.

As already stated, nine other slaves followed our wagon, as it moved off. They had no hats on; some were bare-footed,—they had not stopped to get anything; but, as soon as they saw a chance to get away, they went just as they were at the moment. Aunt Kitty was brave and forethoughtful, for during the week we were gone she had baked and cooked a large amount of substantial food that would keep us from starving while on our journey.

At the first road crossing, the two soldiers thought they saw a large troop of soldiers in the distance, and they galloped ahead of us at full speed; but, on arriving at the spot, they found that what they had thought soldiers were only a herd of cattle. They rode on to the next crossing, we following as we conveniently could. Each poor slave was busy with his thoughts and his prayers. Now and then one would hear a moan or a word from some of the party. All were scared, even though the soldiers were with us. We came to the next cross road, and passed that safely. Our fear was that the McGees might get the neighborhood to join them and pursue us, or send the home guards after us; but Providence was seemingly smiling upon us at last, for no one followed or molested us. We moved on all night, until we came to a creek, at four o'clock in the morning of Monday. The banks of the creek were very steep, and as the horses and wagon went down into the stream, the mattress on top of the wagon, upon which my wife and her sister's children were sitting, was thrown off into the water. Immediately the horses stopped, and became balky. It was such a warm night that they did not want to move on out of the water, and would not start, either, until they got ready. As soon as the soldiers saw the mattress slide off with my wife and the children, one of them plunged into the water with his horse, and, in a minute, brought them all out. All had a good ducking—indeed it seemed like a baptism by immersion. The drenched ones were wrapped in old blankets; and, after an hour's delay, we were again on our way. The soldiers said: "Now we must leave you; the time is coming when we must be in camp for roll call. If you are not at our camp when roll call is over, we will come back and see about you." We gave them each the second ten dollars, as agreed upon, and just as they rode to the top of the hill they left us. We had a clear sweep from this point, and we came into Senatobia about nine o'clock in the forenoon. Our two soldier friends, who had brought us out so safely, came out of camp to see us. They cheered us, and seemed glad that they had rendered us service. We stopped at the camp until we had dried our clothes and had some breakfast; and, then, we made our way to Memphis.

OUT OF BONDAGE AT LAST.

MY WIFE AND HER sister were shoeless, and the latter had no hat on—
she had hurried out of the house in such excitement that she thought
of nothing but getting away. Having to walk some of the way, as all
could not ride in the wagon at the same time, we were all tired, dirty
and rest-broken, and, on the whole, a pitiful crowd to look at, as we
came into the city. One venerable old man, bent with age, whose ebony
face shone with delight, came running out into the road as we appeared,
exclaiming: "Oh! here dey come, God bless 'em! Poor chil'en! they
come fannin." We used large palm leaves to fan ourselves with, as we
were so warm. Those nine souls that followed us walked the whole distance, arriving shortly after we did. Thousands of others, in search of
the freedom of which they had so long dreamed, flocked into the city of
refuge, some having walked hundreds of miles.

It was appropriately the 4th of July when we arrived; and, aside from
the citizens of Memphis, hundreds of colored refugees thronged the
streets. Everywhere you looked you could see soldiers. Such a day I don't
believe Memphis will ever see again—when so large and so motley a
crowd will come together. Our two soldier rescuers looked us up after
we were in Memphis, and seemed truly glad that we had attained our
freedom, and that they had been instrumental in it. Only one thing we
regret, and that is that we did not learn their names; but we were in so
much trouble, and so absorbed in the business which we had in hand—
so excited by the perils of our undertaking, that we never thought to ask
them their names, or to what regiment they belonged. Then, after we
got to Memphis, though we were most grateful for the service which
they had rendered us, we were still so excited by our new condition and
surroundings that we thought of little else, and forgot that we had no
means of establishing, at a later time, the identity of those to whom we
owed so much. Freedom, that we had so long looked for, had come at
last; and we gave praise to God, blessing the day when we met those two
heroes. It is true that we should have been free, sooner or later; still, but
for their assistance, my wife and I might never have met again. If I could
not have gone back, which I could never have done alone, until long
after, such changes might have occurred as would have separated us for
years, if not forever. Thousands were separated in this manner—men
escaping to the Union lines, hoping to make a way to return for their

families; but, failing in this, and not daring to return alone, never saw their wives or children more. Thanks to God, we were guided to these brave soldiers, and so escaped from so cruel a fate.

A WORD FOR MY OLD MASTER.

In closing this account of my years of bondage, it is, perhaps, but justice to say of my old master that he was in some respects kinder and more humane than many other slaveholders. He fed well, and all had enough to wear, such as it was. It is true that the material was coarse, but it was suited to the season, and, therefore, comfortable, which could not truthfully be said of the clothing of the slaves of other planters. Not a few of these did not have sufficient clothes to keep them warm in winter; nor did they have sufficient nourishing and wholesome food. But while my master showed these virtues, similar to those which a provident farmer would show in the care of his dumb brutes, he lacked in that humane feeling which should have kept him from buying and selling human beings and parting kindred—which should have made it impossible for him to have permitted the lashing, beating and lacerating of his slaves, much more the hiring of an irresponsible brute, by the year, to perform this barbarous service for him. The McGees were charitable—as they interpreted the word—were always ready to contribute to educational and missionary funds, while denying, under the severest penalties, all education to those most needing it, and all true missionary effort—the spiritual enlightenment for which they were famishing. Then our masters lacked that fervent charity, the love of Christ in the heart, which if they had possessed they could not have treated us as they did. They would have remembered the golden rule: "Do unto others as ye would that men should do to you." Possessing absolute power over the bodies and souls of their slaves, and grown rich from their unrequited toil, they became possessed by the demon of avarice and pride, and lost sight of the most vital of the Christly qualities.

Louis Hughes, *Thirty Years a Slave. From Bondage to Freedom. The Institution of Slavery as Seen on the Plantation and in the Home of the Planter* (Milwaukee, WI: South Side Printing Company, 1897), 111–190.

20

Remembering Slavery and the Civil War in Kentucky

"Life and History"
Rev. Elijah P. Marrs
1885

Marrs joined the 12th United States Colored Heavy Artillery on September 26, 1864, in Louisville, Kentucky, and during his service rose to the rank of sergeant. His extraordinary life as a slave, soldier, businessman, civil rights advocate, and, after the war, a Baptist minister, has few equals. His memoir testifies to the resourcefulness and courage of the former slaves who sought freedom, fought for it, and spent their postwar lives defending it against the Klan and other enemies. Indeed, Kentucky proved especially virulent in its opposition to black freedom. It was a border state and loyal to the Union, and the Emancipation Proclamation did not free any of the more than 225,000 slaves there. White Kentuckians resisted the Union army's attempt to employ their slaves, demanded the return of every fugitive slave in army hands, and used every means in their power, from intimidation to murder, to prevent the recruitment of slaves into the Union army. When the state's governor heard that the army intended to recruit black troops in his state, he informed military officials that "Ky will never see another day of peace."

If anything, Marrs's memoir underplayed the level of hatred aimed at men like himself in Kentucky and the dangers he faced as a soldier. Although his unit had successfully negotiated a safe and temporary surrender to rebels—men who likely sought escape as much as the black troops they had captured—this event made Marrs and his comrades some of the luckiest black soldiers of the war. Wounded black troops that had been captured after the Battle of Saltville, which included men from Camp Nelson, where Marrs was stationed, proved not so fortunate. Enraged rebel troops shot many of the wounded men in their hospital beds. White Kentuckians, while loyal to the Union, wanted no part of black recruitment. Nevertheless, nearly 60 percent of the state's black men of military age joined the army, an astonishing figure. After the war, as Marrs recorded, the Klan and other white paramilitary terrorist organizations sought vengeance on those whom they could not retain as slaves. Richard D. Sears, *Camp Nelson, Kentucky: A Civil War History* (Lexington, KY: University Press of Kentucky, 2002); Berlin et al., *Freedom: The Wartime Genesis of Free Labor: The Upper South*, 625–638.

HISTORY OF THE REV. ELIJAH P. MARRS.

I WAS BORN JANUARY, 1840, in Shelby County, Kentucky, twenty miles east of the city of Louisville; and my parents, Andrew and Frances Marrs, were born in Culpepper County, Virginia. My father was born in 1810. I am unable to tell when my mother was born; but, I think, about the year 1815. My father, who is yet living, is seventy-five years old. My mother belonged to a man by the name of Jesse Robinson. My father was a free man; my mother was a slave, hence I was born a slave. On the farm where I was reared there were about thirty slaves. I remember, when I was but four years old, how I used to steal away from home and stay until the dark would drive me in. The white boys and colored boys would leave home soon in the morning and rove the woods through during the summer time.

We had the dog-kennel for our hiding-place, and often the whole family would be in an uproar to know where we were. We would get a flogging when we returned, but the next day we would be gone again. After I became seven or eight years old I was made a dining-room boy. I remember how Brother Henry and I used to steal the biscuits off the plates while carrying them into the dining-room, and how they would burn us while hot in our pockets. In those days the colored people hardly knew the taste of wheat bread. The white boys used to make trades with the colored boys; for instance, I would have a marble he wanted; he would say to me, "I will give you a seldom for that marble." He meant that he would give me a biscuit with butter on it; that he would save a portion of what he was to eat to pay his debt.

I left the dining-room and went to the corn-field. I could tell of many romances of the field, but this little book will not allow it. It was a source of pleasure for me to leave the house and go to the field, where I could skip, hop, and jump to my heart's delight. We boys, in the time of plowing, as a general thing, only had the corn to plow over once a week. This we knew, hence we would lash our horses from morning until night, and get through sometimes by the middle of the week, and would then spend the remainder of the week in roving and roaming up and down the creek, fishing, etc. Our master was not hard on us, and allowed us generally to do as we pleased after his own work was done, and we enjoyed the privilege granted to us. I was a cow-boy in the meantime, and for six successive years I, with my mother, attended to the dairy.

My mother was very severe on me. She used to whip me nearly every night for the misdemeanors of the day. She would wait till I had undressed, and then attended to her loving boy as she used to call me.

Mothers were necessarily compelled to be severe on their children to keep them from talking too much. Many a poor mother has been whipped nearly to death on account of their children telling the white children things, who would then go and tell their mothers or fathers. My mother always told me what she was going to whip me before commencing, and would talk to me while she was whipping me. I only got one whipping from father, and that I richly deserved. I would blush to tell the cause of that whipping in this book, but it was a good one. He was always my friend when I thought trouble was in the air; he was my only refuge; when he failed to plead for me my hopes fled.

Very early in life I took up the idea that I wanted to learn to read and write. I was convinced that there would be something for me to do in the future that I could not accomplish by remaining in ignorance. I had heard so much about freedom, and of the colored people running off and going to Canada, that my mind was busy with this subject even in my young days. I sought the aid of the white boys, who did all they could in teaching me. They did not know that it was dangerous for a slave to read and write. I availed myself of every opportunity, daily I carried my book in my pocket, and every chance that offered would be learning my A, B, C's. Soon I learned to read. After this the white people would send me daily to the post-office, at Simpsonville, Ky., a distance of two miles, when I would read the address of the letters; I also would read the newspapers the best I could. There was an old colored man on the place by the name of Ham Graves, who opened a night school, beginning at 10 o'clock at night. I attended his school one year and learned how to write my name and read writing. On every gate-post around the stable, as on the plowhandles, you could see where I had been trying to write. Of course, I did not know the danger of it, and that fools' names like fools' faces are always seen in public places.

I am unable to tell the day or year when I became a Christian, but it was about the year 1851. Well do I remember the time when I went to a Methodist class meeting, and heard them all telling the experience of grace. I was then quite small. They talked about how good the Lord had been to them. I sat and listened. I cried and wondered why I could not talk that way too. I could not understand it. I had peculiar ideas as to what religion was. The Rev. R. Bain came over to our house one morning to see my father. He said to him, "Andy, I believe in my soul I've got religion." My father replied, but I have forgotten his answer. I went off wondering what he meant. My thoughts ran high; I thought that if he had religion he at least ought to know it; yet I hadn't the remotest idea what he meant. Yet I thought it was something very solemn, for he was crying. When he said that he believed that he had religion, I thought it was something written on a piece of paper, hence he ought to know it, yet the thought came back to me as to the cause of his crying. This thought haunted me. In going after my cows I would ask myself the question, "What did he mean?" My mind grew more active, but the mystery I could not comprehend. I had great faith in my father, and I thought he could whip a world, yet I saw him crying. Father said to Rev. Bain, "God is good; He saved me from hell." Hark! I began to fear though only eleven years old. A thought came to me to seek that which had been found by my father. "Seek and ye shall find," I had heard Bro. Bain remark, but how and in what way should I seek, and hopes I had none as to the consummation of my desires. My head was bowed down in sorrow. They watched me at home, and one would ask the other, "What is the matter with Elijah?" They could not tell. I hardly knew what was the matter with myself. Nature had taught me that I was a sinner. I wanted some instruction what to do. I was ignorant. I had heard many a prayer from mother and father and old Brother Bullitt, but none of them gave me any promise.

Instruction, teaching, was what I most needed. One day I was sent out into the field to cut corn-stalks with one of my young masters. He looked at me, and he saw that I was sin sick. He, being a Christian, took me in hand and told me that I was a sinner, and that Jesus Christ died to save sinners, and all I had to do was to believe that Jesus Christ was able to save. He told me about hell and its horrors. From morning to evening he talked. I prayed the best I could after I left him. I prayed during that week, and had a special place to pray every morning, when I went after the cows, about a mile from home, under a June apple-tree. Sunday came and I went to church and heard old Brother James Venable preach from this text, "Escape for your life." I was struck with conviction, and lingered along until Rev. Charles Wells, who was then pastor of the Colored Baptist Church, Simpsonville, commenced a protracted meeting. Shortly after the commencement of the meeting I professed faith in Christ. Oh how well I remember the time when Jesus freed me! Then, after I had found Christ, I had to go to Old Mass and Old Miss to get permission to join the Church. They consented, and then came the time to be baptized. It was extremely cold, and the streams covered with ice an inch thick. I had to again ask permission to be baptized, and with tears in their eyes my request was granted. Rev. Wells buried about fifty souls that day in the liquid grave. Thank God that I was saved!

There was something on Robinson place that was an exception to the general rule. There were forty-two in family, and all members of the Church who were above ten years of age, and all Baptists save one old colored lady, Robinson himself having been a deacon in the Baptist Church for about forty years. After my conversion and baptism I was permitted to attend Sunday-school and study the Word of God for myself. My master then removed all objections to my learning how to read, and said he wanted all the boys to learn how to read the Bible, it being against the laws of the State to write. We had to steal that portion of our education, and I did my share of it I suppose. Only a few of the white people would let their slaves attend the Sunday-school, hence I became an active member in it.

At the age of seventeen I made my first attempt at courting. There was a beautiful young lady living in Boston [Kentucky] by the name of Mary Malone. My brother, who was older than I, persuaded me to accompany him on a visit to her one day. We had a very good time, especially so to me. It was my first love affair, and when the young lady addressed me in such endearing terms as "my little pet—my little sweetheart"—I neglected to see that the declining sun was fast nearing the western horizon, and that I was a long way from home. Alas! before I got there the sun had long disappeared. Mother was waiting anxiously for me—waiting as a mother alone can wait—doubt, fear, and anger each struggling for supremacy. Suffice it to say, I was whipped up stairs and down again, and when she gave me a rest I promised to no more a courting go until I was of maturer age. My brother was permitted to go scot-free. I thought that he at least should have shared the burden of suffering with me, but such was not the case. I thought it best, however, to quietly rest on my oars until I had passed my teens.

My next love was Miss Ella Freeman, now Ella Johnson, whom I loved dearly. At that time I was twenty-one years of age. The war between the North and South was upon us, and ideas of freedom began to steal across my brain, and my mind was active with the probabilities of being able some day to put into actual practice the scattering thoughts of my earlier years. I would read the newspapers as I would bring them from the post-office, and I kept the colored population of the neighborhood well posted as to the prevailing news.

Robinson's was general headquarters for the negroes, and I would read to them for hours at a time. It soon became known that I was reading to the slaves of the neighborhood, and that I was also familiar with the pen. At this time the county was full of rebels, and it was not long until they heard of me. I was branded as the Shelby County negro clerk. My owner took me to task one day and warned me of the danger I was incurring if I should be caught by the rebels. One thing that gave me some notoriety was the fact that nearly all the colored soldiers who had enlisted prior to myself sent their letters to their wives, sons, and daughters, addressed to my care. My owner cautioned me in regard to this matter, and even made me take his horse and ride to Boston, and to write to all my friends in the army, cautioning them against addressing any more letters to my care. This I did, but it put no stop to the letters. The colored soldiers had confidence in me, and knew that their letters would be faithfully delivered.

I remember the morning I made up my mind to join the United States Army. I started to Simpsonville, and walking along I met many of my old comrades on the Shelbyville Pike. I told them of my determination, and asked all who desired to join my company to roll his coat sleeves above his elbows, and to let them remain so during the day. I marshaled my forces that day and night. I had twenty-seven men, all told, and I was elected their captain to lead them to Louisville. Our headquarters were at the colored church. During the day some one brought the news that the rebels were in Simpsonville, and that they were preparing to make a raid upon the church. For a time this news created a panic—women screamed, jumped out the windows, crying "Murder!"—strong men ran pell-mell over the women and took to the woods. I, myself, crowded into the corner of the church, and Captain Marrs was about, for the time being, to throw up the sponge. But I did not despair. I picked up courage and rallied my men, and news soon came that the report was false. We held a council of war, and the conclusion of the boys was, that where I would lead they would follow. I said to them we might as well go; that if we staid at home we would be murdered; that if we joined the army and were slain in battle, we would at least die in fighting for principle and freedom.

During all this excitement no white face was to be seen. Night came, and Rev. Sandy Bullitt, son of Deacon John Bullitt, who had been drafted into the U.S. Army, was to preach his farewell sermon. The house was crowded to suffocation. He preached one of the most powerful sermons I have ever heard before or since. He was a preacher of the Gospel that none need be ashamed of. His name as a faithful minister of the Gospel was often afterwards mentioned by the white chaplains of the army.

It was known by nearly every one present that night that there were a number of young men in the house who were preparing to leave for the army, and they the best in the neighborhood, consequently there was great weeping and mourning—the wife for husband, the maiden for her sweetheart. Such a demonstration of sorrow I have never seen, before or since.

After a many adieu I formed my men in line, twenty-seven in number, and marched them some two miles to Robinson's, where I was raised. I arrived there at about 10 o'clock at night, and I stationed my men around until I could make arrangements to get them something to eat. I went into the house where old Aunt Beller, as we used to call her, staid, who always had on hand something good to eat. She gave me what she had, which I took and gave to the men. Then I went into my mother's room where I had concealed about $300 in money, which I had saved during slave times. I took about $200 of it and left the remainder for mother. She being asleep it was my intention to steal off without arousing her, but in getting my money I awakened her, when she screamed at the top of her voice. I immediately ran out of the door, rejoined my comrades, and we took up our march for the army. We had on the place a large Newfoundland dog, and he followed in our tracks for nearly a half mile.

Our arms consisted of twenty-six war clubs and one old rusty pistol, the property of the captain. There was one place on our route we dreaded, and that was Middletown, through which the colored people seldom passed with safety. When we got within two miles of the place I ordered my men to circle to the left until we got past the town, when we returned to the Pike, striking it in front of Womack's big woods. At this place we heard the rumbling of vehicles coming at full speed, as we supposed, towards us. I at once ordered the men to lie down in a ditch by the roadside, where we remained some twenty-five minutes, but hearing nothing further I ordered my men to arise and we took up our line of march.

Day was now breaking, and in one half hour we were within the lines of the Union Army, and by eight o'clock we were at the recruiting office in the city of Louisville. Here we found Mr. George Womack, the Provost Marshal, in whose dark woods we had taken shelter the night before. By twelve o'clock the owner of every man of us was in the city hunting his slaves, but we had all enlisted save one boy, who was considered too young.

I enlisted on the 26th day of September, 1864, and was immediately marched out Third Street to Taylor Barracks, and assigned to Company L, Twelfth U. S. Colored Artillery.[1] My first night in the barracks was anything but a pleasant one, and an accident occurred that so jarred my nerves that I wished I had never heard of the war. Our bunks were arranged in tiers of three, one above the other. I occupied the top one. During the night the man who occupied the middle one accidentally discharged his revolver. The ball passed downward, striking the man below in the head and killing him almost instantly. In less than two hours afterwards the body of the man shot was robbed of three hundred dollars that he had received that day as a substitute. This was the experience of the first eight hours of my soldier life, and it naturally caused my mind to revert back to my old home and to those I had left behind. I thought it would have been better had I remained there, than to be in the position I then was, liable to be slain at any moment. My fears in a measure overcame me. I prayed, I cried, I said, "How long, how long, O Lord, shall it be before I am delivered from this thraldom?" The shock was more than I thought I could bear; but I was in for it, and I knew there was no way of getting out of it. In due time I dosed off to sleep, only to dream of what had happened in the former part of the night, with other horrible things, and was only too glad to waken in the morning and find them not true.

When the sun came up from behind the eastern hills I looked towards home, and thought of my old mother and father I had left behind. I said "Lord! shall I ever see them more? I commit them into thy hands." I remembered the poet: "The Lord has promised good to me; his Word my hopes secure!"

Breakfast time came, the tattoo was beat, and the men formed into line. I was not disobedient to the call. The Orderly Sergeant called the roll, and when he called "Marrs, Elijah," I promptly answered. I can stand this said I, and like a man, with cup, pan, and spoon, marched up to the window and received my rations. It is true I thought of my mother's sweet voice when she used to call me to dine, but "pshaw!" said I, "this is better than slavery, though I do march in line to the tap of the drum." I felt freedom in my bones, and when I saw the American eagle, with outspread wings, upon the American flag, with the motto, "*E Pluribus Unum*," the thought came to me, "Give me liberty or give me death." Then all fear banished. I had quit thinking as a child and had commenced to think as a man. I had in camp some reputation as a writer, though I had little confidence in myself, coming as I did just out of the bondage of slavery. I appeared, however, to be above the average of those in our quarters, and many former friends who had joined the army before me employed me to do their writing.

Soon the officers learned that there was a little fellow from Shelby County that was skilled in the use of the pen, and they sought to find me. They found me surrounded by a number of the men, each waiting his turn to have a letter written home. The officers soon made known their wishes, which was to find a man who was a penman who they wished as a Duty Sergeant. The mere mention of such a thing made me quake with fear, as I knew no more about tactics than a newborn babe. This I told them, but they insisted, and I accepted the position as a non-commissioned officer, with the understanding that they would give me personal instruction in army tactics. At their headquarters I had a consultation with them respecting my duties as a non-commissioned officer. Lieut. Bassworth [Drake S. Boswarth] was my chief instructor, together with Lieut. [Sidney A.] Vaughn. Early the next day I was assigned as Third Duty Sergeant, Co. L. 12th U. S. Heavy Artillery.

An incident occurred on the third night of my enlistment that should not be passed over in this little book. We were all new men, and we soon expected to be sent to the front. We had just left our homes, and though out of slavery we loved the place of our birth; and while we could not help thinking of home, sweet home, yet we were loth to return, and a thought seemed to come to the mind of every Christian, that though the Civil War between the North and South had separated us from home and friends, yet the protecting hand of the United Government of God was still over us all. Hence some of the new recruits proposed that we have prayer and preaching in the barracks that night. We selected Rev. Sandy Bullitt to officiate, the same brother who preached the night I left for the army, and who had been drafted from the same neighborhood that I came from. Night came, and all arrangements had been made for the meeting. Rev. Bullitt mounted the rostrum and preached one of his wonderful sermons. His effort wrought the greatest excitement—he, in a measure, set the camp on fire. Strong men, who had never before been known to bow, fell on their knees for prayer. Over three hundred took part in the exercises, and some men were so overcome as to lay all night as if in a trance. Officers came to see what was the matter, but could only look and say, "Surely God is with those people."

The next night many professed Christ. Praise God for his goodness, I thought, for it extends to the end of the world. His love nerves the Christian to action, and moves them to feel his power, however weak the subject may be. After this meeting I felt myself to be a free man in both soul and body.

The fourth day I was ordered by the commanding officer to take a squad of men and go to Tenth and Broadway streets, and clear off ground for the erection of barracks. While I felt myself a free man and an U.S. soldier, still must I move at the command of a white man, and

I said to myself is my condition any better now than before I entered the army? But the idea would come to me that I was a soldier fighting for my freedom, and this thought filled my heart with joy. I thought, too, that the time will come when no man can say to me come and go, and I be forced to obey.

We were in camp at Taylor Barracks three weeks, when we received orders to report at Camp Nelson.[2] Some rejoiced, whilst others wept, the latter thinking we were going on a fighting tour. We went by the way of Lexington, and arrived at Camp Nelson without the loss of a man. The barracks being crowded, we were assigned to tents, mine being pitched beside the bullpen.

Whilst passing through Lexington I became acquainted with a young lady named Emma—. Our love was mutual. She followed me to Camp Nelson, in the neighborhood of which she found employment. She invited me to see her; but it should be at night, after her daily duties were done. One night I called, and not seeing her, presumed her to be in some other portion of the house, and walked in without announcement. My entrance alarmed some one in the adjacent room, whose cries of "murder" hurried me back to camp, with the resolution of never seeing Emma again. The last I heard of poor Emma was that she was dead. Her last thoughts were of me, and her last request was to her kind lady employer to send me her only portrait. She was my first love, and was too early called away. Sweet spirit, which nothing can banish from an unforgetful heart—who never looked upon sin and seldom on sorrow—why should thy memory be so precious to me now? Never again has come to my heart that gladness that seemed to brighten thine—never more has beamed upon me the soft glory which seemed to shine from thy blessed eyes! Often coming up from the struggles of passion and from the midst of the world's temptations, the remembrance of thee and thy virtues burst upon me as a vision, and I feel purified, sanctified, and strengthened by thy presence, and with an increased vigor renew my labors in the upholding of the Cross of Christ. Emma, farewell! Thy name may not be written on a tombstone, but thy memory is enshrined within a heart!

Sitting in camp one bright sunny day, surrounded by my comrades, for whom I was writing letters home, I was very agreeably surprised by meeting with my brother [H. C. Marrs], who had joined the army some six weeks before I did. I had not heard from him since his enlistment, but I knew that his regiment had been ordered to Saltville [Virginia]. He had gone as far as Cumberland Gap, when he became sick, and had been ordered back. My brother at that time was Orderly Sergeant, and the man who was detailed to fill his place was killed at the battle of Saltville, and within the walls of the fort. My brother was afterwards promoted to the rank of Sergeant Major, and served in this capacity until mustered out of service.

Our stay at Camp Nelson was not altogether devoid of excitement, and this event being my first actual experience in the science of war, is now more vivid to my memory, as I presume it is to my comrades who were with me, than subsequent events of the war. One night the news reached the camp that the rebels were in Danville, Ky., and in about forty minutes afterwards Gen. S[peed]. S[mith]. Fry, accompanied by about fifty men, came galloping into camp with all speed. The alarm was at once given, the long roll of the drum was beaten, and every man roused and ordered to prepare for battle. We were at once marched to the various forts surrounding the camp, and though up to that time we had only been drilled in infantry tactics, we were commanded to man the cannons. It is true we belonged to the Heavy Artillery, but had never been drilled in the tactics thereof. Nos. 1, 2, 3, and 5, however, soon learned their positions at the cannon, and while apparently paying attention to their work, could not keep their eyes from peering into the darkness beyond the river, from which direction they thought they heard the clang of swords and the clattering of horses coming upon us.

Day broke, however, and no enemy was in sight, so we marched back to camp in great glee, as much so as if we had met the enemy and gained a great victory.

In connection with our stay at Camp Nelson I must mention the name of Sergeant Major Geo. Thomas,[3] who was and is yet an intimate friend of mine. He was a genial companion and a good officer. His many acts of kindness to his men will long be remembered by them as his friendship is by me. He was the only man in the regiment, white or colored, who understood vocal music sufficiently well to teach it, and he and myself, by permission, formed regular classes among the men, which we would teach at designated times in vocal music and in the rudiments of English during our entire stay at Camp Nelson.

After a stay of some weeks at Camp Nelson, we were ordered to Russellville, Ky. It was thought now that we were on our way to the front.

Many of us would have preferred remaining at Camp Nelson, but the command was to march. We began to pack up on the morning of November 24, 1864, and we were marched on foot to Lexington, there being no railroad. I shall never forget that day. It was my first long march, and I had to carry my knapsack, my gun, my sword, and army equipments. Though late in the year, the sun seemed to shine with equal force as in the hottest days of July, and the heat was oppressive and overpowering. The roads were inches deep in dust, and it filled my eyes, mouth and ears. Our thirst was intolerable, and no water was to be had save the stagnated water we would find along the line of our march. To this we would drive the horses, and of it fill our canteens. The use of this water so weakened me that I became completely prostrated and had to cry for help. Lieut. Bossworth, who was an old soldier, and who took pride in aiding and assisting his men, came to my relief, took my equipments, transferred them to his own back, and resumed his march with as light a foot as he had started with in the morning.

By sunset we arrived at Lexington, tired and fagged out, having marched a distance of nineteen miles. We expected to get our usual rations of bread, and meat, and coffee, but we did not get it. No provision had been made for our arrival, and nothing could be had but hard tack and water, off of which we made our supper.

After supper I retired. My sleeping apartment was an old hog car, but I was so stiff and so worn out from the effects of the march of the day that I was soon asleep and dreaming of home and friends. I thought I had returned—I saw my father's fond looks of delight—felt on my cheek my mother's warm kiss—even the cows that I was wont to drive from pasture seemed to welcome me back. I again strolled along the stream on whose mossy banks I had often laid and fished—again was in the old church listening to Bro. Bullitt's farewell sermon—once more on my march to freedom and the army—again with beloved Emma.

The morning's drum-beat dispelled the happy vision, and the stern reality of my situation was before me. But little time elapsed before we were off for Louisville, where we arrived about 2 P.M. On arriving we were met at the depot by an army of women of all classes, white and colored, each with her basket. They had hams, chickens, pies, and everything that was good for the inner man, but unfortunately for us they were all for sale and we unable to buy. Our Captain finally came among us, and told us to "Press it." It was not long before we understood what he meant. We were like hungry wolves, and so soon as the idea of "pressing" dawned upon us the eatables disappeared like magic. Each man helped himself to such dainties as suited his taste. As for my part I was more modest than many others and contented myself with some ham and bread. Some, to use the common expression, "went the whole hog," and took basket and all. It was the first time I had ever been guilty of anything of this kind, and was extremely awkward at the business, but my hunger urged me on, and I only did that which the others did, and that with the connivance of our Captain.

The next morning at six we took up our line of march for the Nashville Depot, the boys singing as we marched through the streets of Louisville, "I wish I was in Dixie's land." Many of our old friends, as we marched at the tap of the drum, watched us with tears of sorrow in their eyes, while their lips muttered prayers to God that we might be able to return and enjoy that liberty which had for so long a time been hoped for by our fore-parents, and for which we were now to imperil our lives.

In due time we were on board the train and off for Russellville. We were in open cars, hence we had a very good view of the country through which we passed, and as I gazed upon the hills and dales, the fields and forests, I could not keep from thinking of the beautiful part of the State in which I was reared, its green fields and pastures, and as to the probabilities of my ever seeing them again.

We arrived in Russellville all safe and sound. We marched up into town and took up our quarters in an old stable. By this time I began to realize the fact that for a man to be a good soldier, he must subject himself to innumerable hardships. Each man at once set himself to work to make for himself a sleeping bunk, which was indispensable. It was in this sleeping-place I had my first spell of sickness, which lasted some three weeks. During my sickness I prayed to God for aid and comfort in my affliction, and it seemed that my prayer was granted, for there visited me a kind lady in the person of Miss Henrietta Forees. She, with others, had sought the camp to render aid to any who should be sick and needing help. She and others visited me regularly, supplied me with nourishing food, and to their kind offices, and the hope they inspired within my heart, I believe I am indebted for my recovery. I frequently offered up thanks to God for leading unto me such ministering angels, and thought of how good the Lord is to those that loved Him—to those that put their trust and faith in Jesus.

Though the life of a soldier is a hard and rugged one, full of temptations, yet I tried ever to keep God and his teachings before me, though I found it often an up-hill business. In the company I belonged to there were only two professed Christians beside myself, viz.: George Thomas and Jacob Stone. They, like myself, had been brought up by Christian parents, and the moral training they received had left its impress upon their minds. We frequently communed with one another, and resolved that however evil our associations we would remain steadfast to the principles and teachings of our parents, come what would. I have already passed over my childhood days, yet I hope it will not be thought out of place here to say that in all my life I never swore an oath, never danced, never played a card, nor got drunk—save in one single instance, and then there was extenuating circumstances connected therewith. It was on a Christmas morning, the beginning of the week of the year that all bound men looked forward to for rest, frolic, and pleasure. I was but a small boy, and in company with one of about the same age. We were persuaded by an old man to drink some whisky. Its effects soon told upon us, and on our road home there were but few mudholes that we did not tumble into. It was my first and last attempt at drinking.

At camp in Russellville I was surrounded by men whose daily habit was to brag, bully, and brow-beat, and it illy fared with anyone who was too timid to stand up for himself. They spent most of their leisure hours in jumping, wrestling, and playing marbles. In my younger days I was very fond of athletic sports of all kinds, and in the matter of jumping and wrestling very few could be found who were my superior, and I have never yet met with a man who could put me on my back. Of course, to vary the dull monotony of camp life, I indulged in these sports, and attained quite a reputation as a wrestler, so much so, that when any new wrestler appeared, the little red-shirt Sergeant was immediately hunted up to down him. I wore a red shirt while at camp in Russellville. One instance I will relate.

There was a man in camp by the name of Nick Kiger. All the men feared him in a rough and tumble wrestle as we used to call it. Now-a-days they have designated it as catch-and-catch can. Without my knowledge a match was made between him and myself. I was sent for, and at once responded to the call. He looked upon me with as much contempt as did Goliath upon David, and hooted at the idea of my being able to cope with him. Nevertheless we took our positions, and the signal being given we commenced the contest. In almost the twinkling of an eye he was sprawling on his back some five feet in my rear. I at once walked away, leaving our Company boys to rejoice over my victory. I think this was my last play of that kind.

Sunday was our day for rest, pleasure, and religious exercises, we being free from the labor of regular drill. It was, however, our general inspection day, and each man was up by daybreak and busily at work brushing his clothes, cleaning his gun and other equipments, so as to be ready for general inspection at half-past nine o'clock A.M. His non-appearance in the ranks, or even if there, his dress and arms not being scrupulously clean and coming up to a certain standard, he could certainly reckon on the guard-house as being his home for the balance of the day. No excuse, no explanation would be taken in palliation of the offense—he was marched off, his voice uttering all the oaths known to his vocabulary.

After the best portion of the Lord's Day having been spent as before mentioned, the men are marched back to their quarters, when some five or six passes are given to a company by its captain, when the rest were required to attend chapel services. This latter duty was one that gave me infinite pleasure in performing. The inspection drill I would have gladly omitted, but I was a soldier, and stern duty required that I should be present.

During our sojourn at Russellville we received the news of [Gen. John B.] Hood's attack on General [George H.] Thomas at Nashville, the 15th day of December, 1864, and of his defeat and retreat. A portion of Hood's command, however, had crossed the Cumberland River and attacked the Seventeenth Kentucky Calvary, which latter fell back upon us in the wildest confusion. The town was full of the defeated and flying cavalrymen. We, at the same time, received orders to at once march to Bowling Green. It was near 12 o'clock when we received the order, and we were all preparing our dinners. Everything at once was turned into confusion—men here, and everywhere, each trying to get at a dinner pot containing soup that he might not be compelled to commence the march upon an empty stomach. Then came the rattling of swords, the shouldering of knapsacks, the order to fall into ranks, and we were soon on our march to Bowling Green, a distance of about forty-five miles. We numbered, all told, one hundred and forty men, and as we were well aware that we had been ordered to Bowling Green in apprehension of an attack upon us from the same body of rebels who had defeated the Seventeenth Kentucky Cavalry, we were not without misgivings as to our safe arrival at that point without coming in contact with the enemy, more especially so as we imagined we were marching inside of the enemy's line. We marched, without halting, a distance of twenty miles, when we went into camp at an old school-house. One-half of the men were immediately placed on guard, and the others slept on their arms, as we were expecting an attack at any time.

We passed, however, a quiet night, and at early dawn we were on our way to Bowling Green. The nearer we approached this place, and the greater the distance we placed betwixt ourselves and Russellville, the more exuberant were we in spirits, and many the jokes perpetrated relative to the dangers encountered during our midnight flight. At two o'-clock P.M. we arrived at Bowling Green, and at once reported at headquarters. There we heard of Hood's defeat, when we at once gave three cheers for General Thomas and his valiant and victorious troops.

We remained at Bowling Green for some few days, and as cold weather was approaching we prepared for winter quarters. Every stable and out-house in the town had been taken possession of, our company occupying an old school-house, and we crowding it from floor to rafters. As for myself, individually, I took an apartment to myself, which I did after the manner of the ground-hog. I dug me a hole in the ground, covered it with boards and earth, and with straw and my blanket I was comfortably fixed during the short time we remained at Bowling Green.

Soon, however, we received marching orders, and contrary to our wish and expectation we were ordered to Munfordsville instead of to Nashville. On our way we met with General [James B.] Steedman's Cavalry, who were hurrying to the front to assist in the pursuit of the defeated and flying enemy.

A march of two days brought us to Munfordsville. While there at least twelve thousand prisoners of war passed through on their way to Louisville, and under guard of colored troops. After a stay of some few days at Munfordsville, we were again on the move, our destination being Glasgow, Ky. We arrived at Glasgow Junction at about 5 o'clock P.M., where we camped in a grove. No sooner had the boys stacked arms than they began to forage for something to eat, as provisions were not too plentiful with us. It was not long before some six or seven shoats were brought in, which were soon killed. As we had no facilities for cleaning them by scalding, they were at once skinned and preparations made for a grand supper. While thus engaged, a man riding at full speed informed us that the rebels had taken possession of Glasgow and that they were then on their march towards us. It was then a time for getting up and doing, which everyone seemed to have done—that is, to get a slice of pork before falling into line. The rain at this time was falling in torrents, but we at once marched back to the Junction, where a halt was called and a consultation had between the Lieutenants and Sergeants as to what had best be done under the circumstances. It was finally resolved that we should go on to Cave City, and we again took up our line of march. It was still raining and the night was so very dark that it was impossible to see where we were going. We trudged along, however, through mud and slush up to our knees, till near midnight, when we were suddenly brought to a stand by a voice in our front calling upon us to "Halt!" We imagined at once that we had fallen into the hands of the very party we were fleeing from, and to say that we were frightened is a poor expression to describe the state of our feelings. Our officers, as well as ourselves, were so dumbfounded as to be unable to speak, and it was only after a second call to "Halt! Who goes there?"—that our Lieutenant found his voice and courage to use it. At the words "Advance and give the countersign," the Lieutenant called upon some one to go in advance with him, whereupon I volunteered to accompany him, and we started forward. As we approached the sentinel, as he afterwards proved to be, and who by the way was as much alarmed as we ourselves, we were ordered to advance with our arms down, which we did until we discovered that each party was clothed in the Federal uniform.

The party proved to be one, who, like ourselves, were fleeing from the rebels at Glasgow, they, too, having been ordered to that point, but discovered the town to be in their possession. That we were all made happy at the result of our surprise it is needless to say, and the men of both companies cried, laughed, and rejoiced that our meeting had not been with our common enemy.

We rested all night on our arms, and kept a bright look out until daylight. It being on the day before Christmas, and our courage having somewhat risen with our increased numbers, and our desire to be in Glasgow on Christmas day, we concluded we would strike out for the Glasgow rebels. We accordingly took up our line of march, and along as miserable a road as could be found anywhere in Kentucky. It was extremely muddy, and it seemed to be up a succession of hills, one upon another, for a distance of five miles. We trudged our way along until about five o'clock in the evening, when, upon turning an angular rock which projected itself across the road, we saw in the edge of a long pasture a squad of rebels. I called the attention of our Captain to them, who at once gave the command to halt. Almost instantly the rebels disappeared. As night was approaching, and we not familiar with the country surrounding us, nor the strength of the enemy, we concluded to go into camp for the night, which we did, in a neighboring wood. Food being somewhat scarce, a portion of our company was detailed to go out foraging, or "pressing" as we called it, an other portion placed on guard, while the others were given permission to sleep if they so desired. During the night the foraging party returned, with more or less provisions. A member of my mess by the name of J. George was fortunate enough to obtain a bucket of flour, which he brought to my tent, and we soon had it converted into dough and baking before the fire. With this and some bacon we had a nice supper.

We kept a bright look out during the night for an attack should one be made, but the night passed off quietly. With the morning we made our preparations to enter Glasgow, the town we had turned our backs upon two days before. As we approached the town we saw, at some distance off, a man waiving the Union flag, but whether it was waived to signal us that the rebels were lying in ambush for us or not I never knew. So soon as our Captain perceived it he ordered us to give three cheers to the old flag, which were given with a will. Just at this juncture of affairs, the rebels, who were secreted on a hill just above, opened fire upon us. We returned the fire, and after several rounds Sergeant Thomas, with a portion of the company, charged the hill and drove the enemy from it at the point of the bayonet. Another body of the rebels appearing in another direction, the remainder of the company charged upon them, and they at once fled.

The enemy having been dispersed, we filed into marching order and entered the town. As I have said before, it was Christmas Day, and it seemed that all the colored people throughout the county had collected in town that day. I never before saw so many of them congregated together in so small a place. As we neared the center of the town we saw quite a crowd in and about the court-house, and a body of white men from this point were seen rapidly approaching us, as if bent on a hostile demonstration. Our Lieutenant at once dismounted, and gave orders that if a single shot was fired upon us, we should immediately return the fire, regardless of who we should kill. Seeing that we were ready for any exigency that might arise, the crowd dispersed in various directions. Upon inquiry as to the locality and direction of the fort, everyone seemed loth and unwilling to give the desired information. Finally a little white boy was prevailed on to tell us, when we shouldered arms, and marched in the direction indicated.

We found the fort without difficulty. It was one that had been built by [Gen. Braxton] Bragg when he invaded Kentucky, and stood upon the edge of the town. As we entered the fort the rebels entered the town from the other side, and dividing themselves, one party held the town, and the other by a circuitous route placed themselves between the fort and the open country. Not knowing of this movement on the part of the enemy, we sent out a detachment to scour the country for something to eat. To our surprise and discomfiture it was driven back to the fort in a very few minutes, and we soon realized the melancholy fact that we were surrounded and hemmed in on all sides. Not being strong enough in point of numbers to leave the fort and make an attack, we could do nothing but await results. The nearest Federal Soldiers to us were those at Cave City, but they were there guarding supplies, so we could expect no relief from that quarter. Desperation gave us courage, however, and we resolved to do the best we could and fight ourselves out if necessary. We rested on our arms that night expecting an attack, but none was made. Next morning we were informed that the rebels were marching upon us in force. We knew, in this case, we would in time be forced to surrender, as we only numbered seventy-five men, all told; but we were resolved to give them a taste of our metal before being compelled so to do. We accordingly kept the breastworks manned from early dawn till dusk, but no rebels put in an appearance, though we were satisfied they were not far away. That night we again slept on our arms, but everything passed off quietly. The next day we began laying plans to get ourselves out of the awkward position we were in, and when night set in we quietly stole out of the fort, in Indian file passed through the enemy's lines, and took up our march for Elizabethtown, where we arrived after a three days' tramp, and without the loss of a man. Our escape was a miraculous one, and the boldness of the attempt was what gave to it success. It is true we were fired upon once or twice during the night, whilst wending our way around the rebel camps, but we were so scatteringly drawn out that no man was hit.

On our arrival at Elizabethtown we found the place guarded by one or two companies of white soldiers; also two companies of colored. We took up our quarters in an old school-house near the center of the town, and separate from the other troops. We could hear the rebels all around swearing vengeance, and especially against us. So we placed on duty a guard of thirty men, while the remainder of us slept. The rebels had doubtless heard of our "pressing" proclivities. I know of no other reason for the bitter hate they seemed to manifest towards our company.

At eight o'clock in the morning, after breakfast, we marched for Hardinsburg, Ky., a distance of about forty miles from Elizabethtown. The first day we traversed about twenty miles, when we camped for the night, stationed our guards, and threw out our pickets. It had been raining hard all day, and every man was drenched to the skin. I made my bed of old sticks, leaves, and moss, and I also built me a good fire. I was soon sound asleep. How long I slept I do not know, but I suddenly found myself in an upright position, with fire all over me. The fire had communicated with my bed, which was now one solid mass of fire. I soon extinguished myself, or rather the fire that was on me, and found myself minus of eyebrows, as also a good portion of the hair of my head. I scrambled around in the rain, however, collected and made me another bed, and slept the remainder of the night in better luck. That night the guard discovered some one spying around the camp and captured him before he could make his escape. We kept him under guard until daylight, when he claimed to be a neighboring citizen, attracted to the camp by our fires. He sent for some of his friends to prove the correctness of his statement, and we permitted him to depart, but I afterwards saw him in the rebel army.

After breakfast we again took up our line of march for Hardinsburg. This was on Thursday, March 5, 1865. At about 3 o'clock, P.M., we arrived at a place called Big Springs. As we entered one end of the town the rebels retreated out the other. On this date and at this place trouble to Company L began its work. Up to this time we had many adventures, but we had passed safely through them all. The enemy was now around and before us, and we felt that in the future we would have work to do. We at once marched up to the Baptist Church (white), took possession of it, and built our fires. It had been raining hard all day, and the men were wet, hungry, and tired. The first thing we did was to inspect our guns, and on doing so found that there were only nine guns in the entire company that were in good condition. We remedied the matter as far as we were able, loaded our guns, and knowing that the rebels were in the neighborhood, were on our guard to prevent surprise. After placing the guard, two of our men, Corporal Harriway and W. Nichols, stole off from camp and went down into the town. They were soon surrounded by rebels, who took from them their arms and accoutrements, and compelled them to flee for their lives. William Nichols succeeded in reaching the church. Not so with poor Harriway. As he jumped upon the fence surrounding it he fell mortally wounded upon the outside, while a perfect shower of bullets were rained against the sides of the church. At the time of the shooting I was engaged in parching corn, and stooping down over the fire. Behind me was a man of our company named Henry Adcock, who was about seven feet high, with weight proportionately great. At the sound of the bullets upon the sides of the church he did not take time to go around me, but on to me and over the fire he went, out of the church and away. On getting to my feet I was literally covered with mud and ashes, so much so, that I was hardly recognized by our Lieutenant, who at once commanded me to take twenty men and proceed in one direction, while Jacob Stone was to take twenty men and proceed in another. We were to meet at a point on the top of a hill. When we arrived at our meeting-place, the enemy could be seen, but they were in full retreat, and we did not care to assume the responsibility of following them without further orders. We therefore returned back to camp to hold a council of war as what it was best to do. We were thirty miles from any of our own troops, and we knew there remained for us only one of three things to do—fight, run, or surrender. We resolved to fight it out. Night was now upon us. It was asked, "Who will take thirty men and guard the lines?" I answered the call. The enemy proved troublesome during the night, making several attempts to capture our guards, but were each time driven off by my men.

The next night, Friday, January 6, 1865, we rested on our arms, but there was no one to molest us, and we who were on guard duty done our share of bragging over our previous night's exploits. A deep snow had fallen during that day. I was again made Sergeant of the guard, with thirty men under my command. About midnight the rebels endeavored to steal upon our guards. On one of the beats was a soldier named Oglesby, who, as the rebels advanced, gave the alarm, and I quickly formed my men in line to repulse an attack. The guard informed me that one of the enemy had entered a little house in the neighborhood. I marched up in front of the door and opened fire on the rebel, when he broke and ran, succeeding in making his escape, though one of our boys informed me that when I fired upon the fleeing man, he jumped back twenty feet. On the same night Corporal Elijah Dagner and I heard the rebels talking in a grove near by, and creeping along by the side of a fence until within fair distance, we opened fire upon them, when they at once fled.

On Saturday, the 7th, the sun shone out brightly. We were engaged in talking over the best way to get back to our regiment in safety. We decided on enjoying ourselves, and visiting the outskirts of town we gathered up our chickens and turkeys and provided ourselves with a bountiful dinner and supper, which served to cheer us on our march. Saturday night we rested in peace, no one appearing to molest us.

Sunday, the 8th of January, 1865, dawned upon us. Oh, what a lovely morning! The sun seemed to have put on all of his beauty, and the effect was noticeable upon all of us. The boys were all merry, singing with right good will their favorite army songs, and enjoying themselves fully. "No Rebs. last night, boys! They've got enough of old Company L, you bet!" is a sample of expressions heard on all sides.

Breakfast being over, and I having been appointed to take down the names of new recruits, who were coming in rapidly, about 7 o'clock I commenced forming them in line to march down to my headquarters for enrollment and to report to the commanding officer. Just as we were crossing the road, one of my recruits exclaimed, "Lord, God! Look at the rebels!" I turned to look toward the enemy, and I have never seen one of my recruits since. As I glanced down the road at the enemy, their line appeared to be about two miles long. Our Lieutenant commanded the company to fall out, and for two hours the opposing forces remained there, intently watching each other, but neither making an offensive movement. As we were not the attacking party, we awaited their action, and finally the rebel General [John S.] Williams, a Baptist preacher, who was in command of the forces of the enemy, accompanied by one of his staff officers, advanced, bearing a white flag, the remainder of his staff being stationed at about five hundred yards distance.

Our Lieutenant asked who would go down with him to meet the truce party, and Sergeant Thomas and myself volunteered at once for the duty. Advancing, Gen. Williams handed us a paper containing the words: "We demand an unconditional surrender." The Lieutenant read it and turned it over to me. Having read it, I shook my head in the negative, Sergeant Thomas doing the same. The General gave his horse what the Christians sometimes call "a short rein for a quick turn," and in five minutes he was back again among his own men. With a quick, sharp command from him, his men speedily spread out in every direction, and in an hour's time we were completely hemmed in on all sides. We quickly realized our position, but rather than surrender unconditionally we preferred to die fighting. When they had tightened their lines they again demanded an unconditional surrender, which we again refused. They drew gradually nearer and nearer, and we could see from the cupola of the church, wherein we had taken refuge, that they outnumbered us twenty to one, and were still coming from the surrounding hills in great numbers. A third time they repeated their demand for a surrender, threatening us with bloody consequences if we refused. We trembled, but refused to accede to their demand. At length the rebels procured a stack of hay, and placing it on a wagon on the hill-side, prepared to ignite it and run it down against the church for the purpose of burning us out. Sharpshooters had been placed so as to command every window, and our situation was indeed hazardous. Word was sent us that they would give us ten minutes in which to comply with their terms.

"Here is a test. What must we do?" said the Lieutenant. I said, "No surrender." So said Thomas and Stone. But hark! It is all over in three minutes. Lieutenant Love, in a moment of time almost, drew up our terms of surrender in the following language:

"We will surrender our men to you on the following terms: That you immediately parole us and give us a safeguard to our regiment, and that we turn over to you all of our munitions of war."

No sooner was the message borne to them than they accepted it. As soon as it was understood among our men that we were to surrender several incidents worthy of note occurred. Henry Graves, a young man who entered the army with me, attempted to escape by running. I caught him by the collar of the coat and drew him back into the house. He said that he would rather die than surrender. Another man in my company, Corporal A. Jackson, said to be the bravest man in the command, was so badly frightened at the idea of surrendering that he jerked off his stripes and attempted to dispossess me of mine. I told him if the enemy killed me it would be with my stripes on.

When the time came for us to march on the field to turn over our arms to our captors, about twenty of the rebel officers met us, shook hands with us, and talked as if nothing unpleasant had happened. There was one exception, in the case of a fellow among them who was drunk and felt that he ought to kill somebody. He was quickly placed under arrest and sent to the rear. We formed in line, marched out on the field, and after turning over our arms, proceeded back to our quarters and then down into the town, where we were paroled.

On the Thursday night previous to the occurrence of the foregoing incidents I had shot a man who was trying to steal upon one of our guards. Some of the rebels were going through our crowd inquiring for the man who did the shooting. I was the first man to deny all knowledge of it. All of my bravery had fled.

By 8 o'clock at night we had all been paroled and were ready to start on our journey. The night was dark and the snow deep, but the rebels lighted us out of town by the flames of our own wagons and ambulances.

The day I was captured, the 8th of January, 1865, will always be remembered by me. The night we left, the General ordered that those who were sick should be permitted to ride. I claimed to be sick, and four of us got on one mule. After we had reached the woods, our mule shied at a stump and spilled us off in the snow.

At midnight we went into camp, and our captors quartered us at a Union man's house. He had just killed his hogs and he was ordered to give us all we wanted to eat. The gentleman came into camp and informed us we could have all we wanted to eat, as he had plenty. That night I made my bed under the snow. Just before day we all arose from our snowy beds and set about preparing breakfast. I remember when the last hoecake was baked, I jerked it from the griddle and appropriated it to my own use.

The rebels quickly formed us in line and we were off for E. Town. The trouble with me was, that as the United States troops did not know that we were prisoners, and we were to march into town without their being made aware of our true character, I feared our troops would be fired on by them. The nearer we approached the lines the more frightened I became, but at last, without an accident, we arrived in town, when it proved that neither our own troops nor the rebel citizens knew who we were. The latter, presuming we were rebels, began to hand out clothes, thinking we had captured the town and all the Union soldiers in it.

We marched down to the camp with the rebel General Williams and Lieutenant String in front. The soldiers stood ready to make a charge when ordered. Major Bailey, the commander of the post, was a brave and dashing officer. The rebel General told him the conditions of the surrender of Company L; that according to promise he turned the men over to the Union troops, and asked for six hours' time in which to take his own departure. Major Bailey, a Dutchman, said:

"Me gives you zix hours to get out in. If any other force come, me don't gives you information."

At the same time he sent a dispatch to Muldraugh's Hill, and in twenty minutes we could hear the car-wheels rolling, and one hour from that time not a rebel could be seen in all the plain.

At night the rebels attempted to retaliate, but were driven off. It was reported that numbers of them were killed that night.

We received arms, marched the next day, and went into camp on Muldraugh's Hill, where we lived on half rations for two weeks—two hard-tacks, one ounce of meat, and a cup of rye coffee without sugar. This was a trying time for poor me. I wondered, the day I was made prisoner, whether I would ever be a free man again. While I was a prisoner I looked at myself and asked myself whether it was me or not.

We left Muldraugh's Hill about the last of January, 1865, on our second tramp to Bowling Green, where we went into quarters just under the hill from Fort Smith. That is now a reservoir. It was in that city I received many honors.

One night the news came that the rebels were advancing on the town. The commander of the post ordered me to take a platoon of men and march them up to Fort Smith; also Battery A, and place it in the gateway, while each Sergeant held his place. After drilling my men for about half an hour, I commanded them to lie down, in which position they watched throughout the entire night. At the dawn of day, as we were preparing to march back to the Barracks, I chanced to glance under our cannon and to my very great surprise I found the grape and canister with which we had loaded our cannon lying on the ground, it having rolled out of the gun after it had been loaded. If the rebels had attacked us they could have marched directly through the gate without the loss of a man; for if we had fired our cannon it would have been nothing more than a blank cartridge discharge, doing no execution. This discovery I kept to myself lest we should be disciplined for our negligence.

One day while I was on duty and walking around and giving instructions to the men I saw some one over in a thick grove not a great distance from the camp. He seemed to be watching our movements, at the same time endeavoring to keep himself concealed. I at once took a guard with me, and by a sharp flank movement I was on to him before he was aware of our presence. He proved to be a rebel lieutenant. We brought him into camp turned him over to the commanding officers.

After Hood's defeat, and during the time our soldiers occupied Nashville, frequent furloughs were given to the colored soldiers to return to Kentucky to see their wives and families. One of them stopped at Bowling Green, his wife living about five miles distant, on the other side of Barren River. He informed our commanding officer, [Lt.] Col. [Walter S.] Babcock, that the parties she belonged to had been treating her very cruelly, and to some extent on account of he, her husband, being in the army. The Colonel immediately sent for me, informed me of these facts, and ordered me to take a guard of ten men to accompany the soldier, who acted as our guide, and to bring the woman into camp; and further, that if the man who owned her had anything to say about it or offered any resistance, to put a ball into one ear so that it might come out of the other. When he said this I imagined that I was clothed with authority to do whatsoever I pleased on my trip. I got my men together as soon as possible, and crossed the Barren River, but instead of at once proceeding to the man's house on foot as we were ordered to do, I concluded that we would go by water, and at once commenced to look around for means of transportation. We soon discovered a small boat that was lying at the wharf, which we took possession of at once, and ordered the captain of the craft to take us nine miles down the river. This he refused to do, and as I did not propose to have my orders disobeyed, I concluded I would take charge of the boat myself, and at once placed myself at the wheel. I was not equal to the emergency, as the wheel refused to do my bidding. Some of the other boys tried it, but their failure equaled my own. I had determined, however, to make the journey by river, and as we could do nothing with the larger boat, we "pressed" into service two skiffs, and started on our trip. We had not proceeded a great way before we were fired upon by the rebels from the southern side of the river. We at once, with great haste, rowed to the opposite shore, where we arrived in safety, abandoned the skiffs, and returned the enemy's fire at long range, the rebels being on one side of the river and we on the other. We remained out from camp until dark, when we made a forced march for our quarters.

We arrived in camp at about 10 o'clock. We claimed to have had a brush with the enemy, and that we had obtained a great and signal victory, but our victory was in beating a hasty retreat. The next morning I reported to the commander of the post as to the result of our expedition. But, unfortunately, advices had already reached his ears of our retreat, my attempt to capture the boat, which was already in the service of the Government, and of our taking the two skiffs. For these offenses I came very near losing my office, but luckily I escaped with a reprimand. From this time forward I was an obedient officer, and never attempted to do anything without I had special orders so to do from my superiors.

The next day twenty soldiers were mounted and sent in search of the same woman who had been sent after on the day previous. They went to the house of her owner, but the woman had fled to parts unknown.

About this time I had become very expert in drilling, and as our regiment was fast filling up, I was assigned to the special duty of drilling Company K. One day while drilling I noticed that the Captain of the company was watching me very intently and with considerable interest. I was drilling the company in the Zouave drill. After looking at the varied and numerous movements for some length of time he called me to him and asked where on earth I had ever learned to drill men in that style? I replied that it was a drill originally my own. He said that it was very good, but he thought it best that I should drill the men in the old way. I had the men doubling up in such a manner that he could not comprehend the beauty of the movements; besides, he did not wish to take the trouble to learn them.

I remember an incident that happened while we were stationed in Bowling Green that is worthy of notice. In our quarters was an old man who was in the habit of sitting around the fire, sleeping in that position night after night. The boys were disposed to tantalize and annoy him, one man in particular going to the extreme of carrying stones to his own

bunk and amusing himself by pelting the old man at intervals, sometimes almost knocking him out of his chair. I informed our Captain and
inaugurated a plan to catch and punish the offender. I arranged with the
Captain to be on the watch, and about midnight, when our man cast
the first stone, the Captain walked in and ordered every man to turn
out. Officers and men promptly obeyed the order, the culprit (Lewis)
among the number, but the latter quickly disappeared through the door
and was absent until a search revealed a number of stones in his bunk.
Thinking everything was all right, Lewis returned to his quarters, and
when confronted by the inquiry as to his whereabouts, he said he had
been to see a lady. The proof of his guilt were shown to him and our
Captain ordered the punishment. I was ordered to tie him up. Taking
my belt, I threw it over a joist, and with the aid of a twine string I had
him in a few moments standing on his toes. The string broke and Lewis
came down with a crash, laughing heartily meanwhile. The Captain,
greatly annoyed, told him his laughter would soon be turned to mourning, and ordered me to again tie him up, and to keep him suspended for
twenty minutes. Under this punishment, the poor fellow wept and
moaned, and at length fainted, and after about ten minutes had elapsed
I cut him down. The lesson was a salutary one, for, from that time on,
we had in our company no more obedient soldier. He expressed the
greatest love for me, and was ever after prompt in the discharge of every
duty. I loved the soldiers over whom I was placed and I believed they
loved me, as I would not have them punished unless for a flagrant
breach of discipline. I remember one night when one of our soldiers
came and informed me that two of our men were in a certain forbidden
place. As I was Sergeant of the guard it was my duty to look after them,
and taking three of my men I soon had them under arrest. They offered
me fifty dollars if I would not report them to the officer of the day. I indignantly declined to accept their bribe and moved off with them toward the guard-house. Before reaching there, however, I relented, and
turning them loose, told them to retire at once to their quarters. This,
of course, was not a true soldierly act, but I felt that the good of the service would not be greatly promoted by their punishment, and that the
life of no man depended upon their being brought into camp.

While in Bowling Green I gained many friends among the citizens.
Some of the most valued of these were Mrs. Ewing, Mrs. Frances Kersy,
Mrs. King, Rev. Mr. G. Graham, Miss Johnson, Mr. Johnson, the famous

blacksmith; Mrs. Nealy, a lady with whom I boarded; Mr. Benj. Bibb, now a citizen of Louisville; Mr. George Bleaky, of Louisville, Mrs. Cook, and a host of others too numerous to mention. Their hospitalities were frequently enjoyed by me.

I remember the time our men went out on a scout and brought in ten rebels as prisoners. A sergeant being asked for to escort them to Louisville, I volunteered and was placed in charge of them. We were soon at the train, on boarding which I found four thousand veteran soldiers on their way home to be mustered out of the service. I was ordered to turn my prisoners over to these, and as they swore vengeance against the rebels, the latter begged that I might be permitted to go with them. I was, however, ordered back to camp.

A train on the way to Louisville was thrown from the track by the enemy, in 1865, the coaches were burned, and the passengers robbed. I was again chosen to go, and with twenty men proceeded to Glasgow Junction to succor the passengers on board the wrecked train. The night was dark and dreary, not a star could be seen, and the train traveled slowly. Arriving at the scene of trouble, we found all quiet, with not a rebel in sight. The citizens had fled to the woods, the cars were burned to ashes, and the ground was strewn with the debris of the destroyed train. We lay upon our arms all night, momentarily expecting an attack, and at daybreak moved off to Bowling Green. Of course, when we returned to our quarters we had more to tell of than had really occurred, but with soldiers that was not unusual.

My efficiency as a sergeant had proven to the officers that I was capable, and as a consequence I was ordered to report to headquarters for assignment to more important duties. At this time hundreds of women and children, the wives and families of men who had gone into war, had flocked into Bowling Green for protection, their former masters having driven them from their homes.[4] They sought that protection at our headquarters, and I was detailed to collect them together and look after their needs. I made my headquarters in the old colored Methodist Church on the hill, my duties requiring that I should see that their rations were duly distributed among them, and power was conferred upon me to punish the unruly. Unfortunately, the General Government did not provide them with clothing, and as some of these poor people were driven from their homes without even a second garment, their condition was pitiable in the extreme, as in four weeks' time many of them were unable to hide their nakedness. They looked to me as if I were their Saviour. Whatever happened in camp to disturb or annoy them, the story was at once detailed to me, and I was expected to remedy every evil. Sometimes fifteen or twenty would engage in a broil, and the weaker party would invariably come to me for protection. On these oc-casions I would call a court-martial, sit as judge, examine witnesses, and condemn the guilty to such punishment as in my judgment the offense deserved; as a rule, that was the last of it. There were in camp two or three old women who were always in some row. These I would talk to, and tell them they ought to act as mothers to the younger women, in which they would coincide, but before long would again be in trouble. They used to say of me:

"God knows dat's a good child! God mus' be wid him, kase he couldn't act as he do wid dese niggers."

They were in camp in Bowling Green for six months, when orders were received to transfer them to Camp Nelson,[5] and I was directed to canvass the town and ascertain who among them would go. I set out one morning betimes, with my little book in hand, to take down the names of those willing to go. Many of them had a grave misapprehension of my object and fled at my approach, but after considerable trouble I gath-ered together about 750, the majority of those having no place of shel-ter. They embraced all ages, from the child six months to the woman eighty years. Among them were some of the prettiest girls I ever saw, and every shade of color was represented in the multitude.

Captain [Cyrus C.] Palmer, myself, and ten men were detailed to go with them, and leaving Bowling Green at 7 o'clock at night we arrived in Louisville the next morning at the same hour. But one accident marred the pleasure of the journey, and that was when, awaking in the night, I found three women piled up on my head. Arriving in the city, we found it full of soldiers, and had great difficulty in making our way through the streets. At 5 P.M. we were off for Lexington and arrived there in due time. Late in the night Captain Palmer had passed through the city without leaving orders for me. We had no provisions, our sup-plies having been left on the L. & N. Road. The women and children were almost famished for want of food, the children even eating dirt. I spent all the means I had for the poor sufferers, and then called upon the commander of the Post, General [Stephen Gano] Burbridge. He agreed to furnish us with one ration apiece, and at one o'clock I received orders to march the women around to Morgan's old negro pen, where we found everything heart could desire. It was astonishing how the colored ladies of Lexington stole these little children in order to take care of them. Some of the women gave their children away in order to get rid of them.

An incident occurred in the camp on the morning we arrived that was very amusing. Two white men came in, and producing bottles, dipped them repeatedly into the spring on the grounds. The women came running to me, asserting that the men had placed poison in the water, and as matters did look somewhat suspicious, I compelled the men to fill their bottles from the spring, stir up a substance that could be seen in the bottom of one of them, and drink a quantity of the liquid. I then placed them under surveillance for an hour to see what effect the drink would have upon them, and as no bad results came of it, it was concluded they were innocent, and they were allowed to depart.

At 5 o'clock P.M. we were off for camp, where we arrived about 11 o'clock. I was angry, for we were compelled to walk nearly all the way from Nicholasville to the camp. On arriving, the guard ordered me to halt, which I refused to do at the risk of my life. How often I have been frightened about it since!

Marching my people around to headquarters, I there met Captain Palmer for the first time since leaving Louisville. Down through the streets of the City of Refuge we went, the scene presented being a beautiful one. Every door was open, and in each of them stood some one with a torch in hand to light us on our way. There was no room for us in the neat little cottages, but abundant shelter had been provided in tents for my troop of females, two families being assigned to each tent. It was late in the night, and I was compelled to leave them in the hands of the Lord and under the care of the commanding officer. Mounting a stump, I delivered to them a neat little speech, wishing them well, which called forth such expressions as they would make to a father. With many tears I bade them adieu, telling them to trust in God, who was able to do more for them than I could. They clung to my coat-tail, and I remembered the scripture that says, "The time will come when seven women will take hold of one man." I did not know but what that time had come, but I was not prepared to stand it.

I formed my men in line and marched to the Soldier's Home,[6] where we demanded our supper. The cook soon served us a supper in fine style, which made me feel happy temporarily. I had the first happy night's rest I had enjoyed since leaving Bowling Green, as the case of these poor women and children were off my mind.

The next morning I met Captain Palmer, and he instructed me to give passes to those who desired to visit the ladies. I did so, and that was the last I seen of the Captain until I arrived in Bowling Green.

I gave one of the men a pass to go home and see his mother, who lived about five miles from Camp Nelson. While there the rebels made a raid on the place, and he moved back to camp on double-quick time.

Camp Nelson was overrun with troops at that time, and the place looked gay. Thousands of people were coming in from all directions, seeking their freedom. It was equal to the forum at Rome. All they had to do was to get there and they were free.

Col. Bridgewater[7] was commander of the Post, and a brave one he was. As I said, Captain Palmer had left me without instructions. I remained here contented for three days, and then applied to Col. Bridgewater for transportation. He told me to go back to the Soldier's Home and eat good victuals; that I should not be hurt; that Captain Palmer should suffer for the way he had treated me.

In ten days, however, we struck a line of march for Nicholasville, Ky., where we arrived about 5 o'clock in the afternoon. There was a circus in town, and the proprietor engaged me and my men to guard the inside ring for him, for which I received compensation. The next morning we were off for Lexington, where we arrived on Saturday night. On Sunday morning we reached Louisville, where I expected to meet my mother and father. I had written to them to meet me on my return to the city, and they had been waiting for a week, expecting me on every train, but the conduct of Captain Palmer prevented my coming, and they returned home with sad hearts at not seeing the boy they loved so well. However, on Sunday I had a fine time in greeting old friends I had not seen since I enlisted, among them many young ladies to whom I had paid my regards before I enlisted, and included in the number my late wife, of whom I will speak hereafter. I done my share of boasting that day.

At 7 o'clock. P.M. we were to leave for Bowling Green. Great crowds of people, both male and female, followed us to the train. Tramp! Tramp! Some of us thought that would be our last visit to the city where we enlisted. The girls cried and we, too, wept, for we thought that would be the last time we should ever meet.

The police, in the midst of this scene, ordered us out of the depot. My tears were dried at once, and I ordered the boys to charge bayonets. The police fled in every direction, so in the sight of my friends I gained a victory. I was then ready to take my departure, and leave them to carry the news of my victory over civil officers. Ding-dong! All aboard! We kiss each other good-bye, and are off for Bowling Green.

Soon after my arrival here I was appointed, temporarily, Regimental Quartermaster Sergeant, with my headquarters at the Commissary Department, near the depot. One day, while I was off duty, about five thousand soldiers came up from Nashville and stopped over in Bowling Green for two rations. I was out on a visit, and the soldiers missed their dinner. For this piece of negligence I was severely censured. While I held this office I had a fine time. I was allowed to occupy quarters in town and boarded with Mrs. Nealey, a worthy lady, and one who will ever be remembered by me. Her daughter, the wife of Mr. Benjamin Bibb, was an amiable lady, of rare qualities.

While stationed here the son of my old boss, A. Robinson, visited the city to see me. It was three days before he found me, and then he was preparing to leave town for home. We had a joyous time together. I took him through my department and showed him what I thought were all the places of interest. We talked freely of old slave times without a show of prejudice on either side. He bought me a box of cigars, he bade me adieu, and I have never seen him more.

While in camp, and seeing joyous times for soldiers, religion began to grow cold. One day, on the river bank, I met Bro. Swift Johnson. I had never seen him before. He said to me, "You look like a Christian." I told him I was. He grasped my hand, and we rejoiced together that we were not ashamed to own our God. We proposed to have a meeting in our barracks. He said in his company he was the only man who would own Christ. On mentioning the matter to my captain, he said he would be glad if we would hold meetings. That night we had a glorious prayer meeting. Bro. Johnson prayed, I followed, and Thomas also prayed. Bro. Johnson then talked to the sinners and the presence of the Lord was made manifest. Bless His name! How sweet it is to think of Him!

The day of the surrender of Lee was a grand one with Company L and all the troops in Bowling Green. The war was now over, and the thoughts of going home and being free men filled all hearts with joy. Men were shouting, some crying, and others praying, "O Freedom! how

I love thee! Long have I prayed for thee, and at last thou hast come! May I enter into thy joy and rest!"

Almost before we had time to stop smiling, the sad, sad news came, on Sunday morning, that Abraham Lincoln, whom we almost esteemed as a God, had been assassinated by the notorious J. Wilkes Booth. Gen. R. E. Lee surrendered to Gen. U. S. Grant on the 9th day of April and Abraham Lincoln was assassinated on the 14th of April, 1865. The morning the news reached us I had ten men and was patrolling the suburbs of the town. I marched my men out on the plain and sat down and wept. We remained there until nightfall, and then returned to town and joined with the men in camp in sorrowing over our loss. Our Moses had been slain, and we knew not what the future had in store for us. I had recourse to prayer. I threw myself on the strong arm of God, and felt that He would bring me through.

We stayed in Bowling Green during the year 1865 until fall, and then received orders to proceed to Columbus, Ky. I shall never forget the day I left. My friends accompanied me to the depot, bringing a bountiful supply of provisions, cigars, and everything necessary to make a soldier comfortable. My provisions were sufficient in quantity to last me five weeks. I bade adieu to my Bowling Green friends and boarded the train for Louisville, on reaching which place I was again assigned to my company. George Thomas was made Sergeant Major, Jacob Stone appointed Orderly Sergeant, and I was assigned to the position of Regimental Quartermaster. Our men camped on the plain near town, while I was sent with a company of men to guard the boat upon which our rations were to be shipped. I slept on the lower deck, and this night was a dreary one for me, for the mosquitoes had so used me that the soldiers, on seeing me, were about to break ranks, but were soon brought to time by the Captain.

About 2 o'clock we got aboard of the boat, bound for Columbus, Ky. We started on Sunday and arrived at our destination on the following Tuesday evening at about 3 o'clock—slow traveling. It rained all the time, and I had to sleep on the hurricane roof. Lee had surrendered and Marrs was pretty near ready to do the same thing.

We remained there a part of the winter of 1865, when I was again relieved from active duty. My principal business was to look after the sick in our quarters, and march those who were able to go, up to the doctor's quarters for examination. The rest of my time was devoted to looking after matters in general. I helped to throw out of the Mississippi River the cannon balls the rebels had thrown in at that point where they had been driven from Columbus. I stood on the banks of the Mississippi and looked over into Missouri, on the little town called Belmont, where, it was said, when Gen. Grant fought and routed the enemy, they fell like beating apples from a full tree.

We were ordered, finally, to leave Columbus and go to Paducah, Ky., to relieve the Fourth U. S. Colored Artillery stationed there.[8] We rejoiced at the change, for our men were dying off rapidly in our unhealthy locality. Here I was assigned to duty as master of a wagon train, with three horses to care for. One day, while going out to where the men were engaged in cutting wood, I met three rebels coming toward me at a sweeping gallop. I was approaching them at the same speed. They swore vengeance and passed on. It made me think the war was being renewed. I went on to the woods and ordered one-half of the men to do the chopping, while the balance stood guard.

Soon after this I was taken sick. One of the men that went away with me had been on guard duty in town, and he had by chance caught the small-pox from the citizens. He was brought to the camp, when every soldier immediately fled, and left him sitting in the yard by himself. I told the doctor I would never leave him, and took him to my own quarters, where I sat up with him all night by myself. Such a night I never experienced before or since. He was flighty, and imagined Satan had him in his clutches. He would cry out, "Oh, take him away! I see the chains in his hands! Look at him!" and to keep him in bed I was compelled to sit on him and hold him down. Death had laid his icy hands on him, and though I prayed with him it did no good. He had sinned away the day of grace, and, as the poet says, made his bed in hell. Poor J. D. Brown! I never expect to see him again. His soul is housed in hell. The next morning he was removed to the eruptive hospital, and I felt that I had played the part of a man by standing by a friend. The next day as the drum tapped for dinner a pain struck me in the head and I fell to the earth as dead. The small-pox had me. I was picked up and carried to my room, and the next morning it was found that I had a genuine case of the disease. I was removed to the hospital, there to remain and wrestle with the loathsome malady, but thank God, I was only compelled to keep my bed a few weeks. After I had sufficiently recovered to attend to business, I was solicited to remain to assist the doctor and watch over the medical department. This I refused to do, and was sent back to the camp and reassigned to duty as wagon-master. At the same time I was allowed by the commander of the Post to make extra money with the wagon train by hauling for the citizens of the town when the teams had nothing else to do. This was called a mess-house. In this business I made $300 in six weeks.

I applied for a furlough to go home, which was granted. About this time the Fifth Cavalry,[9] of which my brother, H. C. Marrs, was Sergeant Major, was mustered out of service at Helena, Arkansas, and he came by and we made the journey home together. Arriving in Louisville, we found the city and suburbs full of Gen. [William T.] Sherman's troops, there for the purpose of being mustered out.

I mounted the stage for Shelbyville, for there were no cars running to Shelbyville in those days. I started with my stripes on, and when at Gilman's Point some of Sherman's men, stationed there, said to me, "Oh, Sergeant, I pity your case to night." I went on to Shelbyville, where I met my father, mother, sisters, and brother. You may know we had a happy reunion. We talked and cried, and friends gathered from all parts of the city to greet me. In the midst of our glee a fire broke out in the upper end of the city and everybody was excited. Without thought that I was among my enemies I pulled off my weapons, kept on my uniform, and ran toward the fire with all speed. I worked with might and main to save the property. So soon, however, as the fire was subdued, my presence was noticed, and I was at once attacked by three men. One of them remarked with an oath "Yonder is a negro officer of the army," at the same time they rushed upon me with drawn knives. Mother threw herself in between me and them, but we soon pushed her aside, when we had a desperate hand to hand conflict, I retreating and defending myself as best I could. I was armed only with a heavy stick, which I had picked up by chance when the fight first commenced, and the knowledge of the sword exercise I had acquired in the army came in good play on this occasion. It was near half a mile down the road to my father's house, and we fought this entire distance. The front part of my clothing was literally hacked to pieces, but I sustained no bodily injury. When we reached a point in the road opposite to my father's house I at once wheeled and ran into the gate, around the house, and into the back door, when I seized upon my pistols, threw open the front door, and opened fire upon them. They at once fled and were soon beyond the reach of my bullets. My father, mother, and sister at once became very much alarmed as to my safety, they believing that my antagonists, reinforced by others, would return and attack us during the night. I had come to stay, however, but I took the precaution to stand guard throughout the entire night.

I remained in Shelbyville three weeks, and I enjoyed myself to my heart's content. The ladies and gentlemen showed me every attention, and entertainments were almost nightly given in honor of my presence. One incident occurred during my stay at Shelbyville that will not be out of place in speaking of these entertainments. I had been in attendance at one of them, and was escorting a young lady home. She had a remarkable fair complexion, was extremely handsome, and was richly and tastefully attired. It was near midnight, and we were passing along one of the principal streets. All at once we were hailed by some one on the opposite side of the street, who started across towards us. I at once drew my pistol and leveled it at him, which, as soon as he saw, compelled him to make a hurried retreat. The young lady was speechless, for at least five minutes, from the fright occasioned by the occurrence. I had no further trouble after this while I remained in Shelbyville.

One week before my time was out I took my departure for Paducah, to rejoin my regiment, and upon my arrival entered at once upon the duties of my office. I was thus engaged but a short time, when I was sent for by my Major and Captain, who desired to know whether I would like promotion to Quartermaster Sergeant. I expressed a desire for the office, but before my appointment was consummated, orders came for our march to Louisville to be mustered out. This was joyful news to us, and with one accord our men raised the grand old song of "Home, sweet home! There's no place like home!"

All aboard for Louisville, where we arrived on the 20th of April, 1866, and were mustered out on the 24th of the same month.

My friends on the day of my discharge from the service made me a present of a suit of clothes costing $105, a gift highly appreciated. This ends the history of my war life. I have written more in this book of my war campaign than I expected to do, but I think it will prove pleasant to my friends to have had something to say of the part our soldiers took, though it was on a small scale, in the late civil war.

As I have referred thus far only to the *ante bellum* days and to the period covered by the war, I propose now to speak of my life since the close of the conflict, and I trust it will prove interesting to those who may read it.

When I arrived home from the army I immediately set about perfecting plans to make a living for myself and to help my father and mother along in life. But I must not forget to speak of my old grandmother, whom I loved so well, and who was yet with her owners. I was deeply interested in her, and determined to have her make her home with my family. She belonged to Goodnough's, near Simpsonville, Ky., and I procured a wagon and went after her. The white people with whom she lived, whom she had nursed in their young days, loved her dearly and were unwilling to part with her, but I insisted on caring for her in her old age and took her home with me. She lived but a few years, dying at the good old age of ninety years, giving God the glory.

I now began to think about business matters, and consulting with my brother, H. C. Marrs, we formed a copartnership. We purchased harness, a two-horse wagon, one four-horse wagon, and I purchased for my own use a horse, saddle, and bridle. He was to engage in teaming with the wagons, while I attended to raising a crop. For eight successive months he had as much hauling as he could do at eight dollars per day. We rose early in the morning, and attended to our horses, and by daylight were ready for business. While he drove the teams I looked after my crop, having, in connection with Mr. Benj. Burley, rented a field of twenty-five acres. The Lord prospered us greatly, and we reaped an abundant harvest.

My friends, at this time, knowing what I had endeavored to do for them in the past, importuned me to go to Simpsonville and engage in the teaching of their children, but this I did not feel myself competent to do. Their persuasions, however, finally induced me to leave the cornfield and enter the school-room to labor for the development of my race. Oh, how I love them! I opened the school under the auspices of Wilkerson Bullitt, Isaac Simpson, and Benj. Elmore, as trustees, on September 1, 1866. The trustees employed me at a salary of twenty-five dollars a month, and at this time we had no aid from the Freedman's Bureau, the parents paying one dollar per month for each child. The trustees were generous and kind to me, making many presents as a reward for my labor. I shall ever remember them as faithful friends.

Simpsonville was not only my first field in school-teaching, but it was in that neighborhood I was converted and became a member of the Baptist Church.

I remember an incident that occurred while I was in Simpsonville. One night, while all were asleep, the K. K. K. rode into town, some of them mounted on horses, some on mules, and others on asses. They were provided with tin horns, old tin pans, drums, bells, etc., and made a terrible din. Coming into the yard of the house where I lived, they dismounted and began stripping the trees of switches, as if preparing to come into the house to administer a flogging to every one of us. I stole down stairs, and, armed with my old pistol, stationed myself in a chimney corner, prepared to fight my way through should occasion demand it. They made threats of some sort, which I could not hear, but finally they rode off, my back was saved, and I felt mightily relieved. The women were terribly frightened, and as I was an ex-soldier they thought I had frightened the party away, and looked upon me as their saviour. I went to my room again and went to bed, but all of the men and women came and crouched around me for protection.

I was a perfect curiosity to the white people of Simpsonville, simply because I was the first colored school-teacher they had ever seen, and yet I was no stranger to them, for just three years from the time I left Simpsonville, a slave, to join the United States Army, I returned a free man and a school teacher. They would come to visit me and stare, and wonder at the change, and this was especially the case with my original owners. They said I ought to thank them for what I knew. I did, in part. They would send me sums to solve, such as $146 + 12 - 19 + 200$, and the like, to see if I really knew anything. Then when I would work them out they would say to my colored friends, "That Elijah is a smart nigger!"

One day, while the school children were at play, during recess, some one fired a shot among them. I saw the man who did the shooting, and going to him, charged him with the offense. He denied it, and raised a club to strike me, when I retreated to the school-room, glad to get away alive, for, though the war was over, the K. K. K. was in full blast, and no man was safe from their depredations.

I had some very bright pupils in my school at Simpsonville. One young man, by the name of Wells, very attentive to his studies, and a very apt pupil, afterward learned telegraphy, but his color debarred him from obtaining employment, and he is now a policeman in the city of Indianapolis. The total number of scholars on the roll in that school was one hundred and fifty. I closed my connection with the school in my native town after having very good results.

My brother had been teaching school in Lagrange, on the L., C. & L. R. R., and was solicited to take charge of one at Lexington, which was held in Braxton's Church, on Main Street. I took charge of his school September 1, 1867, under trustees Dennis Roberts, Palmer Berry, and Albert Sanders. At that time there was considerable denominational strife between the Methodists and Baptists, which culminated in a division of the school and the formation of two distinct organizations, the Methodist school being under the trusteeship of A. Sanders, and that of the Baptists' controlled by Dennis Roberts and P. Berry. During the whole controversy I was neutral, taking sides with neither party. The first school was at this time under the protection of the Freedman's Bureau, receiving aid from it, and the new order of things brought about many differences, which were not easy of settlement. Both parties claimed aid from the Bureau, and as only one was entitled to it, much trouble was experienced in adjusting the matter. The agent of the Bureau, then stationed in Louisville, was written to by both parties, and in November, 1867, the following reply was received:

"To A. SANDERS, DENNIS ROBERTS, AND OTHERS:

"Yours is at hand. I would suggest to you to call a meeting and have an election, and let all those who want Marrs vote for him, and those who do not, vote for who they want. But I think you had better keep Marrs.

I. CATLIN,
"Brevet Col. and B. Agent."

In compliance with this suggestion, the trustees met, held an election, and I received all but three votes. I still remained neutral, for I knew if I took part in the fuss it would hurt me financially. The school was divided, one hundred of the pupils remaining with me, and only seven seceding. It was a glorious victory for me, and the result was that my friends done more for me afterwards than they would have done had the school remained undivided. The Lord seemed to guide me all through the struggle. The Bureau decided to divide the school fund. I was to receive fifteen dollars per month and the other teacher ten dollars. The parents of my pupils agreed to pay me seventy-five cents for each of them per month, and altogether I was very handsomely compensated for my services.

When the time came to make out a monthly report, I did so, and sent it into the Bureau. The teacher of the other school did the same. In three days afterwards I received the following letter from the agent at Louisville:

"E. P. MARRS, TEACHER OF THE BAPTIST SCHOOL, LA-GRANGE, KY.:

"Your report for this month is correct, but the report from the other school is so incorrect that nothing can be made out of it. You go around to the other school and show that teacher how to make out her report or she will not get any money from this office. Show this as your authority.

I. CATLIN.
"DECEMBER, 1867."

Up to this time she had been my enemy, but this bit of authority made us friends and we so remained.

I will recall an incident that happened while I was teaching school at Lagrange. It was not connected with the school, but with politics. In 1869, when we were to cast our ballot for the first time, Judge Wheat, a Republican, had announced himself an independent candidate for Judge of the Shelby County Court.

I had written my first political letter to the Louisville Commercial, saying that now we, as a race, were about to cast our ballot for the first time in life, and that we would cast it for weal or woe. I warned my people not to vote the Democratic ticket, but to give their suffrage to Judge Wheat, the Republican nominee. This enraged the Republicans of Shelby County. They sent a man to Lagrange to induce me to withdraw my letter, but this I refused to do. I thought if Judge Wheat sought our suffrage he had no right to be ashamed of us.

While I was at home in Shelbyville, the Republicans held a secret meeting at the colored Baptist Church for the purpose of shaking up things for the election. It was intended that none but the colored Republicans should know anything of the proceedings or objects of this gathering. I was made secretary of the meeting. On Saturday a reporter called on me and desired to know something in regard to the meeting. Without thought I gave him the information asked for, telling him that we had resolved to support Judge Wheat in the election on the following Monday. Before daylight on election day the proceedings of our meeting had been printed on slips and circulated in every district in the county, the charge being made that Judge Wheat was the candidate of the negro party. This only had the effect of combining the colored voters in support of Judge Wheat and produced no bad results.

During my four years residence in Lagrange I made many friends. Among those I valued most highly were Elder Warren Lewis, Moses Berry, a former pupil and now a teacher in one of the public schools of Missouri; Frank James, Salathiel Berry, Susan Davis, Mrs. Berry, Alice James, Josie Sutton, Annie and William Wilson, Eliza Barber; Caroline, Washington and Mary Bullit; Mrs. Annie Lewis, and a host of others. Of Elder Warren Lewis I can say much in commendation. When at his house, I received every courtesy, and nothing was too good for me. Elder Lewis, his wife, and Susan Davis presented to my wife and myself a beautiful bouquet on our marriage day.

While teaching in Lagrange I had occasion to go out into the country one evening to visit some of my pupils and stay all night with them. The latter lived adjacent with some white people by the name of Whitesides. They had never seen a colored school teacher, and, from their actions, one would have supposed they had never come in contact with a white one either. They had heard of my coming and were all in the yard of the house, awaiting my coming with, apparently, as much curiosity as if I were President of the United States. As I walked into the yard, I heard one of them say, "Thar he is now!" Another said, "Take keer, Ann, let me see him for God's sake!" I underwent this ordeal as I marched down to the quarters of the colored people, the crowd following and stationing themselves about the door of the house when I reached it. Finally, one of them asked:

"Teacher, can you read?"

I answered in the affirmative.

"Well, I wish you'd read some for me."

I took a book and read a portion of it to them, much to their surprise. They were wonderfully astonished that a colored school teacher could read.

At the close of my second session in Lagrange I again went to Shelbyville. One night, sitting at home, thinking over measures for the development of my race, I proposed to my brother that we form an Agricultural and Mechanical Association. To his inquiry as to how we should proceed in the matter, I suggested that we endeavor to obtain fifty subscribers to the project, at fifteen dollars each, making a total of $750, and organize at once. He agreeing, we immediately went to work canvassing, and in a fortnight we had the men with the money. A company was formed, with H. C. Marrs as President, and myself as Secretary. The next business was to procure a site for our enterprise, and James Flint, John Tyree, and myself were appointed a committee for that purpose. We purchased from Mr. Beard 42½ acres of ground at a cost of $4,200. The President and Secretary were appointed a committee to go to Louisville and select premiums. A fair for colored people was a new and novel venture in that section, and hence the greatest interest was taken in it, and visitors from far and near were present to witness our first attempt. It is, perhaps, needless to say it was a success. Our fondest expectations were exceeded, and our inaugural meeting netted us $3,000. Of this money $1,500 was paid on our property[.] The second year's receipts were $2,300, the third, $1,800, and the fourth, $1,300, a gradual decrease. When I found that interest in the matter was on the wane, I sold out to Mr. Silas Ford in the fall of 1874. During the four years of my connection with the enterprise I held the office of Secretary, and on my withdrawal turned over my books to my successor, Lewis Lawson.

We turn again to Lagrange. During my stay here as a teacher, I was superintendent of the Sunday-school, and for four years did what I conceived a great moral work, among the children, teaching them the Word of God. At times my school numbered one hundred and fifty pupils. I was also secretary of the Loyal League, organized at Lagrange by Prof. W. L. Yancey for protection against the K. K. K.

I was the first colored man elected President of the Republican Club of Oldham County, in 1869. I was the first colored man to take the stump for the Republican party in Oldham. I was the first colored man to propose a celebration in honor of the passage of the Fifteenth Amendment to the Constitution of the United States. This was a great occasion. Thirty-seven girls in the procession represented the States, and the whole affair was a grand one. Col. Sam. McKee was the orator of the occasion.

I am the man of whom the Lagrange correspondent of the Shelby Sentinel wrote, saying that after the celebration he observed a colored man whose perspiration would make good ink, and who was ruling the negroes politically.

While in Lagrange, sitting at the fireside of Elder W. Lewis one beautiful fall night, we heard the windows of the house broken in and a general uproar. The K. K. K. was upon us. I told the women to get behind the chimney for safety. The irons were hot upon the stove, and I used them freely in repelling the assault. Mr. Roberts ran to his bed for a pistol, but was struck on the head with a stone and fell back. Mrs. R. attempted to reach it, when she, too, was struck and forced to retire. Mr. Roberts, Sr., finally made his way to the bed and secured the weapon, and would have made short work of our assailants had the pistol been loaded. The K. K. K. did not know this, however, for when they saw it they fled. I followed them up to where I boarded, and securing my old gun I returned to Mr. Lewis'. About midnight they came again, and as they got near me I called to them to halt and then fired. They immediately fled, never to return.

About this time I became somewhat dissatisfied, and desired very much to leave Lagrange, and having made up my mind to that effect I intended doing so without any one being aware of my resolve until the moment of my departure. It leaked out in some way, however, when the citizens, both white and colored, held a meeting on the 20th of November, 1878, and subscribed and paid over to me $150.00 extra to remain with them another year. May God ever bless such true friends as they proved themselves to me.

While teaching in Lagrange a bright-eyed boy of seven years, named Henry Weeden,[10] was one of my pupils. I feel that I would fail to do justice to a worthy scholar if I do not refer to him in this book. He was very attentive to his studies and always knew his lessons. Before he was twenty-one years old he became the editor of a newspaper—Zion's Advocate, a Methodist publication. He has held many honorable positions in Zion Methodist Church, and is now a letter-carrier in Louisville, Ky.

During my career as teacher in Lagrange I had under my supervision, at different times, three hundred children, and when I left there it was with the consciousness of having done my duty as a Christian and a teacher.

In 1870, when I left Lagrange, it was for the purpose of taking charge of a school at Newcastle, Henry County, Ky. I opened on the first Monday in January of that year with fifty scholars, and under the supervision of the following as a board of trustees: George Grigsby, Emanuel Bennett, Milton Hurley, London Clifton, and Esquire Hamilton. I can say of these men, as I have said of others, that they were faithful to their trust and never faltered when a duty was to be performed.

On reaching New Castle my first thought was concerning my status with the church, and I at once wrote to Simpsonville for my letter. On receiving it I united with the church at New Castle, of which the late Rev. A. Taylor was pastor. He was a man whom we all loved and esteemed as a minister of the Gospel. Peace to his ashes!

While in New Castle, during the year 1871, I became an active worker in the church and Sunday-school, and did what I could for the development of the minds of the children and older people. In the winter I taught school day and night.

At that time Henry County was overrun with the K. K. K., and a colored man in public business dared not go five miles outside of the city for fear of assassination. Public court day always attracted large crowds of country people to town. One day one of the K. K. K. called to me and invited me to enter a stable with him. There was no one near, and as I feared to disobey, I entered with him. He at once evinced a desire to raise a fuss with me, and asked me to drink with him. This I at first refused to do, when he, with an oath, exclaimed, "What! you nigger! You won't drink with a white man? I'll show you, sir!" That was enough for me. I turned the bottle up and pretended to drink. Thinking I had done so, he was satisfied and soon left me alone.

I then called the colored men together and organized a society for self-protection, calling ourselves the Loyal League. Of this society I was secretary, and we were always in readiness for any duty. For three years I slept with a pistol under my head, an Enfield rifle at my side, and a corn-knife at the door, but I never had occasion to use them.

My stay in New Castle was a pleasant one. School closed on the first of June, and, as usual, I had my closing exercises. This proved a financial success, netting $105.

The trustees and citizens generally of Lagrange now sent me a proposition to return to them and teach for another session. This I assented to, providing the people of New Castle would release me, and the Lagrange friends would insure a liberal support.

My term being thus closed in New Castle, I returned to my home in Shelbyville for the purpose of marrying, and on the 3d day of August, 1871, I was united to Miss Julia Gray, the ceremony being performed by Rev. Simon Grigsby, brother of Deacon George Grigsby, of New Castle, Henry County. My wife's mother, Harriet Gray, done all she could to make the nuptials a grand affair. There were eight attendants, friends of myself and wife. These were Mr. Lewis Lawson and Miss Mary Griffith, Mr. Andrew Ellis and Miss Ida Houghs, Mr. Salathiel Berry and Miss Kittie Wilson, Mr. Leonard Taylor and Miss Jennie Gray.

Mrs. Julia Tevis, proprietress of Science Hill College,[11] Shelbyville, was a great friend to my wife, and brought the school girls to witness the ceremony. They set the table, and aided in every way to make the occasion a pleasant one. Mrs. Tevis made my wife some handsome presents, and afterward presented me with about sixty books. In doing so she said:

"Elijah, I want to say to you that I have been teaching school for fifty years, and there is not a day but what I learn something; and I want you to take these books and apply yourself to study."

I have never forgotten her words. They are to me like words engraved on brass.

Before I married I became a believer in the old saying that we should not catch a bird before we had a cage to put it in. God had prospered me, and I had bought a place on Main Street, Shelbyville, built a two-story frame house and fitted it up. I then went out, caught my bird, and early one morning had my wagons at the door of my mother-in-law's house ready to move my wife to her new home. We remained here during the summer months, and it was indeed a happy season for us.

In September, 1871, according to promise, I returned to Lagrange and was received cordially by the warmhearted people there.

I remember an incident that occurred while my wife and I were located at Lagrange. For the purpose of tantalizing my new wife I concluded I would remain away from home one night, not letting her know of my intentions or whereabouts. I did so and she had the whole town in an uproar, looking for me, while I was quietly sojourning with Rev. Warren Lewis. When I arrived at home the next morning I found it was not so funny as I had anticipated, as my wife was almost crazy with the thought that I had been killed. I never tried that again.

I finished my last school term in Lagrange and once more returned to New Castle, where I again opened school on the first of January, 1872. On my arrival with my wife the citizens greeted us heartily, and as it was our intention to go to housekeeping they presented us with a sufficiency of meat, sugar, coffee, etc., to last us for three months. Soon after my arrival I was again elected Superintendent of the Sunday-school, composed of two hundred scholars, with ten teachers and five officers. The labor of the Sunday-school was always one of my greatest delights. We held it in the morning, and the evening was devoted to the singing school. We soon concluded to buy us an organ, and in less than a month after our school passed a resolution to buy one, we had it in our possession and paid for. Our day school was all that could be expected of it during this year. At the close of the school, June, 1873, we had quite an interesting and entertaining exhibition. It was witnessed by a great many persons, they coming from all directions. It was said that every vehicle within a radius of sixteen miles of New Castle was brought into service by those who attended the closing exercises of my school, which was pronounced by all to be a perfect success. The receipts at the door exceeded $100. The receipts from these exhibitions were used by me for spending money during the summer months.

Elijah P. Marrs, *Life and History of the Rev. Elijah P. Marrs, First Pastor of Beargrass Baptist Church, and Author* (Louisville, KY: The Bradley & Gilbert Company, 1885), 9–93.

---

1. The 12th Regiment, Colored Heavy Artillery was organized at Camp Nelson, Kentucky, near Louisville, in July 1864, and mustered out of the army in April 1866. It was the largest of the seven or more black regiments organized at Camp Nelson. Wilson, *The Black Phalanx*, 465; Sears, *Camp Nelson, Kentucky*, xxxix.

2. Camp Nelson, near Lexington, Kentucky, was established by Union forces in the spring and summer of 1863 and became the largest recruiting depot in the state. At its height, the camp housed thousands of soldiers, their families, and refugees on about 4,000 acres of land, with 300 military buildings and 97 cottages for black refugees. Sears, *Camp Nelson, Kentucky*, lvii; Berlin et al., *Freedom: The Wartime Genesis of Free Labor: The Upper South*, 2:626, 668–671.

3. George Thomas, a corporal in Battery L of the 12th USCHA, was from Nelson County, Kentucky, and enlisted in the fall of 1864. He was promoted to sergeant major at the end of the war. Sears, *Camp Nelson, Kentucky*, 231–232.

4. Since early 1862, Bowling Green, near the Tennessee border, had been occupied by Union forces. The area quickly became a magnet for escaping slaves. Black Union troops brought their families to the military post, hav-

ing nowhere else to go, and the meager rations handed out to them and former slaves kept them alive. But conditions steadily declined and even in July 1865, Union forces reported that the former slaves at Bowling Green "are living here in most destitute, and miserable condition[s]. . . a great many have already died." Berlin et al., *Freedom: The Wartime Genesis of Free Labor: The Upper South*, 626, 704–705.

5. Camp Nelson drew thousands of former slaves and the families of slaves-turned-soldiers seeking relief. The men built temporary shelters and the women, receiving little or nothing from the government, earned a pittance washing clothes for the soldiers. The camp's commander, Gen. Speed Smith Fry, disdained their presence and periodically expelled the refugees, but in 1864 about 400 remained. In an especially frigid November 1864, Fry expelled all refugees from Camp Nelson, even the families of his own men. Officers and Northern relief agencies protested the cruel mandate and compelled Fry to reverse his order. Hundreds of additional ex-slave women and children poured into the camp seeking the food and few supplies that the government now offered. Fugitives continued to arrive well into 1865, as former masters turned out their slaves that they refused to support. Conditions for the former slaves, despite the ordered appearance of the camp, did not improve. Between April 16 and July 16, 1865, 103 women and 409 children died there. Berlin et al., *Freedom: The Wartime Genesis of Free Labor: The Upper South*, 635–636; Sears, *Camp Nelson, Kentucky*, lii–liii, lvii.

6. A Soldier's Home, operated by the Western Sanitary Commission, was located in Columbus, Kentucky. Marrs probably refers to the Soldiers' Home located at Camp Nelson, erected in the winter of 1863–1864. Run by the United States Sanitary Commission, the facility first served white refugees from east Tennessee and southeastern Kentucky. Support for wounded and sick soldiers began in March 1864. Berlin, et al., *Freedom: The Wartime Genesis of Free Labor: The Upper South*, 640–641; Sears, *Camp Nelson, Kentucky*, xxxii–xxxiii.

7. Capt. James H. Bridgewater commanded a company of scouts, not the whole of Camp Nelson. *Official Records*, vol. 39:120, 273.

8. The 4th U.S. Colored Artillery, organized at Columbus, Kentucky, was originally designated the 2nd Tennessee. It became the 3rd Tennessee in March 1864 and finally the 4th Heavy Artillery the next April. It remained active until February 1866. Wilson, *The Black Phalanx*, 465.

9. The 5th U.S. Colored Cavalry, organized at Camp Nelson, Kentucky, in October 1864, fought in four significant engagements before mustering out of service in March 1866. Wilson, *The Black Phalanx*, 464.

10. Henry Clay Weeden, born in Oldham County, Kentucky, was an author,

businessmen, and editor. In addition to *Zion's Banner*, an AMEZ Church publication, he edited the *Christian Index*, the *Bulletin*, and the *Argus*, and he managed the Louisville office of the *Appeal*. He also wrote and published *Weeden's History of the Colored People of Louisville* (1892). James de T. Abajian, comp., *Blacks in Selected Newspapers, Censuses and Other Sources: An Index to Names and Subjects*, 3 vols. (Boston: G.K. Hall, 1977), 3:623; Randall K. Burkett, Nancy Hall Burkett, Henry Louis Gates, Jr., eds., *Black Biography, 1790–1950*, 3 vols. (Alexandria, VA: Chadwyck-Healey, 1991).

11. Julia Tevis founded the Science Hill Female Academy in 1825. She and her husband, Rev. John Tevis, operated the school together until his death in 1860. In 1879 his wife sold the school to the Poynter family who maintained it until its closing in 1939. Tevis's friendship with Marrs was highly unusual, and the school's appearance at his wedding was even more so. Julia A. H. Tevis, *Sixty Years in a School-room: An Autobiography of Mrs. Julia A. Trevis, Principal of Science Hill Female Academy: To Which Is Prefixed an Autobiographical Sketch of Rev. John Trevis* (Cincinnati, OH: Western Methodist Book Concern, 1878); www.filsonhistorical.org.

21

War, Race, and Remembering

Iola Leroy
Frances Ellen Watkins Harper
1893

In the end, the war was all about race. In much of the black writing of the postwar period black historians, poets, and writers such as Frances Ellen Watkins Harper, Paul Lawrence Dunbar, and Charles Chestnut focused on the character of American race-relations and its meaning in light of the Civil War. They used many standard literary conventions and stereotypes—albeit certainly with a twist—to maintain a black literary voice in the national debates over race. Although the white race game compelled African Americans to place issues of identity at the center of their concerns, black writers took up the challenge with enormous vigor and passion and in ways that exposed the deepest recesses of American culture. Those who wrote about the black soldier and slavery adopted the forms and narrations available to them that would appeal to the widest audience. The tradition of the slave narrative and the theme of the "tragic octoroon," long familiar to white and black readers, achieved new importance as white interest in securing democracy for African Americans declined. In the deft hands of the sixty-seven-year-old Harper, antebellum sentimentality and the demand for racial justice powerfully merged in her novel *Iola Leroy*.

An antislavery lecturer since the 1850s and an advocate of women's rights, Harper continued her public role after the Civil War. In an especially heroic act, she toured the South lecturing to whites and blacks, even charming one rebel veteran who found her "remarkable—as sweet as any woman's voice we have ever heard." A courageous woman who had won an interracial audience, Harper revived and revised the antebellum convention of the "tragic octoroon," the white-appearing woman who attracts the love of a white man who later discovers his lover's "true" identity, to expose the irrationality of American racial notions. With a variety of subplots and stock figures, the book positively portrays black characters, male and female, emphasizing their loyalty, trust, honesty, and heroism. Her book reflected the hopes and aspirations of Civil War–era blacks like herself, and spoke directly to the continuing racial conflicts of the post-Reconstruction period that refused to die. Donald Yacovone, "Sacred Land Regained: Francis Ellen Watkins Harper and 'The Massachusetts Fifty-Fourth,' A Lost Poem," *Pennsylvania History* 62 (Winter 1995):98; Hazel V. Carby, "Introduction," Frances Ellen Watkins Harper, *Iola Leroy, or Shadows Uplifted* (Boston: Beacon Press, 1987); Dickson D. Bruce, Jr., *Black American Writings from the Nadir: The Evolution of Literary Tradition, 1877–1915* (Baton Rouge, LA: Louisiana State University Press, 1989), 16–18, 89–91, 173–185.

CHAPTER III
UNCLE DANIEL'S STORY

THE UNION HAD SNAPPED asunder because it lacked the cohesion of justice, and the Nation was destined to pass through the crucible of disaster and defeat, till she was ready to clasp hands with the negro and march abreast with him to freedom and victory.

THE UNION army was encamping a few miles from C——, in North Carolina. Robert, being well posted on the condition of affairs, had stealthily contrived to call a meeting in Uncle Daniel's cabin. Uncle Daniel's wife had gone to bed as a sick sister, and they held a prayer-meeting by her bedside. It was a little risky, but as Mr. Thurston did not encourage the visits of the patrollers, and heartily detested having them prying into his cabins, there was not much danger of molestation.

"Well, Uncle Daniel, we want to hear your story, and see if you have made up your mind to go with us," said Robert, after he had been seated a few minutes in Uncle Daniel's cabin.

"No chillen, I've no objection to finishin' my story, but I ain't made up my mind to leave the place till Marse Robert gits back."

"You were telling us about Marse Robert's mother. How did you get along after she died?"

"Arter she war gone, ole Marster's folks come to look arter things. But eberything war lef' to Marse Robert, an' he wouldn't do widout me. Dat chile war allers at my heels. I couldn't stir widout him, an' when he missed me, he'd fret an' cry so I had ter stay wid him; an' wen he went to school, I had ter carry him in de mornin' and bring him home in de ebenin'. An' I learned him to hunt squirrels, an' rabbits, an' ketch fish, an' set traps for birds. I beliebs he lob'd me better dan any ob his kin.' An' he showed me how to read."

"Well," said Tom, "ef he lob'd you so much, why didn't he set you free?"

"Marse Robert tole me, ef he died fust he war gwine ter leave me free—dat I shuld neber sarve any one else."

"Oh, sho!" said Tom, "promises, like pie crusts, is made to be broken. I don't trust non ob dem. I'se been yere dese fifteen years, an' I'se neber foun' any troof in dem. An' I'se gwine wid dem North men soon's I gits a chance. An' ef you knowed what's good fer you, you'd go, too."

"No, Tom; I can't go. When Marster Robert went to de front, he called me to him an' said: 'Uncle Daniel,' an' he was drefful pale when he said it, 'I are gwine to de war, an' I want yer to take keer of my wife an' chillen, jis' like yer used to take keer of me wen yer called me your little boy.' Well, dat jis' got to me, an' I couldn't help cryin', to save my life."

"I specs," said Tom, "your tear bags must lie mighty close to your eyes. I wouldn't cry ef dem Yankees would make ebery one ob dem go to de front, an' stay dere foreber. Dey'd only be gittin' back what dey's been doin' to us."

"Marster Robert war nebber bad to me. An' I beliebs in stannin' by dem dat stans by you. Arter Miss Anna died, I had great 'sponsibilities on my shoulders; but I war orful lonesome, an' thought I'd like to git a wife. But dere warn't a gal on de plantation, an' nowhere's roun', dat filled de bill. So I jis' waited, an' 'tended to Marse Robert till he war ole 'nough to go to college. Wen he went, he allers 'membered me in de letters he used to write his grandma. Wen he war gone, I war lonesomer dan eber. But, one day, I jis' seed de gal dat took de rag off de bush. Gundover had jis' brought her from de up-country. She war putty as a picture!" he exclaimed, looking findly at his wife, who still bore traces of great beauty. "She had putty hair, putty eyes, putty mouth. She war putty all over; an' she know'd how to put on style."

"O, Daniel," said Aunt Katie, half chidingly, "how you do talk."

"Why, its true. I 'member when you war de puttiest gal in dese diggins; when nobody could top your cotton."

"I don't," said Aunt Katie.

"Well, I do. Now, let me go on wid my story. De fust time I seed her, I sez to myself, 'Dat's de gal for me, an' I means to hab her ef I kin git her.' So I scraped 'quaintance wid her, and axed her ef she would hab me ef our marsters would let us. I warn't 'fraid 'bout Marse Robert, but I warn't quite shore 'bout Gundover. So when Marse Robert com'd home, I axed him, an' he larf'd an' said, 'All right,' an' dat he would speak to ole Gundover 'bout it. He didn't relish it bery much, but he didn't like to 'fuse Marse Robert. He wouldn't sell her, for she tended his dairy, an' war mighty handy 'bout de house. He said, I mought marry her an' come to see her wheneber Marse Robert would gib me a pass. I wanted him to sell her, but he wouldn't hear to it, so I had to put up wid what I could git. Marse Robert war mighty good to me, but ole Gundover's wife war de meanest woman dat I eber did see. She used to go out on de plantation an' boss things like a man. Arter I war married, I had a baby. It war de dearest, cutest little thing you eber did see; but, pore thing, it got sick and died. It died 'bout three o'clock; and in de mornin', Katie, habbin her cows to milk, lef' her dead baby in de cabin. When she com'd back from milkin' her thirty cows, an' went to look for her pore little baby, some one had been to her cabin an' took'd de pore chile away an' put it in de groun'. Pore Katie, she didn't eben hab a chance to kiss her baby 'fore it war burioed. Ole Gundover's wife has been dead thirty years, an' she didn't die a day too soon. An' my little baby has gone to glory, an' is wingin' wid the angels an' a lookin' out for us. One ob de las' things ole Gundover's wife did 'fore she died war to order a woman whipped 'cause she com'd to de field a little late when her husband war sick, an' she had stopped to tend him. Dat mornin' she war taken sick wid de fever, an' in a few days she war gone out like de snuff ob a candle. She lef' several sons, an' I specs she would almos' turn ober in her grave ef she know'd she had ten culled granchillen somewhar down in de lower kentry."

"Isn't it funny," said Robert, "how these white folks look down on colored people, an' then mix up with them?"

"Marster war away when Miss 'Liza treated my Katie so mean, an' when I tole him 'bout it, he war tearin' mad, an' went ober an' saw ole

Gundover, an' foun' out he war hard up for money, an' he bought Katie and brought her home to lib wid me, and we's been a libin in clover eber sence. Marster Robert has been mighty good to me. He stood by me in my troubles, an' now his trouble's come, I'm a gwine to stan' by him. I used to think Gundover's wife war jealous ob my Katie. She war so much puttier. Gundover's wife coudn't tech my Katie wid a ten foot pole."

"But, Aunt Katie, you have had your trials," said Robert, now that Daniel had finished his story; "don't you feel bitter towards these people who are fighting to keep you in slavery?"

Aunt Katie turned her face towards the speaker. It was a thoughtful intelligent face, saintly and calm. A face which expressed the idea of a soul which had been fearfully tempest tossed, but had passed through suffering into peace. Very touching was the look of resignation and hope which overspread her features as she replied, with the simple child-like faith which she had learned in the darkest hour, "The Lord says, we must forgive." And with her that thought, as coming from the lips of Divine Love, was enough to settle the whole question of forgiveness of injuries and love to enemies.

"Well," said Thomas Anderson, turning to Uncle Daniel, "we can't count on yer to go wid us?"

"Boys," said Uncle Daniel, and there was grief in his voice, "I'se mighty glad you hab a chance for your freedom; but, ez I tole yer, I promised Marse Robert I would stay, an' I mus' be as good as my word. Don't you youngsters stay for an ole stager like me. I'm ole an' mos' worn out. Freedom wouldn't do much for me, but I want you all to be as free as the birds; so, you chillen, take your freedom when you kin get it."

"But, Uncle Dan'el, you won't say nothin' bout our going, will you?" said the youngest of the company.

Uncle Daniel slowly arose. There was a mournful flash in his eye, a tremor of emotion in his voice, as he said, "Look yere, boys, de boy dat axed dat question war a new comer on dis plantation, but some ob you's bin here all ob your lives; did you eber know ob Uncle Dan'el gittin' any on you inter trouble?"

"No, no," exclaimed a chorus of voices, "but many's de time you've held off de blows wen de oberseer got too mean, an' cruelized us too much, qwen Marse Robert war away. An' wen he got back, you made him settle de oberseer's hash."

"Well, boys," said Uncle Daniel, with an air of mournful dignity, "I'se de same Uncle Dan'el I eber war. Ef any ob you wants to go, I habben't a word to say agin it. I specs dem Yankees be all right, but I knows Marse Robert, an' I don't know dem, an' I ain't a gwine ter throw away dirty water 'til I gits clean."

"Well, Uncle Ben," said Robert, addressing a stalwart man whose towering form and darkly flashing eye told that slavery had failed to put the crouch in his shoulders or general abjectness into his demeanor, "you will go with us, for sure, won't you?"

"Yes," spoke up Tom Anderson, " 'cause de trader's done took your wife, an' got her for his'n now."

As Ben Tunnel looked at the speaker, a spasm of agony and anger darkened his face and distorted his features, as if the blood of some strong race were stirring with sudden vigor through his veins. He clutched his hands together, as if he were struggling with an invisible foe, and for a moment he remained silent. Then suddenly raising his head, he exclaimed, "Boys, there's not one of you loves freedom more than I do, but—"

"But what?" said Tom. "Do you think white folks is your bes' friends?"

"I'll think so when I lose my senses."

"Well, now, I don't belieb you're 'fraid, not de way I yeard you talkin' to de oberseer wen he war threatnin' to hit your mudder. He saw you meant business, an' he let her alone. But, what's to hinder you from gwine wid us?"

"My mother," he replied, in a low, firm voice. "That is the only thing that keeps me from going. If it had not been for her, I would have gone long ago. She's all I've got, an' I'm all she's got."

It was touching to see the sorrow on the strong face, to detect the pathos and indignation in his voice, as he said, "I used to love Mirandy as I love my life. I thought the sun rose and set in her. I never saw a handsomer woman than she was. But she fooled me all over the face and eyes, and took up with that hell-hound of a trader, Lukens; an' he gave her a chance to live easy, to wear fine clothes, an' be waited on like a lady. I thought at first I would go crazy, but my poor mammy did all she could to comfort me. She would tell me there were as good fish in the sea as were ever caught out of it. Many a time I've laid my poor head on her lap, when it seemed as if my brain was on fire and my heart was almost ready to burst. But in course of time I got over the worst of it; an'

Mirandy is the first an' last woman that ever fooled me. But that dear old mammy of mine, I mean to stick by her as long as there is a piece of her. I can't go over to the army an' leave her behind, for if I did, an' anything should happen, I would never forgive myself."

"But couldn't you take her with you," said Robert, "the soldiers said we could bring our women."

"It isn't that. The Union army is several miles from here, an' my poor mammy is so skeery that, if I were trying to get her away and any of them Secesh would overtake us, an' begin to question us, she would get skeered almost to death, an' break down an' begin to cry, an' then the fat would be in the fire. So, while I love freedom more than a child loves its mother's milk, I've made up my mind to stay on the plantation. I wish, from the bottom of my heart, I could go. But I can't take her along with me, an' I don't want to be free and leave her behind in slavery. I was only five years old when my master and, as I believe, father, sold us both here to this lower country, an' we've been here ever since. It's no use talking, I won't leave her to be run over by everybody."

A few evenings after this interview, the Union soldiers entered the town of C——, and established their headquarters near the home of Thomas Anderson.

Out of the little company, almost every one deserted to the Union army, leaving Uncle Daniel faithful to his trust, and Ben Tunnel hushing his heart's deep aspirations for freedom in a passionate devotion to his timid and affectionate mother.

CHAPTER IV
ARRIVAL OF THE UNION ARMY

A FEW EVENINGS before the stampede of Robert and his friends to the army, and as he sat alone in his room reading the latest news from the paper he had secreted, he heard a cautious tread and a low tap at his window. He opened the door quietly and whispered:—

"Anything new, Tom?"

"Yes."

"What is it? Come in."

"Well, I'se done bin seen dem Yankees, an' dere ain't a bit of troof in dem stories I'se bin yerin 'bout 'em."

"Where did you see 'em?"

"Down in de woods whar Marster tole us to hide. Yesterday ole Marse sent for me to come in de settin'-room. An' what do you think? Instead ob makin' me stan' wid my hat in my han' while he went froo a whole rigamarole, he axed me to sit down, an' he tole me he 'spected de Yankees would want us to go inter de army, an' dey would put us in front whar we'd all git killed; an' I tole him I didn't want to go, I didn't want to git all momached up. An' den he he said we'd better go down in de woods an' hide. Massa Tom and Frank said we'd better go as quick as eber we could. Dey said dem Yankees would put us in dere wagons and make us haul like we war mules. Marse Tom ain't libin at de great house jis' now. He's keepin' bachellar's hall."

"Didn't he go to the battle?"

"No; he foun' a pore white man who war hard up for money, an' he got him to go."

"But, Tom, you didn't believe these stories about the Yankees. Tom and Frank can lie as fast as horses can trot. They wanted to scare you, and keep you from going to the Union army."

"I knows dat now, but I didn't 'spect so den."

"Well, when did you see the soldiers? Where are they? And what did they say to you?"

"Dey's right down in Gundover's woods. An' de Gineral's got his headquarters almos' next door to our house."

"That near? Oh, you don't say so!"

"Yes, I do. An', oh golly, ain't I so glad! I jis' stole yere to told you all 'bout it. Yesterday mornin' I war splittin' some wood to git my breakfas', an' I met one ob dem Yankee sogers. Well, I war so skeered, my heart flew right up in my mouf, but I made my manners to him and said, "Good mornin', Massa.' He said, 'Good mornin'; but don't call me "massa."' Dat war de fust white man I eber seed dat didn't want ter be called 'massa,' eben ef he war as pore as Job's turkey. Den I begin to feel right sheepish, an' he axed me ef my marster war at home, an' ef he war a Reb. I tole him he hadn't gone to de war, but he war Secesh all froo, inside and outside. He war too ole to go to de war, but dat he war all de time gruntin' an' groanin', an' I 'spected he'd grunt hisself to death."

"What did he say?"

"He said he specs he'll grunt worser dan dat fore dey get froo wid him. Den he axed me ef I would hab some breakfas,' an' I said, "No, t'ank you, sir.' An' I war jis' as hungry as a dorg, but I war 'feared to eat. I war 'feared he war gwine to pizen me."

"Poison you! don't you know the Yankees are our best friends?"

"Well, ef dat's so, I'se mighty glad, cause de woods is full ob dem."

"Now, Tom, I thought you had cut your eye-teeth long enough not to let them Anderson boys fool you. Tom, you must not think because a white man says a thing, it must be so, and that a colored man's word is no account 'longside of his. Tom, if ever we get our freedom, we've got to learn to trust each other and stick together if we would be a people. Somebody else can read the papers as well as Marse Tom and Frank. My ole Miss knows I can read the papers, an' she never tries to scare me with big whoppers 'bout the Yankees. She knows she can't catch ole birds with chaff, so she is just as sweet as a peach to her Bobby. But as soon as I get a chance I will play her a trick the devil never did."

"What's that?"

"I'll leave her. I ain't forgot how she sold my mother from me. Many a night I have cried myself to sleep, thinking about her, and when I get free I mean to hunt her up."

"Well, I ain't tole you all. De gemman said he war 'cruiting for de army; dat Massa Linkum had set us all free, an' dat he wanted some more sogers to put down dem Secesh; dat we should all hab our freedom, our wages, an' some kind ob money. I couldn't call it like he did."

"Bounty money," said Robert.

"Yes, dat's jis' what he called it, bounty money. An' I said dat I war in for dat, teeth and toe-nails."

Robert Johnson's heart gave a great bound. Was that so? Had that army, with freedom emblazoned on its banners, come at last to offer them deliverance if they would accept it? Was it a bright, beautiful dream, or a blessed reality soon to be grasped by his willing hands? His heart grew buoyant with hope; the lightness of his heart gave elasticity to his step and sent the blood rejoicingly through his veins. Freedom was almost in his grasp, and the future was growing rose-tinted and rainbow-hued. All the ties which bound him to his home were as ropes of sand, now that freedom had come so near.

When the army was afar off, he had appeared to be light-hearted and content with his lot. If asked if he desired his freedom, he would have answered, very naively, that he was eating his white bread and believed in letting well enough alone; he had no intention of jumping from the

frying-pan into the fire. But in the depths of his soul the love of freedom was an all-absorbing passion; only danger had taught him caution.
He had heard of terrible vengeance being heaped upon the heads of
some who had sought their freedom and failed in the attempt. Robert
knew that he might abandon hope if he incurred the wrath of men
whose overthrow was only a question of time. It would have been madness and folly for him to have attempted an insurrection against slavery, with the words of [Gen. George B.] McClellan ringing in his ears:
"If you rise I shall put you down with an iron hand,"[1] and with the home
guards ready to quench his aspirations for freedom with bayonets and
blood. What could a set of unarmed and undisciplined men do against
the fearful odds which beset their path?

Robert waited eagerly and hopefully his chance to join the Union
army; and was ready and willing to do anything required of him by
which he could earn his freedom and prove his manhood. He conducted
his plans with the greatest secrecy. A few faithful and trusted friends
stood ready to desert with him when the Union army came within hail-
ing distance. When it came, there was a stampede to its ranks of men
ready to serve in any capacity, to labor in the tents, fight on the fields,
or act as scouts. It was a strange sight to see these black men rallying
around the Stars and Stripes, when white men were trampling them under foot and riddling them with bullets.

CHAPTER V
THE RELEASE OF IOLA LEROY

"WELL, BOYS," said Robert to his trusted friends, as they gathered together at a meeting in Gundover's woods, almost under the shadow of
the Union army, "how many of you are ready to join the army and fight
for your freedom."

"All ob us."

"The soldiers," continued Robert, "are camped right at the edge of
the town. The General has his headquarters in the heart of the town,
and one of the officers told me yesterday that the President had set us
all free, and that as many as wanted to join the army could come along
to the camp. So I thought, boys, that I would come and tell you. Now,
you can take your bag and baggage, and get out of here as soon as you
choose."

"We'll be ready by daylight," said Tom. "It won't take me long to pack up," looking down at his seedy clothes, with a laugh. "I specs ole Marse'll be real lonesome when I'm gone. An' won't he be hoppin' mad when he finds I'm a goner? I specs he'll hate it like pizen."

"O, well," said Robert, "the best of friends must part. Don't let it grieve you."

"I'se gwine to take my wife an' chillen," said one of the company.

"I'se got hobody but myself," said Tom; "but dere's a mighty putty young gal dere at Marse Tom's. I wish I could git her away. Dey tells me dey's been sellin' her all ober de kentry; but dat she's a reg'lar spitfire; dey can't lead nor dribe her."

"Do you think she would go with us?" said Robert.

"I think she's jis' dying to go. Dey say dey can't do nuffin wid her. Marse Tom's got his match dis time, and I'se glad ob it. I jis' glories in her spunk."

"How did she come there?"

"Oh, Marse bought her ob de trader to keep house for him. But ef you seed dem putty white han's ob hern you'd never tink she kept her own house, let 'lone anybody else's."

"Do you think you can get her away?"

"I don't know; 'cause Marse Tom, keeps her mighty close. My! but she's putty. Beautiful long hair comes way down her back; putty blue eyes, an' jis' ez white ez anybody's in dis place. I'd jis' wish you could see her yoresef. I heerd Marse Tom talkin' 'bout her las' night to his brudder; tellin' him she war mighty airish, but he meant to break her in."

An angry curse rose to the lips of Robert, but he repressed it and muttered to himself, "Graceless scamp, he ought to have his neck stretched." Then turning to Tom, said:—

"Get her, if you possibly can, but you must be mighty mum about it."

"Trus' me for dat," said Tom.

Tom was very anxious to get word to the beautiful but intractable girl who was held in durance vile by her reckless and selfish master, who had tried in vain to drag her down to his own level of sin and shame. But all Tom's efforts were in vain. Finally he applied to the Commander of the post, who immediately gave orders for her release. The next day Tom had the satisfaction of knowing that Iolay Leroy had been taken as a trembling dove from the gory vulture's nest and given a place of security. She was taken immediately to the General's headquarters. The General was much impressed by her modest demeanor, and surprised to see the refinement and beauty she possessed. Could it be possible that this young and beautiful girl had been a chattel, with no power to protect herself from the highest insults that lawless brutality could inflict upon innocent and defenseless womanhood? Could he ever again glory in his American citizenship, when any white man, no matter how coarse, cruel, or brutal, could buy or sell her for the basest purposes? Was it not true that the cause of a hapless people had become entangled with the lightnings of heaven, and dragged down retribution upon the land?

The field hospital was needing gentle, womanly ministrations, and Iola Leroy, released from the hands of her tormentors, was given a place as nurse; a position to which she adapted herself with a deep sense of relief. Tom was doubly gratified at the success of his endeavors, which had resulted in the rescue of the beautiful young girl and the discomfiture of his young master who, in the words of Tom, "was mad enough to bite his head off" (a rather difficult physical feat).

Iola, freed from her master's clutches, applied herself readily to her appointed tasks. The beautiful, girlish face was full of tender earnestness. The fresh, young voice was strangely sympathetic, as if some great sorrow had bound her heart in loving compassion to every sufferer who needed her gentle ministrations.

Tom Anderson was a man of herculean strength and remarkable courage. But, on account of physical defects, instead of enlisting as a soldier, he was forced to remain a servant, although he felt as if every nerve in his right arm was tingling to strike a blow for freedom. He was well versed in the lay of the country, having often driven his master's cotton to market when he was a field hand. After he became a coachman, he had become acquainted with the different roads and localities of the country. Besides, he had often accompanied his young masters on their hunting and fishing expeditions. Although he could not fight in the army, he proved an invaluable helper. When tents were to be pitched, none were more ready to help than he. When burdens were to be borne, none were more willing to bend beneath them than Thomas Anderson. When the battle-field was to be searched for the wounded and dying, no hand was more tender in its ministrations of kindness than his. As a general factotum in the army, he was ever ready and willing to serve anywhere and at any time, and to gather information from every possible source which could be of any service to the Union army. As a Pagan might worship a distant star and wish to call it his own, so he loved Iola. And he never thought he could do too much for the soldiers who had rescued her and were bringing deliverance to his race.

"What do you think of Miss Iola?" Robert asked him one day, as they were talking together.

"I jis' think dat she's splendid. Las' week I had to take some of our pore boys to de hospital, an' she war dere, lookin' sweet an' putty ez an angel, a nussin' dem pore boys, an' ez good to one ez de oder. It looks to me ez ef dey raley lob'd her shadder. She sits by 'em so patient, an' writes 'em sech nice letters to der frens, an' yit she looks so heart-broken an' pitiful, it jis' gits to me, an' makes me mos' ready to cry. I'm so glad dat Marse Tom had to gib her up. He war too mean to eat good victuals."

"He ought," said Robert, "to be made to live on herrings' heads and cold potatoes. It makes my blood boil just to think that he was going to have that lovely looking young girl whipped for his devilment. He ought to be ashamed to hold up his head among respectable people."

"I tell you, Bob, de debil will neber git his own till he gits him. When I seed how he war treating her I neber rested till I got her away. He buyed her, he said, for his housekeeper; as many gals as dere war on de plantation, why didn't he git one ob dem to keep house, an' not dat nice lookin' young lady? Her han's look ez ef she neber did a day's work in her life. One day when he com'd down to breakfas,' he chucked her under de chin, an' tried to put his arm roun' her waist. But she jis' frew it off like a chunk ob fire. She looked like a snake had bit her. Her eyes fairly spit fire. Her face got red ez blood, an' den she turned so pale I thought she war gwine to faint, but she didn't, an' I yered her say, 'I'll die fust.' I war mad 'nough to stan' on my head. I could had tore'd him all to pieces wen he said he'd hab her whipped."

"Did he do it?"

"I don't know. But he's mean 'nough to do enythin'. Why, dey say she war sole seben times in six weeks, 'cause she's so putty, but dat she war game to de las'."

"Well, Tom," said Robert, "getting that girl away was one of the best things you ever did in your life."

"I think so, too. Not dat I specs enytin' ob it. I don't spose she would think ob an ugly chap like me; but it does me good to know dat Marse Tom ain't got her."

CHAPTER VI
ROBERT JOHNSON'S PROMOTION AND RELIGION

ROBERT JOHNSON, BEING ABLE to meet the army requirements, was enlisted as a substitute to help fill out out the quota of a Northern regiment. With his intelligence, courage, and prompt obedience, he rose from the ranks and became a lieutenant of a colored company. He was daring, without being rash; prompt, but not thoughtless; firm, without being harsh. Kind and devoted to the company he drilled, he soon won the respect of his superior officers and the love of his comrades.

"Johnson," said a young officer, Captain Sybil, of Maine, who had become attached to Robert, "what is the use of your saying you're a colored man, when you are as white as I am, and as brave a man as there is among us. Why not quit this company, and take your place in the army just the same as a white man? I know your chances for promotion would be better."

"Captain, you may doubt my word, but to-day I would rather be a lieutenant in my company than a captain in yours."

"I don't understand you."

"Well, Captain, when a man's been colored all his life it comes a little hard for him to get white all at once. Were I to try it, I would feel like a cat in a strange garret. Captain, I think my place is where I am most needed. You do not need me in your ranks, and my company does. They are excellent fighters, but they need a leader. To silence a battery, to capture a flag, to take a fortification, they will rush into the jaws of death."

"Yes, I have often wondered at their bravery."

"Captain, these battles put them on their mettle. They have been so long taught that they are nothing and nobody, that they seem glad to prove they are something and somebody."

"But, Johnson, you do not look like them, you do not talk like them. It is a burning shame to have held such a man as you in slavery."

"I don't think it was any worse to have held me in slavery than the blackest man in the South."

"You are right, Johnson. The color of a man's skin has nothing to do with the possession of his rights."

"Now, there is Tom Anderson," said Robert, "he is just as black as black can be. He has been bought and sold like a beast, and yet there is not a braver man in all the company. I know him well. He is a noble-hearted fellow. True as steel. I love him like a brother. And I believe Tom would risk his life for me any day. He don't know anything about his father or mother. He was sold from them before he could remember. He can read a little. He used to take lessons from a white gardener in Virginia. He would go between the hours of 9 P.M. and 4 A.M. He got a book of his own, tore it up, greased the pages, and hid them in his hat. Then if his master had ever knocked his hat off he would have thought them greasy papers, and not that Tom was carrying his library on his head. I had another friend who lived near us. When he was nineteen years old he did not know how many letters there were in the A B C's. One night, when his work was done, his boss came into his cabin and saw him with a book in his hand. He threatened to give him five hundred lashes if he caught him again with a book, and said he hadn't work enough to do. He was getting out logs, and his task was ten logs a day. His employer threatened to increase it to twelve. He said it just harassed him; it set him on fire. He thought there must be something good in that book if the white man didn't want him to learn. One day he had an errand in the kitchen, and he heard one of the colored girls going over the A B C's. Here was the key to the forbidden knowledge. She had heard the white children saying them, and picked them up by heart, but did not know them by sight. He was not content with that, but sold his cap for a book and wore a cloth on his head instead. He got the sounds of the letters by heart, then cut off the bark of a tree, carved the letters on the smooth inside, and learned them. He wanted to learn how to write. He had charge of a warehouse where he had a chance to see the size and form of letters. He made the beach of the river his copybook, and thus he learned to write. Tom never got very far with his learning, but I used to get the papers and tell him all I knew about the war."

"How did you get the papers?"

"I used to have very good privileges for a slave. All of our owners were not alike. Some of them were quite clever, and others were worse than git out. I used to get the morning papers to sell to the boarders and others, and when I got them I would contrive to hide a paper, and let some of the fellow-servants know how things were going on. And our owners thought we cared nothing about what was going on."

"How was that? I thought you were not allowed to hold meetings unless a white man were present."

"That was so. But we contrived to hold secret metings in spite of their caution. We knew whom we could trust. My ole Miss wasn't mean like some of them. She never wanted the patrollers around prowling in our cabins, and poking their noses into our business. Her husband was an awful drunkard. He ran through every cent he could lay his hands on, and she was forced to do somthing to keep the wolf from the door, so she set up a boarding-house. But she didn't take in Tom, Dick, and Harry. Nobody but the big bugs stopped with her. She taught me to read and write, and to cast up accounts. It was so handy for her to have some one who could figure up her accounts, and read or write a note, if she were from home and wanted the like done. She once told her cousin how I could write and figure up. And what do you think her cousin said?"

"'Pleased,' I suppose, 'to hear it.'"

"Not a bit of it. She said, if I belonged to her, she would cut off my thumbs; her husband said, 'Oh, then he couldn't pick cotton.' As to my poor thumbs, it did not seem to be taken into account what it would cost me to lose them. My ole Miss used to have a lot of books. She would let me read any one of them except a novel. She wanted to take care of my soul, but she wasn't taking care of her own."

"Wasn't she religious?"

"She went for it. I suppose she was as good as most of them. She said her prayers and went to church, but I don't know that that made her any better. I never did take much stock in white folks' religion."

"Why, Robert, I'm afraid you are something of an infidel."

"No, Captain, I believe in the real, genuine religion. I ain't got much myself, but I respect them that have. We had on our place a dear, old saint, named Aunt Kizzy. She was a happy soul. She had seen hard times, but was what I call a living epistle. I've heard tell how her only child had been sold from her, when the man who bought herself did not want to buy her child. Poor little fellow! he was only two years old. I asked her one day how she felt when her child was taken away. 'I felt,' she said, 'as if I was going to my grave. But I knew if I couldn't get justice here, I could get it in another world.'"

"That was faith," said Captain Sybil, as if speaking to himself, "a patient waiting for death to redress the wrongs of life."

"Many a time," continued Robert, "have I heard her humming to herself in the kitchen and saying, 'I has my trials, ups and downs, but it won't allers be so. I specs one day to wing and wing wid de angels, Hallelujah! Den I specs to hear a voice sayin', "Poor ole Kizzy, she's done de bes' she kin. Go down, Gabriel, an' tote her in." Den I specs to out on my golden slippers, my long white robe, an' my starry crown, an' walk dem golden streets, Hallelujah!' I've known that dear, old soul to travel going on two miles, after her work was done, to have some one read to her. Her favorite chapter began with, 'Let not your heart be troubled, ye believe in God, believe also in Me.'"

"I have been deeply impressed," said Captain Sybil, "with the child-like faith of some of these people. I do not mean to say that they are consistent Christians, but I do think that this faith has in a measure underlain the life of the race. It has been a golden thread woven amid the somber tissues of their lives. A ray of light shimmering amid the gloom of their condition. And what would they have been without it?"

"I don't know. But I know what she was with it. And I believe if there are any saints in glory, Aunt Kizzy is one of them."

"She is dead, then?"

"Yes, went all right, singing and rejoicing until the last, 'Troubles over, troubles over, and den my troubles will be over. We'll walk de golden streets all 'roun' in de New Jerusalem.' Now, Captain, that's the kind of religion that I want. Not that kind which could ride to church on Sundays, and talk so solemn with the minister about heaven and good things, then come home and light down on the servants like a thousand of bricks. I have no use for it. I don't believe in it. I never did and I never will. If any man wants to save my soul he ain't got to beat my body. That ain't the kind of religion I'm looking for. I ain't got a bit of use for it. Now, Captain, ain't I right?"

"Well, yes, Robert, I think you are more than half right. You ought to know my dear, old mother who lives in Maine. We have had colored company at our house, and I never saw her show the least difference between her colored and white guests. She is a Quaker preacher, and don't believe in war, but when the rest of the young men went to the front, I wanted to go also. So I thought it all over, and there seemed to be no way out of slavery except through war. I had been taught to hate war and detest slavery. Now the time had come when I could not help the war, but I could strike a blow for freedom. So I told my mother I was going to the front, that I expected to be killed, but I went to free the slave. It went hard with her. But I thought that I ought to come, and I believe my mother's prayers are following me."

"Captain," said Robert, rising, "I am glad that I have heard your story. I think that some of these Northern soldiers do two things—hate slavery and hate niggers."

"I am afraid that is so with some of them. They would rather be whipped by Rebels than conquer with negroes. Oh, I heard a soldier," said Captain Sybil, "say, when the colored men were being enlisted, that he would break his sword and resign. But he didn't do either. After Colonel [Robert Gould] Shaw led his charge at Fort Wagner, and died in the conflict, he got bravely over his prejudices. The conduct of the colored troops there and elsewhere has done much to turn public opinion in their favor. I suppose any white soldier would rather have his black substitute receive the bullets than himself."

CHAPTER VII
TOM ANDERSON'S DEATH

"WHERE IS TOM?" asked Captain Sybil; "I have not seen him for several hours."

"He's gone down the sound with some of the soldiers," replied Robert. "They wanted Tom to row them."

"I am afraid those boys will get into trouble, and the Rebs will pick them off." responded Sybil.

"O, I hope not," answered Robert.

"I hope not, too; but those boys are too venturesome."

"Tom knows the lay of the land better than any of us," said Robert. "He is the most wide-awake and gamiest man I know. I reckon when the war is over Tom will be a preacher. Did you ever hear him pray?"

"No; is he good at that?"

"First-rate," continued Robert. "It would do you good to hear him. He don't allow any cursing and swearing when he's around. And what he says is law and gospel with the boys. But he's so good-natured; and they can't get mad at him."

"Yes, Robert, there is not a man in our regiment I would sooner trust than Tom. Last night, when he brought in that wounded scout, he couldn't have been more tender if he had been a woman. How gratefully the poor fellow looked in Tom's face as he laid him down so carefully and staunched the blood which had been spurting out of him. Tom seemed to know it was an artery which had been cut, and he did just the right thing to stop the bleeding. He knew there wasn't a moment to be lost. He wasn't going to wait for the doctor. I have often heard that colored people are ungrateful, but I don't think Tom's worst enemy would say that about him."

"Captain," said Robert, with a tone of bitterness in his voice, "what had we to be grateful for? For ages of poverty, ignorance, and slavery? I think if anybody should be grateful, it is the people who have enslaved us and lived off our labor for generations. Captain, I used to know a poor old woman who couldn't bear to hear any one play on the piano."

"Is that so? Why, I always heard that colored people were a musical race."

"So we are; but that poor woman's daughter was sold, and her mistress took the money to buy a piano. Her mother could never bear to hear a sound from it."

"Poor woman!" exclaimed Captain Sybil, sympathetically; "I suppose it seemed as if the wail of her daughter was blending with the tone of the instrument. I think, Robert, there is a great deal more in the colored people than we give thm credit for. Did you know Captain Sellers?"

"The officer who escaped from prison and got back to our lines?" asked Robert.

"Yes. Well, he had quite an experience in trying to escape. He came to an aged couple, who hid him in their cabin and shared their humble food with him. They gave him some corn-bread, bacon, and coffee which he thought was made of scorched bran. But he said that he never ate a meal that he relished more than the one he took with them. Just before he went they knelt down and prayed with him. It seemed as if his very hair stood on his head, their prayer was so solemn. As he was going away the man took some shingles and nailed them on his shoes to throw the bloodhounds off his track. I don't think he will ever cease to feel kindly towards colored people. I do wonder what has become of the boys? What can keep them so long?"

Just as Captain Sybil and Robert were wondering at the delay of Tom and the soldiers they heard the measured tred of men who were slowly bearing a burden. They were carrying Tom Anderson to the hospital, fearfully wounded, and nigh to death. His face was distorted, and the blood was streaming from his wounds. His respiration was faint, his pulse hurried, as if life were trembling on its frailest cords.

Robert and Captain Sybil hastened at once towards the wounded man. On Robert's face was a look of intense anguish, as he bent pityingly over his friend.

"O, this is dreadful! How did it happen?" cried Robert.

Captain Sybil, pressing anxiously forward, repeated Robert's question.

"Captain," said one of the young soldiers, advancing and saluting his superior officer, "we were all in the boat when it struck against a mud bank, and there was not strength enough among us to shove her back into the water. Just then the Rebels opened fire upon us. For awhile we lay down in the boat, but still they kept firing. Tom took in the whole situation, and said: 'Some one must die to get us out of this. I might's well be him as any. You are soldiers and can fight. If they kill me, it is nuthin'.' So Tom leaped out to shove the boat into the water. Just then the Rebel bullets began to rain around him. He received seven or eight of them, and I'm afraid there is no hope for him."

"O, Tom, I wish you hadn't gone. O, Tom! Tom!" cried Robert, in tones of agony.

A gleam of grateful recognition passed over the drawn features of Tom, as the wail of his friend fell on his ear. He attempted to speak, but he words died upon his lips, and he became unconscious.

"Well," said Captain Sybil, "put him in one of the best wards. Give him into Miss Leroy's care. If good nursing can win him back to life, he shall not want for any care or pains that she can bestow. Send immediately for Dr. Gresham."

Robert followed his friend into the hospital, tenderly and carefully helped to lay him down, and remained awhile, gazing in silent grief upon the sufferer. Then he turned to go, leaving him in the hands of Iola, but hoping against hope that his wounds would not be fatal.

With tender devotion Iola watched her faithful friend. He recognized her when restored to consciousness, and her presence was as balm to his wounds. He smiled faintly, took her hand in his, stroked it tenderly, looked wistfully into her face, and said, "Miss Iola, I ain't long fer dis! I'se 'most home!"

"Oh, no," said Iola, "I hope that you will soon get over this trouble, and live many long and happy days."

"No, Miss Iola, it's all ober wid me. I'se gwine to glory; gwine to glory; gwine to ring them charmin' bells. Tell all de boys to met me in heben; dat dey mus' 'list in de hebenly war."

"O, Mr. Tom," said Iola, tenderly, "do not talk of leaving me. You are the best friend I have had since I was torn from my mother. I should be so lonely without you."

"Dere's a frien' dat sticks closer dan a brudder. He will be wid yer in de sixt' trial, an' in de sebbent' he'll not fo'sake yer."

"Yes," answered Iola, "I know that. He is all our dependence. But I can't help grieving when I see you suffering so. But, dear friend, be quiet, and try to go to sleep."

"I'll do enythin' fer yer, Miss Iola."

Tom closed his eyes and lay quiet. Tenderly and anxiously Iola watched over him as the hours waned away. The doctor came, shook his head gravely, and turning to Iola, said, "There is no hope, but do what you can to alleviate his sufferings."

As Iola gazed upon the kind but homely features of Tom, she saw his eyes open and an unexpressed desire upon his face.

Tenderly and sadly bending over him, with tears in her dark, luminous eyes, she said, "Is there anything I can do for you?"

"Yes," said Tom, with laboring breath; "let me hole yore han', an' sing 'Ober Jordan inter glory' an' 'We'll anchor bye and bye.'"

Iola laid her hand gently in the rough palm of the dying man, and, with a tremulous voice, sang the parting hymns.

Tenderly she wiped the death damps from his dusky brow, and imprinted upon it a farewell kiss. Gratitude and affection lit up the dying eye, which seemed to be gazing into the enternities. Just then Robert entered the room, and, seating himself quietly by Tom's bedside, read the death signs in his face.

"Good-bye, Robert," said Tom, "meet me in de kingdom." Suddenly a look of recognition and rapture lit up his face, and he murmured, "Angels, bright angels, all's well, all's well!"

Slowly his hand released its pressure, a peaceful calm overspread his countenance, and without a sigh or murmur Thomas Anderson, Iola's faithful and devoted friend, passed away, leaving the world so much poorer for her than it was before. Just then Dr. Gresham, the hospital physician, came to the bedside, felt for the pulse which would never throb again, and sat down in silence by the cot.

"What do you think, Doctor," said Iola, "has he fainted?"

"No," said the doctor, "poor fellow! he is dead."

Iola bowed her head in silent sorrow, and then relieved the anguish of her heart by a flood of tears. Robert rose, and sorrowfully left the room.

Iola, with tearful eyes and aching heart, clasped the cold hands over the still breast, closed the waxen lid over the eye which had once beamed with kindness or flashed with courage, and then went back, after the burial, to her daily round of duties, feeling the sad missing of something from her life.

CHAPTER VIII
THE MYSTIFIED DOCTOR

"COLONEL," said Dr. Gresham to Col. Robinson, the commander of the post, "I am perfectly mystified by Miss Leroy."

"What is the matter with her?" asked Col. Robinson. "Is she not faithful to her duties and obedient to your directions?"

"Faithful is not the word to express her tireless energy and devotion to her work," responded Dr. Gresham. "She must have been a born nurse to put such enthusiasm into her work."

"Why, Doctor, what is the matter with you? You talk like a lover."

A faint blush rose to the cheek of Dr. Gresham as he smiled, and said, "Oh! come now, Colonel, can't a man praise a woman without being in love with her?"

"Of course he can," said Col. Robinson; "but I know where such admiration is apt to lead. I've been there myself. But Doctor, had you not better defer your love-making till you're out of the woods?"

"I assure you, Colonel, I am not thinking of love or courtship. That is the business of the drawing-room, and not of the camp. But she did mystify me last night."

"How so?" asked Col. Robinson.

"When Tom was dying," responded the doctor, "I saw that beautiful and refined young lady bend over and kiss him. When she found that he was dead, she just cried as if her heart was breaking. Well, that was a new thing to me. I can eat with colored people, walk, talk, and fight with them, but kissing them is something I don't hanker after."

"And yet you saw Miss Leroy do it?"

"Yes; and that puzzles me. She is one of the most refined and lady-like women I ever saw. I hear she is a refugee, but she does not look like other refugees who have come to our camp. Her accent is slightly Southern, but her manner is Northern. She is self-respecting without being supercilious; quiet, without being dull. Her voice is low and sweet, yet at times there are tones of such passionate tenderness in it that you would think some great sorrow has darkened and overshadowed her life. Without being the least gloomy, her face at times is pervaded by an air of inexpressible sadness. I sometimes watch her when she is not aware that I am looking at her, and it seems as if a whole volume was depicted on her countenance. When she smiles, there is a longing in her eyes which is never satisfied. I cannot understand how a Southern lady, whose education and manners stamp her as a woman of fine culture and good breeding, could consent to occupy the position she so faithfully holds. It is a mystery I cannot solve. Can you?"

"I think I can," answered Col. Robinson.

"Will you tell me?" queried the doctor.

"Yes, on one condition."

"What is it?"

"Everlasting silence."

"I promise," said the doctor. "The secret between us shall be as deep as the sea."

"She has not requested secrecy, but at present, for her sake, I do not wish the secret revealed. Miss Leroy was a slave."

"Oh, no," said Dr. Gresham, starting to his feet, "it can't be so! A woman as white as she a slave?"

"Yes, it is so," continued the colonel. "In these States the child follows the condition of its mother. This beautiful and accomplished girl was held by one of the worst Rebels in town. Tom told me of it and I issued orders for her release."

"Well, well! Is that so?" said Dr. Gresham, thoughtfully stroking his beard. "Wonders will never cease. Why, I was just beginning to think seriously of her."

"What's to hinder your continuing to think?" asked Col. Robinson.

"What you tell me changes the whole complexion of affairs," replied the doctor.

"If that be so I am glad I told you before you got head over heels in love."

"Yes," said Dr. Gresham, absently.

Dr. Gresham was a member of a wealthy and aristocratic family, proud of its lineage, which it could trace through generations of good blood to its ancestral isle. He had become deeply interested in Iola before he had heard her story, but after it had been revealed to him he tried to banish her from his mind; but his constant observation of her only increased his interest and admiration. The deep pathos of her story, the tenderness of her minsitrations, bestowed alike on black and white, and the sad loneliness of her condition, awakened within him a desire to defend and protect her all through her future life. The fierce clashing of war had not taken all the romance out of his nature. In Iola he saw realized his ideal of the woman whom he was willing to marry. A woman, tender, strong, and courageous, and rescued only by the strong arm of his Government from a fate worse than death. She was young in years, but old in sorrow; one whom a sad destiny had changed from a light-hearted girl to a heroic woman. As he observed her, he detected an undertone of sorrow in her most cheerful words, and observed a quick flushing and sudden paling of her cheek, as if she were living over scenes that were thrilling her soul with indignation or chilling her heart with horror. As nurse and physician, Iola and Dr. Gresham were constantly thrown together. His friends sent him magazines and books, which he gladly shared with her. The hospital was a sad place. Mangled forms, stricken down in the flush of their prime and energy; pale young corpses, sacrificed on the altar of slavery, constantly drained on her sympathies. Dr. Gresham was glad to have some reading matter which might divert her mind from the memories of her mournful past, and also furnish them both with interesting themes of conversation in their moments of relaxation from the harrowing scenes through which they were constantly passing. Without any effort or consciousness on her part, his friendship ripened into love. To him her presence was a pleasure, her absence a privation; and her loneliness drew deeply upon his sympathy. He would have merited his own self-contempt if, by word or deed, he had done anything to take advantage of her situation. All the manhood and chivalry of his nature rose in her behalf, and, after carefully revolving the matter, he resolved to win her for his bride, bury her secret in his Northern home, and hide from his aristocratic relations all knowledge of her mournful past. One day he said to Iola:—

"This hospital life is telling on you. Your strength is failing, and although you possess a wonderful amount of physical endurance, you must not forget that saints have bodies and dwell in tabernacles of clay, just the same as we common mortals."

"Compliments aside," she said, smiling; "what are you driving at, Doctor?"

"I mean," he replied, "that you are running down, and if you do not quit and take some rest you will be our patient instead of our nurse.

You'd better take a furlough, go North, and return after the first frost."

"Doctor, if that is your only remedy," replied Iola, "I am afraid that I am destined to die at my post. I have no special friends in the North, and no home but this in the South. I am homeless and alone."

There was something so sad, almost depairing in her tones, in the drooping of her head, and the quivering of her lip, that they stirred Dr. Gresham's heart with sudden pity, and, drawing nearer to her, he said, "Miss Leroy, you need not be all alone. Let me claim the privilege of making your life bright and happy. Iola, I have loved you ever since I have seen your devotion to our poor, sick boys. How faithfully you, a young and gracious girl, have stood at your post and performed your duties. And now I ask, will you not permit me to clasp hands with you for life? I do not ask for a hasty reply. Give yourself time to think over what I have proposed."

Frances Ellen Watkins Harper, *Iola Leroy, or Shadows Uplifted*, 2nd ed. (Philadelphia, 1893), 24–60.

---

1. McClellan and generals Benjamin F. Butler and Robert Patterson—and others—all offered to assist slave owners in "crushing" any slave insurrections. At the outset of the war, the army, the War Department, and the Lincoln administration also demanded that all fugitive slaves of loyal masters be returned to their owners and all fugitive slaves be excluded from Union lines. Had a slave insurrection occurred within reach of the Army of the Potomac, General McClellan certainly would have suppressed it. Berlin et al, eds. *Freedom: The Destruction of Slavery*, 1:12–13, 353–357, 496.

The House of Bondage
Octavia V. Rogers Albert
1890

Octavia V. R. Albert (1853–1890), born a slave in Macon County, Georgia, was a remarkable woman. She attended Atlanta University and taught school in Montezuma, Georgia, before marrying an African American minister and moving to Houma, Louisiana, in 1874. Four years later, she began interviewing the former slaves of her neighborhood who came to her home for food and educational instruction. The information she gathered and the interviews she recorded are important precursors of the famed WPA interviews of the depression era and, though far fewer in number, they may in some ways be even more valuable. She knew her interviewees better than those who worked for the WPA, and, as an African American and a former slave herself, she could win a measure of trust impossible for any whites to achieve.

Her interviews were first published in 1890 in the *Southwestern Christian Advocate,* an organ of the Methodist Episcopal Church. The paper was one of the few of its kind with an African American editor and a substantial white audience. Although Albert died before her stories came out as *The House of Bondage,* she clearly intended to publish them in a book. While she wished to reach black and white readers in New Orleans, she also hoped for a national audience, and when the book came out in 1891, simultaneous publication in Cincinnati and New York helped her book reach that goal. The foreword by Bishop Willard Mallalieu of Boston, like the white endorsements that appeared in the antebellum slave narratives, lent an air of credibility to Albert's book and helped give it legitimacy in the eyes of whites—the very people that Albert primarily hoped to reach.

The House of Bondage sought to counteract the work of writers like Thomas Nelson Page, who idealized the days of slavery—by then more than a generation removed from public consciousness. By the time of Albert's book, most Americans had gotten their understanding of American slavery from Uncle Remus, not Uncle Tom. To Page and others of the popular "plantation school of thought," the antebellum era of the South represented a chivalrous ideal when respect and order reigned, African Americans were happy and well cared for in slavery, and the troubled days of the postwar years and its "race problems" did not exist. Thus, Bishop Mallalieu struck exactly the right tone in his foreword. "The truth is that slavery is the product of human greed and lust and oppression, and not of God's ordering. Then it is well to write about slavery that the American people may know from what depths of disgrace and infamy they rose when, guided by the hand of God, they broke every yoke and let the oppressed go free."

In the following two selected chapters from the end of Albert's book, she brings the story of slavery through the history of black ser-

vice in the Civil War to the hopeful and harrowing days of Reconstruction and after. In the mouth of Douglass Wilson, a pseudonym or
composite of former black Union soldiers in Louisiana, Albert is able
to explain briefly and creatively how slaves came to be men and heroes
in the war. She then reminds her readers of how the Ku Klux Klan's
reign of terror extinguished the lives of countless blacks and their white
allies for doing nothing more than seeking education and raising themselves out of the mire of slavery. For a popular audience unfamiliar with
the ordeal of African Americans, Albert wished to honor the men who
braved bullets on the battlefield and on their way to the ballot box and
school room. While admitting that the African American Reconstruction governments may have had flaws, they shimmered brilliantly in light
of the Democratic "redeemer" ones that followed. Their endlessly corrupt white officials cost the public millions of dollars. "If our people did
so well when only a few years removed from the house of bondage"
where they could neither read not write, Albert's interviewee stated,
"what may we not expect of them with the advances they have since
made and are making?" The piece concludes with a positive assessment
of the achievements of African Americans in education, religion, the
professions, and business. Albert also wished to counter the newest
emigrationist movement, this time to Kansas, asserting that the best
hope for the future was an integrationist one. In that, her dreams were
not far distant from many of our own. John Blassingame, ed., *Slave Testimony: Two Centuries of Letters, Speeches, Interviews, and Autobiographies*
(Baton Rouge, LA: Louisiana State University Press, 1977), lxi; Frances
Smith Foster, "Introduction," Octavia V. Rogers Albert, *The House of
Bondage, or Charlotte Brooks and Other Slaves* (New York: Oxford University Press, 1988).

CHAPTER XVII.
A COLORED SOLDIER.

AFTER MY CONVERSATION with Uncle Cephas in the last chapter I did
not get to see any one particularly for a month or more who could add
materially to my story any thing that might interest you; but during the
succeeding summer, after this last conversation, I met Colonel Douglass
Wilson,[1] a colored man of considerable prominence, not only in
Louisiana, but in the nation. He and his family and my husband, daugh-

ter, and I were spending a vacation at Bay St. Louis, Mississippi, a very popular watering-place on the Mississippi Sound. He and my husband were very great friends, and used to visit each other during our stay there. One day I said to him:

"Colonel, from what I have heard you say and learned of you generally, as a public man, you must have a rich experience touching occurrences before, during, and since the war among our people. I have made the matter one of deep study, and I know your story would delight almost any one. Don't keep all the good things to yourself; tell us about them sometime."

"Yes," said he, "my experience is a rich and varied one, and I am so constantly telling it every-where and on every occasion that I fear sometimes that people will say that I have a hobby."

"I assure you," said I, "you will never hear that from me, because I believe we should not only treasure these things, but should transmit them to our children's children. That's what the Lord commanded Israel to do in reference to their deliverance from Egyptian bondage, and I verily believe that the same is his will concerning us and our bondage and deliverance in this country. After thirty-three centuries the Jews are more faithful in the observance of the facts connected with their bondage and deliverance than we are in those touching ours, although our deliverance took place scarcely a quarter of a century ago."

"You are right, Mrs. Albert," replied the colonel, "and that is my principal reason for so heartily concurring with those of our leading colored men who are doing all in their power to induce all of our people in this country to unite every year in the observance of January 1 as National Emancipation Day. There can be no doubt that that is the day every true American should celebrate as National Emancipation Day, as that was the day on which Mr. Lincoln's ever-memorable proclamation of freedom was issued—January 1, 1863."

"Colonel, let me ask you, were you ever a slave?"

"A slave? Why, yes; I was a slave until Mr. Lincoln's proclamation of freedom. It found me, however, on the battle-field at Port Hudson, La., where the colored troops fought so nobly as to extort from their chief officers such praises as were showered upon few soldiers at any time or place. I was there in the hottest of the fight, when Captain [Andre] Caillioux, that valiant negro, fell, one whose praises can never be too loudly proclaimed. If ever patriotic heroism deserved to be honored in stately marble or in brass that of Captain Caillioux deserves to be, and the American people will have never redeemed their gratitude to genuine patriotism until that debt is paid. I was there, yes, ma'am, when, with one arm dangling in his sleeve, the brave captain waved his comrades on to the bloody conflict with the other. I was there, too, and heard the lion-hearted color-bearer, [Sgt. Anselmas] Planciancois, when he received the regimental colors from his superior officer, and, grasping them with a firm and manly hand, assured him that he would 'return with those colors from the sweeping, bloody fray with honor, or report to God the reason why.' The recital of these things fires all the military ardor in my soul. From that day to the close of the war 'Remember Port Hudson' was the talismanic watchword that ever inspired our regiment to the highest degree of heroism. But Port Hudson was only one of a hundred battle-fields whereon the colored soldier demonstrated his valor. There were Fort Pillow, Fort Wagner, Chickamauga, Fort Blakely, Fort Donelson, Lake Providence, Pulaski, Waterproof, Appomattox, and a hundred others. The verdict was that 'the colored troops fought nobly.'[2]

"O, yes, I was a slave, but I became a soldier, too, and fought for freedom and the Union, and I am proud of it. But I want to tell you that this last war exploded many false notions in the minds of our Southern people, and in some of our Northern neighbors, too. They used to say, 'The negro doesn't care to be set free, and but for Northern meddlers you would never hear any complaints from him.' They said, 'If you free him he will die out;' but I tell you he is the liveliest corpse this nation has ever handled. He is multiplying faster than any people in this country. When it was proposed to make a soldier out of him, why, they said, 'He can't fight.' But what was the universal verdict at the close of every battle? Why, he fought like a demon. After the war they said, 'O, he can't learn!' But what mean these laurels that he is getting at Yale, Cornell, Dartmouth, and other colleges over white competitors? Whether he wanted freedom or not is beautifully illustrated in a story that came under my observation.

"Among thousands of contrabands, as they were called, that flocked into the Union lines, as the Yankees captured various sections in the South, were a very aged man and his wife. The slaves were escaping from the old plantations in every direction. So one morning a planter out near Vicksburg, Miss., went out into his negro quarters, and, addressing this aged patriarch, now bent under the weight of over three-score and ten years, said, 'Uncle Si, I don't suppose you are going off to those hateful Yankees, too, are you?' 'O no, marster,' he said, 'I'se gwine to stay right here with you.' Next morning the planter visited the quarters again, when he found that every one of his slaves, not excepting even Uncle Si and his wife, Aunt Cindy, had gone to the Yankees during the night. Searching out in the woods for them, he finally came upon Uncle Si, just inside the Union line. Aunt Cindy was stretched out on the bare ground, dead, and Uncle Si was bending over her, weeping. She had died from the exposure and hardship incident upon the making of their escape. Addressing Uncle Si, the planter said, 'Uncle Si, why on earth did you so cruelly bring Aunt Cindy here for, through all of such hardship, thereby causing her death?' Lifting up his eyes and looking his master full in the face, he answered, 'I couldn't help it, master; but then, you see, she died free.'"

"Colonel, tell me something about the Kuklux. Did you know anything about them? They were said to be very bad and numerous in Georgia and South Carolina."

"That's true; at that time they were very bad and numerous in both Georgia and South Carolina, but they were equally bad in Louisiana, Mississippi, Texas, and, in fact, throughout the South. They were known in some places as the White Camelias, the White Cohort, and other such names, but after all they were nothing more nor less than the Confederate army that had surrendered at Appomattox that was really continuing a sort of guerrilla warfare against Union men and the poor freedmen. This was what made the task of reconstruction such a difficult one throughout the South. The Kuklux were determined that the colored people, if now free, should not enjoy their freedom, but should remain in a condition of peonage. To accomplish their purpose they heaped all sorts of indignities upon the Northern white missionary preachers and teachers that followed the march of the Union lines to organize our people in church relations and to establish schools among them. Not only were they socially ostracized, but they were maltreated, whipped, mobbed, and massacred by wholesale.

"I remember, just now, the case of Mr. Joel Brinkley, who was taken out of his school-house, right before his scholars, in broad day-time, and caned half to death by a mob of nearly a hundred of those hyenas. After that they gave him five hours in which to leave the town of Springdale, where he was teaching. After he started off they thought they ought to have killed him, so they started off after him to catch him, and they followed him for ten days, trying to catch him. He had to hide in the swamps, sleep in the cane-rows and ditches and under negro cabins to save his life. A reward of five hundred dollars was offered for his apprehension and delivery into their hands, but the Lord was with him, and he finally reached New Orleans in safety, where he could continue in the same line of work with a little more security. I have often heard him tell of how kindly the colored people treated him when he was then fleeing for his life. They were the only friends he could trust. They would hide him under their cabins and in their hay-lofts, and feed him there until it was safe for him to journey on farther. From them, too, he could learn of the whereabouts of the human hounds that were pursuing him for his life. Mr. Brinkley, however, was fortunate to have gotten away with his life, notwithstanding the fact that he thereby contracted terrible constitutional troubles, from which he suffered many years. Hundreds of others were killed outright, their churches or schoolhouses burnt down, and their families driven away. They were equally murdered, however, some instantly, while others, like Mr. Brinkley, died a slower death."

CHAPTER XVIII.
NEGRO GOVERNMENT.

"IF THE KUKLUX treated the missionaries in that manner you must not imagine that they left the colored people and their children unharmed. Thousands of colored men and women throughout the South were in like manner whipped and shot down like dogs, in the fields and in their cabins. The recital of some of the experiences of those days is enough to chill your blood and raise your hair on ends. The horrors of those days can scarcely be imagined by those who know nothing about it. Why, madam, you ought to have been down here in 1868. That was the year in which [U. S.] Grant and [Schuyler] Colfax ran for President and Vice-President, against [Horatio] Seymour and [Francis P.] Blair. A perfect reign of terror existed all over the South; and the colored people who attempted to vote were shot down like dogs every-where. There was such a reign of terrorism in many States of the South that the Congress of the United States refused to count the bloody electoral votes of several of the Southern States. Two years before that, in July, 1866, there was a constitutional convention in New Orleans, to frame a constitution whereby the State of Louisiana might be reconstructed and readmitted into the Union. On the 30th day of that month, I believe it was, a fearful riot was instituted by those fire-eaters, and the result was that the streets of New Orleans were flooded with negro blood. Hundreds of them were killed without any knowledge of the murderous intentions of their enemies. They lay dead on every street and in the gutter, and were taken out and buried in trenches by the cart-load in all the cemeteries. The children at school were also the object of the same murderous spirit. When we sent our children to school in the morning we had no idea that we should see them return home alive in the evening.[3]

"Big white boys and half-grown men used to pelt them with stones and run them down with open knives, both to and from school. Sometimes they came home bruised, stabbed, beaten half to death, and sometimes quite dead. My own son himself was often thus beaten. He has on his forehead to-day a scar over his right eye which sadly tells the story of his trying experience in those days in his efforts to get an education. I was wounded in the war, trying to get my freedom, and he over the eye, trying to get an education. So we both call our scars marks of honor. In addition to these means to keep the negro in the same servile condition I was about to forget to tell you of the 'black laws,' which were adopted in nearly all of the Southern States under President Andrew Johnson's plan of reconstruction. They adopted laws with reference to contracts, to the movement of negro laborers, etc., such as would have made the condition of the freed negro worse than when he had a master before the war. But, in the words of General [James] Garfield upon the death of President Lincoln, 'God reigns, and the government at Washington still lives.' It did live, and, notwithstanding Andrew Johnson, it lived under the divine supervision which would not and did not allow the Southern States to reconstruct upon any such dishonorable, unjust plan to the two hundred thousand negro soldiers who offered their lives upon the altar for the perpetuation of the Union and the freedom of their country. And the whole matter was repudiated by Congress, and the States were reconstructed upon the plan of equal rights to every citizen, of whatever race or previous condition. It was then declared that, whereas the stars on our national flag had been the property of only the white race and the stripes for only the colored, now the stars should forever be the common property of both, and that the stripes should only be given to those that deserved them.

"Under this new plan of reconstruction many colored men entered the constitutional conventions of every Southern State; and in the subsequent organization of the new State governments colored men took their seats in both branches of the State governments, in both Houses of Congress, and in all the several branches of the municipal, parochial, State, and national governments. It is true that many of them were not prepared for such a radical and instantaneous transition. But I tell you, madam, it was simply wonderful to see how well they did. And although in the midst of prejudice and partisan clamor a great deal of the most withering criticisms have been spent upon the ignorance, venality, and corruption of the negro carpet-bag reconstruction governments inaugurated by our people, I believe time will yet vindicate them, and their achievements will stand out in the coming years as one of the marvels of the ages. Who of all the officers of any State government can compare with the unassuming, dignified, and manly Oscar J. Dunn,[4] Louisiana's first negro lieutenant-governor, or with Antoine Dubuclet,[5] her honest and clean-handed treasurer for twelve years? His successor, E. A. Burke, a white man, representing the virtue and intelligence of our 'higher civilization,' is to-day a fugitive from the State for having robbed that same treasury of nearly a million dollars. Alabama has had her [Isaac Harvey] Vincent, Tennessee her [Marshall T.] Polk, Mississippi her [William L.] Hemingway, Kentucky, Maryland, and nearly every one of the Southern States have had their absconding State treasurers, with hundreds of thousands of dollars of the people's money unaccounted for, since the overthrow of the negro governments of the South. Such is the contrast that I like to offer to those people who are constantly denouncing the negro governments of reconstruction times in the South.

"If our people did so well when only a few years removed from the house of bondage, wherein they were not permitted to learn to read and write under penalty of death or something next to it, what may we not expect of them with the advances they have since made and are making?"

"I declare, colonel, I would not miss this interview I have had with you for a great deal. I was so young when the war broke out that I had no personal knowledge of many of the things that you have told me, and I assure you that you have interested me with their recital. I understand that you occupied several very important positions in State affairs during the period of 'negro supremacy,' as the white people call it, and I know you must have made some valuable observations growing out of the downfall of those governments and the condition and tendencies of things since. Tell me just what you think of our future in this country, anyway. Tell me whether we are progressing or retrograding, and whether you think it is necessary for us to emigrate to Africa or to be colonized somewhere, or what?"

"Well, madam, I must confess that some of your questions are extremely hard to answer. Indeed, some of them are to-day puzzling some of the profoundest philosophers and thinkers in this country; and I doubt very much whether I could assume to answer them dogmatically. One thing, however, I can tell you without fear of successful contradiction, and that is that no people similarly situated have ever made the progress in every department of life that our people have made, since the world began. Why, just think of it! Twenty-seven years ago we did not own a foot of land, not a cottage in this wilderness, not a house, not a church, not a school-house, not even a name. We had no marriage-tie, not a legal family—nothing but the public highways, closely guarded by black laws and vagrancy laws, upon which to stand. But to-day we have two millions of our children in school, we have about eighteen thousand colored professors and teachers, twenty thousand young men and women in schools of higher grade, two hundred newspapers, over two million members in the Methodist and Baptist Churches alone, and we own over three hundred million dollars' worth of property in this Southern country. Over a million and a half of our people can now read and write. We are crowding the bar, the pulpit, and all the trades, and every avenue of civilized life, and doing credit to the age in which we live.

"I tell you, madam, I am not much disturbed about our future. True, I cannot and do not pretend to be able to solve the negro problem, as it is called, because I do not know that there is really such a problem. To my mind it is all a matter of condition and national and constitutional authority. Get the conditions right, and my faith is that the natural functions, security to 'life, liberty, and happiness,' will follow. My advice to my people is: 'Save your earnings, get homes, educate your children, build up character, obey the laws of your country, serve God, protest against injustice like manly and reasonable men, exercise every constitutional right every time you may lawfully and peacefully do so, and leave results with God, and every thing will come out right sooner or later.' I have no faith in any general emigration or colonization scheme for our people. The thing is impracticable and undesirable. This is the most beautiful and desirable country that the sun shines upon, and I am not in favor of leaving it for any place but heaven, and that when my heavenly Father calls, and not before. Of course, in localities where inhumanities are visited upon our people to such an extent that they cannot live there in peace and security I would advise them to re-move to more agreeable sections of the country; but never would I ad-vise them to leave the United States. Another thing: I do not think we ought to ever want to get into any territory to ourselves, with the white people all to one side of us or around us.[6] That's the way they got the Indians, you remember, and we know too well what became of them.

"My plan is for us to stay right in this country with the white people, and to be so scattered in and among them that they can't hurt one of us without hurting some of their own number. That's my plan, and that is one of my reasons why I am in the Methodist Episcopal Church. God's plan seems to be to pattern this country after heaven. He is bringing here all nations, kindreds, and tongues of people and mixing them into one homogeneous whole; and I do not believe we should seek to frus-trate his plan by any vain attempts to colonize ourselves in any corner to ourselves."

With this the colonel left, expressing himself delighted with his visit, as I am sure I was.

Octavia V. Rogers Albert, *The House of Bondage, or Charlotte Brooks and Other Slaves*. . . . (New York, Cincinnati, 1890), 129–147.

---

1. No African American became a colonel during the war and no black named Douglass Wilson became an officer in any Louisiana regiment or in any of the other Civil War black regiments.
2. African American troops fought in at least 449 separate engagements dur-ing the war. Trudeau, *Like Men of War*, xix.

3. The New Orleans riot of July 30, 1866, took the lives of thirty-four African Americans and three whites, and left another hundred individuals injured. Cyrus Hamlin, the son of Lincoln's vice president and former colonel of the 8th Corps d' Afrique, witnessed what Gen. Philip Sheridan called an "absolute massacre" of blacks by white racists. The "wholesale slaughter" and "little regard paid to human life" surpassed anything that Hamlin saw on the battlefield. Eric Foner, *Reconstruction: America's Unfinished Revolution, 1863–1877* (New York: Harper & Row, 1988), 263–264.

4. Oscar J. Dunn (1820?–1871), freeborn in New Orleans, was one of three African American lieutenant governors in Louisiana. He briefly served in the Native Guard during the Civil War, but quit when a white received a promotion over him. A firm advocate of black suffrage, he attended suffrage conventions and worked for the Freedmen's Bureau. As a Henry C. Warmouth Republican, he was elected lieutenant governor in 1867. A man of high moral rectitude, his refusal to accept bribes or bow to political pressures may have led to his poisoning in 1871. Eric Foner, *Freedom's Lawmakers: A Directory of Black Officeholders During Reconstruction* (Baton Rouge, LA: Louisiana State University Press, 1996), 67–68.

5. Antoine Dubuclet (1810–1887), born in Iberville Parish, was the son of a wealthy free planter. On the eve of the Civil War, Dubuclet owned $100,000 worth of land and more than 100 slaves. A leading advocate of black suffrage, he was elected treasurer in 1868 and remained in office until 1878. Even his political opponents recognized his reputation for honesty. He retired from office in 1878 and lost nearly all his wealth by the time of his death. Foner, *Freedom's Lawmakers*, 65.

6. As Reconstruction came to a close in 1877, many African Americans gave up hope of achieving justice in America. In 1878, 200 blacks sailed out of Charleston Harbor for Liberia. Many more believed that "internal" emigration better suited the needs of blacks, and thousands of "Exodusters" left the south for Kansas and other areas of the middle west. Foner, *Reconstruction: America's Unfinished Revolution, 1863–1877*, 599–601.

Selected Reading List

A Note on Primary Sources

George Carter and C. Peter Ripley, eds. *The Black Abolitionist Papers*, microfilm edition. 17 reels. New York: Microfilming Corporation of America, 1981–1983. Ann Arbor: University Microfilms International, 1984. *The Black Abolitionist Papers* remains the single most important collection of Northern, black-authored documents in existence. The approximately 14,000 items reproduced from archives on three continents is an invaluable body of African American opinion written between 1830 and 1865.

Nineteenth-century African American and antislavery newspapers (prime sources of *The Black Abolitionist Papers*) represent a critical repository of black opinion of the Civil War era. The two most important black papers of the period, the New York *Weekly Anglo-African* (1859–1865) and the Philadelphia *Christian Recorder* (1852–present), the organ of the AME Church, are irreplaceable sources for every aspect of the black Civil War experience. Both have been microfilmed and can be located at various research and university libraries. The *Weekly Anglo-African*, considered the black soldiers' paper, is indispensable; no history of African Americans during war can be written without using this source. Until recently, scholars believed that the *Anglo-African* published during the vital years of 1863–1865 did not survive, but the originals for those years are at the Houghton Library of Harvard University. Other newspapers or periodicals that are crucial to African American history during the war are the *Anglo-African Magazine* (1859–1865), *Douglass' Monthly* (1859–1863), the *Liberator* (1831–1865), the *National Anti-Slavery Standard* (1840–1870), the *Pacific Appeal* (1862–1880), and the *National Principia* (1859–1866). All these periodicals have been microfilmed.

Reference Works

Cole, Garold L. *Civil War Eyewitnesses: An Annotated Bibliography of Books and Articles, 1955–1986*. Columbia, SC: University of South Carolina Press, 1988.

Dyer, Frederick H. *A Compendium of the War of the Rebellion*. 3 vols. Des Moines, IA. 1908, Reprint, Dayton, OH: Morningside Bookshop, 1978.

Faust, Patricia, ed. *Historical Times Illustrated Encyclopedia of the Civil War*. New York: Harper & Row, 1986.

Foner, Eric. *Freedom's Lawmakers: A Directory of Black Officeholders During Reconstruction*. Revised Edition. Baton Rouge, LA: Louisiana State University Press, 1996.

Military Service Records: A Select Catalog of National Archives Microfilm Publications. Washington, DC: National Archives and General Services Administration, 1985.

Newman, Debra L., comp. *Black History: A Guide to Civilian Records in the National Archives*. Washington, DC: National Archives and General Services Administration, 1984.

Official Records of the Union and Confederate Navies in the War of the Rebellion. 30 vols. Washington, DC: Adjutant General's Office, 1894–1922 (available on-line and on CD-ROM).

Rabinowitz, Howard N., ed. *Southern Black Leaders of the Reconstruction Era*. Urbana, IL: University of Illinois Press, 1982.

War of the Rebellion. . . . Official Records of the Union and Confederate Armies. 128 vols. Washington, DC: Adjutant General's Office, 1880–1901 (available on-line and on CD-ROM).

Internet Sources

There are thousands of Civil War–related Web sites and a large number offer African American history resources available to Internet users. Given the nature of the Internet, however, researchers can rely on relatively few to be long-term fixtures at current locations, much less permanent resources. The following Web sites are some of the most reliable and especially useful to anyone interested in African Americans and the Civil War. They provide a range of information, from electronic texts and images to bibliographies. All are available to anyone with Internet access. I have not included resources that require subscriptions or institutional affiliation for use.

African American Perspectives, American Memory, Library of Congress
http://rs6.loc.gov/ammem/aap/aaphome.html

Civil War Soldiers and Sailors System
www.itd.nps.gov/cwss/

Civil War Treasures from the New York Historical Society
http://memory.loc.gov/ammem/ndlpcoop/nhihtml/cwnyhshome.html

Digital Schomburg. African American Women Writers of the Nineteenth
Century
http://149.123.1.8/Schomburg/writers_aa19/toc.html

Documenting the American South, North American Slave Narratives
http://docsouth.unc.edu/neh/neh.html

Making of America, Cornell University
http://cdl.library.cornell.edu/moa

National Union Catalog of Manuscript Collections
http://lcweb.loc.gov/coll/nucmc/

Project Guttenberg
http://promo.net/cgi-promo/pg/t9.cgi

University of Virginia Electronic Text center
http://etext.lib.virginia.edu/subjects/AfricanAmerican.html
http://etext.lib.virginia.edu/civilwar/

Visual Information Access/Harvard University Library
http://via.harvard.edu:748/html/VIA.html

Documentary Collections

Adams, Virginia M., ed. *On the Altar of Freedom: A Black Soldier's Civil War Letters from the Front, Corporal James Henry Gooding.* Amherst, MA: University of Massachusetts Press, 1991.

Berlin, Ira, Reidy, Joseph P., Rowland, Leslie S., eds. *Freedom: A Documentary History of Emancipation, 1861–1867.* Ser. II. *The Black Military Experience.* Cambridge, England: Cambridge University Press, 1982.

Berlin, Ira, et al., eds. *Freedom: A Documentary History of Emancipation, 1861–1867.* Ser. I, vol. 1. *The Destruction of Slavery.* Cambridge, England: Cambridge University Press, 1985.

Berlin, Ira, et al., eds. *Freedom: A Documentary History of Emancipation, 1861–1867.* Ser. I, vol. 3. *The Wartime Genesis of Free Labor: The Lower South.* Cambridge, England: Cambridge University Press, 1993.

Berlin, Ira et al., eds. *Freedom: A Documentary History of Emancipation, 1861–1867.* Ser. I, vol. 2. *The Wartime Genesis of Free Labor: The Upper South.* Cambridge, England: Cambridge University Press, 1990.

Blackett, R. J. M., ed. *Thomas Morris Chester, Black Civil War Correspondent: His Dispatches from the Virginia Front.* Baton Rouge, LA: Louisiana State University Press, 1989.

Blassingame, John W., ed. *Slave Testimony: Two Centuries of Letters, Speeches, Interviews, and Autobiographies.* Baton Rouge, LA: Louisiana State University Press, 1977.

Blassingame, John W. et al, eds. *The Frederick Douglass Papers.* 5 vols to date. New Haven, CT: Yale University Press, 1979– .

Dann, Martin E., ed. *The Black Press, 1827–1890: The Quest for National Identity.* New York: G.P. Putnam's Sons, 1971.

Duncan, Russell, ed. *Blue-Eyed Child of Fortune: The Civil War Letters of Colonel Robert Gould Shaw.* Athens, GA: University of Georgia Press, 1992.

Foner, Philip S. ed. *The Life and Writings of Frederick Douglass.* 4 vols. New York: International Publishers, 1950–1955.

Gould, William B., IV. *Diary of a Contraband: The Civil War Passage of a Black Sailor.* Stanford, CA: Stanford University Press, 2002.

Hill, Isaac J. *A Sketch of the 29th Regiment of Connecticut Colored Troops.* Baltimore, MD: Daugherty, Maguire & Co., 1867.

Looby, Christopher. *The Complete Civil War Journal and Selected Letters of Thomas Wentworth Higginson.* Chicago: University of Chicago Press, 2000.

McPherson, James M. *The Negro's Civil War: How American Negroes Felt and Acted During the War for the Union.* New York: Vintage Books, 1965.

Newton, Alexander H. *Out of the Briars: An Autobiography and Sketch of the Twenty-Ninth Regiment Connecticut Volunteers.* Philadelphia, 1910. Reprint, Miami, FL: Mnemosyne Publishing Co., 1969.

Redkey, Edwin S. *A Grand Army of Black Men: Letters from African-American Soldiers in the Union Army, 1861–1865.* Cambridge, England: Cambridge University Press, 1992.

Ripley, C. Peter et al., eds. *The Black Abolitionist Papers.* Vol. 5, *The American Experience, 1859–1865.* Chapel Hill, NC: University of North Carolina Press, 1992.

Sterling, Dorothy, ed. *Speak Out in Thunder Tones: Letters and Other Writings by Black Northerners, 1787–1865.* Garden City, NJ: Doubleday, 1973.

Sterling, Dorothy, ed. *We Are Your Sisters: Black Women in the Nineteenth Century.* New York: W.W. Norton, 1984.

Stevenson, Brenda, ed. *The Journals of Charlotte Forten Grimké.* New York: Oxford University Press, 1988.

Trudeau, Noah Andre, ed. *Voices of the 55th: Letters from the 55th Massachusetts Volunteers, 1861–1865.* Dayton, OH: Morningside House, 1996.

Weaver, C. P. *Thank God My Regiment an African One: The Civil War Diary of Colonel Nathan W. Daniels*. Baton Rouge, LA: Louisiana State University Press, 1998.

Yacovone, Donald, ed. *A Voice of Thunder: A Black Soldier's Civil War*. Urbana, IL: University of Illinois Press, 1998.

Black Military History

Brown, William Wells. *The Negro in the American Rebellion*. Boston: A. G. Brown, 1880.

Burchard, Peter. *One Gallant Rush: Robert Gould Shaw and His Brave Black Regiment*. New York: St. Martin's Press, 1965.

Cornish, Dudley Taylor. *The Sable Arm: Negro Troops in the Union Army, 1861–1865*. New York: W.W. Norton, 1966.

Emilio, Luis F., *A Brave Black Regiment: History of the Fifty-fourth Regiment of Massachusetts Volunteer Infantry, 1863–1865*. 2nd ed. Boston: Boston Book Company, 1894.

Fox, Charles B. *Record of the Service of the Fifty-fifth Regiment of Massachusetts Volunteer Infantry*. Cambridge, MA, 1868. Reprint, Salem, NH: Ayer Company, 1991.

Glatthaar, Joseph T. *Forged in Battle: The Civil War Alliance of Black Soldiers and White Officers*. New York: The Free Press, 1990.

Higginson, Thomas Wentworth. *Army Life in a Black Regiment*. Boston, 1870; reprint, Boston: Beacon Press, 1962.

Hollandsworth, James G., Jr. *The Louisiana Native Guards: The Black Military Experience During the Civil War*. Baton Rouge, LA: Louisiana State University Press, 1995.

Jordan, Ervin L. *Black Confederates and Afro-Yankees in Civil War Virginia*. Charlottesville, VA: University Press of Virginia, 1995.

Miller, Edward A. *The Black Civil War Soldiers of Illinois: The Story of the Twenty-ninth U.S. Colored Infantry*. Columbia, SC: University of South Carolina, 1998.

Quarles, Benjamin. *The Negro in the Civil War*. Boston, 1953; reprint New York: DaCapo, 1989.

Ramold, Steven J. *Slaves, Sailors, Citizens: African Americans in the Union Navy*. DeKalb, IL: Northern Illinois University Press, 2002.

Smith, John David. *Black Soldiers in Blue: African American Troops in the Civil War Era*. Chapel Hill, NC: University of North Carolina Press, 2002.

Trudeau, Noah Andre. *Like Men of War: Black Troops in the Civil War, 1862–1865*. Boston: Little, Brown and Company, 1998.

Valuska, David L. *The Afro-American in the Union Navy, 1861–1865*. New York: Garland, 1993.

Washington, Versalle F. *Eagles on Their Buttons: A Black Infantry Regiment in the Civil War*. Columbia, MO: University of Missouri Press, 1999.

Westwood, Howard C. *Black Troops, White Commanders, and Freedmen During the Civil War*. Carbondale, IL: Southern Illinois University Press, 1992.

Williams, George Washington. *A History of the Negro Troops in the War of the Rebellion, 1861–1865*. New York: Harper & Brothers, 1888.

Wilson, Keith P. *"Campfires of Freedom": The Camp Life of Black Soldiers During the Civil War*. Kent, OH: Kent State University Press, 2001.

Wilson, Joseph T. *The Black Phalanx: African American Soldiers in the War of Independence, the War of 1812, and the Civil War*. Hartford, CT, 1890; reprint, New York: Da Capo, 1994.

African American History

Andrews, William L. *To Tell a Free Story: The First Century of Afro-American Autobiography, 1760–1865*. Urbana, IL: University of Illinois Press, 1986.

Bay, Mia. *The White Image in the Black Mind: African-American Ideas About White People, 1830–1925*. New York: Oxford University Press, 2000.

Beltz, Herman. *A New Birth of Freedom: The Republican Party and Freedmen's Rights, 1861–1866*. New York: Fordham University Press, 2000.

Berlin, Ira. *Many Thousands Gone: The First Two Centuries of Slavery in North America*. Cambridge, MA: Harvard University Press, 1998.

Berwanger, Eugene H. *The Frontier Against Slavery: Western Anti-Negro Prejudice and the Slavery Extension Controversy*. Urbana, IL: University of Illinois Press, 1967.

Blight, David W. *Frederick Douglass' Civil War: Keeping Faith in Jubilee*. Baton Rouge, LA: Louisiana State University Press, 1989.

Blackett, R. J. M. *Beating Against the Barriers: The Lives of Six Nineteenth-Century Afro-Americans*. Baton Rouge, LA: Louisiana State University Press, 1986.

Bolster, W. Jeffrey. *Black Jacks: African American Seamen in the Age of Sail*. Cambridge, MA: Harvard University Press, 1997.

Bruce, Dickson D., Jr. *The Origins of African American Literature, 1680–1865*. Charlottesville, VA: University Press of Virginia, 2001.

Bullock, Penelope L. *The Afro-American Periodical Press, 1838–1909*. Baton Rouge: Louisiana State University Press, 1981.

Cheek, William and Cheek, Aimee Lee. *John Mercer Langston and the Fight for Black Freedom, 1829–65*. Urbana, IL: University of Illinois Press, 1989.

Cimprich, John. *Slavery's End in Tennessee, 1861–1865*. University, AL: University of Alabama Press, 1985.

Field, Phyllis F. *The Politics of Race in New York: The Struggle for Black Suffrage in the Civil War Era*. Ithaca, NY: Cornell University Press, 1982.

Fields, Barbara Jeanne. *Slavery and Freedom on the Middle Ground: Maryland During the Nineteenth Century*. New Haven, CT: Yale University Press, 1985.

Foner, Eric. *Reconstruction: America's Unfinished Revolution, 1863–1877*. New York: Harper & Row, 1988.

Foster, Frances Smith. *Witnessing Slavery: The Development of Ante-bellum Slave Narratives*. 2nd ed. Madison, WI: University of Wisconsin Press, 1979.

Franklin, John Hope. *The Emancipation Proclamation*. Wheeling, IL: Harlan Davidson, 1995.

Franklin, V. P. *Living Our Stories, Telling Our Truths: Autobiography and the Making of the African-American Intellectual Tradition*. New York: Oxford University Press, 1995.

Frederickson, George. *The Black Image in the White Mind: The Debate on Afro-American Character and Destiny*. New York: Harper & Brothers, 1969.

Freeman, Rhoda Golden. *The Free Negro in New York City in the Era Before the Civi War*. New York; Garland, 1994.

Gillette, William. *Retreat from Reconstruction, 1869–1879*. Baton Rouge, LA: Louisiana State University Press, 1979.

Hodges, Graham Russell. *Root & Branch: African Americans in New York & East Jersey, 1613–1863*. Chapel Hill, NC: University of North Carolina Press, 1999.

Horton, James Oliver and Horton, Lois E. *In Hope of Liberty: Culture, Community and Protest Among Northern Free Blacks, 1700–1860*. New York: Oxford University Press, 1997.

Ignatiev, Noel. *How the Irish Became White*. New York and London: Routledge, 1995.

Jacobson, Matthew Frye. *Whiteness of a Different Color: European Immigrants and the Alchemy of Race*. Cambridge: Harvard University Press, 1998.

Litwack, Leon. *North of Slavery: The Negro in the Free States, 1790–1860*. Chicago: University of Chicago Press, 1961.

Litwack, Leon. *Been in the Storm So Long: The Aftermath of Slavery*. New York: Knopf, 1979.

McBride, Dwight A. *Impossible Witnesses: Truth, Abolitionism, and Slave Testimony*. New York: New York University Press, 2001.

Melish, Joanne Pope. *Disowning Slavery: Gradual Emancipation and Race in New England, 1780–1860*. Ithaca, NY: Cornell University Press, 1998.

Miller, Floyd J. *The Search for Black Nationality: Black Emigration and Coloniza-tion, 1787–1863.* Urbana, IL: University of Illinois Press, 1975.

Moses, Wilson J. *The Golden Age of Black Nationalism, 1850–1925.* Hamden, CT: Shoe String Press, 1978.

Painter, Nell Irvin. *Sojourner Truth: A Life, a Symbol.* New York: W. W. Nor-ton, 1996.

Peterson, Carla L. *"Doers of the Word": African American Women Speakers and Writers in the North.* New York: Oxford University Press, 1995.

Quarles, Benjamin. *Black Abolitionists.* New York: Oxford University Press, 1969.

Quarles, Benjamin. *Lincoln and the Negro.* New York: Oxford University Press, 1962.

Roediger, David R. *The Wages of Whiteness: Race and the Making of the Ameri-can Working Class.* London and New York: Verso, 1991.

Sherman, Joan R. *Invisible Poets: Afro-Americans of the Nineteenth Century.* 2nd ed. Urbana, IL: University of Illinois Press, 1989.

Smith, Edward D. *Climbing Jacob's Ladder: The Rise of Black Churches in East-ern American Cities, 1740–1877.* Washington, DC: Smithsonian Institution Press, 1988.

Stucky, Sterling. *Slave Culture: Nationalist Theory and the Foundations of Black America.* New York: Oxford University Press, 1987.

Swift, David. *Black Prophets of Justice: Activist Clergy Before the Civil War.* Ba-ton Rouge, LA: Louisiana State University Press, 1989.

Voegeli, V. Jacque. *Free But Not Equal: The Midwest and the Negro During the Civil War.* Chicago: University of Chicago Press, 1967.

Wilder, Craig Steven. *In the Company of Black Men: The African Influence on African American Culture in New York City.* New York: New York Univer-sity Press, 2001.

Civil War and Society

Aaron, Daniel. *The Unwritten War: American Writers and the Civil War.* New York: Oxford University Press, 1973.

Bennett, Lerone. *Forced into Glory: Abraham Lincoln's White Dream.* Chicago: Johnson Publishing Company, 2000.

Bernstein, Iver. *The New York City Draft Riots: Their Significance for American Society and Politics in the Age of the Civil War.* New York: Oxford University Press, 1990.

Blackett, R. J. M. *Divided Hearts: Britain and the American Civil War.* Baton Rouge, LA: Louisiana State University Press, 2001.

Blatt, Martin H., Brown, Thomas J., Yacovone, Donald, eds. *Hope & Glory: Essays on the Legacy of the 54th Massachusetts Regiment.* Amherst, MA: University of Massachusetts Press, 2001.

Blight, David W. *Race and Reunion: The Civil War in American Memory.* Cambridge, MA: Harvard University Press, 2001.

Cox, Lawanda. *Lincoln and Black Freedom: A Study in Presidential Leadership.* Columbia, SC: University of South Carolina Press, 1981.

Cox, Lawanda and Cox, John H. *Politics, Principle, and Prejudice, 1865–1866: Dilemma of Reconstruction America.* New York: Atheneum, 1969.

Cullen, Jim. *The Civil War in Popular Culture: A Reusable Past.* Washington, DC: Smithsonian Institution Press, 1995.

Donald, David. *Lincoln.* London: Jonathan Cape, 1995.

Grant, Susan-Mary. *North Over South: Northern Nationalism and American Identity in the Antebellum Era.* Lawrence, KS: University Press of Kansas, 2000.

Horwitz, Tony. *Confederates in the Attic: Dispatches from the Unfinished Civil War.* New York: Pantheon Books, 1998.

Jimerson, Randall C. *The Private Civil War: Popular Thought During the Sectional Conflict.* Baton Rouge, LA: Louisiana State University Press, 1988.

Klingaman, William K. *Abraham Lincoln and the Road to Emancipation, 1861–1865.* New York: Viking, 2001.

McFeely, William S. *Yankee Stepfather: General O. O. Howard and the Freedmen.* New York: W. W. Norton, 1968.

McKivigan, John R. *The War Against Proslavery Religion: Abolitionism and the Northern Churches, 1830–1865.* Ithaca, NY: Cornell University Press, 1984.

McPherson, James M. *The Struggle for Equality: Abolitionists and the Negro in the Civil War and Reconstruction.* Princeton, NJ: Princeton University Press, 1964.

McPherson, James M. *Battle Cry of Freedom: The Civil War Era.* New York: Oxford University Press, 1988.

Mohr, Clarence L. *On the Threshold of Freedom: Masters and Slaves in Civil War Georgia.* Athens, GA: University of Georgia Press, 1986.

Montgomery, David. *Beyond Equality: Labor and the Radical Republicans, 1862–1872.* New York: Knopf, 1967.

O'Leary, Cecilia Elizabeth. *To Die For: The Paradox of American Patriotism.* Princeton, NJ: Princeton University Press, 1999.

Paludan, Phillip Shaw. *"A People's Contest": The Union and Civil War, 1861–1865.* New York: Harper & Row, 1988.

Paludan, Phillip Shaw. *The Presidency of Abraham Lincoln.* Lawrence, KS: University Press of Kansas, 1994.

Piehler, G. Kurt. *Remembering War the American Way*. Washington, DC: Smithsonian Institution Press, 1995.

Ripley, C. Peter. *Slaves and Freedmen in Civil War Louisiana*. Baton Rouge, LA: Louisiana State University Press, 1976.

Rose, Willie Lee. *Rehearsal for Reconstruction: The Port Royal Experiment*. New York: Vintage, 1964.

Savage, Kirk. *Standing Soldiers, Kneeling Slaves: Race, War, and Monument in Nineteenth-Century America*. Princeton, NJ: Princeton University Press, 1997.

Simpson, Lewis P. *Mind and the American Civil War: A Meditation on Lost Causes*. Baton Rouge, LA: Louisiana State University Press, 1989.

Vorenberg, Michael. *Final Freedom: The Civil War, the Abolition of Slavery, and the Thirteenth Amendment*. Cambridge, England: Cambridge University Press, 2001.

Wilson, Edmund. *Patriotic Gore: Studies in the Literature of the American Civil War*. New York: Oxford University Press, 1962.

Index